E M BOUNDS
THE CLASSIC COLLECTION
ON
PRAYER

E M BOUNDS
THE CLASSIC COLLECTION
ON
PRAYER

REVISED IN MODERN ENGLISH BY
HAROLD J. CHADWICK

Bridge-Logos

Gainesville, FL 32614 USA

Bridge-Logos, Gainesville, FL 32614
Copyright © 2001 by Bridge-Logos Publishers

Printed in the United States of America.

04 01   2   1

Library of Congress Catalog Card Number: 2001098625
International Standard Book Number: 0-88270-888-0

Unless otherwise indicated, the Scripture quotations in this publication are from the *King James Version*.

Scripture quotations marked (RSV) are taken from *The Holy Bible: Containing the Old Testament and The New Testaments: Revised Standard Version*. Copyright ©1973 by American Bible Society. Used by permission.

Scripture quotations marked (NKJV) are taken from *The New King James Version*. Copyright ©1997, 1980, 1982, Thomas Nelson Inc., Publishers. Used by permission.

Table of Contents

Book 3: The Possibilities of Prayer

Book 4: The Reality of Prayer

Book 5: The Weapon of Prayer

Book 6: The Purpose of Prayer

Book 7: The Power of Prayer

Book 8: Prayer and Praying Saints

BIOGRAPHY

E.M. BOUNDS

Edward McKendree (E.M.) Bounds
August 15, 1835 - August 24, 1913

*"Man is looking for better methods. God is looking for better men.
Men are God's methods."*

E. M. Bounds

E. M. Bounds once wrote "Elijah learned new and higher lessons of prayer while hidden away by God and with God ..." Clearly Bounds must have understood the ramifications of "new and higher lessons," because he, too, was a man hidden away by God and with God. He was a son, a husband and father, a gold miner, a lawyer, a pastor, a Confederate Army chaplain, a writer, a community leader, and a friend and neighbor. But the enduring legacy of E.M. Bounds is that he was first and foremost God's man. He was a man of prayer.

Edward McKendree Bounds was born on August 15, 1835 to Thomas J. and Hatty Bounds in Shelby County, Missouri. His middle name, McKendree, came from the famous Methodist circuit rider, Bishop William McKendree, who planted churches from the Atlantic coast to Missouri. The name was a prophetic choice, for Edward would grow up to serve God in a quiet, powerful ministry that still resonates today through his writings.

Bounds may have started his life with a pastor's name, but his early career did not reflect a pastor's path. His father died of tuberculosis when Edward was only fourteen years old. On their own and thrilled with tales of "There's gold in them thar hills," he and his elder brother Charles heeded the call: "Go west, young man, go west!" Together they left their home in Missouri and traveled to Mesquite Canyon in California to seek their fortune in mining and panning for gold. But the promise of wealth soon faded into backbreaking work and crushing disappointment. Not only that, but living among miners wrenched the boys from their tender Methodist upbringing in Missouri into the grimy, gritty moral degradation of Western boomtowns. Surprisingly, they lasted four years. Edward and his brother might not have struck gold, but he set his sights on greater treasure. He turned to the God of his youth.

When he returned home, Edward, as many young men did, studied law. In fact, he excelled at it. He was the youngest man ever admitted to the bar in Missouri. With all his drive and ambition, his practice was highly successful. But his restless heart longed for something else.

That "something else" soon revealed itself. The Great Spiritual Awakening of 1857-58 reached northern Missouri. The Methodist Episcopal Church South in La Grange, Missouri, sponsored a meeting with Evangelist Smith Thomas. Edward was there. That night, enfolded in the preaching and praying, his spirit was ignited and more: his heart was moved to answer God's call for full-time Christian ministry. After only five years in practice, he locked the door of his law firm and walked away ... straight into the service of God. He enrolled in Centenary Seminary of the Methodist Episcopal Church South in Palmyra. Two years later he graduated. He was ordained in 1859.

His first pastorate was in Brunswick, Missouri, but his idyllic life as a country pastor with a red brick church was to be short-lived. The Civil War, which had seemed so far away from the daily life of peaceful Brunswick, roared into Missouri. On May 10, 1861, Union troops imprisoned the State Guard in St. Louis and captured the Arsenal. Their rampage took the lives of twenty-eight civilians, including a seventeen-year-old boy who was deliberately drowned by Union soldiers in the Grand River. Reverend Bounds officiated at his funeral. Later Bounds would personally witness the brutal execution of fifty-five more innocent civilians, and officiate yet one more funeral. His despair grew. When he was asked to sign the Oath of Allegiance, he had no moral choice but to refuse. His conscience would not permit him to support the federal government that butchered the Constitution as well as the citizens who lived within its protection, and condoned the atrocities he was witnessing. His courage would have consequences.

In the autumn of 1861, six months after the start of the Civil War, Union troops thundered up on their horses, stormed the church where Bounds worked quietly, and took him into custody. Obviously a man of peace, his only crimes were that he hadn't signed the Oath of Allegiance, and had once publicly spoken on his opposition of Union troops commandeering churches. In punishment, he was beaten and thrown into federal prison at St. Louis. To describe conditions as harsh is to understate the next few months of his life. This horror might have destroyed a lesser man, but Bounds embraced prison as a wonderful opportunity to serve God, to minister to the Confederate prisoners who shared his dank existence. The reputation of this godly man spread quickly. Early the next year, when prisoners were exchanged, Bounds was transported to Arkansas, released and ordered to stay out of Missouri forever. But Bounds knew he would have to return home.

Bounds walked out of prison and continued walking ... over 200 miles to Pinebluff, where he purchased a mule and continued his journey. His single-minded mission was to join the Confederate Army and defend his beloved Missouri—not with a rifle, but with prayer. On February 7, 1863, he joined the Confederate Army, Company B of the Third Missouri Infantry, where he served as a chaplain.

Against the dark and bloody backdrop of the Civil War, in a country torn apart by moral issues so inflammatory that they pitted brother against brother on the battlefield, a gentle man of God rose.

Rather than reward Bounds for his faithful tenure in prison with a safe desk job back home in Missouri, the Confederate Army assigned him to a unit on the front line. Rebel Chaplain Bounds was assigned to General John Bell Hood's Army of Tennessee. At first, Bounds found it difficult to preach to battle-weary veterans who were accustomed to chaplains who would preach about faith at night at the campfire, but run home when the fighting broke out the next day. Bounds, however, was a "battle-weary veteran" in his own right. As a fatherless boy, he had been toughened up by the rough and tumble California miners and later by harsh conditions in prison in St. Louis. Additionally, his faith wasn't one of speech. It was one of practice. From the first volley fired to the last, Bounds stood side by side with his fellow soldiers, shouting encouragement and praying for their safety. The men were won over.

Their affection is apparent in the fact that they teased him. Bounds was short in stature: just over five feet tall. With a full pack bowing his slim shoulders, he was nearly dwarfed by the load. His men good-naturedly nicknamed him "the walking bundle."

But any small bit of good-natured fun would soon vanish. Life changed forever at the Battle of Franklin, Tennessee. On November 30, 1864, Bounds' commanding officer, General Hood, ordered his troops to attack entrenched Union forces under General Schofield near Franklin, Tennessee. Eighteen thousand Rebels stormed Union lines in a battle still etched in history as one of the most brutal and possibly ill conceived in the Civil War. Called "The Gettysburg of the West," Franklin was one of the few battles fought in the dark of night in the Civil War. It was also one of the smallest battlefields of the war (only 2 miles long and $1^{1}/_{2}$ miles wide). The main battle began around 4:00 PM and wound down around 9:00 PM. In six bloody hours General Hood's Army suffered over 6,000 casualties.

"(Franklin) is the blackest page in the history of the War of the Lost Cause. It was the bloodiest battle of modern times in any war. It was the finishing stroke to the Independence of the Southern Confederacy. I was there. I saw it."—Sam Watkins, 1st Tennessee Infantry

Union soldiers took prisoners from among the soldiers they didn't slaughter, and among them was Chaplain Bounds, suffering himself from a severe gash across his forehead from a Union saber. For two horrific weeks following the defeat, injured and exhausted Bounds dug mass graves and buried friends and comrades with whom he had served and to whom he had ministered. Still, his spirit would not be broken. While he dug and hauled corpses, he offered support to fellow prisoners of war, sang hymns out loud, and quoted Scripture. At the end of two weeks, when the dead were buried, the Union Army released most of their captives on the condition that they return home and vow to not rejoin the fighting.

Bounds complied and returned to Missouri, but an important part of his heart remained in Franklin, Tennessee, with the treasured friends he had buried. He would return not to fight, but to make right something that was horribly wrong.

Early in 1865, Bounds left Missouri and returned to Franklin. He was haunted by the disrespectful way that his men had been buried: in mass graves. These were friends whom he loved, not faceless, nameless corpses. These were brave soldiers. These were husbands and fathers and brothers and men who deserved better. He arrived in Franklin with dogged determination and a plan to properly bury his men and honor their lives. By summer, he convinced a local farmer, McGavock, to donate a small parcel of land near the hills of Carter Farm. It probably didn't take much convincing.

Land very near the Carter Farm was a logical choice for the Confederate Cemetery, because, for the Carter family, that battle had been both personal and tragic. The Federal Army had actually commandeered their home as their general's headquarters. At that time, the Carter Farm consisted of 288 acres on the south edge of Franklin. During the hours of fighting, the Carter family took refuge in their basement. Twenty-three men, women and children huddled in the dark while the suicidal defense of Franklin stormed above them. The head of the family, Fountain Branch Carter, a 67-year old widower, had seen three of his sons fight for the Confederacy. One son, Theodrick (Tod), was serving as an aid for General T.B. Smith on the battlefield and saw his home for the first time in three years. Crying out, "Follow me, boys! I'm almost home," Captain Tod Carter was mortally wounded and died two days later at the Carter House.

After the battle, as with so many homes in Franklin, the parlor of the Carter House had been converted into a Confederate field hospital. The Carter House was purchased by the State of Tennessee in 1951 and first opened to the public in 1953. Today, it's a Registered Historic Landmark dedicated to all Americans who fought in this battle ... among them E.M. Bounds.

Under Bounds' direction and with the Carter family's generosity, one thousand four hundred and ninety-six Confederate solders were exhumed from the mass graves of the prison camp that summer and given proper, individual, Christian burials. Bounds even raised enough money to pay local men to care for their graves. He made a list of all the men from Missouri now buried at Carter Farm and published it in Missouri newspapers to inform their families. He also stayed in touch with those families he could find, and helped their children get scholarships so that they could attend school. A man who had been a fatherless boy understood the hardships of fatherless children.

Bounds carried that list of men from Missouri in his wallet for forty-eight years, until the day he died.

While in Franklin, although Bounds concentrated on the exhumation and burial of his men, he couldn't escape noticing that a pall hung over the entire town. Perhaps they were exhausted and shell-shocked from all the death and destruction of the Union invasion. Even though it was a dominantly Christian community, there was no spirit of joy. No love. No hope. There was also no Methodist minister to turn it all around ... until Edward M. Bounds stepped up.

Bounds took over as pastor of Franklin's Methodist Episcopal Church. Of course, he had his usual duties as a pastor, his usual responsibilities to his congregation, but his eye was on the larger picture. He entreated God to show him a way to lift the sorrow and darkness that engulfed the entire town. Then one day God answered his prayer with an idea: Bounds would call the men of the town to join him in prayer every Tuesday evening in the town square and cry out to God for their city. Even if the idea might have seemed far-fetched and frankly much too simplistic to work, the men gave it a try. For months, every Tuesday evening, they would gather on their knees in the town square and pray that the sorrow and darkness would lift. Slowly, surely it worked.

For over a year this faithful band called upon the Lord until God finally answered by fire. The revival came down without any previous announcement or plan, and without the pastor sending for an evangelist to help him. Not only did Franklin, Tennessee, begin to heal, but God began to touch hearts and awaken spirits all over town. Bounds' own congregation exploded from a few faithful believers to over five hundred.

Within two years, Bounds knew that his work in Franklin was completed. He had buried his friends, and he had been God's servant in lifting the town by bringing its people to their knees in prayer.

There could be no doubt that God had given Bounds a commission for intercessory prayer, and gifts for building and reviving churches. Bounds was sure-handed and fervent, but was not always popular with other ministers. He said, "Revivals are among the charter rights of the Church. A revival means a heartbroken pastor. A revival means a church on its knees confessing its sins— the sins of the individual and of the Church—confessing the sins of the times and of the community."

W. H. Hodge, the pastor who would later become his trusted friend and assistant, and who is responsible for putting most of Bounds' writings into print, remarked, "His constant call for revival annoyed those who believed that the Church was essentially sound …" Undaunted, he prayed without ceasing for the sanctification of preachers, revival of the Church in North America and the spread of holiness among Christians. Bounds spent a minimum of three to four hours a day in concentrated prayer. "Sometimes the venerable mystic would lie flat on his back and talk to God, but many hours were spent on his knees or lying face down where he could be heard weeping …"

Hodge generously offers a private glimpse into Bounds' prayer life. He writes, "I have been among many ministers and slept in the same room with them for several years. They prayed, but I was never impressed with any special praying among them until one day a small man with gray hair and an eye like an eagle came along. We had a ten-day convention. We had some fine preachers around the home, and one of them was assigned to my room. I was surprised early next morning to see a man bathing himself before day and then see him get down and begin to pray. I said to myself, 'He will not disturb us, but will soon finish.' He kept on softly for hours, interceding and weeping softly for me and my indifference, and for all the ministers of God. He spoke the next day on prayer. I became interested, for I was young in the ministry, and had often desired to meet with a man of God that prayed like the saints of the Apostolic age. Next morning he was up praying again, and for ten days he was up early praying for hours. I became intensely interested and thanked God for sending him. 'At last,' I said, 'I have found a man that really prays. I shall never let him go.' He drew me to him with hooks of steel."

When Bounds' intercessory work in Franklin, Tennessee, was complete, he moved on to Alabama. On September 19, 1876, at the age of forty-one, he married Emma Elizabeth Barnett. They had three children. Nine years later, at the age of thirty, Emma passed away. At age fifty-two, after two years of grieving for Emma, he found love and happiness again when he married her cousin, Harriet A. Barnett. He and Harriet were blessed with four more children. But as sometimes happens in life, tragedy visited their home. Edward, Jr., his son with Emma, become sick and died. Then infant Charles, his son with Harriet, died.

On June 7, 1890, Reverend Bounds accepted the position as Assistant Editor of the Methodist Episcopal Church South's official publication, *The Christian Advocate*. But his uncompromising views on holiness and the role of pastors put him into philosophical conflict with the members of the National Conference. He simply could not support the material he was being asked to help publish. Worse, he could not support his own church. Within four years, he was forced to resign, rather than to compromise.

"And I will give you pastors according to mine heart, which shall feed you with knowledge and understanding" Jeremiah 3:15.

He refused severance pay, and quietly left *The Christian Advocate* and moved his family to Washington, Georgia. If the Bounds' family's financial future looked bleak, it was for only a moment. Bounds might have essentially severed ties with his own Methodist Episcopal church, but he had attracted the attention of other denominations that shared his uncompromising stance. He immediately began to receive invitations for speaking engagements in ministry. Wherever he preached, crowds of people hungry for truth gathered, and revival ignited their spirits.

For the last nineteen years of his life, E.M. Bounds devoted himself to intercessory prayer. He was deeply burdened because of the backslidden condition of his church, the corruption and self-interest of his fellow ministers, the moral decay of the government, and for the lost souls of his people. He spent a minimum of three to four hours each morning in prayer. In fact, with regard to Bounds' commitment to intercessory prayer, there is a good story that Bounds scholars tell. It seems that at the end of the day, when the rest of his neighborhood would fall into slumber, Bounds would frequently, quietly slip out of his home and wander the lamp-lit streets until he finally selected a house. He would stand in the street in front of the house or move onto the front yard, where he would devote himself to impassioned prayer for several hours on behalf of the occupants unaware. Local police on patrol were so accustomed to finding this quiet man walking the streets at night and standing too close to people's homes that they no longer bothered to "check him out." They knew this man in the shadows was not an intruder or a voyeur or a criminal. No, it was merely Brother Bounds, praying for people who probably never even knew he was there in the night.

Although Bounds was a very human man with very human triumphs and tragedies, his legacy—the gift—he left to all who would come after him is that he was a man of prayer. Filtered through the perspective afforded us by history, it's interesting, even perplexing, to note that he never attracted a large following during his lifetime. In spite of his scholarship, faithfulness, authorship and unusually heroic and colorful life in forty-six years of ministry, he was largely unknown. Today, most evangelicals regard E.M. Bounds as an important authority on prayer, but during his lifetime, only two of his eight books on prayer were even published. Among his works are *Power Through Prayer, Prayer and Praying Men, The Essentials of Prayer,* and *The Possibilities of Prayer.*

E.M. Bounds died on August 24, 1913, at his home in Washington, Georgia, at the age of seventy-eight. Just as surely as his soul entered immortality, his work endures—a triumphant partnership between glorious God and a faithful, humble servant.

PHOTO GALLERY

Edward McKendree (E.M.) Bounds
August 15, 1835 - August 24, 1913

The youthful Bounds and his elder brother Charles left their home in Missouri and traveled to Mesquite Canyon in California to seek their fortune in mining and panning for gold.

E.M. Bounds served as a Confederate Army Chaplain during the Civil War.

The harsh circumstances Bounds encountered early in his life prepared him to minister to the battle-weary troops in the final days of the war. He stood side by side in battle with his fellow soldiers, shouting encouragement and praying for their safety, winning the men over completely.

The Confederate Troops suffered a bloody defeat at the Battle of Franklin, Tennessee. As a result, Bounds was captured and held as a prisoner of war for a short time.

The Federal Army commandeered the Carter Family home as its headquarters. At that time, the Carter Farm consisted of 288 acres on the south edge of Franklin. After the battle, the parlor of the Carter House was converted into a Confederate field hospital.

The Confederate cemetery in Franklin, Tennessee, is located near the hills of the Carter Farm on a small parcel of land donated by a local farmer, McGavock.

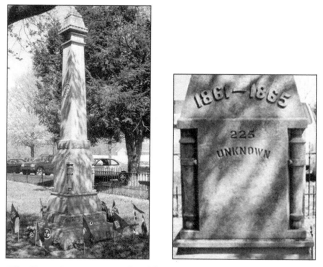

The Carter House was purchased by the State of Tennessee in 1951 and first opened to the public in 1953. Today, it's a Registered Historic Landmark dedicated to all Americans who fought in this battle . . . among them E.M. Bounds.

BOOK I

THE NECESSITY OF PRAYER

I

Prayer and Faith

A DEAR FRIEND OF MINE *who was quite a lover of the chase, told me the following story: "Rising early one morning," he said, "I heard the baying of a score of deerhounds in pursuit of their quarry. Looking away to a broad, open field in front of me, I saw a young fawn making its way across, and giving signs, moreover, that its race was well-nigh run. Reaching the rails of the enclosure, it leaped over and crouched within ten feet from where I stood. A moment later two of the hounds came over, when the fawn ran in my direction and pushed its head between my legs. I lifted the little thing to my breast, and, swinging round and round, fought off the dogs. I felt, just then, that all the dogs in the West could not, and should not capture that fawn after its weakness had appealed to my strength." So is it, when human helplessness appeals to Almighty God. Well do I remember when the hounds of sin were after my soul, until, at last, I ran into the arms of Almighty God.* (A. C. Dixon)

In any study of the principles, and procedure of prayer, of its activities and enterprises, first place must necessarily be given to faith. It is the initial quality in the heart of any Christian who attempts to talk to the Unseen. We must, out of sheer helplessness, stretch forth hands of faith. We must believe, where we cannot prove. In the ultimate issue, prayer is simply faith, claiming its natural yet marvelous prerogatives—faith taking possession of its illimitable inheritance [in Christ]. True godliness is just as true, steady, and persevering in the realm of faith as it is in the province of prayer. Moreover: when faith ceases to pray, it ceases to live.

FAITH DOES THE IMPOSSIBLE

Faith does the impossible because it brings God to undertake for us, and nothing is impossible with God. How great—without qualification or limitation—is the power of faith! If doubt be banished from the heart, and unbelief made stranger there, what we ask of God shall surely come to pass, and a believer hath vouchsafed to him "whatsoever he saith."

Prayer projects faith on God, and God on the world. Only God can move mountains, but faith and prayer move God. In His cursing of the fig tree, our Lord demonstrated His power. Following that, He proceeded to declare that large powers were committed to faith and prayer, not in order to kill but to make alive, not to blast but to bless.

At this point in our study, we turn to a saying of our Lord, which there is need to emphasize, since it is the very keystone of the arch of faith and prayer.

"Therefore I say unto you, What things soever ye desire when ye pray, believe that ye receive them, and ye shall have them."[1]

We should ponder well that statement—"Believe that ye receive them, and ye shall have them." Here is described a faith that realizes, that appropriates, that takes. Such faith is a consciousness of the Divine, an experienced communion, a realized certainty.

Is [your] faith growing or declining as the years go by? Does [your] faith stand strong and four square these days, as iniquity abounds and the love of many grows cold? Does [your] faith maintain its hold, as religion tends to become a mere formality and worldliness increasingly prevails? The question of our Lord may appropriately be ours: "When the Son of Man cometh," He asks, "shall He find faith on the earth?"[2] We believe that He will, and it is our job today to see to it that the lamp of faith is trimmed and burning, lest He come who shall come, and that very soon.

FAITH IS FOUNDATION OF CHRISTIAN CHARACTER

Faith is the foundation of Christian character and the security of the soul. When Jesus was looking forward to Peter's denial, and cautioning him against it, He said to His disciple:

Simon, Simon, behold, Satan hath desired to have you, to sift you as wheat; but I have prayed for thee, that thy faith fall not.[3]

Our Lord was declaring a central truth—it was Peter's faith He was seeking to guard, for He well knew that when faith is broken down the foundations of spiritual life give way, and the entire structure of religious experience falls. It was Peter's faith that needed guarding. Hence Christ's concern for the welfare of His disciple's soul, and His determination to fortify Peter's faith by His own all-prevailing prayer.

4

In his second epistle, Peter has this idea in mind when speaking of growth in grace as a measure of safety in the Christian life, and as implying fruitfulness.

> And beside this, giving all diligence, add to your faith virtue; and to virtue knowledge; And to knowledge temperance; and to temperance patience; and to patience godliness.4

Of this additive process, faith was the starting point—the basis of the other graces of the Spirit. Faith was the foundation on which other things were to be built. Peter does not direct his readers to add to works or gifts or virtues but to faith. Much depends on starting correctly in this business of growing in grace. There is a divine order, of which Peter was aware. So he goes on to declare that we are to be even more diligent to make our call and election sure.[5] Our election is made certain by adding to [our] faith, which, in turn, is done by constant, earnest, praying. Thus faith is kept alive by prayer, and every step taken in this adding of grace to grace is accompanied by prayer.

FAITH THAT CENTERS ITSELF ON A POWERFUL PERSON

The faith that creates powerful praying is the faith that centers itself on a powerful person. Faith in Christ's ability to do and to do greatly is the faith that prays greatly. Thus the leper laid hold upon the power of Christ. "Lord, if Thou wilt," he cried, "Thou canst make me clean."[6] In this instance, we are shown how faith centered in Christ's ability to do, and how it secured the healing power.

It was concerning this very point that Jesus questioned the blind men who came to Him for healing:

> "Believe ye that I am able to do this?" He asks. "They said unto Him, Yea, Lord. Then touched He their eyes, saying, According to your faith be it unto you."[7]

To inspire faith in His ability to do, Jesus left behind Him that last, great, statement, which, in the final analysis, is a ringing challenge to faith: "All [8]power is given unto Me in heaven and in earth."[9]

SUCH FAITH IS OBEDIENT

Faith goes when it is commanded, as did the nobleman who came to Jesus because his son was grievously sick.[10]

SUCH FAITH ACTS

Like the man who was born blind, it goes to wash in the pool of Siloam when told to wash.[11] Like Peter on [the lake of] Gennesaret it casts the net where Jesus commands, instantly, without question or doubt. It takes away the stone from the grave of Lazarus promptly.[12]

A praying faith keeps the commandments of God and does those things that are well pleasing in His sight.[13] It asks, "Lord, what wilt Thou have me to do?"[14] and answers quickly, "Speak, Lord, Thy servant heareth."[15] Obedience helps faith, and faith, in turn, helps obedience. To do God's will is essential to true faith, and faith is necessary to unquestioning obedience.

FAITH OFTEN CALLED TO WAIT PATIENTLY

Yet faith is very often called upon to wait patiently before God, and is prepared for God's seeming delays in answering prayer. Faith does not grow disheartened because prayer is not immediately honored. It takes God at His Word, and lets Him take what time He chooses in fulfilling His purposes, and in carrying on His work. There is bound to be much delay and long days of waiting for true faith, but faith accepts the conditions. It knows there will be delays in answering prayer, and regards such delays as times of testing. During that time it is privileged to show its mettle, and the unyielding stuff that it is made of.

The case of Lazarus was an instance of where there was delay, where the faith of two good women was sorely tried. [You know the story,] Lazarus was critically ill and his sisters sent for Jesus. But, without any known reason, our Lord delayed His going to the relief of His sick friend. The plea was urgent and touching, "Lord, behold, he whom Thou lovest is sick."[16] But the Master wasn't moved by it, and the women's earnest request seemed to fall on deaf ears. What a trial to faith! Furthermore: our Lord's tardiness appeared to bring about hopeless disaster. While Jesus tarried, Lazarus died. But Jesus' delay was in the interests of a greater good.

Finally, Jesus starts His journey to the home in Bethany, [saying to His perplexed disciples], "Lazarus is dead. And I am glad for your sakes, that I was not there, to the intent ye may believe; nevertheless let us go unto him."[17]

Fear not, O tempted and tried believer, Jesus will come, if patience is exercised and faith holds fast. His delay will serve to make His coming the more richly blessed. Pray on. Wait on. You cannot fail. If Christ delays, wait for Him. In His own good time, He will come, and will not tarry.

DELAY IS OFTEN THE TEST AND THE STRENGTH OF FAITH

How much patience is required when these times of testing come! Yet faith gathers strength by waiting and praying. Patience has its perfect work in the school of delay. In some instances, delay is the most essential part of the prayer. God has to do many things before He can give the final answer—things that are essential to the lasting good of the one who is requesting favor at His hands.

Jacob prayed with purpose and intensity to be delivered from Esau. But before that prayer could be answered, there was much to be done with and for Jacob. Both he and Esau must be changed. Jacob had to be made into a new man before Esau could be. Jacob had to be converted to God before Esau could be converted to Jacob.

A WONDERFUL PRAYER PROMISE

Among the large and enlightening utterances of Jesus concerning prayer, none is more arresting than this:

> Verily, verily, I say unto you, He that believeth on Me, the works that I do shall he do also; and greater works than these shall he do; because I go unto My Father. And whatsoever ye shall ask in My Name, that will I do, that the Father may be glorified in the Son. If ye shall ask anything in My Name, I will do it.[18]

How wonderful are these statements of what God will do in answer to prayer! Of how great importance are these ringing words, prefaced as they are with the most solemn verily![19] Faith in Christ is the basis of all working, and of all praying. All wonderful works depend on wonderful praying, and all praying is done in the name of Jesus Christ. This praying in the name of Jesus is an amazing lesson of wondrous simplicity! All other conditions are without value, everything else is renounced, save Jesus only. The name of Christ—the person of our Lord and savior Jesus Christ—must be supremely sovereign in the time and presentation of prayer.

If Jesus dwells at the fountain of my life, if the currents of His life have displaced and superseded all self-currents, if unquestionable obedience to Him is the inspiration and force of every movement of my life, then He can safely commit the praying to my will, and pledge Himself, by an obligation as profound as His own nature, that whatsoever I ask will be granted. Nothing can be clearer, more distinct, more unlimited both in application and extent, than the exhortation and urging of Jesus, "Have faith in God."[20]

FAITH COVERS ALL NEEDS

Faith covers temporal as well as spiritual needs. Faith dispels all undue anxiety and needless care about what will be eaten, what will be drunk, what will be worn. Faith lives in the present, and considers the day as having sufficient troubles of its own.[21] It lives day by day, and dispels all fears for tomorrow. Faith brings great ease of mind and perfect peace of heart.

> Thou wilt keep him in perfect peace whose mind is stayed on Thee: because he trusted in Thee.[22]

When we pray, "Give us this day our daily bread,"[23] we are, in a measure, shutting tomorrow out of our prayer. We do not live in tomorrow but in today. We do not seek tomorrow's grace or tomorrow's bread. Those who live in the present time thrive best and get most out of life. They pray best who pray for today's needs, not for tomorrow's, which may render our prayers unnecessary and redundant by not existing at all!

True prayers are born of present trials and present needs. Bread for today is bread enough. Bread given for today is the strongest sort of pledge that there will be bread tomorrow. Victory today is the assurance of victory tomorrow. Our prayers need to be focused upon the present. We must trust God today and leave tomorrow entirely with Him. The present is ours, the future belongs to God. Prayer is the task and duty of each recurring day— daily prayer for daily needs.

As every day demands its bread, so every day demands its prayer. No amount of praying done today will be sufficient for tomorrow's praying. On the other hand, no praying for tomorrow is of any great value to us today. Today's manna is what we need—tomorrow God will see that our needs are supplied. This is the faith that God seeks to inspire. So leave tomorrow with its cares, its needs, its troubles, in God's hands. There is no storing tomorrow's grace or tomorrow's praying—neither is there any storing of today's grace to meet tomorrow's necessities. We cannot have tomorrow's grace, we cannot eat tomorrow's bread, we cannot do tomorrow's praying. "Sufficient unto the day is the evil thereof,"[24] and most assuredly, if we possess faith, sufficient unto the day will be the good, also.

Endnotes

1 Mark 11:24
2 Luke 18:8
3 Luke 22:31
4 2 Peter 1:5-6
5 Therefore, brethren, be even more diligent to make your call and election sure, for if you do these things you will never stumble (2 Peter 1:10, NKJV).
6 Matthew 8:2
7 Matthew 9:28-29
8 Greek: *exousia*, which means authority.
9 And Jesus came and spoke to them, saying, "All authority has been given to Me in heaven and on earth" (Matthew 28:18, NKJV).
10 John 4:46-50
11 John 9:7
12 John 11:39-41
13 1 John 3:22
14 Acts 9:6
15 1 Samuel 3:9-10
16 John 11:3
17 John 11:14-15
18 John 14:12-14
19 *verily*: in truth, in fact, truly
20 Mark 11:22
21 "Therefore do not worry about tomorrow, for tomorrow will worry about its own things. Sufficient for the day is its own trouble" (Matthew 6:34, NKJV).

22 Isaiah 26:3
23 Matthew 6:11
24 Matthew 6:34

2

Prayer and Faith (Continued)

T HE GUESTS AT A *certain hotel were being rendered uncomfortable by repeated strumming on a piano, done by a little girl who possessed no knowledge of music. They complained to the proprietor with a view to having the annoyance stopped. "I am sorry you are annoyed," he said. "But the girl is the child of one of my very best guests. I can scarcely ask her not to touch the piano. But her father, who is away for a day or so, will return tomorrow. You can then approach him, and have the matter set right." When the father returned, he found his daughter in the reception-room and, as usual, thumping on the piano. He walked up behind the child and, putting his arms over her shoulders, took her hands in his, and produced some most beautiful music. Thus it may be with us, and thus it will be, some coming day. Just now we can produce little but clamor and disharmony, but one day the Lord Jesus will take hold of our hands of faith and prayer and use them to bring forth the music of the skies.* (Author unknown)

Genuine, authentic, faith must be definite and free of doubt. Not simply general in character; not a mere belief in the being, goodness, and power of God, but a faith that believes "that those things which he saith shall come to pass." As the faith is specific, so the answer is likewise definite: "He shall have whatsoever he saith."[1] Faith and prayer select the things, and God commits Himself to do the very things that faith and persevering prayer determine and petition Him to accomplish.

The American *Revised Version* [of the Bible] renders the twenty-fourth verse of the eleventh chapter of Mark, this way: "Therefore I say unto you,

All things whatsoever ye pray and ask for, believe that ye receive them, and ye shall have them." Perfect faith has always in its keeping what perfect prayer asks for. How large and unqualified is the area of operation—*the all things whatsoever!* How definite and specific the promise—*ye shall have them!*

OUR CHIEF CONCERN

Our chief concern is with our faith—the problems of its growth, and the activities of its vigorous maturity. A faith that grasps and holds in its keeping the very things it asks for, without wavering, doubt, or fear—that is the faith we need. Such faith in the process and practice of prayer is as a pearl of great price.[2]

The statement of our Lord about faith and prayer quoted above is of supreme importance. Faith must be definite and specific—an unqualified, unmistakable, request for the things asked for. It is not to be a vague, indefinite, shadowy thing. It must be something more than an abstract belief in God's willingness and ability to do for us. It is to be a definite, specific, asking for—and expecting the things for which we ask. Note how Mark 11:23 reads.

And shall not doubt in his heart, but shall believe that those things which he saith shall come to pass; he shall have whatever he saith.

Just so far as the faith and the asking is definite, so also will the answer be. The giving is not to be something other than the things prayed for—it is to be the actual things sought and named. "He shall have whatsoever he saith." It is all imperative, "He shall have." The granting is to be unlimited, both in quality and in quantity.

FAITH AND PRAYER

Faith and prayer select the subjects for petition, thereby determining what God is to do. "He shall have whatsoever he saith." God holds Himself ready to supply exactly, and fully, all the requests of faith and prayer. If the petition to God is made clear, specific, and definite, God will fill it exactly in accordance with the presented terms.

Faith is not an abstract belief in the Word of God, nor a mere mental conviction, nor a simple agreement of the understanding and will. Neither is it a passive acceptance of facts, however sacred or thorough. Faith is an operation of God, a divine illumination, a holy energy implanted by the Word of God and the Spirit in the human soul. It is a spiritual, divine principle that takes of the supernatural and makes it a thing capable of being understood by the faculties of time and sense.

FAITH DEALS WITH GOD

Faith deals with God and is conscious of God. It deals with the Lord Jesus Christ and sees in Him a Savior. It deals with God's Word, and lays hold of the truth. It deals with the Spirit of God, and is energized and inspired by His holy fire. God is the great objective of faith, for faith rests its whole weight on His Word. Faith is not an aimless act of the soul, but a looking to God and a resting upon His promises. Just as love and hope always have an objective so, also, has faith. Faith is not believing just anything; it is believing God, resting in Him, trusting His Word.

FAITH GIVES BIRTH TO PRAYER

Faith gives birth to prayer, and grows stronger, strikes deeper, rises higher, in the efforts and struggles of mighty petitioning. "Faith is the substance of things hoped for,"[3] the assurance and realization of the inheritance of the saints. Faith is also humble and persevering. It can wait and pray; it can stay on its knees, or lie in the dust. It is the one great condition of prayer. The lack of it lies at the root of all poor praying, feeble praying, little praying, unanswered praying.

THE NATURE AND MEANING OF FAITH

The nature and meaning of faith is more demonstrable in what it does than it is by reason of any definition given it. So if we turn to the record of faith given us in that great honor roll that constitutes the eleventh chapter of Hebrews, we see something of the wonderful results of faith. What a glorious list it is—one of great men and women of faith! What marvelous achievements are recorded there and set to the credit of faith! The inspired writer, exhausting his resources in cataloging the Old Testament saints who were such notable examples of wonderful faith, finally exclaims:

And what more shall I say? For the time would fail me to tell of Gideon and Barak and Samson and Jephthah, also of David and Samuel and the prophets.[4]

And then the writer of Hebrews goes on again, in a wonderful strain, telling of the unrecorded exploits brought about through the faith of the men and women of old, "of whom the world was not worthy." "All these," he says, "obtained a good report through faith." [5]

THE CHURCH NEEDS GREAT SAINTS OF MIGHTY FAITH

What a day of glorious achievements would dawn for the Church and the world if there could be reproduced a race of saints of like mighty faith, of like wonderful praying! It is not the intellectually great that the Church needs. Neither is it men and women of wealth that the times demand. It is not people of great social influence that this day requires. Above everybody and everything else, it is Christians of faith, Christians of mighty prayer, men and women like the saints and heroes listed in Hebrews, who "obtained a good report through faith," that the Church and the whole wide world of humanity needs.

Many people today obtain a good report because of their money-giving, their great mental gifts and talents. But there are few who obtain a "good report" because of their great faith in God, or because of the wonderful things that are being brought about through their great praying. Today, as much as at any time, we need men and women of great faith and who are great in prayer. These are the two cardinal virtues that make Christians great in the eyes of God, the two things that create conditions of real spiritual success in the life and work of the Church. It is our chief concern to see that we maintain a faith of the quality and structure that counts before God. A faith that grasps and holds in its keeping the things for which it asks, without doubt and without fear.

DOUBT AND FEAR

Doubt and fear are the twin foes of faith. Sometimes they actually usurp the place of faith, and although we pray, it is a restless and anxious prayer that we offer—uneasy and often complaining. Peter failed to walk on [the waters of] Gennesaret because he let the waves break over him [emotionally] and swamp the power of his faith. Taking his eyes from the Lord and looking fearfully at the water all about him, he began to sink and had to cry for help: "Lord, save me."[6]

Doubts should never be cherished, nor fears harbored. Never cherish the delusion that you are a martyr to fear and doubt. It is no credit to any Christian's mental capacity to cherish doubt of God, and no comfort can possibly derive from such a thought. Our eyes should be taken off self, removed from our own weakness, and allowed to rest implicitly upon God's strength. "Cast not away therefore your confidence, which hath great recompense of reward." A simple, confiding, faith, living day by day and casting its burden on the Lord each hour of the day will dissipate fear, drive away misgiving, and deliver from doubt:

> Be careful for nothing, but in every thing by supplication and prayer with thanksgiving let your requests be made known unto God.[7]

That is the divine cure for all fear, anxiety, and undue concern of soul—all of which are closely akin to doubt and unbelief. This is the divine prescription for securing "the peace of God, which passeth all understanding,"[8] and keeps the heart and mind in quietness and peace.

GUARD AGAINST UNBELIEF

All of us need to mark well and heed the caution given in Hebrews:

> "Take heed, brethren, lest there be in any of you an evil heart of unbelief, in departing from the living God."[9]

We need to guard against unbelief as we would against an enemy. Faith needs to be cultivated. We need to keep on praying, "Lord, increase our faith,"[10] for faith is susceptible of increase. Paul's tribute to the Thessalonians was that their faith grew exceedingly.[11] Faith is increased by exercise, by being put into use. It is nourished by painful trials.

> That the trial of your faith, being much more precious than of gold that perisheth, though it be tried with fire, might be found unto praise and honour and glory at the appearing of Jesus Christ.[12]

How faith grows

Faith grows by reading and meditating upon the Word of God. Most, and best of all, faith thrives in an atmosphere of prayer.

It would be well if all of us were to stop and ask ourselves: "Have I faith in God? Have I real faith—faith that keeps me in perfect peace about the things of earth and the things of heaven?"

This is the most important question a person can put forth and expect to be answered. But there is another question closely related to it in significance and importance: "Do I really pray to God so that He hears me and answers my prayers, and do I truly pray to God so that I get direct from God the things I ask of Him?"

Augustus Caesar and pastors

It was claimed for Augustus Caesar that he found Rome a city of wood, and left it a city of marble. Pastors who succeed in changing their people from a prayerless to a prayerful people have done a greater work than did Augustus in changing a city from wood to marble. After all, this is the prime work of pastors. Primarily, they are dealing with prayerless Christians—with Christians of whom it is said, "God is not in all their thoughts." Pastors meet such Christians everywhere, and all the time. Their main business, therefore, is to turn those Christians from being forgetful of God, from being devoid of faith, from being prayerless, so that they become Christians who habitually pray, who believe in God, remember Him, and do His will. Pastors are not sent to merely induce people to join the Church, nor merely to get them to do better. They are sent to get people to pray, to trust God, and to keep God always before their eyes so that they may not sin against Him.

The work of the ministry

The work of the ministry is to change unbelieving sinners into praying and believing saints. The call goes forth by divine authority, "Believe on the Lord Jesus Christ, and thou shalt be saved."[13] We catch a glimpse of the tremendous importance of faith and of the great value God has set upon it, when we remember that He has made it the one indispensable condition of being saved. "By grace are ye saved, through faith."[14] So when we contemplate the great importance of prayer, we find faith standing immediately by its side. By faith are we saved, and by faith we stay saved. Prayer introduces us to a life of faith. Paul declared that the life he lived, he lived by faith in the Son of God, who loved him and gave Himself for him[15]—that he walked by faith and not by sight.[16]

PRAYER DEPENDENT UPON FAITH

Prayer is absolutely dependent upon faith. It has virtually no existence apart from it, and accomplishes nothing unless it is its inseparable companion. Faith makes prayer effectual, and in a certain important sense, must precede it.

> For he that cometh to God must believe that He is, and that He is a rewarder of them that diligently seek Him.[17]

Before prayer ever starts toward God; before its petition is chosen, before its requests are made known, faith must have gone on ahead. It must have asserted its belief in the existence of God, and must have given its agreement to the gracious truth that God "is a rewarder of them that diligently seek Him." This is the primary step in praying. In this regard, while faith does not bring the blessing, yet it puts prayer in a position to ask for it. And it leads to another step toward realization by aiding the petitioner to believe that God is able and willing to bless.

FAITH STARTS PRAYER WORKING

Faith starts prayer to work—clears the way to the mercy seat. First of all, it gives assurance that there is a mercy seat, and that there our high priest awaits those who pray and their prayers. Faith opens the way for prayer to approach God. But it does more—it accompanies prayer at every step it takes. It is prayer's inseparable companion, and when requests are made to God it is faith that turns the asking into obtaining. Faith naturally follows prayer, for the spiritual life into which a believer is led by prayer is a life of faith. The one prominent characteristic of the experience into which believers are brought through prayer is not a life of works, but of faith.

FAITH MAKES PRAYER STRONG

Faith makes prayer strong, and gives it patience to wait on God. Faith believes that God is a rewarder. No truth is more clearly revealed in the Scriptures than this, and none is more encouraging. Even the closet has its promised reward: "He that seeth in secret, shall reward thee openly."[18] The most insignificant service rendered to a disciple in the name of the Lord receives its reward. To this precious truth, faith heartily agrees.

Yet faith is narrowed down to one particular thing—it does not believe that God will reward everybody, nor that He is a rewarder of all who pray, but that He is a rewarder of them that diligently seek Him. Faith rests its case on diligent prayer, and gives assurance and encouragement to diligent seekers after God, for it is they alone who are richly rewarded when they pray.

FAITH AND PRAYER INSEPARABLE

We constantly need to be reminded that faith is the one inseparable condition of successful praying. There are other considerations entering into the exercise, but faith is the final, indispensable, condition of true praying. As it is written in a familiar, primary, declaration: "Without faith, it is impossible to please Him."[19] James puts this truth very plainly.

If any of you lack wisdom, let him ask of God, that giveth to all men liberally, and upbraideth not, and it shall be given him. But let him ask in faith, nothing wavering. For he that wavereth is like a wave of the sea driven with the wind and tossed. For let not that man think that he shall receive any thing of the Lord.[20]

DOUBTING HINDERS EFFECTIVE PRAYER

Doubting is always forbidden because it stands as an enemy to faith and hinders effective praying. In his first epistle to Timothy, Paul gives us an invaluable truth about the conditions of successful praying. He says, "I will therefore that men pray everywhere, lifting up holy hands, without wrath and doubting."[21]

All questioning must be watched for and avoided. Fear and uncertainty have no place in true praying. Faith must assert itself and command these enemies of prayer to depart.

Too much authority cannot be attributed to faith, but prayer is the scepter by which it communicates its power. There is much spiritual wisdom in the following advice written by an eminent old divine.

"Would you be freed from the bondage to corruption?" he asks. "Would you grow in grace in general and grow in grace in particular? If you would, your way is plain. Ask of God more faith. Beg of Him morning, and noon and night, while you walk by the way, while you sit in the house, when you lie down and when you rise up. Beg of Him simply to impress divine things more deeply on your heart, to give you more and more of the substance of things hoped for and of the evidence of things not seen."[22]

THE SCRIPTURES ENCOURAGE PRAYER

Great incentives to pray are furnished in the holy Scriptures, and our Lord closes His teaching about prayer with the assurance and promise of heaven.[23] The presence of Jesus Christ in heaven, the preparation for His saints that He is making there, and the assurance that He will come again to receive them[24] greatly help the weariness of praying, strengthen its conflicts, and sweeten its difficult work! These things are the star of hope to prayer, the wiping away of its tears, the putting of the fragrance of heaven into the bitterness of its cry. The spirit of a pilgrim makes praying easier. An earth-bound, earth-satisfied, spirit cannot pray. In a heart like that the flame of spiritual desire has either gone out or is burning faintly. The wings of its faith are clipped, its eyes are filmed, its tongue silenced. But those who wait continually upon the Lord in unswerving faith and unceasing prayer, do renew their strength, do mount up with wings as eagles, do run and are not weary, do walk and not faint.[25]

Endnotes

1 Mark 11:23
2 Matthew 13:46
3 Hebrews 11:1
4 Hebrews 11:32, NKJV
5 Hebrews 11:38-39
6 Matthew 14:30
7 Philippians 4:6
8 Philippians 4:7
9 Hebrews 3:12
10 Luke 17:5
11 2 Thessalonians 1:3
12 1 Peter 1:7
13 Acts 16:31
14 Ephesians 2:8
15 Galatians 2:20 (KVJ says, "the faith of the son of God")
16 2 Corinthians 5:7
17 Hebrews 11:6
18 Matthew 6:4
19 Hebrews 11:6
20 James 1:5-7
21 1 Timothy 2:8
22 Hebrews 11:1
23 Probably Matthew 6:20-21
24 John 14:1-3
25 Isaiah 40:31

3

Prayer and Trust

ONE EVENING I LEFT *my office in New York, with a bitterly cold wind in my face. I had with me, (as I thought) my thick, warm muffler, but when I proceeded to button-up against the storm, I found that it was gone. I turned back, looked along the streets, searched my office, but in vain. I realized, then, that I must have dropped it, and prayed God that I might find it; for such was the state of the weather, that it would be running a great risk to proceed without it. I looked, again, up and down the surrounding streets, but without success. Suddenly, I saw a man on the opposite side of the road holding out something in his hand. I crossed over and asked him if that was my muffler? He handed it to me saying, "It was blown to me by the wind." He who rides upon the storm, had used the wind as a means of answering prayer. (William Horst)*

Prayer does not stand alone. It is not an isolated duty and independent principle. It lives in association with other Christian duties, is wedded to other principles, and is a partner with other graces. But prayer is inseparably joined to faith. Faith gives prayer color and tone, shapes its character, and secures its results.

Trust is faith that has become absolute, confirmed, and completed. When all is said and done, there is a sort of uncertain undertaking in faith and its exercise. But trust is firm belief, it is faith in full flower. Trust is a conscious act, a fact that we are aware of. According to the scriptural concept, it is the eye of the new-born soul, and the ear of the renewed soul. It is the feeling of the soul—the spiritual eye, the ear, the taste, the feeling.

All these have to do with trust. How bright, distinct, conscious, powerful, and above all scriptural is such a trust! How different from many forms of modern belief, that are so feeble, dry, and cold! These new faith movements bring no consciousness of their presence, no "Joy unspeakable and full of glory"[1] results from their exercise. For the most part they are adventures in the uncertainties of the soul. There is no safe and sure trust in anything. The whole transaction takes place in the realm of maybe and perhaps.

TRUST IS MORE THAN FEELING

Trust, like life, is feeling, though much more than feeling. An unfelt life is a contradiction, and an unfelt trust is a wrong name, a delusion, a contradiction. Trust is the most felt of all attributes. It is all feeling, and it works only by love. An unfelt love is as impossible as an unfelt trust. The trust that we are now speaking about is a conviction. An unfelt conviction? How absurd!

Trust sees God doing things here and now. But even more. It rises to a high place, and looking into the invisible and eternal realizes that God has done things—and regards those things as being already done. Trust brings eternity into the history and happenings of time, transforms the substance of hope into realization, and changes promise into present possession. We know when we trust just like we know when we see, just like we are conscious of our sense of touch. Trust sees, receives, holds. Trust is its own witness.

OFTEN FAITH IS TOO WEAK

Yet, quite often faith is too weak to immediately obtain God's greatest good. So it has to wait in loving, strong, prayerful, earnest obedience, until it grows in strength, and is able to bring the eternal down into the realms of experience and time.

To this purpose, trust masses all its forces. Then here it holds.[2] And in the struggle, trust's grasp becomes mightier and embraces for itself all that God has done for it in His eternal wisdom and abundance of grace.

In the matter of waiting in mighty prayer, faith rises to its highest level and becomes indeed the gift of God. It becomes the blessed condition and expression of the soul, which is obtained by a constant communion with God and untiring petition to Him.

Jesus Christ clearly taught that faith was the condition on which prayer was answered. When our Lord had cursed the fig tree, the disciples were very surprised that the tree had actually withered, and their remarks indicated their disbelief. It was then that Jesus said to them, "Have faith in God."

For verily I say unto you, That whosoever shall say unto this mountain, Be thou removed, and be thou cast into the sea, and shall not doubt in his heart, but shall believe that those things which he saith shall come to pass, he shall have whatsoever he saith. Therefore I say unto you, What things soever ye desire, when ye pray, believe that ye receive them, and ye shall have them.

TRUST GROWS MOST THROUGH PRAYER

There is nowhere that trust grows so readily and richly as in the prayer closet. Its growth and development are rapid and wholesome when prayers are kept regularly and well. When these times of prayer are vigorous and full and free, trust grows exceedingly.[3] The eye and presence of God give vigorous life to trust, just as the eye and presence of the sun make fruit and flower grow, and all things become glad and bright with fuller life.

"Have faith in God" and "trust in the Lord"[4] form the keynote and foundation of prayer. Primarily, it is not trust in the Word of God, but rather trust in the person of God.[5] For trust in the person of God must precede trust in the Word of God. "Ye believe in God, believe also in Me,"[6] is the demand our Lord makes on the personal trust of His disciples. The person of Jesus Christ must be central to the eye of trust. Jesus sought to impress this great truth upon Martha when her brother lay dead in their home at Bethany. Martha asserted her belief in her brother's resurrection.

Martha saith unto Him, "I know that he shall rise again in the resurrection at the last day.[7]"

Jesus then lifts her trust clear above the mere fact of resurrection to His own person by telling her:

I am the resurrection, and the life: he that believeth in Me, though he were dead, yet shall he live: And whosoever liveth and believeth in Me shall never die. Believest thou this? She saith unto Him, 'Yea, Lord: I believe that Thou art the Christ, the Son of God, which should come into the world.'[8]

Trust in a historical fact or a mere record may be a very passive thing, but trust in a person invigorates the quality, develops it, and infuses it with love. The trust that infuses prayer centers in a Person.

Trust goes even further than this. The trust that inspires our prayer must be not only trust in the person of God, and of Christ, but in their ability and willingness to grant the thing prayed for. It is not only, "Trust ye in the LORD," but, also, "for in the LORD Jehovah is everlasting strength."[9]

The trust that our Lord taught as a condition of effective prayer is not of the head but of the heart. It is trust that "does not doubt not in his heart."[10] Such trust has the divine assurance that it shall be honored with large and satisfying answers. The strong promise of our Lord brings faith down to the present, and counts on a present answer.

DO WE BELIEVE WITHOUT A DOUBT?

When we pray, do we believe that we receive the answer then and there, and not just sometime in the future? That is the teaching of this inspiring Scripture. How we need to pray, "Lord, increase our faith,"[11] until doubt be gone and unquestioning trust claims the promised blessings as its very own.

This is no easy condition. It is reached only after many failures, after much praying, waiting, after many trials of faith. May our faith increase until we realize and receive all the fullness that there is in the name of Jesus Christ, which guarantees to do so much.

TRUST IS THE FOUNDATION OF PRAYING

Our Lord puts trust as the very foundation of praying. The background of prayer is trust. The whole of Christ's ministry and work was dependent on unquestioning trust in His Father. The center of trust is God. Mountains of difficulties and all hindrances to prayer are moved out of the way by trust and its powerful helper—faith. When trust is perfect and without doubt, prayer is simply the outstretched hand expecting to receive. Trust perfected, is prayer perfected. Trust looks to receive the thing asked for—and gets it. Trust is not a belief that God can bless, that He will bless, but that He does bless, here and now. Trust always operates in the present tense. Hope looks toward the future. Trust looks to the present. Hope expects. Trust possesses. Trust receives what prayer acquires. So what prayer needs at all times is abiding and abundant trust.

The disciples woeful lack of trust and resulting failure to do what they were sent out to do,[12] is seen in the case of the lunatic son. He was brought by his father to nine of the disciples while their Master was on the Mount of Transfiguration. A boy who was sadly afflicted was brought to these men to be cured of his sickness. They had been commissioned to do this very kind of work. This was a part of their mission. They attempted to cast out the demon from the boy but conspicuously failed. The demon was too much for them. They were humiliated at their failure and filled with shame, while their enemies were in triumph. During the confusion caused by their failure, Jesus draws near. He is informed of the circumstances,[13] and told of the conditions connected with the problem. Here is the succeeding account:

> He answereth him, and saith, O faithless generation, how long shall I be with you? how long shall I suffer you? bring him unto me. And they brought him unto him: and when he saw him, straightway the spirit tare him; and he fell on the ground, and wallowed foaming. And he asked his father, How long is it ago since this came unto him? And he said, Of a child. And ofttimes it hath cast him into

the fire, and into the waters, to destroy him: but if thou canst do any thing, have compassion on us, and help us. Jesus said unto him, If thou canst believe, all things are possible to him that believeth. And straightway the father of the child cried out, and said with tears, Lord, I believe; help thou mine unbelief. When Jesus saw that the people came running together, he rebuked the foul spirit, saying unto him, Thou dumb and deaf spirit, I charge thee, come out of him, and enter no more into him. And the spirit cried, and rent him sore, and came out of him: and he was as one dead; insomuch that many said, He is dead. But Jesus took him by the hand, and lifted him up; and he arose. And when he was come into the house, his disciples asked him privately, Why could not we cast him out? And he said unto them, This kind can come forth by nothing, but by prayer and fasting.[14]

WHERE WAS THE DIFFICULTY WITH THESE DISCIPLES?

They had neglected cultivating their faith by prayer [and fasting], and so their trust utterly failed. They did not trust God, or Christ, or the authenticity of His mission, or their own. It has been that way many times since, in many crises in God's Church. Failure has resulted from a lack of trust and a weakness of faith—and both caused by a neglect of prayer. Many failures in revival efforts have been traceable to the same cause. Faith had not been nurtured and made powerful by prayer. Neglect of the inner chamber is the solution of most spiritual failure. This is as true of our personal struggles with the devil as was the case when we went forth to attempt to cast out demons. Being much on our knees in private communion with God is the only guarantee that we will have Him with us in our personal struggles or in our efforts to convert sinners.

Whenever people came to Him, our Lord put trust in Him and the divinity of His mission in the forefront. He gave no definition of trust, and provided no theological discussion or analysis of it. He knew that people would see what faith was by what faith did. They would see from its free exercise that trust grew up spontaneously in His presence. It was the product of His work, His power, and His Person. These furnished and created an atmosphere most favorable for its exercise and development. Trust is altogether too splendidly simple for verbal definition, and too hearty and spontaneous for theological terminology. The very simplicity of trust is that which staggers many people. They look away for some great thing to come to pass, while all the time "the word is nigh thee, even in thy mouth, and in thy heart."[15]

PRAYER ASKED, FAITH RECEIVED

When the saddening news of his daughter's death was brought to Jairus, our Lord said, "Be not afraid, only believe."[16]

To the woman with the issue of blood, who stood tremblingly before Him, He said, "Daughter, thy faith hath made thee whole; go in peace, and be whole of thy plague."[17]

As the two blind men followed Him, pressing their way into the house, He said, "According to your faith be it unto you. And their eyes were opened."[18]

When the paralytic was let down through the roof of the house where Jesus was teaching and placed before Him by four of his friends, it is recorded this way: "And Jesus seeing their faith said unto the sick of the palsy; Son, be of good cheer; thy sins be forgiven thee."[19]

When Jesus dismissed the centurion whose servant was seriously ill, and who had come to Jesus with the prayer that He speak the healing word, without even going to his house, He did it this way: "And Jesus said unto the centurion, Go thy way; and as thou hast believed, so be it done unto thee. And his servant was healed in the selfsame hour."[20]

When the poor leper fell at the feet of Jesus and cried out for relief, "Lord, if Thou wilt, Thou canst make me clean,"[21] Jesus immediately granted his request, and the man glorified Him with a loud voice. Then Jesus said to him, "Arise, go thy way; thy faith hath made thee whole."[22]

The Syrophenician woman came to Jesus about her afflicted daughter, making the case her own with the prayer, "Lord, help me," and persisted in a heroic struggle of faith. Jesus honors her faith and prayer, saying, "O woman, great is thy faith: be it unto thee even as thou wilt. And her daughter was made whole from that very hour."[23]

After the disciples had utterly failed to cast the devil out of the epileptic boy, the father of the stricken lad came to Jesus with the sad and almost despairing cry, "If Thou canst do anything, have compassion on us and help us." But Jesus replied, "If thou canst believe, all things are possible to him that believeth."[24]

Blind Bartimaeus sitting by the wayside hears our Lord is passing by, and cries out pitifully and almost despairingly, "Jesus, Thou son of David, have mercy on me."[25] The keen ears of our Lord immediately catch the sound of prayer, and after healing him, He says, "Go thy way; thy faith hath made thee whole. And immediately he received his sight, and followed Jesus in the way."[26]

To the weeping penitent woman washing His feet with her tears and wiping them with the hair of her head, Jesus speaks cheering, soul-comforting, words: "Thy faith hath saved thee; go in peace."[27]

One day Jesus healed ten lepers at one time in answer to their united prayer, "Jesus, Master, have mercy on us." He told them to go and show themselves to the priests. "And it came to pass, that, as they went, they were cleansed."[28]

Endnotes

1 1 Peter 1:8
2 Ephesians 6:13-14
3 2 Thessalonians 1:3
4 Philippians 2:19, 24
5 Romans 4:20-21
6 John 14:1
7 John 11:24
8 John 11:25-27
9 Isaiah 26:4
10 Mark 11:23
11 Luke 17:5
12 Matthew 10:1; Mark 3:15; Luke 9:1
13 Mark 9:17-18
14 Mark 9:19-29
15 Romans 10:8
16 Mark 5:36
17 Mark 5:34
18 Matthew 9:29-30
19 Matthew 9:2
20 Matthew 8:13
21 Matthew 8:2
22 Luke 17:19 — This is from the story of the ten lepers, not the story of the one leper recorded in Matthew.
23 Matthew 15:28
24 Mark 9:23
25 Mark 10:47
26 Mark 10:52
27 Luke 7:50
28 Luke 17:14

4

Prayer and Desire

THERE ARE THOSE WHO *will mock me, and tell me to stick to my trade as a cobbler, and not trouble my mind with philosophy and theology. But the truth of God did so burn in my bones, that I took my pen in hand and began to set down what I had seen.* (Jacob Behmen)

Desire is not merely a simple wish, it is a deep seated craving, an intense onging for attainment. In the realm of spiritual affairs, it is an important accompaniment to prayer. It is so important that one might almost say that desire is an absolute essential of prayer. Desire precedes prayer, accompanies it, is followed by it. Desire goes before prayer, and is created and intensified by it. Prayer is the oral expression of desire. If prayer is asking God for something, then prayer must be expressed. Prayer comes out into the open. Desire is silent. Prayer is heard, desire is unheard. The deeper the desire, the stronger the prayer. Without desire, prayer is a meaningless mumble of words. Indifferent formal praying with no heart, no feeling, no real desire accompanying it, is to be shunned like a pestilence. Its exercise is a waste of precious time, and no real blessing is gained from it.

PRAY EVEN IF DESIRE IS ABSENT

Nevertheless, even if it is discovered that desire is honestly absent, we should pray anyway. We should pray. The "should" comes in so that both desire and expression are cultivated. God's Word commands it. Our judgment tells us we should pray—to pray whether we feel like it or not—and not to allow our feelings to determine our habits of prayer. In such circumstance, we should pray for the desire to pray, for such a desire is God-given and heaven-born. We should pray for desire. Then, when desire has been given, we should pray according to its dictates. Lack of spiritual desire should grieve us, and lead us to mourn its absence. We should seek earnestly that it be given so that our praying from then on will be an expression of "the soul's sincere desire."

A sense of need creates, or should create, earnest desire. The stronger the sense of need before God, the greater should be the desire, and more earnest the prayer. The "poor in spirit"[1] are the most competent to pray.

Hunger is an active sense of physical need. It prompts the request for bread. In the same way, the inward consciousness of spiritual need creates desire, and desire expresses itself in prayer. Desire is an inward longing for something that we do not possess and that we need. It is something that God has promised, and that we may obtain by earnest prayer at His throne of grace.[2]

SPIRITUAL DESIRE IS EVIDENCE OF THE NEW BIRTH

Carried to a higher degree, spiritual desire is the evidence of the new birth. It is born in the renewed soul: "As newborn babes, desire the sincere milk of the word, that ye may grow thereby."[3]

The absence of this holy desire in the heart is reasonable proof that there has been either a decline in spiritual joy, or that the new birth has never taken place. "Blessed are they which do hunger and thirst after righteousness: for they shall be filled."[4]

These heaven-given appetites are the proof of a renewed heart—the evidence of a stirring spiritual life. Physical appetites are the attributes of a living body, not a corpse. Spiritual desires belong to a soul made alive to God. As the renewed soul hungers and thirsts after righteousness, these holy inward desires break out into earnest, petitioning, prayer.

In prayer we are shut up to the name, merit, and intercessory virtue of Jesus Christ, our great High Priest. Probing down below the accompanying conditions and forces in prayer, we come to its vital basis, which is found in the human heart. It is not simply our need, it is the heart's yearning for what we need, and for which we feel impelled to pray. Desire is the will in action. It is a strong, conscious, longing, that is aroused in the inner nature for some great good. Desire exalts the object of its longing, and fixes the mind on it. It has choice, focus, and fire in it. Based on these, prayer is clearly stated and specific. It knows its need, feels and sees the thing that will meet it, and hurries to obtain it.

PRAYER HELPED BY DEVOUT MEDITATION

Holy desire is greatly helped by devout meditation. Meditation on our spiritual need, and on God's readiness and ability to supply it,[5] helps desire to grow. Engaging in serious thought before praying increases desire, makes it more insistent, and tends to save us from the menace of private prayer—wandering thoughts. We fail much more in desire than in its outward expression. We keep the form while the inner life fades and almost dies.

One might well ask whether the weakness of our desires for God, the Holy Spirit, and for all the fullness of Christ, is not the reason for our little praying? Do we really feel these inward yearning of desire after heavenly treasures? Do the inbred groanings[6] of desire stir our souls to mighty wrestlings? How sad for us! The fire burns altogether too low. The flaming heat of the soul has been turned down until it is barely lukewarm. It should be noted that this was the central cause of the sad and desperate condition of the Laodicean Christians. Of them, the awful condemnation is written that they were, "rich, and increased in goods and had need of nothing," and yet did not know that they "were wretched, and miserable, and poor, and blind."[7]

HAVE WE A BURNING DESIRE IN PRAYER?

Again, we might well ask, "have we that desire that presses us to close communion with God, that is filled with unutterable burnings, and that holds us there through the agony of an intense and soul-stirred petition? Our hearts very much need to be worked over, not only to get the evil out of them, but to get the good into them. The foundation and inspiration of the incoming good is strong, driving, desire. This holy and burning fire in the soul awakens the interest of heaven, attracts the attention of God, and places the exhaustless riches of divine grace at the disposal of those who have it.

The dampening of the fire of holy desire is destructive to the vital and aggressive forces in Church life. God requires that He be represented by a fiery Church, or He is not in any proper sense, represented at all. God Himself is all on fire.[8] So if His Church is to be like Him, it must also be at white heat. The only things about which His Church can afford to be on fire are the great and eternal interests of heaven-born, God-given, Christianity. Yet holy desire does not need to be loud and noisy to be consuming. Our Lord was the incarnate opposite of nervous excitability, the absolute opposite of intolerant or clamorous speech, yet the zeal of God's house consumed Him. The world is still feeling the glow of His fierce, consuming, fire, and responding to it with an ever-increasing readiness and response.

A lack of zeal in prayer is the sure sign of a lack of depth and of intensity of desire. The absence of intense desire is a sure sign of God's absence from the heart! To decrease fervor is to withdraw from God. He can, and does, tolerate many things in the way of infirmity and error in His children. He can, and will pardon sin when a repentant person prays. But two things He will not tolerate—insincerity and lukewarmness. Lack of heart and lack of heat are two things He loathes, and to the Laodiceans He said, in terms of unmistakable severity and condemnation, "I would thou wert cold or hot. So then because thou art lukewarm, and neither cold nor hot, I will spue thee out of My mouth."[9]

GOD'S JUDGMENT FOR LACK OF FIRE

This was God's expressed judgment on the lack of fire in one of the seven churches. It is also His indictment against individual Christians for the fatal lack of sacred zeal. In prayer, fire is the motivating power. Religious principles that do not come out of fire have neither force nor effect. Fire is the wing on which faith ascends. Red hot fervency is the soul of prayer. It was the "fervent, effectual prayer"[10] that availed much. Love is kindled in a flame, and passion is its life. Fire is the air that true Christian experience breathes. It feeds on fire, and can withstand anything but a feeble flame. It dies chilled and starved to its core when the surrounding atmosphere is lukewarm or cold.

TRUE PRAYER MUST BE ON FIRE

Christian life and character need to be all on fire. Lack of spiritual heat creates more unfaithfulness than lack of faith. Not to be overwhelmingly interested in the things of heaven is not to be interested in them at all. The fiery souls are those who conquer in the day of battle. They are those from whom the kingdom of heaven permits violence, and who take it by force.[11] The citadel of God is taken only by those who storm it in dreadful earnestness, and besiege it with fiery, unceasing, zeal.

Nothing short of being red hot for God can keep the glow of heaven in our hearts these chilly days. The early Methodists had no heating apparatus in their churches. They said that the flame in the pew and the fire in the pulpit must be sufficient to keep them warm. In this day and age, we need to have the live coal from God's altar and the consuming flame from heaven glowing in our hearts. This flame is not mental power or fleshly energy. It is intense, dross-removing, divine fire in the soul.[12] It is the very essence of the Spirit of God.

No extensive learning, no purity of diction, no width of mental outlook, no flowers of fine speech, no grace of person, can make up for lack of fire. Prayer ascends by fire. Fire gives prayer access as well as wings, acceptance as well as energy. There is no incense without fire—and no prayer without it.

STRONG DESIRE IS THE BASIS OF UNCEASING PRAYER

It is not a shallow, fickle, inclination, but a strong yearning, an unquenchable desire that impregnates, glows, burns, and fixes the heart. It is the flame of a present and active principle mounting up to God. It is zeal propelled by desire that burns its way to the throne of grace[13] and obtains its petition. It is the persistence of desire that gives triumph to the conflict in a great struggle of prayer.[14] It is the burden of a heavy desire that sobers, makes restless, and reduces to silence the soul that has just emerged from mighty wrestlings. It is the embracing character of desire that arms prayer with a thousand pleas, and robes it with an invincible courage and an all-conquering power.

The Syrophenician woman is an object lesson of desire, set in its need, and unstoppable in its intensity and unyielding boldness. The persistent widow represents desire gaining its end through obstacles impossible to weaker motives.[15]

STRONG DESIRE REFUSES TO LET GO

Prayer is not the rehearsal of a mere performance. Neither is it an indefinite, scattered, petition. Desire kindles the soul and holds it to the thing it is seeking. Prayer is an essential phase of spiritual habit, but it ceases to be prayer when carried on by habit alone. It is depth and intensity of spiritual desire that give intensity and depth to prayer. The soul cannot be lazy when some great desire fires and inflames it. The urgency of our desire holds us to the thing we desire with a tenacity that refuses to be lessened or loosened. It stays and pleads and persists, and refuses to let go until the blessing has been granted.

> Lord, I cannot let Thee go,
> Till a blessing Thou bestow;
> Do not turn away Thy face;
> Mine's an urgent, pressing, case.

WEAKNESS OF SPIRITUAL DESIRE

The secret of timidity, lack of insistent petitions, and lack of courage and strength in prayer, lies in the weakness of spiritual desire. Not praying is the fearful sign of that desire having ceased to live. That person whose desire for God no longer presses into the inner chamber, has turned from Him. There can be no successful praying without consuming desire. Of course, there can be much seeming to pray without desire of any kind.

Many things may be listed and much ground covered. But does desire compile the list? Does desire map out the region to be covered? On the answer hangs the issue of whether our petitioning is babbling or prayer. Desire is intense, but narrow; it cannot spread itself over a wide area. It wants a few things, but it wants them badly. So badly, in fact, that nothing but God's willingness to answer can bring it relief or content.

DESIRE FOCUSES ON A SINGLE OBJECTIVE

There may be many things desired, but they are specifically and individually felt and expressed. David did not yearn for everything; nor did he allow his desires to spread out everywhere and hit nothing. Here is the way his desires ran and found expression: "One thing have I desired of the Lord, that will I seek after; that I may dwell in the house of the Lord all the days of my life, to behold the beauty of the Lord, and to enquire in His temple."[16]

It is this singleness of desire, this definite yearning, that counts in praying, and drives prayer directly to the core and center of supply.

In the Beatitudes Jesus voiced the words that directly bear upon the inborn desires of a renewed soul, and the promise that they will be granted: "Blessed are they which do hunger and thirst after righteousness: for they shall be filled."[17]

This, then, is the basis of prayer that compels an answer—that strong inward desire has entered into the spiritual appetite, and demands to be satisfied. Alas for us! It is altogether too true and frequent that our prayers operate in the dry region of a mere wish, or in the leafless area of a memorized prayer. Sometimes our prayers are merely overused expressions of set phrases and traditional elements, out of which the freshness and life left many years ago.

Without desire there is no burden of soul, no sense of need, no passion, no vision, no strength, no glow of faith. There is no mighty pressure, no holding on to God with a deathless, despairing, grasp: "I will not let Thee go, except Thou bless me."[18] There is no total self-abandonment as there was with Moses. Lost in the grip of a desperate, uncontrollable, and all-consuming plea, he cried: "Yet now, if Thou wilt forgive their sin—; and if not, blot me, I pray Thee, out of Thy book which Thou has written."[19] Or as there was with John Knox when he pleaded, "Give me Scotland, or I die!"

God draws close to the praying soul

God draws extremely near to the praying soul. To see God, to know God, and to live for God—these form the objective of all true praying. So, praying is, after all, inspired to seek after God. Prayer desire is on fire to see God, and to have clearer, fuller, sweeter, and richer revelations of God. To those who so pray, the Bible becomes a new Bible and Christ a new Savior by the light and revelation of the inner chamber.

We repeat and repeat again, that burning desire—ever increasing—for the best and most powerful gifts and graces of the Spirit of God, is the legitimate heritage of true and effectual praying. Self and service cannot be divorced. They cannot possibly be separated. More than that, desire must be made intensely personal and centered on God with an insatiable hungering and thirsting after Him and His righteousness. "My soul thirsteth for God, the living God."[20] The indispensable requirement for all true praying is a deeply seated desire that seeks after God Himself, and remains unsatisfied until the choicest gifts in heaven have been richly and abundantly granted.

Endnotes

1 Matthew 5:3
2 Hebrews 4:16
3 I Peter 2:2
4 Matthew 5:6
5 Philippians 4:19
6 Romans 8:26
7 Revelation 3:17
8 Hebrews 12:29
9 Revelation 3:15-16
10 James 5:16
11 Matthew 11:12
12 Proverbs 25:4, Isaiah 1:25
13 Hebrews 4:16
14 Luke 11:5-8, 18:1-8
15 Matthew 15:22-28
16 Psalm 27:4
17 Matthew 5:6
18 Genesis 32:26
19 Exodus 32:32
20 Psalm 42:2

5

Prayer and Fervency

S T. TERESA ROSE OFF *her deathbed to finish her work. She inspected, with all her quickness of eye and love of order the whole of the house in which she had been carried to die. She saw everything put into its proper place, and every one answering to their proper order, after which she attended the divine offices of the day. She then went back to her bed, summoned her daughters around her . . . and, with the most penitential of David's penitential prayers upon her tongue, Teresa of Jesus went forth to meet her Bridegroom.*
(Alexander Whyte)

Prayer without intense feeling stakes nothing on the issue, because it has nothing to stake. It comes with empty hands. Hands that are listless as well as empty, and that have never learned the lesson of clinging to the Cross.

Passionless prayer, prayer that lacks fervency, has no heart in it—it is an empty thing, an unfit vessel. Heart, soul, and life must find place in all real praying. Heaven must be made to feel the force of this crying unto God.

Paul was a notable example of a person who possessed a fervent spirit of prayer. His petitioning was all-consuming, centered immovably upon the object of his desire and the God who was able to meet it.

PRAYERS MUST BE RED HOT

It is the fervent prayer that is effective and that prevails. Coldness of spirit hinders praying—prayer cannot live in a cold atmosphere. Chilly surroundings freeze out petitioning, and dry up the springs of supplication. It takes fire to make prayers go. A warm soul creates an atmosphere favorable to prayer, because it is favorable to fervency. Prayer ascends to heaven by fire. Yet fire is not commotion, and heat is not noise. Heat is intensity—something that glows and burns. Heaven is a mighty poor market for ice.

GOD WANTS WARM-HEARTED SERVANTS

The Holy Spirit comes as a fire to dwell in us. We are to be baptized with the Holy Ghost and with fire.[1] Fervency is warmth of soul. An unemotional temperament is highly detrimental to vital experience. If our religion does not set us on fire, it is because we have frozen hearts. God dwells in a flame,[2] the Holy Ghost descends in fire.[3] To be absorbed in God's will, to be so greatly in earnest about doing it that our whole being takes fire, is the qualifying condition of the person who would engage in effective prayer.

Our Lord warns us against feeble praying. "Men ought always to pray, and not to faint."[4] That means we are to have enough fervency to carry us through the severe and long periods of pleading prayer. Fire makes us alert and vigilant, and brings us through more than conquerors.[5] The atmosphere about us is too heavily charged with resisting forces for limp and lazy prayers to make headway. It takes heat, and fervency, and meteoric fire to push through to the upper heavens where God dwells with His saints in light.[6]

Many of the great Bible characters were notable examples of fervency of spirit when seeking God. The Psalmist declares with great earnestness: "My soul breaketh for the longing that it hath unto Thy judgments at all times."[7] What strong desires of heart are here! What earnest soul longings for the Word of the living God!

An even greater fervency is expressed by him in another place: "As the hart panteth after the water brooks, so panteth my soul after Thee, O God. My soul thirsteth for God, for the living God: when shall I come and appear before God?"[8] That is the word of a man who lived in a state of grace that had been deeply and supernaturally created in his soul.

FERVENCY COUNTS BEFORE GOD IN PRAYER

Fervency before God counts in the hour of prayer, and finds a speedy and rich reward at His hands. The Psalmist gives us this statement of what God had done for the king as his heart turned toward his Lord: "Thou hast given him his heart's desire, and hast not withholden the request of his lips."[9]

At another time, he addressed himself directly to God in making his request: "Lord, all my desire is before Thee; and my groaning is not hid from Thee."[10]

What an encouraging thought! Our inward groanings, our secret desires, our heart-longings, are not hidden from the eyes of Him with whom we have to deal in prayer. The motivation to fervency of spirit before God is precisely the same as it is for continued and earnest prayer.

While fervency is not prayer, yet it comes from an earnest soul and is precious in the sight of God. Fervency in prayer is the forerunner of what God will do by way of answer. God stands pledged to give us the desire of our hearts in proportion to the fervency of spirit we exhibit when seeking His face in prayer.

FERVENCY COMES FROM THE HEART

Fervency is located in the heart, not in the brain or the intellectual faculties of the mind. Fervency, therefore, is not an expression of the intellect. Fervency of spirit is something that is far above poetical fancy or sentimental imagery. It is something else besides mere selection that contrasts like with dislike. Fervency is the throb and movement of the emotional nature.

It is not in our power, perhaps, to create fervency of spirit at will, but we can ask God to implant it. Then it is ours to nourish and cherish, to guard against extinction, to prevent its reduction in amount or decline in quality. The process of personal salvation is not only to pray, to express our desires to God, but to acquire a fervent spirit and seek by all proper means to cultivate it. It is never out of place to ask God to create within us and keep alive the spirit of fervent prayer.

FERVENCY HAS TO DO WITH GOD

Fervency has to do with God, just as prayer has to do with Him. Desire always has an objective. If we desire at all, we desire something. The degree of zeal with which we fashion our spiritual desires, will always serve to determine the earnestness of our praying. In this relation, Adoniram Judson says:

> A travailing spirit, the throes of a great burdened desire, belongs to prayer. A fervency strong enough to drive away sleep, which devotes and inflames the spirit, and which retires all earthly ties, all this belongs to wrestling, prevailing prayer. The Spirit, the power, the air, and food of prayer is in such a spirit.

Prayer must be clothed with fervency, strength, and power. When centered on God, it is the force that determines the amount of Himself He gives for earthly good. Christians who are fervent in spirit are determined to attain righteousness, truth, grace, and all other sublime and powerful graces that adorn the character of the authentic, unquestioned, child of God.[11]

By the mouth of the prophet Hanani, God once declared the following message to Asa king of Judah, who at one time had been true to Him but had lost his faith because of success and material prosperity: "The eyes of the Lord run to and fro throughout the whole earth, to shew Himself strong in the behalf of them whose heart is perfect toward Him. Herein hast thou done foolishly: therefore from henceforth thou shalt have wars."[12]

God had heard Asa's prayer in early life, but because he had given up the life of prayer and simple faith disaster and trouble came.

STRIVE IN PRAYER

In Romans 15:30, we have the word "strive" in the request that Paul made for prayers for his work. "Now I beseech you, brethren, for the Lord Jesus Christ's sake, and for the love of the Spirit, that ye strive together with me in your prayers to God for me."

In Colossians 4:12, we have the same word, but translated differently: "Epaphras, who is one of you, a servant of Christ, saluteth you, always labouring fervently for you in prayers." Paul charged the Romans to "strive together with him in prayer"—that is, to help him in his struggle of prayer. The word means to enter into a contest, to fight against adversaries. It also means to exert strong effort or energy to obtain something.

TRUST TAKES OVER FROM FAITH

These recorded instances of the exercise and reward of faith, let us easily see that in almost every instance faith was united with trust until the former was swallowed up in the latter. It is hard to properly distinguish the specific activities of these two qualities, faith and trust. But without question there is a point at which faith is relieved of its burden, so to speak. It is a point where trust comes along and says, "You have done your part, the rest is mine!"

In the incident of the barren fig tree, our Lord transfers the marvelous power of faith to His disciples. To their exclamation, "How soon is the fig tree withered away!" He replied:

If ye have faith, and doubt not, ye shall not only do this which is done to the fig tree, but also if ye shall say unto this mountain, Be thou removed, and be thou cast into the sea; it shall be done. And all things, whatsoever ye shall ask in prayer, believing, ye shall receive."[13]

When Christian believers obtain faith of such magnificent proportions as these, they enter the realm of unquestioning trust. They stand without a tremor on the highest point of their spiritual outreach. They have attained faith's genuine top stone—unswerving, unalterable, unalienable trust in the power of the living God.

Endnotes

1 Luke 3:16
2 Deuteronomy 4:24; Hebrews 12:29
3 Acts 2:1-4

4 Luke 18:1
5 Romans 8:37
6 Colossians 1:12
7 Psalm 119:20
8 Psalm 42:1-2
9 Psalm 21:2
10 Psalm 38:9
11 Philippians 3:12-16
12 2 Chronicles 16:9
13 Matthew 21:21-22

6

Persistent Prayer

HOW GLIBLY WE TALK *of praying without ceasing! Yet we are quite apt to quit, if our prayer remains unanswered but one week or month! We assume that by a stroke of His arm or an action of His will, God will give us what we ask. It never seems to dawn on us, that He is the Master of nature, as of grace, and that, sometimes He chooses one way, and sometimes another in which to do His work. It takes years, sometimes, to answer a prayer and when it is answered, and we look backward we can see that it was. But God knows all the time, and it is His will that we pray, and pray, and still pray, and so come to know, what it is to pray without ceasing.* (Author unknown)

Our Lord Jesus declared that "men ought always to pray and not to faint."[1] The parable in which His words occur was taught with the intention of saving Christians from faintheartedness and weakness in prayer. Our Lord was teaching that negligence must be guarded against, and persistence nurtured and encouraged. We cannot have two opinions concerning the importance of exercising this indispensable quality in our praying.

Persistent prayer is a mighty movement of the soul toward God. It is a stirring of the deepest forces of the soul toward the throne of heavenly grace. It is the ability to hold on, press on, and wait. Restless desire, restful patience, and strength to hold on are all contained in it. It is not an incident or a performance, but a passion of soul. It is not a half-needed want, but a sheer necessity.

The wrestling quality in persistent prayers does not spring from physical force or fleshly energy. It is not an impulse of energy, not a mere earnestness of soul, It is an inwrought force, a faculty implanted and aroused by the Holy Spirit. In effect, it is the intercession of the Spirit of God in us.[2] It is also "the effectual, fervent prayer, which availeth much."[4] The divine Spirit infusing every element within us with the energy of His own striving is the essential part of the persistence that urges our praying at the mercy seat to continue until the fire falls and the blessing comes down. This wrestling in prayer may not be loud or intensely emotional, but quiet, tenacious, and urgent. When there are no visible outlets for its mighty forces, it may even be silent, inward, prayer.

PRAYER DISTINGUISHES THE CHILDREN OF GOD

Nothing distinguishes the children of God so clearly and strongly as prayer. It is the one infallible mark and test of being a Christian. Christian people are prayerful. The worldly-minded are prayerless. Christians call on God. The worldly ignore God and do not call on His name. But even Christians need to cultivate continual prayer. Prayer must be habitual, but much more than a habit. It is duty, yet one that rises far above and goes beyond the ordinary meaning of the word. It is the expression of a relation to God, a yearning for divine communion. It is the outward and upward flow of the inward life toward its original fountain. It is an assertion of the soul's paternity, a claiming of the sonship that links a Christian to the eternal Father.[4]

Prayer has everything to do with molding the soul into the image of God.[5] It has everything to do with enhancing and enlarging the measure of divine grace.[6] It has everything to do with bringing the soul into complete communion with God. It has everything to do with enriching, broadening, and maturing the soul's experience of God. That person who does not pray cannot possibly be called a Christian. By no possible pretext can such a person claim any right to the name or its implied significance. The person who does not pray is a sinner, pure and simple. For prayer is the only way in which the soul of a person can enter into fellowship and communion with the source of all Christlike spirit and energy. Therefore, a person who does not pray is not of the household of faith.

ONE PHASE OF PRAYER

In this study however, we are concerned with one phase of prayer—persistence. This is the pressing of our desires upon God with urgency and perseverance. It is praying with that tenacity and tension that neither relaxes nor ceases until its plea is heard, and its cause is won.

Christians who have clear views of God, scriptural concepts of the divine character, appreciate their privilege of approach to God, and understand their inward need of all that God has for them, will be eager, outspoken, and persistent. In God's Word, the duty of prayer itself is advocated in terms that are barely stronger than those in which the necessity for its persistence is stated. The praying that influences God is declared to be that of the fervent, effectual, outpouring of a righteous person.[7] It is prayer on fire, with no feeble, flickering, flame, no momentary flash, but shining with a vigorous and steady glow.

EXAMPLES OF PERSISTENT PRAYER

The repeated intercessions of Abraham for the salvation of Sodom and Gomorrah are an early example of the necessity for persistent praying and the benefit obtained from it.[8] Jacob's wrestling with the angel all night[9] gives significant emphasis to the power of a dogged perseverance in praying. It shows how persistence succeeds in spiritual things just as effectively as it does in matters relating to time and sense.

As we have noted elsewhere, Moses prayed forty days and forty nights, seeking to stay the wrath of God against Israel,[10] and his example and success are a stimulus to present-day faith in its darkest hour. Elijah repeated and urged his prayer seven times before the rain cloud appeared above the horizon, heralding the success of his prayer and the victory of his faith.[11] On one occasion Daniel fasted and pressed his case for three weeks before the answer and the blessing came.[12]

During His earthly life the blessed Savior spent many nights in prayer.[13] In Gethsemane, He presented the same petition three times with unabated, urgent, yet submissive persistence.[14] His prayer involved every element of His soul and brought forth tears and bloody sweat.[15] His life crises were distinctly marked, and his life victories all won in hours of persistent prayer. Even so, the servants are not greater than their Lord.[16]

THE PARABLE OF THE PERSISTENT WIDOW

The parable of the persistent Widow is a classic of insistent prayer. We do well to refresh our memory of it at this point in our study:

And He spake a parable unto them to this end, that men ought always to pray, and not to faint; saying, There was in a city a judge, which feared not God, neither regarded man: and there was a widow in that city; and she came unto him, saying, Avenge me of my adversary. And he would not for a while: but afterward he said within himself, Though I fear not God nor regard man; yet because this widow troubleth me, I will avenge her, lest by her continual coming she weary me. And the Lord said, Hear what the unjust judge saith. And shall not God avenge His own elect, which cry day and night unto Him, though He bear long with them? I tell you He will avenge them speedily.[17]

This parable stresses the central truth of persistent prayer. The widow presses her case until the unjust judge yields. If this parable does not teach the necessity for persistence, it has neither purpose nor instruction in it. Take this one thought away, and you have nothing left worth recording.

Beyond all objection, Christ intended it to stand as an evidence of the need that exists for insistent, persistent, prayer.

THE SYROPHENICIAN WOMAN

We have the same teaching emphasized in the story of the Syrophenician woman who came to Jesus on behalf of her daughter. Here, persistence is demonstrated—not with insolence, but with the persuasive clothing of humility, sincerity, and fervency. We are given a glimpse of a woman's persistent faith, a woman's bitter grief, and a woman's spiritual insight. The Master went into that Sidonian country so that this truth might be recorded for all time. There is no plea so effective as persistent prayer, and none to which God surrenders Himself so fully and so freely.

The persistence of this distressed mother won her the victory and the answer to her request. Yet instead of being an offence to the Savior, it drew from Him a word of wonder and [18]glad surprise: "O woman, great is thy faith! Be it unto thee, even as thou wilt."

NO PERSISTENCE, NO PRAYER

Christians who do not press their plea, do not pray at all. Cold prayers have no claim on heaven, and no hearing in the courts above. Fire is the life of prayer, and heaven is reached by flaming persistence rising in an ascending scale.

Going back to the case of the persistent widow, we see that her widowhood, friendlessness, and weakness were of no concern to the unjust judge. Persistence was everything. "Because this widow troubleth me," he said, "I will avenge her speedily, lest she weary me." It was entirely because the widow imposed upon the time and attention of the unjust judge that her case was won.

God waits patiently as His elect cry to Him day and night. He is moved by their requests a million times more than was this unjust judge. A limit is set to His waiting by the persistent praying of His people, and the answer richly given.[19] God finds in His praying child the faith that stays and cries, and He honors it by permitting its further exercise so that it is strengthened and enriched. Then He rewards it by granting its request in abundance and decisively.

SUCCESSFUL PERSISTENCE

The case of the Syrophenician woman previously referred to is a notable instance of successful persistence.[20] It is one that is highly encouraging to all who would pray successfully. It was a remarkable instance of insisting and persevering to ultimate victory in the face of almost insuperable obstacles and hindrances. But the woman surmounted them all by heroic faith and persistent spirit that were as remarkable as they were successful. Jesus had gone over into her country, "and would have no man know it."[21] But she breaks through His purpose, violates His privacy, attracts His attention, and pours out to Him a moving appeal of need and faith. Her heart was in her prayer.

At first, Jesus appears to pay no attention to her agony, and ignores her cry for relief. He gives her neither eye, nor ear, nor word. Deep and chilling silence greets her impassioned cry. But she is not turned aside or disheartened. She holds on. Offended at her unseemly cries, the disciples try to get the Lord to send her away, but are silenced by the Lord's declaring that the woman is entirely outside the scope of His mission and His ministry.

But the woman is not daunted by hearing that she is barred from the benefits of His mission. It serves only to lend intensity and increased boldness to her approach to Christ. She came closer, cutting her prayer in half, and falling at His feet. Then, worshipping Him she blended her daughter's case with her own need, and cried, "Lord, help me!" This cry won her case—her daughter was healed that same hour. Hopeful, urgent, and unwearied, she stays near the Master, insisting and praying until the answer is given. What a study in persistence, in earnestness, in insistence. They were promoted and propelled under conditions that would have discouraged any but a heroic and persistent soul.

In these parables of persistent praying, our Lord shows for our information and encouragement the serious difficulties that stand in the way of prayer. At the same time, He teaches that persistency conquers all adverse circumstances and gains a victory over a whole host of hindrances. He teaches, moreover, that an answer to prayer is conditional upon the amount of faith that goes into the petition. To test this, He delays the answer. Those who pray superficially sink into silence when the answer is delayed. But the person of persistent prayer hangs on and on. The Lord recognizes and honors such faith, and gives a rich and abundant answer to this faith-evidencing persistent prayer.

Endnotes

1 Luke 18:1
2 Romans 8:26
3 James 5:16
4 Romans 8:15; Galatians 4:6
5 2 Corinthians 3:18; Colossians 1:15
6 Hebrews 4:16; James 4:6
7 James 5:16
8 Genesis 18:22-32
9 Actually, Jacob did not wrestle with the angel, the angel wrestled with Jacob—a significant difference: "And Jacob was left alone; and there wrestled a man with him until the breaking of the day" (Genesis 32:24).

10 Deuteronomy 9:13-19
11 I Kings 18:41-45
12 Daniel 10:1-14
13 Luke 6:12
14 Matthew 26:44
15 Luke 22:44
16 John 13:16
17 Luke 18:1-8
18 Matthew 15:28
19 Philippians 4:19
20 Matthew 15:21-28
21 Mark 7:24

7

Persistent Prayer (continued)

TWO-THIRDS OF THE *praying we do, is for that which would give us the greatest possible pleasure to receive. It is a sort of spiritual self-indulgence in which we engage, and as a consequence is the exact opposite of self-discipline. God knows all this, and keeps His children asking. In process of time—His time—our petitions take on another aspect, and we, another spiritual approach. God keeps us praying until, in His wisdom, He deigns to answer. And no matter how long it may be before He speaks, it is, even then, far earlier than we have a right to expect or hope to deserve.* (Author Unknown)

The purpose of Christ's teachings is to declare that Christians are to pray earnestly—pray with an earnestness that cannot be denied. Heaven has listening ears only for the wholehearted, and the deeply earnest. Energy, courage, and persistent perseverance must back the prayers that heaven respects and God hears. All these qualities of soul, so essential to effective praying are brought out in the parable of the man who went to his friend for three loaves of bread at midnight.[1] The man went on his errand with confidence. Friendship promised him success. His plea was urgent—he could not go back empty-handed. The flat refusal embarrassed and surprised him. Here even friendship failed! But there was something yet to be tried—stern resolution and fixed determination. He would stay and press his demand until the door was opened and the request granted. This he proceeded to do, and by force of persistence secured what his ordinary petition had failed to obtain.

The success this man achieved in the face of a flat denial was used by the Savior to illustrate the necessity for insistence in supplicating the throne of heavenly grace. When the answer is not immediately given, the praying Christian must gather courage at each delay and advance in urgency until the answer comes. The answer is assured if we but have the faith to press our petition with vigorous faith.

Negligence, faint-heartedness, impatience, or timidity is fatal to our prayers. Waiting for our persistent and insistent prayers is the Father's heart, the Father's hand, the Father's infinite power, the Father's infinite willingness to hear and give to His children.

PERSISTENT PRAYING IS THE HEART MOVING TOWARD GOD

Persistent praying is the earnest, inward, movement of the heart toward God. It is throwing the entire force of the spiritual person into the exercise of prayer. Isaiah lamented that no one stirred himself up to take hold of God.[2] Much praying was done in Isaiah's time, but it was too easy, indifferent, and complacent. There were no mighty movements of souls toward God. There was no array of sanctified energies bent on reaching and grappling with God, to draw from Him the treasures of His grace. Forceless prayers have no power to overcome difficulties, win marked results, or gain complete victories. We must win God before we can win our plea.

Isaiah looked forward with hopeful eyes to the day when religion would flourish, when there would be times of real praying. When those times came, the watchmen would not reduce their vigilance, but cry day and night. And those who were the Lord's remembrancers would give Him no rest.[3] Their urgent, persistent efforts would keep all spiritual interests involved, and make increasing calls on God's exhaustless treasures.

PERSISTENT PRAYING NEVER QUITS

Persistent praying never faints or grows weary. It is never discouraged. It never yields to cowardice. It is motivated and sustained by a hope that knows no despair, and a faith that will not let go. Persistent praying has patience to wait and strength to continue. It never prepares itself to quit praying, and refuses to rise from its knees until an answer is received.

The familiar and encouraging words of that great missionary, Adoniram Judson, is the testimony of a man who was persistent in prayer. He says, "I was never deeply interested in any object, never prayed sincerely and earnestly for it, but that it came at some time, no matter how distant the day. Somehow, in some shape, probably the last I would have devised, it came."

"Ask, and ye shall receive. Seek, and ye shall find. Knock, and it shall be opened unto you."[4] These are the ringing challenges of our Lord in regard to prayer. His indication is that true praying must stay and advance in effort and urgency until the prayer is answered and the desired blessing is received.

By the order in which He places the three words—ask, seek, knock—Jesus urges the necessity of persistence in prayer. Asking, seeking, knocking, are ascending rungs in the ladder of successful prayer. No principle is more definitely enforced by Christ than that prevailing prayer must have in it the quality that waits and perseveres, the courage that never surrenders, the patience that never grows tired, and the resolution that never wavers.

THREE QUALITIES OF PERSISTENCE

Persistence is made up of intensity, perseverance, and patience. The seeming delay in answering prayer is the foundation and heart of persistence. In Matthew we have the first recorded instance of a miracle being worked on a blind person. It is an illustration of the way in which our Lord appeared not to listen at once to those who sought Him. But the two blind men continued their crying and followed Him with their continual petition, saying, "Thou Son of David, have mercy on us."[5] But He did not answer them, and went into the house. Yet the needy ones followed Him and, finally, gained their plea and their eyesight.

The case of blind Bartimaeus is a notable one in many ways. It is especially remarkable for the show of persistence that this blind man exhibited in appealing to our Lord. If his first cries were done as Jesus entered into Jericho—as it seems to have been—and he continued them until Jesus came out of the place, it is an even stronger illustration of the necessity of persistent prayer and the success that comes to those who stake their all on Christ, and give Him no peace until He grants them their hearts' desire.

Mark puts the whole incident graphically before us.[6] At first, Jesus seems not to hear. The crowd rebukes the noisy shouts of Bartimaeus. Despite the seeming unconcern of our Lord, however, and despite the rebuke of an impatient and quick-tempered crowd, the blind beggar still cries. In fact, he increases the loudness of his cry until Jesus is impressed and moved. Finally, the crowd, and Jesus, listen to the beggar's plea and speak in favor of his cause. He gains his case. His persistence wins even in the face of apparent neglect on the part of Jesus, and despite opposition and rebuke from the surrounding crowd. His persistence won where half-hearted indifference would surely have failed.

PERSISTENT PRAYER IS ABSOLUTELY NECESSARY

Faith has its function in connection with prayer, and, of course, is inseparably associated with persistence. But the latter quality drives the prayer to the believing point. A persistent spirit brings a Christian to the place where faith takes hold, claims, and appropriates the blessing.

The absolute necessity of persistent prayer is plainly set forth in the Word of God, and needs to be stated and restated today. We are apt to overlook this vital truth. Love of ease and spiritual and religious laziness all operate against this type of petitioning. Our praying, however, needs to be pressed and pursued with an energy that never tires, a persistency that will not be denied, and a courage that never fails.

We have need, too, to give thought to that mysterious fact of prayer—the certainty that there will be delays, denials, and seeming failures, in connection with its exercise. We are to prepare for these, endure them, and not cease in our urgent praying. When the conflict gets stronger, a brave soldier displays a greater courage than in the earlier stages of the battle. So do praying Christians. When delay and denial face them, they increase their earnest asking and do not stop until the answer comes.

MOSES AN OUTSTANDING EXAMPLE OF PERSISTENT PRAYER

Moses provides an outstanding example of persistence in prayer. Instead of allowing his nearness to God and his intimacy with Him to dispense with the necessity for persistence, he regards them as making him better able to exercise it. When Israel set up the golden calf, the wrath of God burned hot against them. Bent on executing justice, Jehovah said to Moses when revealing what He purposed doing, "Let Me alone!"[7] But Moses would not let Him alone. He threw himself down before the Lord in an agony of intercession in behalf of the sinning Israelites, and for forty days and nights, fasted and prayed.[8] What a season of persistent prayer was that!

Jehovah was angry with Aaron, also, who had acted as leader in this idolatrous business of the golden calf. But Moses prayed for Aaron as well as for the Israelites.[9] Had he not, both Israel and Aaron would have perished under the consuming fire of God's wrath.

That long season of pleading before God left its mighty impression on Moses. He had been in close relation with God before that, but his character never attained the greatness that marked it in the days and years following this long season of persistent intercession.

There can be no question but that persistent prayer moves God and heightens Christian character! If we were more with God in this great mandate of intercession, our face would shine more brightly, and our life and service would be more richly endowed with the qualities that earn the goodwill of humanity and bring glory to the name of God.

Endnotes

1 Luke 11:5-8
2 Isaiah 64:7
3 Isaiah 62:5-7
4 Matthew 7:7
5 Matthew 9:27
6 Mark 10:46-52
7 Exodus 32:10
8 Deuteronomy 9:18-19
9 Deuteronomy 9:20

8

Prayer, Character, and Conduct

GENERAL CHARLES JAMES GORDON, *the hero of Khartoum, was a truly Christian soldier. Shut up in the Sudanese town he gallantly held out for one year, but, finally, was overcome and slain. On his memorial in Westminster Abbey are these words, "He gave his money to the poor; his sympathy to the sorrowing; his life to his country and his soul to God."* (Homer W. Hodge)

Prayer governs conduct, and conduct makes character. Conduct is what we do, character, is what we are. Conduct is the outward life. Character is the unseen life that is hidden within, yet shown by what is seen. Conduct is external—seen from the outside. Character is internal—operating within. In the economy of grace, conduct is the offspring of character. Character is the state of the heart. Conduct is its outward expression. Character is the root of the tree. Conduct is the fruit it bears.

Prayer is related to all the gifts of grace. To character and conduct its relation is that of a helper. Prayer helps to establish character and fashion conduct, and both depend on prayer for their successful continuance. There may be a certain degree of moral character and conduct independent of prayer, but there cannot be anything like distinctive religious character and Christian conduct without it. Prayer helps where all other aids fail. The more we pray the better we are, and the purer and better our lives become.

CHRISTIAN CHARACTER AND CONDUCT

The very end and purpose of the atoning work of Christ is to create religious character and make Christian conduct.

Who gave Himself for us, that He might redeem us from all iniquity, and purify unto Himself a peculiar people, zealous of good works.[1]

In Christ's teaching, it is not simply works of charity and deeds of mercy that He insists upon, but inward spiritual character. This much is demanded, and nothing short of it will suffice.

In the study of Paul's epistles, there is one thing which that out clearly and unmistakably—the insistence on holiness of heart and righteousness of life. Paul does not try to promote what is termed "personal work," and the leading theme of his letters is not deeds of charity. It is the condition of the human heart and the blamelessness of the personal life that form the burden of his writings.

Character and conduct are preeminent elsewhere in the Scriptures, too. The Christian religion deals with people who are devoid of spiritual character and unholy in life. It aims so to change them so that they become holy in heart and righteous in life. It aims to change bad people into good people. It deals with inward badness, and works to change it into inward goodness.

PRAYER CHANGES CHARACTER AND CONDUCT

Here is where prayer enters and demonstrates its wonderful effectiveness and fruit. Prayer drives toward this specific end. In fact, without prayer, no such supernatural change in moral character can ever be effected. The change from badness to goodness is not brought about "by works of righteousness that we have done." It is brought about according to God's mercy, which saves us "by the washing of regeneration." This marvelous change is brought to pass through earnest, persistent, faithful, prayer. Any alleged form of Christianity that does not create this change in the hearts of people is a delusion and a snare.

One of the effects of prayer is to change the character and conduct of people. In countless instances change has been brought about by prayer. By so doing prayer has proved its divinity. Just as it is a function of prayer to effect this, so it is the prime work of the Church to take hold of evil people and make them good. Its mission is to change human nature. It does so by changing character, influencing behavior, and revolutionizing conduct. The Church is presumed to be righteous, and should be engaged in turning people to righteousness.

PRIMARY DUTY OF THE CHURCH

The Church is God's manufacturing plant on earth, and its primary duty is to create and nurture righteousness of character. This is its very first business. Primarily, its work is not to acquire members, or amass numbers, or bring in money, or engage in deeds of charity and works of mercy. Its primary work is to produce righteousness of character, and purity of the outward life.

A product reflects and partakes of the character of the manufacturing plant that makes it. A righteous Church with a righteous purpose makes righteous people. Prayer produces cleanliness of heart and purity of life. It can produce nothing else. Unrighteous conduct is born of prayerlessness—the two go hand-in-hand. Prayer and sinning cannot keep company with each other. One or the other must necessarily stop. Get people to pray, and they will quit sinning. Prayer creates a distaste for sinning, and so works upon the heart that doing evil becomes repulsive. It lifts the entire nature to a reverent contemplation of high and holy things.

PRAYER IS BASED ON CHARACTER

What we are with God determines our influence with Him. It was the inner character and not the outward appearance of such men as Abraham, Job, David, Moses, and all others who had such great influence with God in Old Testament days. Today, it is not so much our words as what we really are that counts with God. Conduct affects character, of course, and counts for much in our praying.

At the same time, character affects conduct to a far greater extent, and has a superior influence over prayer. Our inner life not only gives color to our praying, but also to our body. Bad living means bad praying and, in the end, no praying at all. We pray feebly because we live feebly. The stream of prayer cannot rise higher than the fountain of living. The force of the prayer closet is made up of the energy that flows from the merging streams of living. The weakness of living grows out of the shallowness and shoddiness of character.

Feebleness of living reflects its weakness and listlessness in the praying hours. We simply cannot talk strongly, intimately, and confidently to God unless we are living faithfully and truly for Him. The prayer closet cannot become sanctified to God when the life is foreign to His precepts and purpose. We must learn this lesson well—righteous character and Christlike conduct give us a peculiar and preferential standing in prayer before God. His holy Word gives special emphasis to the part conduct has in imparting value to our praying:

> Then shalt thou call and the Lord shall answer; thou shalt cry, and He shall say, Here I am. If thou take away from the midst of thee the yoke, the putting forth of the finger, and speaking vanity.[2]

The wickedness of Israel and their heinous practices were definitely cited by Isaiah as the reason why God would turn His ears away from their prayers: "And when ye spread forth your hands, I will hide mine eyes from you: yea, when ye make many prayers, I will not hear: your hands are full of blood."[3]

The same sad truth was declared by the Lord through the mouth of Jeremiah: "Therefore pray not thou for this people, neither lift up a cry or prayer for them: for I will not hear them in the time that they cry unto Me for their trouble."[4]

It is plainly stated here that unholy conduct is a bar to successful praying. Just as it is clearly implied that to have full access to God in prayer, there must be a total abandonment of conscious and premeditated sin.

LIFT UP HOLY HANDS

We are directed to pray, "lifting up holy hands, without wrath and doubting."[5] We must pass the days of our life here in a strict abstaining from evil if we are to retain our privilege of calling upon the Father. There is no process by which we can divorce praying from conduct.

And whatsoever we ask, we receive of him, because we keep his commandments, and do those things that are pleasing in his sight.[6]

James strongly declares that Christians ask and receive not because they ask amiss, and seek only to gratify their selfish desires.[7]

Our Lord's command, "Watch ye therefore, and pray always,"[8] is to cover and guard all our conduct. This is so that we may come to our prayer closet with all its force secured by a vigilant guard kept over our lives.

And take heed to yourselves, lest at any time your hearts be overcharged with surfeiting, and drunkenness, and cares of this life, and so that day come upon you unawares.[9]

Quite often, Christian experience caves in on the rock of conduct. Beautiful theories are marred by ugly lives. The most difficult thing about piety, since it is the most impressive, is to be able to live it. It is the life that counts. Thus every part of our religious experience and our praying suffer from bad living.

PREACHERS SHOULD PREACH BY THEIR LIVES

In primitive times preachers were charged to preach by their lives or not preach at all. In the same way today, Christians everywhere should be charged to pray by their lives or not pray at all. The most effective preaching is not that which is heard from the pulpit, but that which is proclaimed by living quietly, humbly, and consistently—thus exhibiting its excellencies in the home and in the community. Example preaches a far more effective sermon than doctrine. Even in the pulpit, the best preaching is that which is fortified by godly living in the preacher.

The most effective work done by the pew is preceded by, and accompanied with, holiness of life, and separation from the world and sin.[10] Some of the strongest appeals are made with mute lips—by godly fathers and saintly mothers. Such parents fear God, love His cause, and daily exhibit to their children and others about them the beauties and excellencies of Christian life and conduct.

The best–prepared and most eloquent sermon can be marred and rendered ineffective by questionable practices in the preacher. The most active church workers can have the labor of their hands weakened by worldliness of spirit and inconsistency of life. Ministers preach by their lives and not by their words. Sermons are delivered not so much in and from a pulpit as they are in tempers, actions, and the thousand and one incidents that crowd the pathway of daily life.

Of course, the prayer of repentance is acceptable to God. He delights in hearing the cries of penitent sinners. But repentance involves not only sorrow for sin, but the turning away from wrongdoing, and the learning to do well. A repentance that does not produce a change in character and conduct, is a mere sham that should deceive no one. Old things must pass away, all things must become new.[11]

EFFECTIVE PRAYING

Praying that does not result in right thinking and right living, is a farce. We have missed the whole concern of prayer if it fails to purge character and correct conduct. We have failed entirely to apprehend the virtue of prayer if it does not bring about the revolutionizing of the life. In the very nature of things, we must quit praying or our bad conduct. Cold, formal, praying may exist side by side with bad conduct, but such praying in the estimation of God is no praying at all. Our praying advances in power only so far as it corrects the life. Growing in purity and devotion to God will make and be a more prayerful life.

The character of the inner life is a condition of effective praying. As the life is, so the praying will be. An inconsistent life obstructs praying and neutralizes what little praying we may do. It is always "the prayer of the righteous man which availeth much."[12] Indeed, we could go further and declare that it is only the prayer of the righteous that avails anything at all—at any time. To have an eye to God's glory, be possessed by an earnest desire to please Him in all our ways, possess hands busy in His service, and have feet swift to run in the way of His commandments, these give weight, influence, and power to prayer and secure an audience with God. The oppressive burdens of our lives often break the force of our praying, and are like doors of brass in the face of prayer.

PRAYING OUT OF A CLEAN HEART

Praying must come out of a clean heart and be presented and urged with the "lifting up of holy hands."[13] It must be fortified by a life that aims unceasingly to obey God, to attain conformity to the divine law, and to come into submission to the divine will.

Let it not be forgotten that while life is a condition of prayer, prayer is also the condition of righteous living. Prayer promotes righteous living, and is the one great aid to uprightness of heart and life. The fruit of real praying is right living. Praying sets Christians who pray to the great business of "working out [their] salvation with fear and trembling."[14] It causes them to watch their temper, conversation, and conduct. Makes them "walk circumspectly . . . redeeming the time."[15] Enables them to "walk worthy of the vocation wherewith they are called, with all lowliness and meekness."[16]And gives them a high incentive to pursue their pilgrimage consistently by "shunning every evil way, and walking in the good."[17]

Endnotes

1 Titus 2:14
2 Isaiah 58:9
3 Isaiah 1:15
4 Jeremiah 11:14
5 1 Timothy 2:8
6 1 John 3:22
7 James 4:3
8 Luke 21:36
9 Luke 21:34
10 2 Corinthians 6:17
11 2 Corinthians 5:17
12 James 5:16
13 1 Timothy 2:8
14 Philippians 2:12
15 Ephesians 5:15-16
16 Ephesians 4:1-2
17 No Scripture reference could be found for this quotation, so it is undoubtedly from some source other than the Bible.

9

Prayer and Obedience

A N OBEDIENCE DISCOVERED ITSELF *in Fletcher of Madeley, which I wish I could describe or imitate. It produced in him a ready mind to embrace every cross with alacrity and pleasure. He had a singular love for the lambs of the flock, and applied himself with the greatest diligence to their instruction, for which he had a peculiar gift. . . . All his intercourse with me was so mingled with prayer and praise, that every employment, and every meal was, as it were, perfumed therewith."* (John Wesley)

Under the Mosaic law, obedience was looked upon as being "better than sacrifice, and to hearken than the fat of rams."[1] In Deuteronomy 5:29, Moses records Almighty God declaring Himself to this very quality in a manner that left no doubt as to the importance He laid upon its exercise. Referring to the waywardness of His people He cries:

> O that there were such a heart in them, that they would fear Me, and keep all My commandments always, that it might be well with them, and with their children forever.

Unquestionably obedience is a high virtue, a soldier quality. It belongs preeminently to the soldier. It is the soldiers first and last lesson, and they must learn how to practice it all the time without questioning or complaining. Moreover, obedience is faith in action, and the outflow and test of love. "He that hath My commandments, and keepeth them, he it is that loveth Me."[2]

If ye keep My commandments, ye shall abide in My love; even as I have kept My Father's commandments, and abide in His love.[3]

What a marvelous statement of the relationship created and maintained by obedience! The Son of God is held in the bosom of the Father's love by virtue of His obedience! What enables the Son of God to ever abide in His Father's love is revealed in His own statement, "For I do always those things that please Him."[4]

THE GIFT OF THE HOLY SPIRIT DEPENDS ON OBEDIENCE

The gift of the Holy Spirit in full measure and in richer experience, depends upon loving obedience: "If ye love Me, keep My commandments," is the Master's word. "And I will pray the Father, and He shall give you another Comforter, that He may abide with you for ever."[5]

Obedience to God is a condition of spiritual wisdom, inward satisfaction, and steadiness of heart. "If ye be willing and obedient, ye shall eat the good of the land."[6] Obedience opens the gates of the Holy City, and gives access to the tree of life.[7]

Blessed are they that do His commandments, that they may have right to the tree of life, and may enter in through the gates, into the city.[8]

WHAT IS OBEDIENCE?

Obedience is doing God's will—keeping His commandments. Keeping how many of the commandments constitutes obedience? Keeping half of them and breaking the other half, is that real obedience? Keeping all the commandments but one, is that obedience? On this point, James is very clear. "Whosoever shall keep the whole law, and yet offend in one point, he is guilty of all."[9]

The spirit that prompts a person to break one commandment is the spirit that may move that person to break them all. God's commandments are a unit, and to break one strikes at the principle that underlies and runs through the whole. The person who does not hesitate to break a single commandment, would—more than likely—under the same stress and surrounded by the same circumstances break them all.

UNIVERSAL OBEDIENCE DEMANDED

Universal obedience of every human being is demanded. Nothing short of unquestioning obedience will satisfy God, and the keeping of all His commandments is the demonstration of it that God requires. But can we keep all of God's commandments? Can we receive moral ability that will enable us to obey every one of them? Certainly we can. Every indication is that through prayer we can obtain the ability to do this very thing.

Does God give commandments that people cannot obey? Is He so arbitrary, so severe, so unloving, as to issue commandments that cannot be obeyed? The answer is that in all the records of holy Scripture not a single instance is recorded of God having commanded any person to do a thing that was beyond their power. Is God so unjust and so inconsiderate as to require something of us that we are unable to do? Surely not. To infer it is to slander the character of God.

Let us think about this for a moment. Do earthly parents require their children to do things that they cannot do? Where is the father who would even think of being so unjust and so tyrannical? Is God less kind and just than faulty, earthly, parents? Are they better and more just than a perfect God? Such a thought is utterly foolish and irrational!

OBEDIENCE IS LOVE IN ACTION

In principle, obedience to God is the same quality as obedience to earthly parents. In general, it implies the giving up of one's own way and following that of another, surrendering the will to the will of another, and submitting oneself to the authority and requirements of a parent. Commands that are from our heavenly Father or our earthly father are love-directing, and all such commands are in the best interests of those who are commanded. God's commands are not issued in severity nor tyranny. They are always issued in love and in our interests, and so it is important for us to heed and obey them. In other words, God has issued His commands to us to contribute to our good. It pays, therefore, to be obedient. Obedience brings its own reward. God has ordained it so. Since He has, even human reason can realize that He would never demand something that is out of our power to do.

Obedience is love fulfilling every command, and thereby expressing itself. Obedience, therefore, is not a hard demand made upon us, any more than is the service a husband gives his wife or a wife gives her husband. Love delights to obey and please the one it loves. There are no hardships in love. There may be strictness, but no weariness. There are no impossible tasks for love.

OBEDIENCE MOTIVATED BY LOVE

In a simple and matter-of-fact way the apostle John says, "And whatsoever we ask, we receive of Him, because we keep His commandments, and do those things that are pleasing in His sight."[10]

This is obedience running ahead of every command. It is love obeying by anticipation. Those who declare that people are bound to commit iniquity because of environment, heredity, or tendency, are highly wrong, and even sin. God's commands are not grievous.[11] Their ways are pleasant and their paths peaceful. The task that falls to obedience is not a hard one. "For My yoke is easy, and My burden is light."[12]

It is far away from our heavenly Father to demand impossibilities of His children. It is possible to please Him in all things, for He is not hard to please. He is neither a hard master, nor an stern Lord, "taking up that I laid not down, and reaping that I did not sow."[13] Thank God it is possible for every child of God to please their heavenly Father! It is really much easier to please Him than to please people. Moreover, we may know when we please Him. This is the witness of the Spirit[14]—the inward divine assurance given to all the children of God that they are doing their Father's will, and that their ways are well-pleasing in His sight.

GOD'S COMMANDMENTS ARE RIGHTEOUS

God's commandments are righteous and founded in justice and wisdom. "Wherefore the law is holy, and the commandment holy, and just, and good." [15]"Just and true are Thy ways, Thou King of saints."[16] God's commandments, then, can be obeyed by all who seek the grace that enable them to obey.[17] These commandments must be obeyed. God's government is at stake. God's children are under obligation to obey Him— disobedience cannot be permitted. The spirit of rebellion is the very essence of sin.[18] It is a denial of God's authority that God cannot tolerate. He never has done so, and a declaration of His attitude toward disobedience was part of the reason the Son of the Highest was made manifest in the world.

For what the law could not do, in that it was weak through the flesh, God sending His own Son in the likeness of sinful flesh, and for sin, condemned sin in the flesh: that the righteousness of the law might be fulfilled in us, who walk not after the flesh, but after the Spirit.[19]

SUFFICIENT GRACE TO OBEY

If any should complain that humanity under the fall is too weak and helpless to obey these high commands of God, the answer is that through the atonement of Christ humanity is made able to obey. The atonement is God's "Enabling Act". In regeneration and through the agency of the Holy Spirit, God works in us and bestows sufficient enabling grace for all that is required of us under the atonement. This grace is furnished without measure in answer to prayer. So at the same time that God commands, He stands pledged to give us all the necessary strength of will and grace of soul to meet His demands.[20] Since this is true, we are without excuse for our disobedience. And we are highly at fault for refusing or failing to obtain the necessary grace by which we may serve the Lord with reverence and godly fear.[21]

Those who declare it to be impossible to keep God's commandments strangely overlook one important consideration. That consideration is the vital truth that states that through prayer and faith our nature is changed and we are made partakers of the divine nature.[22] Also, that all reluctance to obey God it taken out of us, and our natural inability to keep God's commandments because by our fallen and helpless state is gloriously removed. By this radical change that is worked in our moral nature, we receive power to obey God in every way and to yield full and glad allegiance. Thus we can say, "I delight to do Thy will, O my God."[23] God removes the rebellion that is part of our natural person, and blessedly gives us a heart that gladly obeys His Word.

There is no denying that unrenewed people with all the disabilities of the Fall upon them cannot obey God. But to declare that, after one is renewed by the Holy Spirit, has received a new nature, and become a child of the King, he cannot obey God, is to assume a ridiculous attitude, and to display, moreover, a lamentable ignorance of the work and implications of the Atonement.

Unquestioning and perfect obedience is the state to which the person of prayer is called. "Lifting up holy hands, without wrath and doubting,"[24] is the condition of obedient praying. Here inward faithfulness and love, together with outward cleanness, are put down as coexisting requirements of acceptable praying.

John gives the reason for answered prayer in the passage previously quoted: "And whatsoever we ask we receive of Him because we keep His commandments and do those things which are pleasing in His sight."[25]

Since John says that keeping of God's commandments is the reason He answers prayer, it is reasonable to assume that we can keep God's commandments, can do those things that are pleasing to Him. Do you think God would make the keeping of His commandments a condition of effective prayer if He knew we could not keep them? Of course not!

OBEDIENCE CAN PRAY WITH BOLDNESS

Obedience can ask with boldness at the throne of grace, and those who are obedient are the only ones who can ask in that way. Disobedient Christians are timid in their approach and hesitant in their supplication. They are stopped by reason of their wrongdoing. Praying obedient children come into the presence of their father with confidence and boldness. Their consciousness of obedience gives them courage and frees them from the dread created by disobedience.

To do God's will without delay is the joy and privilege of the successful praying person. It is those who have clean hands and a pure heart that can pray with confidence.[26] In the Sermon on the Mount, Jesus said, "Not every one that saith unto me, Lord, Lord, shall enter into the kingdom of heaven, but he that doeth the will of My Father which is in heaven."[27]

To this great statement may be added another: "If ye keep My commandments ye shall abide in My love, even as I have kept my Father's commandments, and abide in His love."[28]

OBEDIENCE AND PRAYER

"The Christian's trade," says Luther, "is prayer." But Christians have another trade to learn before they proceed to learn the secrets of the trade of prayer. They must learn well the trade of perfect obedience to the Father's will. Obedience follows love, and prayer follows obedience. The business of the real observance of God's commandments inseparably accompanies the business of real praying.

Those who have been disobedient may pray. They may pray for pardoning mercy and the peace of their soul. They may come to God's footstool with tears, with confession, with penitent heart, and God will hear them and answer their prayer. This kind of praying does not belong to the child of God, however, but to the penitent sinner who has no other way by which to approach God. It is the possession of the unjustified soul, not of those who have been saved and reconciled to God.

An obedient life helps prayer. It speeds prayer to the throne. God cannot help hearing the prayer of an obedient child. He always has heard His obedient children when they have prayed. Unquestioning obedience counts much in the sight of God, at the throne of heavenly grace. It acts like the converging tides of many rivers, and gives volume and fullness of flow as well as power to the prayer closet. An obedient life is not simply a reformed life. It is not the old life primed and repainted. Neither is it a churchgoing life or a good covering of activities. And it is not an external conformation to the dictates of public morality. Far more than all this is combined in a truly obedient Christian, God-fearing life.

A LIFE OF FULL OBEDIENCE

A life of full obedience—one that is settled on the most intimate terms with God, with the will in full conformity to God's will, and the outward actions showing the fruit of righteousness—offers no obstruction to the inner closet. Instead, it lifts up and sustains the hands of prayer like Aaron and Hur did for Moses.

If you have an earnest desire to pray well, you must learn how to obey well. If you have a desire to learn to pray, then you must have an earnest desire to learn how to do God's will. If you desire to pray to God, you must first have a consuming desire to obey Him. If you want free access to God in prayer, then every obstacle of sin or disobedience must be removed. God delights in the prayers of obedient children. Requests, coming from the lips of those who delight to do His will, reach His ears with great swiftness, and incline Him to answer them promptly and abundantly.

Tears have no value in themselves. Yet they have their uses in prayer. Tears should baptize our place of supplication. Those who have never wept concerning their sins, has never really prayed over their sins. Sometimes tears are a penitent's only plea. But tears are for the past, for the sin and the wrongdoing. There is another step and stage waiting to be taken. It is that of unquestioning obedience. Until it is taken, prayer for blessing and continued sustenance will be of no use.

DISOBEDIENCE AND SIN

Throughout the Scriptures God is shown disapproving disobedience and condemning sin. This is as true in the lives of His elect as it is in the lives of sinners. Nowhere does He approve sin or excuse disobedience. God always puts the emphasis upon obeying His commands. Obeying them brings blessing, disobeying them brings disaster.[29]

This is true in the Word of God from the beginning to the end. It is because of this, that the people of prayer in the Scriptures had such influence with God. Obedient people have always been the closest to God. They are the ones who have prayed well and have received great things from God—who by prayer have brought great things to pass.

OBEDIENCE COUNTS IN PRAYER

Obedience to God counts tremendously in the realm of prayer. This fact cannot be emphasized too much or too often. To plead for a Christian faith that tolerates sinning is to cut the ground from under the feet of effective praying. To excuse sinning by the plea that obedience to God is not possible to unregenerate people is to discount the character of the new birth, and to place people where effective praying is not possible. Jesus asked a very pertinent and personal question that struck right to the core of disobedience when He said, "Why call ye Me, Lord, Lord, and do not the things I say?"[30]

Christians who pray must obey. If they want to get anything out of their prayers, they must be in perfect harmony with God. Prayer puts a spirit of obedience into those who sincerely pray, for the spirit of disobedience is not of God and belongs not to God's praying hosts.[31]

An obedient life is a great help to prayer. In fact, an obedient life is a necessity to prayer—to prayer that accomplishes things. The absence of an obedient life makes prayer an empty performance—something wrongly named. Penitent sinners seek pardon and salvation and have an answer to their prayers even with a life stained and corrupted with sin. But God's royal intercessors come before Him with royal lives. Holy living promotes holy praying—God's intercessors "lift up holy hands,"[32] the symbols of righteous, obedient, lives.

Endnotes

1 I Samuel 15:22
2 John 14:21
3 John 15:10
4 John 8:29
5 John 14:15-16
6 Isaiah 1:19
7 Revelation 2:7
8 Revelation 22:14
9 James 2:10
10 I John 3:22
11 I John 5:3

12 Matthew 11:30
13 Luke 19:22
14 Romans 8:16   -
15 Romans 7:12
16 Revelation 15:3
17 2 Corinthians 12:9
18 I Samuel 15:23
19 Romans 8:3-4
20 John 10:18
21 Hebrews 12:28
22 2 Peter 1:4
23 Psalm 40:8
24 I Timothy 2:8
25 I John 3:22
26 Psalm 24:3-4
27 Matthew 7:21
28 John 15:10
29 See the Old Covenant blessings and curses in Deuteronomy 28.
30 Luke 6:46
31 Ephesians 2:2
32 I Timothy 2:8

10

Prayer and Obedience (Continued)

MANY EXEMPLARY MEN HAVE *I known, holy in heart and life, within my four score years. But one equal to John Fletcher—one so inwardly and outwardly obedient and devoted to God—I have not known.* (John Wesley)

It is important to note that the praying to which such transcendent position is given and to which great results are attributed, is not simply the saying of prayers, but holy praying. It is the "prayers of the saints,"[1] the prayers of the holy men and women of God. It is the Christians who are wholly devoted to God, entirely separated from sin, and fully separated unto God, who are doing such praying and give it energy and flame. These are the ones who always give energy, force, and strength to praying.

JESUS ABOVE ALL OTHERS IN PRAYING

Our Lord Jesus Christ was above all others in praying because He was above all others in saintliness. Wings are given to faith and energy to prayer by an entire dedication to God—a full surrender that carries with it the whole being in a flame of holy consecration. This opens the door to the throne of grace, and brings strong influence to bear on Almighty God.

The "lifting up of holy hands"[2] is essential to Christly praying. It is not, however, a holiness that only dedicates a closet to God, that sets apart merely an hour to Him, but a consecration that takes hold of the entire person and dedicates the whole life to God.

Our Lord Jesus Christ, "holy, harmless, undefiled, separate from sinners,"[3] had full liberty of approach and ready access to God in prayer. He had this free and full access because of His unquestioning obedience to His Father. Throughout His earthly life, His supreme care and desire was to do the will of His Father. This fact, coupled with another—the consciousness of having so lived His life—gave Him confidence and assurance. That enabled Him to draw near to the throne of grace with unbounded confidence born of obedience—obedience that promised acceptance, audience, and answer.

LOVING OBEDIENCE

Loving obedience puts us where we can "ask anything in His name," with the assurance, that "He will do it."[4] Loving obedience brings us into the prayer realm, and makes us beneficiaries of the wealth of Christ and the riches of His grace.[5] All this is through the coming of the Holy Spirit who will abide with us and be in us. Cheerful obedience to God, qualifies us to pray effectively.

This obedience that qualifies and is the forerunner to prayer must be loving, constant, always doing the Father's will, and cheerfully following the path of God's commands.

In the instance of King Hezekiah, it was a potent plea that changed God's decree that he should die and not live. The stricken ruler called upon God to remember that he had walked before Him in truth and with a perfect heart. This counted with God. He listened carefully to the petition and, as a result, death's approach to Hezekiah was barred for fifteen years.[6]

OBEDIENCE LEARNED IN THE SCHOOL OF SUFFERING

Jesus learned obedience in the school of suffering.[7] At the same time, He learned prayer in the school of obedience. Just as it is the prayer of a righteous person that "availeth much,"[8] so it is righteousness that is obedience to God. Righteous Christians are obedient Christians. They can pray effectively, therefore, and can accomplish great things when they go to their knees.

Remember, true praying is not mere sentiment, poetry, or eloquent speech, and does not consist of saying sweetly, "Lord, Lord." Prayer is not a mere form of words. It is not just calling upon a name. Prayer is obedience. It is founded on the unyielding rock of obedience to God. Only those who obey have the right to pray. The doing must be behind the praying. It is the constant doing of God's will in daily life that gives prayer its power, as our Lord plainly taught:

> Not every one which saith unto Me, Lord, Lord, shall enter into the kingdom of heaven; but he that doeth the will of My Father which is in heaven. Many will say unto Me in that day, Lord, Lord, have we not prophesied in Thy Name? and in Thy Name have cast out devils? and in Thy Name done many wonderful works? And then will I profess unto them, I never knew you: depart from Me, ye that worketh iniquity.[9]

No name, however precious and powerful, can protect and give efficiency to prayer that is not accompanied by doing God's will. Neither can the doing without the praying protect from divine disapproval. If the will of God does not master the life, the praying will be nothing but sickly sentiment. If prayer does not inspire, sanctify, and direct our work, then self-will enters and ruins both work and worker.

MISCONCEPTIONS OF PRAYER

There are many great misconceptions of the true elements and functions of prayer! There are many who earnestly desire to obtain an answer to their prayers, but who go unrewarded and unblessed. They fix their minds on some promise of God, and then try by force of stubborn perseverance to summon faith enough to lay hold on it and claim it. This fixing of the mind on some great promise may avail in strengthening faith. But persistent and urgent prayer that expects and waits till faith grows exceedingly[10] must be added to the promise. There is no one who is able and competent to do such praying except the person who willingly, cheerfully, and continually obeys God!

FAITH IS THE ATTITUDE OF THE SOUL

In its highest form, faith is the attitude and the act of a person surrendered to God—one in whom His Word and His Spirit dwells. It is true that faith must exist in some form or another in order to inspire praying. But in its strongest form and largest results, faith is the fruit of prayer. It is true that faith increases the ability and the efficiency of prayer, but it is likewise true that prayer increases the ability and efficiency of faith. Prayer and faith work, act, and react one upon the other.

Obedience to God helps faith as no other attribute possibly can. When obedience is based upon unquestioning recognition of the validity and supremacy of God's commands, faith ceases to be an almost superhuman task. It requires no straining to exercise it. Obedience to God makes it easy to believe and trust God. When the spirit of obedience fully saturates the soul, the will is perfectly surrendered to God, and there is a fixed, unalterable, purpose to obey God, faith almost believes itself. Faith then becomes almost automatic. After obedience it is the next natural step, and it is easily and willingly taken. The difficulty in prayer is not with faith but with obedience, which is faith's foundation.

LACK OF OBEDIENCE BREAKS DOWN PRAYER

If we want to pray well and get the most out of our praying, we must look carefully at our obedience, at the secret sources of our actions, and at the loyalty of our heart to God. Obedience is the groundwork of effective praying. It is that which brings us near to God.

The lack of obedience in our lives breaks down our praying. Quite often our life is in revolt and this places us where praying is almost impossible, except to obtain pardoning mercy. Disobedient living produces mighty poor praying. Disobedience shuts the door of the inner closet, and bars the way to the Holy of Holies. No Christian can pray—really pray—who does not obey.

The will must be surrendered to God as a primary condition of all successful praying. Everything about us gets its coloring from our innermost character. Character is made and conduct is controlled by our secret. The will, therefore, plays an important part in all successful praying. When the will is not wholly and fully surrendered to God, there can be no praying in its richest and truest sense. This unswerving loyalty to God is an utterly indispensable condition of the best, truest, and most effective praying. We have simply got to:

Trust and obey—
For there's no other way
To be happy in Jesus
But to trust, and obey!"[11]

Endnotes

1 Revelation 8:4
2 I Timothy 2:8
3 Hebrews 7:26
4 John 14:13-14
5 Ephesians 1:7, 2:7; Philippians 4:19
6 2 Kings 20:1-6
7 Hebrews 5:8
8 James 5:16
9 Matthew 7:21-23
10 2 Thessalonians 1:3
11 From the hymn "Trust and Obey" by John H. Sammis and Daniel B. Towner.

II

Prayer and Vigilance

DAVID BRAINERD WAS PURSUED *by unearthly adversaries, who were resolved to rob him of his reward. He knew he must never quit his armor, but lie down to rest with his corselet laced. The stains that marred the perfection of his lustrous dress, the spots of rust on his gleaming shield, are imperceptible to us, but they were to him the source of much sorrow and ardency of yearning.* (The Life of David Brainerd)

The description of the Christian soldier given by Paul in the sixth chapter of his letter to the Ephesians is compact and comprehensive. The soldier is shown as being always in the conflict, which has many varying seasons—seasons of prosperity and adversity, light and darkness, victory and defeat. As Christian soldiers, we are to pray in all seasons and with all prayer. This to be added to the armor which we are to wear into battle. At all times, we are to have the full armor of prayer. If we are to fight to win, we must pray much. Only by this means are we enabled to defeat our long-established enemy, the devil, and his forces. "Praying always with all prayer"[1] is the divine instruction given to us. This means in all seasons and in all manner of praying.

Christian soldiers who are fighting the good fight of faith[2] have access to a place of retreat, where they continually go for prayer. "Praying always with all prayer," is a clear statement of the pressing need of much praying. Also, of the need for many kinds of praying by those who in fighting the good fight of faith would in the end win over all their foes.

The *Revised Standard Version* of the Bible puts it this way:

Pray in the Spirit at all times in every prayer and supplication. To that end keep alert and always persevere in supplication for all the saints. Pray also for me, so that when I speak, a message may be given to me to make known with boldness the mystery of the gospel, for which I am an ambassador in chains.[3]

SPIRITUAL WARFARE

It cannot be said too often that the life of a Christian is a warfare, an intense conflict, a lifelong contest. Furthermore, it is a battle waged against invisible foes who are ever alert and ever seeking to entrap, deceive, and ruin the souls of people. The life to which the holy Scripture calls Christians is no picnic or holiday excursion. It is not entertainment or a pleasure trip. It involves effort, wrestling, and struggling. It demands putting forth the full energy of your spirit in order to frustrate the foe and be in the end more than a conqueror. It is no flower-strewn path, no rose-scented affair. From start to finish, it is war. It is a battle, not a game. From the moment they first draw their swords, Christian warriors are compelled to "endure hardness, as a good soldier of Jesus Christ."[4]

What a misconception many people have of the Christian life! How little the average church members appear to know of the character of the conflict and its demands upon them! How ignorant they seem to be of the enemies they must encounter if they are to serve God faithfully, succeed in getting to heaven, and receive the crown of life![5] They scarcely seem to realize that the world, the flesh, and the devil will oppose their onward march—and will totally defeat them unless they give themselves to constant vigilance and unceasing prayer.

WE WRESTLE NOT AGAINST FLESH AND BLOOD

Christian soldiers wrestle not against flesh and blood, but against spiritual wickedness in high places.[6] Or, as some margin references read, "wicked spirits in high places." What a fearful array of forces are set against those who would make their way through the wilderness of this world to the gates of the Celestial City! It is no surprise, therefore, to find Paul, who understood the character of the Christian life so well, carefully and plainly urging us to "take up the whole armor of God," and to pray "always with all prayer and supplication in the Spirit."[7] Paul thoroughly knew the evilness and number of the foes that the disciples of the Lord must encounter. Our present generation of Christians would be much wiser if all professors of our faith could be convinced to realize this all-important and vital truth—a truth that is absolutely indispensable to a successful Christian life.

It is just at this point in today's Christianity that we find its greatest defect. There is little to nothing of the soldier element in it. The discipline, self-denial, spirit of hardship, determination, that belong to military life and are so prominent in it are lacking in Christianity. Yet the Christian life *is* warfare from beginning to end.

PAUL'S DIRECTIONS TO CHRISTIAN SOLDIERS

How comprehensive, pointed, and striking are all of Paul's directions to Christian soldiers who are determined to defeat the devil. First of all, they must have a clear idea of the character of the life on which they have entered. Then, they must know something of their foe—the adversary of their immortal soul. They must know their enemy's strength, skill, and evilness. Knowing something of the character of the enemy, and realizing the need of preparation to overcome them, they are prepared to hear the Apostle's decisive conclusion:

Finally, my brethren, be strong in the Lord, and in the power of His might. Put on the whole armor of God, that ye may be able to stand against the wiles of the devil. . . . Wherefore, take unto you the whole armor of God, that ye may be able to stand in the evil day, and having done all, to stand.[8]

All these directions end in a climax, and that climax is prayer. How can brave warriors for Christ be made braver still? How can strong soldiers be made stronger still? How can victorious battlers be made still more victorious? Here are Paul's clear and specific directions to that end: "Praying always with all prayer and supplication in the Spirit, and watching thereunto with all perseverance and supplication for all saints."[9]

Prayer, and more prayer, adds to the fighting qualities and the more certain victories of God's good warriors. The power of prayer is most forceful on the battlefield in the middle of the noise and fury of the conflict. Paul was preeminently a soldier of the Cross. For him, life was no flowery bed of ease. He was no dress-parade, holiday soldier, whose only business was to put on a uniform for special occasions. His was a life of intense conflict, the facing of many adversaries, the exercise of unsleeping vigilance and constant effort. When the end of his life and battle were in sight, we hear him chanting his final song of victory: "I have fought a good fight."[10] Reading between the lines, we can easily see that he was more than a conqueror!

THE NATURE OF A SOLDIER'S LIFE

In his letter to the Romans, Paul indicates the nature of his soldier-life, and gives us some views of the kind of praying needed for such a career. He writes:

Now I beseech you, brethren, for the Lord Jesus Christ's sake, and for the love of the Spirit, that ye strive together with me in your prayers to God for me; that I may be delivered from them that do not believe in Judea.

Paul had enemies in Judea—enemies who surrounded and opposed him in the form of unbelieving people. Added to other burdensome reasons, this led him to urge the Roman Christians to "strive together" with him in prayer. That word "strive" indicates wrestling—putting forth great effort. This is the kind of effort and spirit that must possess Christian soldiers.

Here is Paul, a great soldier in a great struggle, faced by evil forces who seek his ruin. His spiritual strength is nearly gone. What reinforcements can he count on? What can give help and bring success to a warrior in such a pressing emergency? It is a critical moment in the conflict. What force can be added to the energy of his own prayers? The answer is: the prayers of others—the prayers of his brothers and sisters in Rome. He believes these will bring him additional aid so that he can win his fight and overcome his adversaries.

PRAY ALWAYS

Christian soldiers are to pray at all times and under all circumstances. Their praying must be arranged to cover their times of peace as well as their hours of active conflict. It must be available in their marching and their fighting. Prayer must strengthen all effort, saturate all ventures, decide all issues. Christian soldiers must be as intense in their praying as in their fighting, for their victories will depend much more on their praying than on their fighting. Fervent supplication must be added to steady resolve. Prayer and supplication must supplement the armor of God. The Holy Spirit must aid the supplication with His own strenuous plea, and the soldiers must pray in the Spirit. In this, as in other forms of warfare, eternal vigilance is the price of victory. So watchfulness and persistent perseverance must mark every activity of Christian warriors.

Our battle prayers must reflect our profound concern for the success and well-being of the whole army. The battle is not altogether a personal matter. Victory cannot be achieved for self alone. There is a sense in which the entire army of Christ is involved. The cause of God, His saints, their woes and trials, their duties and crosses—all should find a voice and a pleader in Christian soldiers when they pray. We dare not limit our praying to ourselves. Nothing dries up spiritual rivers so certainly and completely, nothing poisons the fountain of spiritual life so effectively, and nothing acts in such deadly fashion as selfish praying.

OUR ARMOR IS USELESS WITHOUT PRAYER

Note carefully that our Christian armor is of no use to us unless prayer is added. This is the pivot, the connecting link of the armor of God. This holds it together and makes it effective. God's true soldiers plan their campaigns, arrange their battle-forces, and engage in conflict with prayer. Prayer is all important and absolutely essential to victory—it should so saturate the life that every breath is a petition, every sigh a supplication. Christian soldiers must always be fighting. Out of sheer necessity, therefore, they should always be praying.

Christian soldiers are forced to be constantly on guard duty and always watching for danger. They are faced by a foe who never sleeps, who is always alert, and ever prepared to take advantage of the changing fortunes of war. Watchfulness is a cardinal principle with Christ's warriors. "Watch and pray"[11] forever sounds in their ears. They cannot dare to be asleep at their post. Such carelessness brings them not only under the displeasure of the Captain of their salvation, but exposes them to added danger. Watchfulness, therefore, is absolutely required for the soldiers of the Lord.

WATCHFULNESS

In the New Testament, there are three different words that are translated "watch." The first means "absence of sleep," and implies a wakeful frame of mind, as opposed to listlessness. It is a command to keep awake, attentive, steady, and vigilant. The second word means "fully awake." It is a state induced by some rousing,[12] active, cautious effort, lest through carelessness or laziness some destructive disaster should suddenly occur. The third word means "to be calm and collected in spirit," unemotional, untouched by tranquilizing or clouding influences, watching for all snares and enticements.

All three definitions are used by Paul. Two of them are used in connection with prayer. Intensified watchfulness is required for prayer. Watchfulness must guard and cover the whole spiritual person, and prepare the person for prayer. Everything resembling unpreparedness or non-vigilance is death to prayer.

In his letter to the Ephesians, Paul gives prominence to the duty of constant watchfulness: "Watching thereunto with all perseverance and supplication."[13] Watch, he says, watch, WATCH! "And what I say unto you I say unto all, Watch."[14]

WAKEFULNESS IS THE PRICE OF VICTORY

Sleepless wakefulness is the price we must pay for victory over our spiritual foes. Rest assured that the devil never falls asleep. He always "walketh about, seeking whom he may devour.[15]" Just as a shepherd must never be careless and unwatchful lest the wolf devour the sheep, so Christian soldiers must always have their eyes wide open—showing that they possess a spirit that neither slumbers nor grows careless. The inseparable companions and safeguards of prayer are vigilance, watchfulness, and a mounted guard.[16] In writing to the Colossians, Paul groups these inseparable qualities together: "Continue in prayer, and watch in the same with thanksgiving."[17]

When will Christians more thoroughly learn the twofold lesson that they are called to a great warfare, and that in order to get the victory they must give themselves to unsleeping watchfulness and unceasing prayer? "Be sober, be vigilant," says Peter, "because your adversary, the devil, as a roaring lion walketh about, seeking whom he may devour."[18]

THE MILITANT HOST

God's church is a militant host. Its warfare is with unseen forces of evil. God's people compose an army fighting to establish His kingdom in the earth. Their aim is to destroy the kingdom of Satan and to erect the Kingdom of God over its ruins, which is "righteousness, and peace, and joy in the Holy Ghost."[19] This militant army is composed of individual soldiers of the Cross, the armor of God is its defense, and prayer is the added power that crowns it all.

> Stand then in His great might,
> With all His strength endued;
> But take, to arm you for the fight,
> The shield and sword of God.

Prayer is too simple and too obvious a duty to need definition. Necessity gives being and shape to prayer. Its importance is so absolute that the breadth and intensity of the lives of Christian soldiers should be filled of prayer. The entire life of a Christian soldier—its being, intention, implication, and action—are all dependent on its being a life of prayer. Without prayer—no matter what else they have—the lives of Christian will be feeble and ineffective, and make them easy prey for their spiritual enemies.

NO CHRISTIAN INFLUENCE WITHOUT PRAYER

If prayer does not have a high place in our lives, our Christian experience will be without spirit and our influence will be dry and lifeless. Without prayer the Christian graces will wither and die. We may also add that without, prayer preaching is dull and useless and the Gospel loses its wings and its power. Christ is the lawgiver of prayer, and Paul is His apostle of prayer. Both declare prayer's primary importance and demonstrate its indispensibility. Their prayer-directions cover all places, include all times, and encompass all things. How, then, can Christian soldiers hope or dream of victory unless they are fortified by prayer's power? How can they fail, if in addition to putting on the armor of God, they are at all times and seasons "Praying always with all prayer and supplication in the Spirit, and watching thereunto with all perseverance and supplication for all saints"?[20]

Endnotes

1 Ephesians 6:18
2 2 Timothy 4:7
3 Ephesians 6:18-20a
4 2 Timothy 2:3
5 2 Timothy 4:7-8
6 Ephesians 6:12
7 Ephesians 6:13, 18
8 Ephesians 6:10-11, 13
9 Ephesians 6:18
10 2 Timothy 4:7
11 Matthew 26:41
12 Phrase removed: "which faculty excited to attention and interest,"
13 Ephesians 6:18
14 Mark 13:37
15 I Peter 5:8
16 A mounted guard in Bounds' day was like a mounted police officer today.
17 Colossians 4:2
18 I Peter 5:8
19 Romans 14:17
20 Ephesians 6:18

12

Prayer and the Word of God

W E CONSTANTLY ENCOUNTER IN *the Scriptures such words as 'field,' 'seed,' 'sower,' 'reaper,' 'seed-time,' 'harvest'! Employing such metaphors interprets a fact of nature by a parable of grace. The field is the world and the good seed is the Word of God .Whether the Word is spoken or written, it is the power of God unto salvation.[1] In our work of evangelism, the whole world is our field, every creature the object of effort, and every book and tract a seed of God.* (David Fant Jr.)

God's Word is a record of prayer—of praying men and women and their achievements, of the divine sanction of prayer, and of the encouragement given to those who pray. No one can read the instances, commands, examples, and the many various statements that concern themselves with prayer, without realizing that the cause of God and the success of His work in this world are committed to prayer. Praying men and women have been God's representatives on earth, but prayerless men and women have never been used by Him.

A reverence for God's holy name is closely related to a high regard for His Word. The hallowing of God's Name, the ability to do His will on earth as it is done in heaven, and the establishment and glory of God's kingdom are as much involved in prayer as when Jesus taught His disciples the universal prayer.[2] That Christians "ought always to pray and not to faint"[3] is as fundamental to God's cause today as when Jesus Christ enshrined that great truth in the immortal settings of the parable of the persistent widow.[4]

God's house is called "the house of prayer"[5] because prayer is the most important of its holy offices. By the same token, the Bible may be called the book of prayer. Prayer is the great theme and content of its message to humanity.

PRAYER AND THE WORD

God's Word is the basis and the directory of the prayer of faith. "Let the word of Christ dwell in you richly in all wisdom," says Paul, "teaching and admonishing one another in psalms and hymns and spiritual songs, singing with grace in your hearts to the Lord."[6]

As this word of Christ dwelling in us richly is transformed and absorbed, it flows forth in praying. Faith is constructed of the Word and the Spirit, and faith is the body and substance of prayer.

In many of its aspects, prayer is dependent upon the Word of God. Jesus said, "If ye abide in Me, and My words abide in you, ye shall ask what ye will, and it shall be done unto you."[7]

The Word of God is the support upon which the lever of prayer is placed, and by which things are mightily moved. God has committed Himself, His purpose, and His promise to prayer. His Word becomes the basis and the inspiration of our praying. There are also circumstances under which persistent prayer may obtain an addition or enlargement of God's promises. It is said of the old saints that "through faith" they "obtained promises."[8] There would seem to be in prayer the capacity for going even beyond the Word—of getting even beyond God's promise into His very presence.

Jacob did not so much wrestle with a promise as with the Promiser. We must take hold of the Promiser, lest the promise prove invalid. Prayer may well be defined as the force that vitalizes and energizes the Word of God by taking hold of God Himself. By taking hold of the Promiser, prayer brings forth the promise again and makes it personal. "There is none . . . that stirreth up himself to take hold of Me"[9] is God's sad lament. "Let him take hold of My strength, that he may make peace with Me, is God's recipe for prayer.[10]

PRAYER OF FAITH AND PRAYER OF SUBMISSION

By scriptural authority, prayer may be divided into the prayer of faith and the prayer of submission. The prayer of faith is based on the written Word, for "faith cometh by hearing, and hearing by the Word of God."[11] It is certain to receive its answer—the very thing for which it prays.

The prayer of submission is without a definite word of promise, so to speak. It takes hold of God with a lowly and contrite spirit, and asks and pleads with Him for what the soul desires. Abraham had no definite promise that God would spare Sodom.[12] Moses had no definite promise that God would spare Israel—on the contrary, there was the declaration of

His wrath and of His purpose to destroy. But the devoted leader gained his plea with God when he interceded for the Israelites with incessant prayers and many tears.[13] Daniel had no definite promise that God would reveal to him the meaning of the king's dream, but he prayed specifically, and God answered definitely.[14]

The Word of God is made effective and operative by the process and practice of prayer. The Word of the Lord came to Elijah, "Go, shew thyself to Ahab; and I will send rain on the earth."[15] Elijah showed himself to Ahab, but the answer to his prayer did not come until he had pressed his fiery prayer upon the Lord seven times.[16]

Paul had the definite promise from Christ, who said to him, "I will deliver you from the Jewish people, as well as from the Gentiles, to whom I now send you."[17] Yet we find him exhorting the Romans in an urgent and solemn manner concerning this very matter: "Now I beseech you, brethren, for the Lord Jesus Christ's sake, and for the love of the Spirit, that ye strive together with me in your prayers to God for me; That I may be delivered from them that do not believe in Judea; and that my service which I have for Jerusalem may be accepted of the saints."[18]

THE WORD AND PRAYER

The Word of God is a great help in prayer. If it is lodged and written in our hearts, it will create an outpouring current of prayer that is full and irresistible. Promises stored in the heart are the fuel from which prayer receives life and warmth. Just as the oil that is stored in the earth ministers to our comfort on stormy days and wintry nights. The Word of God is the food by which prayer is nourished and made strong. Like people, prayer cannot live by bread alone, "but by every word that proceedeth out of the mouth of God."[19]

Unless the living forces of prayer are supplied by God's Word, even earnest prayer, though it may even be strong and noisy in its urgency, is, in reality, flabby, lifeless, and empty. The absence of living force in praying can be traced to the absence of a constant supply of God's Word to repair the waste and renew the life. Those who would learn to pray well must first study God's Word, and store it in their memory and thoughts.

When we consult God's Word, we find that no duty is more binding and more exacting than that of prayer. But we also discover that no privilege is more exalted and no habit is more richly acknowledged by God. No promises are more radiant, more numerous, more definite, more often repeated than those that are attached to prayer. "All things, whatsoever"[20] are received by prayer because "all things whatsoever" are promised. There is no limit to the provisions included in the promises to prayer, and nothing is excluded from its promises. "For every one that asketh receiveth."[21] The word of our Lord is to this all-embracing effect: "If ye shall ask any thing in My name, I will do it."[22]

PROMISES AND PRAYER

Here are some of the comprehensive and exhaustive statements of the Word of God about prayer, the things to be received by prayer, and the strong promise made to answer prayer:

"Pray without ceasing;"[23] "continue in prayer;"[24] "continuing instant in prayer;"[25] "in everything by prayer, let your request be made known unto God;"[26] "always to pray, and not to faint;"[27] "men [should] pray everywhere;"[28] "praying always with all prayer and supplication."[29]

What clear and strong statements these are—put into the divine record to furnish us with a sure basis of faith and to urge, constrain, and encourage us to pray! How wide the range of prayer given to us in the divine revelation! How these Scriptures inspire us to seek the God of prayer with all our needs and all our burdens!

In addition to these statements left on record for our encouragement, the sacred pages teem with facts, examples, incidents, and observations, stressing the importance and the absolute necessity of prayer, and putting emphasis on its all-prevailing power.

PUTTING THE PROMISES TO THE TEST

The furthest reach and full benefit of the rich promises of the Word of God should humbly be received by us and be put to the test. The world will never receive the full benefits of the Gospel until this is done. Neither Christian experience nor Christian living will be what they should be until these divine promises have been fully tested by those who pray. By prayer we bring these promises of God's holy will into the realm of the actual and the real. Prayer is the philosopher's stone that transmutes them into gold.[30]

If asked what is to be done to make God's promises real, the answer is—we must pray until the words of the promise are brought unto fulfillment.

God's promises are altogether too large to be mastered by random praying. When we examine ourselves, we all too often discover that our praying does not rise to the demands of the situation. It is so limited that it acts as little more than a mere oasis amid the waste and desert of the world's sin. In our praying, who of us measures up to this promise of our Lord?

Verily, verily, I say unto you, He that believeth on Me, the works that I do shall he do also; and greater works than these shall he do, because I go to My Father.[31]

How comprehensive, how far reaching, how all-embracing! How much is here for the glory of God, how much for the good of humanity! How much for the manifestation of Christ's enthroned power, how much for the reward of abundant faith! And how great and gracious are the results that can be made to increase by the exercise of persistent, believing, prayer!

Look, for a moment, at another of God's great promises, and discover how we may be supported by the Word as we pray, and on what firm ground we may stand on which to make our petitions to our God. "If ye abide in Me, and My words abide in you, ye shall ask what ye will, and it shall be done unto you."[32]

In these comprehensive words, God turns Himself over to the will of His people. When Christ becomes our all-in-all, prayer lays God's treasures at our feet. Primitive Christianity had an easy and practical solution of the situation, and got all that God had to give. That simple, brief, solution is recorded in John's first letter: "Whatsoever we ask, we receive of Him, because we keep His commandments, and do those things which are pleasing in His sight."[33]

WHAT PRAYER DOES

Prayer coupled with loving obedience is the way to put God to the test, and to make prayer answer all requests and all things. Prayer joined to the Word of God hallows and makes sacred all of God's gifts. Prayer is not simply to get things from God, but to make those things holy that already have been received from Him. It is not merely to get a blessing, but also to be able to give a blessing. Prayer makes common things holy and secular things sacred. It receives things from God with thanksgiving and hallows them with thankful hearts and devoted service.

In his first letter to Timothy, Paul gives us these words: "For every creature of God is good, and nothing to be refused, if it be received with thanksgiving: For it is sanctified by the word of God and prayer."[34]

That is a statement that says 'no' to mere self-denial. God's good gifts are to be holy, not only by God's creative power but, also, by prayer. We receive them, appropriate them, and sanctify them by prayer.

KNOWING AND DOING GOD'S WILL

Doing God's will and having His Word abiding in us is an unbreakable principle of effective praying. But it may be asked, "How are we to know what God's will is?" The answer is simple—by studying His Word, by hiding it in our hearts, and by letting the Word dwell in us richly. "The entrance of Thy words, giveth light."[35]

To know God's will in prayer, we must be filled with God's Spirit, who makes intercession for the saints, and in the saints, according to the will of God.[36] To be filled with God's Spirit, to be filled with God's Word, is to know God's will. It is to be put into a frame of mind and state of heart that will enable us to read and interpret rightly the purposes of the Infinite. Our hearts filled with the Word and the Spirit gives us insight into the will of the Father, and enables us to rightly discern His will. It puts within us a disposition of mind and heart to make His will the guide and compass of our lives.

Epaphras prayed that the Colossians might stand "perfect and complete in all the will of God."[37] This is proof positive that not only may we know the will of God, but that we may know *all* the will of God. And not only may we know all the will of God, but we may do *all* the will of God. Also, we can do all the will of God habitually, as a settled manner of conduct, not just occasionally or on impulse. Still further, it shows us that we may not only do the will of God externally, but cheerfully from the heart—without reluctance or secret distaste or any drawing or holding back from the intimate presence of the Lord.

Endnotes

1 Romans 1:16
2 Matthew 6:9-13
3 Luke 18:1
4 Luke 18:1-8
5 Matthew 21:13
6 Colossians 3:16
7 John 15:7
8 Hebrews 11:33
9 Isaiah 64:7
10 Isaiah 27:5
11 Romans 10:17
12 Genesis 18:16-33
13 Deuteronomy 9:12-19
14 Daniel 2:1-45
15 I Kings 18:1
16 I Kings 18:41-44
17 Acts 26:17 (NKJV)
18 Romans 15:30-31
19 Matthew 4:4
20 Matthew 21:22
21 Luke 11:10
22 John 14:14
23 I Thessalonians 5:17
24 Colossians 4:2
25 Romans 12:12
26 Philippians 4:6
27 Luke 18:1
28 I Timothy 2:8
29 Ephesians 6:18
30 Figuratively, the "philosopher's stone" is a substance thought to be capable of regenerating people spiritually. Practitioners of alchemy believed that it was possible to change other metals or stones into gold.
31 John 14:12
32 John 15:7
33 I John 4:22
34 I Timothy 4:4
35 Psalm 119:130
36 Romans 8:26
37 Colossians 4:12

13

Prayer and the Word of God (Continued)

SOME YEARS AGO A *man was traveling in the wilds of Kentucky. He had with him a large sum of money and was well armed. He stayed at a log-house one night, but was much concerned about the rough appearance of the men who came and went from the house. He retired early but not to sleep. At midnight he heard the dogs barking furiously and the sound of someone entering the cabin. Peering through a crack in the boards of his room, he saw a stranger with a gun in his hand. Another man sat before the fire. The traveler concluded they were planning to rob him, and prepared to defend himself and his property. Presently, however, the newcomer took down a copy of the Bible, read a chapter aloud, and then knelt down and prayed. The traveler dismissed his fears, put his revolver away, and laid down and slept peacefully until the morning light. All because a Bible was in the cabin, and its owner a man of prayer.* (Rev. F. F. Shoup)

Prayer has all to do with the success of the preaching of the Word. Paul clearly teaches this in that familiar and pressing request he made to the Thessalonians: "Finally, brethren, pray for us that the Word of the Lord may have free course, and be glorified."[1]

Prayer opens the way for the Word of God to run without being slowed down or stopped. It creates the atmosphere that is favorable to the word accomplishing its purpose. Prayer puts wheels under God's Word, and gives wings to the angel of the Lord: "having the everlasting Gospel to preach unto them that dwell on the earth, and to every nation, and kindred, and tongue, and people."[2] Prayer greatly helps the Word of the Lord.

THE PARABLE OF THE SOWER

The parable of the sower is a notable study of preaching, showing its differing effects and describing the diversity of hearers. The wayside hearers are a legion. The soil lies totally unprepared by either previous thought or prayer. Consequently, the devil easily takes away the seed—the Word of God. He scatters all good impressions and makes the work of the sower fruitless. If those who hear the Word would prepare the ground of their hearts beforehand by prayer and meditation,[3] much of today's sowing would produce the fruit it should.

It is the same with the stony-ground hearers, and the thorny-ground hearers. Although the Word lodges in their hearts and begins to sprout, it is all lost because the Word is not followed by prayer, watchfulness, or cultivation. The good-ground hearers benefit from the sowing because their minds have been prepared to receive the seed. Also, after hearing the Word they have cultivated the seed sown in their hearts by the exercise of prayer. All this gives special emphasis to the conclusion of this striking parable: "Take heed therefore how ye hear."[4] To take heed how we hear, we need to give ourselves continually to prayer.

We have got to believe that underlying God's Word is prayer, and that its final success depends upon it. In the book of Isaiah we read, "So shall my word be that goeth forth out of my mouth: it shall not return unto me void, but it shall accomplish that which I please, and it shall prosper in the thing whereto I sent it.[5]

THE WORD OF GOD

In Psalm 19, David magnifies the Word of God in six statements concerning it. It converts the soul, makes wise the simple, rejoices the heart, enlightens the eyes, endures eternally, and is altogether true and righteous.[6] The Word of God is perfect, sure, right, pure. It both searches and purifies the heart. It is no surprise, therefore, that after considering the deep spirituality of the Word of God, its power to search the inner nature of a person, and its deep purity, the Psalmist should close his dissertation with this passage:

> Who can understand his errors? cleanse thou me from secret faults. Keep back thy servant also from presumptuous sins; let them not have dominion over me: then shall I be upright, and I shall be innocent from the great transgression. Let the words of my mouth, and the meditation of my heart, be acceptable in thy sight, O Lord, my strength, and my redeemer.[7]

James recognizes the deep spirituality of the Word and its inherent saving power in the following exhortation: "Wherefore lay apart all filthiness and superfluity of naughtiness, and receive with meekness the engrafted word, which is able to save your souls."[8]

Peter talks along the same line when describing the saving power of the Word of God: "Being born again, not of corruptible seed, but of incorruptible, by the word of God, which liveth and abideth forever."[9]

Not only does Peter speak of being born again by the incorruptible Word of God, but he informs us that to grow in grace we must be like new-born babes, desiring or feeding upon the "sincere milk of the Word."[10]

That is not to say, however, that the mere form of words as they occur in the Bible have in them any saving power.[11] But we should always remember that the Word of God is impregnated with the Holy Spirit. So just as there is a divine element in the words of Scripture, so also is the same divine element to be found in all true preaching of the Word, which is able to save and convert the soul.

PRAYER CREATES A LOVE FOR THE WORD OF GOD

Prayer invariably creates a love for the Word of God and causes people to read it. Prayer leads people to obey the Word of God, and puts a joy unspeakable[12] into the heart of those who obey. Praying people and Bible-reading people are the same sort of folk. The God of the Bible and the God of prayer are one. God speaks to the person by the Bible. The person speaks to God by prayer. One reads the Bible to discover God's will, and prays in order to receive power to do that will. Bible-reading and praying are the distinguishing traits of those who strive to know and please God. Prayer creates a love for the Scriptures and causes people to read the Bible. It also causes them to visit the house of God to hear the Scriptures expounded. Churchgoing is closely connected with the Bible, not so much because the Bible cautions us against "forsaking the assembling of ourselves together, as the manner of some is," but because in God's house His chosen ministers declare the Word explain the Scriptures, and enforce their teachings upon the hearers. In those who practice it, prayer also develops a resolve not to forsake the house of God.

Prayer creates a church-going conscience, a church-loving heart, and a church-supporting spirit. It is the praying people who make it a matter of conscience to attend the preaching of the Word, who delight in its reading and exposition, and who support it with their influence and their means. Prayer exalts the Word of God and gives it preeminence in the estimation of those who faithfully and wholeheartedly call upon the name of the Lord.

PRAYER AND PSALM 119

Prayer draws its very life from the Bible, and has no standing ground outside of the authority of the Scriptures. Its very existence and character is dependent on revelation made by God to humanity in His holy Word. In turn, prayer exalts this same revelation and turns people toward that

Word. The nature, necessity, and all-comprehending character of prayer, is based on the Word of God.

Psalm 119 is a directory of God's Word. With only three or four exceptions, each verse contains a word that identifies or establishes the Word of God. Quite often the writer breaks out into supplication—several times praying, "Teach me Thy statutes."[13] He is so deeply impressed with the wonders of God's Word, and with the need for divine light to see and understand the wonderful things recorded in it, that he fervently prays, "Open Thou mine eyes, that I may behold wondrous things out of Thy law."[14]

From the opening of this wonderful Psalm to its close, prayer and God's Word are intertwined. Almost every phase of God's Word is touched upon by this inspired writer. So thoroughly convinced was the Psalmist of the deep spiritual power of the Word of God that he makes this declaration: "Thy word have I hid in my heart that I might not sin against Thee."[15]

Here the Psalmist found his protection against sinning—by having God's Word hidden in his heart, and having his whole being thoroughly impregnated with that Word. Having been brought completely under the Word's gentle and gracious influence, he was given the ability to walk back and forth on the earth safe from the attack of the evil one, and fortified against a tendency to wander out of the way.

We find, furthermore, the power of prayer to create a real love for the Scriptures, and to put within people a nature that takes pleasure in the Word. In holy ecstasy David cries, "O, how I love Thy law! It is my meditation all the day."[16] And again: "How sweet are Thy words to my taste! Yea, sweeter than honey to my taste."[17]

READING THE WORD OF GOD

Do we want to have a love for God's Word? Then let us give ourselves continually to prayer. Those who would have a heart for the reading of the Bible must not—dare not—forget to pray. Christians of whom it can be said, their "delight is in the law of the Lord,"[18] are the ones who can truly say, "I delight to visit the place of prayer." No person loves the Bible who does not love to pray. No person loves to pray who does not delight in the law—the Word—of the Lord.

Our Lord was a person of prayer, and He magnified the Word of God, quoting often from the Scriptures. Right through His earthly life, Jesus observed Sabbath-keeping, churchgoing, and the reading of the Word of God. Intermingled with it all were His prayers: "And He came to Nazareth, where He had been brought up: and, as His custom was, He went into the synagogue on the Sabbath Day, and stood up to read."[19]

Let it be said that no two things are more essential to a spirit-filled life than Bible-reading and secret prayer. And no two things are more helpful to growth in grace, to getting the largest joy out of a Christian life, and to establishing one in the ways of eternal peace. The neglect of these all-important duties will result in leanness of soul, loss of joy, absence of peace, dryness of spirit, and decay in all that pertains to spiritual life. Neglecting these things paves the way for apostasy, and gives the evil one an advantage that he is not likely to ignore. Reading God's Word regularly, and praying habitually in the secret place of the Most High,[20] puts us where we are absolutely safe from the attacks of the enemy of souls, and guarantees us salvation and final victory through the overcoming power of the Lamb.

Endnotes

1 I Thessalonians 3:1
2 Revelation 14:6
3 Jeremiah 4:3
4 Luke 8:18
5 Isaiah 55:11
6 Psalm 19:7-9
7 Psalm 19:12-14
8 James 1:21
9 I Peter 1:23
10 I Peter 2:2
11 John 5:39-40
12 I Peter 1:8
13 Psalm 119:12
14 Psalm 119:18
15 Psalm 119:11
16 Psalm 119:97
17 Psalm 119:103
18 Psalm 1:2
19 Luke 4:16
20 Psalm 91:11

14

Prayer and the House of God

And dear to me the loud "Amen,"
Which echoes through the blest abode—
Which swells, and sinks, then swells again,
Dies on the walls—but lives with God!

PRAYER IS RELATED TO places, times, occasions, and circumstances. It has to do with God and with everything that is related to God, and it has an intimate and special relationship to His house. A church is a sacred place, set apart from all unhallowed and secular uses, for the worship of God. As worship is prayer, the house of God is a place set apart for worship. It is no common place. It is where God dwells, where He meets with His people, and where He delights in the worship of His saints.

Prayer is always in place in the house of God. When prayer is a stranger there, then it ceases to be God's house at all. Our Lord put special emphasis upon what the church was when He cast out the buyers and sellers in the Temple, repeating the words from Isaiah, "It is written, My house shall be called the house of prayer."[1] He makes prayer more important than everything else in the house of God. Those who sidetrack prayer or seek to minimize it and give it a secondary place, pervert the Church of God and make it something less and other than it is ordained to be.[2]

PRAYER IS PERFECTLY AT HOME IN THE HOUSE OF GOD

Prayer is not a stranger or a mere guest in the house of God—it belongs there. It has a peculiar attraction and relationship to the place. Moreover, it has a divine right to be there, having been set in the Church by divine authority and approval.

The inner chamber is a sacred place for personal worship. The house of God is a holy place for united worship. The prayer-closet is for individual prayer. The house of God is for mutual prayer, concerted prayer, united prayer. Yet even in the house of God there is the element of private worship, since God's people are to worship Him and pray to Him personally even in public worship. The Church is for the united prayer of closely related, yet individual, believers.

THE LIFE, POWER, AND GLORY OF THE CHURCH IS PRAYER

The life of Church members is dependent on prayer. The presence of God is obtained and retained by prayer. Even the place where the Church gathers is made sacred by its ministry. Without it, the Church is lifeless and powerless. Without it, even the building itself is nothing more than any other structure. Prayer converts even the bricks, concrete, and lumber, into a sanctuary—a holy of holies where the Shekinah[3] dwells. Prayer separates the building, in spirit and in purpose, from all other structures. Prayer gives a peculiar sacredness to the building, sanctifies it, sets it apart for God, conserves it from all common, ordinary, and secular affairs.

With prayer, the house of God becomes a divine sanctuary, even though it might seem to lack everything else. As the Tabernacle in the wilderness moved from place to place, it was always the holy of holies because prayer was there. Without prayer, a church building may be costly, perfect in all its furnishings, beautiful for situation,[4] and attractive to the eye, but it is lowered to human status with nothing divine in it.

A CHURCH IS DEAD WITHOUT PRAYER

Without prayer, a church is like a body without spirit—it is a dead, inanimate thing. A church with prayer in it has God in it. When prayer is set aside, God is set aside. When prayer becomes an unfamiliar practice, then God Himself is a stranger there.

Since God's house is a house of prayer, it is God's intention that people leave their homes and go to meet Him in His own house. The church building is especially set apart for prayer. Because God has made a special promise to meet His people there, it is their duty to go there for that specific purpose. Prayer should be the chief attraction for all spiritually minded church-goers. Admittedly, the preaching of the Word has an important place in the house of God, but prayer is the predominating, distinguishing, feature. It is not that all other places are sinful or evil in themselves or in their uses. But they are secular and human and have no special concept of God in them.

The Church is essentially religious and divine. Therefore, its buildings and the work done in them should be of the same nature. The work done in other places is done without special reference to God. He is not specifically recognized or called upon. In the Church, however, God is acknowledged, and nothing is done without Him. Prayer is the one distinguishing mark of the house of God. As prayer (in the name of Jesus Christ) distinguishes Christians from all who are not Christians, so prayer distinguishes God's house from all other houses. It is a place where faithful believers meet with their Lord.

THE SCHOOLHOUSE OF PRAYER

Since God's house is preeminently a house of prayer, prayer should enter into and undergird—support and strengthen—everything that is undertaken there. Prayer belongs to every sort of work appertaining to the Church of God. God's house is a house where the business of praying is carried on, and so it is a place where the business of making praying people out of prayerless people is done. The house of God is a divine workshop, and there the work of prayer goes on. Or the house of God is a divine schoolhouse in which the lesson of prayer is taught—the place where men and women learn to pray, and where they graduate from the school of prayer.[5]

Any church that calls itself the house of God but does not magnify prayer, put prayer in the forefront of its activities, or teach the great lesson of prayer, should change its teaching to conform to the divine pattern, or change the name of its building to something other than a house of prayer.

JOSIAH AND THE BOOK OF THE LAW

In the process of renovating the temple in about B.C. 621, a copy of the book of the law (either the Book of Deuteronomy or, more likely, the entire Pentateuch, the first five books of the Bible) was found. Evidently Manasseh or Amon had destroyed other copies so that the discovery of this one constituted an important find. Hilkiah the high priest shared his discovery with Shaphan who also read it.

After reporting on the progress of the restoration to Josiah, Shaphan informed the king of this important discovery and read it to him. How long that book had been there, we do not know. But upon hearing what God required of His people and comparing it with how far they had departed from His will, Josiah tore his clothes in distress and wept.

Then Josiah thought of God, and commanded Hilkiah to go and make inquiry of the Lord. Such neglect of the Word of the Law was too serious a matter to be treated lightly, and God must be sought and repentance made by the king and the nation.

> Go ye, enquire of the Lord for me, and for the people, and for all Judah, concerning the words of this book that is found: for great is the wrath of the Lord that is kindled against us, because our fathers have not hearkened unto the words of this book, to do according unto all that which is written concerning us.[6]

But that was not all. Josiah was determined to promote a revival of religion in his kingdom, so he gathered all the elders of Jerusalem and Judah together, for that purpose. When they had come together, the king went into the house of the Lord and read to them all the words of the book of the covenant that was found in the house of the Lord.[7]

With this righteous king, God's Word was of great importance. He esteemed it at its proper worth, and considered a knowledge of it to be of such grave importance that it required consulting God in prayer about it. Further, it warranted gathering together the notables of his kingdom so that he and they could be instructed out of God's Book concerning God's Law.

EZRA AND THE BOOK OF THE LAW

When Ezra had returned from Babylon and was seeking the reconstruction of his nation, the people themselves were concerned about the situation. On one occasion, the priests, Levites, and people assembled together as one person before the water gate.

And all the people gathered themselves together as one man into the street that was before the water gate; and they spake unto Ezra the scribe to bring the book of the law of Moses, which the Lord had commanded to Israel. And Ezra the priest brought the law before the congregation both of men and women, and all that could hear with understanding, upon the first day of the seventh month. And he read therein before the street that was before the water gate from the morning until midday, before the men and the women, and those that could understand; and the ears of all the people were attentive unto the book of the law.[8]

This was Bible reading day in Judah—a real revival of Scripture study. The leaders read the law before the people, whose ears were keen to hear what God had to say to them out of the book of the law. But it was not only a Bible-reading day. It was a time when real Bible preaching was done, as the following passage indicates: "So they read in the book in the law of God distinctly, and gave the sense, and caused them to understand the reading."[9]

THE SCRIPTURAL DEFINITION OF PREACHING

Here then is the Scriptural definition of preaching. No better definition can be given. To read the Word of God distinctly—so that the people could hear and understand the words read. Not to mumble the words, nor read them in an undertone or indistinctly, but boldly and clearly. That was the way it was done in Jerusalem on this great day. Moreover, the sense of the words was made clear in the meeting held before the water gate. The people were treated to a high type of expository preaching. That was true Bible preaching—preaching of a sort that is sorely needed, today so that God's Word will have the effect it should on the hearts of the people. This meeting in Jerusalem surely contains a lesson that all of today's Bible teachers should learn and heed.

No one having any knowledge of the existing facts will deny the comparative lack of expository preaching in the pulpit today. And surely there are none who will not deplore the lack. Topical preaching, controversial preaching, historical preaching, and other similar forms of sermons perhaps have their rightful uses. But expository preaching, the prayerful expounding of the Word of God, is preaching that is preaching—pulpit effort par excellence.

PREACHING AND PRAYING

For its successful accomplishment, however, a preacher must be a person of prayer. For every hour spent studying, two hours should be spent upon the knees. For every hour devoted to an obscure passage of holy Scripture, two hours should be spent in getting your words and thoughts from God. Pray that God will give you the message, and then pray that God will be in the message. Prayer and preaching, preaching and prayer! They cannot be separated. The ancient cry was, "To your tents, O Israel!"[10] The modern cry should be, "To your knees, O preachers, to your knees!"

Endnotes

1 Matthew 21:13

2 In this and other Pure Gold Classics, the word Church is capitalized when referring to the universal Church, the mystical body of Christ, and is lowercased when referring to a local church or building.

3 *Shekinah*: A visible manifestation of the divine presence.

4 Psalm 48:2

5 For further reading along this line, see the Pure Gold Classic, *With Christ in the School of Prayer* by Andrew Murray, ©1999, by Bridge-Logos Publishers.

6 2 Kings 22:1-13

7 2 Kings 23:1-2

8 Nehemiah 8:1-3

9 Nehemiah 8:8

10 1 Kings 12:16

BOOK 2

THE ESSENTIALS OF PRAYER

I

Prayer Takes in the Entire Person

HENRY CLAY TRUMBULL SPOKE *forth the Infinite in the terms of our world, and the Eternal in the forms of our human life. Some years ago, on a ferry-boat, I met a gentleman who knew him, and I told him that when I had last seen Dr. Trumbull, a fortnight before, he had spoken of him. "Oh, yes." said my friend, "he was a great Christian, so real, so intense. He was at my home years ago and we were talking about prayer." "Why, Trumbull," I said, "you don't mean to say if you lost a pencil you would pray about it, and ask God to help you find it?" "Of course I would; of course I would," was his instant and excited reply. Of course he would. Was not his faith a real thing? Like the Savior, he put his doctrine strongly by taking an extreme illustration to embody his principle, but the principle was fundamental. He did trust God in everything. And the Father honored the trust of His child.* (Robert E. Speer)

Prayer has to do with the entire person. Prayer takes in the person's entire being, mind, soul, and body. It takes the entire person to pray, and prayer affects the entire person in its gracious results. As the whole nature of a person enters into prayer, so also all that belongs to the person is the beneficiary of prayer. All of the person receives benefits in prayer. The whole person must be given to God in praying. The largest results in praying come to those who give themselves, all of themselves and all that belongs to them, to God. This is the secret of full consecration, and this is a condition of successful praying, and the sort of praying that brings the largest fruits.

The people of ancient times who were successful in prayer, who brought the largest things to pass, who moved God to do great things, were those who were entirely given over to God in their praying. God wants, and must have, all that there is in us in answering our prayers. He must have whole-hearted people through whom to work out His purposes and plans concerning humanity. God must have people in their entirety. No double-minded person need apply. No vacillating person can be used. No person with a divided allegiance to God, the world, and self, can do the praying that is needed.

HOLINESS IS WHOLENESS

Holiness is wholeness, and so God wants holy people, people whole-hearted and true, for His service and for the work of praying. "And the very God of peace sanctify you wholly; and I pray God your whole spirit and soul and body be preserved blameless unto the coming of our Lord Jesus Christ"[1] These are the sort of people God wants for leaders of the hosts of Israel, and these are the kind out of which the praying class is formed.

A person is a trinity in one, and yet neither a trinity nor a dual creature when praying, but a unit. A person is one in all the essentials and acts and attitudes of piety. Soul, spirit, and body are to unite in all things pertaining to life and godliness.

THE BODY IN PRAYER

The body is the first part of us that engages in prayer, since it assumes the praying attitude in prayer. Prostration of the body is appropriate in praying as well as prostration of the soul. The attitude of the body counts much in prayer, although it is true that the heart may be haughty and lifted up, the mind listless and wandering, and the praying a mere form, even while the knees are bent in prayer.

Daniel kneeled three times a day in prayer.[2] Solomon kneeled in prayer at the dedication of the temple.[3] Our Lord in Gethsemane prostrated Himself in that memorable season of praying just before His betrayal.[4] Where there is earnest and faithful praying, the body always takes on the form most suited to the state of the soul at the time. In that, the body joins the soul in praying.

The entire person must pray. The whole person, life, heart, temper, and mind, are in it. Each and all join in the prayer exercise. Doubt, double-mindedness, division of the affections, are all foreign to the prayer closet. Undefiled character and conduct, made whiter than snow, are mighty powers, and are the most pleasing beauties for the closet hour and the struggles of prayer.

THE MIND IN PRAYER

A loyal intellect must plan and add the energy and fire of its undoubting and undivided faith to the time of prayer. The mind necessarily enters into the praying. First of all, it takes thought to pray. The intellect teaches us we ought to pray. By serious thinking beforehand, the mind prepares itself for approaching a throne of grace.[5] Thought goes before entrance into the closet and prepares the way for true praying. It considers what will be asked for in the closet hour.

True praying does not leave to the inspiration of the hour, what will be the requests of that hour. Praying is asking for something definite of God, so the thought beforehand should be, "What shall I ask for at this hour?" By this, all vain, evil, and frivolous thoughts are eliminated, and the mind is given over entirely to God. It thinks only of Him, of what is needed, and what has been received in the past. When prayer takes hold of the entire person, it does not leave out the mind.

The very first step in prayer is a mental one. The disciples took that first step when they said to Jesus at one time, "Lord, teach us to pray."[6] We must be taught through the intellect. So only to the degree that the intellect is given up to God in prayer will we be able to learn well and easily the lesson of prayer.

THE WHOLE PERSON IN PRAYER

Paul spreads the nature of prayer over the whole person. It must be so. It takes the whole person to embrace in its god-like sympathies the entire race of humanity—the sorrows, the sins, and the death of Adam's fallen race. It takes the whole person to run parallel with God's high and sublime will in saving humankind. It takes the whole person to stand with our Lord Jesus Christ as the one Mediator between God and sinful humanity. This is the doctrine Paul teaches in his prayer directory in the second chapter of his first letter to Timothy.

Nowhere does it appear so clearly that it requires all parts of a person's being to pray than in this teaching of Paul. It takes the whole person to pray until all the storms that agitate the soul are calmed to a great calm—until the stormy winds and waves cease by a God-like spell. It takes the whole person to pray until cruel tyrants and unjust rulers are changed in their natures and lives, as well as in their governing qualities—or until they cease to rule. It requires the entire person in prayer until stern, proud, and unspiritual ecclesiastics become gentle, lowly, and spiritual. It takes the entire person in prayer until godliness and seriousness bear rule in church and in state, in home and in business, in public and in private life.

IT IS A PERSON'S BUSINESS TO PRAY

It is a person's business to pray, and it takes courageous people to do it. It is a godly business to pray and it takes godly people to do it. It is godly people who give over themselves entirely to prayer. Prayer is far-reaching in its influence and gracious effects. It is intense and profound business that deals with God and His plans and purposes, and it takes whole-hearted people to do it. No half-hearted, half-brained, half-spirited effort will do for this serious, all-important, heavenly business. The whole heart, the whole brain, the whole spirit, must be in the matter of praying, which is so mightily able to affect the characters and destinies of people.

The answer of Jesus to the scribe as to what was the first and greatest commandment was: "The Lord our God is one Lord; And thou shalt love the Lord thy God with all thy heart, and with thy soul, and with all thy mind, and with all thy strength."[7]

In one word, the entire person without reservation must love God. So it takes the same entire person to do the praying that God requires of people. All the powers of a person must be engaged in it. God cannot tolerate a divided heart in the love He requires of people, and neither can He bear with a divided person in prayer.

WHOLE-HEART PRAYING

In the Psalm 119, the Psalmist teaches this very truth in these words, "Blessed are they that keep his testimonies, and that seek him with the whole heart."[8] It takes whole-hearted people to keep God's commandments and it demands the same sort of people to seek God. These are the people that the psalmist says are counted "blessed." God's approval rests upon these whole-hearted ones.

Bringing the case closer home to himself, the Psalmist makes this statement about his own manner in prayer: "With my whole heart have I sought thee; O let me not wander from thy commandments."[9] Further on he gives us his prayer for a wise and understanding heart, and tells us his purposes concerning the keeping of God's law: "Give me understanding and I shall keep thy law; Yea, I shall observe it with my whole heart."[10]

Just as it requires a whole heart given to God to gladly and fully obey God's commandments, so it takes a whole heart to do effective praying. Because it requires the whole person to pray, praying is no easy task. Praying is far more than simply bending the knee and saying a few words mechanically or from memory.

> 'Tis not enough to bend the knee,
> And words of prayer to say;
> The heart must with the lips agree,
> Or else we do not pray.

PRAYERS OF JESUS

Praying is no light and superficial exercise. While children should be taught early to pray, praying is no child's task. Prayer draws upon the whole nature of a person. Prayer engages all the powers of a person's moral and spiritual nature. It is this that explains somewhat the praying of our Lord described in Hebrews 5:7:

Who in the days of his flesh, when he had offered up prayers and
supplications, with strong crying and tears, unto him that was able
to save him from death, and was heard in that he feared.

It takes only a moment's thought to see how such praying of our Lord
drew mightily upon all the powers of His being, and called into exercise
every part of His nature. This is the praying that brings the soul close to
God and that brings God down to earth.

Body, soul, and spirit are taxed and brought under tribute to prayer.
David Brainerd makes this record of his praying: "God enabled me to
agonize in prayer until I was wet with perspiration, though in the shade and
in a cool place."

The Son of God in Gethsemane was in an agony of prayer that
engaged His whole being:

And when he was at the place, he said unto them, Pray that ye enter
not into temptation. And he was withdrawn from them about a
stone's cast, and kneeled down, and prayed, Saying, Father, if thou
be willing, remove this cup from me: nevertheless not my will, but
thine, be done. And there appeared an angel unto him from heaven,
strengthening him. And being in an agony he prayed more earnestly:
and his sweat was as it were great drops of blood falling down to
the ground.[11]

Here was praying that laid its hands on every part of our Lord's nature,
which called forth all the powers of his soul, His mind and His body. This
was praying which took in the entire man.

PRAYERS OF PAUL

Paul was acquainted with this kind of praying. In writing to the Roman
Christians, he urges them to pray with him in this way: "Now I beseech
you, brethren, for the Lord Jesus Christ's sake, and for the love of the
Spirit, that ye strive together with me in your prayers to God for me."[12]

The words "strive together with me," tells of Paul's praying and how
much he put into it. It is not a feeble request, not a little thing, this sort of
praying, this "striving" is the nature of war, a conflict to win, a great battle
to be fought. Like a soldier, the praying Christian fights a life-and-death
struggle. Honor, immortality, and eternal life are all in it. This is praying
as the athlete struggles for mastery and the crown, and as he wrestles or
runs a race. Everything depends on the skill and strength put in it. Energy,
intensity, swiftness, every power of the athlete's nature is in it. Every power
is quickened and strained to its utmost. Littleness, half-heartedness,
weakness, and laziness are all absent.

THE WHOLE PERSON BENEFITS

Just as it takes the whole person to pray successfully, so in turn the whole person receives the benefits of such praying. As every part of a person's complex being enters into true praying, so every part of that same nature receives blessings from God in answer to such praying. This kind of praying engages our undivided hearts, our whole desires, our full consent to be the Lord's.

God sees to it that when the whole person prays the whole person is blessed. The person's body takes in the good of praying, for much praying is done specifically for the body. Food and raiment, health and bodily strength, come in answer to prayer. Clear mental action, right thinking, an enlightened understanding, and safe reasoning powers, come from praying. Divine guidance means God so moving and impressing the mind that we shall make wise and safe decisions. "The meek will He guide in judgment."[13]

PRAYING PREACHERS

Many praying preachers have been greatly helped just at this point. The unction of the Holy One that comes upon the preacher invigorates the mind, loosens up thought, and gives utterance. This is the explanation of former days when men and women of very limited education had such wonderful liberty of the Spirit in praying and in preaching. Their thoughts flowed as a stream of water. Their entire intellectual machinery felt the impulse of the divine Spirit's gracious influences.

And, of course, the soul receives large benefits in this sort of praying. Thousands can testify to this statement. So we repeat, that as the entire person comes into play in true, earnest, effective praying, so the entire person—soul, mind, and body—receives the benefits of prayer.

Endnotes

1 I Thessalonians 5:23
2 Daniel 6:10
3 I Kings 8:54
4 Matthew 26:39; Mark 14:35
5 Hebrews 4:16
6 Luke 11:1
7 Luke 10:27
8 Psalm 119:2
9 Psalm 119:10
10 Psalm 119:34
11 Luke 22:40-44
12 Romans 15:30
13 Psalm 25:9

2

Prayer and Humility

IF TWO ANGELS WERE *to receive at the same moment a commission from God, one to go down and rule earth's grandest empire, the other to go and sweep the streets of its meanest village, it would be a matter of entire indifference to each which service fell to his lot, the post of ruler or the post of scavenger; for the joy of the angels lies only in obedience to God's will, and with equal joy they would lift a Lazarus in his rags to Abraham's bosom, or be a chariot of fire to carry an Elijah home.* (John Newton)

To be humble is to have a low estimate of one's self.[1] It is to be modest, lowly, with a disposition to seek obscurity. Humility keeps itself from the public gaze. It does not seek publicity or hunt for high places—and it does not care for prominence. Humility is retiring in its nature. Self-abasement belongs to humility. It is given to self-depreciation. It never exalts itself in the eyes of others or in the eyes of itself. Modesty is one of its most prominent characteristics.

In humility there is a total absence of pride, and it is at the furthest distance from anything like self-conceit. There is no self-praise in humility. Rather it has the disposition to praise others. "In honor preferring one another."[2] It is not given to self-exaltation. Humility does not love the uppermost seats or aspire to the high places. It is willing to take the lowliest seat and prefers those places where it will be unnoticed. The prayer of humility is after this fashion:

Never let the world break in,
Fix a mighty gulf between;
Keep me humble and unknown,
Prized and loved by God alone.

Humility does not have its eyes on self, but on God and others. It is poor in spirit, meek in behavior, lowly in heart. "With all lowliness and meekness, with long-suffering, forbearing one another in love."[3]

THE PHARISEE AND PUBLICAN

The parable of the Pharisee and publican is a sermon in brief on humility and self-praise. The Pharisee, given over to self-conceit, wrapped up in himself, seeing only his own self-righteous deeds, catalogs his virtues before God while despising the poor publican who stands far off. He exalts himself, gives himself over to self-praise, and is self-centered. Because of this, he goes away unjustified, condemned, and rejected by God.

The publican sees no good in himself, is overwhelmed with self-depreciation, far removed from anything that would take any credit for any good in himself, and does not presume even to lift his eyes to heaven. With downcast eyes he smites himself on his breast and cries out, "God be merciful to me, a sinner."[4]

With great preciseness, our Lord gives us the sequel of the story of these two men—one utterly devoid of humility, and the other utterly submerged in the spirit of self-depreciation and lowliness of mind.

I tell you this man went down to his house justified rather than the other; for every one that exalteth himself shall be abased; and he that humbleth himself shall be exalted.[5]

HUMILITY OF THE HEART

God puts a great price on humility of heart. It is good to be clothed with humility as with a garment. It is written, "God resisteth the proud, but giveth grace unto the humble."[6] That which brings the praying soul near to God is humility of heart. That which gives wings to prayer is lowliness of mind. That which gives ready access to the throne of grace is self-depreciation. Pride, self-esteem, and self-praise effectively shut the door of prayer. Those who would come to God must approach Him with self hid from their eyes. They must not be puffed-up with self-conceit, or be possessed with an over-estimate of their virtues and good works.

Humility is a rare Christian grace, of great price in the courts of heaven. entering into and being an inseparable condition of effective praying. It gives access to God when other qualities fail. It takes many descriptions to describe it, and many definitions to define it. It is a rare and retiring grace. Its full portrait is found only in the Lord Jesus Christ. Our prayers must be set low before they can ever rise high. Our prayers must have much of the dust of humility on them before they can ever have much of the glory of heaven in them. In our Lord's teaching, humility has great prominence in His system of religion, and is a distinguishing feature of His character. So much so, that to leave it out of His lesson on prayer would be improper, would not agree with His character, and would not fit into His religious system.

PRAYING WITHOUT PRAYING

The parable of the Pharisee and publican stands out in such bold relief that we must again refer to it. The Pharisee seemed to be accustomed to prayer. Certainly he should have known by that time how to pray. But like many others, he seemed never to have learned this invaluable lesson. He leaves business and business hours and walks with steady and fixed steps up to the house of prayer. The position and place are well-chosen by him. There is the sacred place, the sacred hour, and the sacred name, each and all invoked by this seemingly praying man. But this ecclesiastic praying, though schooled in prayer by training and by habit, prays not. Words are uttered by him, but words are not prayer. God hears his words only to condemn him. A death-chill has come from those formal lips of prayer— a death-curse from God is on his words of prayer. Pride has entirely poisoned the prayer offering of that hour. His entire praying has been impregnated with self-praise, self-congratulation, and self-exaltation. That hour of going to the temple has had no worship whatever in it.

On the other hand, the publican is smitten with a deep sense of his sins and his inward sinfulness. He realizes how poor in spirit he is, and how utterly devoid of anything like righteousness, goodness, or any quality that would commend him to God. His pride is completely blasted and dead, and he falls down with humiliation and despair before God, uttering a sharp cry for mercy for his sins and his guilt. A sense of sin and a realization of complete unworthiness has fixed the roots of humility deep into his soul, and has driven self and eye and heart downward into the dust.

This is the picture of pride versus humility in praying. Here we are shown two things in sharp contrast. First, the utter worthlessness of self-righteousness, self-exaltation, and self-praise in praying. Second, the great value, the beauty and the divine commendation that comes to humility of heart, self-depreciation, and self-condemnation when a soul comes before God in prayer.

THE GROUND OF HUMILITY IS PRAYING GROUND

Happy are those who have no righteousness of their own to plead and no goodness of their own of which to boast. Humility flourishes in the soil of a true and deep sense of our sinfulness and our nothingness. Nowhere does humility grow so vigorously and so rapidly and shine so brilliantly as when it feels utterly guilty, confesses all sin, and trusts all grace. "I the chief of sinners am, but Jesus died for me."[7] That is praying ground, the ground of humility—low down, seemingly far away, but in reality brought near by the blood of the Lord Jesus Christ. God dwells in the lowly places with the contrite and humble.[8] He makes such lowly places the high places to the praying soul.

> Let the world their virtue boast,
> Their works of righteousness;
> I, a wretch undone and lost,
> Am freely saved by grace;
> Other tide I disclaim,
> This, only this, is all my plea,
> I the chief of sinners am,
> But Jesus died for me.

HUMILITY INDISPENSABLE FOR TRUE PRAYER

Humility is an indispensable requirement of true prayer. It must be an attribute, a characteristic, of prayer. Humility must be in the praying character as light is in the sun. Prayer has no beginning, no ending, no being, without humility. As a ship is made for the sea, so prayer is made for humility, and humility is made for prayer.

Humility is not isolated from self, nor does it ignore thought about self. It is a many-phased principle. Humility is born by looking at God and His holiness, and then looking at self and human unholiness. Humility loves obscurity and silence, dreads applause, esteems the virtues of others, excuses their faults with mildness, easily pardons injuries, fears contempt less and less, and sees baseness and falsehood in pride.

A true nobleness and greatness are in humility. It knows and reveres the inestimable riches of the Cross, and the humiliations of Jesus Christ. It fears the luster of those virtues admired by people, and loves those that are more secret and prized by God. It draws comfort even from its own defects, through the humiliation that they cause. It prefers any degree of contrition before it prefers the light of the world.

Somewhat like this description is that definable grace of humility that is so perfectly drawn in the publican's prayer, and so entirely absent from the prayer of the Pharisee. It takes many sittings to make a good picture of it.

HUMILITY AND A LIFE OF PRAYER

Humility holds in its keeping the very life of prayer. Neither pride nor vanity can pray. Humility, though, is much more than the absence of vanity and pride. It is a positive quality, a substantial force, that energizes prayer. There is no power in prayer to ascend to heaven without it. Humility springs from a lowly estimate of ourselves and what we deserve. The Pharisee prayed without praying, though well schooled and in the habit of praying, because there was no humility in his prayer. The publican prayed, though banned by the public and receiving no encouragement from the Church because he prayed in humility.

To be clothed with humility is to be clothed with a praying garment. Humility is feeling little because we are little. Humility is realizing our unworthiness because we are unworthy. It is feeling and declaring ourselves to be sinners because we are sinners. Kneeling shows the attitude of prayer, because it speaks of humility.

The Pharisee's proud estimate of himself and his supreme contempt for his neighbor closed the gates of prayer to him, while humility opened wide those gates to the defamed and reviled publican.

That fearful saying of our Lord about the works of big religious workers in the latter part of the Sermon on the Mount, is in response to proud estimates of work and wrong estimates of prayer:

> Many shall say unto me in that day, Lord, Lord, have we not prophesied in thy name? and in thy name cast out devils? and in thy name done many wonderful works? And then will I profess unto them, I never knew you: depart from me, ye that work iniquity.[9]

Humility is the first and last attribute of Christly religion, and the first and last attribute of Christly praying. There is no Christ without humility. There is no praying without humility. If you would learn well the art of praying, then learn well the lesson of humility.

THE ATTITUDE OF HUMILITY

How graceful and imperative does the attitude of humility become to us! Humility is one of the unchanging and exacting attitudes of prayer. Dust, ashes, earth upon the head, sackcloth for the body, and fasting for the appetites, were the symbols of humility for the Old Testament saints. Sackcloth, fasting ,and ashes brought Daniel a lowliness before God, and brought Gabriel to him. The angels are fond of the sackcloth-and-ashes people.

How lowly was the attitude of Abraham, the friend of God, when pleading for God to stay His wrath against Sodom! "Behold now, I have taken upon me to speak unto the Lord, which am but dust and ashes."[10] With what humility does Solomon appear before God! His grandeur is abased, and his glory and majesty are retired as he assumes the rightful attitude before God: "I am but a little child: I know not how to go out or come in."[11]

The pride of doing sends its poison all through our praying. The same pride of being infects all our prayers, no matter how well-worded they may be. It was this lack of humility, this self-applauding, this self-exaltation, that kept the most religious man of Christ's day from being accepted of God. The same thing will keep us in this day from being accepted of Him.

O that now I might decrease!
O that all I am might cease!
Let me into nothing fall!
Let my Lord be all in all.

Endnotes

1 Some say that true humility is not to think little of one's self, but to think of one's self not at all.
2 Romans 12:10
3 Ephesians 4:2
4 Luke 18:13
5 Luke 18:14
6 James 4:6
7 1 Timothy 1:15
8 Isaiah 57:15
9 Matthew 7:22-23
10 Genesis 18:27
11 1 Kings 3:7

3

Prayer and Devotion

ONCE AS I RODE *out into the woods for my health, in 1737, having alighted from my horse in a retired place, as my manner commonly had been to walk for divine contemplation and prayer, I had a view that for me was extraordinary, of the glory of the Son of God. As near as I can judge, this continued about an hour; and kept me the greater part of the time in a flood of tears and weeping aloud. I felt an ardency of soul to be what I know not otherwise how to express, emptied and annihilated; to love Him with a holy and pure love; to serve and follow Him; to be perfectly sanctified and made pure with a divine and heavenly purity.* (Jonathan Edwards)

Devotion has a religious signification. The root meaning of *devotion* is to devote to a sacred use. So devotion in its true sense has to do with religious worship. It stands intimately connected with true prayer.

Devotion is the particular frame of mind found in a person entirely devoted to God. It is the spirit of reverence, awe, and godly fear. It is a state of heart that appears before God in prayer and worship. It is foreign to everything like lightness of spirit, and is opposed to levity, noise, and bluster. Devotion dwells in the realm of quietness and is still before God. It is serious, thoughtful, meditative.

Devotion belongs to the inner life and lives in the closet, but also appears in the public services of the sanctuary. It is a part of the very spirit of true worship, and is of the nature of the spirit of prayer.

Devotion belongs to the devout person, whose thoughts and feelings are devoted to God. Such a person has a mind given up wholly to religion, and possesses a strong affection for God and an ardent love for His house. Cornelius was "a devout man, and one that feared God with all his house, which gave much alms to the people, and prayed to God alway."[1] "Devout men carried Stephen to his burial."[2] "One Ananias, a devout man according to the law,"[3] was sent to Saul when he was blind, to tell him what the Lord would have him do. God can wonderfully use such people, for devout people are His chosen agents in carrying forward His plans.

PRAYER AND DEVOTION

Prayer promotes the spirit of devotion, and devotion is favorable to the best praying. Devotion furthers prayer and helps to drive prayer home to the goal that it seeks. Prayer thrives in the atmosphere of true devotion. It is easy to pray when in the spirit of devotion. The attitude of mind and the state of heart implied in devotion make prayer effective in reaching the throne of grace. God dwells where the spirit of devotion resides. All the graces of the Spirit are nourished and grow well in the environment created by devotion. Indeed, these graces grow nowhere else but there. The absence of a devotional spirit means death to the graces born in a renewed heart. True worship finds pleasant reception in the atmosphere made by a spirit of devotion. While prayer is helpful to devotion, devotion reacts on prayer and helps us to pray.

Devotion engages the heart in prayer. It is not an easy task for the lips to try to pray while the heart is absent from it. The charge that God at one time made against His ancient Israel was that they honored Him with their lips while their hearts were far from Him.[4]

The very essence of prayer is the spirit of devotion. Without devotion prayer is an empty form, a vain round of words. Sad to say, much of this kind of prayer prevails today in the Church. This is a busy age, bustling and active, and this bustling spirit has invaded the Church of God. Its religious performances are many. The Church works at religion with the order, precision, and force of real machinery. But too often it works with the heartlessness of the machine. There is much of the treadmill movement in our ceaseless round and routine of religious doings. We pray without praying. We sing without singing with the Spirit and the understanding.[5] We have music without the praise of God being in it or near it. We go to Church by habit, and come home all too gladly when the benediction is pronounced. We read our accustomed chapter in the Bible, and feel quite relieved when the task is done. We say our prayers mechanically from memory, like a schoolboy recites his lesson, and are not sorry when the "Amen" is spoken.

Religion and the heart

Religion has to do with everything but our hearts. It engages our hands and feet, it takes hold of our voices, it lays its hands on our money, it affects even the postures of our bodies. It does not, however, take hold of our affections, our desires, our zeal, and make us serious, desperately in earnest, and cause us to be quiet and worshipful in the presence of God. Social attractions draw us to the house of God, not the spirit of the occasion. Church membership keeps us to some degree decent in outward conduct and with some shadow of loyalty to our baptismal vows, but the heart is not in the thing. It remains cold, formal, and unimpressed amid all this outward performance, while we give ourselves over to self-congratulation that we are doing wonderfully well religiously.

Why all these sad defects in our piety? Why this modern perversion of the true nature of the religion of Jesus Christ? Why is the modern type of religion so much like a jewel case with the precious jewels gone? Why so much of this handling religion with the hands, often unsoiled, and so little of it felt in the heart and witnessed in the life?

The spirit of devotion

The great lack of modern religion is the spirit of devotion. We hear sermons in the same spirit with which we listen to a lecture or hear a speech. We visit the house of God just as if it were a common place, on a level with the theatre, the lecture room, or the forum. We do not look upon the minister of God as the divinely-called minister of God, but merely as a sort of public speaker, on a plane with the politician, the lawyer, the average speech maker, or the lecturer. Oh, how the spirit of true and genuine devotion would radically change all this for the better! We handle sacred things just as if they were the things of the world. Even the sacrament of the Lord's Supper has become a mere religious performance. There is no preparation for it beforehand, and no meditation and prayer afterward. Even the sacrament of baptism has lost much of its solemnity and degenerated into a mere form with nothing specially in it.

We need the spirit of devotion to not only salt our secularities but to make praying real prayers. We need to put the spirit of devotion into Monday's business as well as in Sunday's worship. We need the spirit of devotion to recollect always the presence of God, to be always doing the will of God, and to direct all things always to the glory of God.

The spirit of devotion puts God in all things. It puts God not merely in our praying and church going, but in all the concerns of life. "Whether therefore ye eat, or drink, or whatsoever ye do, do all to the glory of God."[6] The spirit of devotion makes the common things of earth sacred, and the little things great. With this spirit of devotion, we go to business on Monday directed and inspired by the very same influence by which we went to Church on Sunday. The spirit of devotion makes a Sabbath out of Saturday and transforms the shop and the office into a temple of God.

The spirit of devotion removes religion from being a thin veneer, and puts it into the very life and being of our souls. With it, religion ceases to be doing a mere work and becomes a heart, sending its rich blood through every artery and beating with the pulsations of vigorous and radiant life.

The spirit of devotion is not merely the aroma of religion, but the stalk and stem on which religion grows. It is the salt that penetrates and makes flavorful all religious acts. It is the sugar that sweetens duty, self-denial, and sacrifice. It is the bright coloring that relieves the dullness of religious performances. It dispels frivolity and drives away all shallow forms of worship, and makes worship a serious and deep-seated service that saturates body, soul, and spirit with its heavenly infusion. Let us ask in all seriousness, has this highest angel of heaven, this heavenly spirit of devotion, this brightest and best angel of earth, left us? When the angel of devotion has gone, the angel of prayer has lost its wings, and it becomes a deformed and loveless thing.

THE PASSION OF DEVOTION IN PRAYER

In Revelation 4:8 we read: "And they rest not day and night, saying, Holy, holy, holy, Lord God Almighty, which was, and is, and is to come." The inspiration and center of their rapturous devotion is the holiness of God. That holiness of God claims their attention and inflames their devotion. There is nothing cold, nothing dull, nothing wearisome about them or their heavenly worship. "They rest not day and night." What zeal! What unweary ardor and ceaseless rapture! The ministry of prayer, if it is anything worthy of the name, is a ministry of passion, a ministry of unwearied and intense longing after God and after His holiness.

The spirit of devotion pervades the saints in heaven and characterizes the worship of heaven's angelic intelligences. No creatures lacking devotion are in that heavenly world. God is there, and His very presence creates the spirit of reverence, of awe, and of godly fear. If we would be partakers with them after death, we must first learn the spirit of devotion on earth before we get there.

These living creatures in their restless, tireless, attitude after God, and their rapt devotion to His holiness, are the perfect symbols and illustrations of true prayer and its passion. Prayer must be aflame. Its passion must consume. Prayer without intense emotion is as a sun without light or heat, or as a flower without beauty or fragrance. A soul devoted to God is a fervent soul, and prayer is the creature of that flame. Those only can truly pray who are all aglow for holiness, for God, and for heaven.

ACTIVITY AND DEVOTION

Activity is not strength. Work is not zeal. Moving about is not devotion. Activity often is the unrecognized symptom of spiritual weakness. It may be hurtful to piety when made the substitute for real devotion in worship. The colt is much more active than its mother, but she is the wheel-horse of the team, pulling the load without noise or bluster or show. The child is more active than the father or mother, either of whom may be bearing the rule and burdens of an empire upon their heart and shoulders. Enthusiasm is more active than faith, though it cannot remove mountains or call into action any of the omnipotent forces that faith can command.

A feeble, lively, showy religious activity may spring from many causes. There is much running around, much stirring about, much going here and there, in today's church life. But sad to say, the spirit of genuine, heartfelt, devotion is strangely lacking. If there is real spiritual life, a deep-toned activity will spring from it. But it is an activity springing from strength and not from weakness. It is an activity that has deep roots that are many and strong.

In the nature of things, religion must show much of its growth above ground. Much will be seen and be evident to the eye. The flower and fruit of a holy life, abounding in good works, must be seen. It cannot be otherwise. But the surface growth must be based on a vigorous growth of unseen life and hidden roots. The roots of religion that is seen on the outside must go deep down in the renewed nature. The external must have a deep internal groundwork.

113

There must be much of the invisible and the underground growth, or else the life will be feeble and short-lived, and the external growth sickly and fruitless.

WAITING ON GOD

In the book of the prophet Isaiah these words are written:

They that wait on the Lord shall renew their strength; they shall mount up with wings as eagles; they shall run, and not be weary; and they shall walk, and not faint.[7]

This is the origin—the source—of the whole matter of activity and strength of the most energetic, exhaustless, and untiring nature. All this is the result of waiting on God.

There may be much of activity that is caused by training, created by enthusiasm or the weakness of the flesh, or the inspiration of explosive, short-lived, forces. Activity is often at the expense of more solid, useful, elements, and generally results in a total neglect of prayer. To be too busy with God's work to commune with God, to be busy with doing church work without taking time to talk to God about His work, is the highway to backsliding. Many people have walked that highway to the hurt of their immortal souls.

Notwithstanding great activity, great enthusiasm, and much approval for the work, the work and the activity will be nothing but blindness without the cultivation and the maturity of the graces of prayer.

Endnotes

1 Acts 10:2
2 Acts 8:2
3 Acts 22:12
4 Isaiah 29:13
5 1 Corinthians 14:15
6 1 Corinthians 10:31
7 Isaiah 40:31

4

Prayer, Praise, and Thanksgiving

D<small>R. A. J. GORDON</small> *describes the impression made upon his mind by intercourse with Joseph Rabinowitz, whom Dr. Delitzsch considered the most remarkable Jewish convert since Saul of Tarsus: 'We shall not soon forget the radiance that would come into his face as he expounded the Messianic Psalms at our morning or evening worship, and how, as here and there he caught a glimpse of the suffering or glorified Christ, he would suddenly lift his hands and his eyes to heaven in a burst of adoration, exclaiming with Thomas after he had seen the nail-prints, "My Lord, and my God."'* (D. M. McIntyre)

Prayer, praise, and thanksgiving all go together. A close relationship exists between them. Praise and thanksgiving are so near alike that it is not easy to distinguish between them or define them separately. The Scriptures join these three things together. Many are the causes for thanksgiving and praise. The Psalms are filled with many songs of praise and hymns of thanksgiving, all pointing back to the results of prayer.

Thanksgiving includes gratitude. In fact, thanksgiving is but the expression of an inward conscious gratitude to God for mercies received. Gratitude is an inward emotion of the soul involuntarily arising in it, while thanksgiving is the voluntary expression of gratitude.

Thanksgiving is oral, positive, active. It is the giving out of something to God. Thanksgiving comes out into the open. Gratitude is secret, silent, negative, passive, not showing its existing until expressed in praise and thanksgiving. Gratitude is felt in the heart. Thanksgiving is the expression of that inward feeling.

Thanksgiving is just what the word itself signifies—the giving of thanks to God. It is giving something to God in words that we feel in our heart for blessings we've received. Gratitude arises from thinking about the goodness of God. It is created by serious meditation on what God has done for us. Both gratitude and thanksgiving point to and have to do with God and His mercies. The heart is consciously grateful to God. The soul gives expression to that heartfelt gratitude to God in words or acts.

Gratitude is born of meditation on God's grace and mercy. "The Lord hath done great things for us, whereof we are glad."[1] Here we see the value of serious meditation. "My meditation of him shall be sweet."[2] Praise is produced by gratitude and a conscious obligation to God for mercies given. As we think of past mercies, the heart is inwardly moved to gratitude.

I love to think on mercies past,
And future good implore;
And all my cares and sorrows cast
On Him whom I adore.

LOVE IS THE CHILD OF GRATITUDE

Love grows as gratitude is felt, and then breaks out into praise and thanksgiving to God: "I love the Lord, because he hath heard my voice and my supplication."[3] Answered prayers cause gratitude, and gratitude brings forth a love that declares it will not cease praying: "Because he hath inclined his ear unto me, therefore will I call upon him as long as I live."[4] Gratitude and love move to larger and increased praying.

Paul appeals to the Romans to dedicate themselves wholly to God, a living sacrifice, and the compelling motive is the mercies of God:

I beseech you therefore, brethren, by the mercies of God, that ye present your bodies a living sacrifice, holy, acceptable unto God, which is your reasonable service.[5]

Consideration of God's mercies not only creates gratitude, but causes a large consecration to God of all we have and are. So that prayer, thanksgiving, and consecration are all linked inseparably together.

Gratitude and thanksgiving always look back at the past, though they may also take in the present. But prayer always looks to the future. Thanksgiving deals with things already received. Prayer deals with things desired, asked for, and expected.[6] Prayer turns to gratitude and praise when the things asked for have been granted by God. As prayer brings things to us that create gratitude and thanksgiving, so praise and gratitude promote prayer and cause more and better praying.

Gratitude and thanksgiving forever stand opposed to all murmurings at God's dealings with us, and all complaining about our conditions. Gratitude and murmuring never abide in the same heart at the same time.

An unappreciative spirit has no fellowship with gratitude and praise. True prayer corrects complaining and promotes gratitude and thanksgiving. Dissatisfaction at one's conditions, and a disposition to be discontented with things that come to us in the providence of God, are enemies to gratitude and thanksgiving.

COMPLAINERS ARE UNGRATEFUL PEOPLE

Appreciative men and women have neither the time nor disposition to stop and complain. The destructive force in the wilderness-journey of the Israelites on their way to Canaan was their proneness to murmur and complain against God and Moses—and sometimes against Aaron. For this, God was several times greatly grieved, and it took the strong praying of Moses to avert God's wrath because of these murmurings.[7]

The absence of gratitude left no room nor disposition for praise and thanksgiving, just as it is always so. But when these same Israelites were brought through the Red Sea as on dry land, while their enemies were destroyed by the waters, there was a song of praise led by Miriam, the sister of Moses. One of the leading sins of these Israelites was forgetting God and His mercies because of their ungrateful souls. This brought forth murmurings and lack of praise, as it always does.

When Paul wrote to the Colossians to let the word of Christ dwell in their hearts richly and to let the peace of God rule there, he said to them, "and be ye thankful," and adds, "admonishing one another in psalms and hymns and spiritual songs, singing with grace in your hearts to the Lord."[8]

Later in his later, he joins prayer and thanksgiving together: "Continue in prayer, and watch in the same with thanksgiving."[9]

Writing to the Thessalonians, he again unites prayer and thanksgiving: "Rejoice evermore. Pray without ceasing. In every thing give thanks, for this is the will of God in Christ Jesus concerning you."[10]

> We thank Thee, Lord of heaven and earth,
> Who hast preserved us from our birth;
> Redeemed us oft from death and dread,
> And with Thy gifts our table spread.

Wherever there is true prayer, there thanksgiving and gratitude stand close by, ready to respond to the answer when it comes. For as prayer brings the answer, so the answer brings forth gratitude and praise. As prayer sets God to work, so answered prayer sets thanksgiving to work. Thanksgiving follows answered prayer just as day follows night.

True prayer and gratitude lead to full consecration, and consecration leads to more praying and better praying. A consecrated life is both a prayer life and a thanksgiving life.

THE SPIRIT OF PRAISE

The spirit of praise was once the boast of the primitive Church. This spirit lived in the tabernacles of these early Christians, as a cloud of glory out of which God shone and spoke. It filled their temples with the perfume of costly, flaming, incense. That this spirit of praise is sadly deficient in today's congregations must be evident to every careful observer. That it is a mighty force in projecting the Gospel and its saving power must be equally evident.

To restore the spirit of praise to our congregations should be one of the main concerns of every true pastor. The normal state of the Church is set forth in the declaration made to God: "Praise waiteth for thee, O God, in Sion: and unto thee shall the vow be performed."[11]

Praise is so distinctly and definitely wedded to prayer, so inseparably joined, that they cannot be divorced. Praise is dependent on prayer for its full volume and its sweetest melody.

Singing is one method of praise, not the highest it is true, but it is the ordinary and usual form. The singing service in our churches has much to do with praise, for according to the character of the singing will be the genuineness or the measure of praise. The singing may be so directed as to have in it elements that degrade and corrupt prayer. It may be so directed as to drive away everything like thanksgiving and praise. Much of modern singing in our churches is entirely foreign to anything like hearty, sincere, praise to God.

THE SPIRIT OF PRAYER

The spirit of prayer and of true praise go hand in hand. Both are often entirely dissipated by the flippant, thoughtless, light singing in our congregations. Much of the singing lacks serious thought and is devoid of everything like a devotional spirit. Its lustiness and sparkle may not only dissipate all the essential features of worship, but may substitute the flesh for the spirit.

Giving thanks is the very life of prayer. It is its fragrance and music, its poetry and its crown. Prayer bringing the desired answer breaks out into praise and thanksgiving. So that whatever interferes with and injures the spirit of prayer necessarily hurts and drives away the spirit of praise.

The heart must have the grace of prayer in it to sing the praise of God. Spiritual singing is not to be done by musical taste or talent, but by the grace of God in the heart. Nothing helps praise so mightily as a gracious revival of true religion in a church. The conscious presence of God inspires song. The angels and the glorified ones in heaven do not need artistic music directors to lead them, nor do they care for paid choirs to chime in with their heavenly doxologies of praise and worship. They are not dependent upon singing schools to teach them the notes. Their singing involuntarily breaks forth from the heart.

GOD'S PRESENCE

God is immediately present in the heavenly assemblies of the angels and the spirits of just men made perfect.[12] His glorious presence creates the song, teaches the singing, and saturates their notes of praise. It is so on earth.

God's presence gives birth to singing and thanksgiving, while the absence of God from our congregations is the death of song—or what amounts to the same, singing made lifeless, cold, and formal. His conscious presence in our churches would bring back the days of praise and would restore the full chorus of song.

Where grace abounds, song abounds. When God is in the heart, heaven is present and melody is there, and the lips overflow out of the abundance of the heart. This is as true in the private life of the believer as it is so in the congregations of the saints. The decay of singing, the dying down of the spirit of praise in song, means the decline of grace in the heart and the absence of God's presence from the people.

PURPOSE OF SINGING

The main design of all singing is for God's ear—to attract His attention and to please Him. It is "to the Lord,"[13] for His glory and to His honor. Certainly it is not for the glorification of the paid choir, to exalt the wonderful musical powers of the singers, or is it to draw the people to the church. It is for the glory of God and the good of the souls of the congregation. How far, however, has the singing in today's churches departed from this idea! It is no surprise that there is no life, no power, no unction, no spirit, in much of the church's singing heard in this day. It is sacrilege for any but the sanctified hearts and holy lips to direct the singing part of the service of God's house of prayer.

Much of the singing in churches would do credit to the opera house and theater, and might satisfy as mere entertainment that is pleasing to the ear, but as a part of real worship, having in it the spirit of praise and prayer, it is a fraud, an imposition on spiritually minded people, and entirely unacceptable to God. The cry should go out afresh, "Let all the people praise thee, O God,"[14] for "it is good to sing praises unto our God; for it is pleasant; and praise is comely."[15]

MUSIC OF PRAISE

The music of praise—for there is real music of soul in praise—is too hopeful and happy to be denied. All these are in the "giving of thanks." In Philippians, prayer is called "requests."

"Let your requests be made known unto God" describes prayer as asking for a gift, giving prominence to the thing asked for, and making it emphatic. It is something to be given by God and received by us, and not something to be done by us. All this is closely connected with gratitude to God: "with thanksgiving, let your requests be made known unto God."[16]

PRAYING ACCORDING TO SPECIAL NEEDS

God does much for us in answer to prayer, but we need from Him many gifts, and for them we are to make special prayer. According to our special needs, so must our praying be. We are to be special and particular and bring to the knowledge of God by prayer, supplication, and thanksgiving, our specific requests—the things we need, the things we greatly desire. Especially important, thanksgiving must accompanying all these requests.

It is indeed a pleasing thought that what we are called upon to do on earth, to praise and give thanks, the angels in heaven and the redeemed spirits of the saints are doing also. It is still further pleasing to contemplate the glorious hope that what God wants us to do on earth, we will be engaged in doing throughout eternity. Praise and thanksgiving will be our blessed employment while we are in heaven. Never will we grow weary of this pleasing task.

Joseph Addison sets before us in verse this pleasing prospect:

> Through every period of my life
> Thy goodness I'll pursue;
> And after death, in distant worlds,
> The pleasing theme renew.

> Through all eternity to Thee
> A grateful song I'll raise;
> But Oh! eternity's too short
> To utter all Thy praise.

Endnotes

1 Psalm 126:3
2 Psalm 104:34
3 Psalm 116:1
4 Psalm 116:2
5 Romans 12:1
6 Mark 11:24
7 Exodus 32:10-14; Numbers 16:41-48
8 Colossians 13:15a-16
9 Colossians 4:2
10 I Thessalonians 5:16-18
11 Psalm 65:1
12 Hebrews 12:22-23
13 Ephesians 5:19
14 Psalm 67:5
15 Psalm 147:1
16 Philippians 4:6

5

Prayer and Trouble

It may not be today,
That God Himself shall wipe our tears away,
Nor, hope deferred, may it be yet tomorrow
He'll take away our cup of earthly sorrow;
But, precious promise, He has said He will,
If we but trust Him fully—and be still.

We, too, as He, may fall, and die unknown;
And e'en the place we fell be all unshown,
But eyes omniscient will mark the spot
Till empires perish and the world's forgot.
Then they who bore the yoke and drank the cup
In fadeless glory shall the Lord raise up.

God's word is ever good; His will is best:—
The yoke, the heart all broken—and then rest.
(Claudius L. Chilton)

TROUBLE AND PRAYER ARE closely related to each other. Prayer is of great value to trouble. Trouble often drives people to God in prayer, while prayer is but the voice of people in trouble. There is great value in prayer in the time of trouble. Prayer often delivers out of trouble, and even more so gives strength to bear trouble, ministers comfort in trouble, and produces patience in the midst of trouble. Wise are they in the day of trouble who know their true source of strength and do not fail to pray.

Trouble belongs to the present state of humankind on earth. "Man that is born of a woman is of few days, and full of trouble."[1] Trouble is common to everyone. There is no exception in any age or climate or station. Rich and poor alike, the educated and the ignorant, one and all are partakers of this sad and painful inheritance of the fall of humanity. "There hath no temptation taken you but such as is common to man."[2] The "day of trouble"[3] dawns on every one at some time in his life. "The evil days come and the years draw nigh"[4] when the heart feels its heavy pressure.

The view of life that expects nothing but sunshine and looks only for ease, pleasure, and flowers is entirely false and shows supreme ignorance. It is this class of people who are so sadly disappointed and surprised when trouble breaks into their lives. They are the ones who know not God,[5] who know nothing of His disciplinary dealings with His people, and who are prayerless.

What an infinite variety there is in the troubles of life! How diversified the experiences of people in the school of trouble! No two people have the same troubles under like environments. God deals with no two of His children in the same way. Since God varies His treatment of His children, trouble is varied. God does not repeat Himself. He does not run in a rut. He doesn't have one pattern for every child. Each trouble is proportioned to each child. We are each dealt with according to our own peculiar case.

TROUBLE IS GOD'S SERVANT

Trouble is God's servant, doing His will. Trouble is under the control of Almighty God, and is one of His most efficient agents in fulfilling His purposes and in perfecting His saints. God's hand is in every trouble that breaks into the lives of people. Not that He directly and arbitrarily orders every unpleasant experience of life. Not that He is personally responsible for every painful and afflicting thing that comes into the lives of His people. But no trouble is ever turned loose in this world and comes into the life of saint or sinner that does not come with God's permission. Trouble is only allowed to exist and do its painful work with God's hand in it or on it, carrying out His gracious designs of redemption.

All things are under God's control. Trouble is neither above God nor beyond His control. It is not something in life independent of God. No matter from what source it springs or from where it comes, God is sufficiently wise and able to lay His hand upon it without assuming responsibility for its origin. He knows exactly how to work it into His plans and purposes concerning the highest welfare of His saints. This is the explanation of that gracious statement in Romans, so often quoted, but the depth of whose meaning has rarely been measured, "And we know that all things work together for good to them that love God, to them who are the called according to His purpose."[6]

Even the evils brought about by the forces of nature are His servants, carrying out His will and fulfilling His designs. God even says that the locusts, the cankerworm, and the caterpillar are His servants. He calls them "My great army,"[7] and uses them to correct His people and discipline them.

TROUBLE IS PART OF GOD'S DISCIPLINE

Trouble belongs to the disciplinary part of the moral government of God. This is a life of probation. It is a season of trial. Trouble is not punishment. It is what the Scriptures call "chastening." "Whom the Lord loveth he chasteneth, and scourgeth every son whom He receiveth."[8]

Speaking accurately, punishment does not belong to this life. Punishment for sin will take place in the next world. God's dealings with people in this world are of the nature of discipline. They are corrective processes in His plans concerning humanity. It is because of this that prayer comes in when trouble arises. Prayer belongs to the discipline of life.

Trouble is neither sinful in itself, nor the evidence of sin. The good and bad alike experience trouble. As the rain falls alike on the just and unjust,[9] so drought likewise comes to the righteous and the unrighteous. Trouble is no evidence whatever of God's displeasure. There are Scripture instances without number disproving any such idea. Job is a case in point, where God bore clear testimony to his deep piety, and yet God permitted Satan to afflict him beyond any other person for wise and beneficial purposes. Trouble has no power in itself to interfere with the relations of a saint to God. "Who shall separate us from the love of Christ? shall tribulation, or distress, or persecution, or famine, or nakedness, or peril, or sword?"[10]

TEMPTATION, TRIAL, AND TROUBLE

There are three words used to describe the processes of Divine discipline that are practically the same: temptation, trial, and trouble. Yet there are differences between them.

Temptation is a suggestion to do evil that comes from the devil or a person's carnal nature.[11]

Trial is testing.[12] It is that which proves us, tests us, and makes us stronger and better when we submit to the trial and work together with God in it. "My brethren, count it all joy when ye fall into divers temptations; Knowing this, that the trying of your faith worketh patience."[13]

Peter speaks along the same line:

> Wherein ye greatly rejoice, though now for a season, if need be, ye are in heaviness through manifold temptations: That the trial of your faith, being much more precious than of gold that perisheth, though it be tried with fire, might be found unto praise and honor and glory at the appearing of Jesus Christ.

Trouble covers all the painful, sorrowing, and grievous events of life. Yet temptations and trials might really become troubles. So that all evil days in life might well be classed under the heading of the "time of trouble."[14] Such days of trouble are the lot of all people. It is enough to know that trouble, no matter from what source it comes, becomes in God's hand His own agent to accomplish His gracious work concerning those who submit patiently to Him—recognizing Him in prayer and working together with Him.

TROUBLE DOES NOT COME BY CHANCE OR ACCIDENT

Let us settle down at once to the idea that trouble does not come by chance or by what people call accident. "Although affliction cometh not forth of the dust, neither doth trouble spring out of the ground; yet man is born unto trouble, as the sparks fly upward."[15] Trouble naturally belongs to God's moral government, and is one of His invaluable agents in governing the world.

When we realize this, we can better understand much that is recorded in the Scriptures, and can have a clearer concept of God's dealings with ancient Israel. In God's dealings with them, we find what is called a history of divine providence, and providence always embraces trouble. No one can understand the story of Joseph and his old father Jacob unless he takes into the account trouble and its various functions. God takes account of trouble when He says through His prophet Isaiah, "Comfort ye, comfort ye my people, saith your God. Speak ye comfortably to Jerusalem, and cry unto her, that her warfare is accomplished, that her iniquity is pardoned."[16]

There is a distinct note of comfort in the Gospels for the praying saints of the Lord, and it is a wise minister in divine things who knows how to minister this comfort to the brokenhearted and sad people of earth. Jesus Himself said to His disheartened disciples, "I will not leave you comfortless."[17]

RELATIONSHIP OF PRAYER TO TROUBLE

All the foregoing has been said that we may rightly appreciate the relationship of prayer to trouble. In the time of trouble, where does prayer come in? The Psalmist tells us: "Call upon me in the day of trouble: I will deliver thee, and thou shalt glorify me."[18] Prayer is the most appropriate thing for a soul to do in the "time of trouble." Prayer recognizes God in the day of trouble. "It is the Lord; let Him do what seemeth Him good." Prayer sees God's hand in trouble, and prays about it.

Nothing more truly shows us our helplessness than when trouble comes. It brings the strong person low. It discloses our weakness. It brings a sense of helplessness. Blessed is the person who knows how to turn to God in "the time of trouble." If trouble is of the Lord, then the most natural thing to do is to carry the trouble to the Lord, and seek grace and patience and submission. It is the time to inquire in the trouble, "Lord, what wilt thou have me to do?"[19] How natural and reasonable for the soul that is oppressed, broken, and bruised to bow low at the footstool of mercy and seek the face of God. Nowhere is a soul in trouble more likely to find comfort than in the closet.

Unfortunately, trouble does not always drive people to God in prayer. When trouble bends our spirit down and grieves our heart, it is a sad state if we do not know where trouble comes from or know how to pray about it. Blessed are those who are driven by trouble to their knees in prayer!

> Trials must and will befall;
> But with humble faith to see
> Love inscribed upon them all—
> This is happiness to me.
>
> Trials make the promise sweet,
> Trials give new life to prayer;
> Bring me to my Savior's feet,
> Lay me low, and keep me there.

PRAYER BRINGS COMFORT DURING TIMES OF TROUBLE

Prayer in the time of trouble brings comfort, help, hope, and blessings. Although these do not remove the trouble, they enable the saint to better bear it and to submit to the will of God. Prayer opens the eyes to see God's hand in trouble. Prayer does not interpret God's providences, but it does justify them and recognize God in them. Prayer enables us to see wise ends in trouble. Prayer in trouble drives us away from unbelief, saves us from doubt, and delivers from all vain and foolish questionings because of our painful experiences. Let us not lose sight of the tribute paid to Job when all his troubles came to the highest point: "In all this Job sinned not, nor charged God foolishly."[20]

Alas! for vain, ignorant people who have no faith in God and know nothing of God's disciplinary processes in dealing with people. They charge God foolishly when troubles come, and are tempted to "curse God."[21] How silly and vain are the complaining, murmurings, and rebellion of Christians in the time of trouble! They need to read again the story of the children of Israel in the wilderness.

How useless is all our fretting and worrying over trouble, as if such unhappy actions on our part could change things. "And which of you with taking thought can add to his stature one cubit?"[22] How much wiser, how much better, how much easier to bear life's troubles when we take everything to God in prayer?

125

TROUBLES OFTEN A BLESSING IN DISGUISE

Trouble has wise ends for the praying ones, and they find it so. Happy are those who, like the Psalmist, find that their troubles have been blessings in disguise. "It is good for me that I have been afflicted; that I might learn thy statutes. . . . I know, O LORD, that thy judgments are right, and that thou in faithfulness hast afflicted me."[23]

> O who could bear life's stormy doom,
> Did not Thy wing of love
> Come brightly wafting through the gloom
> Our peace branch from above.

> Then sorrow, touched by Thee, grows bright,
> With more than rapture's ray;
> As darkness shows us worlds of light
> We never saw by day.

It is conceded, of course, that some troubles are really imaginary. They have no existence other than in the mind. Some are anticipated troubles, which never arrive at our door. Others are past troubles, and there is much foolishness in worrying over them. Present troubles are the ones requiring attention and demanding prayer. "Sufficient unto the day is the evil thereof."[24]

THE ORIGINS OF TROUBLES

Some troubles are self-originated. We are their authors. Some of these originate involuntarily with us, some arise from our ignorance, some come from our carelessness. All this can be readily admitted without breaking the force of the statement that they are the subjects of prayer, and should drive us to prayer.

What parents cast off their child who cries to them when because of his own carelessness he has stumbled and fallen and hurt itself? Does not the cry of the child attract the ears of the parents even though the child is to blame for the accident? "Whatever things ye desire"[25] takes in every event of life, even though we are responsible for some of the events.

Some troubles are human in their origin. They arise from second causes. They originate with others and we are the sufferers. This is a world where often the innocent suffer the consequences of the acts of others. This is a part of life's incidents. Who has not at some time suffered at the hands of others? But even these are allowed to come in the order of God's providence, are permitted to break into our lives for beneficial ends, and may be prayed over. Why should we not carry our hurts, wrongs, and losses that are caused by the acts of others to God in prayer? Are such things outside the realm of prayer? Are they exceptions to the rule of prayer? Not at all. God can and will lay His hand upon all such events in answer to prayer, and cause them to work for us "a far more exceeding and eternal weight of glory."[26]

Nearly all of Paul's troubles arose from wicked and unreasonable men. Read the story as he gives it in 2 Corinthians 11:23-33.

Some troubles are directly of Satanic origin. Quite all of Job's troubles were the offspring of the devil's scheme to break down Job's integrity, to make him charge God foolishly, and to curse God. But are these not to be recognized in prayer? Are they to be excluded from God's disciplinary processes? Job did not do so. Hear him in those familiar words. "The Lord gave, and the Lord hath taken away; blessed be the name of the Lord."[27]

What a comfort it is to see God in all of life's events! What a relief to a broken, sorrowing, heart to see God's hand in sorrow! What a source of relief prayer is in unburdening the heart in grief!

> O Thou who driest the mourner's tear,
> How dark this world would be,
> If, when deceived and wounded here,
> We could not fly to Thee?
>
> The friends who in our sunshine live,
> When winter comes are flown,
> And he who has but tears to give,
> Must weep those tears alone.
>
> But Thou wilt heal the broken heart,
> Which, like the plants that throw
> Their fragrance from the wounded part,
> Breathes sweetness out of woe.

TWO VALUABLE TRUTHS

But when we survey all the sources from which trouble comes, it shows two invaluable truths.

First, our troubles are of the Lord. They come with His consent. He is in all of them, and is interested in us when they press and bruise us.

Second, it does not matter what the origin of our troubles—ourselves, people, devils, or even God Himself. We can take them all to God in prayer, pray over them, and seek to get the greatest spiritual benefits out of them.

PRAYER IN TIME OF TROUBLE

Prayer in the time of trouble tends to bring our spirit into perfect subjection to the will of God, causes our will to be conformed to God's will, keeps us from all complaining about our circumstances, and delivers us from everything like a rebellious heart or a spirit critical of the Lord.

Prayer sanctifies trouble to our highest good. Prayer so prepares the heart that it softens under the disciplining hand of God. Prayer places us where God can bring to us the greatest good, spiritual and eternal. Prayer allows God to freely work with us and in us in the day of trouble. Prayer removes everything in the way of trouble, bringing to us the sweetest, highest, and greatest good. Prayer permits God's servant—trouble—to accomplish its mission in us, with us, and for us.

The end of trouble is always good in the mind of God. If trouble fails in its mission, it is either because of prayerlessness or unbelief or both. Being in harmony with God in the dispensations of His providence, always makes trouble a blessing.

The good or evil of trouble is always determined by the spirit in which it is received. Trouble proves a blessing or a curse according to how it is received and treated by us. It either softens or hardens us. It either draws us to prayer and to God, or it drives us from God and from the closet. Trouble hardened Pharaoh till finally it had no effect on him, only to make him more desperate and to drive him further from God. The same sun that softens wax—hardens clay. The same sun that melts the ice—dries the moisture from the earth.

Just as there is an infinite variety of trouble, there is an infinite variety of prayer. Prayer has to do with everything that concerns us, with everybody with whom we have to do, and has to do with all times. But prayer especially has to do with trouble. "This poor man cried, and the LORD heard him, and saved him out of all his troubles."[28] O the blessedness, the help, the comfort of prayer in the day of trouble! How marvelous are the promises of God to us in the time of trouble!

Because he hath set his love upon me, therefore will I deliver him: I will set him on high, because he hath known my name. He shall call upon me, and I will answer him: I will be with him in trouble; I will deliver him and honor him.[29]

> If pain afflict, or wrongs oppress,
> If cares distract, or fears dismay;
> If guilt deject, if sin distress,
> In every case, still watch and pray.

How rich in its sweetness, how far-reaching in the realm of trouble, and how cheering to faith are the words of promise that God speaks to His believing, praying saints by the mouth of Isaiah:

But now thus saith the Lord that created thee, O Jacob, and he that formed thee, O Israel, Fear not: for I have redeemed thee, I have called thee by thy name; thou art mine. When thou passest through the waters, I will be with thee; and through the rivers, they shall not overflow thee: when thou walkest through the fire, thou shalt not be burned; neither shall the flame kindle upon thee. For I am the Lord thy God, the Holy One of Israel, thy Savior.[30]

Endnotes

1 Job 14:1
2 1 Corinthians 10:13
3 Psalm 50:15
4 Paraphrase or reversal of Ecclesiastes 12:1
5 Expression found in 2 Thessalonians 1:8, but not in sense used by Bounds.
6 Romans 8:28
7 Joel 2:25b
8 Hebrews 12:6
9 Matthew 5:45
10 Romans 8:35
11 James 1:13
12 Genesis 22:1, NKJV
13 James 1:2-3
14 Psalm 27:5; Daniel 12:1
15 Job 5:6-7
16 Isaiah 40:1-2a
17 John 14:18
18 Psalm 50:15
19 Acts 9:6
20 Job 1:22
21 Job 2:9
22 Luke 12:25
23 Psalm 119:71, 75
24 Matthew 6:34b
25 Mark 11:24
26 2 Corinthians 4:17
27 Job 1:21
28 Psalm 34:6
29 Psalm 91:14-15
30 Isaiah 43:1-3

6

Prayer and Trouble (Continued)

M Y FIRST MESSAGE FOR *heavenly relief went singing over millions of miles of space in 1869, and brought relief to my troubled heart. But, thanks be to Him, I have received many delightful and helpful answers during the last fifty years. I would think the commerce of the skies had gone into bankruptcy if I did not hear frequently, since I have learned how to ask and how to receive.* (H. W. Hodge)

In the New Testament there are three words used that embrace trouble: *tribulation, suffering,* and *affliction.* The words differ somewhat, but each of them mean "trouble" of some kind. Our Lord put His disciples on notice that they could expect tribulation in this life. He taught them that tribulation belonged to this world, they could not hope to escape it, and they would not be carried through this life on flowery beds of ease. How hard to learn this plain and clear lesson! "In the world ye shall have tribulation: but be of good cheer; I have overcome the world."[1] This is the encouragement. As He had overcome the world and its tribulations, so might they do the same.

Paul taught the same lesson throughout his ministry. When confirming the souls of the saints and exhorting them to continue in the faith, he told them that, "we must through much tribulation enter into the kingdom of God."[2] He knew this by his own experience, for his pathway was anything but smooth and flowery.

Paul uses the word "suffering" to describe the troubles of life in that comforting passage where he contrasts life's troubles with the final glory of

131

heaven. This glory will be the reward of all who patiently endure the troubles brought by divine providence.

> For I reckon that the sufferings of this present time are not worthy to be compared with the glory which shall be revealed in us.[3]

It is also Paul who speaks of the afflictions that come to the people of God in this world, and says they are light in comparison with the measure of glory awaiting all who are submissive, patient, and faithful in all their troubles.

> For our light affliction, which is but for a moment, worketh for us a far more exceeding and eternal weight of glory.[4]

But our present afflictions can work for us only as we cooperate with God in prayer. Since God works through prayer, it is only through prayer that He can accomplish His highest ends for us. His providence works with greatest effect with those who pray. They understand the uses of trouble and its gracious designs. The greatest value in trouble comes to those who bow lowest before the throne.

PRAYER AND TRIBULATION

In urging patience in tribulation, Paul connects it directly with prayer, as if prayer alone would place us where we could be patient when tribulation comes. "Rejoicing in hope; patient in tribulation; continuing [steadfastly] in prayer."[5] Here he couples tribulation and prayer, showing their close relationship and the worth of prayer in creating and developing patience in tribulation. In fact, there can be no patience manifested when trouble comes except when secured through instant and continued prayer. Patience is learned and practiced in the school of prayer.

Prayer brings us into that state of grace where tribulation is not only endured, but where there is under it a spirit of rejoicing. In showing the gracious benefits of justification, Paul says,

> And not only so, but we glory in tribulation also: knowing that tribulation worketh patience; And patience, experience; and experience, hope; And hope maketh not ashamed; because the love of God is shed abroad in our hearts by the Holy Ghost which is given unto us.[6]

What a chain of graces are here set forth as coming from tribulation! What successive steps to a high state of religious experience! What rich fruits result from even painful tribulation!

Peter writes essentially the same thing in his first letter. In his strong prayer for those Christians to whom he writes, he shows that suffering and the highest state of grace are closely connected. He states that it is through suffering that we are to be brought to those higher regions of Christian experience.

But the God of all grace, who hath called us into his eternal glory by Christ Jesus, after that ye have suffered a while, make you perfect, stablish, strengthen settle you.[7]

SAINTS PURIFIED IN THE FIRE OF SUFFERING

It is in the fires of suffering that God purifies His saints and brings them to the highest things. It is in the furnace their faith is tested, their patience is tried, and they are developed in all those rich virtues that make up Christian character. It is while they are passing through deep waters that He shows how close He can come to His praying, believing saints.

It takes faith of a high order and a Christian experience far above the average religion of this day to count it joy when we are called to pass through tribulation. God's highest aim in dealing with His people is in developing Christian character. He is after creating in us those rich virtues that belong to our Lord Jesus Christ. He is seeking to make us like Himself. It is not so much work that He wants in us. It is not greatness. It is the presence in us of patience, meekness, and submission to the divine will. He wants praying saints who bring everything to Him. He seeks to create His own image in us.

Trouble in some form tends to do this very thing, for this is the end and aim of trouble. This is its work. This is the task it is called to perform. It is not a chance incident in life, but has a design in view. That is because there is an all-wise designer behind it who makes trouble His agent to bring forth the largest results.

The writer of the letter to the Hebrews gives us a perfect directory of trouble—comprehensive, clear, and worth studying. Here is "chastisement," another word for trouble, coming from a Father's hand, showing God is in all the sad and afflictive events of life. Here is its nature and its gracious design. It is not punishment in the accurate meaning of that word, but the means God employs to correct and discipline His children in dealing with them on earth.

It is then that we have the evidence of being His people—namely, the presence of chastisement. The ultimate end is that we "may be partakers of his holiness," which is but another way of saying that all this disciplinary process is to the end that God may make us like Himself. What an encouragement, too, that chastisement is no evidence of anger or displeasure on God's part, but is the strong proof of His love. Let us read the entire directory on this important subject:

And ye have forgotten the exhortation which speaketh unto you as unto children, My son, despise not thou the chastening of the Lord, nor faint when thou art rebuked of him: For whom the Lord loveth he chasteneth, and scourgeth every son whom he receiveth. If ye endure chastening, God dealeth with you as with sons; for what son is he whom the father chasteneth not? But if ye be without chastisement, whereof all are partakers, then are ye bastards, and not sons.

Furthermore we have had fathers of our flesh which corrected us, and we gave them reverence: shall we not much rather be in subjection unto the Father of spirits, and live? For they verily for a few days chastened us after their own pleasure; but he for our profit, that we might be partakers of his holiness. Now no chastening for the present seemeth to be joyous, but grievous: nevertheless afterward it yieldeth the peaceable fruit of righteousness unto them which are exercised thereby.[8]

TROUBLE HAS VARIED USES

Just as prayer is wide in its range, taking in everything, so trouble is infinitely varied in its uses and designs. It takes trouble sometimes to get attention, to stop people in the busy rush of life, and to awaken them to a sense of their helplessness and their need and sinfulness. Not until King Manasseh was bound with thorns and carried away into a foreign land and got into deep trouble was he awakened and brought back to God. It was then he humbled himself and began to call upon God.[9]

The prodigal son was independent and self-sufficient when in prosperity. But when money and friends left and he began to be in need, he "came to himself,"[10] and decided to return to his father's house with prayer and confession on his lips. By the use of trouble, God has gotten the attention of many people, caused them to consider their ways, and brought them to remember him. Blessed is trouble when it accomplishes this in people!

It is for this, among other reasons, that Job says:

Behold, happy is the man whom God correcteth: therefore despise not thou the chastening of the Almighty: For he maketh sore, and bindeth up: he woundeth, and his hands make whole. He shall deliver thee in six troubles: yea, in seven there shall no evil touch thee.[11]

TROUBLE MAKES THE EARTH UNDESIRABLE

One thing more might be mentioned—trouble makes earth undesirable and causes heaven to loom up large in the horizon of hope. There is a world where trouble never comes. But the path of tribulation leads to that world. Those who are there went there through tribulation. What a world set before our longing eyes. It greatly appeals to our hopes when sorrows sweep over us like a hurricane. Hear John as he talks about it and those who are there:

> And one of the elders answered, saying unto me, What are these which are arrayed in white robes? and whence came they? And I said unto him, Sir, thou knowest. And he said to me, These are they which came out of great tribulation, and have washed their robes, and made them white in the blood of the Lamb.

> They shall hunger no more, neither thirst any more; neither shall the sun light on them, nor any heat. For the Lamb which is in the midst of the throne shall feed them, and shall lead them unto living fountains of waters: and God shall wipe away all tears from their eyes.[12]

> There I shall bathe my weary soul,
> In seas of heavenly rest,
> And not a wave of trouble roll,
> Across my peaceful breast.

Oh, children of God, you who have suffered, who have been sorely tried, whose sad experiences have often brought broken spirits and bleeding hearts, cheer up! God is in all your troubles, and He will see that all will "work together for good"—if you will be patient, submissive, and prayerful.

Endnotes

1 John 16:33b
2 Acts 14:22
3 Romans 8:18
4 2 Corinthians 4:17
5 Romans 12:12
6 Romans 5:3-5
7 1 Peter 5:10
8 Hebrews 12:5-11
9 2 Chronicles 33:1-13
10 Luke 15:17
11 Job 5:17-19
12 Revelation 7:13-14, 16-17

7

Prayer and God's Work

IF JACOB'S DESIRE HAD *been given him in time for him to get a good night's sleep he might never have become the prince of prayers we know today. If Hannah's prayer for a son had been answered at the time she set for herself, the nation might never have known the mighty man of God it found in Samuel. Hannah wanted only a son, but God wanted more. He wanted a prophet, and a savior, and a ruler for His people. Someone said that "God had to get a woman before He could get a man." This woman He got in Hannah precisely by those weeks and months and years there came a woman with a vision like God's, with tempered soul and gentle spirit and a seasoned will, prepared to be the kind of a mother for the kind of a man God knew the nation needed.* (W. E. Binderwolf)

God has a great work on hand in this world. This work is involved in the plan of salvation. It embraces redemption and providence. God is governing this world and its intelligent beings for His glory and their good. What, then, is God's work in this world? Rather, what is the end He seeks in His great work? It is nothing short of holiness of heart and life in the children of fallen Adam. Human beings are a fallen race, born with an evil nature, unholy tendencies, sinful desires. Human beings are unholy by nature, because they are born that way. "They go astray as soon as they are born, speaking lies."[1]

God's entire plan is to take hold of fallen humanity and to seek to change it and make it holy. God's work is to make holy people out of unholy people. This is the purpose for which Christ came into the world:

For this purpose was the Son of God manifested that he might destroy the works of the devil.[2]

God is holy in nature and in all His ways, and He wants to make us like Himself.

As he which hath called you is holy, so be ye holy in all manner of conversation; Because it is written, Be ye holy; for I am holy.[3]

This is being Christlike. This is following Jesus Christ. This is the aim of all Christian effort. This is the earnest, heartfelt, desire of every truly regenerated soul. This is what should be constantly and earnestly prayed for— that we may be made holy.

Not that we must make ourselves holy, but we must be cleansed from all sin by the precious atoning blood of Christ, and be made holy by the direct agency of the Holy Spirit. Not that we are to do holy, but rather to be holy. Being must precede doing. First be, then do. First, obtain a holy heart, then live a holy life. For this high and gracious end God, has made the most ample provisions in the atoning work of our Lord and through the agency of the Holy Spirit.

The work of God in the world is the implantation, the growth, and the perfection of holiness in His people. Keep this ever in mind. But we might ask:

Is this work advancing in the Church?

Are men and women being made holy?

Is today's Church engaged in the business of making holy men and women?

These are not vain and speculative questions. They are practical, pertinent, and all important.

HOLINESS AND MINISTERS

The present-day Church has vast machinery. Its activities are great, and its material prosperity is unparalleled. The name of Christianity is widespread and well-known. Much money comes into the Lord's treasury and is paid out. But here are the questions:

Does the work of holiness keep pace with all this?

Is the burden of the prayers of Church people to be made holy?

Are our preachers really holy men and women?

Or to go back a little further, are they hungering and thirsting after righteousness, desiring the sincere milk of the Word that they may grow thereby?

Are they really seeking to be holy ministers?

Of course intelligent men and women are greatly needed in the pulpit, but prior to that, and primary to it, is the fact that we need holy ministers to stand before dying people and proclaim the salvation of God to them.

Ministers, like laypeople, and no more so than laypeople, must be holy in life, in conversation, and in disposition. They must be examples to the flock of God in all things. They are to preach and speak more by their lives than their voices. Ministers in the pulpit are needed to be spotless in life, and wise and prudent in behavior: "blameless and harmless . . . in the midst of a crooked and perverse nation," among whom they are to "shine as lights in the world."[4] Are our preachers of this type of people? We are simply asking the question. Make up your own judgment. Is the work of holiness making progress among our preachers?

HOLINESS AND LAYPEOPLE

Are our leading laypeople examples of holiness?

Are they seeking holiness of heart and life?

Are they praying men and women, ever praying that God would fashion them according to His pattern of holiness?

Are their business ways without stain of sin, and their gains free from the taint of wrong-doing?

Have they the foundation of solid honesty, and does uprightness bring them into elevation and influence?

Does business activity and integrity run parallel with religious activity and Christian principles?

Then, while we are pursuing our investigation, seeking light as to whether the work of God among His people is making progress, let us ask a few questions that the Scriptures direct to women.[5]

Are the leading women of our churches dead to the fashions of this world, separated from the world, not conformed to the world's maxims and customs?

Is their behavior in keeping with holiness?

Do they teach the young women by word and life the lessons of soberness, obedience, and home-keeping?

Are our women noted for their praying habits?

Are they patterns of prayer?

How searching are all these questions? And will any one dare say they are impertinent and out of place? If God's work be to make men and women holy, and He has made ample provisions in the law of prayer of doing this very thing, why should it be thought impertinent and useless to put forth such personal and pointed questions as these? They have to do directly with the work and with its progress and its perfection. They go to the very root of the disease. They hit the spot.

We might as well face the situation now. There is no use to shut our eyes to real facts. If the church does not do this sort of work—if the church does not advance its members in holiness of heart and life—then all our show of activities and all our display of church work are a delusion and a snare.

But let us ask another large and important class of people in our churches, who are the hope of the Christian Church of the future, to whom all eyes are turned–are our young men and women growing in sober-mindedness and reverence, and in all those graces that have their root in the renewed heart—those things that mark solid and permanent advancement in the Christian life? If we are not growing in holiness, then we are doing nothing Christian or abiding.

MATERIAL PROSPERITY

Material prosperity is not the infallible sign of spiritual prosperity. The former may exist while the latter is significantly absent. Material prosperity may easily blind the eyes of church leaders, so much so that they will make it a substitute for spiritual prosperity. How great the need to watch that point! Prosperity in money matters does not signify growth in holiness. The seasons of material prosperity are rarely seasons of spiritual advance, either to the individual or to the church. It is so easy to lose sight of God when goods increase. It is so easy to lean on human agencies and cease praying and relying upon God when material prosperity comes to a church.[6]

To make sure that the work of God is progressing, and that we are growing in holiness, and if the Church is making advances on the lines of deep spirituality, if we are a praying people, noted for our prayer habits, if our people are hungering after holiness—then let us ask these questions:

Why do we now have so few mighty outpourings of the Holy Spirit on our churches?

Why is it that so few of our revivals spring from the life of the pastor, who is noted for deep spirituality, or the life of our church?

Is the Lord's hand shortened that He cannot save?

Is His ear heavy that He cannot hear?

Why is it that in order to have so-called revivals, we must have outside influence—such as the reputation and sensation of some renowned evangelist, singer, or musical group?

Why is it that our pastors are not sufficiently spiritual, holy, and in communion with God that they cannot hold their own revival services, and have large outpourings of the Holy Spirit on the church, the community, and on themselves?

There can be but one solution for all this state of things. We have cultivated other things to the neglect of the work of holiness. We have permitted our minds to be preoccupied with material things in the church. Unfortunately, whether designedly or not, we have substituted the external for the internal. We have put that which is seen to the front, and shut out that which is unseen. It is all too true in the Church that we are much further advanced in material matters than in spiritual matters.

HOLINESS AND PRAYER

But the cause of this sad state of things may be traced further back. It is largely due to the decay of prayer. For with the decline of the work of holiness there has come a decline in the business of praying. As praying and holiness go together, so the decline of one means the decline of the other. Excuse it if we may, justify the present state of things if we will, yet it is all too clear that the emphasis in the work of today's Church is not put on prayer. At the same time, the emphasis has been taken from the great work of God started in the atonement—holiness of heart and life. The Church is not turning out praying men and women because the Church is not intently engaged in the one great work of holiness.

At one time, John Wesley saw that there was a noticeable decline in the work of holiness, and he spent some time looking for the cause. If we are as honest and spiritual as he was, we will now see the same causes operating to stop God's work among us. In a letter to his brother, Charles, he comes directly to the point, and makes short, incisive, work of it. Here is how he begins his letter:

> What has hindered the work? I want to consider this. And must we not first say, we are the chief. If we were more holy in heart and life, thoroughly devoted to God, would not all the preachers catch fire, and carry it with them, throughout the land?
>
> Is not the next hindrance the littleness of grace (rather than of gifts) in a considerable part of our preachers? They have not the whole mind that was in Christ. They do not steadily walk as He walked. And, therefore, the hand of the Lord is stayed, though not altogether—He does still work. But it is not in such a degree as He surely would, were they holy as He that has sent them is holy.
>
> Is not the third hindrance the littleness of grace in the generality of our people? Therefore, they pray little, and with little fervency for a general blessing. And, therefore, their prayer has little power with God. It does not, as once, shut and open heaven.
>
> Add to this, that as there is much of the spirit of the world in their hearts, so there is much conformity to the world in their lives. They ought to be bright and shining lights, but they neither burn nor shine. They are not true to the rules they profess to observe. They

are not holy in all manner of conversation. Nay, many of them are salt that has lost its savor, the little savor they once had. Wherewith then shall the rest of the land be seasoned? What wonder that their neighbors are as unholy as ever?

John Wesley strikes the spot. He hits the center. He grades the cause. He freely confesses that he and Charles are the first cause in this decline of holiness. The chief ones occupy positions of responsibility. As they go, so goes the Church. They give color to the Church. They largely determine its character and its work. What holiness should mark these chief leaders? What zeal should ever characterize them? What prayerfulness should be seen in them! How influential they ought to be with God! If the head be weak, then the whole body will feel the stroke.

The pastors come next in Wesley's catalog. When the chief shepherds and those who are under them stop their advance in holiness, the panic will reach to the end of the line. As a rule, as the pastors are, so are the people. If the pastors are prayerless, the people will be prayerless also. If the preachers are silent upon the work of holiness, then there will be no hungering and thirsting after holiness in the laypeople. If the preachers are careless about obtaining the highest and best God has for them in Christian experience, then the people will be careless to the same degree.

One statement of Wesley needs to be repeated with emphasis. The littleness of grace, rather than the smallness of gifts,—this is largely the case with the preachers. It may be stated as an axiom: The work of God fails more for the lack of grace than for the want of gifts. It is more than this. It is more than this because a full supply of grace brings an increase of gifts. It may be repeated that small results; a low experience; a low religious life, and pointless, powerless preaching always flow from a lack of grace. And a lack of grace flows from a lack of praying. Great grace comes from great praying.

> What is our calling's glorious hope
> But inward holiness?
> For this to Jesus I look up,
> I calmly wait for this.

> I wait till He shall touch me clean,
> Shall life and power impart;
> Give me the faith that casts out sin,
> And purifies the heart.

GOD WORKS THROUGH PEOPLE

In carrying on His great work in the world, God works through human agents. He works through His Church collectively and through His people individually. In order that they may be effective agents, they must be "vessels unto honor, sanctified, and meet for the Master's use, and prepared unto every good work."[7] God works most effectively through holy men and women. His work makes progress in the hands of praying men and women. Peter tells us that husbands who might not be reached by the Word of God, might be won by the conversation of their wives. It is those who are "blameless and harmless, the sons of God,"[8] who can hold forth the word of life "in the midst of a crooked and perverse nation."

The world judges Christianity not by what the Bible says, but by how Christians live. Christians are the Bible that sinners read. These are the epistles to be read by all.[9] "By their fruits ye shall know them."[10] The emphasis, therefore, is to be placed upon holiness of life. But, unfortunately, in today's Church emphasis has been placed elsewhere. In selecting church workers and choosing ecclesiastical officers, the quality of holiness is not considered. The praying fitness seems not to be taken into account, when it was just otherwise in all of God's movements and in all of His plans. He looked for holy people, those noted for their praying habits. Prayer leaders are scarce. Prayer conduct is not counted as the highest qualification for offices in the church.

WHY SO LITTLE IS ACCOMPLISHED

We cannot wonder that so little is accomplished in the great work in the world that God has in hand. The fact is that it is surprising so much has been done with such feeble, defective, agents. "Holiness to the Lord"[11] needs again to be written on the banners of the Church. Once more it needs to be sounded out in the ears of modern Christians. "Follow peace with all men, and holiness, without which no man shall see the Lord."[12]

Let it be said again and again that this is the divine standard of Christianity. Nothing short of this will satisfy God's requirement. How great is the danger of deception at this point! How near one can come to being right and yet be wrong! Some can come very near to pronouncing the test word "Shibboleth," but they miss it.[13] "Many will say unto me in that day, Lord, Lord, " says Jesus Christ, but He further states that He will then say to them, "I never knew you: depart from me, ye that work iniquity."[14]

Christians can do many good things and yet not be holy in heart and righteous in conduct. They can do many good things and lack that spiritual quality of heart called holiness. How great the need of hearing the words of Paul guarding us against self-deception in the great work of personal salvation:

Be not deceived; God is not mocked: for whatsoever a man soweth, that shall he also reap.[15]

O may I still from sin depart;
A wise and understanding heart,
Jesus, to me to be given;
And let me through thy Spirit know
To glorify my God below,
And find my way to heaven.

Endnotes

1 Psalm 58:3
2 I John 3:8
3 I Peter 1:15-16
4 Philippians 2:15
5 It should be noted that Bounds wrote this book around the end of the 1800s—occupations and customs for women have changed since then, although God's commandment for holiness in both women and men has not.
6 Deuteronomy 8:17-18
7 2 Timothy 2:21
8 Philippians 2:15
9 2 Corinthians 3:2
10 Matthew 7:22
11 Exodus 28:36
12 Hebrews 12:14
13 Judges 12:6
14 Matthew 7:22a-23
15 Galatians 6:7

8

Prayer and Consecration

EUDAMIDAS, A CITIZEN OF *Corinth, died in poverty; but having two wealthy friends, Arctæus and Carixenus, left the following testament:*

In virtue of my last will, I bequeath to Arctæus my mother and to Carixenus my daughter to be taken home to their houses and supported for the remainder of their lives.

This testament occasioned much mirth and laughter. The two legatees were pleased and affectionately executed the will. If heathens trusted each other, why should not I cherish a far greater confidence in my beloved Master, Jesus? I hereby, therefore, nominate Him my sole heir, consigning to Him my soul and my children and sisters, that He may adopt, protect, and provide for them by His mighty power unto salvation. The whole residue of the estate shall be entrusted to His holy counsel. (Gotthold)

When we study the many facets of prayer, we are surprised at the number of things with which it is connected. There is no phase of human life that it does not affect, and it has to do with everything affecting human salvation. Prayer and consecration are closely related. Prayer leads up to and governs consecration. Prayer precedes consecration, accompanies it, and is a direct result of it. Much goes under the name of consecration that has no consecration in it. Much of today's consecration is defective, superficial, and spurious—worth nothing so far as the function and purpose of consecration are concerned. Popular consecration is sadly at fault because it has little or no prayer in it. No consecration is worth anything that is not the direct fruit of much praying, and that fails to bring one into a life of prayer. Prayer is the one thing prominent in a consecrated life.

Consecration is much more than a life of so-called service. First of all, it is a life of personal holiness. It is that which brings spiritual power into the heart and enlivens the entire inner person. It is a life that always recognizes God and is given up to true prayer.

Full consecration is the highest type of Christian life. It is the one divine standard of experience, of living, and of service. It is the one thing at which the believer should aim. Nothing short of entire consecration must satisfy us.

Never are we to be contented until we are fully and entirely the Lord's by our own consent. Praying naturally and involuntarily leads up to this act of consent.

Consecration is the voluntary and set dedication of one's self to God, an offering definitely made, and made without any reservation whatever. It is first of all the setting apart to God of all we are, all we have, and all we expect to have or be. It is not so much the giving of ourselves to the Church, or the mere engaging in some line of Church work. Almighty God is in view and He is the end of all consecration. It is a separation of ourselves to God, a devoting to Him all that we are and have for a sacred use. Some things may be devoted to a special purpose, but it is not consecration in the true sense. Consecration has a sacred nature. It is devoted to holy ends. It is the voluntary putting of ourselves in God's hands to be used sacredly, holily, with sanctifying goals in view.

CONSECRATION IS SEPARATION FROM THE WORLD

Consecration is not so much setting ourselves apart from sinful things and wicked ends. It is separating ourselves from worldly, secular, and even legitimate things—if they come in conflict with God's plans, that He might put us to holy use. It is the devoting of all we have to God for His own specific use. It is a separation from things questionable, or even legitimate, when the choice is to be made between the things of this life and the claims of God.

The consecration that meets God's demands and that He accepts is to be full and complete, with no mental reservation and with nothing withheld. It cannot be partial, any more than a whole burnt offering[1] in Old Testament times could have been partial. The whole animal had to be offered in sacrifice. To reserve any part of the animal would have seriously reduced the value of the offering. So to make a half-hearted, partial, consecration is to make no consecration at all. It is to fail utterly in securing God's acceptance. Consecration involves our whole being, all we have and all that we are. Everything is definitely and voluntarily placed in God's hands for His supreme use.

CONSECRATION IS NOT ALL THERE IS IN HOLINESS

Many make serious mistakes at this point. Consecration makes us relatively holy. We are holy only in the sense that we are now closely related to God in a manner we were not related before this. Consecration is the human side of holiness. In this sense, it is self-sanctification, and only in this sense. Sanctification or holiness in its truest and highest sense is divine. It is the act of the Holy Spirit working in the heart, making it clean and putting into it a higher degree of the fruits of the Spirit.

This distinction is clearly set forth and kept in view by Moses in Leviticus, where he shows the human and the divine side of sanctification or holiness:

> Sanctify yourselves therefore and be ye holy: for I am the Lord your God. And ye shall keep my statutes, and do them: I am the LORD which sanctify you.[2]

Here they were to sanctify themselves, and then in the next word they were told that it is the LORD that sanctifies them.

God does not consecrate us to His service. We do not sanctify ourselves in this highest sense. Here is the two-fold meaning of sanctification, and a distinction that needs to be always kept in mind.

Consecration is the intelligent, voluntary, act of the believer, and is the direct result of praying. No prayerless person ever conceives the idea of a full consecration. Prayerlessness and consecration have nothing whatever in common. A life of prayer naturally leads up to full consecration. It leads nowhere else. In fact, a life of prayer is satisfied with nothing else but an entire dedication of one's self to God. Consecration recognizes fully God's ownership of us. It cheerfully agrees with the truth set forth by Paul:

> Ye are not your own. For ye are bought with a price: therefore glorify God in your body, and in your spirit, which are God's.[3]

TRUE PRAYING LEADS TO CONSECRATION

It cannot reach any other destination. It is bound to run into this depot. This is its natural result This is the sort of work that praying turns out. Praying makes consecrated people. It cannot make any other sort. It drives to this end. It aims at this very purpose.

As prayer leads up to and brings forth full consecration, so prayer entirely saturates a consecrated life. The prayer life and the consecrated life are intimate companions. They are sun and sunshine, inseparable. Prayer enters into every phase of a consecrated life. A prayerless life that claims consecration is a misnomer—a counterfeit.

CONSECRATION MEANS A LIFE OF PRAYER

Consecration involves yourself apart to a life of prayer. It means not only to pray, but to pray habitually, and to pray more effectively. It is the consecrated Christians who accomplish most by their praying. God must hear the Christian wholly given up to God. God cannot deny the requests of those who have renounced all claims to themselves, and who have wholly dedicated themselves to God and His service.

This act of consecrated Christians puts them "on praying ground and pleading terms"[4] with God. It puts them in reach of God in prayer. It places them where they can get hold of God, and where they can influence God to do things that He would not otherwise do. Consecration brings answers to prayer. God can depend upon consecrated Christians. God can afford to commit Himself in prayer to those who have fully committed themselves to God. Those who give all to God will get all from God. Having given all to God, they can claim all that God has for them.

Prayer is the condition of full consecration, so prayer is the habit and rule of those who have dedicated themselves wholly to God. Prayer is developing in the consecrated life. Prayer is no strange thing in such a life. There is a peculiar affinity between prayer and consecration, for both recognize God, both submit to God, and both have their aim and end in God. Prayer is part and parcel of the consecrated life. Prayer is the constant, inseparable, and intimate companion of consecration. They walk and talk together.

MODERN CONSECRATION

There is much talk today of 'consecration', and many are termed 'consecrated people' who do not really know about consecrated living. Much modern consecration falls far below the Scripture standard. In the same way that there is much praying today without any real prayer in it, there is much so-called consecration in the Church that has no real consecration in it. Much that passes for consecration in the Church and receives the praise of superficial, formal professors, totally misses the mark.

In the Church today, there is much hurrying to and fro, here and there, much fuss and feathers, much going about and doing many things, and those who busy themselves in this way are often called consecrated men and women. The central trouble with all this false consecration is that there is no prayer in it. Neither is it in any sense the direct result of praying. People can do many excellent and commendable things in the Church and be utter strangers to a life of consecration, just as they can do many things and be prayerless.

THE TEST OF CONSECRATION

Here is the true test of consecration. It is a life of prayer. Unless prayer is preeminent, unless prayer is foremost, the consecration is faulty, deceptive, falsely named. Does the Christian pray? That is the test-question of every so-called consecrated saint. Is that Christian a person of prayer? No consecration is worth a thought if it is devoid of prayer. Even more— if it is not preeminently and primarily a life of prayer.

God wants consecrated Christians because they can pray and will pray. He can use consecrated people because He can use praying people. Prayerless people are in His way, hinder Him, and prevent the success of His cause. In the same way, unconsecrated people are useless to Him and hinder Him in carrying out His gracious plans and executing His noble purposes in redemption. God wants consecrated people because He wants praying people. Consecration and prayer meet in the same person. Prayer is the tool with which the consecrated person works.

Consecrated Christians are the agents through whom prayer works. Prayer helps consecrated Christians to maintain their attitude of consecration, keeps them alive to God, and aids them in doing the work to which they are called and to which they have given themselves. Consecration helps to produce prayer.

> Let Him to whom we now belong
> His sovereign right assert;
> And take up every thankful song,
> And every loving heart.
>
> He justly claims us for His own,
> Who bought us with a price;
> The Christian lives to Christ alone,
> To Christ alone he dies.

PRIMARY PURPOSE OF CONSECRATION IS NOT SERVICE

We must insist upon it that the primary purpose of consecration is not service, in the ordinary sense of that word. Service in the minds of most means nothing more than engaging in some of the many forms of modern church activities. There are a multitude of such activities, enough to engage the time and mind of anyone—even more than enough. Some of these may be good, others not so good.

Today's Church is filled with machinery, organizations, committees, departments, and societies. So much so, that the power it has is altogether insufficient to run the machinery, or to furnish life sufficient to do all this external work. Consecration has a much higher and nobler end than merely to expend itself in these external things.

Consecration aims at the right sort of service—the Scriptural kind. It seeks to serve God, true, but in an entirely different form than that which is in the minds of today's church leaders and workers. Here is the very first sort of service mentioned by Zachariah, the father of John the Baptist, in his wonderful prophecy and statement in Luke:

> That he would grant unto us, that we being delivered out of the hand of our enemies might serve him without fear, In holiness and righteousness before Him, all the days of our life.[5]

Here we have the idea of "serving God in holiness and righteousness all the days of our life."

The same kind of service is mentioned in Luke's strong tribute to the father and mother of John the Baptist before his birth:

And they were both righteous before God, walking in all the co mmandments and ordinances of the Lord blameless.[6]

In writing to the Philippians, Paul strikes the same keynote in putting the emphasis on blamelessness of life:

Do all things without murmurings and disputings: That ye may be blameless and harmless, the sons of God, without rebuke, in the midst of a crooked and perverse nation, among whom ye shine as lights in the world; Holding forth the word of life.[7]

We must mention a truth that is strangely overlooked in these days by what are called 'personal workers'. In the letters of Paul and others, it is not church activities that are brought to the front, but the Christian's personal life. It is good behavior, righteous conduct, holy living, godly conversation, right tempers—things that belong primarily to the personal life in Christianity. Everywhere this is emphasized, put in the forefront, made much of and insisted on. Christianity first of all puts one to living right. Christianity shows itself in the life. It is in this way that Christianity is to prove its reality, its sincerity, and its divine origin.

> So let our lips and lives express
> The holy Gospel we profess;
> So let our works and virtues shine
> To prove the doctrine all Divine.
> Thus shall we best proclaim abroad
> The honors of our Savior God;
> When the salvation reigns within
> And grace subdues the power of sin.

THE FIRST OBJECT OF CONSECRATION

The first great object of consecration is holiness of heart and of life. It is to glorify God. This can be done in no more effect way than by a holy life flowing from a heart cleansed from all sin. The great burden of heart pressed on every one who becomes a Christian lies right here. We are always to keep this in mind. To develop this kind of life and this kind of heart, we are to watch, pray, and diligently use all the means of grace available to us. Christians who are truly and fully consecrated, live holy lives. They seek after holiness of heart, and are not satisfied without it. For this very purpose they consecrate themselves to God. They give themselves entirely over to God in order to be holy in heart and in life.

Holiness of heart and of life is thoroughly saturated with prayer, and so consecration and prayer are closely allied in personal Christianity. It takes prayer to bring a person into a consecrated life of holiness to the Lord, and it takes prayer to maintain such a life. Without much prayer, such a life of holiness will break down. Holy people are praying people. Holiness of heart and life puts people to praying. Consecration puts people to praying in earnest.

Prayerless people are strangers to anything like holiness of heart and cleanness of heart. Those who are unfamiliar with the closet are not at all interested in consecration and holiness. Holiness thrives in the place of secret prayer. The environments of the closet of prayer are favorable to its being and its culture. In the closet holiness is found. Consecration brings one into holiness of heart, and prayer stands close by when it is done.

THE SPIRIT OF CONSECRATION IS THE SPIRIT OF PRAYER

The law of consecration is the law of prayer. Both laws work in perfect harmony without the slightest jar or discord. Consecration is the practical expression of true prayer. Christians who are consecrated are known by their praying habits. Consecration thus expresses itself in prayer. Those who are not interested in prayer have no interest in consecration. Prayer first creates an interest in consecration, then brings the praying person into a state of heart where consecration is the subject of delight.

The consecrated soul is the happiest soul. There is no friction between a soul that is fully given over to God and God's will. The perfect agreement of the two wills brings rest of soul, absence of friction, and the presence of perfect peace.

> Lord, in the strength of grace,
> With a glad heart and free,
> Myself, my residue of days,
> I consecrate to Thee.
> Thy ransomed servant, I
> Restore to Thee Thy own;
> And from this moment, live or die,
> To serve my God alone.

Endnotes

1 Psalm 51:19
2 Leviticus 20:7-8
3 1 Corinthians 6:19b-20
4 source unknown

5 Luke 1:74-75
6 Luke 1:6
7 Philippians 2:14-16a

9

Prayer and a Definite Christian Standard

THE ANGEL GABRIEL DESCRIBED *Him as 'that holy thing' before He was born. As He was, so are we, in our measure, in this world.* (Dr. Alexander White)

Much of the feebleness, barrenness, and deficiency of Christianity results from the failure to have a scriptural and reasonable standard in Christianity by which to shape character and measure results. This largely results from the omission of prayer or the failure to put prayer as the standard. We cannot possibly mark our advances in Christianity if there is no point to which we are definitely advancing. There must always be something definite before the mind's eye at which we are aiming and to which we are driving. We cannot contrast shapeliness with unshapeliness if there be no pattern after which to model. Neither can there be inspiration if there be no high end to stimulate us.

Many Christians are disjointed and aimless because they have no pattern before them after which conduct and character are to be shaped. They just move on aimlessly, their minds in a cloudy state, no pattern in view, no point in sight, no standard after which they are striving. There is no standard by which to value and gauge their efforts—no magnet to fill their eyes, quicken their steps, draw them toward it, and keep them steady.

All this vague idea of Christianity grows out of loose notions about prayer. Prayer makes the standard of Christianity clear and definite. In fact, prayer itself is a very definite thing. It aims at something specific and has a mark at which it aims. It aims at the sweetest Christian experience.

The praying ones want all that God has in store for them. They are not satisfied with a low Christian life—superficial, vague, and indefinite. The praying ones are not only after a "deeper work of grace," but want the very deepest work of grace promised. They are not after being saved from some sin, but saved from all sin, both inward and outward. They are after not only deliverance from sinning, but from sin itself—from its being, power, and pollution. They are after holiness of heart and life.

PRAYER SEEKS THE HIGHEST CHRISTIAN LIFE

Prayer believes in, and seeks for the very highest Christian life set before us in the Word of God. Prayer is the condition of that life. Prayer points out the only pathway to such a life. The standard of a Christian life is the standard of prayer. Prayer is so vital, so essential, so far-reaching, that it enters into all Christianity, and sets the standard clear and definite before the eye. The degree of our estimate of prayer fixes our ideas of the standard of a Christian life. The standard of Biblical Christianity is the standard of prayer. The more there is of prayer in the life, the more definite and the higher our notions of Christianity.

The Scriptures alone make the standard of Christian life and experience. When we make our own standard, there is delusion and falsehood in our desires. Convenience and pleasure then form the rule, and that is always a fleshly and low rule. From it, all the fundamental principles of a Christ-like Christianity are left out. Any standard of Christianity that has in it provision for the flesh is unscriptural and harmful.

DO NOT LET OTHERS SET YOUR STANDARD OF CHRISTIANITY

We must not let others set the standard of Christianity for us. When we allow others to set our standard of Christianity, it is generally deficient. When someone is imitated the defects of that person are transferred to the imitator more often than the virtues, and the second edition of the person becomes marred.

The most serious damage caused by determining what Christianity is by what others say, is in allowing the current opinions and grade of Christianity to shape our Christian opinions and characters. Adoniram Judson once wrote to a friend, "Let me beg you not to rest contented with the commonplace Christianity that is now so prevalent."

Commonplace Christianity is pleasing to flesh and blood. There is no self-denial in it, no cross bearing, no self-crucifixion. It is good enough for our neighbors, so why should we be different and strict? Others are living on a low plane, on a compromising level, living as the world lives. Why should we be peculiar and zealous of good works?[1] Why should we fight to win heaven while so many are sailing there on flowery beds of ease?

But are the easy-going, careless, sauntering crowds who live prayerless lives going to heaven? Is heaven a fit place for non-praying, loose-living, ease-loving people?

PAUL'S CAUTION ABOUT A LOW STANDARD

Paul gives the following caution about using the jolly, pleasure-seeking, religious company all about us as the standard for measuring our Christianity:

> For we dare not make ourselves of the number, or compare ourselves with some that commend themselves: but they measuring themselves by themselves, and comparing themselves among themselves, are not wise. But we will not boast of things without our measure, but according to the measure of the rule which God hath distributed to us, a measure to reach even unto you.[2]

No standard of Christianity that leaves prayer out is worth a moment's consideration. No standard that does not make prayer the main thing in Christianity is worth thinking about. Prayer is so necessary, so fundamental in God's plan, so important to everything in Christian life, that it enters into all Biblical Christianity. Prayer itself is a standard—definite, emphatic, scriptural. A life of prayer is the divine rule. This is the pattern in the same way that our Lord, being a person of prayer, is the one pattern for us to copy. Prayer fashions the pattern of a Christian life. Prayer is the measure. Prayer molds the life.

The vague, indefinite, popular view of Christianity has no prayer in it. Prayer is entirely left out of its program, or put so low down and made so insignificant, that it hardly is worth mentioning. The human standard of Christianity has no prayer about it.

WE ARE TO AIM AT GOD'S STANDARD

It is God's standard that we are to aim at, not that of people. It is not what people say, their opinions, but what the Scriptures say. Loose notions of Christianity grow out of low notions of prayer. Prayerlessness creates loose, cloudy, and indefinite views of what Christianity is. Aimless living and prayerlessness go hand in hand. Prayer sets something definite in the mind. Prayer seeks after something specific.

The more definite our views as to the nature and need of prayer, the more definite our views of the Christian experience and right living will be. A low standard of Christianity always has a low standard of praying.

THE ONLY TRUE STANDARD

The Scriptures always set before us the one standard of full consecration to God. This is the divine rule. This is the human side of this standard. The sacrifice acceptable to God must be a complete one, entire, a whole burnt offering. This is the measure laid down in God's Word. Nothing less than this can be pleasing to God. Nothing half-hearted can please Him. "A living sacrifice,"[3] holy and perfect in all its parts is the measurement of our service to God. A full renunciation of self, a free recognition of God's right to us, and a sincere offering of all to Him—this is the divine requirement. There is nothing indefinite in that, and there is nothing in it that is governed by the opinions of others or affected by how people live about us.

A life of prayer is included in a full consecration, and prayer leads up to the point where a complete consecration is made to God. Consecration is but the silent expression of prayer. The highest Christian standard is the measure of prayer and self-dedication to God. The prayer-life and the consecrated life are partners in Christianity. They are so closely allied they are never separated. Prayer is the natural outflow of a truly consecrated life. The measure of consecration is the measure of real prayer.

NO PARTIAL CONSECRATION PLEASING TO GOD

No consecration is pleasing to God that is not perfect in all its parts, just as no burnt offering of an Israelite was ever acceptable to God unless it was a "whole burnt offering."[4] A consecration of this sort, after this divine measurement, has in it as a basic principle, the business of praying. Consecration is made to God. Prayer has to do with God. Consecration is putting one's self entirely at the disposal of God. God wants and commands all His consecrated ones to be praying ones. This is the one definite standard at which we must aim. Lower than this we cannot afford to seek.

A scriptural standard of Christianity includes a clear Christian experience. Christianity is nothing if not experimental. Christianity appeals to the inner consciousness. It is an experience if it is anything at all, and an experience in addition to a Christian life. There is the internal part of Christianity as well as the external. Not only are we told to "work out your own salvation with fear and trembling," but "it is God which worketh in you both to will and to do of His good pleasure."[5] There is a "good work in you," as well as a life outside to be lived.

The new birth is a definite Christian experience, proved by infallible marks, and appealing to the inner consciousness. The witness of the Spirit is not an indefinite, vague, something, but is a definite, clear, inward assurance given by the Holy Spirit that we are the children of God.[6] In fact, everything belonging to Christian experience is clear and definite, bringing conscious joy, peace, and love. This is the divine standard of Christianity, a standard attained by earnest, constant, prayer—and a Christian experience kept alive and enlarged by the same means of prayer.

AN END TO BE GAINED

Directing effort toward a definite end to be gained is important in every pursuit of life in order to give unity, energy, and steadiness to it. In the Christian life, such an end is all important. Without a high standard before us to be gained, for which we are earnestly seeking, weariness will weaken effort, and past experience will decay into mere sentiment or be hardened into cold, loveless, ritual.

"Therefore leaving the principles of the doctrine of Christ, let us go on unto perfection."[7] The present ground we occupy must be held by making advances, and all the future must be covered and brightened by it. In Christianity, we must not only go on, we must know where we are going—what our goal is.

It is essential that in going on in the Christian experience we have something definite in view, and strike out for that one point. To always go on and not know to what place we are going is altogether too vague and indefinite, and is like a person who starts out on a journey and does not have any destination in view.

It is important that we do not lose sight of the starting point in a Christian life, and that we measure the steps already taken. But it is likewise necessary that the end be kept in view, and that the steps necessary to reach that goal always be kept before our eyes.

Endnotes

1 Titus 2:14
2 2 Corinthians 10:12-13
3 Romans 12:1
4 Psalm 51:19
5 Philippians 2:12a-13
6 Romans 8:16
7 Hebrews 6:1

10

Prayer Born of Compassion

OPEN YOUR NEW TESTAMENT, *take it with you to your knees, and set Jesus Christ out of it before you. Are you like David in the sixty-third Psalm? Is your soul thirsting for God, and is your flesh longing for God in a dry and thirsty land where no water is? Then set Jesus at the well of Samaria before the eyes of your thirsty heart And, again set Him before your heart when He stood on the last day, that great day of the feast, and cried, saying, 'If any man thirst let him come to me and drink.' Or, are you like David after the matter of Uriah? "For day and night thy hand was heavy upon me: my moisture is turned into the drought of summer."[1] Then set Him before you who says: "I am not come to call the righteous, but sinners to repentance.[2] . . . They that are whole need not a physician, but they that are sick."[3] Or are you the unhappy father of a prodigal son? Then, set your Father in heaven always before you: and set the Son of God always before you as He composes and preaches the parable of all parables for you and your son.* (Dr. Alexander White)

We speak here especially of spiritual compassion, that which is born in a renewed heart, and which finds hospitality there. This compassion has in it the quality of mercy, is of the nature of pity, and moves the soul with the tenderness of feeling for others. Compassion is moved at the sight of sin, sorrow, and suffering. It stands opposite of indifference to the needs and troubles of others. It is far removed from insensibility and hardness of heart. Compassion stands besides sympathy for others.

That which excites and develops compassion and puts it to work is the sight of multitudes in need and distress—those who are helpless to relieve themselves. Helplessness especially appeals to compassion. Compassion is silent but does not remain secluded. It goes out at the sight of trouble, sin, and need.

Compassion runs out first in earnest prayer for those for whom it has sympathy. Prayer for others is born of a sympathetic heart. Prayer is natural and almost spontaneous when compassion is born in the heart. Prayer belongs to the compassionate person.

There is a certain compassion that belongs to the natural person, which expends its force in simple gifts to those in need, and is not to be despised. But spiritual compassion, the kind born in a renewed heart, is Christlike in its nature, deeper, broader, and more prayer-like. Christlike compassion always moves to prayer. This sort of compassion goes beyond the relief of mere bodily needs and saying, "Be ye warmed and filled."[4] It reaches deeper down and goes much further.

COMPASSION IS NOT BLIND

We should say, rather, that compassion is not born of blindness. Those who have compassion of soul, first of all have eyes to see the things that excite compassion. Those who have no eyes to see the exceeding sinfulness of sin, the needs and troubles of humanity, will never have compassion on humanity. It is written of our Lord that, "when he saw the multitudes, he was moved with compassion on them."[5] First, seeing the multitudes with their hunger, their troubles, and their helpless condition, then compassion. Then prayer for the multitudes. Hard of heart and far from being Christlike are those who see the multitudes and are unmoved by the sight of their sad state, unhappiness, and peril. They have no heart of prayer for people.

Compassion may not always move people, but is always moved toward people. Compassion may not always turn people to God, but it will and does turn God to people. Where it is most helpless to relieve the needs of others, it can at least break out into prayer to God for others. Compassion is never indifferent, selfish, and forgetful of others. Compassion has alone to do with others. The fact that the multitudes were as sheep having no shepherd was the one thing that appealed to our Lord's compassionate nature. Then their hunger moved Him, and the sight of the sufferings and diseases of the multitudes stirred the pity of His heart.

Father of mercies, send Thy grace
All powerful from above,
To form in our obedient souls
The image of Thy love.
O may our sympathizing breasts

That generous pleasure know;
Kindly to share in others' joy,
And weep for others' woe.

COMPASSION FOR SINNERS

But compassion has not only to do with the body and its disabilities and needs. The soul's distressing state, its needs and danger, all appeal to compassion. The highest state of grace is known by the infallible mark of compassion for poor sinners. This sort of compassion belongs to grace, and sees not just the bodies of people. It also sees their immortal spirits soiled by sin, unhappy in their condition without God, and in imminent peril of being forever lost. When compassion beholds this sight of dying people hurrying to the judgment seat of God, it breaks out into intercessions for sinful souls. It is then that compassion speaks in this way:

But feeble my compassion proves,
And can but weep where most it loves;
Thy own all saving arm employ,
And turn these drops of grief to joy.

GOD'S COMPASSION

The Prophet Jeremiah declares this about God, giving the reason why sinners are not consumed by His wrath: "It is of the LORD's mercies that we are not consumed, because His compassions fail not."

It is this divine quality in us that makes us so much like God. So we find the Psalmist describing the righteous person who is pronounced blessed by God: "He is gracious, and full of compassion, and righteous."[6]

To give great encouragement to repentant sinners, the psalmist records some of the striking attributes of God's character: "The Lord is gracious and full of compassion; slow to anger, and of great mercy."[7]

It is no wonder, then, that we find it recorded several times of our Lord while He was on earth that "he was moved with compassion."[8] Can anyone doubt that His compassion moved Him to pray for those suffering, sorrowing ones who came across His pathway?

PAUL'S COMPASSION

Paul was wonderfully interested in the spiritual welfare of his Jewish brethren–and his heart was strangely warmed with tender compassion for their salvation, even though he was mistreated and greatly persecuted by them. In writing to the Romans, he says this about himself:

I say the truth in Christ, I lie not, my conscience also bearing me witness in the Holy Ghost, That I have great heaviness and continual sorrow in my heart. For I could wish that myself were accursed from Christ for my brethren, my kinsmen according to the flesh.[9]

What marvelous compassion is here described for Paul's own nation! What wonder that a little later on he records his desire and prayer: "Brethren, my heart's desire and prayer to God for Israel is, that they might be saved."[10]

JESUS' COMPASSION

We have an interesting case in Matthew that gives us an account of what excited so greatly the compassion of our Lord at one time:

> But when He saw the multitudes, He was moved with compassion on them, because they fainted, and were scattered abroad, as sheep having no shepherd. Then saith He unto His disciples, The harvest truly is plenteous, but the laborers are few; Pray ye therefore the Lord of the harvest, that He will send forth laborers into His harvest.[11]

This parallels the story of our Lord when he called His disciples away to rest awhile, from the ceaseless contact with the people who desired healing and teaching. But they couldn't escape because the multitudes preceded Him. Christ's compassions were moved, when he saw the crowd's hurt. He charged the disciples to go to God in prayer and ask Him to send forth laborers into His harvest.

THE HARVEST IS READY, BUT LABORERS ARE LACKING

Here is the urgency of prayer enforced by the compassions of our Lord. It is prayer born of compassion for perishing humanity. Prayer is pressed on the Church for laborers to be sent into the harvest of the Lord. The harvest will go to waste and perish without the laborers, but the laborers must be God-chosen, God-sent, and God-commissioned. God, however, does not send these laborers into His harvest without prayer. The failure of the laborers is owing to the failure of prayer. The lack of laborers in the harvest is due to the fact that the Church fails to pray for laborers according to His command.

The ingathering of the harvests of earth for the granaries of heaven is dependent on the prayers of God's people. Prayer obtains the quantity and quality of laborers for all the needs of the harvest. God's chosen laborers, God's endowed laborers, and God's thrust-forth laborers, are the only ones who will truly go. When they go, they will be filled with Christlike compassion and endued with Christlike power Their going will accomplish the work, for they were obtained by prayer. Christ's people on their knees with Christ's compassion in their hearts for dying souls that are exposed to eternal peril, is the pledge of laborers in sufficient numbers and character to meet the needs of earth and the purposes of heaven.

GOD CHOOSES THE LABORERS

God is sovereign on earth and in heaven, and the choice of laborers in His harvest He delegates to no one else. Prayer honors Him as sovereign and moves Him to His wise and holy selection. We will have to put prayer to the front before the fields of paganism will be successfully harvested for Christ. God knows His people, and He likewise knows full well His work. Prayer gets God to send forth the best people, the most fit people, and the people best qualified to work in the harvest. Moving the missionary cause by forces this side of God has been its ruin, its weakness, and its failure. Compassion for the world of sinners fallen in Adam but redeemed in Christ will move the Church to pray for them, and stir the Church to pray the Lord of the harvest to send forth laborers into His harvest.

> Lord of the harvest hear
> Thy needy servants' cry;
> Answer our faith's effectual prayer,
> And all our wants supply.
>
> Convert and send forth more
> Into Thy Church abroad;
> And let them speak Thy word of power,
> As workers with their God.

THE LORD'S COMPASSION NEVER FAILS

What a comfort and what hope there is to fill our breasts when we think of one in Heaven who ever lives to intercede for us, because "His compassions fail not!"[12] Above everything else, we have a compassionate Savior, one "Who can have compassion on the ignorant, and on them that are out of the way; for that he himself also is compassed with infirmity."[13]

The compassion of our Lord well fits Him for being the great high priest of Adam's fallen, lost, and helpless race.

If the Lord is filled with such compassion that it moves Him at the Father's right hand to intercede for us, then by every token we should have the same compassion on the ignorant and those who are out of the way of salvation. The fact that they are, therefore, exposed to divine wrath should move us to pray for them. We will be praying for them to the same measure that we are compassionate. Compassion does not expend its force in simply saying, "Be ye warmed and filled,"[14] but drives us to our knees in prayer for those who need Christ and His grace.

> The Son of God in tears
> The wondering angels see;
> Be thou astonished, O my soul!
> He shed those tears for thee.

He wept that we might weep;
Each sin demands a tear;
In heaven alone no sin is found,
And there's no weeping there.

Jesus Christ was altogether human. He was the divine Son of God, and at the same time was the human Son of God. Christ had a preeminently human side, and there compassion reigned. He was tempted in all points as we are, yet without sin.[15] At one time the flesh seems to have weakened under the fearful strain upon Him, and He must have inwardly shrunk under the pain and pull of His flesh! Looking up to heaven, He almost prayed, "Father, save me from this hour." But His spirit strengthened and held: "but for this cause came I unto this hour."[16] Only those can solve this mystery who have followed their Lord in difficulties, sorrows, and pain and learned that, "the spirit indeed is willing, but the flesh is weak."[17]

All this prepared our Lord to be a compassionate Savior. It is no sin to feel the pain and realize the darkness on the path into which God leads. It is only human to cry out against the pain, terror, and desolation of a dreaded, but needed hour. It is divine to cry out to God in that hour, even while shrinking and sinking down, "For this cause came I unto this hour."

Shall I fail through the weakness of the flesh? No. "Father, glorify thy name."[18] How strong and true it makes us to have a bright North Star to guide us to the glory of God!

Endnotes

1 Psalm 32:4
2 Matthew 9:13b
3 Matthew 9:12b
4 James 2:16
5 Matthew 9:36
6 Psalm 112:4
7 Psalm 145:8
8 Matthew 9:36, 14:14, 18:27; Mark 1:41, 6:34
9 Romans 9:1-3
10 Romans 10:1
11 Matthew 9:36-38
12 Lamentations 3:22
13 Hebrews 5:2
14 James 2:16
15 Hebrews 4:15
16 John 12:27
17 Matthew 26:41
18 John 12:28a

11

Concerted Prayer

A TOURIST, IN CLIMBING AN *Alpine summit, finds himself tied by a strong rope to his trusty guide, and to three of his fellow-tourists. As they skirt a perilous precipice he cannot pray, "Lord, hold up my goings in a safe path, that my footsteps slip not,*[1] *but as to my guide and companions, they must look out for themselves." The only proper prayer in such a case is, "Lord, hold up our goings in a safe path; for if one slips all of us may perish."* (H. Clay Trumbull)

The pious Quesnel says that "God is found in union and agreement. Nothing is more effective than this in prayer." Intercessions combine with prayers and supplications. The word *intercession* does not mean necessarily prayer in relation to others. It means a coming together, a falling in with a most intimate friend for free, unrestrained, communion. It implies prayer that is free, familiar, and bold.

Our Lord deals with this question of the unity and agreement of prayer in the eighteenth chapter of Matthew. He deals with the benefit and energy resulting from the coming together of prayer forces. The prayer principle and the prayer promise will be best understood in the connection in which it was made by our Lord:

> Moreover if thy brother shall trespass against thee, go and tell him his fault between thee and him alone: if he shall hear thee, thou hast gained thy brother. But if he will not hear thee, then take with thee one or two more, that in the mouth of two or three witnesses every word may be established.

And if he shall neglect to hear them, tell it unto the church: but if he neglect to hear the church, let him be unto thee as an heathen man and a publican.

Verily I say unto you, Whatsoever ye shall bind on earth shall be bound in heaven: and whatsoever ye shall loose on earth shall be loosed in heaven. Again I say unto you, That if two of you shall agree on earth as touching any thing that they shall ask, it shall be done for them of my Father which is in heaven. For where two or three are gathered together in my name, there am I in the midst of them.[2]

This represents the church in prayer to enforce discipline, so that its members who have committed faults may yield readily to the disciplinary process. In addition, it is the church called together in a unity of prayer in order to repair the waste and friction created by the cutting off of a church offender. This last direction as to a unity of prayer is that the whole matter may be referred to Almighty God for His approval and ratification.

PRAYER AND THE CHURCH

All this means is that the main, concluding, and all powerful agency in the church is prayer. Whether it is used to thrust out laborers into God's earthly harvest fields as we have read in Matthew, or to exclude from the church a violator of unity, law, and order who will not listen to the other members or repent and confess the fault.

It means that church discipline, now a lost art in today's Christianity, must go hand in hand with prayer. The church that has no disposition to separate wrongdoers from the congregation, and that has no excommunication spirit for incorrigible offenders against law and order, will have no communication with God. Church purity must precede the church's prayers. The unity of discipline in the church precedes the unity of prayers by the church.

Let it be noted with emphasis that a church that is careless of discipline will be careless in praying. A church that tolerates evildoers in its communion, will cease to pray, will cease to pray with agreement, and will cease to be a church gathered together in prayer in Christ's name.

CHURCH DISCIPLINE IN THE SCRIPTURES

This matter of church discipline is an important one in the Scriptures. It is the duty of the church to watch over the spiritual and moral life of its members. The church is an organization for mutual help, and it is charged with the watchful care of all of its members. Disorderly conduct cannot be passed by unnoticed. The course of procedure in such cases is clearly given in the eighteenth chapter of Matthew, which has just been referred to.

Furthermore, in Galatians 6:1 Paul gives specific directions concerning those who fall into sin in the church: "Brethren, if a man be overtaken in a fault, ye which are spiritual restore such a one in the spirit of meekness, considering thyself lest thou also be tempted."

The work of the church is not only to seek members, but also to watch over and guard them after they have entered the church. If any are overtaken by sin, they must be sought out. If they cannot be cured of their faults, then expulsion must take place. This is the doctrine our Lord lays down.

It is somewhat striking that although the church at Ephesus had left its first love and sadly declined in vital godliness and in those things that make up spiritual life, it still receives credit for this good quality: "Thou canst not bear them which are evil."[3]

By contrast, the church at Pergamos was admonished because it had among its membership those who taught hurtful doctrines that were a stumbling-block to others. It was not so much that such characters were in the church, but that they were tolerated. The impression is that the church leaders were blind to the presence of such harmful characters, and so were unfit to administer discipline. This unfitness was an unfailing sign of prayerlessness in the membership. There was no union of prayer effort looking to cleansing the church and keeping it clean.

This disciplinary idea stands out prominently in the apostle Paul's writings to the churches. The church at Corinth had a notorious case of fornication where a man had been intimate with his step-mother, and the church had been careless about this iniquity. Paul rather sharply reproved the church and gave a clear command about what they were to do: "Therefore put away from among yourselves that wicked person."[4] Here Paul demanded agreement of action on the part of praying people.

Even as good a church as that at Thessalonica needed instruction and caution on this matter of looking after disorderly persons. So we read Paul saying to them: "Now we command you, brethren, in the name of our Lord Jesus Christ, that ye withdraw yourselves from every brother that walketh disorderly."[5]

GOD DOES NOT TOLERATE CHURCHES THAT TOLERATE EVIL

Notice this. It is not the mere presence of disorderly persons in a church that merits the displeasure of God. It is when they are tolerated under the mistaken plea of bearing with them, and no steps are taken either to cure them of their evil practices or exclude them from the fellowship of the church.

This glaring neglect on the part of the church of its wayward members is a sad sign of a lack of praying. For a praying church that is given to mutual praying, agreement praying, is keen to discern when a member is overtaken in a fault, and seeks either to restore or remove the person, if the person refuses to repent.

Much of this is caused by a lack of spiritual vision on the part of church leaders. The Lord once asked through the Prophet Isaiah the very pertinent, suggestive question, "Who is blind, but my servant?"[6] This blindness in leadership of the church is no more evident than in this problem of evildoers in the church. The church is to care for them and attempt to restore them. But if the effort to restore them fails, the church is to withdraw fellowship from them and let them be "as an heathen man and a publican."[7]

The truth, however, is that there is such a desire for members in the church today that the leaders and preachers have entirely lost sight of the members who have violated Christian principles, and who are living in open disregard of God's Word. The goal now is quantity in membership, not quality. The purity of the church is put in the background in the craze to secure numbers, and to pad the church rolls and make large figures in statistical columns. Prayer, much prayer, mutual prayer, would bring the church back to scriptural standards. It would also purge the church of many wrongdoers, and might even cure many of their evil lives.

PRAYER AND CHURCH DISCIPLINE

Prayer and church discipline are not new revelations of the Christian dispensation. These two things had a high place in the Jewish Church. Instances are too numerous to mention all of them.

Ezra is a case in point. When he returned from the captivity, he found a sad and distressing condition of things among the Lord's people who were left in the land. They had not separated themselves from the surrounding heathen people, and had intermarried with them, contrary to God's commands. Those high in the Church office were also involved—the priests and the Levites. Ezra was greatly moved at the account given to him, and tore his garments and wept and prayed.[8]

Evildoers in the church did not meet his approval. Therefore, he did not shut his eyes to them or excuse them or compromise the situation. When he had finished confessing the sins of the people and his praying, the people assembled themselves before him and joined him in a covenant agreement to put away from them their evil doings. They wept and prayed in unity with Ezra.[9]

The result was that the people thoroughly repented of their transgressions, and Israel was reformed. Praying and a good man, who was neither blind nor unconcerned, did the deed.

Of Ezra it is written, "for he mourned because of the guilt of those from the captivity."[10] So it is with every praying person in the church who has eyes to see the transgression of evildoers in the church, who has a heart to grieve over them, and who has a spirit so concerned about the church that they pray about it.

Blessed is that church who has praying leaders who can see what is disorderly in the church, who are grieved about it, and who put forth their hands to correct the evils that harm God's cause and impede its progress. One point in the indictment against those "that are at ease in Zion,"[11] referred to by Amos, is that "they are not grieved for the affliction of Joseph."[12]

This same indictment could be brought against today's church. They are not grieved because the members are engulfed in a craze for worldly, carnal things—nor when there are those in the Church walking openly in disorder, whose lives scandalize Christianity and Christ. Obviously, such leaders do not pray over the matter, for praying would create a spirit of concern in them for these evildoers, and would drive away the spirit of unconcern that possesses them.

PRAYERLESS CHURCH LEADERS AND CARELESS PASTORS

It would be well for prayerless church leaders and careless pastors to read the account of the man with the inkhorn in the 9th chapter of Ezekiel. God instructed the prophet to send through the city certain men who would destroy those in the city because of the great evils found there. But certain persons were to be spared. These were the ones who "that sigh and that cry for all the abominations that be done in the midst" of the city.[13] The man with the inkhorn was to mark every one of these sighers and criers so that they would escape the impending destruction.[14] Please note that the instructions were that the slaying of those who did not sigh and cry should "begin at my sanctuary."[15]

What a lesson for non-praying, unconcerned, leaders of the modern church! How few there are who "sigh and cry" today for abominations in the land, and who are grieved over the desolations of Zion! What need there is for "two or three to be gathered together"[16] in a unity of prayer over these conditions, and to weep and pray in the secret place for the sins in Zion!

UNITY AND AGREEMENT IN PRAYER

This unity of prayer, this agreement in praying, taught by our Lord in the eighteenth chapter of Matthew, finds proof and illustration elsewhere. This was the kind of praying that Paul referred to in his request to the church in Rome.

> Now I beseech you, brethren, for the Lord Jesus Christ's sake, and for the love of the Spirit, that ye strive together with me in your prayers to God for me; That I may be delivered from them that do not believe in Judea; and that my service which I have for Jerusalem may be accepted of the saints.[17]

Here is unity in prayer, prayer by agreement, and prayer drives directly at deliverance from unbelieving and evil people. It is the same kind of prayer urged by our Lord,[18] with the end purpose being practically the same—deliverance from unbelieving people. That deliverance is to be accomplished either by bringing them to repentance or by exclusion from the church.

The same idea is found in Paul's letter to the Thessalonians: "Finally, brethren, pray for us, that the word of the Lord may have free course, and be glorified, even as it is with you: And that we may be delivered from unreasonable and wicked men: for all men have not faith."[19]

United prayer is requested by an apostle for, among other things, deliverance from wicked men—the same thing the church of God needs in this day. By the Thessalonians joining their prayers to Paul's, there was the desired end of riddance from those who were harmful to the church of God and who were a hindrance to the free flowing of the Word of the Lord.

CHURCH DISCIPLINE TODAY

Let us ask ourselves: Are there not in today's church those who are a positive hindrance to the Word of the Lord flowing freely? What better course is there than to jointly pray over the problem—using first the Christ-given course of discipline to save them, but removing them from the body if that fails?

Does that seem like a harsh course? Then our Lord was guilty of harshness Himself, for He ends His directions by saying, "But if he neglect to hear the church, let him be unto thee as an heathen man and a publican."[20]

This is no more harsh than is the act of the skilful surgeon, who sees the whole body and its members endangered by a gangrenous limb, and severs the limb from the body for the good of the whole. It is no more harsh than it was for the captain and crew of the vessel on which Jonah was found to cast the fleeing prophet overboard when the storm arose because of him and threatened to destroy everyone onboard.

Church discipline that seems harsh is obedience to God, is for the welfare of the Church, and is the highest wisdom.

Endnotes

1 Psalm 17:5
2 Matthew 15:18-20
3 Ephesians 2:2
4 1 Corinthians 5:13
5 2 Thessalonians 3:6
6 Isaiah 42:19a
7 Matthew 18:17
8 Ezra 9:1-15
9 Ezra 10:1
10 Ezra 10:6a
11 Amos 6:1a

12 Amos 6:6b
13 Ezekiel 9:4b
14 Ezekiel 9:1-4
15 Ezekiel 9:6a
16 Matthew 18:20
17 Romans 15:30-31
18 Matthew 18:15-17
19 2 Thessalonians 3:1-2
20 Matthew 18:17

12

The Universality of Prayer

IT TAKES MORE OF *the power of the Spirit to make the farm, the home, the office, the store, the shop, holy than it does to make the Church holy. It takes more of the power of the Spirit to make Saturday holy than to make Sunday holy. It takes much more of the power of the Spirit to make money for God than it does to make a talk for God, much more to live a great life for God than to preach a great sermon.* (Edwards M. Bounds)

Prayer is far-reaching in its influence and worldwide in its effects. It touches people's interest in time and eternity. It lays hold upon God and moves Him to interfere in the affairs of earth. It moves the angels to minister to people in this life. It restrains and defeats the devil in his schemes to ruin humanity. Prayer goes everywhere and lays its hand upon everything.

There is a universality in prayer. When we talk about prayer and its work we must use universal terms. It is individual in its application and benefits, but it is general and worldwide in its good influences. It blesses people in every event of life, furnishes them help in every emergency, and gives them comfort in every trouble. There is no experience through which people are called to go without prayer.

THE MANY SIDES OF UNIVERSAL PRAYER

When we speak of the universality of prayer, we discover many sides to it. First, it may be remarked that everyone ought to pray. Prayer is intended for everyone, because everyone needs God and needs what God has and what prayer only can secure. As everyone is called upon to pray everywhere, by consequence everyone must pray for people everywhere.

Universal terms are used when people are commanded to pray, while there is a promise in universal terms to all who call upon God for pardon, mercy, and help:

> For there is no difference . . . for the same Lord over all is rich unto all that call upon him. For whosoever shall call upon the name of the Lord shall be saved.[1]

There is no difference in the state of sin in which people are found, and everyone needs the saving grace of God that alone can bless them. Since this saving grace is obtained only in answer to prayer, everyone is called upon to pray because of their need for salvation.

It is a rule of scriptural interpretation that whenever a command is given with no limitation, it is universal in its binding force—that is, it applies to everyone. So the words of the Lord in Isaiah are to everyone:

> Seek ye the Lord while he may be found, call ye upon him while he is near: Let the wicked forsake his way, and the unrighteous man his thoughts: and let him return unto the Lord, and he will have mercy upon him; and to our God, for he will abundantly pardon.[2]

Since wickedness is universal and pardon is needed by everyone, everyone must seek the Lord while He may be found, and must call upon Him while He is near. Prayer belongs to everyone because everyone is redeemed only in Christ. It is a privilege for everyone to pray, but it is no less an obligation for them to call upon God. No sinner is kept from the mercy seat. All are welcomed to approach the throne of grace with all their needs and distresses, with all their sins and burdens.

> Come all the world, come, sinner thou,
> All things in Christ are ready now.

Whenever poor sinners repent and look to God for mercy, no matter where they are or what their guilt and sinfulness, the eyes of God are upon them and His ears are opened to their prayers.

But people may pray everywhere, since God is accessible in every climate and under all circumstances. "I will therefore that men pray everywhere, lifting up holy hands, without wrath and doubting."[3]

No locality is too distant from God on earth to reach heaven. No place is so remote that God cannot see and hear one who looks toward Him and seeks His face. Oliver Holden puts into a hymn these words:

> Then, my soul, in every strait,
> To Thy Father come and wait;
> He will answer every prayer;
> God is present everywhere.

THERE ARE SOME PLACES WHERE PRAYER IS INAPPROPRIATE

There is just this modification of the idea that one can pray everywhere. Prayer would not be proper in some places because of the evil business carried on in them, the environment that grows out of the place itself, and the moral character of those who work there and those who support it. For instance, saloons, theatres, opera houses, gambling halls and casinos, dance halls and nightclubs, and other similar places of worldly amusement. Prayer is so much out of place at such places that no one would ever presume to pray. Prayer would be regarded as an intrusion by the owners, patrons, and supporters of such places. Furthermore, those who attend such places are not praying people. They belong almost entirely to the prayerless crowd of worldlings—those absorbed by worldly pursuits and pleasures.

Since we are to pray everywhere, it obviously means that we are not to patronize places where we cannot pray. To pray everywhere is to pray in all legitimate places, and to attend especially those places where prayer is welcome, and is given a gracious hospitality. To pray everywhere is to preserve the spirit of prayer in places of business, in our association with people, and in the privacy of the home amid all of its domestic cares.

THE UNIVERSAL PRAYER

The model prayer of our Lord, referred to as "The Lord's Prayer," is the universal prayer, because it is especially adapted to everyone everywhere in all circumstances and times of need. It can be put in the mouths of all people in all nations, and in all times. It is a model of praying that needs no amendment or alteration for every family, people, and nation.

Furthermore, prayer has its universal application in that everyone is to be the subject of prayer. Everyone everywhere is to be prayed for. Prayer must take in all of Adam's fallen race because everyone is fallen in Adam, redeemed in Christ, and benefited by prayers for them. This is Paul's doctrine in his prayer directions:

> I exhort therefore, that, first of all, supplications, prayers, intercessions, and giving of thanks, be made for all men.[4]

There is, therefore, strong scriptural justification for reaching out and embracing everyone in our prayers. We are commanded to pray for them, and the reason given is that Christ gave Himself a ransom for everyone,[5] and everyone is provisionally a beneficiary of the atoning death of Jesus Christ. That is, atonement has been provided for everyone, and anyone can obtain it by faith in Christ.[6]

Prayer also has a universal side in that all things that concern us are to be prayed about. Everything that is for our good—physically, socially, intellectually, spiritually, and eternally—are subjects of prayer.

PRAYERS FOR EVERYONE

Before we consider this phase of prayer, however, let us look again at the universal prayer for everyone. As a special class to be prayed for, there are those who control the government or who rule the Church. Prayer has mighty powers. It makes good rulers, and makes them better rulers. It restrains the lawless and the tyrants. Rulers are to be prayed for. They are not out of the reach and the control of prayer, because they are not out of the reach and control of God. Wicked Nero was on the throne of Rome when Paul wrote these words to Timothy, urging prayer for those in authority.

Christian lips are to breathe prayers for the cruel and infamous rulers as well as for the righteous and kind. Prayer is to be as far-reaching as the human race extends. Humanity is to burden our hearts as we pray, and our thoughts are to be concerned with everyone when we approach the throne of grace. In our praying hours, everyone must have a place. The needs and distresses of the entire race are to broaden and make tender our sympathies and inflame our petitions. No small-minded person can pray. No person with narrow views of God, of His plan to save people, and of the universal needs of all people can pray effectually. It takes a broad-minded person who understands God and His purposes in the atonement to pray well. No cynic can pray. Prayer is the godliest philanthropy, as well as giant-great-heartedness. Prayer comes from a big heart filled with thoughts about all people, and with sympathies for everyone.

PRAYER AND GOD'S WILL

Prayer runs parallel with the will of God, "who will have all men to be saved, and to come unto the knowledge of the truth."[7] It reaches up to heaven and brings heaven down to earth. Prayer has in its hands a double blessing. It rewards those who pray, and blesses those who are prayed for. It brings peace to warring passions and calms warring elements. Tranquility is the happy fruit of true praying. There is an inner calm that comes to person who prays—and an outer calm as well. Prayer creates "a quiet and peaceable life in all godliness and honesty."[8]

Right praying not only makes life beautiful in peace, but fragrant in righteousness and powerful in influence. Honesty, gravity, integrity, and strength in character are the natural and essential fruits of prayer.

It is this kind of world-wide, large-hearted, unselfish praying that pleases God well, and that is acceptable in His sight, because it cooperates with His will and runs in gracious streams to all people and to each person. It is this kind of praying that Christ Jesus did when on earth, and the same kind that He is now doing at His Father's right hand in heaven as our mighty intercessor. He is the pattern of prayer. He is between God and humanity—the one mediator, who gave Himself a ransom for everyone and for each one.

So it is that true prayer links itself to the will of God, and runs in streams of concern, compassion, and intercession for humanity. As Jesus Christ died for everyone involved in the fall, so prayer girdles everyone and gives itself for the benefit of everyone. Like our one mediator between God and humanity, the person who prays stands midway between God and people with "prayers and supplications with strong crying and tears."[9]

Prayer holds in its grasp the movements of the race of human beings, and embraces the destinies of people for all eternity. The king and the beggar are both affected by it. It touches heaven and moves earth.

Your guides and brethren bear
Forever on your mind;
Extend the arms of mighty prayer
In grasping all mankind.

Endnotes

1 Romans 10:12-13
2 Isaiah 55:6-7
3 1 Timothy 2:8
4 1 Timothy 2:1
5 1 Timothy 2:6
6 Romans 5:1, 10:9-10; Ephesians 2:8
7 1 Timothy 2:4
8 1 Timothy 2:2
9 Hebrews 5:7

13

Prayers and Missions

ONE DAY, ABOUT THIS TIME, *I heard an unusual bleating amongst my few remaining goats, as if they were being killed or tortured. I rushed to the goat-house and found myself instantly surrounded by a band of armed men. The snare had caught me, their weapons were raised, and I expected the next moment to die. But God moved me to talk to them firmly and kindly; I warned them of their sin and its punishment; I showed them that only my love and pity led me to remain there seeking their good, and that if they killed me they killed their best friend. I further assured them I was not afraid to die, for at death my Savior would take me to heaven and that I would be far happier than on earth; and that my only desire to live was to make them happy by teaching them to love Jesus Christ my Lord. I then lifted up my hands and eyes to the heavens and prayed aloud for Jesus to bless all my Tannese and to protect me or take me to heaven as He saw to be for the best. One after another they slipped away from me and Jesus restrained them again. Did ever a mother run more quickly to protect her crying child in danger's hour than the Lord Jesus hastens to answer believing prayer and send help to His servants in His own good time and way, so far as it shall be for their good and His glory.* (John G. Paton)

Missions mean the giving of the Gospel to those of Adam's fallen race who have never heard of Christ and His atoning death. It means giving to others the opportunity to hear of salvation through our Lord Jesus Christ, and allowing others to have a chance to receive and accept the blessings of the Gospel, as we have it in Christianized lands. It means that those who enjoy the benefits of the Gospel give these same religious advantages and Gospel privileges to all of humankind. Prayer is the servant of missions.

The success of all real missionary effort is dependent on prayer. The life and spirit of missions are the life and spirit of prayer. Both prayer and missions were born in the divine mind, they are close companions. Prayer creates and makes missions successful, while missions lean heavily on prayer. In Psalm 72, which deals with the Messiah, it is stated that "prayer also shall be made for him continually."[1] Prayer would be made for His coming to save humanity, and prayer would be made for the success of the plan of salvation that He would come to set in action.

THE SPIRIT OF JESUS CHRIST IS THE SPIRIT OF MISSIONS

Our Lord Jesus Christ was Himself the first missionary. His promise and advent composed the first missionary movement. The missionary spirit is not simply a phase of the Gospel, not a mere feature of the plan of salvation, but is its very spirit and life. The missionary movement is the Church of Jesus Christ marching in militant array, with the design of possessing the whole world of humankind for Christ. Whoever is touched by the Spirit of God is fired by the missionary spirit. An anti-missionary Christian is a contradiction in terms. We might say that it would be impossible to be an anti-missionary Christian because of the impossibility for the divine and human forces to put people in such a state as not to align them with the missionary cause. Missionary impulse is the heartbeat of our Lord Jesus Christ, sending the vital forces of Himself through the whole body of the Church. The spiritual life of God's people rises or falls with the force of those heartbeats. When these life forces stop, then death starts. Anti-missionary Churches are dead Churches, just as anti-missionary Christians are dead Christians.

If Satan cannot prevent a great movement of God, his craftiest device is to corrupt the movement. If he can put the movement first and the spirit of the movement in the background, he has thoroughly corrupted the movement. Only mighty prayer will save the movement from materialism and keep its spirit strong.

THE KEY OF ALL MISSIONARY SUCCESS IS PRAYER

The key of prayer is in the hands of the home churches. The trophies won by our Lord in heathen lands will be won by praying missionaries, not by professional workers in foreign lands. Success will be won by saintly praying in the churches at home. The home church on her knees fasting and praying is the great base of spiritual supplies, the power of war, and the pledge of victory, in this terrible and final conflict. Financial resources are not the real power of war in this fight. Machinery in itself carries no power to break down heathen walls, open effective doors, and win heathen hearts to Christ. Prayer alone can do the deed.

A praying church through Jesus Christ will give victory on every battlefield in heathen lands just as surely as Aaron and Hur gave victory to Israel through Moses.[2] It is as true in foreign fields as it is in home lands. The praying Church wins the contest. The home church has done only a trivial thing when it has furnished the money to establish missions and support its missionaries. Money is important, but money without prayer is powerless in the face of the darkness, wretchedness, and sin in Christless lands. Prayerless giving breeds barrenness and death. Poor praying at home is the reason for poor results in the foreign field. Prayerless giving is the secret of all crises in the missionary movements of the day, and is the reason for the missionary boards' accumulation of debt.

It is all right to urge Christians to give of their means to the missionary cause. But it is much more important to urge them to give their prayers to the movement. Foreign missions today need the power of prayer more than the power of money. Prayer can make even the poorest of missionary causes succeed, but much money without prayer is powerless on the foreign field.

The missionary age

Protestant Christianity is stirred as it never was before in the line of aggression in pagan lands. The missionary movement has grown so large that it awakens hope, kindles enthusiasm, and demands the attention, if not the interest, of even the coldest and the most lifeless churches. Nearly every church has caught the fever, and the sails of their proposed missionary movements are spread wide to catch the favoring breezes. The danger now, however, is that the missionary movement will go ahead of the missionary spirit. This has always been the peril of the Church—losing the substance in the shade, losing the spirit in the outward shell, priding itself in the mere parade of the movement, and putting the force of effort in the movement and not in the spirit. The magnificence of this movement may not only blind us to the spirit of it, but the spirit that should give life and shape to the movement may be lost in the wealth of the movement, like a sailing vessel once moved rapidly by favoring winds, but now lost from sight as those same winds swell to a storm.

Many of us have heard numerous eloquent and earnest speeches stressing the imperative need of money for missions but few stress the imperative need of prayer. All of our plans and devices are geared to the one goal of raising money, but not to quickening faith and promoting prayer. The common idea among church leaders is that if we get the money, prayer will come as a matter of course, but the very reverse is the truth. If we get the Church to pray, thus securing the spirit of missions, money will come as a matter of course.

Spiritual agencies and spiritual forces, however, never come as a matter of course. If left to the "matter of course" law, spiritual duties, and spiritual factors will surely fall out and die. Only the things that are stressed live and rule in the spiritual realm. Those who give will not necessarily pray. Many in our churches are liberal givers, but are noted for their prayerlessness. One of the evils of the today's missionary movement lies there. Giving is entirely removed from prayer.

PRAYER AND GIVING

Those who truly pray will be moved to give. Praying creates the giving spirit. The praying ones will give liberally and unselfishly. Those who open their closet to God will also open their purse to God. But indifferent, grudging, evaluation-giving kills the very spirit of prayer. There is a relentless law by which emphasizing the material to the neglect of the spiritual retires and discounts the spiritual.

It is truly astonishing how great a part money plays in the modern religious movements, and how little prayer plays in them. In striking contrast with that statement, it is marvelous how little a part money played in primitive Christianity as a factor in spreading the Gospel, and how wonderful a part prayer played in it.

The grace of giving is nowhere cultured to a richer growth than in the closet. If all our missionary boards and trustees were turned into praying bands until the agony of real prayer and travail with Christ for a perishing world came on them, real estate, stocks, and government bonds would be in the market for the spreading of Christ's Gospel among humanity. If the spirit of prayer prevailed, missionary boards whose individual members are worth millions would not be staggering under a load of debt. Neither would great churches have a yearly deficit and a yearly grumbling, grudging, and pressure to pay a beggarly assessment to support a mere handful of missionaries, with the additional humiliation of debating the question of recalling some of them. The ongoing of Christ's kingdom is locked up in the closet of prayer by Christ Himself, and not in the contribution box.

CHRIST'S KINGDOM

Looking down the centuries with the vision of a seer, the prophet Isaiah expresses his purpose to continue in prayer and give God no rest till Christ's kingdom be established among humanity.

For Zion's sake will I not hold my peace, and for Jerusalem's sake I will not rest, until the righteousness thereof go forth as brightness, and the salvation thereof as a lamp that burneth.[3]

Then foretelling the final success of the Christian Church, he says:

And the Gentiles shall see Thy righteousness, and all kings Thy glory: and thou shalt be called by a new name, which the mouth of the LORD shall name.[4]

Then the LORD Himself, by the mouth of this evangelical prophet, declares as follows:

I have set watchmen upon thy walls, O Jerusalem, which shall never hold their peace day nor night: ye that make mention of the Lord, keep not silence, And give Him no rest, till He establish, and till He make Jerusalem a praise in the earth.[5]

In the margin of some Bibles it reads, "Ye that are the Lord's remembrancers." The idea is that these praying ones are those who remind Him of what He has promised, and who give Him no rest till Christ's kingdom is established in the earth.

One of the leading petitions in the Lord's Prayer deals with the same question of establishing God's kingdom and the progress of the Gospel when it states "Thy kingdom come," and then adds the words, "Thy will be done in earth, as it is in heaven."

BIRTH OF THE MISSIONARY MOVEMENT

The missionary movement in the apostolic Church was born in an atmosphere of fasting and prayer. That same movement was on the housetop where Peter went to pray and God showed him His divine purpose to extend the privileges of the Gospel to all people, and to break down the partition between Jew and Gentile.

But more specifically, Paul and Barnabas were called to the missionary field at Antioch when the church there had fasted and prayed. It was then the Holy Spirit answered from heaven and said, "Separate me Barnabas and Saul for the work whereunto I have called them."[6]

Please note this was not the call to the ministry of Paul and Barnabas, but more particularly their definite call to the foreign field. Paul had been called to the ministry years before this at the time of his conversion. This was a subsequent call to a work born of special and continued prayer in the church at Antioch. God calls people not only to the ministry, but to be missionaries. Missionary work is God's work. It is the God-called Christians who are to do it. These are the kind of missionaries who have worked well and successfully in the past, and who will do the work in the future—or it will not be done.

PRAYING MISSIONARIES AND A PRAYING CHURCH

It is praying missionaries who are needed for the work, and it is a praying church who sends them out. Their prayers are prophecies of the success that is promised in the Scriptures. The sort of religion to be exported by missionaries is the praying sort. The religion to which the heathen world is to be converted to is a religion of prayer, and a religion of prayer to the true God. The heathen world already prays to its idols and false gods. But they are to be taught by praying missionaries, sent out by a praying Church, to cast away their idols and to begin calling upon the name of the Lord Jesus Christ.

A prayerless church cannot send a praying religion to heathen lands. just as prayerless missionaries cannot bring heathen idolaters who do not know our God, to their knees in true prayer, until the missionaries become preeminently people of prayer. It takes praying people at home to do God's work, and it take praying missionaries to bring those who sit in darkness to the light.

The most noted and most successful missionaries have been men and women of prayer. David Livingstone, William Taylor, Adoniram Judson, Henry Martyn, Amy Carmichael, Hudson Taylor, and many more form a band of illustrious praying men and women whose image and influence still live where they labored. No prayerless Christian is wanted for this job. Above everything else, the primary qualification for every missionary is prayer. Let that one be, above everything else, a person of prayer. When the crowning day comes and the records are made up and read at the great judgment day, then it will appear how well praying men and women worked in the hard fields of the heathen, and how much was due to them in laying the foundations of Christianity in those fields.

THE POWER OF PRAYER

The one only thing that gives worldwide power to this Gospel is prayer, and the spread of this Gospel depends on prayer. The energy that is to give it marvelous momentum and conquering power over all its malignant and powerful foes is the energy of prayer.

The fortunes of the kingdom of Jesus Christ are not made by the feebleness of its enemies. They are strong and bitter and have always been strong and always will be. But mighty prayer is the one great spiritual force that will enable the Lord Jesus Christ to enter into full possession of His kingdom. It will secure for Him the heathen as His inheritance, and the uttermost part of the earth for His possession.

It is prayer that will enable Christ to break His enemies with a rod of iron, that will make these enemies tremble in their pride and power. They are but frail potter's vessels to be broken in pieces by one stroke of His hand. A person who can pray is the mightiest instrument Christ has in this world. A praying Church is stronger than all the gates of hades.

God's decree for the glory of His Son's kingdom is dependent on prayer for its fulfillment: "Ask of me, and I shall give thee the heathen for thine inheritance, and the uttermost parts of the earth for thy possession."[7] God the Father gives to His Son only through prayer. The reason why the Church has not received more in the missionary work in which it is engaged is the lack of prayer. "Ye have not, because ye ask not."[8]

Every dispensation that foreshadows the coming of Christ when the world has been evangelized, rests upon these constitutional provisions— God's decree, His promises, and prayer. However far away that day of victory is by distance or time, or however vague the shadowy type, prayer is the essential condition on which the dispensation becomes strong, typical, and representative. From Abraham, the first of the nation of the Israelites and the friend of God, down to the dispensation of the Holy Spirit, this has been true.

> The nations call! From sea to sea
> Extends the thrilling cry,
> "Come over, Christians, if there be,
> And help us, ere we die."
>
> Our hearts, O Lord, the summons feel;
> Let hand with heart combine,
> And answer to the world's appeal,
> By giving 'that is thine.

THE LORD'S PLAN FOR SECURING WORKERS

Our Lord's plan for securing workers in the foreign missionary field is the same plan He set into action for obtaining preachers. It is by praying. It is the prayer plan as distinguished from all human-made plans. These mission workers are to be "sent people." God must send them. They are God-called and divinely moved to this great work. They are inwardly moved to enter the harvest fields of the world and gather sheaves for the heavenly granaries. People do not choose to be missionaries any more than they choose to be preachers. God sends out laborers in His harvest field in answer to the prayers of His Church. Here is the divine plan as set forth by our Lord:

> But when He saw the multitudes, He was moved with compassion on them, because they fainted, and were scattered abroad, as sheep having no shepherd. Then saith He unto His disciples, The harvest truly is plenteous, but the laborers are few; Pray ye therefore the Lord of the harvest, that He will send forth laborers into His harvest.[9]

It is the business of the home church to do the praying. It is the Lord's business to call and send forth the laborers. The Lord does not do the praying. The Church does not do the calling. Our Lord's compassions were aroused by the sight of weary, hungry, and scattered multitudes that were exposed to evils, like sheep having no shepherd. In the same way, when the

Church has eyes to truly see the vast multitudes of earth's inhabitants—descendants of Adam, weary in soul, living in darkness, and wretched and sinful—it will it be moved to compassion and begin to pray to the Lord of the harvest to send forth laborers into His harvest.

MISSIONARIES AND MINISTERS BORN OF PRAYING PEOPLE

A praying church creates laborers in the harvest field of the world. The scarcity of missionaries indicates a non-praying church. It is all right to send trained people to the foreign field, but first of all they must be God-sent. The sending is the fruit of prayer. Since praying people caused them to be sent, the workers in turn must be praying people. The prime mission of these praying missionaries is to convert prayerless unbelievers into praying people. Prayer is the proof of their calling, their divine credentials, and their work.

Those who are not praying people at home need the one thing that makes them fit to become a mission worker abroad. Those who have not the spirit that moves them toward sinners at home, will hardly have a spirit of compassion for sinners abroad. Missionaries are not made of people who are failures at home. Those who would be a person of prayer abroad must, before anything else, be a person of prayer in their home church. If they are not engaged in turning sinners away from prayerless ways at home, they will hardly succeed in turning away unbelievers in foreign lands from their prayerless ways. In other words, it takes the same spiritual qualifications for being a home worker as it does for being a foreign worker.

God in His own way, in answer to the prayers of His Church, calls people into His harvest fields. Sad will be the day when missionary boards and churches overlook that fundamental fact and send out their own chosen men and women independent of God.

Is the harvest great? Are the laborers few? Then "pray ye therefore the Lord of the harvest, that He will send forth laborers into His harvest." Oh, that a great wave of prayer would sweep over the Church asking God to send out a great army of laborers into the needy harvest fields of the earth! No danger of the Lord of the harvest sending out too many laborers and crowding the fields. He who calls will most certainly provide the means for supporting those whom He calls and sends forth.

THE MISSIONARY MOVEMENT'S GREAT NEED

The one great need in the modern missionary movement is intercessors. They were scarce in the days of Isaiah. This was God's statement of wonder at the lack: "And He saw that there was no man, and wondered that there was no intercessor."[10]

Even so today there is a great need of intercessors. First, intercessors for the needy harvest fields of earth, born of a godly compassion for the thousands without the Gospel. Second, intercessors for laborers to be sent forth by God into the needy fields of earth.

Endnotes

1 Psalm 72:15
2 Exodus 17:12
3 Isaiah 62:1
4 Isaiah 62:2
5 Isaiah 62:6-7
6 Acts 13:2
7 Psalm 2:8
8 James 4:2b
9 Matthew 9:36-38
10 Isaiah 59:16

Book 3

The Possibilities of Prayer

I

The Ministry of Prayer

"PRAYER SHOULD BE THE *breath of our breathing, the thought of our thinking, the soul of our feeling, and the life of our living, the sound of our hearing, the growth of our growing." Prayer in its magnitude is length without end, width without bounds, height without top, and depth without bottom. Illimitable in its breadth, exhaustless in height, fathomless in depths and infinite in extension.* (Homer W. Hodge)

The ministry of prayer has been the peculiar distinction of all of God's saints. This has been the secret of their power. The energy and the soul of their work has been the closet. Our need of help is so great—our natural inability to always judge kindly, justly, and truly, and to live the Golden Rule—that prayer is commanded by Christ to enable us to act in all these things according to God's will. By prayer, the ability is obtained to feel the law of love, speak according to the law of love, and do everything in harmony with the law of love.

God can help us. God is our Father. We need God's good things to help us to "do justly, to love mercy, and to walk humbly before God."[1] We need God's aid to act neighborly, wisely, and nobly, and to judge truly and charitably. God's help to do all these things in God's way is obtained by prayer. "Ask, and it shall be given you; seek, and ye shall find; knock, and it shall be opened unto you."[2]

CONTINUING IN PRAYER

In the marvelous output of Christian graces and duties that are the result of giving ourselves wholly to God, it is recorded in Romans, "continuing instant in prayer," preceded by "rejoicing in hope, patient in tribulation," followed by, "distributing to the necessity of the saints, given to hospitality."[3] Paul thus writes as if these rich and rare graces and unselfish duties—so sweet, bright, generous, and unselfish—had for their center and source the ability to pray.

This is the same word that is used of the prayer of the disciples that ushered in Pentecost with all of its rich and glorious blessings of the Holy Spirit. In Colossians, Paul presses the word into the service of prayer again, "Continue in prayer, and watch in the same with thanksgiving." In its background and root, the word *continue* means strong, the ability to stay and persevere steadfast, to hold fast and firm, to give constant attention to.

In Acts it is translated, "Give ourselves continually to prayer."[4] There is in it constancy, courage, untiring perseverance. It means giving the kind of close attention and deep concern to a thing that will make it conspicuous and controlling.

This is an advance in demand on "continue." Prayer is to be incessant, without intermission, and steadfast. There is to be no check in desire, in spirit, or in action. The spirit and the life are to be always in the attitude of prayer. The knees may not always be bent, the lips may not always be vocal with words of prayer, but the spirit is always in the act and communication of prayer.

THE CLOSET SPIRIT

There should be no change of life or spirit for closet hours. The closet spirit should sweetly rule and adjust all times and occasions. Our activities and work should be performed in the same spirit that makes our devotion and closet time sacred. "Without intermission, incessantly, steadfast," describes a richness and energy—unabated and ceaseless strength and fullness of effort. It is like the full and exhaustless and spontaneous flow of an artesian stream. Touch the children of God who so understand prayer, at any point and any time, and a full current of prayer is seen flowing from them.

But all these untold benefits, of which the Holy Spirit is made to us the conveyor, go back in their disposition and results to prayer. The coming of the Holy Spirit and His great grace is not conditioned on a little process and a mere performance of prayer. It results from prayer set on fire, unquenchable desire, a sense of need that cannot be denied, and a fixed determination that will never let go or faint until it wins the greatest good and gets the best and last blessing God has in store for us.

Christ Jesus, our great high priest—forever blessed and adored be His name—was a gracious comforter, a faithful guide, a gifted teacher, a fearless advocate, a devoted friend, and an all-powerful intercessor. The other "Comforter,"[5] the Holy Spirit, comes into all these blessed relations

of fellowship, authority, and aid, with all the tenderness, sweetness, fullness, and efficiency of Jesus.

JESUS, A HIGH PRIEST OF PRAYER

Was Jesus a high priest of prayer? Did He offer prayers and supplications, with strong crying and tears, unto God?[6] Did He seek the silence, solitude, and darkness so that He might pray unheard and unseen except by heaven in His supplications for humanity with God?[7] In His position as our high priest at the right hand of God, does He not ever live to make intercession for us?[8]

Then how truly does the other Comforter, the Holy Spirit, represent Jesus Christ as our intercessor![9] This Comforter does not plant Himself in the waste of the mountain or far away in the night, but in the chill and the night of the human heart to rouse it to the struggle, and to teach it the need and form of prayer. The divine Comforter, the Spirit of truth, puts into the human heart the burden of earth's mighty needs, and makes the human lips give voice to its mute and unutterable groanings!

What a mighty person of prayer is the Holy Spirit! How He quenches every flame in the heart but the flame of heavenly desire! How He quiets, like a weaned child, all our self-will—until in will, brain, heart, and by mouth, we pray only as He prays. "The Spirit . . . maketh intercession for the saints according to the will of God."[10]

Endnotes

1 Micah 6:8
2 Matthew 7:7
3 Romans 12:12-13
4 Acts 6:4
5 John 14:16
6 Hebrews 5:7
7 Luke 6:12
8 Romans 8:34
9 Romans 8:26
10 Romans 8:27

2

Prayer and the Promises

YOU NEED NOT UTTERLY *despair even of those who for the present "turn again and rend you."*[1] *For if all your arguments and persuasives fail, there is yet another remedy left, and one that is frequently found effectual, when no other method avails. This is prayer. Therefore, whatsoever you desire or want, either for others or for your own soul, "Ask, and it shall be given you."*[2] (John Wesley)

Without the promise, prayer is eccentric and baseless. Without prayer, the promise is dim, voiceless, shadowy, and impersonal. The promise makes prayer dauntless and irresistible. The apostle Peter said that God has given to us "exceeding great and precious promises."[3] "Precious" and "exceeding great" promises they are, and for this very cause we are to "add to our faith,"[4] and supply virtue. It is the addition that makes the promises current and beneficial to us. It is prayer that makes the promises mighty, precious, and practical. The apostle Paul did not hesitate to declare that God's grace so richly promised was made operative and efficient by prayer. "Ye also helping together by prayer for us."[5]

THE PROMISES OF GOD

The promises of God are "exceeding great and precious." These are words that clearly indicate the promises are of great value and broad reach, and as grounds upon which to base our expectations in praying. However exceeding great and precious they are, their realization, and the possibility and condition of that realization, are based on prayer. How glorious are these promises to the believing saints and to the whole Church! How the brightness and bloom, the fruitage and cloudless midday glory of the future, beam on us through the promises of God! Yet these promises never brought hope to bloom or fruit to a prayerless heart. Neither could these promises, were they a thousand times increased in number and preciousness, bring millennium glory to a prayerless Church. Prayer makes the promise rich, fruitful, and a conscious reality.

Prayer as a spiritual energy, and demonstrated in its enlarged and mighty working, makes way for and brings into practical realization the promises of God.

God's promises cover all things that pertain to life and godliness,[6] which relate to body and soul and have to do with time and eternity. These promises bless the present and stretch out in their benefits to the unlimited and eternal future. Prayer holds these promises in keeping and in fruition. Promises are God's golden fruit that is plucked by the hand of prayer. Promises are God's incorruptible seed that is sown and tilled by prayer.

Prayer and the promises are interdependent. The promise inspires and energizes prayer, but prayer focuses the promise, and gives it realization and location. The promise is like the blessed rain falling in full showers. Prayer is like the pipes that transmit, preserve, and direct the rain. It directs the until they become local and personal—and bless, refresh, and fertilize. Prayer takes hold of the promise and conducts it to its marvelous ends, removes the obstacles, and makes a highway for the promise to its glorious fulfillment.

While God's promises are "exceeding great and precious," they are specific, clear, and personal. How pointed and plain God's promise to Abraham:

> And the angel of the Lord called unto Abraham out of heaven the second time, And said, By myself have I sworn, saith the Lord, for because thou hast done this thing, and hast not withheld thy son, thine only son: That in blessing I will bless thee, and in multiplying I will multiply thy seed as the stars of the heaven, and as the sand which is upon the sea shore; and thy seed shall possess the gate of his enemies; And in thy seed shall all the nations of the earth be blessed; because thou hast obeyed my voice.[7]

ISAAC'S PRAYING

But Rebekah, through whom the promise is to flow, is childless. Her barren womb forms an obstacle to the fulfillment of God's promise. But in the course of time children are born to her. Isaac becomes a man of prayer through whom the promise is to be realized, and so we read, "And Isaac intreated the Lord for his wife, because she was barren: and the Lord was intreated of him, and Rebekah his wife conceived."[8] Isaac's praying opened the way for the fulfillment of God's promise, and carried it on to its marvelous fulfillment, and made the promise effectual in bringing forth marvelous results.

JACOB'S PRAYING

God spoke to Jacob and made definite promises to him: "Return unto the land of thy fathers, and to thy kindred; and I will be with thee."[9] Jacob promptly moves out on the promise, but Esau confronts him with his awakened vengeance and his murderous intention, more dreadful because of the long years it spent festering. Jacob throws himself directly on God's promise by a night of prayer. First, he prays quietly and calmly, then when the stillness, loneliness, and darkness of the night are upon him, he makes the all-night wrestling prayer.

> With thee I mean all night to stay,
> And wrestle till the break of day.

God's person is involved, His promise is at stake, and much is involved in the issue. Esau's temper, conduct, and character are also involved. It is a notable occasion. Much depends upon it. Jacob pursues his case and presses his plea with great struggles and hard wrestling. It is the highest form of importunity. But the victory is gained at last. His name and nature are changed and he becomes a new and different man. Jacob himself is saved first of all. He is blessed in his life and soul. But more still is accomplished. Esau undergoes a radical change of mind. He who came forth with hate and revenge in his heart against his own brother, seeking Jacob's destruction, is strangely and wonderfully affected. He is changed and his whole attitude toward his brother becomes radically different. When the two brothers meet, love takes the place of fear and hate, and they vie with each other in showing true brotherly affection.

The promise of God is fulfilled. But it took that all night of importunate praying to do the deed. It took that fearful night of wrestling on Jacob's part to make the promise sure and cause it to bear fruit. Prayer brought about the marvelous deed. Prayer of the same kind will produce like results in this day. It was God's promise and Jacob's praying that crowned and crowded the results so wondrously.

ELIJAH'S PRAYERS

"Go, show thyself to Ahab; and I will send rain on the earth,"[10] was God's command and promise to His servant Elijah after the terrible famine had cursed the land. Many glorious results marked that day of heroic faith and dauntless courage on Elijah's part. The sublime issue with Israel had been successful, the fire had fallen, Israel had been reclaimed, the prophets of Baal had been killed, but there was no rain. The one thing, the only thing, that God had promised had not been given. The day was declining, and the awestruck crowds were faint and yet held by an invisible hand.

Elijah turns from Israel to God and from Baal to the one source of help for a final issue and a final victory. But seven times is the restless eagerness of the prophet stayed. Not till the seventh repeated time is his vigilance rewarded and the promise pressed to its final fulfillment. Elijah's fiery, relentless, praying bore to its triumphant results the promise of God, and rain descended in full showers.[11]

> Thy promise, Lord, is ever sure,
> And they that in Thy house would dwell
> That happy station to secure,
> Must still in holiness excel.

FEEBLE, LITTLE PRAYERS

Our prayers are too little and feeble to execute the purposes or to claim the promises of God with appropriating power. Marvelous purposes need marvelous praying to execute them. Miracle-making promises need miracle-making praying to obtain them. Only divine praying can operate divine promises or carry out divine purposes. How great, how sublime, and how exalted are the promises God makes to His people! How eternal are the purposes of God! Why are we so impoverished in experience and so low in life when God's promises are so "exceeding great and precious"? Why do the eternal purposes of God move so slowly? Why are they so poorly executed? Our failure to appropriate the divine promises and rest our faith on them and pray believingly is the solution. "We have not, because we ask not. . . We ask, and receive not, because we ask amiss."[12]

PRAYERS BASED ON GOD'S PURPOSE AND PROMISE

Prayer is based on the purpose and promise of God. Prayer is submission to God. Prayer has no sigh of disloyalty against God's will. It may cry out against the bitterness and the dread weight of an hour of unutterable anguish: "O My Father, If it be possible, let this cup pass from me." But it is surcharged with the sweetest and promptest submission: "nevertheless not as I will, but as Thou wilt."[13]

Prayer in its usual uniform and deep current is conscious conformity to God's will, based upon the direct promise of God's Word, and under the illumination and application of the Holy Spirit. Nothing is surer than that the Word of God is the sure foundation of prayer. We pray just as we believe God's Word. Prayer is based directly and specifically upon God's revealed promises in Christ Jesus. It has no other ground upon which to base its plea. All else is shadowy, sandy, and fickle. Not our feelings, not our merits, not our works, but God's promise is the basis of faith and the solid ground of prayer.

> Now I have found the ground wherein
> Sure my soul's anchor may remain;
> The wounds of Jesus—for my sin,
> Before the world's foundation slain.

God's promises are dependent and conditioned upon prayer to appropriate them and make them a conscious realization. The promises are inwrought in us, appropriated by us, and held in the arms of faith by prayer. Let it be noted that prayer gives the promises their efficiency, directs and appropriates them, and utilizes them. Prayer puts the promises to practical and present uses. Prayer puts the promises as the seed in the fruit-producing soil. Promises are general like the rain. Prayer embodies, precipitates, and directs them for personal use. Prayer goes by faith into the great fruit orchard of God's exceedingly great and precious promises, and with hand and heart picks the ripest and richest fruit. Like electricity, the promises may sparkle and dazzle and yet be impotent for good until these dynamic, life-giving, currents are chained by prayer, and are made the mighty forces that move and bless.

Endnotes

1 Matthew 7:6
2 Matthew 7:7
3 2 Peter 1:4
4 2 Peter 1:5
5 2 Corinthians 1:11
6 2 Peter 1:3
7 Genesis 22:15-18
8 Genesis 25:21
9 Genesis 31:3
10 1 Kings 18:1
11 1 Kings 18:41-45
12 James 4:2-3, paraphrase
13 Matthew 26:39

3

Prayer and the Promises (Continued)

EVERY PROMISE OF SCRIPTURE *is a writing of God, which may be pleaded before Him with this reasonable request: "Do as Thou hast said." The Creator will not cheat His creature who depends upon His truth; and, far more, the Heavenly Father will not break His word to His own child. "Remember the word unto Thy servant, on which Thou hast caused me to hope," is most prevalent pleading. It is a double argument: It is Thy Word, wilt Thou not keep it? Why hast Thou spoken of it if Thou wilt not make it good? Thou hast caused me to hope in it; wilt Thou disappoint the hope which Thou hast Thyself begotten in me?* (C. H. Spurgeon)

The great promises find their fulfillment along the lines of prayer. They inspire prayer, and through prayer the promises flow out to their full realization and bear their ripest fruit.

The magnificent and sanctifying promise in Ezekiel that finds its full, ripe, and richest fruit in the New Testament, is an illustration of how the promise waits on prayer:

> Then will I sprinkle clean water upon you, and ye shall be clean: from all your filthiness, and from all your idols, will I cleanse you. A new heart also will I give you, and a new spirit will I put within you: and I will take away the stony heart out of your flesh, and I will give you an heart of flesh. And I will put my spirit within you, and cause you to walk in my statutes, and ye shall keep my judgments, and do them. And ye shall dwell in the land that I gave to your fathers; and ye shall be my people, and I will be your God.[1]

Concerning this promise and work, God definitely says, "I will yet for this be inquired of by the house of Israel, to do it for them."[2]

The more truly people have prayed for these rich things, the more fully they have entered into this exceeding great and precious promise. In the initial and final results, as well as in all the processes, realization of the promise is entirely dependent on prayer.

Give me a new, a perfect heart,
From doubt, and fear, and sorrow free;
The mind which was in Christ impart,
And let my spirit cleave to thee.

O take this heart of stone away!
Thy sway it doth not, cannot own;
In me no longer let it stay;
O take away this heart of stone!

No new heart ever throbbed with the pulsations of divine life in a person who never prayed with a contrite spirit for that precious boon of a perfect heart of love and cleanness. God never has put His Spirit into the realm of a human heart that has never invoked by ardent praying the coming and indwelling of the Holy Spirit. A prayerless spirit has no affinity for a clean heart. Prayer and a pure heart go hand in hand. Purity of heart follows praying, while prayer is the natural, spontaneous, outpouring of a heart made clean by the blood of Jesus Christ.

GOD'S PERSONAL AND SPECIFIC PROMISES

In this connection, let it be noted that God's promises are always personal and specific. They are not general, indefinite, or vague. They do not have to do with multitudes and classes of people in a mass, but are directed to individuals. They deal with persons. Each believer can claim the promise as their own. God deals with each one personally. So that every saint can put the promises to the test. "Prove me now herewith, saith the LORD of hosts."[3] No need of generalizing or of being lost in vagueness. Praying saints have the right to put their hand upon the promise and claim it for their own, one made especially to them, and one intended to embrace all their present and future needs.

Though troubles assail,
And dangers affright,
Though friends should all fail,
And foes all unite,
Yet one thing secures us,
Whatever betide,

The promise assures us,
The Lord will provide.

Almighty God once said through the prophet about the captivity of Israel and of its ending, "after seventy years be accomplished at Babylon, I will visit you, and perform my good word toward you, in causing you to return to this place."[4]

But this strong and definite promise of God was accompanied by these words, coupling the promise with prayer: "Then shall ye call upon me, and ye shall go and pray unto me, and I will hearken unto you. And ye shall seek me, and find me, when ye shall search for me with all your heart."[5]

PROMISE DEPENDENT ON PRAYER

This seems to indicate very clearly that the promise was dependent for its fulfillment on prayer. In Daniel we have this record: "I, Daniel, understood by books the number of the years, whereof the word of the Lord came to Jeremiah the prophet, that he would accomplish seventy years in the desolations of Jerusalem."[6]

So as the time of the captivity was expiring, Daniel set himself in mighty prayer so that the promise would be fulfilled and the captivity be brought to an end. It was God's promise by Jeremiah and Daniel's praying that broke the chains of Babylonian captivity, set Israel free, and brought God's ancient people back to their native land. The promise and prayer went together to carry out God's purpose and execute His plans.

JOHN THE BAPTIST

God had promised through His prophets that the coming Messiah would have a forerunner. How many homes and wombs in Israel had longed to have this great honor come to them! Perhaps Zacharias[7] and Elizabeth were the only ones who were trying to realize by prayer this great dignity and blessing. At least we do know that as the angel announced to Zacharias the coming of this great person, he said to him, "thy prayer is heard."[8] It was then that the word of the Lord, as spoken by the prophets, and the prayer of the old priest and his wife brought John the Baptist into the withered womb and childless home of Zacharias and Elizabeth.

PAUL BEFORE AGRIPPA

When Paul was making his defense before King Agrippa after his arrest in Jerusalem, he stated about the promise given to him and engraved on his apostolic commission: "I will deliver you from the Jewish people, as well as from the Gentiles, to whom I now send you."[9] How did Paul make this promise effective? How did he make the promise real? Here is the answer. Troubled grievously by Jew and Gentile, he writes to the Christians at Rome with a pressing request for prayer: "Now I beseech you, brethren, for the Lord Jesus Christ's sake, and for the love of the Spirit, that ye strive together with me in your prayers to God for me; That I may be delivered from them that do not believe in Judea; and that my service which I have for Jerusalem may be accepted of the saints."[10]

Their prayers united with his were to secure his deliverance and secure his safety, and were also to make the apostolic promise vital and cause it to be fully realized.

Everything sanctified by the Word and prayer

All is to be sanctified and realized by the Word of God and prayer.[11] God's deep and wide river of promise will turn to vapor or stagnate like the Salt Sea if we do not utilize these promises by prayer, and receive their full and life-giving waters into our hearts.

The promise of the Holy Spirit to the disciples was in a very marked way the "promise of the Father,"[12] but it was only realized after many days of continued and persistent praying. The promise was clear and definite that the disciples would be endued with power from on high, but as a condition of receiving that power of the Holy Spirit, they were instructed to "tarry in the city of Jerusalem, until ye be endued with power from on high."[13] The fulfillment of the promise depended upon the "tarrying." The promise of being "endued with power" was made sure by prayer. Prayer sealed it to glorious results. So we find it written, "These all continued with one accord in prayer and supplication, with the women."[14] It is significant that it was while they were praying, resting their expectations on the certainty of the promise, that the Holy Spirit fell upon them and "they were all filled with the Holy Ghost."[15] The promise and the prayer went hand in hand.

The promise of the Holy Spirit

After Jesus Christ made this large and definite promise to His disciples, He ascended to heaven and was seated at His Father's right hand of exaltation and power. Yet the promise given by Him of sending the Holy Spirit was not fulfilled by His enthronement alone, or the promise alone, or by the fact that the Prophet Joel had foretold with transported raptures of the bright day of the Spirit's coming. It also was not that the Spirit's coming was the only hope of God's cause in this world. All these all-powerful and all-engaging reasons were not the immediate cause that brought forth the coming of the Holy Spirit. The solution is found in the attitude of the disciples. The answer is found in the fact that the disciples spent several days in that upper room in earnest, specific, continued prayer. It was prayer that brought to pass the famous day of Pentecost. And as it was then, so it can be now. Prayer can bring a Pentecost in this day if there is the same kind of praying, for the promise has not exhausted its power and vitality. The "promise of the Father" still holds good for today's disciples.

Mighty united, continued, earnest prayer for nearly two weeks brought the Holy Spirit to the Church and to the world in Pentecostal glory and power. The same kind of prayer will do the same now.

> Lord God, the Holy Ghost,
> In this accepted hour;
> As on the day of Pentecost,
> Descend in all Thy power.

> We meet with one accord,
> In our appointed place,
> And wait the promise of our Lord,
> The Spirit of all grace.

GOD'S PROMISE TO SINNERS

It must not be passed by that the promises of God to sinners, of every kind and degree, are equally sure and steadfast, and are made real and true by the earnest cries of all who truly repent.[16] God's promises to the unsaved when they repent and seek God are realized in answer to the prayers of broken-hearted sinners, just as the promises to believers are realized in answer to their prayers. The promise of pardon and peace was the basis of the prayers of Saul of Tarsus during those days of darkness and distress in the house of Judas, when the Lord told Ananias in order to lessens his fears about Saul the persecutor of the Church, "behold, he prayeth."[17]

In Isaiah, the promise of mercy and an abundant pardon is tied up with seeking God and calling upon Him:

> Seek ye the Lord while he may be found, call ye upon him while he is near: Let the wicked forsake his way, and the unrighteous man his thoughts: and let him return unto the Lord, and he will have mercy upon him; and to our God, for he will abundantly pardon.[18]

Praying sinners receive mercy because their prayer is grounded on the promise of pardon made by Him whose right it is to pardon guilty sinners. The repentant seeker after God obtains mercy because there is a definite promise of mercy to all who seek the Lord in repentance and faith. Prayer always brings forgiveness to the seeking soul. The abundant pardon is dependent upon the promise made real by the promise of God to the sinner.

SALVATION PROMISED TO THE ONE WHO BELIEVES

While salvation is promised to the one who believes, the believing sinner is always a praying sinner. God has no promise of pardon for a prayerless sinner—just as He has no promise for the prayerless professor of religion. "Behold, he prayeth" is not only the unfailing sign of sincerity and the evidence that the sinner is proceeding in the right way to find God, but it is the unfailing prophecy of an abundant pardon. Get sinners to praying according to God's promise, and they are near the kingdom of God. The very best sign of returning prodigals is that they confess their sins and begin to ask for the lowliest place in their father's house.

It is God's promise of mercy and forgiveness that gives poor sinners hope. This encourages them to pray. This moves them in distress to cry out, "Jesus, thou Son of David, have mercy on me."[19]

> Thy promise is my only plea,
> With this I venture nigh;
> Thou call'st the burdened soul to Thee,
> And such, O Lord, am I.

How large are the promises made to the saint! How great the promises given to poor, hungry-hearted, lost sinners, ruined by the fall! Prayer has arms sufficient to encompass them all and prove them. How great an encouragement to all souls are the promises of God! How firm the ground on which to rest our faith! How stimulating to prayer! What firm ground on which to base our pleas in praying!

> The Lord hath promised good to me,
> His word my hope secures;
> He will my shield and portion be
> As long as life endures.

Endnotes

1 Ezekiel 36:25-28
2 Ezekiel 36:37
3 Malachi 3:10
4 Jeremiah 29:10
5 Jeremiah 29:12-13
6 Daniel 9:2-3
7 KJV spelling—name spelled *Zechariah* in other versions.
8 Luke 1:13
9 Acts 26:17, NKJV
10 Romans 15:30-31
11 1 Timothy 4:5
12 Acts 1:4
13 Luke 24:49
14 Acts 1:14
15 Acts 2:4
16 Acts 2:38, 3:19
17 Acts 9:11
18 Isaiah 55:6-7
19 Mark 10:47

4

Possibilities of Prayer

THE HOLY GHOST COMES *down into our hearts sometimes in prayer with a beam from heaven, whereby we see more at once of God and His glory, more astounding thoughts and enlarged apprehensions of God, many beams meeting in one and falling to the center of our hearts. By these coming downs or divine influxes, God slides into our hearts by beams of Himself. We come not to have communion with God by way of many broken thoughts put together, but there is a contraction of many beams from heaven, which is shed into our souls, so that we know more of God and have more communion with Him in a quarter-hour than we could know in a year by the way of wisdom only.* (Thomas Goodwin)

How vast are the possibilities of prayer! How wide is its reach! What great things are accomplished by this divinely appointed means of grace! It lays its hand on Almighty God and moves Him to do what He would not otherwise do if prayer was not offered. It brings things to pass that would never otherwise occur. The story of prayer is the story of great achievements. Prayer is a wonderful power placed by Almighty God in the hands of His saints, which may be used to accomplish great purposes and to achieve unusual results. Prayer reaches to everything, takes in all things great and small that are promised by God to the human race. The only limits to prayer are the promises of God and His ability to fulfill those promises. "Open thy mouth wide, and I will fill it."[I]

PRAYER'S ACHIEVEMENT RECORD

The records of prayer's achievements are encouraging to faith, cheering to the expectations of saints, and an inspiration to all who would pray and test its value. Prayer is no mere untried theory. It is not some strange unique scheme concocted in the brains of people and set on foot by them—an invention that has never been tried nor put to the test. Prayer is a divine arrangement in the moral government of God. It is designed for the benefit of people, and intended as a means for furthering the interests of His cause on earth and carrying out His gracious purposes in redemption and providence. Prayer proves itself. It is capable of proving its power by those who pray. Prayer needs no proof other than its accomplishments. "If any man will do his will, he shall know of the doctrine, whether it be of God." If people want to know the power of prayer, if they want to know what it will do, let them pray. Let them put prayer to the test.

What a breadth is given to prayer! What heights it reaches! It is the breathing of a soul inflamed for God, and inflamed for humanity. It goes as far as the Gospel goes, and is as wide, compassionate, and prayerful as that Gospel is.

How much prayer do all the non-Christian areas of earth demand in order to enlighten them, impress them with the gospel, and move them toward God and His Son Jesus Christ? Had the professed disciples of Christ prayed in the past as they should have done, the centuries would not have found these area still bound in sin and death.

THE UNBELIEF OF CHRISTIANS

Alas! how the unbelief of Christians has limited the power of God to work through prayer! What limitations have disciples of Jesus Christ put upon prayer by their prayerlessness! How the Church and its neglect of prayer has hedged about the Gospel and shut up doors of access!

Prayer possibilities open doors for the entrance of the Gospel: "Withal praying also for us, that God would open unto us a door of utterance."[2] Prayer opened for the apostles doors of utterance, created opportunities, and made openings to preach the Gospel. The appeal by prayer was to God, because God was moved by prayer. God was thereby moved to do His own work in an enlarged way and by new ways. Prayer possibility gives not only great power, and opens doors to the Gospel, but gives facility as well to the Gospel. Prayer makes the Gospel not only move fast, but move with glorious fastness. A Gospel projected by the mighty energies of prayer is neither slow, lazy, nor dull. It moves with God's power, with God's radiance, and with angelic swiftness.

"Brethren, pray for us, that the word of the Lord may have free course, and be glorified,"[3] is the request of the apostle Paul, whose faith reached to the possibilities of prayer for the preached Word. The Gospel moves altogether too slowly, often timidly, and with feeble steps. What will make this Gospel go rapidly like a race runner? What will give this Gospel divine radiance and glory, and cause it to move worthy of God and of Christ? The answer is at hand. Prayer, more prayer, and better prayer will do the deed. This means of grace will give fast going, splendor, and divinity to the Gospel.

THE POSSIBILITIES OF PRAYER

The possibilities of prayer reach to all things. Whatever concerns humanity's highest welfare, and whatever has to do with God's plans and purposes concerning people on earth, is a subject for prayer. "Whatsoever ye shall ask"[4] embraces all that concerns us or the people of the world and God. Whatever is left out of "whatsoever" is left out of prayer. Where will we draw the lines that leave out or that will limit the word "whatsoever"? Define it, and search out and publish the things that the word does not include. If "whatsoever" does not include all things, then add to it the word "anything." "If ye shall ask anything in my name, I will do it."[5]

What riches of grace, what spiritual and temporal blessings, what good for time and eternity would have been ours had we learned the possibilities of prayer and our faith had taken in the wide range of God's promises to answer prayer! What blessings on our times and what furtherance to God's cause if we had learned how to pray with large expectations! Who will rise up in this generation and teach the Church this lesson? It is a child's lesson in simplicity, but who has learned it well enough to put prayer to the test? It is a great lesson in its matchless and universal good. The possibilities of prayer are unspeakable, but who has learned the lesson of prayer that realizes and measures up to these possibilities?

FRIENDSHIP WITH CHRIST

In His discourse in John, our Lord seems to connect friendship for Him with that of prayer, and His choosing of His disciples seemed to have been with a design that through prayer they should bear much fruit.

> Ye are my friends, if ye do whatsoever I command you. . . . Ye have not chosen me, but I have chosen you, and ordained you, that ye should go and bring forth fruit, and that your fruit should remain: that whatsoever ye shall ask of the Father in my name, he may give it you.[6]

Jesus puts fruit-bearing and fruit-remaining—ripe, unwithered, and rich fruit—as a necessary part in prayer coming to its full possibilities so that the Father might give whatsoever is asked. Here we have again the undefined and unlimited word, "whatsoever," as covering the rights and the things for which we are to pray in the possibilities of prayer.

We have still another declaration from Jesus:

And in that day ye shall ask me nothing. Verily, verily, I say unto you, Whatsoever ye shall ask the Father in my name, he will give it you. Hitherto have ye asked nothing in my name: ask, and ye shall receive, that your joy may be full.[7]

Here is a very definite exhortation from our Lord to largeness in praying. Here we are definitely urged by Him to ask for large things, and urged with the dignity and solemnity indicated by the double amen, "verily, verily."[8] Why these marvelous urgencies in this last recorded and vital conversation of our Lord with His disciples? The answer is that our Lord might prepare them for the New Covenant, in which prayer was to have such marvelous results, and in which prayer was to be the chief agency to preserve His Gospel and make it aggressive.

BEARING FRUIT

In our Lord's language to His disciples about choosing them that should bear fruit—that affluent statement of our Lord—He clearly teaches us that this matter of praying and fruit-bearing is not a petty business of our choice, or a secondary matter in relation to other matters. He has chosen us for this very business of praying. He had especially in mind our praying, and He has chosen us of His own divine selection. He expects us, therefore, to do this one thing of praying and to do it intelligently and well. For before that He says that He made us His friends and brought us into bosom confidence with Him, and also into free and full conference with Him. The main object of choosing us as His disciples and of friendship for Him was that we might be better able to bear the fruit of prayer.

Let us not forget that we are noting the possibilities of the true praying ones. "Anything" is the word of area and circumference. How far it reaches we may not know. How wide it spreads, our minds fail to discover. What is there that is not within its reach? Why does Jesus repeat and exhaust these words, all-inclusive and boundless words, if He does not desire to emphasize the unbounded magnificence and unlimited benefit of prayer? Why does He press people to pray if it is not so that our very poverty might be enriched and our limitless inheritance by prayer be secured?

GOD ANSWERS PRAYER

We affirm with absolute certainty that Almighty God answers prayer. The vast possibilities and the urgent necessity of prayer lie in this stupendous fact that God hears and answers prayer— hears and answers all prayer. He hears and answers every prayer where the true conditions of praying are met. Either this is so or it is not. If not, then there is nothing in prayer. Then prayer is but the recitation of words, a mere verbal performance, an empty ceremony. Then prayer is an altogether useless exercise. But if what we have said is true, then there are vast possibilities in prayer. Then it is far reaching in its scope and wide in its range. Then it is true that prayer can lay its hand upon Almighty God and move Him to do great and wonderful things.

The benefits, possibilities, and necessity of prayer are not merely subjective but are peculiarly objective in their character. Prayer aims at a definite object. Prayer has a direct design in view. Prayer always has something specific before the mind's eye. There may be some subjective benefits that come from praying, but this is altogether secondary and incidental. Prayer always drives directly at an object and seeks to secure a desired end. Prayer is asking, seeking, and knocking[9] at a door for something we do not have, that we desire, and that God has promised to us.

Prayer is a direct address to God. "In everything . . . let your requests be made known unto God."[10] Prayer secures blessings, and makes people better because it reaches the ear of God. Prayer is only for the betterment of people when it has affected God and moved Him to do something for them. Prayer affects people by affecting God. Prayer moves people because it moves God to move people. Prayer influences people by influencing God to influence them. Prayer moves the hand that moves the world.

> That power is prayer, which soars on high,
> Through Jesus to the throne;
> And moves the hand which moves the world,
> To bring salvation down.

POSSIBILITIES OF PRAYER RARELY REALIZED

The utmost possibilities of prayer have rarely been realized. The promises of God are so great to those who truly pray. He puts Himself so fully into the hands of the praying ones, that it almost staggers our faith and causes us to hesitate with astonishment. His promise to answer, to do, and to give "all things," "anything," "whatsoever," and "all things whatsoever," are so large, so great, so exceedingly broad, that we stand back in amazement and give ourselves to questioning and doubt. We stagger "at the promise through unbelief."[11] The promises of God to prayer have been reduced by us to match our little faith and have been brought down to the low level of our narrow notions about God's ability, generosity, and resources. Let us always keep in mind and never for one moment allow ourselves to doubt the statement that God means what He says in all of His promises.

GOD'S TRUTHFULNESS AT STAKE

God's promises are His own word. His truthfulness is at stake in them. To question them is to doubt His truthfulness. He cannot afford to prove faithless to His word. "In hope of eternal life, which God, that cannot lie, promised before the world began."[12] His promises are for plain people, and He means to do for all who pray just what He says He will do. "For He is faithful that promised."[13]

Unfortunately, we have failed to lay ourselves out in praying. We have "limited the Holy One of Israel."[14] The ability to pray can be obtained by the grace and power of the Holy Spirit, but it demands so strenuous and high a character that it is a rare thing for a man or woman to be on praying ground and on pleading terms with God. It is as true today as it was in the days of Elijah—"the effectual fervent prayer of a righteous man availeth much."[15] No one knows how much such a prayer avails!

THE POSSIBILITIES OF FAITH

The possibilities of prayer are the possibilities of faith. Prayer and faith are connected twins. One heart animates them both. Faith is always praying. Prayer is always believing. Faith must have a voice by which it can speak. Prayer is the voice of faith. Faith must receive. Prayer is the hand of faith stretched out to receive. Prayer must rise and soar. Faith must give prayer the wings to fly and soar. Prayer must have an audience with God. Faith opens the door, and access and audience are given. Prayer asks. Faith lays its hand on the thing asked for.

God's omnipotent power is the basis of omnipotent faith and omnipotent praying. "All things are possible to him that believeth,"[16] and "all things whatsoever" are given to those who pray. God's decree of Hezekiah's coming death yields readily to Hezekiah's faith and prayer.[17] When God's promise and our praying are united by faith, then "nothing shall be impossible."[18]

Persistent prayer is so all-powerful and irresistible that it obtains promises—or wins where the prospect and the promise seem to be against it. In fact, the New Testament promises include all things in heaven and in earth. By His promises, God puts all things He possesses into our hands. Prayer and faith put us in possession of this boundless inheritance.

FAILURE TO PRAY

Prayer is not an indifferent or a small thing. It is not a sweet little privilege. It is a great privilege, far-reaching in its effects. Failure to pray involves losses far beyond the person who neglects it. Prayer is not a mere episode of the Christian life. Rather the whole life is a preparation for and the result of prayer. In its condition, prayer is the sum of Christianity. Faith is but a channel of prayer. Faith gives it wings and swiftness. Prayer is the lungs through which holiness breathes. Prayer is not only the language of spiritual life, but makes its very essence and forms its real character.

O for a faith that will not shrink
Though pressed by every foe;
That will not tremble on the brink
Of any earthly woe.
Lord, give us such a faith as this,
And then, whate'er may come,
We'll taste e'en here, the hallowed bliss
Of our eternal home.

Endnotes

1 Psalm 81:10
2 Colossians 4:3
3 1 Thessalonians 3:1
4 Matthew 21:22
5 John 14:14
6 John 15:14, 16
7 John 16:23-24
8 The double usage of *verily* or *truly* was reserved for statements of extreme importance or urgency.
9 Matthew 7:7
10 Philippians 4:6
11 Romans 4:20
12 Titus 1:2
13 Hebrews 10:23
14 Psalm 78:41
15 James 5:16
16 Mark 9:23
17 2 Kings 20:1-11
18 Matthew 17:20

5

Prayer Possibilities

T HOSE WHO HAVE THE *spirit of prayer have the highest interest in the court of heaven. And the only way to retain it is to keep it in constant employment. Apostasy begins in the closet. No one ever backslid from the life and power of Christianity who continued constant and fervent in private prayer. The person who prays without ceasing is likely to rejoice evermore.* (Adam Clarke)

After a comprehensive and cursory view of the possibilities of prayer, as mapped out in the previous chapter, it is important to descend to specifics—to Bible facts and principles concerning this great subject. What are the possibilities of prayer as disclosed by divine revelation? The necessity of prayer and its being are coexistent with humanity. Nature, even before a clear and full revelation, cries out in prayer. Humanity is, therefore prayer is. God is, therefore prayer is. Prayer is born of the instincts, needs, cravings, and the very being of every person.

SOLOMON'S PRAYER

The prayer of Solomon at the dedication of the temple is the product of inspired wisdom and piety, and gives a lucid and powerful view of prayer in the wideness of its range, the minuteness of its details, and its abounding possibilities and urgent necessity. How minute and exactly comprehending is this prayer! National and individual blessings are in it, and temporal and spiritual good is embraced by it. National calamities, individual sins, sickness, exile, famine, war, pestilence, mildew, drought, insects, damage to crops, whatever affects agriculture, enemies—whatever sickness, one's own misery, one's own guilt, one's own sin—one and all are in this prayer, and all are for prayer.

For all these evils, prayer is the one universal remedy. Pure praying remedies all ills, cures all diseases, relieves all situations—no matter how desperate, disastrous, fearful, and despairing. Prayer to God, pure praying, relieves dreadful situations because God can relieve when no one else can. Nothing is too hard for God.[1] No cause is hopeless that God undertakes. No case is mortal when Almighty God is the physician.[2] No conditions are despairing that can deter or defy God.

Almighty God heard this prayer of Solomon, and committed Himself to undertake, relieve, and remedy the problem if real praying is done—despite all adverse and relentless conditions. He will always relieve, answer, and bless if people will pray from the heart, and if they will give themselves to real, true praying.

After Solomon had finished his magnificent, unlimited, and all-comprehending prayer, this is what God said to him:

> And the Lord appeared to Solomon by night, and said unto him, I have heard thy prayer, and have chosen this place to myself for an house of sacrifice. If I shut up heaven that there be no rain, or if I command the locusts to devour the land, or if I send pestilence among my people; If my people, which are called by my name, shall humble themselves, and pray, and seek my face, and turn from their wicked ways; then will I hear from heaven, and will forgive their sin, and will heal their land. Now mine eyes shall be open, and mine ears attent[3] unto the prayer that is made in this place. For now have I chosen and sanctified this house, that my name may be there for ever: and mine eyes and mine heart shall be there perpetually.[4]

GOD CAN WITHHOLD NOTHING FROM FAITH AND PRAYER

God put no limit to His ability to save through true praying. No hopeless conditions, accumulation of difficulties, or desperation in distance or circumstance can hinder the success of real prayer. The possibilities of prayer are linked to the infinite righteousness and omnipotent power of God. There is nothing too hard for God to do. God has pledged that if we ask Him we shall receive. God can withhold nothing from faith and prayer.

The thing surpasses all my thought,
But faithful is my Lord;
Through unbelief I stagger not,
For God hath spoke the word.
Faith, mighty faith, the promise sees,
And looks to that alone;

Laughs at impossibilities,
And cries, "It shall be done!"

PRAYER HAS FAR-REACHING POSSIBILITIES

The many statements of God's Word fully set forth the possibilities and far-reaching nature of prayer. How full of sympathy and tenderness! "Call upon me in the day of trouble: I will deliver thee, and thou shalt glorify me."[5] Again, read the cheering words: "He shall call upon me, and I will answer him: I will be with him in trouble; I will deliver him, and honour him."[6]

How diversified the range of trouble! How almost infinite its extent! How universal and dire its conditions! How despairing its waves! Yet the range of prayer is as great as trouble, as universal as sorrow, as infinite as grief. Prayer can relieve all these evils that come to us. There is no tear that prayer cannot wipe away or dry up. There is no depression of spirits that it cannot relieve and elevate. There is no despair that it cannot dispel.

"Call unto me, and I will answer thee, and shew thee great and mighty things, which thou knowest not."[7] How broad these words of the Lord, how great the promise, how cheering to faith! They really challenge the faith of the saint. Prayer always brings God to our relief to bless and to aid, and brings marvelous revelations of His power. What impossibilities are there with God? Name them. The angel said to the virgin Mary, "For with God nothing shall be impossible." And all the possibilities in God are in prayer.

THE PROPHET SAMUEL

The prophet Samuel fully illustrates the possibility and the necessity of prayer. He himself was the beneficiary of the greatness of faith and prayer in a mother who knew what praying meant. His mother Hannah was a childless woman of quality in character and piety. Not having a child was a source of worry, weakness, and grief for her. She went to God for relief, and prayed and poured out her soul before the LORD. She persisted in her praying—in fact, she multiplied her praying to such an extent that to old Eli she seemed to be intoxicated, almost beside herself in the intensity of her supplications.[8] She was specific in her prayers. She wanted a man child, and for a man child she prayed.[9]

God was specific in His answer. A man child God gave her, but a special man, a prophet. He was the creation of prayer, and became himself a man of prayer. He was a mighty intercessor, especially in emergencies in the history of God's people. The epitome of his life and character is found in the statement, "Samuel cried unto the LORD for Israel; and the Lord heard him."[10] The victory was complete, and the Ebenezer was the memorial of the possibilities and necessity of prayer.[11]

At another time, Samuel called unto the Lord, and thunder and rain came out of season in wheat harvest.[12] Here are some statements concerning this mighty intercessor who knew how to pray, and whom God always regarded when he prayed: "He cried unto the Lord all night."[13]

Once when speaking to the Lord's people he said, "Moreover as for me, God forbid that I should sin against the LORD in ceasing to pray for you."[14]

These great occasions show how this great prophet of Israel made prayer a habit, and that this was a notable and conspicuous characteristic of his dispensation. Prayer was no strange exercise to Samuel. He was accustomed to it. He was in the habit of praying, knew the way to God, and received answers from God. Through him and his praying, God's cause was brought out of its low, depressed, condition, and a great national revival began, of which David was one of its fruits.

Samuel was one of the notable men of the old dispensation who stood out prominently as one who had great influence with God in prayer. God could not deny him anything he asked of Him. Samuel's praying always affected God, and moved God to do what would not have otherwise been done had he not prayed. Samuel stands out as a striking illustration of the possibilities of prayer. He shows conclusively the achievements of prayer.

THE CONQUERING FORCE OF PRAYER

Jacob is an illustration of the commanding and conquering forces of prayer. God came to him as an antagonist. He grappled Jacob, and shook him as if he were in the embrace of a deadly foe. Jacob, who underhandedly took away Esau's birthright and blessings, had no eyes to see God. His perverted principles, and his deliberate overreaching and wrong-doing, had blinded his vision.

To reach God, know God, and conquer God was the demand of this critical hour. Jacob was alone, and all night witnessed to the intensity of the struggle, its changing issues, and its veering fortunes, as well as the receding and advancing lines in the conflict. Here was the strength of weakness, the power of self-despair, the energy of perseverance, the elevation of humility, and the victory of surrender. Jacob's salvation issued from the forces that he massed in that all-night conflict.[15]

He prayed and wept and pleaded until the fiery hate of Esau's heart died and it was softened into love. A greater miracle was wrought on Jacob than on Esau. His name, character, and destiny were all changed by that all-night praying. Here is the record of the results of that night's praying struggle: "As a prince hast thou power with God and with men, and hast prevailed."[16] "By his strength he had power with God: Yea, he had power over the angel, and prevailed."[17] What forces lie in persistent prayer! What mighty results are gained by it in one night's struggle in praying! God is affected and changed in attitude, and two men are transformed in character and destiny.

Endnotes

1 Genesis 18:14; Jeremiah 32:27
2 Exodus 15:26b
3 attentive
4 2 Chronicles 7:12-16
5 Psalm 50:15
6 Psalm 91:15
7 Jeremiah 33:3
8 1 Samuel 1:9-18
9 1 Samuel 1:11
10 1 Samuel 7:9
11 1 Samuel 7:12
12 1 Samuel 12:17
13 1 Samuel 15:11b
14 1 Samuel 12:23
15 Genesis 32:24
16 Genesis 32:28
17 Hosea 12:3b-4a

6

Prayer Possibilities (Continued)

SATAN DREADS NOTHING BUT *prayer. The Church that lost its Christ was full of good works. Activities are multiplied that meditation may be ousted, and organizations are increased that prayer may have no chance. Souls may be lost in good works, as surely as in evil ways. The one concern of the devil is to keep the saints from praying. He fears nothing from prayerless studies, prayerless work, prayerless religion. He laughs at our toil, mocks at our wisdom, but trembles when we pray.* (Samuel Chadwick)

The possibilities of prayer are seen in its results in temporal matters. Prayer reaches to everything that concerns people, whether it be body, mind, or soul. Prayer embraces the very smallest things of life. Prayer takes in the wants of the body, food, raiment, business, finances. Everything that belongs to this life, as well as those things that have to do with the eternal interests of the soul. Its achievements are seen not only in the large things of earth, but more especially in what might be called the little things of life. It brings to pass not only large things, speaking after the manner of people, but also the small things.

Temporal matters are of a lower order than the spiritual, but they concern us greatly. Our temporal interests make up a great part of our lives. They are the main source of our cares and worries. They have much to do with our Christianity. We have bodies that have wants, pains, disabilities, and limitations. What concerns our bodies necessarily engages our minds. These are subjects of prayer, and prayer takes in all of them, and great are the accomplishments of prayer in this realm of our king.

Our temporal matters have much to do with our health and happiness. They form our relations. They are tests of honesty and belong to the sphere of justice and righteousness. Not to pray about temporal matters is to leave God out of the largest sphere of our being. Those who cannot pray in everything, as we are charged to do by Paul in Philippians,[1] has never learned in any true sense the nature and worth of prayer. To leave business and time out of prayer is to leave religion and eternity out of it.

PRAYING FOR TEMPORAL AND SPIRITUAL MATTERS

Those who do not pray about temporal matters cannot pray with confidence about spiritual matters. Those who do not put God by prayer into their struggling toil for daily bread will never put Him in their struggle for heaven. Those who do not cover and supply the wants of the body by prayer will never cover and supply the wants of their soul. Both body and soul are dependent on God, and prayer is but the crying expression of that dependence.

The Syrophenician woman prayed for health for her daughter. In fact, the Old Testament is but the record of God in dealing with His people through the divine appointment of prayer. Abraham prayed that Sodom might be saved from destruction. Abraham's servant prayed and received God's direction in choosing a wife for Isaac. Hannah prayed and Samuel was given to her. Elijah prayed and no rain came for three years. He prayed again and the clouds gave rain. Hezekiah was saved from a mortal sickness by his praying. Jacob's praying saved him from Esau's revenge. The Old Testament is a history of prayer for temporal blessings as well as for spiritual blessings.

PRAYER COVERAGE: SPIRITUAL AND TEMPORAL

In the New Testament, we have the same principles illustrated and enforced. Prayer in this section of God's Word covers the whole realm of both temporal and spiritual good. In His universal prayer for humanity, our Lord puts in the petition for every climate, age, and condition: "Give us this day our daily bread."[2] This embraces all necessary earthly good.

In the Sermon on the Mount, a whole section is taken up by our Lord about food and raiment. In it, He cautions against undue care or anxiety for these things, and encourages a faith that takes in and claims all these necessary bodily comforts and necessities. This teaching stands in close connection with His teachings about prayer. Food and raiment are taught as subjects of prayer. Not for one moment is it even hinted that they are things beneath the notice of a great God, nor too material and earthly for such a spiritual exercise as prayer.

The Syrophenician woman prayed for the health of her daughter. Peter prayed for Dorcas to be brought back to life. When Paul was on his way to Rome and cast upon the island of Melita,[3] he prayed for the father of

Publius who was sick with a fever, and God healed him. Paul urged the Christians at Rome to strive with him together in prayer that he might be delivered from evil people.[4]

When Peter was put in prison by Herod, the Church was instant in prayer that Peter might be delivered from the prison, and God honored the praying of these early Christians.[5] In his letter to Gaius, John said, "Beloved, I pray that you may prosper in all things and be in health, just as your soul prospers."[6]

The divine instructions in James says: "Is any among you afflicted? let him pray. . . . Is anyone among you sick? Let him call for the elders of the church, and let them pray over him, anointing him with oil in the name of the Lord."[7]

In writing to the Philippians, Paul says: "Be careful for nothing; but in every thing by prayer and supplication with thanksgiving let your requests be made known unto God."[8]

PRAY FOR ALL THINGS

This provides for all kinds of cares—business cares, home cares, body cares, and soul cares. All are to be brought to God by prayer, and at the throne of grace[9] our minds and souls are to be unburdened of all that affects us or causes anxiety or uneasiness. These words of Paul stand in close connection with what he says about temporal matters especially: "But I rejoiced in the Lord greatly, that now at the last your care of me hath flourished again; wherein ye were also careful, but ye lacked opportunity. Not that I speak in respect of want: for I have learned, in whatsoever state I am, therewith to be content."[10]

Paul closes his letter to these Christians with words that embrace all temporal needs as well as spiritual wants: "But my God shall supply all your need according to his riches in glory by Christ Jesus."[11]

UNBELIEF IN PRAYER FOR ALL THINGS

Unbelief in the doctrine that prayer covers all things that have to do with the body and business affairs breeds undue anxiety about earth's affairs, causes unnecessary worry, and creates very unhappy states of mind. We would save ourselves much needless care if we simply believed in prayer as the means of relieving those cares, and would learn the happy art of casting all our cares in prayer upon God who cares for us.[12] Unbelief in God as one who is concerned about even the smallest affairs that affect our happiness and comfort limits the Holy One of Israel,[13] and makes our lives altogether empty of real happiness and sweet contentment.

CASE STUDY: THE DISCIPLES VS. THE DEMONS

In the story of the disciples failure to cast the demon out of a man's son who was brought to them while Jesus was on the Mount of

Transfiguration, we have a suggestive lesson of the unity of faith, prayer, and fasting—and of the failure to reach the possibilities and obligations of such an occasion.[14] The disciples should have cast the demon out of the boy. They had been sent out to do this very work, and had been empowered by their Lord and Master to do it.[15] Yet they conspicuously failed. Christ reproved them sharply for not doing it. They had been sent out on this very specific mission. This one thing was specified by our Lord when He sent them out.

Their failure brought shame and confusion on them, and discredited their Lord and Master and His cause. They brought Him into disrepute, and reflected very seriously upon the cause that they represented. Their faith to cast out the demon had noticeably failed, simply because it had not been nurtured by prayer and fasting. Failure to pray broke the ability of faith, and failure came because they had not the energy of a strong authoritative faith.

The promise reads, and we cannot too often refer to it, for it is the very basis of our faith and the ground on which we stand when we pray: "All things, whatsoever ye shall ask in prayer, believing, ye shall receive."[16] What enumeration table can tabulate, itemize, and aggregate "all things whatsoever"? The possibilities of prayer and faith go to the length of an endless chain, and cover an immeasurable area.

THE FAITH CHAPTER

The writer of the book of Hebrews seems almost to grow weary with trying to specify the examples and wonderful exploits of faith, so he pauses a moment and then gives us almost unheard-of achievements of prayer and faith as exemplified by the Old Testament saints. Here is what he says.

> And what shall I more say? for the time would fail me to tell of Gideon, and of Barak, and of Samson, and of Jephthae; of David also, and Samuel, and of the prophets: Who through faith subdued kingdoms, wrought righteousness, obtained promises, stopped the mouths of lions, Quenched the violence of fire, escaped the edge of the sword, out of weakness were made strong, waxed valiant in fight, turned to flight the armies of the aliens. Women received their dead raised to life again: and others were tortured, not accepting deliverance; that they might obtain a better resurrection.[17]

What an illustrious record this is! What marvelous accomplishments, brought about not by armies or by superhuman strength, but all accomplished simply by men and women noted alone for their faith and prayer! Hand in hand with these records of faith's unlimited range are the illustrious records of prayer, for they are all one. Faith has never won a victory or gained a crown where prayer was not the weapon of the victory, and where prayer did not jewel the crown. If "all things are possible to him that believeth,"[18] then all things are possible to those who pray.

> Depend on him; thou canst not fail;
> Make all thy wants and wishes known:
> Fear not; his merits must prevail;
> Ask but in faith, it shall be done.

Endnotes

1 Philippians 4:6
2 Matthew 6:11
3 Malta
4 Romans 15:30-31
5 Acts 12:1-19
6 3 John 1:2, NKJV
7 James 5:13a-14
8 Philippians 4:6
9 Hebrews 4:16
10 Philippians 4:10-11
11 Philippians 4:19
12 1 Peter 5:7
13 Psalm 78:41
14 Mark 9:14-29
15 Mark 6:7
16 Matthew 21:22
17 Hebrews 11:32-35
18 Mark 9:23

7

Prayer's Wide Range

NOTHING SO PLEASES GOD *in connection with our prayer as our praise, and nothing so blesses the man who prays as the praise which he offers. I got a great blessing once in China in this connection. I had received bad and sad news from home, and deep shadows had covered my soul. I prayed, but the darkness did not vanish. I summoned myself to endure, but the darkness only deepened. Just then I went to an inland station and saw on the wall of the mission home these words: "Try Thanksgiving." I did, and in a moment every shadow was gone, not to return. Yes, the Psalmist was right, "It is a good thing to give thanks unto the Lord."*[1] (Henry W. Frost)

The possibilities of prayer are gauged by faith in God's ability to do. Faith is the one prime condition by which God works. Faith is the one prime condition by which people pray. Faith draws on God to its full extent. Faith gives character to prayer. A feeble faith has always brought forth feeble praying. Vigorous faith creates vigorous praying. At the close of a parable in which He stressed the necessity of vigorous praying—"And he spake a parable unto them to this end, that men always ought to pray, and not to faint"—Christ asked this pointed question, "Nevertheless, when the Son of Man cometh, shall he find faith on the earth?"[2]

IF YOU CAN BELIEVE

In the case of the demon-oppressed child that the father brought first to the disciples, who could not cure him, and then to the Lord Jesus Christ, the father cried out with all the pain of declining faith and great sorrow, "If thou canst do any thing, have compassion on us, and help us." Jesus replied, "If thou canst believe, all things are possible to him that believeth."[3] The healing turned on the faith in the ability of Christ to heal the boy. The ability to do was in Christ essentially and eternally, but the doing of the thing turned on the ability of the father's faith. Great faith enables Christ to do great things.

We need a quickening faith in God's power. We have hedged God in until we have little faith in His power. We have conditioned the exercise of His power until we have a little God, and a little faith in a little God.

UNBELIEF LIMITS GOD

The only condition that restrains God's power and limits His action is unbelief.[4] He is not limited in action or restrained by the conditions that limit people.

The conditions of time, place, nearness, ability, and all others that could possibly be named upon which the actions of people hinge, have no bearing on God. If people will look to God and cry to Him with true prayer, He will hear and can deliver—no matter how dreadful the condition or how impossible it seems to be to correct.

Strange how God has to school His people in His ability to do! He made a promise to Abraham and Sarah that Isaac would be born. Abraham was nearly one hundred years old, and Sarah was barren by natural defect, and was also beyond the age of having children. She laughed at the thought of having a child as preposterous. The LORD asked, "Wherefore did Sarah laugh? . . . Is anything too hard for the LORD?"[5] Nevertheless, God fulfilled His promise to these old people to the letter.

Moses hesitated to undertake God's purpose to liberate Israel from Egyptian bondage because of his inability to talk well. God stopped him at once by asking several questions.

> And Moses said unto the Lord, O my Lord, I am not eloquent, neither heretofore, nor since thou hast spoken unto thy servant: but I am slow of speech, and of a slow tongue. And the Lord said unto him, Who hath made man's mouth? or who maketh the dumb, or deaf, or the seeing, or the blind? have not I the Lord? Now therefore go, and I will be with thy mouth, and teach thee what thou shalt say.[6]

When God said He would feed the children of Israel a whole month with meat, Moses questioned His ability to do it. The Lord said unto Moses, "Is the Lord's hand waxed short? thou shalt see now whether my word shall come to pass unto thee or not."[7]

NOTHING IS TOO HARD FOR THE LORD TO DO

As Paul declared, God "is able to do exceeding abundantly above all that we can ask or think."[8] Prayer has to do with God, with His ability to do. The possibility of prayer is the measure of God's ability to do.

The "all things," the "all things whatsoever," and the "anything," are all covered by the ability of God. The urgent entreaty reads, "Ask what ye will," because God is able to do anything and all things that my desires may crave, and that He has promised. In God's ability to do, He goes far beyond our ability to ask. Human thoughts, human words, human imaginations, human desires, and human needs, cannot in any way measure God's ability to do.

Prayer in its legitimate possibilities goes out on God Himself. Prayer goes out with faith not only in the promise of God, but faith in God Himself, and in God's ability to do. Prayer goes out not on the promise merely, but obtains promises and creates promises.[9]

Elijah had the promise that God would send the rain, but no promise that He would send the fire. By faith and prayer he obtained the fire as well as the rain, but the fire came first.

Daniel had no specific promise that God would make known to him the dream of the king, but he and his associates joined in united prayer, and God revealed to Daniel the king's dream and the interpretation, and their lives were spared thereby.[10]

Hezekiah had no promise that God would cure him of his desperate sickness that threatened his life. On the contrary, the word of the Lord came to him by the mouth of the prophet, that he should die. He prayed against this decree of Almighty God with faith, however, and he succeeded in obtaining a reversal of God's word and lived.[11]

GOD COMMITS HIMSELF TO PRAYER

God makes it marvelous when He says by the mouth of His prophet Isaiah: "Thus saith the Lord, the Holy One of Israel, and his Maker, Ask me of things to come concerning my sons, and concerning the work of my hands command ye me."[12] In this strong promise in which He commits Himself into the hands of His praying people, He appeals to His great creative power: "I have made the earth, and created man upon it: I, even my hands, have stretched out the heavens, and all their host have I commanded."[13]

The majesty and power of God in making humanity and humanity's world and constantly upholding all things,[14] are always kept before us as the basis of our faith in God, and as assurance and urgency to prayer. Then God calls us away from what He Himself has done, and turns our minds to Himself personally. The infinite glory and power of His person are set before us for contemplation: "Remember ye not the former things, neither consider the things of old."[15]

He declares that He will do a "new thing,"[16] and that He does not have to repeat Himself. All He has done neither limits His doing nor the manner of His doing. Further, if we have prayer and faith, He will so answer our prayers and so work for us that His former work will not be remembered or come into mind. If people would pray as they should pray, the marvels of the past would be more than reproduced. The Gospel would advance with an ease and power it has never known. Doors would be thrown open to the Gospel, and the Word of God would have a conquering force rarely if ever known before.

IF CHRISTIANS PRAYED AS THEY SHOULD

If Christians prayed with strong commanding faith as Christians should, and with earnestness and sincerity, God-called and God-empowered men and women everywhere would be on fire to go and spread the Gospel throughout the world. The Word of the Lord would run and be glorified as never before known. The God-influenced, God-inspired, and God-commissioned would go and kindle the flame of sacred fire for Christ, salvation, and heaven everywhere in all nations. Soon all people would hear the glad tidings of salvation and have an opportunity to receive Jesus Christ as their personal Savior. Let us read another one of those large unlimited statements in God's Word, which are a direct challenge to prayer and faith.

He that spared not his own Son, but delivered him up for us all, how shall he not with him also freely give us all things?[17]

What a basis have we here for prayer and faith—unlimited and immeasurable in breadth, in depth, and in height! The promise to give us all things is backed up by the calling to our mind the fact that God freely gave His only begotten Son for our redemption. Giving His Son is the assurance and guarantee that He will freely give all things to the person who believes and prays.

INSPIRED ASKING

What confidence we have in this divine statement for inspired asking! What holy boldness we have here for the largest asking! No commonplace tameness should restrain our largest asking. Large, larger, and largest asking magnifies grace and adds to God's glory. Feeble asking impoverishes the asker, restrains God's purposes for the greatest good, and obscures His glory.

How enthroned, magnificent, and royal the intercession of our Lord Jesus Christ at His Father's right hand in heaven![18] The benefits of His intercession flow to us through our intercessions. Our intercession should catch by contagion and by necessity the inspiration and largeness of Christ's great work at His Father's right hand. His business and His life are to pray. Our business and our lives should be to pray, and to pray without ceasing. Failure in our intercession affects the fruits His intercession. Lazy, heartless, feeble, and indifferent praying by us mars and hinders the effects of Christ's praying.

Endnotes

1 Psalm 92:1
2 Luke 18:8
3 Mark 9:22b-23
4 Psalm 78:41
5 Genesis 18:13-14a
6 Exodus 4:10-12
7 Numbers 11:23
8 Ephesians 3:20
9 Hebrews 11:33
10 Daniel 2:1-49
11 2 Kings 20:1-11
12 Isaiah 45:11
13 Isaiah 45:12
14 Hebrews 1:3
15 Isaiah 43:18
16 Isaiah 43:19
17 Romans 8:32
18 Hebrews 7:25

8

Facts and History of Prayer

THE PARTICULAR VALUE OF *private prayer consists in being able to approach God with more freedom, and unbosom ourselves more fully than in any other way. Between us and God there are private and personal interests, sins to confess and wants to be supplied, which it would be improper to disclose to the world. This duty is enforced by the example of good people in all ages.* (Amos Binney)

The possibilities of prayer are established by the facts and history of prayer. Facts are stubborn things. Facts are the true things. Theories may be but speculations. Opinions may be wholly at fault. But facts must be deferred to. They cannot be ignored. What are the possibilities of prayer judged by the facts? What is the history of prayer? What does it reveal to us? Prayer has a history that is written in God's Word and recorded in the experiences and lives of God's saints. History is truth teaching by example. We may miss the truth by perverting the history, but the truth is in the facts of history.

> He spake with Abraham at the oak,
> He called Elisha from the plough;
> David he from the sheepfolds took,
> Thy day, thine hour of grace, is now.

GOD REVEALS THE TRUTH BY THE FACTS

God reveals Himself by the facts of religious history. God teaches us His will by the facts and examples of Bible history. God's facts, God's

Word, and God's history are all in perfect harmony, and have much of God in them all. God has ruled the world by prayer, and God still rules the world by the same divinely ordained means.

The possibilities of prayer cover not only individuals but reach to cities and nations. They take in classes and peoples. The praying of Moses was the one thing that stood between the wrath of God against the Israelites, His declared purpose to destroy them, and the execution of that divine purpose. Because of it, the nation of Israel was spared.[1] Notwithstanding, Sodom was not spared, because ten righteous men could not be found inside its limits.[2] Yet the little city of Zoar was spared because Lot prayed for it as he fled from the storm of fire and brimstone that burned up Sodom.[3] Nineveh was saved because the king and its people repented of their evil ways and gave themselves to prayer and fasting.[4]

UNLIMITED POSSIBILITIES OF PRAYER

In his remarkable prayer in his letter to the Ephesians, Paul honors the unlimited possibilities of prayer and glorifies the ability of God to answer prayer. He closes that memorable prayer that is so far-reaching in its petitions, and that sets forth the very deepest religious experience, by declaring that God "is able to do exceeding abundantly above all that we ask or think."[5] He makes prayer all-inclusive—embracing all things great and small. There is no time or place that prayer does not cover and sanctify. All things in earth and in heaven, everything for time and for eternity, are all embraced in prayer. Nothing is too great and nothing is too small to be the subject of prayer. Prayer reaches down to the least things of life and includes the greatest things that concern us.

> If pain afflict or wrongs oppress,
> If cares distract, or fears dismay;
> If guilt deject, or sin distress,
> In every case still watch and pray.

One of the most important, far-reaching, peace-giving, necessary, and practical prayer possibilities we have are contained in Paul's words in Philippians, which state that prayer is a cure for undue care.

> Be careful for nothing; but in every thing by prayer and supplication with thanksgiving let your requests be made known unto God. And the peace of God, which passeth all understanding, shall keep your hearts and minds through Christ Jesus.[6]

CARES ARE THE EPIDEMIC EVIL OF HUMANITY

Cares are universal in their reach. They belong to humanity in its fallen condition. The predisposition to undue anxiety is the natural result of sin. Care comes in all shapes, at all times, and from all sources. It comes to all of every age and station. There are the cares of the home and family, from which there is no escape except in prayer. There are the cares of business, the cares of poverty, and the cares of riches. Ours is an anxious world, and ours is an anxious race. The caution of Paul is well addressed, "be anxious for nothing."[7] This is the divine command. It is given so that we might be able to live above anxiety and be free from undue care. "In every thing by prayer and supplication with thanksgiving let your requests be made known unto God." This is the divinely prescribed remedy for all anxious cares, worry, and inward fretting.

The word *careful* means to be drawn in different directions, distracted, anxious, disturbed, annoyed in spirit. Jesus warned against this very thing in the Sermon on the Mount, where He had earnestly urged His disciples, "Take therefore no thought for the morrow,"[8] in things concerning the needs of the body. He was endeavoring to show them the true secret of a quiet mind—one that is free from anxiety and unnecessary care about food and raiment. Tomorrow's evils were not to be considered. He was simply teaching the same lesson found in Psalm 37:3, "Trust in the Lord, and do good; so shalt thou dwell in the land, and verily thou shalt be fed." In cautioning against the fears of tomorrow's prospective evils and the material wants of the body, our Lord was teaching the great lesson of an unquestioning and childlike confidence in God. "Commit thy way unto the Lord; trust also in him; and he shall bring it to pass."[9]

> "Day by day," the promise reads,
> Daily strength for daily needs
> Cast foreboding fears away;
> Take the manna of today.

Paul's direction is very specific, "Be careful for nothing." Be careful for not one thing. Be careful for not anything, for any condition, chance, or happening. Be troubled about not anything that creates one disturbing anxiety. Have a mind free from all anxieties, cares, fretting, and worries. Cares divide, distract, and bewilder. They destroy unity, energies, and quietness of mind. Cares kill weak piety and weaken strong piety. What great need to guard against them and learn the one secret of their cure—prayer!

What boundless possibilities there are in prayer to remedy the situation of mind that Paul is speaking about! Prayer over everything can quiet every distraction, hush every anxiety, and lift every care from care-enslaved lives and from care-bewildered hearts. Paul's specific direction about prayer is the perfect cure for all the ills created by anxieties, cares, and worries. Only prayer in everything can drive all care away, relieve unnecessary heart burdens, and save from the besetting sin of worrying over things that we cannot help. Only prayer can bring into the heart and mind the "peace which passeth all understanding," and keep the mind and heart at ease and free from troubling care.

WORRIED CHRISTIANS BEAR NEEDLESS BURDENS

Oh, the needless heart burdens held by worried Christians! How few know the real secret of a happy Christian life,[10] one filled with perfect peace, hid from the storms and billows of an anxious care-worn life! Prayer has a possibility of saving us from "carefulness," the ruin of human lives. In writing to the Corinthians Paul says, "I would have you without carefulness."[11] This is the will of God. Prayer has the ability to do this very thing. "Casting all your care upon him; for he careth for you," is the way Peter puts it.[12] The Psalmist says, "Fret not thyself in any wise to do evil."[13] Oh, the blessedness of a heart at ease from all inward care, exempt from undue anxiety, and enjoying the peace of God that passes all understanding!

Paul's directive that includes both God's promise and His purpose, and which immediately precedes his instructions to be "careful for nothing," reads this way:

Rejoice in the Lord alway: and again I say, Rejoice. Let your moderation be known unto all men. The Lord is at hand.[14]

In a world filled with cares of every kind, where temptation is the rule, where there are so many things to try us, how is it possible to rejoice always? We look at the naked, dry command, and we accept it and reverence it as the Word of God, but no joy comes. How are we to let our moderation, our mildness, and our gentleness be universally and always known? We resolve to be gentle and good. We remember the nearness of the Lord, but still we are hasty, quick, hard, and sharp. We listen to the divine charge, "Be careful for nothing," yet we are still anxious, care-worn, care-eaten, and care-tossed.

How can we fulfill the divine Word, so sweet and so large in promise, so beautiful to the eye, and yet so far from being realized? How can we enter upon the rich inheritance of being true, honest, just, pure, and possess lovely things? The recipe is infallible, the remedy is universal, and the cure is unfailing. It is found in the words that we have so often referred to of Paul: "Be careful for nothing; but in every thing by prayer and supplication with thanksgiving let your requests be made known unto God."

IT IS GOD'S WILL THAT WE BE FREE FROM CARES AND WORRIES

This joyous, care-free, peaceful experience that brings the believer into a joyfulness and living simply by faith day by day, is the will of God. Writing to the Thessalonians, Paul tells them: "Rejoice evermore. Pray without ceasing. In every thing give thanks: for this is the will of God in Christ Jesus concerning you."[15] It is God's will that we should find full deliverance from all care and undue anxiety, and He has ordained prayer as the means by which we can reach that happy state of heart.

The *Revised Version* of the Bible makes some changes in the passage of Paul, about which we have been speaking. The reading there is "In nothing be anxious," and "the peace of God shall guard your hearts and your minds." Also, Paul puts the antecedent in the air of prayer, which is "Rejoice in the Lord always." That is, be always glad in the Lord, and be happy with Him. That you may thus be happy, he adds, "Be careful for nothing." This rejoicing is the doorway for prayer and its pathway, too.

The sunshine and buoyancy of joy in the Lord are the strength and boldness of prayer, the praise of its victory. "Moderation" makes the rainbow of prayer. The word means mildness, fairness, gentleness, sweet reasonableness. The *Revised Version* changes it to "forbearance," with the margin reading "gentleness."

What rare ingredients and beautiful colorings! These are colorings and ingredients that make a strong and beautiful character and a wide and positive reputation. A rejoicing, gentle spirit, positive in reputation, is well fitted for prayer, for it is rid of the distractions and unrest of care.

Endnotes

1 Deuteronomy 9:1-19
2 Genesis 18:22-33
3 Genesis 19:18-23
4 Jonah 3:5-10
5 Ephesians 3:20
6 Philippians 4:6-7
7 Philippians 4:6, NKJV
8 Matthew 6:34
9 Psalm 37:5
10 For more reading on this subject, see *The Christian's Secret of a Happy Life* by Hannah Whitall Smith, ©1998 Bridge-Logos
11 I Corinthians 7:32
12 I Peter 5:7
13 Psalm 37:8
14 Philippians 4:4-5
15 I Thessalonians 5:16-18

9

Facts and History of Prayer (Continued)

THE NEGLECT OF PRAYER *is a grand hindrance to holiness. "We have not because we ask not."*[1] *Oh, how meek and gentle, how lowly in heart, how full of love both to God and to man, might you have been at this day, if you had only asked! If you had continued instant in prayer! Ask, that you may thoroughly experience and perfectly practice the whole of that religion which our Lord has so beautifully described in the Sermon on the Mount. (John Wesley)*

It is to the closet Paul directs us to go. The unfailing remedy for all troubling, distressing care is prayer. The place where the Lord is at hand is the closet of prayer. There He is always found, and there He is at hand to bless, deliver, and help. The closet of prayer is the one place where the Lord's presence and power will be more fully realized than any other place.

Paul gives the various terms of prayer, supplication, and giving of thanks as the complement of true praying. The soul must be in all of these spiritual exercises. There must be no half-hearted praying, no reducing its nature, and no lessening its force. Not if we would be freed from this undue anxiety that causes friction and internal distress, and if we would receive the rich fruit of that peace that passes all understanding. The person who prays must be an earnest soul, well-rounded in spiritual attributes.

NOTHING TOO GREAT FOR PRAYER

"In every thing by prayer . . . let your requests be made known unto God,"[2] says Paul. Nothing is too great to be handled in prayer, or to be sought in prayer. Nothing is too small to be weighed in the secret councils of the closet, and nothing is too little for its final arbitration. As care comes from every source, so prayer goes to every source. As there are no small things in prayer, so there are no small things with God. He who counts the hairs of our head, and who is not too lofty and high to notice the little sparrow that falls to the ground, is not too great and high to note everything that concerns the happiness, needs, and safety of His children. Prayer brings God into what people are pleased to term the "little affairs of life." The lives of people are made up of these small matters, and yet how often do great consequences come from small beginnings?

> There is no sorrow, Lord, too light
> To bring in prayer to Thee;
> There is no anxious care too slight
> To wake Thy sympathy.
>
> There is no secret sigh we breathe,
> But meets Thine ear Divine,
> And every cross grows light beneath
> The shadow, Lord, of Thine.

WHATEVER AFFECTS US CONCERNS GOD

As everything by prayer is to be brought to the notice of Almighty God, so we are assured that whatever affects us concerns Him. How all-embracing is this direction about prayer! "In everything by prayer." There is no distinction here between temporal and spiritual things. Such a distinction is against faith, wisdom, and reverence. God rules everything in nature and in grace. People are affected for time and eternity by things secular as well as by things spiritual. Humanity's salvation hangs on its business as well as on its prayers—and business hangs on prayers just as it hangs on diligence.

The chief hindrances to piety and the deadliest temptations of the devil are in business—lying alongside the things of time. The heaviest, most confusing, and most stupefying cares lie beside secular and worldly matters. So prayer is to be made for everything that comes to us and that concerns us, for everything that we want to come to us, and for everything that we do not want to come to us. Prayer blesses all things, brings all things, relieves all things and prevents all things. Everything as well as every place and every hour is to be ordered by prayer. Prayer has in it the possibility to affect everything that affects us. Here are the vast possibilities of prayer.

BITTERNESS OF LIFE IS SWEETENED BY PRAYER

How much is the bitterness of life sweetened by prayer! How are the feeble made strong by prayer! Sickness flees before the health of prayer. Doubts, misgivings, and trembling fears retire before prayer. Wisdom, knowledge, holiness, and heaven are at the command of prayer. Nothing is outside of prayer. It has the power to gain all things in the provision of our Lord Jesus Christ. Paul covers all departments and sweeps the entire field of human concerns, conditions, and happenings by saying, "In everything by prayer."

Supplications and thanksgiving are to be joined with prayer. It is not the dignity of worship, the gorgeousness of ceremonials, the magnificence of its ritual, or the plainness of its sacraments that avail. It is not simply the soul's hallowed and lowly abasement before God, or the speechless awe that benefits in this prayer service. It is the intensity of supplication, the looking and the lifting of the soul in ardent plea to God for the things desired, and for which request is made.

The radiance, gratitude, and utterance of thanksgiving must be there. This is not simply the poetry of praise, but the deep-toned words and prose of thanks. There must be hearty thanks that remembers the past, sees God in it, and voices that recognition in sincere thanksgiving. The hidden depths within must have utterance. The lips must speak the music of the soul. A heart enthused of God, a heart illumined by His presence, a life guided by His right hand, must have something to say for God in gratitude. Such a heart is to recognize God in the events of past life, to exalt God for His goodness, and to honor God who has honored it.

LET YOUR REQUESTS BE MADE KNOWN UNTO GOD

The "requests" must be made known unto God. Silence is not prayer. Prayer is asking God for something that we do not have, that we desire, and that He has promised to give in answer to prayer. Prayer is really verbal asking. Words are in prayer. Strong words and true words are found in prayer. Desires in prayer are put into words. Praying ones are pleaders. They urge their prayers by arguments, promises, and needs.

Sometimes loud words are in prayer. The Psalmist said, "Evening, and morning, and at noon will I pray, and cry aloud."[3] The praying ones want something that they do not have. They want something God has in His possession, and that they can get by praying. They are beggared, bewildered, oppressed, and confused. They are before God in supplication, prayer, and thanksgiving. These are the attitudes, the incense, the paraphernalia, and the fashion of this hour—the court attendance of the soul before God.

ASKING FOR ONE'S SELF

We are in a difficulty. We need something, and we need it badly. Other help has failed. It means a plea for something to be given that has not been done. The request is for the Giver,—not alone His gifts, but Himself. Our requests are to be made known unto God. The requests are to be brought to the knowledge of God. It is then that cares fly away, anxieties disappear, worries depart, and our soul gets at ease. It is then that there steals into the heart "the peace of God that passes all understanding."

> Peace! doubting heart, my God's I am,
> Who formed me man, forbids my fear;
> The Lord hath called me by my name;
> The Lord protects, forever near;
> His blood for me did once atone,
> And still He loves and guards His own.

James has another marvelous description of prayer and its possibilities. It has to do with sickness and health, sin and forgiveness, rain and drought. Here's James' directions for praying:

Is any among you afflicted? let him pray. Is any merry? let him sing psalms. Is any sick among you? let him call for the elders of the church; and let them pray over him, anointing him with oil in the name of the Lord: And the prayer of faith shall save the sick, and the Lord shall raise him up; and if he have committed sins, they shall be forgiven him. Confess your faults one to another, and pray one for another, that ye may be healed. The effectual fervent prayer of a righteous man availeth much. Elias was a man subject to like passions as we are, and he prayed earnestly that it might not rain: and it rained not on the earth by the space of three years and six months. And he prayed again, and the heaven gave rain, and the earth brought forth her fruit.[4]

Here is prayer for one's needs and intercessory prayer for others, prayer for physical needs and spiritual needs, prayer for drought and for rain, prayer for temporal matters and spiritual things. How vast the reach of prayer! How wonderful these words show its possibilities!

REMEDY FOR AFFLICTION AND DEPRESSION

Here is the remedy for affliction and depression of every sort, and here we find the remedy for sickness and for rain in the time of drought. Here is the way to obtain forgiveness of sins. A stroke of prayer paralyzes the energies of nature, stays its clouds, rain, and dew, and blasts field and farm like the simoon.[5] Prayer brings clouds, rain, and fertility to the famished and wasted earth.

"The effectual fervent prayer of a righteous man availeth much" is a general statement of prayer as an energetic force. Two words are used. One signifies power in exercise, operative power, while the other is power as an endowment. Prayer is power and strength—a power and strength that influences God, and is most salutary, widespread, and marvelous in its gracious benefits to humanity. Prayer influences God. The ability of God to do for humanity is the measure of the possibility of prayer.

> Thou art coming to a king,
> Large petitions with thee bring;
> For His grace and power are such
> None can ever ask too much.

Endnotes

1 James 4:2b
2 Philippians 4:6
3 Psalm 55:17
4 James 5:13-18
5 A strong, hot, sand-laden wind of the Sahara and Arabian deserts.

10

Answered Prayer

IN HIS "SOLDIER'S POCKET BOOK," *Lord Wolseley says if a young officer wishes to get on, he must volunteer for the most hazardous duties and take every possible chance of risking his life. It was a spirit and courage like that which was shown in the service of God by a good soldier of Jesus Christ named John McKenzie, who died a few years ago. One evening when he was a lad and eager for work in the Foreign Mission field, he knelt down at the foot of a tree in the Ladies' Walk on the banks of the Lossie at Elgin and offered up this prayer: "O Lord send me to the darkest spot on earth." And God heard him and sent him to South Africa where he labored many years first under the London Missionary Society and then under the British Government as the first Resident Commissioner among the natives of Bechuanaland.* (J. O. Struthers)

It is answered prayer that brings praying out of the realm of dry, dead things, and makes praying a thing of life and power. It is the answer to prayer that brings things to pass, changes the natural trend of things, and orders all things according to the will of God. It is the answer to prayer that takes praying out of the regions of fanaticism, and saves it from being utopian,[1] or from being merely fanciful. It is the answer to prayer that makes praying a power for God and for humanity, and makes praying real and divine. Unanswered prayers are training schools for unbelief, an imposition and a nuisance, irrelevant to God and to humanity.

MILLIONS OF UNANSWERED PRAYERS

Answers to prayer are the only certainty that we have prayed correctly. What marvelous power there is in prayer! What untold miracles it works in this world! What untold benefits to humankind does it secure to those who pray! Why is it that the average prayer by the million is not answered?

The millions of unanswered prayers are not to be solved by the mystery of God's will. We are not the sport of His sovereign power. He is not playing at "make-believe" in His marvelous promises to answer prayer. The complete explanation is found in our wrong praying. "Ye ask, and receive not, because ye ask amiss."[2] If all unanswered prayers were dumped into the ocean, they would come very near filling it. Child of God, can you pray? Are your prayers answered? If not, why not? Answered prayer is the proof of your real praying.

The effectiveness of prayer from a Biblical standpoint lies completely in the answer to prayer. The benefit of prayer has been well and popularly maximized by the saying, "It moves the arm that moves the universe." To get unquestioned answers to prayer is not only important as to the satisfying of our desires, but is the evidence of our abiding in Christ. So getting answers to our prayers is of great importance to us.

PRAYING IS NOT A TEST OF OUR RELATIONSHIP TO GOD

The act of praying may be a real dead performance. It may be the routine of habit. The sure test of our vital connection with Jesus Christ is to pray and receive clear answers, not once or twice but daily. Read our Lord's words in this connection: "If you abide in Me, and My words abide in you, you will ask what you desire, and it shall be done for you."[3]

To God and to us, the answer to prayer is the all-important part of our praying. The answer to prayer, direct and unmistakable, is the evidence of God's being. It proves that God lives, that there is a God, and that He is an intelligent being who is interested in His creatures, and who listens to them when they approach Him in prayer. There is no proof that so clearly demonstrates that God exists than prayer and its answer. This was Elijah's plea: "Hear me, O LORD, hear me, that this people may know that You are the Lord God."[4]

THE PART OF PRAYER THAT GLORIFIES GOD

Unanswered prayers are dumb oracles that leave the praying ones in darkness, doubt, and bewilderment, and which carry no conviction to the unbeliever. It is not the act or the attitude of praying that gives effectiveness to prayer. It is not the abject prostration of the body before God, the passionate or quiet utterance to God, or the exquisite beauty and poetry of the diction of our prayers that do the deed. It is not the marvelous array of argument and eloquence in praying that makes prayer effective. Not one or all of these are the things that glorify God. It is the answer that brings glory to His Name.[5]

Elijah might have prayed on Carmel's heights till that good day with all the fire and energy of his soul. But if no answer had been given, no glory would have come to God. Peter might have shut himself up with Dorcas' dead body until he himself died on his knees. But if no answer had come, no glory to God nor good to the people would have followed. There would have been only doubt, discouragement, and dismay.

PROOF THAT WE ARE RIGHT WITH GOD
Jesus said at the grave of Lazarus:

Father, I thank thee that thou hast heard me. And I knew that thou hearest me always: but because of the people which stand by I said it, that they may believe that thou hast sent me.[6]

The answer to His prayer was the proof of His mission from God. The answer to Elijah's prayer proved the same to the woman whose son he raised to life. She said, "Now by this I know that thou art a man of God."[7] They are highest in the favor of God who have the quickest access and the greatest number of answers to prayer from Almighty God.

Prayer ascends to God by an invariable law—even by more than law: by the will, promise, and presence of a personal God. The answer comes back to earth by all the promise, truth, power, and love of God.

LONGING FOR ANSWERS
What a world of waste there is in praying. What multitudes of prayers have been offered for which no answer is returned, no answer longed for, and no answer is expected! We have been nurturing a false faith and hiding the shame of our loss and inability to pray. This we have done by the false, comforting, excuse that God does not answer directly or objectively, but indirectly and subjectively. We have persuaded ourselves that by some kind of hocus-pocus, of which we are wholly unconscious in its process and its results, we have been made better. Conscious that God has not answered us directly, we have comforted ourselves with the deluding salve that God has in some intangible way, and with unknown results, given us something better. Or we have comforted and nourished our spiritual laziness by saying that it is not God's will to give it to us. Faith, however, teaches God's praying ones that it is God's will to answer prayer. God answers all prayers and every prayer of His true children who truly pray.

> Prayer makes the darkened cloud withdraw,
> Prayer climbs the ladder Jacob saw;
> Gives exercise to faith and love,
> Brings every blessing from above.

The emphasis in the Scriptures is always given to the answer to prayer. All things from God are given in answer to prayer. God Himself, His presence, His gifts, and His grace, one and all, are secured by prayer. The medium by which God communicates with people is prayer. The most real thing in prayer, its very essential end, is the answer it secures. The mere repetition of words in prayer, the counting of beads, the multiplying mere words of prayer as works of duty—as if there was power to receive answers in the number of prayers—is a vain delusion, an empty thing, a useless service. Prayer looks directly to securing an answer. This is its design. It has no other end in view.

COMMUNION WITH GOD

There is sweet fellowship in prayer with our God through His Holy Spirit. There is enjoyment of God in praying, sweet, rich, and strong enjoyment. The graces of the Spirit in the inner soul are nurtured by prayer, kept alive and promoted in their growth by this spiritual exercise. But not one or all of these benefits of prayer have in them the essential end of prayer. Prayer is the divinely appointed channel through which all good and all grace flows to our souls and bodies.

> Prayer is appointed to convey
> The blessings God designs to give.

Prayer is divinely ordained as the means by which all temporal and spiritual good are gained to us. Prayer is not an end in itself. It is not something done to be rested in, something we have done, about which we are to congratulate ourselves. It is a means to an end. It is something we do that brings us something in return, without which the praying is valueless. Prayer always aims at securing an answer.

We are rich and strong, good and holy, and generous and kind by answered prayer. It is not the mere performance, attitude, or words of prayer that bring benefit to us, but it is the answer sent direct from heaven. Conscious and real answers to prayer bring real good to us. This is not praying merely for self or simply for selfish ends. The selfish character cannot exist when the prayer conditions are fulfilled.

It is by these answered prayers that human nature is enriched. The answered prayer brings us into constant and conscious communion with God. It awakens and enlarges gratitude, and excites the melody and lofty inspiration of praise. Answered prayer is the mark of God in our praying. It is the exchange with heaven, and it establishes and realizes a relationship with the unseen. We give our prayers in exchange for the divine blessing. God accepts our prayers through Christ's atoning blood and gives Himself, His presence, and His grace in return.

HOLY AFFECTIONS AND ANSWERED PRAYERS

By the answers to prayer all holy principles are matured—and faith, love, and hope have their enrichment by answered prayer. The answer is found in all true praying. The answer to prayer as a strong aim, a desire expressed, and its expectation and realization give persistence and realization to prayer. It is the fact of the answer that makes the prayer, and that enters into its very being. To seek no answer to prayer takes the desire, aim, and heart out of prayer. It makes praying a dead, tasteless thing fit only for dumb idols. It is the answer that brings praying into Bible regions, and makes it a desire fulfilled. It is a pursuit and interest that clothes it with flesh and blood, and makes it a prayer throbbing with all the true life of prayer. One that is rich with all the paternal relations of giving and receiving, of asking and answering.

GOD HOLDS ALL GOOD IN HIS OWN HANDS

All of God's goodness comes to us through our Lord Jesus Christ because of His atoning merits, by asking it in His name. The only command in which all the others of its class belong is, "Ask . . . seek . . . knock." The sole promise is its counterpart, its necessary equivalent: "It shall be given . . . ye shall find . . . it shall be opened unto you."[8]

God is so much involved in prayer and its hearing and answering, that all of His attributes and being are centered in that great fact. It distinguishes Him as peculiarly beneficent, wonderfully good, and powerfully attractive in His nature. "O thou that hearest prayer, unto thee shall all flesh come."[9]

> Faithful, O Lord, Thy mercies are
> A rock that cannot move;
> A thousand promises declare
> Thy constancy of love.

THE WORD OF GOD GUARANTEES AN ANSWER TO PRAYER

Not only does the Word of God stand as a guarantee for the answer to prayer, but all the attributes of God join together to the same end. God's truthfulness is at stake in the promises to answer prayer. His wisdom, truthfulness, and goodness are involved. God's infinite and inflexible righteousness is pledged to the great end of answering the prayers of those who call upon Him in the time of need. Justice and mercy blend into oneness to secure the answer to prayer. It is significant that the very justice of God comes into play and stands hard by God's faithfulness in the strong promise God makes of the pardon of sins and of cleansing from sin's pollutions. "If we confess our sins, he is faithful and just to forgive us our sins, and to cleanse us from all unrighteousness. "[10]

God's kingly relation to His true children with all of its authority, unites with the fatherly relation and all its tenderness to secure the answer to prayer. Our Lord Jesus Christ is fully committed to the answer of prayer. "And whatsoever ye shall ask in my name, that will I do, that the Father may be glorified in the Son."[11]

ASSURED ANSWERS

The answer to prayer is well assured when that answer is to glorify God the Father! The Lord Jesus Christ is eager to glorify His Father in heaven! He is so eager to answer prayer that always and everywhere brings glory to the Father, that no prayer offered in His name is denied or overlooked by Him. Our Lord Jesus Christ says again, giving fresh assurance to our faith, "If ye shall ask anything in my name, I will do it."[12] Then He says once more, "Ask what ye will, and it shall be done unto you."[13]

> Come, my soul, thy suit prepare,
> Jesus loves to answer prayer;
> He Himself has bid thee pray,
> Therefore will not say thee nay.

Endnotes

1 Excellent or ideal but impractical.
2 James 4:3
3 John 15:7
4 I Kings 18:37
5 John 15:7-8
6 John 11:41b-42
7 I Kings 17:24
8 Matthew 7:7
9 Psalm 65:2
10 I John 1:9
11 John 14:13
12 John 14:14
13 John 15:7

11

Answered Prayer (Continued)

CONSTRAINED AT THE DARKEST *hour to confess humbly that without God's help I was helpless, I vowed a vow in the forest solitude that I would confess His aid before men. A silence as a death was around me; it was midnight, I was weakened by illness, prostrated with fatigue and worn with anxiety for my white and black companions, whose fate was a mystery. In this physical and mental distress I besought God to give me back my people. Nine hours later we were exulting with rapturous joy. In full view of all was the crimson flag with the crescent and beneath its waving folds was the long-lost rear column.* (Henry M. Stanley)

God has committed Himself to us by His Word in our praying. The Word of God is the basis, inspiration, and heart of prayer. Jesus Christ stands as the illustration of God's Word, its unlimited good in promise, and its fulfillment. God takes nothing by halves. He gives nothing by halves. We can have the whole of Him when He has the whole of us. His words of promise are so far-reaching and so all-encompassing that they seem to have deadened our comprehension and have paralyzed our praying. This appears when we consider those large words in which God almost exhausts human language in promises—"whatever" and "anything," and the all-inclusive "whatsoever" and "all things." These great often-repeated promises seem to daze us, and instead of allowing them to move us to asking, testing, and receiving, we turn away full of wonder but with empty hands and empty hearts.

We quote another passage from our Lord's teaching about prayer. By the most solemn verification, He declares, "And in that day ye shall ask me nothing. Verily, verily, I say unto you, Whatsoever ye shall ask the Father in my name, he will give it you. Hitherto have ye asked nothing in my name: ask, and ye shall receive, that your joy may be full."[1]

Twice in this passage He declares the answer, and pledges also that His Father "will give it to you." He then declares with impressive and most suggestive repetition, "ask, and ye shall receive." So strong and so often did Jesus declare and repeat the certainty of the answer as an inducement to pray, and as an inevitable result of prayer, that the apostles held it as being fully and invincibly established. Prayer would be answered, and they considered it to be their main duty to urge and command Christians to pray. So firmly were they established as to the truth of the law of prayer as laid down by our Lord, that they were led to affirm that the answer to prayer was involved in and necessarily bound up with all right praying. God the Father and Jesus Christ His Son are both strongly committed by all the truth of their word and by the fidelity of their character to answer prayer.

SPECIFIC ANSWERS

Not only do these and all the promises pledge Almighty God to answer prayer, but they assure us that the answer will be specific, and that the very thing for which we pray will be given. Jesus said, "what man is there of you, whom if his son ask bread, will he give him a stone? Or if he ask a fish, will he give him a serpent? If ye then, being evil, know how to give good gifts unto your children, how much more shall your Father which is in heaven give good things to them that ask him?"[2]

Our Lord's invariable teaching was that we receive that for which we ask, obtain that for which we seek, and have that door opened at which we knock. This is according to our heavenly Father's direction to us, and His giving to us for our asking. He will not disappoint us by not answering. Also, He will not deny us by giving us some other thing for which we have not asked, by letting us find some other thing for which we have not sought, or by opening to us the wrong door at which we were not knocking. If we ask for bread, He will give us bread. If we ask for an egg, He will give us an egg. If we ask for a fish, He will give us a fish. Not something like bread, but bread itself will be given to us. Not something like a fish, but a fish will be given. Not evil will be given us in answer to prayer, but good.

Though evil in nature, earthly parents give to their children what they ask for—the specific thing asked for in answer to their asking. The encouragement to prayer is transferred from our earthly father to our heavenly Father, from the evil to the supremely good, from the weak to the omnipotent. Our Heavenly Father centers in Himself all the highest conceptions of Fatherhood—able and ready, much more than the best, and most blessed earthly parent. Who can tell how much more? Much more than our earthly parent. He will supply all our needs, give us all good things, and enable us to meet every difficult duty and fulfill every law. Whatever is hard to flesh and blood will be made easy under the full supply of our Father's beneficial and exhaustless help.

Here we have symbolized the necessity of perseverance in prayer and the progressive stages of intentness and effort in the outlay of increasing spiritual force—asking, seeking, knocking. Here is an ascending scale from the mere words of asking to a settled attitude of seeking that results in a determined, insistent, and vigorous direct effort of praying.

Just as God has commanded us to pray always, everywhere, and in everything, so He will answer always, everywhere, and in everything.

GOD HAS COMMITTED HIMSELF TO ANSWER PRAYER

God has plainly and with directness committed Himself to answer prayer. If we fulfill the conditions of prayer, the answer is bound to come. The laws of nature are not so invariable and so inexorable as the promised answer to prayer. The ordinances of nature might fail, but the ordinances of grace can never fail. There are no limitations, no adverse conditions, no weakness, no inability that can or will hinder the answer to prayer. God's doing for us when we pray has no limitations, is not hedged about by conditions in Himself, or in the peculiar circumstances of any particular case. If we really pray, God masters and defies all things and is above all conditions.

God specifically says, "Call unto me, and I will answer thee."[3] There are no limitations, no hedges, no hindrances in the way of God fulfilling the promise. His Word is at stake. His Word is involved. God solemnly promises to answer prayer. Christians are to look for the answer, be inspired by the expectation of the answer, and may with humble boldness demand the answer. God, who cannot lie,[4] is bound to answer. He has voluntarily placed Himself under obligation to answer the prayer of those who truly pray.

> To God your every want
> In instant prayer display;
> Pray always; pray, and never faint;
> Pray, without ceasing, pray.
>
> In fellowship, alone,
> To God with faith draw near;
> Approach His courts, beseech His throne,
> With all the power of prayer.

GOD'S PROMISES WILL BE FULFILLED

The prophets and the people of God of Old Testament times were unshaken in their faith in the absolute certainty of God fulfilling His promises to them. They rested in security on the word of God, and had no doubt whatever to the faithfulness of God in answering prayer or of His willingness or ability. So much so, that their history is marked by repeated asking and receiving at the hands of God,

The same is true of the early Church. They received without question the doctrine their Lord and Master had so often affirmed that the answer to prayer was sure. The certainty of the answer to prayer was as fixed as God's Word was true. The Holy Ghost dispensation was ushered in by the disciples carrying this faith into practice. When Jesus told them to "tarry ye in the city of Jerusalem, until ye be endued with power from on high," they received it as a sure promise that if they obeyed the command, they would certainly receive the divine power. So they tarried in the upper room in prayer for ten days, and the promise was fulfilled. The answer came just as Jesus said.

When Peter and John were arrested for healing the man who sat at the beautiful gate of the temple, they were threatened by the rulers in Jerusalem and then released. "And being let go, they went to their own company."[5] They went to those who were also Christians, those of like minds, and not to people of the world. Still believing in prayer and its effectiveness, they gave themselves to prayer. The prayer itself is recorded in the book of Acts, chapter four. First they recited some facts to the Lord, "And when they had prayed, the place was shaken where they were assembled together; and they were all filled with the Holy Ghost, and they spake the word of God with boldness."[6]

Here they were refilled with the Holy Ghost for this special occasion. The answer to prayer responded to their faith and prayer. The fullness of the Spirit always brings boldness. The cure for fear in the face of the threats of the enemies of the Lord is being filled with the Spirit. This gives power to speak the Word of the Lord with boldness. This gives courage and drives away fear.

Endnotes

1 John 16:23-24
2 Matthew 7:9-11
3 Jeremiah 33:3
4 Titus 1:2
5 Acts 4:23
6 Acts 4:31

12

Answered Prayer (Continued)

A YOUNG MAN HAD BEEN *called to the foreign field. He had not been in the habit of preaching, but he knew one thing, how to prevail with God; and going one day to a friend he said: "I don't see how God can use me on the field. I have no special talent." His friend said: "My brother, God wants men on the field who can pray. There are too many preachers now and too few prayers." He went. In his own room in the early dawn a voice was heard weeping and pleading for souls. All through the day, the shut door and the hush that prevailed made you feel like walking softly, for a soul was wrestling with God. Yet to this home, hungry souls would flock, drawn by some irresistible power. Ah, the mystery was unlocked. In the secret chamber lost souls were pleaded for and claimed. The Holy Ghost knew just where they were and sent them along.* (Hudson Taylor)

We put it to the front. We unfold it on a banner never to be lowered or folded—God does hear and answer prayer. God has always heard and answered prayer. God will forever hear and answer prayer. He is the same yesterday, today, and forever,[1] ever blessed, ever to be adored. Amen. He changes not.[2] He has always answered prayer, and He will ever continue to do so.

To answer prayer is God's universal rule. It is His unchangeable and irrepealable law. It is His invariable, specific, and inviolate promise. The few denials to prayer in the Scriptures are the exceptions to the general rule, suggestive and startling by their fewness and emphasis.

The possibilities of prayer, then, lie in the great truth that is unlimited in its broadness, fathomless in its depths, and exhaustless in its fullness. God answers every prayer from every true soul who truly prays.

God's Word does not say, "Call unto me, and you will thereby be trained into the happy art of knowing how to be denied. Ask, and you will learn sweet patience by getting nothing." Far from it. It is definite, clear, and positive: "Ask, and it shall be given you."[3]

THE PRAYER OF JABEZ

We have this case among many in the Old Testament:

And Jabez called on the God of Israel, saying, Oh that thou wouldest bless me indeed, and enlarge my coast, and that thine hand might be with me, and that thou wouldest keep me from evil, that it may not grieve me! And God granted him that which he requested.[4]

Hannah was distressed in soul because she was childless. Desiring a man child, she went to the house of prayer and prayed. This is the record of the direct answer she received: "For this child I prayed; and the Lord hath given me the petition which I asked of him."[5]

THOSE WHO ASK

God's promises and purposes go direct to the fact of giving for the asking. The answer to our prayers is the motive constantly presented in the Scriptures to encourage us to pray and to quicken us in this spiritual exercise. Take such strong, clear, passages as these:

"Call unto me, and I will answer thee." [6]

"He shall call unto me, and I will answer him." [7]

"Ask, and it shall be given you; seek, and ye shall find; knock, and it shall be opened unto you." [8]

This is Jesus Christ's law of prayer. He does not say, "Ask, and something shall be given you." Nor does He say, "Ask, and you will be trained into piety." He says, instead, that when you ask the very thing you asked for will be given. Jesus does not say, "Knock, and some door will be opened." But the very door at which you are knocking will be opened. To make this doubly sure, Jesus Christ duplicates and reiterates the promise of the answer: "For every one that asketh receiveth; and he that seeketh findeth; and to him that knocketh it shall be opened."[9]

Answered prayer is the spring of love, and is the direct encouragement to pray. "I love the Lord, because he hath heard my voice and my supplications. Because he hath inclined his ear unto me, therefore will I call upon him as long as I live."[10]

CERTAINTY OF GOD'S GIVING

The certainty of the Father's giving is assured by the Father's relation, and by the ability and goodness of the Father. Earthly parents, frail, infirm, and limited in goodness and ability, give when the child asks and seeks. The parental heart responds most readily to the cry for bread. The hunger of the child touches and wins the parent's heart. Being greater in all ways, God our heavenly Father is much more easily and strongly moved by our prayers than the earthly parent. "If ye then, being evil, know how to give good gifts unto your children, how much more shall your Father which is in heaven give good things to them that ask him?"[11] "Much more,"—just as God's goodness, tenderness, and ability exceeds the capability of people to be good and tender.

Just as the asking is specific, so also is the answer specific. The child does not ask for one thing and get another. It does not cry for bread, and get a stone. It does not ask for an egg, and receive a scorpion. It does not ask for a fish, and get a serpent. God demands specific asking. He responds to specific praying by specific giving.

WHAT GOD GIVES

To give the very thing prayed for, and not something else, is fundamental to Christ's law of praying. He never answered a prayer for the cure of blind eyes by curing deaf ears. The very thing prayed for is the very thing that He gives. Those who asks for bread get bread, and not a stone. If they asks for a fish, they receive a fish, and not a serpent. No cry is so pleading and so powerful as the child's cry for bread. The cravings of hunger and the need for food create and propel the crying of the child. Our prayers must be as earnest, as needy, and as desperate as the hungry child's cry for bread. Our praying must be simple, artless, direct, and specific, according to Christ's law of prayer and His teaching of God's fatherhood.

The illustration and enforcement of the law of prayer are found in the specific answers given to prayer. Gethsemane is the only seeming exception. The prayer of Jesus Christ in that awful hour of darkness and pain was conditioned on these words, "If it be possible, let this cup pass from me."[12] But beyond these utterances of our Lord was the soul and life prayer of the willing, suffering, divine victim, "Nevertheless not as I will, but as thou wilt." The prayer was answered, the angel came, strength was imparted, and the meek sufferer in silence drank the bitter cup.

CASE STUDY: TWO UNANSWERED PRAYERS

Two cases of unanswered prayer are recorded in the Scriptures in addition to the Gethsemane prayer of our Lord. The first was that of David for the life of his baby child, but for Almighty God's good reasons the request was not granted.[13] The second was that of Paul for the removal of the thorn in the flesh,[14] which was denied. But we these are notable exceptions to God's rule, as shown in the history of prophet, priest, apostle, and saint recorded in the divine Word. There must have been unrevealed reasons that moved God to veer from His settled and fixed rule to answer prayer by giving the specific thing prayed for.

Our Lord did not hold the Syrophenician woman in the school of unanswered prayer in order to test and mature her faith, neither did He answer her prayer by healing or saving her husband. She asks for the healing of her daughter, and Christ healed the daughter. She received the very thing for which she asked the Lord Jesus Christ. It was in the school of answered prayer that our Lord disciplined and perfected her faith, and it was by giving her a specific answer to her prayer. Her prayer centered on her daughter. She prayed for one thing, the healing of her child. The answer of our Lord centered likewise on the daughter, and He healed her.[15]

WE OFTEN IGNORE GOD'S PROMISES

We tread altogether too gingerly upon the great and precious promises of God, and too often we ignore them wholly. The promise is the ground on which faith stands in asking of God. This is the one basis of prayer. We limit God's ability. We measure God's ability and willingness to answer prayer by the standard of people. We limit the Holy One of Israel.[16] How full of benefits and remedy to suffering humankind are the promises as given us by James in the fifth chapter of his Epistle![17] How personal and involved they make God in prayer! They are a direct challenge to our faith. They are encouraging to large expectations in all the requests we make of God. Prayer affects God in a direct manner, and has its aim and end in affecting Him. Prayer takes hold of God, and induces Him to do large things for us, whether personal or relative, temporal or spiritual, earthly or heavenly.

THE GREAT GAP

The great gap between Bible promises to prayer and the answers from praying is almost unspeakably great, so much so that it is a abundant source of unfaithfulness. It breeds unbelief in prayer as a great moral force, and creates doubt of the effectiveness of prayer. Christianity needs today, above everything else, men and women who can in prayer put God to the test and who can prove His promises. When this happy day for the world begins, it will be earth's brightest day, and will be heaven's dawning day on earth. These are the sort of men and women needed in this modern day in the Church. It is not educated people who are needed for the times. It is not more money that is required. It is not more machinery, more organization, more ecclesiastical laws, but it is men and women who know how to pray. Those who can in prayer lay hold upon God and bring Him down to earth, and move Him to take hold of earth's affairs mightily and put life and power into the Church and into all of its machinery.

The Church and the world greatly need saints who can bridge this wide gap between the praying done and the small number of answers received. Saints are needed whose faith is bold enough and sufficiently far-reaching to put God to the test. The cry comes even now out of heaven to the people of today's Church, as it sounded forth in the days of Malachi: "Prove me now herewith, saith the LORD of hosts." God is waiting to be put to the test by His people in prayer. He delights in being put to the test on His promises. It is His highest pleasure to answer prayer, to prove the reliability of His promises. Nothing worthy of God or of great value to humanity will be accomplished till this is done.

OUR MIRACULOUS GOSPEL

It was projected in the miraculous realm. It cannot be maintained but by the supernatural. Take the supernatural out of our holy Christianity, and its life and power are gone. It then degenerates into a mere mode of morals. The miraculous is divine power. Prayer has in it this same power. Prayer brings this divine power into the ranks of men and women and puts it to work. Prayer brings into the affairs of earth a supernatural element. Our Gospel when truly presented is the power of God.[18] Never was the Church more in need of those who can and will test Almighty God. Never did the Church need more than now those who can raise up everywhere memorials of God's supernatural power, memorials of answers to prayer, memorials of promises fulfilled. These would do more to silence the enemy of souls, the foe of God and the adversary of the Church than any modern scheme or present-day plan for the success of the Gospel. Such memorials reared by praying people would dumbfound God's foes, strengthen weak saints, and would fill strong saints with triumphant rapture.

The most prolific source of unfaithfulness, and that which disgraces and hinders praying, and that which obscures the being and glory of God most effectively, is unanswered prayer. Better not to pray at all than to go through a dead form that secures no answer, brings no glory to God, and supplies no good to people. Nothing so hardens the heart and so blinds us to the unseen and the eternal as this kind of prayerless praying.

Endnotes

1 Hebrews 13:8
2 Malachi 3:6
3 Matthew 7:7
4 I Chronicles 4:10
5 I Samuel 1:27
6 Jeremiah 33:3
7 Psalm 91:15
8 Matthew 7:7
9 Matthew 7:8

10 Psalm 116:1-2
11 Matthew 7:11
12 Matthew 26:39
13 2 Samuel 12:15-19
14 2 Corinthians 7-10
15 Mark 7:24-30
16 Psalm 78:41
17 James 5:13-18
18 Romans 1:16; 1 Thessalonians 1:5

13

Prayer Miracles

GEORGE BENFIELD, A DRIVER *on the Midland Railway, living at Derby, was standing on the footplate oiling his engine, the train being stationary, when his foot slipped; he fell on the space between the lines. He heard the express coming on, and had only time enough to lie full length on the "six-foot" when it rushed by, and he escaped unhurt. He returned to his home in the middle of the night and as he was going upstairs he heard one of his children, a girl about eight years old, crying and sobbing. "Oh, father," she said, "I thought somebody came and told me that you were going to be killed, and I got out of bed and prayed that God would not let you die." Was it only a dream, a coincidence? George Benfield and others believed that he owed his life to that prayer.* (Dean Hole)

The earthly career of our Lord Jesus Christ was no mere episode, a sort of interlude, in His eternal life. What He was and what He did on earth was neither abnormal nor different, but characteristic. What He was and what He did on earth is but the figure and the illustration of what He is and what He is doing in heaven. He is "the same yesterday, and today, and forever."[1] This statement is the divine summary of the eternal unity and changelessness of His character. His earthly life was made up largely of hearing and answering prayer. His heavenly life is devoted to the same divine business. The Old Testament is really the record of God hearing and answering prayer. The whole Bible deals largely with this all important subject.

CHRIST'S MIRACLES ARE OBJECT LESSONS

Christ's miracles are living pictures. They talk to us. They have hands that take hold of us. They teach us many valuable lessons. In their diversity, they refresh us. They show us the matchless power of Jesus Christ, and at the same time reveal to us His marvelous compassion for suffering humanity. These miracles disclose to us His ability to endlessly diversify His operations. God's method in working with humanity is not the same in all cases. He does not administer His grace in rigid ruts. There is endless variety in His movements. There is marvelous diversity in His operations. He does not fashion His creations in the same mold. Just so our Lord is not restricted in His working nor restrained by models. He works independently. He is His own architect. He furnishes His own patterns, which have unlimited variety.

When we examine our Lord's miracles, we discover that quite a number were performed unconditionally. At least there were no conditions accompanying them so far as the divine record shows. To glorify God and to manifest His own glory and power, He often peformed miracles without being asked to do so. Many of His mighty works were performed at the moving of His compassion and at the call of suffering and need, as well as at the call of His power. But a number of them were performed by Him in answer to prayer. Some were wrought in answer to the personal prayers of those who were afflicted. Others were performed in answer to the prayers of the friends of those who were afflicted. Those miracles wrought in answer to prayer are very instructive in the uses of prayer.

FAITH AND PRAYER REQUIRED FOR MIRACLES

In these conditional miracles, faith is foremost and prayer is faith's agent. We have an illustration of the importance of faith as the condition on which the exercise of Jesus' power was based, or the channel through which it flowed, in the incident of a visit He made to Nazareth and its lack of results. Here is the record of the case:

> And he could there do no mighty work, save that he laid his hands upon a few sick folk, and healed them. And he marvelled because of their unbelief.[2]

Those people at Nazareth may have asked our Lord to raise their dead, open the eyes of the blind, or heal the lepers, but it was all in vain.[3] The absence of faith, however much of performance may be seen, restrains the exercise of God's power, paralyzes the arm of Christ, and turns to death all signs of life. Unbelief is the one thing that seriously hinders Almighty God in doing mighty works. Matthew's record of this visit to Nazareth says, "And he did not any mighty works there because of their unbelief." Lack of faith ties the hands of Almighty God in His working among His children. Prayer to Christ must always be based, backed, and impregnated with faith.

RAISING LAZARUS FROM THE DEAD

The miracle of miracles in the earthly career of our Lord, the raising of Lazarus from the dead, was remarkable for its prayer accompaniment. It was really a prayer issue, something after the issue between the prophets of Baal and Elijah. It was not a prayer for help. It was one of thanksgiving and assured confidence. Let us read it:

> And Jesus lifted up His eyes, and said, Father, I thank Thee that Thou hast heard me. And I knew that Thou hearest Me always: but because of the people which stand by I said it, that they may believe that Thou hast sent Me.[4]

It was a prayer mainly for the benefit of those who were present, that they might know that God was with Him because He had answered His prayers, and that faith in God might be radiated in their hearts.

ANSWERED PRAYERS CREATE FAITH

Answered prayers are sometimes the most convincing and faith-creating forces. Unanswered prayers chill the atmosphere and freeze the soil of faith. If Christians knew how to pray so as to have answers to their prayers—immediate, evident, and demonstrative answers from God—faith would be more widely diffused, would become more general, more profound, and a much more mighty force in the world.

The miracle of the healing of the centurion's servant brings to us a valuable lesson of faith and intercessory prayer. The simplicity and strength of the faith of this Roman officer are remarkable, for He believed that it was not necessary for our Lord to go directly to his house in order to have his request granted: "but speak the word only, and my servant shall be healed."[5] Our Lord puts His mark upon this officer's faith by saying, "Verily I say unto you, I have not found so great faith, no, not in Israel."[6] This centurion's statement was an expression of strong faith, and such faith brought the answer promptly.

We get the same invaluable lesson from the prayer miracle of the case of the Syrophenician woman who went to our Lord in behalf of her stricken daughter, making her daughter's case her own by pleading, "Lord, help me."[7] Here was importunity—holding on, pressing her case, refusing to let go or to be denied. It was a strong case of intercessory prayer and its benefits. Our Lord seemingly held her off for a while but at last yielded, and put His seal upon her strong faith: "O woman, great is thy faith: be it unto thee even as thou wilt."[8] What a lesson on praying for others and its large benefits!

INTERCEDING FOR OURSELVES

Individual cases could be named where the afflicted persons interceded for themselves. They are illustrations of wonderful things done by our Lord in answer to the cries of those who were afflicted. As we read the Gospels, the pages fairly glisten with records of our Lord's miracles performed in answer to prayer, showing the wonderful things accomplished by the use of this divinely appointed means of grace.

If we turn back to Old Testament times, we have no lack of instances of prayer miracles. The saints of those days were well acquainted with the power of prayer to move God to do great things. Natural laws did not stand in the way of Almighty God when He was appealed to by His praying ones. What a marvelous record is that of Moses as those successive plagues were visited upon Egypt in the effort to make Pharaoh let the children of Israel go that they might serve God! As one after another of these plagues came, Pharaoh would beseech Moses, "Entreat the LORD your God, that he may take away from me this death only."[9]

The plagues themselves were miracles, and prayer removed them as quickly as they were sent by Almighty God. The same hand that sent these destructive agencies upon Egypt was moved by the prayers of His servant Moses to remove these same plagues. The removal of the plagues in answer to prayer was as remarkable a display of divine power as was the sending of the plagues in the first instance. The removal in answer to prayer would do as much to show God's being and His power as would the plagues themselves.

PRAYER MIRACLES IN OLD TESTAMENT DAYS

God's praying servants had not the least doubt that prayer would work marvelous results and bring the supernatural into the affairs of earth. Miracles and prayer went hand in hand. They were companions. The one was the cause, the other was the effect. The one brought the other into existence. The miracle was the proof that God heard and answered prayer. The miracle was the divine demonstration that God, who was in heaven, was involved in earth's affairs—intervening to help people, and working supernaturally if need be to accomplish His purposes in answer to prayer.

PRAYER MIRACLES IN THE EARLY CHURCH

Looking at the days of the early Church, we find the same divine record of prayer miracles. The sad news came to Peter that Dorcas was dead and he was wanted at Joppa. Promptly he made his way to that place. He put everybody out of the death room, knelt down and prayed, and then with faith said, "Tabitha, arise," and she opened her eyes and sat up.[10] Knee work on the part of Peter did the work. Prayer brought things to pass and saved Dorcas for further work on earth.

Paul was on that noted journey to Rome under guard and had been shipwrecked on an island. The chief man of the island was Publius, and his old father was critically ill of a fever and a bloody discharge. Paul laid his hands on the old man, prayed for him, and God came to the rescue and healed the sick man.[11] Prayer brought the thing desired to pass. God interfered with the laws of nature, either suspending or setting them aside for a season, and answered the prayer of this praying servant of His. The answer to prayer among those heathen people convinced them that a supernatural power was at work among them. In fact, so true was this that many more came to Paul to be healed, and they honored Paul and those with him and gave them many gifts.[12]

Peter was put in prison by Herod, who had killed James with the sword. The young Church was greatly concerned, but they neither lost heart nor gave themselves over to needless fretting and worrying. They had learned before this from where their help came. They had been schooled in the lesson of prayer. God had intervened before in the behalf of His servants when His cause was at stake. So the Church prayed for Peter: "prayer was made without ceasing of the Church unto God for him."[13] An angel on swift wings came to the rescue, and in a marvelous and supernatural way released Peter and left the prison doors locked. Locks and prison doors and an unfriendly king cannot stand in the way of Almighty God when His people cry in prayer to Him. If needed, miracles will be performed in their behalf to fulfill His promises and to carry forward His plans.

SAMSON AND MIRACLES

The Word of God illustrates, enlarges, and confirms the possibilities of prayer by what may be called "prayer miracles." God performed a wonderful work through Samson in enabling him to slay a thousand men with the jawbone of an ass, thereby giving him a great deliverance. Shortly afterward he was abnormally thirsty, and he was unable to obtain any water. It seemed as if he would perish with thirst. God had saved him from the hands of the Philistines, could He not as well save him from thirst? So Samson cried unto the Lord, and "God clave a hollow place that was in the jaw, and there came water thereout; and when he had drunk, his spirit came again, and he revived."[14] God could bring water out of the jaw bone just as well as He could give victory by it to Samson. God could change that which had been death-dealing to His enemies and make it life-giving to His servant. God can and will work a miracle in answer to prayer in order to deliver His friends, sooner than He will work one to destroy His enemies. He does both, however, in answer to prayer.

ALL NATURAL FORCES ARE UNDER GOD'S CONTROL

God did not create the world and put it under law, and then leave it alone to work out its own destiny, unconcerned about the welfare of His intelligent creatures. Natural laws are simply God's laws by which He governs and regulates all things in nature. Nature is nothing but God's servant. God is above nature, not the slave of nature. This being true, God can and will suspend the working of nature's laws. He can suspend them by His almighty hand, and for a time set them aside to fulfill His higher purposes in redemption. It is no violation of nature's laws when, in answer to prayer, He who is above nature makes nature His servant, and causes nature to carry out His plans and purposes.

This is the explanation of that wonderful prayer miracle of Old Testament times, when in the strength and power of the Lord God Joshua commanded the sun and moon to stand still in order to give time to complete the victory over the enemies of Israel. Why should it be thought an incredible thing that the God of nature and of grace should interfere with His own natural laws for a short season in answer to prayer, and for the good of His cause? Is God tied hand and foot? Has He so restricted Himself that He cannot operate the law of prayer? Is the law of nature superior to the law of prayer? Not by any means. He is the God of prayer as well as the God of nature. Both prayer and nature have God as their Maker, their Ruler and their Executor. Prayer is God's servant, just as nature is His servant.

PRAYER FORCE

The prayer force in God's government is as strong as any other force, and all natural and other forces must give way before the force of prayer. Sun, moon, and stars are under God's control in answer to prayer. Rain, sunshine, and drought obey His will. "Fire, and hail; snow, and vapors; stormy wind fulfilling his word."[15] Disease and health are governed by Him. All things in heaven and earth are absolutely under the control of Him who made heaven and earth, and who governs all things according to His own will.

Prayer still works miracles among people and brings to pass great things. It is as true now as when James wrote his Epistle, "The effectual fervent prayer of a righteous man availeth much."[16] When the records of eternity are read out to an assembled world, then it will be revealed how much prayer has accomplished in this world. Little is now seen of the fruits of prayer compared to all that it has accomplished and is accomplishing. At the judgment day, God will reveal the things that were brought to pass in this world through the prayers of the saints. Many occurrences that are now taken as a matter of course will then be seen to have happened because of the Lord's praying ones.

GEORGE MÜLLER

The work of George Müller in Bristol, England, was a miracle of the nineteenth century. It will take the opening of the books at the great judgment day to disclose all he brought about through prayer. His orphanage in which hundreds of fatherless and motherless children were cared for, and for which this godly man never asked anyone for money with which to pay its expenses, is a marvel of modern times. His practice was always to ask God for just what was needed, and the answers that came to him read like a record of apostolic times. He prayed for everything and trusted implicitly to God to supply all his needs. It is a matter of record that never did he, his staff, or the orphans ever lack for any good thing.

It was said at the burial of a holy person who had done much for Christ and suffering humanity, "He prayed up the walls of a hospital, and the hearts of the nurses. He prayed mission stations into being, and missionaries into faith. He prayed open the hearts of the rich, and gold from the most distant lands."

THE CHRISTIAN'S TRADE

Martin Luther is quoted as once saying, "The Christian's trade is praying." For a great reason the preacher's trade should be praying. We fear greatly that many preachers know nothing of this trade of praying, and so they never succeed at this trade. A severe apprenticeship in the trade of praying must be served in order to become qualified in it. Not only is it true that there are few qualified persons at work at this praying trade, but numbers have never even been apprentices at praying. No wonder so little is accomplished by them. God and the supernatural are left out of their programs.

Many do not understand this trade of praying because they have never learned it, and so they do not work at it. Why should many miracles not take place in answer to our prayers? Is the arm of the Lord shortened that He cannot save? Is His ear heavy that He cannot hear? Has prayer lost its power because sin abounds and the love of many has grown cold? Has God changed from what He once was? To all these questions we enter an emphatic 'no'. God can as easily work miracles today through prayer as He did in the days of old. "I am the LORD; I change not."[17] "Is anything too hard for the Lord?"[18]

Those who works miracles by praying will first of all work the chief miracle on themselves. Oh, that we might fully understand the Christian's trade of praying, follow the trade day by day, and gather to ourselves great spiritual wealth!

Endnotes

1 Hebrews 13:8
2 Mark 6:5-6
3 Editor's note: More than likely they did not ask Him to heal any of their sick because of their unbelief, for there is no record of Jesus failing to heal anyone who asked Him.

4 John 11:41b-42
5 Matthew 8:8
6 Matthew 8:10
7 Matthew 15:25
8 Matthew 15:28
9 Exodus 10:17
10 Acts 9:40
11 Acts 28:7-8
12 Acts 28:9-10
13 Acts 12:5
14 Judges 15:19
15 Psalm 148:8
16 James 5:16
17 Malachi 3:6
18 Genesis 18:14

14

Wonders of God Through Prayer

WISDOM AND REVELATION DISTINGUISHED *by experience and Scripture. By experience. Take a weak understanding (but one exceedingly holy), having little knowledge of God by way of discursive wisdom and laying this thing to that, and so knowing God: such a poor soul is oftentimes hardly able to speak wisely and he will know more of God in one prayer than a great scholar (though also very holy) hath known of Him in all his life; God often deals thus with the weak who are very holy; for if such were shut up to knowing God by way of a sanctified reason, large understandings would have infinite advantage of them and they would grow little in grace and holiness; therefore God makes a supply by breaking in upon their spirits by such irradiations as these.* (Thomas Goodwin)

In the fearful contest in this world between God and the devil, between good and evil, and between heaven and hell, prayer is the mighty force for overcoming Satan, giving dominion over sin, and defeating hell. Only praying leaders are to be counted on in this dreadful conflict. Praying men and women alone are to be put to the front. These are the only sort who are able to successfully contend with all the evil forces.

The "prayers of all saints"[1] are a perpetual force against all the powers of darkness. These prayers are a mighty energy in overcoming the world, the flesh, and the devil. Also in shaping the destiny of God's movements to overcome evil and get the victory over the devil and all his works. The character and energy of God's movements lie in prayer. Victory is to come at the end of praying.

THE WONDERS OF GOD

The wonders of God's power are to be kept alive, made real and present, and repeated only by prayer. God is not now so evident in the world, so almighty in manifestation as of old. Not because miracles have passed away, or because God has ceased to work, but because prayer has been deprived of its simplicity, majesty, and power. God still lives, and miracles still live while God lives and acts, for miracles are God's ways of acting. Prayer is dwarfed, withered, and petrified when faith in God is staggered by doubts of His ability, or through the shrinking caused by fear. When faith has a telescopic, far-off, vision of God, prayer works no miracles and brings no marvels of deliverance. But when God is seen by faith's closest, fullest eye prayer creates a history of wonders.

Think about God. Make much of Him until He broadens and fills the horizon of faith. Then prayer will come into its marvelous inheritance of wonders. The marvels of prayer are seen when we remember that God's purposes are changed by prayer, God's vengeance is stopped by prayer, and God's penalty is remitted by prayer. The whole range of God's dealing with humanity is affected by prayer. Prayer is a force that must be increasingly used, a force to which all the events of life should be subjected.

PRAY WITHOUT CEASING

We are commanded to "pray without ceasing,"[2] to pray in everything, and to pray everywhere. These commands of continuity are expressive of the sleepless energy of prayer, of the exhaustless possibilities of prayer, and of its exacting necessity. Prayer can do all things. Prayer must do all things.

> Prayer is the simplest form of speech
> That infant lips can try;
> Prayer the noblest strains that reach
> The majesty on high.

Prayer is asking God for something, and for something that He has promised. Prayer is using the divinely appointed means for obtaining what we need and for accomplishing what God proposes to do on earth.

> Prayer is appointed to convey
> The blessings God designs to give;
> Long as they live should Christians pray,
> They learn to pray when first they live.

Prayer brings to us blessings that we need, that only God can give, and that prayer can alone bring to us.

POSSIBILITIES AND THE NATURE OF PRAYER

In their broadest fullness, the possibilities of prayer are to be found in the very nature of prayer. This service of prayer is not a mere ritual, a ceremony that we go through, or a sort of performance. Prayer is going to God for something needed and desired. Prayer is simply asking God to do for us what He has promised us He will do if we ask Him. The answer is a part of prayer, and is God's part of it. God's doing the thing asked for is as much a part of the prayer as the asking for the thing is prayer. Asking is our part. Giving is God's part. The praying belongs to us. The answer belongs to God.

We makes the plea and God makes the answer. The plea and the answer compose the prayer. God is more ready, more willing, and more anxious to give the answer than we are to give the asking. The possibilities of prayer lie in our ability to ask large things and God's ability to give large things.

THE CHARACTER OF THE PERSON PRAYING

God's only condition and limitation of prayer is found in the character of the person who prays. The measure of our faith and praying is the measure of His giving. As our Lord said to the blind man, "According to your faith be it unto you,"[3] so it is the same in praying: "According to the measure of your asking, be it unto you." God measures the answer according to the prayer. He is limited by the law of prayer in the measure of the answers He gives to prayer. As is the measure of prayer, so will be the answer. The measure of the prayer determines the measure of the answer.

If the person praying has the characteristics that warrant praying, then the possibilities are unlimited. They are declared to be "all things whatsoever."[4] There is no limit in character or kind, in circumference or condition. The person who prays can pray for anything and for everything, and God will give everything and anything. If we limit God in the asking, He will be limited in the giving.

Looking ahead, God declares in His Word that the wonder of wonders will be so great in the last days that everything animate and inanimate will be excited by His power:

> For, behold, I create new heavens and a new earth: and the former shall not be remembered, nor come into mind. But be ye glad and rejoice for ever in that which I create: for, behold, I create Jerusalem a rejoicing, and her people a joy.[5]

DAYS OF MAGNIFICENT PRAYING

But these days of God's mighty working, the days of His magnificent and wonder-creating power, will be days of magnificent praying. "And it shall come to pass, that before they call, I will answer; and while they are yet speaking, I will hear."[6]

It has always been so. God's marvelous, miracle-working, times have been times of marvelous, miracle-working, praying. The greatest thing in God's worship by His own estimate is praying. Its chief service and its distinguishing feature is prayer:

Even them will I bring to my holy mountain, and make them joyful in my house of prayer: their burnt offerings and their sacrifices shall be accepted upon mine altar; for mine house shall be called an house of prayer for all people.[7]

This was true under all the gorgeous rites and parade of ceremonies under the Jewish worship. Sacrifice, offering, and the atoning blood were all to be impregnated with prayer. The smoke of burnt offering and perfumed incense that filled God's house was to be but the flame of prayer, and all of God's people were to be anointed priests to minister at His altar of prayer. So all things were to be done with mighty prayer, because mighty prayer was the result and inspiration of mighty faith. Under the more simple service of the Gospel, it is now much more true in every way.

PRAYER AFFECTS EVERYTHING

The course of nature, movements of the planets, and the clouds have yielded to the influence of prayer. God has changed and checked the order of the sun and the seasons under the mighty energies of prayer. It is only necessary to note the remarkable incident when Joshua, through this divine means of prayer, caused the sun and the moon to stand still so that a more complete victory could be given to the Israel in the battle with the Amorites.[8]

IF WE BELIEVE GOD'S WORD

If we believe God's Word, we are bound to believe that prayer affects God and affects Him mightily, and that prayer avails and avails mightily. There are wonders in prayer because there are wonders in God. Prayer has no mystical influence. It is no mere charm. It has no so-called powers of magic. It is simply making known our requests to God for things agreeable to His will in the name of Jesus Christ. It is just yielding our requests to a Father who knows all things, who has control of all things, and who is able to do all things. Prayer is infinite ignorance trusting to the wisdom of God. Prayer is the voice of need crying out to Him who is inexhaustible in resources. Prayer is helplessness reposing with childlike confidence on the word of its Father in heaven. Prayer is but the verbal expression of a heart of perfect confidence in the infinite wisdom, power, and riches of Almighty God—who has placed at our command in prayer everything we need.

God's Word teaches us how all the gracious results of such gracious times are to come to the world through prayer. God's heart seems to overflow with delight at the prospect of so blessing His people. By the mouth of the prophet Joel, God said:

Fear not, O land; be glad and rejoice: for the Lord will do great things. Be not afraid, ye beasts of the field: for the pastures of the wilderness do spring, for the tree beareth her fruit, the fig tree and the vine do yield their strength. Be glad then, ye children of Zion, and rejoice in the Lord your God: for he hath given you the former rain moderately, and he will cause to come down for you the rain, the former rain, and the latter rain in the first month. And the floors shall be full of wheat, and the fats shall overflow with wine and oil. And I will restore to you the years that the locust hath eaten, the cankerworm, and the caterpiller, and the palmerworm, my great army which I sent among you. And ye shall eat in plenty, and be satisfied, and praise the name of the Lord your God, that hath dealt wondrously with you: and my people shall never be ashamed. And ye shall know that I am in the midst of Israel, and that I am the Lord your God, and none else: and my people shall never be ashamed.[9]

MARVELOUS MATERIAL BLESSINGS

What wonderful material things are these that God proposes to bestow upon His people! They are marvelous temporal blessings He promises to bestow on them. They almost astonish the mind when they are studied. But God does not restrict His large blessings to temporal things. Looking down the ages, He foresees Pentecost, and makes these exceeding great and precious promises concerning the outpouring of the Holy Spirit.

On that great day of Pentecost, Peter quoted these very words from the book of Joel.

And it shall come to pass afterward, that I will pour out my spirit upon all flesh; and your sons and your daughters shall prophesy, your old men shall dream dreams, your young men shall see visions: And also upon the servants and upon the handmaids in those days will I pour out my spirit. And I will shew wonders in the heavens and in the earth, blood, and fire, and pillars of smoke. The sun shall be turned into darkness, and the moon into blood, before the great and the terrible day of the Lord come. And it shall come to pass, that whosoever shall call on the name of the Lord shall be delivered: for in mount Zion and in Jerusalem shall be deliverance, as the Lord hath said, and in the remnant whom the Lord shall call.[10]

But these marvelous blessings will not be bestowed upon the people by sovereign power, or be given unconditionally. God's people must do something prior to such glorious results. Fasting and prayer must play an important part as conditions of receiving such large blessings. By the mouth of the same prophet, God says:

Therefore also now, saith the Lord, turn ye even to me with all your heart, and with fasting, and with weeping, and with mourning: And rend your heart, and not your garments, and turn unto the Lord your God: for he is gracious and merciful, slow to anger, and of great kindness, and repenteth him of the evil. Who knoweth if he will return and repent, and leave a blessing behind him; even a meat offering and a drink offering unto the Lord your God?

Blow the trumpet in Zion, sanctify a fast, call a solemn assembly: Gather the people, sanctify the congregation, assemble the elders, gather the children, and those that suck the breasts: let the bridegroom go forth of his chamber, and the bride out of her closet. Let the priests, the ministers of the Lord, weep between the porch and the altar, and let them say, Spare thy people, O Lord, and give not thine heritage to reproach, that the heathen should rule over them: wherefore should they say among the people, Where is their God?

Then will the Lord be jealous for his land, and pity his people. Yea, the Lord will answer and say unto his people, Behold, I will send you corn, and wine, and oil, and ye shall be satisfied therewith: and I will no more make you a reproach among the heathen.[11]

PRAYER REACHES THE PRESENCE OF GOD

Thus it reaches everywhere, because God is everywhere. Let us read what the inspired psalmist wrote.

If I ascend up into heaven, thou art there: if I make my bed in hell, behold, thou art there. If I take the wings of the morning, and dwell in the uttermost parts of the sea; Even there shall thy hand lead me, and thy right hand shall hold me.[12]

This may be said as truly of prayer as it is said of the God of prayer. The mysteries of death have been penetrated by prayer, and its victims have been brought back to life by the power of prayer—because God reigns over death and prayer reaches where God reigns. Elijah[13] and Elisha[14] both invaded the realms of death by their prayers, and asserted and established the power of God as the power of prayer. By prayer Peter brings back to life the saintly Dorcas to the early Church.[15] Paul, doubtless, exercised the power of prayer as he fell upon and embraced Eutychus who fell out of the window when Paul preached at night.[16]

Our Lord several times clearly declared the far-reaching possibilities and the unlimited nature of prayer as covering "all things whatsoever." The conditions of prayer are exalted into a personal union with Him. That successful praying glorified God was the condition upon which laborers of first quality and sufficient in numbers were to be secured in order to press forward God's work in the world.[17] The giving of all good things is conditioned upon asking for them. The giving of the Holy Spirit to God's children is based upon the asking of the children of God.[18] God's will on earth can only be secured by prayer. Daily bread is obtained and sanctified by prayer. Reverence, forgiveness of sins, deliverance from the evil one, and salvation from temptation are all in the hands of prayer.[19]

The first jeweled foundation Jesus lays as the basic principle of His Church in the Sermon on the Mount reads this way: "Blessed are the poor in spirit: for theirs is the kingdom of heaven."[20] Prayer follows from the inner sense of need, and is the utterance of a deep poverty-stricken spirit. So it is evident that those who are "poor in spirit" are where they can pray and where they do pray.

THE TREMENDOUS FORCE OF PRAYER

Take this picture of prayer and its wonderful possibilities. God's cause is quiet and motionless on the earth. An angel, strong and impatient to be of service, waits round about the throne of God in heaven. Then in order to move things on earth and give impetus to the movements of God's cause in this world, he gathers all the prayers of all God's saints in all ages, and puts them before God. In the same way that Aaron used to cloud, flavor, and sweeten himself with the delicious incense when he entered the holy sanctuary, made awesome by the immediate presence of God.[21] The angel impregnates all the air with that holy offering of prayers, and then takes its fiery body and casts it on the earth.

Note the remarkable result. "There were voices, and thunderings, and lightnings, and an earthquake."[22] What tremendous force is this that has thus convulsed the earth? The answer is that it is the "prayers of the saints," turned loose by the angel round about the throne, who has charge of those prayers. This mighty force is prayer, like the power of earth's mightiest explosive.

Take another fact showing the wonders of prayer brought about by Almighty God in answer to the praying of His true prophet. The nation of God's people was fearfully apostate in head and heart and life. A man of God went to the apostate king with the fearful message that meant so much to the land, "There shall not be rain nor dew these years, but according to my word."[23] From where came this mighty force that can stay the clouds, seal up the rain, and hold back the dew? Who is this who speaks with such authority? Is there any force that can do this on earth? Only one, and that force is prayer, wielded in the hands of a praying prophet of God. It is he who has influence with God and over God in prayer, who thus dares to assume such authority over the forces of nature. This man Elijah is skilled in the use of that tremendous force. "Elijah . . . prayed earnestly that it might not rain: and it rained not on the earth by the space of three years and six months."[24]

THE MIGHTY POWER OF PRAYER

But this is not all the story. He who could by prayer lock up the clouds and seal up the rain, could also unlock the clouds and unseal the rain by the same mighty power of prayer. "And he prayed again, and the heaven gave rain, and the earth gave forth her fruit."[25]

Mighty is the power of prayer. Wonderful are its fruits. Remarkable things are brought to pass by people of prayer. Many are the wonders of prayer worked by God's almighty hand. The evidences of prayer's accomplishments almost stagger us. They challenge our faith. They encourage our expectations when we pray.

From brief examples like this we get a bird's-eye view of the large possibilities of prayer and the urgent necessity of prayer. We see how God commits Himself into the hands of those who truly pray. Great are the wonders of prayer because great is the God who hears and answers prayer. Great are these wonders because great are the rich promises made by a great God to those who pray.

THE IMPORTANCE OF PRAYER

We have seen prayer's far-reaching possibilities and its absolute, unquestioned, necessity. We have also seen that the foregoing particulars and elaboration were required in order to bring the subject more clearly, truly, and strongly before our minds. The Church more than ever needs profound convictions of the vast importance of prayer in doing the work committed to it. More praying must be done and better praying if the Church will be able to perform the difficult, delicate, and responsible task given to it by her Lord and Master. Defeat awaits a non-praying Church. Success is sure to follow a Church given to much prayer. The supernatural element in the Church, without which it must fail, comes only through praying. More time in this busy, bustling age must be given to prayer by a God-called Church. More thought must be given to prayer in this thoughtless, silly age of superficial religion. More heart and soul must be in the praying that is done if the Church would go forth in the strength of its Lord and perform the wonders that is its heritage by divine promise.

> O Spirit of the Living God,
> In all thy plenitude of grace,
> Where'er the foot of man hath trod,
> Descend on our apostate race.
>
> Give tongues of fire and hearts of love,
> To preach the reconciling word,
> Give power and unction from above,
> Where'er the joyful sound is heard.

JOHN WESLEY

It might be in order to give an instance or two in the life of John Wesley, showing some remarkable displays of spiritual power. Many times it is stated this noted man gathered his company together and prayed all night, or until the mighty power of God came upon them. It was at a Watch Night service at Fetter Lane, December 31, 1738, when Charles and John Wesley, along with George Whitfield and others, sat up until after midnight singing and praying. This is the account:

> About three o'clock in the morning, as we were continuing instant in prayer, the power of God came mightily upon us, so that many cried out for exceeding joy, and many fell to the ground. As soon as we had recovered a little from that awe and amazement at the presence of His Majesty, we broke out with one voice, "We praise thee, O God! We acknowledge thee to be the Lord!"

On another occasion, John Wesley gives us this account: "After midnight, about a hundred of us walked home together singing, rejoicing, and praising God."

This godly man often recorded such statements as this, "We continued in ministering the Word and in prayer and praise until morning."

As often as God manifested His power in scriptural times in working wonders through prayer, He has not left Himself without witness in modern times. Prayer brings the Holy Spirit upon people today in answer to persistent, continued, prayer just as it did before Pentecost. The wonders of prayer have not ceased.

Endnotes

1 Revelation 8:3
2 1 Thessalonians 5:17
3 Matthew 9:29
4 Matthew 21:22
5 Isaiah 65:17-18
6 Isaiah 65:24
7 Isaiah 65:7
8 Joshua 10:12-14
9 Joel 2:21-27
10 Joel 2:28-32
11 Joel 2:12-19
12 Psalm 139:8-10
13 1 Kings 17:17-23
14 2 Kings 4:18-35
15 Acts 9:36-41
16 Acts 20:7-12
17 Matthew 9:36-38
18 Luke 11:13

19 Matthew 6:9-13
20 Matthew 5:4
21 Leviticus 16:12-13
22 Revelation 8:5
23 I Kings 17:1
24 James 5:17
25 James 5:18

15

Prayer and Divine Providence

PRAYER AND DIVINE PROVIDENCE are closely related. They stand in close companionship. They cannot possibly be separated. They are so closely connected that to deny one is to abolish the other. Prayer supposes a providence, while providence is the result of and belongs to prayer. All answers to prayer are but the intervention of the providence of God in the affairs of people. Providence has to do especially with praying people. Prayer, providence, and the Holy Spirit are a trinity that cooperate with each other and are in perfect harmony with one another. Prayer is but a request for God through the Holy Spirit to interfere in behalf of the person who prays.

What is termed *providence* is the divine supervision over earth and its affairs. It implies gracious provisions that Almighty God makes for all His creatures, animate and inanimate, intelligent or otherwise. Once we acknowledge that God is the creator and preserver of all humanity and is wise and intelligent, we are logically driven to the conclusion that Almighty God has direct supervision of those whom He has created and preserves. In fact, creation and preservation suppose a supervising providence. What is called divine providence is simply Almighty God governing the world for its best interests, and overseeing everything for the good of humanity.

People talk about a "general providence" as separate from a "special providence." There is no general providence but what is made up of special providences. A general supervision on the part of God supposes a special and individual supervision of each person—indeed, every creature.

GOD IS EVERYWHERE

God is everywhere—watching, supervising, overseeing, governing everything in the highest interest of humanity, and carrying forward His plans and executing His purposes in creation and redemption. He is not an absentee God. He did not make the world with all that is in it, turn it over to so-called natural laws, and then retire into the secret places of the universe with no regard for it or for the working of His laws. His hand is on the throttle. The work is not beyond His control. The earth's inhabitants and its affairs are not running independent of Almighty God.

Any and all providences are special providences, and prayer and these sort of providences work hand in hand. God's hand is in everything. None are beyond Him nor beneath His notice. Not that God orders everything to pass that comes to pass. Each of us is still a free agent, but the wisdom of Almighty God comes out when we remember that while we are free and the devil is abroad in the land, God can supervise and overrule earth's affairs for our good and for His glory, and cause even the wrath of people to praise Him.

Nothing occurs by accident under the supervision of an all-wise and perfectly just God. Nothing happens by chance in God's moral or natural government. God is a God of order and a God of law, but none the less a supervisor in the interest of His intelligent and redeemed creatures. Nothing can take place without the knowledge of God.

> His all surrounding sight surveys
> Our rising and our rest;
> Our public walks, our private ways,
> The secrets of our breasts.

Jesus Christ sets this matter at rest when He says, "Are not two sparrows sold for a farthing? and one of them shall not fall on the ground without your Father. But the very hairs of your head are all numbered. Fear ye not therefore, ye are of more value than many sparrows."[1]

GOD CANNOT BE RULED OUT OF THE WORLD

The doctrine of prayer brings Him directly into the world, and moves Him to a direct intervention with all of this world's affairs.

To rule Almighty God out of the providences of life is to strike a direct blow at prayer and its effectiveness. Nothing takes place in the world without God's consent. Yet it is not in a sense that He either approves everything or is responsible for all things that happen. God is not the author of sin.

The question is sometimes asked, "Is God in everything?" As if there are some things that are outside the government of God and beyond His attention that He is not concerned with. If God is not in everything, what is the Christian doing praying according to Paul's directions to the Philippians? "Be careful for nothing; but in every thing by prayer and supplication with thanksgiving let your requests be made known unto God."[2]

Are we to pray for some things and about things that God has nothing to do with? According to the doctrine that God is not in everything, then we are outside the realm of God when "in everything" we make our requests to God.

What also will we do with that large promise so comforting to all of God's saints in all ages and in all climates, a promise that belongs to prayer and that is embraced in a special providence: "And we know that all things work together for good to them that love God"?[3]

If God is not in everything, then what are the things we are to expect from the "all things" that "work together for good to them that love God"? If God is not in everything in His providence, what are the things that are to be left out of our praying? We can lay it down as a proposition that has a sure foundation, born out by Scripture, that nothing ever comes into the life of God's saints without His consent. God is always there when it occurs. He is not far away. He whose eye is on the sparrow is also upon His saints. His presence that fills the universe is always where His saints are. "Certainly I will be with thee,"[4] is the word of God to every child of His.

THE PROTECTION OF GOD

"The angel of the LORD encampeth round about them that fear Him, and delivereth them."[5] Nothing can touch those who fear God, except with the permission of the angel of the Lord. Nothing can break through the encampment without the permission of the captain of the Lord's hosts.[6] Sorrows, afflictions, needs, trouble, or even death cannot enter this divine encampment without the consent of Almighty God. Even then it is used by God in His plans for the good of His saints and for carrying out His plans and purposes:

> For I am persuaded, that neither death, nor life, nor angels, nor principalities, nor powers, nor things present, nor things to come, Nor height, nor depth, nor any other creature, shall be able to separate us from the love of God, which is in Christ Jesus our Lord.[7]

Evil things that are unpleasant and grievous may come with divine permission, but God is on the spot, His hand is in all of them, and He sees to it that they are woven into His plans. He causes them to be overruled for the good of His people, and eternal good is brought out of them. These things—along with hundreds of others—belong to the disciplinary processes of Almighty God in administering His government for His children.

GOD'S PROVIDENCE

The providence of God reaches as far as the realm of prayer. It has to do with everything for which we pray. Nothing is too small for the eye of God, nothing too insignificant for His notice and His care. God's providence has to do with even the stumbling of the feet of His saints.

> For he shall give his angels charge over thee, to keep thee in all thy ways. They shall bear thee up in their hands, lest thou dash thy foot against a stone.[8]

Read again our Lord's words about the sparrow. He says, "Are not five sparrows sold for two farthings, and not one of them is forgotten before God?"[9] Paul asks the pointed question, "Doth God care for oxen?"[10] His care reaches to the smallest things and has to do with the most insignificant matters that concern humanity. Those who believe in the God of providence are prepared to see His hand in all things that come to them, and can pray over everything.

It is not that the saints who trust the God of providence and take all things to God in prayer can explain the mysteries of divine providence. It is that they recognize God in everything, see Him in all that comes to them, and are ready to say as John said to Peter at the Sea of Galilee, "It is the Lord."[11]

Praying saints do not presume to interpret God's dealings with them or undertake to explain God's providences. They have learned to trust God in the dark as well as in the light, to have faith in God even when "cares like a wild deluge come, and storms of sorrow fall."

"Though He slay me, yet will I trust in Him."[12] Praying saints rest themselves upon the words of Jesus to Peter, "What I do thou knowest not now, but thou shalt know hereafter."[13] None but the praying ones can see God's hands in the providences of life. "Blessed are the pure in heart: for they shall see God."[14] They shall see God here in His providences, in His Word, in His Church. These are they who do not rule God out of earth's affairs, and who believe God intervenes in matters of earth for them.

While God's providence is over all humanity, yet His supervision and administration of His government are peculiarly in the interest of His people.

PRAYER BRINGS GOD'S PROVIDENCE INTO ACTION

Prayer puts God to work in overseeing and directing earth's affairs for the good of people. Prayer opens the way when it is shut up or difficult.

Providence deals more especially with temporal things. It is in this realm that the providence of God shines brightest and is most apparent. It has to do with food and clothing, with business difficulties, with strangely interposing and saving from danger, and with helping in emergencies at very opportune and critical times.

The feeding of the Israelites during the wilderness journey is a striking illustration of the providence of God in taking care of the temporal needs of His people. His dealings with those people show how He provided for them in that long pilgrimage.

> Day by day the manna fell,
> O to learn this lesson well!
> Still by constant mercy fed,
> Give me, Lord, my daily bread.
>
> Day by day the promise reads,
> Daily strength for daily needs;
> Cast foreboding fears away,
> Take the manna of today.

THE SERMON ON THE MOUNT

In the Sermon on the Mount, our Lord teaches this same lesson of a providence that clothes and feeds His people when He says, "Take no thought . . . what ye shall eat, or what ye shall drink; nor yet for your body, what ye shall put on."[15]

He then directs attention to the fact that it is God's providence that feeds the fowls of the air and clothes the lilies of the field, and says that if God does all this for birds and flowers He will surely do it for them.

All of this teaching leads up to the need of a childlike, unquestioning, trust in an overruling providence that looks after the temporal wants of the children of God. Let it be noted especially that all this teaching stands closely connected in the utterances of our Lord with what He says about prayer. By so doing, He closely connects a divine oversight with prayer and its promises.

GOD PROVIDES FOR ELIJAH

We have an impressive lesson on divine providence in the case of Elijah when he was sent to the brook Cherith, where God employed the ravens to feed His prophet. Here was an intervention so plain that God cannot be ruled out of life's temporal things. Before God will allow His servant to want bread, He moves the birds of the air to do His bidding and take care of His prophet.

Nor was this all. When the brook ran dry, God sent Elijah to a poor widow who had just enough meal and oil for the urgent needs of her and her son. Yet she divided with him her last morsel of bread. What was the result? The providence of God intervened, and as long as the drought lasted, the cruse of oil never failed nor did the meal in the barrel give out.[16]

The Old Testament sparkles with illustrations of the provisions of Almighty God for His people, and show clearly God's overruling providence. In fact, the Old Testament is largely the account of a providence that dealt with a peculiar people, anticipating their every temporal need, ministering to them when they were in emergencies, and setting them apart as God's own when they were in trouble.

JOHN NEWTON HYMN

It is worth while to read an old hymn of John Newton's,[17] which has in it so much of the providence of God:

> Though troubles assail, and dangers affright,
> Though friends should all fail, and foes all unite,
> Yet one thing secures me, whatever betide,
> The promise assures us, the Lord will provide.
>
> The birds without barns, or storehouse are fed,
> From them let us learn, to trust for our bread;
> His saints what is fitting, shall ne'er be denied,
> So long as it's written, the Lord will provide.

Many of our old hymns are filled with sentiments in song about a divine providence, and are worthwhile reading and singing even in this day.

GOD AND SORROW

All such events are subjects of prayer, and this is so for the reason that everything that comes into the life of the praying person is in the providence of God, and takes place under His supervising hand. Some would rule God out of the sad and hard things of life. They tell us that God has nothing to do with certain events that bring great grief to us. They say that God is not in the death of children, that they die from natural causes, and that it is but the working of natural laws.

Let us ask what are nature's laws but the laws of God, the laws by which God rules the world? What is nature anyway? Who made nature? There is a need to know that God is above nature, is in control of nature, and is in nature. We need to know that nature or natural laws are but the servants of Almighty God who made these laws and He is directly in them. They are but servants to carry out God's gracious designs, and are made to execute His gracious purposes. The God of providence, the God to whom the Christians pray, and the God who intervenes in behalf of the His children, is above nature, and in perfect and absolute control of all that belongs to nature. No law of nature can crush the life out of even a child without God giving His consent, without such a sad event occurring directly under His all-seeing eye, and without His being immediately present.

David believed this doctrine when he fasted and prayed for the life of his child. For why pray and fast for a baby to be spared if God has nothing to do with its death if it dies?[18]

Moreover, can it be that God who "does care for oxen" and has a direct oversight of the sparrows that fall to the ground, has nothing to do with the going out of this world of an immortal child? Further, even if the death of a child occurs, as some people claim, solely by the operation of the laws of nature, let it be kept in mind that it is a great affliction to the parents of the child. Where do these innocent parents come in under any such doctrine? It becomes a great sorrow to mother and father. Are they not to recognize the hand of God in the death of the child? Is there no providence or divine oversight in the taking away of their child to them?

DAVID AND HIS CHILD

David recognized the facts clearly that God had to do with keeping his child in life, that prayer might avail in saving his child from death, and that when the child died it was because God had ordered it. Prayer and providence in all this affair worked in harmonious cooperation, and David thoroughly understood it.

No child ever dies without the direct permission of Almighty God, and such an event takes place in His providence for wise and beneficial purposes. God works it into His plans concerning the child itself and the parents and all concerned. Moreover, it is a subject of prayer whether the child lives or dies.

In each event of life how clear,
Thy ruling hand I see;
Each blessing to my soul most dear,
Because conferred by Thee.

Endnotes

1 Matthew 10:29-31
2 Philippians 4:6
3 Romans 8:28
4 Exodus 3:12a
5 Psalm 34:7
6 Joshua 5:13-15
7 Romans 8:38-39
8 Psalm 91:11-12
9 Luke 12:6
10 I Corinthians 9:9
11 John 21:7
12 Job 13:15
13 John 13:7
14 Matthew 5:8
15 Matthew 6:25
16 I Kings 17:1-16
17 Author of *Amazing Grace*

18 2 Samuel 12:15-23

16

Prayer and Divine Providence (Continued)

A PROPER IDEA OF PRAYER *is the pouring out of the soul before God,* *with the hand of faith placed on the head of the Sacrificial Offering, imploring mercy, and presenting itself a free-will offering of itself unto God, giving up body, soul, and spirit, to be guided and governed as may seem good to His heavenly wisdom, desiring only perfectly to love Him, and to serve Him with all its powers, at all times, while He has a being.* (Adam Clarke)

Two kinds of providences are seen in God's dealings with people, direct providences and permissive providences. God orders some things, others He permits. But when He permits an affliction or trouble to come into the life of His saint, even though it originates in a wicked mind and is the act of a sinner, before it strikes and affects the saint it becomes God's providence. In other words, God consents to some things in this world, without in the least being responsible for them, or in the least excusing those who originate them. Although many of them are very painful and troublesome, such events or things always become the providence of God to the saint of God. Thus the saint can say in each and all of these sad and distressing experiences, "It is the LORD: let Him do what seemeth Him good."[1] Or with the psalmist, the saint may say, "I was dumb, I opened not my mouth; because Thou didst it."[2]

This was the explanation of all of Job's severe afflictions. They came to him in the providence of God, even though they had their origin in the mind of Satan, who devised them and put them into execution. God gave Satan permission to afflict Job, to take away his property, and to rob him of his children. But Job did not attribute these things to blind chance or accident, or charge them to Satanic agency. Instead he said, "The Lord gave, and the Lord hath taken away; blessed be the name of the LORD." He took these things as coming from his God, whom he feared and served and trusted.

Job spoke similar words to his wife when she left God out of the question, and wickedly told her husband, "curse God, and die." Job replied, "Thou speakest as one of the foolish women speaketh. What! shall we receive good at the hand of God, and shall we not receive evil?"[3]

It is no surprise that with such a view of God's dealings with him that it should be recorded of this man of faith, "In all this did not Job sin with his lips."[4] In another place it is said of him, "In all this Job sinned not, nor charged God foolishly."[5] In nothing concerning God and the events of life do people talk more foolishly and even wickedly than in ignorantly making up their judgments on the providences of God in this world. O that we had saints after the type of Job, who see the hand of God in providence in even severe and extreme afflictions and deprivations, and openly acknowledge God in it.

The sequel to all these painful experiences of Job are but illustrations of that familiar text of Paul, "And we know that all things work together for good to them that love God."[6] Job received back more in the end than was ever taken away from him. He emerged from under these tremendous troubles with victory, and became until this day the exponent and example of great patience and strong faith in God's providences. "Ye have heard of the patience of Job,"[7] rings down the line of divine revelation. God took hold of the evil acts of Satan and worked them into His plans and brought great good out of them. He made evil work out for good without in the least endorsing the evil or conspiring with Satan.

We have the same gracious truth of divine providence evidenced in the story of Joseph and his brethren, who sold him wickedly into Egypt and forsook him and deceived their old father. All this had its origin in their evil minds. Yet when it reached God's plans and purposes, it became God's providence both to Joseph and to the future of Jacob's descendants. Hear Joseph as he spoke to his brethren after he had revealed himself to them down in Egypt. He traces all the painful events back to the mind of God and made them have to do with fulfilling God's purposes concerning Jacob and his posterity:

> Now therefore be not grieved, nor angry with yourselves, that ye sold me hither: for God did send me before you to preserve life. . . And God sent me before you to preserve you a posterity in the earth, and to save your lives by a great deliverance. So now it was not you that sent me hither, but God.[8]

Cowper's well-known hymn might well be read in this connection, but one verse is sufficient just now:

> God moves in a mysterious way,
> His wonders to perform;
> He plants His footsteps in the sea,
> And rides upon the storm.

The very same line of argument appears in the betrayal of our Lord by Judas. Of course it was the wicked act of an evil man, but it never touched our Lord until the Father gave His consent. God took the evil design of Judas and worked it into His own plans for the redemption of the world. It did not excuse Judas in the least that good came out of his wicked act, but it does magnify the wisdom and greatness of God in so overruling it that humanity's redemption was secured. It is always so in God's dealings with people. Things that come to us from second causes are no surprise to God, nor are they beyond His control. His hand can take hold of them in answer to prayer and He can make afflictions, from wherever they may come, work "for us a far more exceeding and eternal weight of glory."

The providence of God goes before His saints, opens the way, removes difficulties, solves problems, and brings deliverance when escape seems hopeless. God brought Israel out of Egypt by the hand of Moses, His chosen leader of that people. They came to the Red Sea. But there were the waters in front, with no crossing or bridges. On one side were high mountains, and behind came the hosts of Pharaoh. Every avenue of escape was closed. There seemed no hope. Despair almost reigned. But there was one way open that people overlooked, and that was the upward way. Moses, a man of prayer and faith in God, was on the ground. This man of prayer, who recognized God in providence, with commanding force spoke to the people and said, "Fear ye not; stand still, and see the salvation of the LORD."[9]

With this he lifted up his rod, and in obedience to divine command stretched his hand over the sea. The waters divided, and the command came forth, "speak unto the children of Israel, that they go forward." Israel went over the sea with dry feet. God had opened a way, and what seemed an impossible emergency was remarkably turned into a wonderful deliverance. This is not the only time God has intervened in behalf of His people when their way was shut up.

The whole history of the Jews is the story of God's providence. The Old Testament cannot be accepted as true without receiving the doctrine of a divine, overruling providence. The Bible is preeminently a divine revelation. It reveals things. It reveals, uncovers, brings to light things concerning God, His character His manner of governing this world and its inhabitants. It reveals things that are not discoverable by human reason, science, or philosophy. The Bible is a book in which God reveals

Himself to humanity. This is particularly true when we consider God's care of His creatures, and His oversight and supervision of the world and its affairs. To dispute the doctrine of providence is to discredit the entire revelation of God's Word. Everywhere the Word reveals God's hand in the affairs of humanity.

The Old Testament especially, but also the New Testament, is the story of prayer and providence. It is the tale of God's dealings with people of faith and prayer in His direct intervention in earth's affairs. Also, with God's manner of supervising the world in the interest of His people, and in carrying forward His work in His plans and purposes in creation and redemption.

Praying saints and God's providence go together. This was thoroughly understood by the praying saints of the Bible. They prayed over everything because God had to do with everything. They took all things to God in prayer because they believed in a divine providence that had to do with all things. They believed in an ever-present God who had not retired into the secret recesses of space to leave His saints and His creatures to the mercy of a tyrant. A tyrant called nature and its laws—blind, unyielding, with no regard for anyone who stood in its way. If that is the correct conception of God, why pray to Him? He is too far away to hear people when they pray, and too unconcerned to trouble Himself about those on earth.

These saints of prayer had an implicit faith in a God of special providence. He was a God who would gladly, promptly, and readily respond to their cries for help in times of need and in seasons of distress.

THE LAWS OF NATURE

The so-called "laws of nature" did not trouble them in the least. God was above nature, in control of nature, and nature was but the servant of Almighty God. Nature's laws were but His own laws, since nature was but the offspring of the divine hand. Laws of nature might be suspended and no evil would result. Everyday the majority of people in the world see the law of gravity being overruled and overcome, and no one is surprised or raises hand or voice in horror at the thought of nature's laws being violated. God is a God of law and order, and all His laws in nature, providence, and grace work together in perfect accord, with no clash or disharmony.

God suspends or overcomes the laws of disease and rain often without or independent of prayer. But quite often He does this in answer to prayer. Prayer for rain or for dry weather is not outside the moral government of God. It is also not asking God to violate any law that He has made, but only asking Him to give rain in His own way, according to His own laws. So also the prayer for the rebuking of disease is not a request at war with law either natural or otherwise, but is a prayer in accordance with the law of prayer. This law was set into operation by Almighty God just as was the so-called natural law that governs rain or controls disease.

Believers in the law of prayer has strong ground on which to base their plea. Those who believe in a divine providence, the companion of prayer, stand equally on strong granite foundations from which they need not be shaken. These twin doctrines stand fast and will abide forever.

> In every condition, in sickness, in health,
> In poverty's vale or abounding in wealth;
> At home or abroad, on the land or the sea,
> As thy days may demand shall thy strength ever be.

Endnotes

1 I Samuel 3:18
2 Psalm 39:9
3 Job 2:10
4 Job 2:10
5 Job I:22
6 Romans 8:28
7 James 5:11
8 Genesis 45:5, 7-8a
9 Exodus 14:13

BOOK 4

THE REALITY OF PRAYER

I

Prayer Is a Princely and Sacred Privilege

I AM THE CREATURE OF *a day, passing through life as an arrow through the air. I am a spirit come from God and returning to God; just hovering over the great gulf; till a few moments hence I am no more seen; I drop into an unchangeable eternity! I want to know one thing, the way to heaven; how to land safe on that happy shore. God Himself has condescended to teach the way; for this end He came from heaven. He hath written it down in a book. O give me that book! At any price give me the Book of God! Lord, is it not Thy word—"If any man lack wisdom, let him ask of God? Thou givest liberally, and upbraidest not. Thou hast said, if any be willing to do Thy will he shall know. I am willing to do; let me know Thy will."* (John Wesley)

The word *prayer* expresses the largest and most comprehensive approach to God. It gives prominence to the element of devotion. It is communion and interaction with God. It is enjoyment of God. It is access to God. Supplication is a more restricted and more intense form of prayer, accompanied by a sense of personal need, limited to seeking in an urgent manner a supply for a pressing need. Supplication is the very soul of prayer in the way of pleading for some one thing, greatly needed, and the need intensely felt.

Intercession is an enlargement in prayer, a going out in broadness and fullness from self to others. It does not primarily center in praying for others, but refers to the freeness, boldness, and childlike confidence of the praying. It is the fullness of confiding influence in the soul's approach to God, unlimited and unhesitating in its access and its demands. This influence and confident trust is to be used for others.

Prayer always and everywhere is an immediate and confiding approach to, and a request of, God the Father. The prayer that is universal and perfect, and is the pattern of all praying, is "Our Father which art in heaven."[1] At the grave of Lazarus, Jesus lifted up His eyes and said, "Father."[2] In His high-priestly prayer, Jesus lifted up His eyes to Heaven, and said, "Father."[3] Personal, familiar, and paternal was all His praying.

His praying was also strong, touching, and tearful. Read these words: "Who in the days of his flesh, when he had offered up prayers and supplications with strong crying and tears unto him that was able to save him from death, and was heard in that he feared."[4]

ASKING OF GOD

In James 1:5, we have asking set forth as prayer: "If any of you lack wisdom, let him ask of God, that giveth to all men liberally, and upbraideth not; and it shall be given him."

Asking of God and receiving from the Lord—direct application to God, immediate connection with God—that is prayer.

In John's first epistle, we have this statement about prayer:

And this is the confidence that we have in him, that, if we ask any thing according to his will, he heareth us: And if we know that he hear us, whatsoever we ask, we know that we have the petitions that we desired of him.[5]

In Philippians we have these words about prayer:

Be careful for nothing; but in every thing by prayer and supplication with thanksgiving let your requests be made known unto God.[6]

WHAT IS GOD'S WILL ABOUT PRAYER?

First of all, it is God's will that we pray. Jesus Christ "spake a parable unto them to this end, that men ought always to pray, and not to faint"[7] Paul writes to young Timothy about the first things that God's people are to do, and the first thing he states is prayer: "I exhort therefore, that, first of all, supplications, prayers, intercessions, and giving of thanks, be made for all men.[8]

In connection with these words, Paul declares that the will of God, and the redemption and mediation of Jesus Christ for the salvation for all people, are all vitally concerned in this matter of prayer. In this, his apostolic authority and solicitude of soul conspire with God's will and Christ's intercession to will that people pray everywhere.

Note how frequently prayer is brought forward in the New Testament: "Continuing instant in prayer."[9] "Pray without ceasing."[10] "Continue in prayer, and watch in the same with thanksgiving."[11] "Be ye therefore sober, and watch unto prayer."[12] Christ's clarion call was "watch and pray."[13] What are all these and others, if it is not the will of God that Christians should pray?

PRAYER COMPLEMENTS AND COOPERATES WITH GOD'S WILL

Prayer is complementary and made efficient when it cooperates with God's will, whose sovereign sway is to run parallel in extent and power with the atonement of Jesus Christ. He, through the Eternal Spirit, by the grace of God, tasted "death for every man."[14] We, through the eternal Spirit, and by the grace of God, pray for every person.

But how do I know that I am praying in the will of God? Every true attempt to pray is in response to the will of God. It may be bungled and untaught by human teachers, but it is acceptable to God because it is in obedience to His will. If I will give myself up to the inspiration of the Spirit of God, who commands me to pray, the details and the petitions of that praying will all fall into harmony with the will of Him who wills that I should pray.

Prayer is no little thing, no selfish and small matter. It does not concern the petty interests of one person. The smallest prayer broadens out by the will of God until it touches all words, conserves all interests, and enhances humanity's greatest wealth, and God's greatest good. God is so concerned that Christians pray that He has promised to answer prayer. He has not promised to do something general if we pray, but He has promised to do the very thing for which we pray.

PRAYER ENTERS INTO ALL THE RELATIONS OF LIFE

Prayer, as taught by Jesus in its essential features, enters into all the relations of life. It sanctifies relationships. To the Jew, the altar was the symbol and place of prayer. The Jew devoted the altar to the worship of God. Jesus Christ takes the altar of prayer and devotes it to supplication for others. How Christ purifies the altar and enlarges it! How He takes it out of the sphere of a mere performance, and makes its virtue to consist, not in the mere act of praying, but in the spirit that actuates us toward people. Our spirit toward folks is of the life of prayer.

We must be at peace with people, and, if possible, have them at peace with us, before we can be at peace with God. Reconciliation with others is the forerunner of reconciliation with God. Our spirit and words must embrace people before they can embrace God. Unity with the believers goes before unity with God. "Therefore if thou bring thy gift to the altar, and there rememberest that thy brother hath ought against thee; Leave there thy gift before the altar, and go thy way; first be reconciled to thy brother, and then come and offer thy gift."[15]

Non-praying is lawlessness, discord, anarchy. Prayer, in the moral government of God, is as strong and far-reaching as the law of gravitation in the material world, and it is as necessary as gravitation to hold things in their proper sphere and in life.

The space occupied by prayer in the Sermon on the Mount speaks of its estimate by Christ and the importance it holds in His system. Many important principles are discussed in a verse or two. The Sermon consists of one hundred and eleven verses, and eighteen are about prayer directly, and others indirectly.

Prayer was one of the cardinal principles of piety in every dispensation and to every child of God. It did not pertain to the business of Christ to originate duties, but to recover, to recast, to spiritualize, and to reinforce those duties that are cardinal and original.

MOSES AND PRAYER

With Moses the great features of prayer are prominent. He never beats the air nor fights a sham battle. The most serious and strenuous business of his serious and strenuous life was prayer. He is much at it with the intense earnestness of his soul. Intimate as he was with God, his intimacy did not lessen the necessity of prayer. This intimacy only brought clearer insight into the nature and necessity of prayer, and led him to see the greater obligations to pray, and to discover the larger results of praying. In reviewing one of the crises through which Israel passed, when the very existence of the nation was imperiled, he writes, "I fell down before the LORD forty days and forty nights."[16] Wonderful praying and wonderful results! Moses knew how to do wonderful praying, and God knew how to give wonderful results.

GOD HEARS AND ANSWERS PRAYER

The whole force of Bible statement is to increase our faith in the doctrine that prayer affects God and secures favors from God, which can be secured in no other way, and that will not be bestowed by God if we do not pray. The whole canon of Bible teaching is to illustrate the great truth that God hears and answers prayer.

One of the great purposes of God in His book is to impress upon us indelibly the great importance, the priceless value, and the absolute necessity of asking God for the things that we need for time and eternity. He urges us by every consideration, and presses and warns us by every interest. He points us to His own Son, turned over to us for our good, as His pledge that prayer will be answered. By this, He teaches us that God is our Father, able to do all things for us and to give all things to us, much more than earthly parents are able or willing to do for their children.

THE BUSINESS OF PRAYER

Let us thoroughly understand ourselves and understand, also, this great business of prayer. Our one great business is prayer, and we will never do it well without fastening to it by an all-binding force. We will never do it well without arranging the best conditions of doing it well. Satan has suffered so much by good praying that all his wily, shrewd, and ensnaring devices will be used to cripple its performances.

We must, by all the fastenings we can find, cable ourselves to prayer. To be loose in time and place is to open the door to Satan. To be exact, prompt, unswerving, and careful in even the little things, is to buttress ourselves against the evil one.

Prayer, by God's own oath, is put in the very stones of God's foundations, as eternal as its companion, "prayer also shall be made for him continually."[17] This is the eternal condition that advances His cause, and makes it powerfully aggressive. Christians are to always pray for it. Its strength, beauty, and aggression lie in their prayers. Its power lies simply in its power to pray. No power is found elsewhere but in its ability to pray. "For mine house shall be called an house of prayer for all people."[18] It is based on prayer, and carried on by the same means.

PRAYER IS A SACRED AND PRINCELY PRIVILEGE

Prayer is a privilege, a sacred, princely privilege. Prayer is a duty, an obligation most binding, and most imperative, which should hold us to it. But prayer is more than a privilege, more than a duty. It is a means, an instrument, a condition. Not to pray is to lose much more than to fail in the exercise and enjoyment of a high or sweet privilege. Not to pray is to fail along lines far more important than even the violation of an obligation.

Prayer is the appointed condition of getting God's aid. This aid is as manifold and illimitable as God's ability, and as varied and exhaustless as our needs. Prayer is the avenue through which God supplies our wants. Prayer is the channel through which all good flows from God to us, and all good from us to others. God is the Christian's Father. Asking and giving are in that relation.

Christians are the ones more immediately concerned in this great work of praying. It ennobles our reason to employ it in prayer. The office and work of prayer is the most divine engagement of our reason. Prayer makes our reason to shine. Intelligence of the highest order approves prayer. They are the wisest who prays the most and the best. Prayer is the school of wisdom as well as of piety.

Prayer is not a picture to handle, admire, and look at. It is not beauty, coloring, shape, attitude, imagination, or genius. These things do not pertain to its character or conduct. It is not poetry nor music. Its inspiration and melody come from heaven. Prayer belongs to the spirit, and at times it possesses the spirit and stirs the spirit with high and holy purposes and resolves.

Endnotes

1 Matthew 6:9; Luke 11:2
2 John 11:41
3 John 17:1
4 Hebrews 5:7
5 I John 5:14-15
6 Philippians 4:6
7 Luke 18:1
8 I Timothy 2:1
9 Romans 12:1
10 I Thessalonians 5:17
11 Colossians 4:2
12 I Peter 4:7
13 Matthew 26:41; Mark 13:33
14 Hebrews 2:9
15 Matthew 5:23-24
16 Deuteronomy 9:25
17 Psalm 72:15
18 Isaiah 56:7b

2

Prayer Fills Our Poverty with God's Riches

FOR TWO HOURS I *struggled on, forsaken of God, and met neither God nor man, all one chilly afternoon. When at last, standing still and looking at Schiehallion clothed in white from top to bottom, this of David shot up into my heart: "Wash me, and I shall be whiter than snow!" In a moment I was with God, or rather God was with me. I walked home with my heart in a flame of fire.* (Alexander Whtye, D.D.)

We have much fine writing and learned talk about the subjective benefits of prayer. We are told how prayer secures its full measure of results, not by affecting God, but by affecting us, by becoming a training school for those who pray. We are taught by such teachers that the province of prayer is not to get, but to train. Prayer thus becomes a mere performance, a drill-sergeant, a school, in which patience, tranquility, and dependence are taught. In this school, denial of prayer is the most valuable teacher.

No matter how well all this may look, and howsoever reasonable it may seem, there is nothing of it in the Bible. The clear and often repeated language of the Bible is that prayer is to be answered by God. That God occupies the relation of a father to us, and that as Father He gives to us when we ask, the exact things for which we ask. The best praying, therefore, is the praying that gets an answer.

The possibilities and necessity of prayer are engraved in the eternal foundations of the Gospel. The relation that is established between the Father and the Son, and the decreed covenant between the two, has prayer as the base of its existence, and is the major requirement for the

301

advancement and success of the Gospel. Prayer is the condition by which all foes are to be overcome and all the inheritance is to be possessed.

These are self-evident truths, though they may be very homely ones. But these are the times when Bible truths need to be stressed, pressed, repeated, and repeated again. The very air is filled with influences, practices, and theories that sap foundations, and the most veritable truths and most self-evident axioms go down by insidious and invisible attacks.

More than this—the tendency of these times is to a pretentious parade of doing, which enfeebles the life and dissipates the spirit of praying. There may be kneeling, and there may be standing in prayerful attitude. There may be much bowing of the head, and yet there may be no serious, real, praying. Prayer is real work. Praying is vital work. Prayer has in its keeping the very heart of worship. There may be the exhibit, circumstance, and pomp of praying, and yet no real praying. There may be much attitude, gesture, and verbiage, but no praying.

WHO CAN APPROACH GOD IN PRAYER?

Who can approach into God's presence in prayer? Who can come before the great God, maker of all worlds, the God and Father of our Lord Jesus Christ, who holds in His hands all good, and who is all powerful and able to do all things? To approach this great God, lowliness, truth, cleanness of hands, and purity of heart are needed and demanded!

Everywhere we are impressed that it is more important and urgent that people pray, than that they be skilled in the theoretical morals of prayer. That is a thing of the heart, not of the schools. It is more of feeling than of words. Praying is the best school in which to learn to pray. Prayer the best dictionary to define the art and nature of praying.

We repeat and repeat. Prayer is not a mere habit, riveted by custom and memory. It is not a routine that we must go through, with its value depending upon the decency and perfection of the performance. Prayer is not a duty that must be performed, to ease obligation and to quiet conscience. Prayer is not mere privilege, a sacred indulgence to be taken advantage of, at leisure, at pleasure, at will, and no serious loss attending its omission.

PRAYER IS A SOLEMN SERVICE

Prayer is a solemn service due to God, an adoration, a worship, an approach to God for some request, the presenting of some desire, the expression of some need to Him who supplies all need, and who satisfies all desires. As a Father, God finds His greatest pleasure in relieving the wants and granting the desires of His children. Prayer is the child's request, not to the winds, nor to the world, but to the Father. Prayer is the outstretched arms of the child for the Father's help. Prayer is the child's cry calling to the Father's ear, the Father's heart, and to the Father's ability. The prayer cry is what the Father is to hear, the Father is to feel, and which the Father is to relieve. Prayer is the seeking of God's great and greatest good, which will not come if we do not pray.

Prayer is an ardent and believing cry to God for some specific thing. God's rule is to answer by giving the specific thing asked for. With it may come much of other gifts and graces. Strength, serenity, sweetness, and faith may come as the bearers of the gifts. But even they come because God hears and answers prayer.

We follow the plain letter and spirit of the Bible when we affirm that God answers prayer, and answers by giving us the very things we desire. The withholding of that which we desire, and the giving of something else, is not the rule, but rare and exceptional. When His children cry for bread He gives them bread.

Revelation does not deal in philosophical subtleties, nor verbal niceties and hair-splitting distinctions. It unfolds relationships, declares principles, and enforces duties. The heart must define, the experience must realize. Paul came on the stage too late to define prayer. That which had been so well done by patriarchs and prophets needed no return to dictionaries. Christ is Himself the illustration and definition of prayer. He prayed as human beings had never prayed. He put prayer on a higher basis, with grander results and simpler being than it had ever known. He taught Paul how to pray by the revelation of Himself, which is the first call to prayer, and the first lesson in praying. Prayer, like love, is too intangible and too heavenly to be held in the gross arms of chilly definitions. It belongs to heaven and to the heart, and not to words and ideas only.

PRAYER IS NOT INVENTED BY PEOPLE

Prayer is no petty invention of people, a fancied relief for fancied ills. Prayer is no dreary performance, dead and death-dealing. It is God's enabling act for people, living and life-giving, joy and joy-giving. Prayer is the contact of a living soul with God. In prayer, God stoops to kiss us, to bless us, and to aid us in everything that God can devise or we can need. Prayer fills our emptiness with God's fullness. It fills our poverty with God's riches. It exchanges our weakness for God's strength. It banishes our littleness with God's greatness. Prayer is God's plan to supply our great and continuous need with God's great and continuous abundance.

What is this prayer to which we are called? It is not a mere form, a child's play. It is serious, difficult work, the manliest, the mightiest work, the most divine work that we can do. Prayer lifts us out of the earthliness and links us with the heavenly. We are never nearer Heaven, nearer God, never more God-like, never in deeper sympathy and truer partnership with Jesus Christ, than when praying. Love, philanthropy, holy affiances—all of them helpful and tender—are born and perfected by prayer.

Prayer is not merely a question of duty, but of salvation. Are sinners people who are not people of prayer? Is not the gift, the inclination, the habit of prayer, one of the elements or characteristics of salvation? Can it be possible to be in affinity with Jesus Christ and not be prayerful? Is it possible to have the Holy Spirit and not have the spirit of prayer? Can one have the new birth and not be born to prayer? Is not the life of the Spirit and the life of prayer coordinate and consistent? Can true love be in the heart that is unschooled in prayer?

TWO KINDS OF PRAYER

We have two kinds of prayer named in the New Testament—prayer and supplication. Prayer denotes prayer in general. Supplication is a more intense and more special form of prayer. These two, supplication and prayer, ought to be combined. Then we would have devotion in its widest and sweetest form, and supplication with its most earnest and personal sense of need.

In Paul's prayer directory in Ephesians 6, we are taught to be always in prayer, as we are always in the battle. The Holy Spirit is to be sought by intense supplication, and our supplications are to be charged by His vitalizing, illuminating, and ennobling energy. Watchfulness is to fit us for this intense praying and intense fighting. Perseverance is an essential element in successful praying, as in every other realm of conflict. The saints universal are to be helped on to victory by the aid of our prayers. Apostolic courage, ability, and success are to be gained by the prayers of the warrior saints everywhere.

It is only those of deep and true vision who can administer prayer. The living creatures in the book of Revelation are described as "full of eyes before and behind . . . full of eyes within."[1] Eyes are for seeing. Clearness, intensity, and perfection of sight are in it. Vigilance and profound insight are in it, the faculty of knowing. It is by prayer that the eyes of our hearts are opened. Clear and profound knowledge of the mysteries of grace is secured by prayer. Those living creatures had eyes "within and without" They were "full of eyes." The highest form of life is intelligent. Ignorance is degrading and low, in the spiritual realm as it is in other realms. Prayer gives us eyes to see God. Prayer is seeing God. The prayer life is knowledge without and within. All vigilance without, all vigilance within. There can be no intelligent prayer without knowledge within. Our inner condition and our inner needs must be felt and known.

IT TAKES PRAYER TO MINISTER

It takes life, the highest form of life, to minister. Prayer is the highest intelligence, the profoundest wisdom, the most vital, the most joyous, the most effective, the most powerful of all vocations. It is life, radiant, transporting, eternal life. Away with dry forms, with dead, cold habits of prayer! Away with sterile routine, with senseless performances and petty playthings in prayer! Let us get at the serious work, the chief business of saints, that of prayer. Let us work at it skillfully. Let us seek to be experts in this great work of praying. Let us be master workers in this high art of praying. Let us be so in the habit of prayer, so devoted to prayer, so filled with its rich spices, so ardent by its holy flame, that all heaven and earth will be perfumed by its aroma, and nations yet in the womb will be blessed by our prayers. Heaven will be fuller and brighter in glorious inhabitants, earth will be better prepared for its bridal day, and Satan robbed of many of his victims, because we have lived to pray.

There is not only a sad and ruinous neglect of any attempt to pray, but there is an immense waste in the false praying that is done, as official praying, state praying, mere habit praying. People cleave to the form and semblance of a thing after the heart and reality have gone out of it. This finds illustrations in many who seem to pray. Formal praying has a strong hold and a strong following.

POURING OUT THE SOUL BEFORE GOD

Hannah's statement to Eli and her defense against his charge of hypocrisy was, I "have poured out my soul before the Lord." God's serious promise to the Jews was, "Then shall ye call upon me, and ye shall go and pray unto me, and I will hearken unto you. And ye shall seek me, and find me, when ye shall search for me with all your heart."[2]

Let all the present day praying be measured by these standards: pouring out the soul before God and seeking with all the heart, and most praying will be found to be mere form, waste, and worthless. James, in effect, says of Elijah that he "prayed with prayer."[3]

THE DESCRIPTION OF PRAYER

In Paul's directions to Timothy about prayer,[4] we have a comprehensive verbal description of prayer in its different departments, or varied manifestations. They are all in the plural form—supplications, prayers, and intercessions. They declare the many sided, endless diversity, and necessity of going beyond the formal simplicity of a single prayer. They press and add prayer upon prayer, supplication to supplication, intercession over and over again, until the combined force of prayers in their most superlative modes, unite their aggregation and pressure with cumulative power to our praying. The unlimited superlative and the unlimited plural are the only measures of prayer.

The one term of prayer is the common and comprehensive one for the act, the duty, the spirit, and the service we call prayer. It is the condensed statement of worship. The heavenly worship does not have the element of prayer so conspicuous. Prayer is the conspicuous, all-important, essence and all-coloring ingredient of earthly worship, while praise is the preeminent, comprehensive, all-coloring, all-inspiring, element of heavenly worship.

Endnotes

1 Revelation 4:6, 8
2 Jeremiah 29:12-13
3 See James 5:16-18
4 I Timothy 2:1

3

Prayer: the Essence of Earthly Worship

WHERE THE SPIRITUAL CONSCIOUSNESS *is concerned—the department which asks the question and demands the evidence—no evidence is competent or relevant except such as is spiritual. Only that which is above matter and above logic can be heard, because the very question at issue is the existence and personality of a spiritual and supernatural God. Only the Spirit himself beareth witness with our spirit. This must be done in a spiritual or supernatural way, or it cannot be done at all.* (C. L. Chilton)

The Jewish law and the prophets know something of God as a Father. they had occasional and imperfect but comforting glimpses of the great truth of God's fatherhood, and of our sonship. Christ lays the foundation of prayer deep and strong with this basic principle. The law of prayer, the right to pray, rests on sonship. Our Father brings us into the closest relationship to God. Prayer is the child's approach, the child's plea, the child's right. It is the law of prayer that looks up, that lifts up the eye to "Our Father which art in heaven."[1] Our Father's house is our home in Heaven. Heavenly citizenship and heavenly homesickness are in prayer. Prayer is an appeal from the lowness, from the emptiness, from the need of earth, to the highness, the fullness, and the all-sufficiency of heaven. Prayer turns the eye and the heart heavenward with a child's longings, a child's trust, and a child's expectancy. To hallow God's name, to speak it with bated breath, to hold it sacred, this also belongs to prayer.

In this connection, it might be said that it is required to dictate to children the necessity of prayer to ensure their salvation. But alas!

Unhappily, it is thought sufficient to tell them there is a heaven and a hell—that they must avoid the latter place and seek to reach the former. Yet they are not taught the easiest way to arrive at salvation. The only way to heaven is by the route of prayer, such prayer of the heart that every one is capable of. It is prayer not of reasonings that are the fruits of study, or of the exercise of the imagination, which fills the mind with wondering objects, but that fails to settle salvation. Rather, it is the simple, confidential, prayer of the child to its Father in heaven.

Poverty of spirit and true praying

"Blessed are the poor in spirit: for theirs is the kingdom of Heaven."[2] The poor means paupers, beggars, those who live on the bounties of others, who live by begging. Christ's people live by asking. Someone has rightly said, "Prayer is the Christian's vital breath." It is the Christian's affluent inheritance, daily annuity.

In His own example, Christ illustrates the nature and necessity of prayer. Everywhere He declares that He who is on God's mission in this world will pray. He is an illustrious example of the principle that the more devoted a person is to God, the more prayerful that person will be. The diviner the person, the more of the Spirit of the Father and of the Son that person has, the more prayerful will that person be. Conversely, it is true that the more prayerful that person is, the more of the Spirit of the Father and of the Son that person will receive.

During the great events and crowning periods of the life of Jesus, we find Him in prayer—at the beginning of His ministry, at the fords of the Jordan, when the Holy Spirit descended upon Him, just prior to the transfiguration, and in the garden of Gethsemane. Well do the words of Peter come in here: "Leaving us an example, that ye should follow His steps."[3]

Prayer and Jesus' miracles

There is an important principle of prayer found in some of the miracles of Christ. It is the progressive nature of the answer to prayer. God does not always give the full answer to prayer all at once, but rather progressively, step by step. Mark describes a case that illustrates this important truth that is too often overlooked.

And he cometh to Bethsaida; and they bring a blind man unto him, and besought him to touch him. And he took the blind man by the hand, and led him out of the town; and when he had spit on his eyes, and put his hands upon him, he asked him if he saw ought. And he looked up, and said, I see men as trees, walking. After that he put his hands again upon his eyes, and made him look up: and he was restored, and saw every man clearly.[4]

At times, He has to take us aside from the world, where He can have us all to Himself, and there speak to and deal with us.

THREE CURES OF BLINDNESS

We have three cures of blindness in the life of our Lord, which illustrate the nature of God's working in answering prayer, and show the exhaustless variety and omnipotence of His working.

In the first case, Christ came incidentally on a blind man at Jerusalem, made clay, softened it by spittle, and smeared it on the man's eyes, and then commanded the man to go and wash in the pool of Siloam.[5] The gracious results lay at the end of his action—washing. The failure to go and wash would have been fatal to the cure. No one, not even the blind man, in this instance, requested the cure.

In the second case, the parties who bring the blind man, back their bringing with earnest prayer for the person's cure. They beseech Christ to simply touch him, as though their faith would relieve the burden of a heavy operation. But He took the man by the hand and led him out of the town and apart from the people. This work was to be done alone and in secret. Jesus spat on the man's eyes and put his hands on them. The response was not complete, a dawning of light, a partial recovery. The first gracious communication only gave him a disordered vision. The second stroke perfected the cure. The man's submissive faith in giving himself up to Christ to be led away into privacy and alone, were prominent features of the cure, as also the gradual reception of sight, and the necessity of a second stroke to finish the perfect work.[6]

The third case was blind Bartimaeus. It was the urgency of faith declaring itself in clamorous utterances, rebuked by those who were following Christ, but intensified and emboldened by opposition.

The first case comes on Christ unawares, the second was brought with specific intent to Him, and the last goes after Christ with irresistible urgency, but was met by the resistance of the multitude and the seeming indifference of Christ. The cure, though, was without the interposition of any agent, no taking by the hand, no gentle or severe touch, no spittle, no clay, no washing—a word only and his sight, full-orbed, came instantly.

Each one had experienced the same divine power, the same blessed results, but with marked diversity in the expression of their faith and the mode of their cure. Suppose, at their meeting, the first had set up the particulars and process of his cure, the spittle, the clay, the washing in Siloam as the only divine process, as the only genuine credentials of a divine work. But such a standard of decisions would have been far from the truth, narrow, and misleading. Not methods, but results, are the tests of the divine work.

Each one could say: "One thing I know, that, whereas I was blind, now I see."[7] The results were conscious results. They knew that Christ did the work. Faith was the instrument, but its exercise was different, and the method of Christ's working was different. The various steps that brought them to the gracious end on their part, and on His part, were strikingly dissimilar at many points.

THE LIMITATIONS OF PRAYER

What are the limitations of prayer? How far do its benefits and possibilities reach? What part of God's dealing with humanity, and with humanity's world, is unaffected by prayer? Do the possibilities of prayer cover all temporal and spiritual good?

The answers to these questions are of transcendental importance. The answer will gauge the effort and results of our praying. The answer will greatly enhance the value of prayer, or will greatly depress prayer. The answer to these important questions are fully covered by Paul's words on prayer:

> Be careful for nothing; but in every thing by prayer and supplication with thanksgiving let your requests be made known unto God.[8]

Endnotes

1 Matthew 6:9
2 Matthew 5:3
3 I Peter 2:21
4 Mark 8:22-25
5 John 9:1-7
6 Mark 8:22-27
7 John 9:25b
8 Philippians 4:6

4

God Has Everything to Do with Prayer

CHRIST IS ALL. *We are complete in Him. He is the answer to every need, the perfect Savior. He needs no decoration to heighten His beauty, no prop to increase His stability, no girding to perfect His strength. Who can gild refined gold, whiten the snow, perfume the rose or heighten the colors of the summer sunset? Who will prop the mountains or help the great deep? It is not Christ and philosophy, nor Christ and money, nor civilization, nor diplomacy, nor science, nor organization. It is Christ alone. He trod the winepress alone. His own arm brought salvation. He is enough. He is the comfort, the strength, the wisdom, the righteousness, the sanctification of all man.* (C. L. Chilton)

Prayer is God's business to which Christians can attend. Prayer is God's necessary business, which only Christians can do, and that Christians must do. Those who belong to God are obliged to pray. They are not obliged to grow rich, nor to make money. They are not obliged to have large success in business. These are incidental, occasional, merely nominal, as far as integrity to Heaven and loyalty to God are concerned. Material successes are immaterial to God. Christians are neither better nor worse with those things or without them. They are not sources of reputation nor elements of character in the heavenly estimates. But to pray, to really pray, is the source of revenue, the basis of reputation, and the element of character in the estimation of God. People are obliged to pray just as they are obliged to be Christians. Prayer is loyalty to God. Non-praying is to reject Christ and to abandon heaven. A life of prayer is the only life that heaven counts.

GOD IS VITALLY CONCERNED THAT WE SHOULD PRAY

We are made better by prayer, and the world is made better by our praying. God does His best work for the world through prayer. God's greatest glory and humanity's highest good are secured by prayer. Prayer forms the godliest men and women and makes the godliest world.

God's promises lie like giant corpses without life, only for decay and dust unless people appropriate and give life to these promises by earnest and prevailing prayer.

A promise is like the unsown seed. The germ of life is in it, but the soil and culture of prayer are necessary to germinate and culture the seed. Prayer is God's life-giving breath. God's purposes move along the pathway made by prayer to their glorious designs. God's purposes are always moving to their high and beneficial ends, but the movement is along the way marked by unceasing prayer. The breath of prayer in Christians is from God.

God has everything to do with prayer, as well as everything to do with the one who prays. To those who pray, and as they pray, the prayer-hour is sacred because it is God's hour. The occasion is sacred because it is the occasion of the soul's approach to God, and of dealing with God. No hour is more hallowed because it is the occasion of the soul's mightiest approach to God, and of the fullest revelation from God. People are godlike and people are blessed, just as it is the hour of prayer that has the most of God in it.

PRAYER MAKES AND MEASURES THE APPROACH OF GOD

They know not God who know not how to pray. They have never seen God whose eyes have not been couched for God in the closet. God's vision place is the closet. His dwelling place is in secret. "He that dwelleth in the secret place of the most High shall abide under the shadow of the Almighty."[1]

They have never studied God who have not had their intellect broadened, strengthened, clarified, and uplifted by prayer. Almighty God commands prayer, God waits on prayer to order His ways, and God delights in prayer. To God, prayer is what the incense was to the Jewish temple. It impregnates everything, perfumes everything, and sweetens everything.

The possibilities of prayer cover the whole purposes of God through Christ. God conditions all gifts in all dispensations to His Son on prayer: "Ask of me," says God the Father to the Son, as that Son was moving earthward on the stupendous enterprise for a world's salvation, "and I shall give thee the heathen for thine inheritance, and the uttermost parts of the earth for thy possession."[2]

Hinging on prayer were all the means and results and successes of that wonderful and divine movement for human salvation. Broad and profound, mysterious and wonderful, was the scheme.

The answer to prayer is assured not only by the promises of God, but by God's relation to us as a Father.

But thou, when thou prayest, enter into thy closet, and when thou hast shut thy door, pray to thy Father which is in secret; and thy Father which seeth in secret shall reward thee openly.[3]

Again, we have these words: "If ye then, being evil, know how to give good gifts unto your children, how much more shall your Father which is in heaven give good things to them that ask him?"[4]

WE ARE ENCOURAGED TO PRAY

God encourages us to pray, not only by the certainty of the answer, but by the generosity of the promise, and the bounty of the giver. How princely the promise! "All things, whatsoever."[5] And when we add anything to that whatsoever[6] promise that covers all things and everything without qualification, exception, or limitation, then the promise is expanded and made minute and specific. The challenge of God to us is "Call unto me, and I will answer thee, and shew thee great and mighty things, which thou knowest not."[7] This includes, like the answer to Solomon's prayer, that which was specifically prayed for, but embraces vastly more of great value and of great necessity.

Almighty God seems to fear we will hesitate to ask largely, because we are apprehensive that we will strain His ability. He declares through Paul that He is "able to do exceeding abundantly above all that we ask or think."[8] He almost paralyses us by giving us a carte blanche, "Ask me of things to come concerning my sons, and concerning the work of my hands command ye me."[9] How He charges, commands, and urges us to pray! He goes beyond promise and says, in essence, "Behold my Son! I have given Him to you." "He that spared not his own Son, but delivered him up for us all, how shall he not with him also freely give us all things?"[10]

God gave us all things in prayer by promise because He had given us all things in His Son. Amazing gift—His Son! Prayer is as unlimited as His own blessed Son. There is nothing on earth or in Heaven, for time or eternity, that God's Son did not secure for us. By prayer, God gives us the vast and matchless inheritance that is ours by virtue of His Son. God charges us to "come boldly unto the throne of grace."[11] God is glorified and Christ is honored by large asking.

GOD DOES NOTHING WITHOUT PRAYER

That which is true of the promises of God is equally true of the purposes of God. We might say that God does nothing without prayer. His most gracious purposes are conditioned on prayer. His marvelous promises in Ezekiel 36 are subject to this qualification and condition: "Thus saith the Lord God; I will yet for this be enquired of by the house of Israel, to do it for them."[12]

In the second Psalm, the purposes of God to His enthroned Christ are decreed on prayer, as has been previously quoted. The decree that promises to Him the heathen for His inheritance relies on prayer for its fulfillment: "Ask of me." We see how sadly the decree has failed in its operation, not because of the weakness of God's purpose, but by the weakness of our praying. It takes God's mighty decree and our mighty praying to bring to pass these glorious results.

In the seventy-second Psalm, we have an insight into the mighty powers of prayer as the force that God moves on the conquest of Christ: "Prayer also shall be made for him continually."[13] In this statement Christ's movements are put into the hands of prayer.

When Christ looked upon the ripened fields of humanity with a sad and sympathizing heart, and saw the great need of laborers, His purposes were for more laborers, and so He charged them, "Pray ye therefore the Lord of the harvest, that he will send forth labourers into his harvest."[14] In Ephesians 3, Paul reminds those believers of the eternal purposes of God, and how he was bowing his knees to God in order that that eternal purpose might be accomplished, and also that they "might be filled with all the fullness of God."[15]

We see in Job how God conditioned His purposes for Job's three friends on Job's praying, and God's purposes in regard to Job were brought about by the same means.

In the first part of Revelation 8, the relation and necessity of saintly prayers to God's plans and operations in executing the salvation of sinners is set forth in rich, expressive, symbol, wherein the angels have to do with the prayers of the saints.

Prayer gives efficiency and utility to the promises. The mighty ongoing of God's purposes rests on prayer. The representatives of the Church in heaven, and of all creation, before the throne of God, "have every one of them golden vials of odours, which are the prayers of saints."[16]

PRAYER IS BASED UPON A RELATIONSHIP

We have said before, and repeat it, that prayer is based not simply upon a promise, but on a relationship. The returning penitent sinner prays on a promise. The child of God prays on the relation of a child. What the father has belongs to the child for present and prospective uses. The child asks, the father gives. The relationship is one of asking and answering, of giving and receiving. The child is dependent upon the father, must look to the father, must ask of the father, and must receive of the father.

We know how with earthly parents asking and giving belong to this relation, and how in the very act of asking and giving, the relationship of parent and child is cemented, sweetened, and enriched. The parents find their wealth of pleasure and satisfaction in giving to an obedient child, and the child finds its wealth in the parent's loving and continuous giving.

HOW PRAYER AFFECTS GOD

God's will, words, and purposes are all subject to review when the mighty powers of prayer come in. How mighty prayer is with God may be seen as He readily sets aside His own fixed and declared purposes in answer to prayer. The whole plan of salvation would have been blocked if Jesus Christ had prayed for the twelve legions of angels to bring dismay and ruin to His enemies.

The fasting and prayers of the Ninevites changed Gods purposes to destroy that wicked city after Jonah had gone there and cried unto the people, "Yet forty days, and Nineveh shall be overthrown."[17]

Almighty God is concerned in our praying. He wills it, He commands it, He inspires it. Jesus Christ in heaven is always praying. Prayer is His law and His life. The Holy Spirit teaches us how to pray. He prays for us "with groanings which cannot be uttered."[18] All these show the deep concern of God in prayer. It discloses very dearly how vital it is to His work in this world, and how far-reaching are its possibilities. Prayer forms the very center of the heart and will of God concerning people. "Rejoice evermore. Pray without ceasing. In every thing give thanks: for this is the will of God in Christ Jesus concerning you."[19]

EVERYTHING REVOLVES AROUND PRAYER

Prayer is the polestar around which rejoicing and thanksgiving revolve. Prayer is the heart sending its full and happy pulsations up to God through the glad currents of joy and thanksgiving.

By prayer, God's name is hallowed. By prayer, God's kingdom comes. By prayer, His kingdom is established in power and made to move with conquering force swifter than the light. By prayer, God's will is done until earth rivals heaven in harmony and beauty. By prayer, daily toil is sanctified and enriched, pardon is secured, and Satan is defeated. Prayer concerns God, and concerns humanity in every way.

God has nothing too good to give in answer to prayer. There is no vengeance pronounced by God so dire that does not yield to prayer. There is no justice so flaming that is not quenched by prayer.

Take the record and attitude of heaven against Saul of Tarsus. That attitude is changed and the record is erased when the astonishing condition is announced, "Behold, he prayeth."[20]

JONAH AND PRAYER

The repentant Jonah is alive and on dry ground, with scarce the taste of the sea or the smell of its weeds about him, after he prayed. "Out of the belly of hell cried I, and thou heardest my voice."[21]

The waters compassed me about, even to the soul: the depth closed me round about, the weeds were wrapped about my head. I went down to the bottoms of the mountains; the earth with her bars was about me for ever: yet hast thou brought up my life from corruption, O Lord my God. When my soul fainted within me I remembered the Lord: and my prayer came in unto thee, into thine holy temple.[22] And the LORD spake unto the fish, and it vomited out Jonah upon the dry land.[23]

PRAYER HAS ALL THE FORCE OF GOD IN IT

Prayer can get anything that God has. Thus prayer has all of its plea and its claim in the name of Jesus Christ, and there is nothing too good or great for God to give that name.

It must be borne in mind that there is no test surer of our being in the family of God than this thing of prayer. God's children pray. They repose in Him for all things. They ask Him for all things—for everything. The faith of the child in the father is proved by the child's asking. It is the answer to prayer that convinces people not only that there is a God, but that He is a God who concerns Himself about people, and about the affairs of this world. Answered prayer brings God near, and assures people of His being. Answered prayer is the credentials of our relation to, and our representation of Him. People cannot represent God who do not get answers to prayer from Him.

THE POSSIBILITIES OF PRAYER FOUND IN THE PROMISES

The possibilities of prayer are found in the unlimited promise, the willingness and power of God to answer prayer, to answer all prayer, to answer every prayer, and to supply fully the unlimited need of humanity. None are so needy as people, none are so able and anxious to supply every need and any need as God.

Preaching should no more fully declare and fulfill the will of God for the salvation of all people, than should the prayers of God's saints declare the same great truth as they struggle in their closet for this sublime end. God's heart is set on the salvation of all people. This concerns God. He has declared this in the death of His Son by an unspeakable voice, and every movement on earth for this end pleases God. So He declares that our prayers for the salvation of everyone are well pleasing in His sight.

The sublime and holy inspiration of pleasing God should ever move us to prayer for everyone. God eyes the closet, and nothing we can do pleases Him better than our large-hearted, ardent, praying for everyone. It is the embodiment and test of our devotion to God's will, and of our sympathetic loyalty to God.

PRAYER IS THE HIGHEST SPIRITUAL WORK

In I Timothy 2:13, the apostle Paul does not descend to a low plane, but presses the necessity of prayer by the most forceful facts. Jesus Christ, a man, the God-man, the highest illustration of manhood, is the mediator between God and humanity. Jesus Christ, this divine man, died for everyone. His life is but an intercession for all people. His death is but a prayer for all people. On earth, Jesus Christ knew no higher law, no holier business, no diviner life, than to plead for people. In Heaven, He knows no more royal estate, no higher theme, than to intercede for people. On earth, He lived and prayed and died for humanity. His life, His death, and His exaltation in Heaven all plead for everyone.

Is there any work, higher work, for the disciple to do than the Lord did? Is there any loftier employment, more honorable, more divine, than to pray for people? To take their woes, their sins, and their perils before God; to be one with Christ? To break the power that binds them, the satanic powers that hold them, and lift them to immortality and eternal life?

Endnotes

1 Psalm 91:1
2 Psalm 2:8
3 Matthew 6:6
4 Matthew 7:11; Luke 11:13
5 Matthew 21:22
6 John 14:13-14
7 Jeremiah 33:3
8 Ephesians 3:20
9 Isaiah 45:11
10 Romans 8:32
11 Hebrews 4:16
12 Ezekiel 36:37
13 Psalm 72:15
14 Matthew 9:38; Luke 10:2
15 Ephesians 3:19
16 Revelation 5:8
17 Jonah 3:4
18 Romans 8:26
19 I Thessalonians 5:16-18
20 Acts 9:11b
21 Jonah 2:2
22 Jonah 2:5-7
23 Jonah 2:10

5

Jesus: the Divine Teacher of Prayer

A FRIEND OF MINE IN *his journey is come to me, and I have nothing to set before him! He knocks again. "Friend! lend me three loaves?" He waits a while and then knocks again. "Friend! I must have three loaves!" "Trouble me not: the door is now shut; I cannot rise and give thee!" He stands still. He turns to go home. He comes back. He knocks again. "Friend!" he cries. He puts his ear to the door. There is a sound inside, and then the light of a candle shines through the hole of the door. The bars of the door are drawn back, and he gets not three loaves only, but as many as he needs. "And I say unto you, Ask and it shall be given you; seek and ye shall find; knock and it shall be opened unto you."* (Alexander Whyte, D.D.)

Jesus Christ was the divine teacher of prayer. Its power and nature had been illustrated by many saints and prophets in Old Testament times, but disciples and teachers of prayer in Jesus' day had lost their inspiration and life. Religiously dead, teachers and superficial ecclesiastics had forgotten what it was to pray. They did much of saying prayers, on state occasions, in public, with much ostentation and parade, but pray they did not. To them it was almost a lost practice. In the multiplicity of saying prayers they had lost the art of praying.

The history of the disciples during the earthly life of our Lord was not marked with much devotion. They were much enamored by their personal association with Christ. They were charmed by His words, excited by His miracles, and were entertained and concerned by the hopes that a selfish interest aroused in His person and mission. Taken up with the superficial and worldly views of His character, they neglected and overlooked the deeper and weightier things that belonged to Him and His mission. The neglect of the most obliging and ordinary duties by them was a noticeable feature in their conduct. So evident and singular was their conduct in this regard, that it became a matter of grave inquiry on one occasion and severe chiding on another.

> And they said unto him, Why do the disciples of John fast often, and make prayers, and likewise the disciples of the Pharisees; but thine eat and drink? And he said unto them, Can ye make the children of the bridechamber fast, while the bridegroom is with them? But the days will come, when the bridegroom shall be taken away from them, and then shall they fast in those days.[1]

In the example and the teaching of Jesus Christ, prayer assumes its normal relation to God's person, God's movements, and God's Son. Jesus Christ was essentially the teacher of prayer by precept and example. We have glimpses of His praying that, like indices, tell how full of prayer the pages, chapters, and volumes of His life were. The epitome that covers not one segment only, but the whole circle of His life and character, is pre-eminently that of prayer! "In the days of his flesh," the divine record reads, "when he had offered up prayers and supplications with strong crying and tears."[2] He was suppliant of all, the intercessor of all intercessors. In lowliest form He approached God, and with strongest pleas He prayed and supplicated.

JESUS TEACHES THE IMPORTANCE OF PRAYER

Jesus Christ teaches the importance of prayer by His urgency to His disciples to pray. But He shows us more than that. He shows how far prayer enters into the purposes of God. We must always keep in mind that the relation of Jesus Christ to God is the relation of asking and giving—the Son ever asking, the Father ever giving. We must never forget that God has put the conquering, inheriting, and expanding forces of Christ's cause in prayer. "Ask of me, and I shall give thee the heathen for thine inheritance, and the uttermost parts of the earth for thy possession."[3]

This was the clause embodying the royal proclamation and the universal condition when the Son was enthroned as the world's mediator, and when He was sent on His mission of receiving grace and power. We very naturally learn from this how Jesus would stress praying as the one sole condition of His receiving His possession and inheritance.

PRAYER IS ALL-INCLUSIVE

Necessarily, lines of thought will cross each other in this study on prayer, and the same Scripture passage or incident will be mentioned more than once, simply because a passage may teach one or more truths. This is the case when we speak of the vast comprehensiveness of prayer. How all-inclusive Jesus Christ makes prayer! It has no limitations in extent or things!

The promises to prayer are Godlike in their magnificence, wideness, and universality. In their nature, these promises have to do with God—with Him in their inspiration, creation, and results. Who but God could say, "And all things, whatsoever ye shall ask in prayer, believing, ye shall receive"?[4]

Who can command and direct "all things, whatsoever" but God? Neither human beings or chance or the law of results are so far lifted above change, limitations, or condition. Neither do they have in them mighty forces that can direct and result all things, as to promise the bestowment and direction of all things.

Whole sections, parables, and incidents were used by Christ to enforce the necessity and importance of prayer. His miracles are but parables of prayer. In nearly all of them prayer figures distinctly, and some features of it are illustrated. The Syrophenician woman[5] is a pre-eminent illustration of the ability and the success of importunity in prayer. The case of blind Bartimaeus[6] has points of suggestion along the same line. Jairus[7] and the centurion[8] illustrate and impress phases of prayer. The parable of the Pharisee and the publican[9] enforce humility in prayer, declare the wondrous results of praying, and show the vanity and worthlessness of wrong praying. The failure to enforce church discipline and the readiness of violating the fellowship, are all used to make an exhibit of far-reaching results of agreed praying, as recorded in Matthew 18:19.

PARTNERING IN PRAYER

It is of prayer in concert that Christ is speaking. Two who agree, two whose hearts have been keyed into perfect symphony by the Holy Spirit. Anything that they shall ask, it shall be done. Christ had been speaking of discipline in the Church, how things were to be kept in unity, and how the fellowship of the Church was to be maintained, by the restoration of the offender or by his exclusion. Members who had been true to the fellowship of Christ, and who were laboring to preserve that fellowship unbroken, would be the ones who agree to make appeals to God in united prayer.

In the Sermon on the Mount,[10] Christ lays down constitutional principles. Types and shadows are retired, and the law of spiritual life is declared. In this foundation law of the Christian system, prayer assumes a conspicuous, if not a paramount, position. It is not only wide, all-commanding, and comprehensive in its own sphere of action and relief, but it is ancillary to all duties. Even the one demanding kindly and discriminating judgment toward others, and also the royal injunction, the Golden Rule of action, these owe their being to prayer.

PRAYER IS A SPIRITUAL LAW

Christ puts prayer among the statutory promises. He does not leave it to natural law. The law of need, demand, and supply, of helplessness, of natural instincts, or the law of sweet, high, attractive privilege—these howsoever strong as motives of action, are not the basis of praying. Christ puts it as spiritual law. His disciples must pray. Not to pray is not simply a privation, an omission, but a positive violation of law, of spiritual life, a crime, bringing disorder and ruin. Prayer is law worldwide and eternity-reaching.

In the Sermon on the Mount, many important utterances are dismissed with a line or a verse, while the subject of prayer occupies a large space. To it, Christ returns again and again. He bases the possibilities and necessities of prayer on the relation of father and child—the child crying for bread, and the father giving that for which the child asks. Prayer and its answer are in the relation of a father to his child. The teaching of Jesus Christ on the nature and necessity of prayer as recorded in His life, is remarkable. He sends His disciples to their closets. Prayer must be a holy exercise, untainted by vanity, or pride. It must be in secret. The disciple must live in secret. God lives there, is sought there, and is found there. The command of Christ as to prayer is that pride and publicity should be shunned. Prayer is to be in private. "But thou, when thou prayest, enter into thy closet, and when thou hast shut thy door, pray to thy Father which is in secret; and thy Father which seeth in secret shall reward thee openly."[11]

THE BEATITUDES

The Beatitudes are not only to enrich and adorn, but they are the material out of which spiritual character is built. The very first one of these fixes prayer in the very foundation of spiritual character, not simply to adorn, but to compose. "Blessed are the poor in spirit." The word "poor" means a pauper, one who lives by begging. The real Christian lives on the bounties of another, whose bounties are received by asking. Prayer then becomes the basis of Christian character, the Christian's business, life, and living. This is Christ's law of prayer, putting it into the very being of the Christian. It is the first step, and the first breath, which is to color and to form all the after life in Christianity. Blessed are the poor ones, for only they can pray.

> Prayer is the Christian's vital breath,
> The Christian's native air;
> His watchword at the gates of death;
> He enters Heaven with prayer.

From praying Christ eliminates all self-sufficiency, all pride, and all spiritual values. The poor in spirit are the praying ones. Beggars are God's princes. They are God's heirs. Christ removes the rubbish of Jewish traditions and glosses from the regulations of the prayer altar.

Ye have heard that it was said by them of old time, Thou shalt not kill; and whosoever shall kill shall be in danger of the judgment: But I say unto you, That whosoever is angry with his brother without a cause shall be in danger of the judgment: and whosoever shall say to his brother, Raca, shall be in danger of the council: but whosoever shall say, Thou fool, shall be in danger of hell fire. Therefore if thou bring thy gift to the altar, and there rememberest that thy brother hath ought against thee; Leave there thy gift before the altar, and go thy way; first be reconciled to thy brother, and then come and offer thy gift.[12]

Those who attempt to pray to God with an angry spirit, with loose and irreverent lips, with an unreconciled heart, and with unsettled neighborly scores, spend their labor for that which is worse than nothing, violate the law of prayer, and add to their sin.

How rigidly exacting is Christ's law of prayer! It goes to the heart, and demands that love be enthroned there, love to other Christians. The sacrifice of prayer must be seasoned and perfumed with love, by love in the inward parts. The law of prayer, its creator and inspirer, is love.

PRAYING MUST BE DONE

God wants it done. He commands it. People need it and people must do it. Something must surely come of praying, for God engages that something shall come out of it, if Christians are in earnest and are persevering in prayer.

After Jesus teaches, "Ask and it shall be given you," etc.,[13] He encourages real praying, and more praying. He repeats with redoubled assurance, "for every one that asketh receiveth." No exception. "Every one." "He that seeketh findeth."[14] Here it is again, sealed and stamped with infinite veracity. Then closed and signed, as well as sealed, with divine attestation, "To him that knocketh it shall be opened." Note how we are encouraged to pray by our relation to God!

If ye then, being evil, know how to give good gifts unto your children, how much more shall your Father which is in heaven give good things to them that ask him?[15]

The relation of prayer to God's work and God's rule in this world, is most fully illustrated by Jesus Christ in both His teaching and His practice. He is first in every way and in everything. Among the rulers of the Church, He is primary in a preeminent way. He has the throne. The golden crown is His in eminent preciousness. The white garments enrobe Him in preeminent whiteness and beauty. In the ministry of prayer, He is a divine example as well as the divine teacher. His example is rich, and His prayer teaching abounds. How imperative the teaching of our Lord when He affirms that "men ought always to pray, and not to faint,"[16] and then presents a striking parable of an unjust judge and a poor widow to illustrate and enforce His teaching. It is a necessity to pray. It is exacting and binding for Christians to always be in prayer. Courage, endurance, and perseverance are demanded that Christians may never faint in prayer. "And shall not God avenge His own elect, which cry day and night unto Him?"[17]

CHRISTIANS MUST PRAY AS CHRIST TAUGHT

This is His strong and indignant questioning and affirmation. Christians must pray according to Christ's teaching. They must not get tired or grow weary in praying. God's character is the assured guarantee that much will come of the persistent praying of true Christians.

Doubtless the praying of our Lord had much to do with the revelation made to Peter and the confession he made to Christ, "Thou art the Christ, the Son of the living God."[18] Prayer mightily affects and molds the circle of our associates. Christ made disciples and kept them disciples by praying. His twelve disciples were much impressed by His praying. No one ever prayed like this man. How different His praying was from the cold, proud, self-righteous praying that they heard and saw on the streets, in the synagogue, and in the Temple.

Endnotes

1 Luke 5:33-35
2 Hebrews 5:7
3 Psalm 2:8
4 Matthew 21:22
5 Mark 7:26
6 Mark 10:46
7 Mark 5:22
8 Matthew 8:5
9 Luke 18:10
10 Matthew 5
11 Matthew 6:6
12 Matthew 5:21-24
13 Matthew 7:7
14 Matthew 7:8
15 Matthew 7:11
16 Luke 18:1
17 Luke 18:7
18 Matthew 16:16

6

Jesus: the Divine Teacher of Prayer
(Continued)

L UKE TELLS US THAT *as Jesus was praying in a certain place, when He ceased, one of His disciples said unto Him, "Lord, teach us to pray." This disciple had heard Jesus preach, but did not feel like saying, "Lord, teach us to preach." He could learn to preach by studying the methods of the Master. But there was something about the praying of Jesus that made the disciple feel that he did not know how to pray; that he had never prayed, and that he could not learn by listening even to the Master as He prayed. There is a profound something about prayer which never lies upon the surface. To learn it, one must go to the depths of the soul, and climb to the heights of God.* (A. C. Dixon, D.D.)

Let it not be forgotten that prayer was one of the great truths that Jesus came into the world to teach and illustrate. It was worth a trip from heaven to earth to teach people this great lesson of prayer. It was great lesson, and a very difficult lesson for people to learn. People are naturally averse to learning this lesson of prayer. The lesson is a very lowly one. None but God can teach it. It is a despised beggary, a sublime and heavenly vocation. The disciples were very stupid scholars, but were quickened to prayer by hearing Him pray and talk about prayer.

The dispensation of Christ's personality, while it was not and could not be the dispensation in its fullest and highest sense of need and dependence. Yet Christ did try to impress on His disciples not only a deep necessity of the necessity of prayer in general, but the importance of prayer to them in their personal and spiritual needs. There came moments to them when they felt the need of a deeper and more thorough schooling in prayer, and of their grave neglect in this regard. One of these hours of deep conviction on their part, and of eager inquiry, was when He was praying at a certain place and time. When they saw Him, they said to Him, "Lord, teach us to pray, as John also taught his disciples."[1]

As they listened to Him praying, they felt very keenly their ignorance and deficiency in praying. Who has not felt the same deficiency and ignorance? Who has not longed for a teacher in the divine art of praying?

The conviction had these twelve men had of their defect in prayer arose from hearing their Lord and Master pray, but likewise from a sense of serious defect even when compared with John the Baptist's training of his disciples in prayer. As they listened to their Lord pray (for unquestionably He must have been seen and heard by them as He prayed), His prayers had a stimulating charm for them. In the presence and hearing of His praying, they felt very keenly their ignorance and deficiency in prayer. Who has not felt the same ignorance and deficiency?

THE SCHOOL OF PRAYER

We do not regret the schooling our Lord gave these twelve men, for in schooling them He schools us. The lesson is one already learned in the law of Christ. But they were so dull, that many patient repetitions were required to instruct them in this divine art of prayer. Likewise, we are so dull and inept that many wearying patient repetition must be given us before we will learn any important lesson in the all-important school of prayer.

This divine teacher of prayer lays Himself out to make it clear and strong that God answers prayer, assuredly, certainly, inevitably. He states repeatedly that it is the duty of the child to ask and to press, and that the Father is obliged to answer, and to give for the asking. In Christ's teaching, prayer is no sterile, vain performance. It is not a mere rite, a form, but a request for an answer, a plea to gain, the seeking of a great good from God. It is a lesson of getting that for which we ask, of finding that for which we seek, and of entering the door at which we knock.

FAILURE AND LACK OF PRAYER

We have a notable occasion when Jesus comes down from the Mount of Transfiguration. He finds His disciples defeated, humiliated, and confused in the presence of their enemies. A father has brought his child possessed with a demon to have the demon cast out. They attempted to do it but failed. They had been commissioned by Jesus and sent to do that very work, but had signally failed. "And when he was come into the house, his disciples asked him privately, Why could not we cast him out? And he said unto them, This kind can come forth by nothing, but by prayer and fasting."[2]

Their faith had not been cultured by prayer. They failed in prayer before they failed in ability to do their work. They failed in faith because they had failed in prayer. The one thing that was necessary to do God's work was prayer. The work that God sends us to do cannot be done without prayer.

FAITH AND PRAYER

In Christ's teaching on prayer we have another pertinent statement. It was in connection with the cursing of the barren fig tree:

> Jesus answered and said unto them, Verily I say unto you, If ye have faith, and doubt not, ye shall not only do this which is done to the fig tree, but also if ye shall say unto this mountain, Be thou removed, and be thou cast into the sea; it shall be done. And all things, whatsoever ye shall ask in prayer, believing, ye shall receive.[3]

In this passage we have faith and prayer, their possibilities and powers conjoined. A fig tree had been blasted to the roots by the word of the Lord Jesus. The power and quickness of the result surprised the disciples. Jesus says to them that it need be no surprise to them or such a difficult work to be done. "If ye have faith," its possibilities to affect will not be confined to the little fig tree, but the gigantic, rock-ribbed, rock-founded mountains can be uprooted and moved into the sea. Prayer is leverage of this great power of faith.

It is well to refer again to the occasion when the heart of our Lord was so deeply moved with compassion as He beheld the multitudes because they fainted and were scattered as having no shepherd. It was then He urged upon His disciples the injunction, "Pray ye therefore the Lord of the harvest, that he will send forth labourers into his harvest,"[4] clearly teaching them that it belonged to God to call into the ministry those whom He will, and that the Holy Spirit does this very work in answer to prayer.

THE NECESSITY OF PRAYER

Prayer is as necessary now as it was then to secure the needed laborers to reap earthly harvests for the heavenly garners. Has God's Church ever learned this lesson of so vital and exacting import? God alone can choose the laborers and thrust them out, and this choosing He does not delegate to human beings, or to a church association or conference. God is moved to this great work of calling laborers into the ministry by prayer. Earthly fields are rotting. They are untilled because prayer is silent. The laborers are few. Fields are not worked because prayer has not worked with God.

We have the prayer promise and the prayer ability put in a distinct form in the higher teachings of prayer by our Lord: "If ye abide in me, and my words abide in you, ye shall ask what ye will, and it shall be done unto you."[5]

Here we have a fixed attitude of life as the condition of prayer. Not simply a fixed attitude of life toward some great principles or purposes, but the fixed attitude and unity of life with Jesus Christ. To live in Him, to dwell there, to be one with Him, to draw all life from Him, to let all life

from Him flow through us—this is the attitude of prayer and the ability
to pray. Abiding in Him cannot be separated from His Word abiding in us.
It must live in us to give birth to and food for prayer. The attitude of the
person of Christ is the condition of prayer.

GOD'S WORD MAGNIFIED ABOVE HIS NAME

The Old Testament saints had been taught that God had magnified His
Word above all His name.[6] New Testament saints must learn fully how to
exalt by perfect obedience that Word issuing from the lips of Him who is
the Word. Praying ones under Christ must learn what praying ones under
Moses had already learned, that "Man shall not live by bread alone, but by
every word that proceedeth out of the mouth of God."[7]

The life of Christ flowing through us and the words of Christ living
in us, these give power to prayer. They breathe the spirit of prayer, and
make the body, blood, and bones of prayer. Then it is Christ praying in me
and through me, and all things that "I will" are the will of God. My will
becomes the law and the answer, for it is written, "ye shall ask what ye will,
and it shall be done unto you."

FRUIT BEARING

Our Lord puts fruit bearing to the front in our praying:

> Ye have not chosen me, but I have chosen you, and ordained you,
> that ye should go and bring forth fruit, and that your fruit should
> remain: that whatsoever ye shall ask of the Father in my name, he
> may give it you.[8]

Barrenness cannot pray. Only fruit bearing capacity and reality can
pray. It is not fruitfulness of the past, but of the present: "that your fruit
should remain." Fruit, the product of life, is the condition of praying. A
life vigorous enough to bear fruit, much fruit, is the condition and the
source of prayer. "And in that day ye shall ask me nothing. Verily, verily, I
say unto you, Whatsoever ye shall ask the Father in my name, he will give
it you. Hitherto have ye asked nothing in my name: ask, and ye shall receive,
that your joy may be full."[9]

"In that day ye shall ask me nothing." It is not solving riddles, not
revealing mysteries, not curious questionings. This is not our attitude, not
our business under the dispensation of the Spirit, but to pray, and to pray
largely. Much true praying increases our joy and God's glory.

"And whatsoever ye shall ask in my name, that will I do,"[10] says Christ,
and the Father will give. Both Father and Son are pledged to give the very
things for which we ask. But the condition is "in His name." This does not
mean that His name is talismanic, to give value by magic. It does not mean
that His name in beautiful settings of pearl will give value to prayer. It is

not that His name perfumed with sentiment and inserted to close our prayers and doings will do the deed.

WORKING IN CHRIST'S NAME

How fearful the statement: "Many will say to me in that day, Lord, Lord, have we not prophesied in thy name? and in thy name have cast out devils? and in thy name done many wonderful works? And then will I profess unto them, I never knew you: depart from me, ye that work iniquity.[11] How blasting the doom of these great workers and doers who claim to work in His name!

It means far more than sentiment, verbiage, and nomenclature. It means to stand in His stead, to bear His nature, to stand for all for which He stood—for righteousness, truth, holiness and zeal. It means to be one with God as He was, one in spirit, in will and in purpose. It means that our praying is singly and solely for God's glory through His Son. It means that we abide in Him, that Christ prays through us, lives in us, and shines out of us—that we pray by the Holy Spirit according to the will of God.

Even amid the darkness of Gethsemane, with the stupor that had settled upon the disciples, we have the sharp warning from Christ to His sluggish disciples, "Watch ye and pray, lest ye enter into temptation. The spirit truly is willing, but the flesh is weak."[12] How needful to hear such a warning, to awaken all our powers, not simply for the great crises of our lives, but as the inseparable and constant attendants of a career marked with perils and dangers on every hand.

PRAYING IN JESUS' NAME

As Christ nears the close of His earthly mission, nearer to the greater and more powerful dispensation of the Spirit, His teaching about prayer takes on a more absorbing and higher form. It has now become a graduating school. His connection with prayer becomes more intimate and more absolute. He becomes in prayer what He is in all else pertaining to our salvation, the beginning and the end, the first and the last. His name becomes all power. Mighty works are to be done by the faith that can pray in His name. Like His nature, His name covers all needs, embraces all worlds, and gets all good.

> Believest thou not that I am in the Father, and the Father in me? the words that I speak unto you I speak not of myself: but the Father that dwelleth in Me, he doeth the works. Believe me that I am in the Father, and the Father in Me: or else believe Me for the very works' sake. Verily, verily, I say unto you, He that believeth on Me, the works that I do shall he do also; and greater works than these shall he do; because I go unto my Father. And whatsoever ye shall ask in My name, that will I do, that the Father may be glorified in the Son. If ye shall ask any thing in My name, I will do it.[13]

The Father, the Son, and the praying person are all bound up together. All things are in Christ, and all things are in prayer in His name. "If ye shall ask anything in My name." The key that unlocks the vast storehouse of God is prayer. The power to do greater works than Christ did, lies in the faith that can grasp His name truly and in true praying.

PRAYER PREVENTS MANY EVILS

In the last of His life, note how He urges prayer as a preventive of the many evils to which they were exposed. In view of the temporal and fearful terrors of the destruction of Jerusalem, He charges them to this effect: "Pray ye that your flight be not in the winter."[14]

Many evils in this life can be escaped by prayer! Many fearful temporal calamities can be mitigated, if not wholly relieved, by prayer! Notice how, amid the excesses and stupefying influences to which we are exposed in this world, Christ charges us to pray:

> And take heed to yourselves, lest at any time your hearts be overcharged with surfeiting, and drunkenness, and cares of this life, and so that day come upon you unawares. For as a snare shall it come on all them that dwell on the face of the whole earth. Watch ye therefore, and pray always, that ye may be accounted worthy to escape all these things that shall come to pass, and to stand before the Son of man.[15]

In view of the uncertainty of the time of Christ's coming to judge, and the uncertainty of our going out of this world, He says: "But of that day and that hour knoweth no man, no, not the angels which are in heaven, neither the Son, but the Father. Take ye heed, watch and pray: for ye know not when the time is.[16]

JESUS' PARTING WORDS AND PRAYER

We have the words of Jesus as given in His last interview with His twelve disciples, found in the Gospel of John, chapters fourteen to seventeen, inclusive. These are true, solemn, parting words. The disciples were to move out into the regions of toil and peril, bereft of the personal presence of their Lord and Master. They were to be impressed that prayer would serve them in everything, and its use and unlimited possibilities would in some measure supply their loss. By it, they would be able to command all the possibilities of Jesus Christ and God the Father.

It was the occasion of momentous interest to Jesus Christ. His work was to receive its climax and crown in His death and His resurrection. His glory and the success of His work and of its execution, under the mastery and direction of the Holy Spirit, was to be committed to His apostles. To them it was an hour of strange wonderment and of peculiar, mysterious, sorrow. They were only too well assured of the fact that Jesus was to leave them. All else was dark and impalpable.

He was to give them His parting words and pray His parting prayer. Solemn, vital, truths were to be the weight and counsel of that hour. He speaks to them of heaven. Young men, strong though they were, yet they could not meet the duties of their preaching life and their apostolic life without the fact, the thought, the hope, and the relish of Heaven. These things were to be present constantly in all sweetness, in all their vigor, in all freshness, in all brightness. He spoke to them about their spiritual and conscious connection with Him, an abiding indwelling, so close and continuous that His own life would flow into them, as the life of the vine flows into the branches. Their lives and their fruitfulness were dependent upon this. Then praying was urged upon them as one of the vital, essential, forces. This was the one thing upon which all the divine force depended, and this was the avenue and agency through which the divine life and power were to be secured and continued in their ministry.

He spoke to them about prayer. He had taught them many lessons upon this all-important subject while they had been together. He seizes this solemn hour to perfect his teaching. They must be made to realize that they have an unlimited and exhaustless storehouse of good in God, and that they can draw on Him at all times and for all things without end. As Paul said in later years to the Philippians, "My God shall supply all your need according to His riches in glory by Christ Jesus."[17]

Endnotes

1 Luke 11:1
2 Mark 9:28-29
3 Matthew 21:21-22
4 Matthew 9:38
5 John 15:7
6 See Psalm 138:2
7 Deuteronomy 8:3; Matthew 4:4
8 John 15:16
9 John 16:23-24
10 John 14:13
11 Matthew 7:22-23
12 Mark 14:38
13 John 14:10-14
14 Matthew 24:20
15 Luke 21:34-36
16 Mark 13:32-33
17 Philippians 4:19

7

Jesus: The Example of Prayer

CHRIST, WHEN HE SAW *that He must die, and that now His time was come, He wore His body out: He cared not, as it were, what became of Him: He wholly spent Himself in preaching all day, and in praying all night, preaching in the temple those terrible parables and praying in the garden such prayers, as the seventeenth of John, and "Thy will be done!" even to a bloody sweat.* (Thomas Goodwin)

The Bible record of the life of Jesus Christ gives only a glance of His busy activities, a small selection of His many words, and only a brief record of His great works. But even in this record we see Him as being much in prayer. Even though busy and exhausted by the severe strain and toils of His life, "in the morning, rising up a great while before day, he went out, and departed into a solitary place, and there prayed."[1]

Alone in the desert and in the darkness with God! Prayer filled the life of our Lord while on earth. His life was a constant stream of incense sweet and perfumed by prayer. When we see how the life of Jesus was one of prayer, then we must conclude that to be like Jesus is to pray like Jesus and live like Jesus. It is a serious life to pray as Jesus prayed.

We cannot follow any chronological order in the praying of Jesus Christ. We do not know what His steps of advance and skill were in the divine art of praying. He is in the act of prayer when we find Him at the fords of the Jordan, when the waters of baptism, at the hands of John the Baptist, are upon Him. So passing over the three years of His ministry, when closing the drama of His life in that terrible baptism of fear, pain, suffering, and shame, we find Him in the spirit and praying. The baptism of the Cross, as well as the baptism of the Jordan, are sanctified by prayer. With the breath of prayer in His last sigh, He commits His spirit to God. In His first recorded utterances, as well as His first acts, we find Him teaching His disciples how to pray as His first lesson, and as their first duty. Under the shadow of the Cross, in the urgency and importance of His last interview with His chosen disciples, He is at the same all-important business, teaching the world's teachers how to pray, trying to make prayerful those lips and hearts out of which were to flow the divine deposits of truth.

JESUS' GREAT WORKS CROWNED WITH PRAYER

The great eras of His life were created and crowned with prayer. What His habits of prayer were during His stay at home and His toil as a carpenter in Nazareth, we have no means of knowing. God has veiled it, and guess and speculation are not only vain and misleading, but proud and foolish. It would be presumptuous searching into that which God has hidden, which would make us seek to be wise above that which was written, trying to lift up the veil with which God has covered His own revelation.

We find Christ in the presence of the famed prophet and preacher. He has left His Nazareth home and His carpenter shop by God's call. He is now at a transitional point. He has moved out to His great work. John's baptism and the baptism of the Holy Ghost are prefatory and are to qualify Him for that work. This epochal and transitional period is marked by prayer.

> Now when all the people were baptized, it came to pass, that Jesus also being baptized, and praying, the heaven was opened, And the Holy Ghost descended in a bodily shape like a dove upon him, and a voice came from heaven, which said, Thou art my beloved Son; in thee I am well pleased.[2]

It is a supreme hour in His history, different and in striking contrast with, but not in opposition to, the past. The descent and abiding of the Holy Spirit in all His fullness, the opening heavens, and the attesting voice that involved God's recognition of His only Son—all these are the result of His praying on that occasion.

WE ARE TO PRAY AS JESUS PRAYED

"As He was praying," so we are to be praying. If we would pray as Christ prayed, we must be as Christ was, and must live as Christ lived. The Christ character, the Christ life, and the Christ spirit, must be ours if we would do the Christ praying, and would have our prayers answered as He had His prayers answered. The business of Christ even now in heaven at His Father's right hand is to pray. Certainly if we are His, if we love Him, if we live for Him, and if we live close to Him, we will catch the spirit of His praying life, both on earth and in heaven. We will learn His trade and carry on His business on earth.

Jesus Christ loved all humanity, He tasted death for all humanity, He intercedes for all humanity. Let us ask then, are we the imitators, the representatives, and the executors of Jesus Christ? Then in our prayers we must run parallel with His atonement in its extent. The atoning blood of Jesus Christ gives sanctity and efficiency to our prayers. As worldwide, as broad, and as human as the man Christ Jesus was, so must be our prayers. The intercessions of Christ's people must give currency and expedition to the work of Christ, carry the atoning blood to its beneficial ends, and help to strike off the chains of sin from every ransomed soul. We must be as praying, as tearful, and as compassionate as was Christ.

PRAYER AFFECTS ALL THINGS

God blesses the person who prays. Those who pray go out on a long voyage for God and are enriched themselves while enriching others. They are blessed themselves while the world is blessed by their praying. To "lead a quiet and peaceable life in all godliness and honesty"[3] is the wealthiest wealth.

The praying of Christ was real. No one prayed as He prayed. Prayer pressed upon Him as a solemn, all-imperative, all-commanding duty, as well as a royal privilege in which all sweetness was condensed, alluring, and absorbing. Prayer was the secret of His power, the law of His life, the inspiration of His toil, and the source of His wealth, His joy, His communion, and His strength.

To Christ Jesus, prayer occupied no secondary place, but was exacting and paramount, a necessity, a life, the satisfying of a restless yearning, and a preparation for heavy responsibilities.

Closeting with His Father in counsel and fellowship, with vigor and in deep joy, all this was His praying. Present trials, future glory, the history of His Church, and the struggles and perils of His disciples in all times and to the very end of time—all these things were born and shaped by His praying.

JESUS' LIFE FILLED WITH PRAYER

Nothing is more conspicuous in the life of our Lord than prayer. His campaigns were arranged and His victories were gained in the struggles and communion of His all-night praying. By prayer He rent the heavens. Moses and Elijah and the transfiguration glory wait on His praying. His miracles and teaching had their power from the same source. Gethsemane's praying crimsoned Calvary with serenity and glory. His high priestly prayer makes the history and hastens the triumph of His Church on earth. What an inspiration and command to pray is the prayer life of Jesus Christ while in this world! What a comment it is on the value, the nature, and the necessity of prayer!

The dispensation of the person of Jesus Christ was a dispensation of prayer. A synopsis of His teaching and practice of prayer was that "Men ought always to pray, and not to faint."[4]

The Jews prayed in the name of their patriarchs and invoked the privileges granted to them by covenant with God. We have a new name and a new covenant, more privileged, powerful, all-comprehensive, authoritative, and more divine. As much as the Son of God is lifted above the patriarchs in divinity, glory, and power, by so much should our praying exceed theirs in range of largeness, glory, and power of results.

JESUS PRAYED TO GOD THE FATHER

He approached God simply and directly in the charmed and revered circle of the Father. The awful, repelling, fear was entirely absent, lost in the supreme confidence of a child.

Jesus Christ crowns His life, works, and teaching with prayer. His Father attested to His relationship and put on Him the glory of answered prayer at His baptism and transfiguration when all other glories were growing dim in the night that settles on Him! What almighty powers are in prayer when we are charged and charged again with but one inspiration and aim! "Father, glorify thy name."[5] This sweetens all, brightens all, conquers all and gets all. "Father, glorify Thy name." That guiding star will illumine the darkest night, calm the wildest storm, and make us brave and true. It is an imperial principle. It will make an imperial Christian.

The range and power of prayer, so clearly shown by Jesus in life and teaching, reveal the great purposes of God. They not only reveal the Son in the reality and fullness of His humanity, but also reveal the Father.

JESUS PRAYED LIKE A CHILD

The spirit of a child was found in Him. At the grave of Lazarus "Jesus lifted up His eyes, and said, Father."[6] Again we hear Him begin His prayer after this fashion: "In that hour Jesus rejoiced in spirit, and said, I thank thee, O Father."[7] So also on other occasions we find Him in prayer addressing God as His Father, assuming the attitude of the child asking something of the Father. What confidence, simplicity, and artlessness! What readiness, freeness, and fullness of approach are all involved in the spirit of a child! What confiding trust, what assurance, what tender interest! What profound solicitudes, and tender sympathy on the Father's part! What respect deepening into reverence! What loving obedience and grateful emotions glow in the child's heart! What divine fellowship and royal intimacy! What sacred and sweet emotions! All these meet in the hour of prayer when the child of God meets His Father in heaven, and when the

Father meets His child! We must live as children if we would ask as children. We must act as children if we would pray as children. The spirit of prayer is born of the child spirit.

The profound reverence in this relation of paternity must forever exclude all lightness, frivolity, and pertness, as well as all undue familiarity. Solemnity and gravity become the hour of prayer. It has been well said:

> The worshipper who invokes God under the name of Father and realizes the gracious and beneficent love of God, must at the same time remember and recognize God's glorious majesty, which is neither annulled nor impaired, but rather supremely intensified through His fatherly love. An appeal to God as Father, if not associated with reverence and homage before the Divine Majesty, would betray a want of understanding of the character of God.

And, we might add, it would show a lack of the attributes of a child. Patriarchs and prophets knew something of the doctrine of the Fatherhood of God to God's family. As someone has said, "they saw it afar off, were persuaded of it, and embraced it." But they did not understand it in all its fullness, "God having provided some better thing for us, that they without us should not be made perfect."[8]

"Behold, he prayeth!"[9] was God's statement of wonderment and surprise to the timid Ananias in regard to Saul of Tarsus. "Behold he prayeth!" applied to Christ has in it far more of wonderment and mystery and surprise. He, the maker of all worlds, the Lord of angels and of humanity, co-equal and co-eternal with the everlasting God, the "brightness of His glory, and the express image of His person,"[10] fresh from his Father's glory and throne, exclaims, "Behold, he prayeth!" To find Him in lowly, dependent, attitude of prayer, the suppliant of all suppliants, His richest legacy and His royal privilege to pray—this is the mystery of all mysteries, the wonder of all wonders.

THE WAY JESUS PRAYED

The writer of Hebrews gives in brief and comprehensive statement the habit of our Lord in prayer—"Who in the days of His flesh, when He had offered up prayers and supplications with strong crying and tears unto Him that was able to save Him from death, and was heard in that He feared."[11] We have in this description of our Lord's praying the outgoing of great spiritual forces. He prayed with "prayers and supplications." It was no formal, tentative, effort. He was intense, personal, and real. He was a pleader for God's good. He was in great need and He must cry with "strong crying," made stronger still by His tears. In an agony the Son of God struggled. His praying was no playing a mere part. His soul was engaged, and all His powers were taxed to a strain. Let us pause and look at Him and learn how to pray in earnest. Let us learn how to win in an agony of prayer that which seems to be withheld from us. *Feared* is a beautiful word. It occurs only twice in the New Testament, the fear of God.

Jesus Christ was always a busy man with His work, but never too busy to pray. The most divine business filled His heart and filled His hands, consumed His time, exhausted His nerves. But with Him even God's work must not crowd out God's praying. Saving people from sin or suffering must not, even with Christ, be substituted for praying. It must not lessen in the least the time or the intensity of these holiest of seasons. He filled the day with working for God. He employed the night with praying to God. The day work made the night praying a necessity. The night praying sanctified and made successful the day work. Too busy to pray gives our religion a Christian burial, it is true, but kills it nevertheless.

In many cases, only the bare, yet important and suggestive, fact is stated that He prayed. In other cases, the very words that came out of His heart and fell from His lips are recorded. The man of prayer by pre-eminence was Jesus Christ. The great events of His life were created by prayer, and all the minor and everyday events of His life were inspired, colored, and impregnated by prayer.

The prayer words of Jesus were sacred words. By them, God speaks to God, and by them God is revealed and prayer is illustrated and enforced. Here is prayer in its purest form and in its mightiest powers. It would seem that earth and heaven would uncover head and open ears most wide to catch the words of Christ's praying. He was truest God and truest man, and the most divine of suppliants, who prayed as never anyone prayed. His prayers are our inspiration and pattern to pray.

Endnotes

1 Mark 1:35
2 Luke 3:21-22
3 I Timothy 2:2
4 Luke 18:1
5 John 12:28
6 John 11:41
7 Luke 10:21
8 Hebrews 11:40
9 Acts 9:11b
10 Hebrews 1:3
11 Hebrews 5:7

8

Prayer Incidents in the Life of Our Lord

THERE WAS A GREAT *cape at the south of Africa and so many storms and so much loss of life until it was called the Cape of Death. One day in 1789 a bold navigator shoved the prow of his vessel into the storms that thundered around it and found a calm sea. He then named it the Cape of Good Hope. So there is a cape that jutted out from earth into the sea of eternity called death. All were afraid of it. All navigators, sooner or later, must contend with these murky waters. But once upon a time, nearly two thousand years ago, a brave navigator from heaven came and drove the prow of His frail humanity bark down into the gloomy waters of this cape and lay under its awful power for three days. Emerging from there, He found it to be the door to endless calm and joy, and now we call it Good Hope.* (John W. Baker)

One of Christ's most impassioned and sublime paeans of prayer and praise is found recorded by both Matthew and Luke, with small verbal contrasts and with some diversity of detail and environments. He is reviewing the poor results of His ministry and remarking upon the feeble responses of people to God's vast outlay of love and mercy. He is arraigning the ingratitude of people to God, and is showing the fearfully destructive results of their indifference with their increased opportunities, favors, and responsibilities.

In the midst of these arraignments, denunciations, and woes, the seventy disciples return to report the results of their mission. They were full of exhilaration at their success, and proved it with no little self-congratulation. The spirit of Jesus was diverted, relieved, and refreshed by their animation, catching somewhat the excitement of their joy, and sharing in their triumph. He rejoiced, gave thanks, and prayed a prayer wonderful for its brevity, inspiration, and revelation:

> In that hour Jesus rejoiced in spirit, and said, I thank thee, O Father, Lord of heaven and earth, that thou hast hid these things from the wise and prudent, and hast revealed them unto babes: even so, Father; for so it seemed good in thy sight. All things are delivered to me of my Father: and no man knoweth who the Son is, but the Father; and who the Father is, but the Son, and he to whom the Son will reveal him.[1]

CHRIST: THE IMAGE OF HIS FATHER

Christ was the "express image of His person."[2] So the spirit of prayer with Christ was to do God's will. His constant affirmation was that He "came to do His Father's will,"[3] and not His own will. When the fearful crisis came in His life in Gethsemane, and all its darkness, direness and dread, with the crushing weight of humanity's sins and sorrows that were pressing down upon Him, His spirit and frame crushed, and almost expiring, then He cried out for relief. Yet it was not His will that was to be followed. It was only an appeal out of weakness and death for God's relief in God's way. God's will was to be the law and the rule of His relief, if relief came.[4]

So those who follow Christ in prayer must have God's will as their law, their rule and their inspiration. In all praying, it is the person who prays. The life and the character flow into the closet. There is a mutual action and reaction. The closet has much to do with making the character, while the character has much to do with making the closet. It is "the effectual fervent prayer of a righteous man [that] availeth much."[5] It is with them who "call on the Lord out of a pure heart"[6] that we are to associate. Christ was the greatest man of prayer because He was the holiest of all people. His character is the praying character. His spirit is the life and power of prayer. The best people of prayer are not judged by their great fluency, their brilliant imagination, their rich gifts, and their fiery ardor, but are those who have imbibed most of the spirit of Christ.

HAVING A CHARACTER LIKE THAT OF CHRIST

It is those whose character is the nearest to a facsimile of Christ upon whom God's power is bestowed and to whom God's person and will are revealed. "Hide these things from the wise and prudent." Those, for instance, who are wise in their own eyes, skilled in letters, cultured, learned, philosophers, teachers, doctors, rabbis. Prudent—one who can put things together, having insight, comprehension, expression. God's revelation of Himself and His will cannot be sought out and understood by reason, intelligence, or great learning. Great people and great minds are neither the channels nor depositories of God's revelation by virtue of their culture, braininess, or wisdom. God's system in redemption and providence is not to be thought out, and open only to the learned and wise. The learned and the wise, following their learning and their wisdom, have always sadly and darkly missed God's thoughts and God's ways.

The condition of receiving God's revelation and of holding God's truth is one of the heart, not one of the head. The ability to receive and search out is like that of the child, the babe, the synonym of docility, innocence, and simplicity. These are the conditions on which God reveals Himself to people. The world by wisdom cannot know God. The world by wisdom can never receive or understand God, because God reveals Himself to people's hearts, not to their heads. Only hearts can ever know God, can feel God, can see God, and can read God in His Book of books. God is not grasped by thought but by feeling. The world gets God by revelation, not by philosophy. It is not apprehension, the mental ability to grasp God, but plasticity, ability to be impressed, that people need. It is not by hard, strong, stern, great reasoning that the world gets God or gets hold of God, but by big, soft, pure hearts. People do not so need light to see God as they need hearts to feel God.

HUMAN WISDOM CANNOT REVEAL GOD'S TRUTH

Human wisdom, great natural talents, and the culture of the schools, howsoever good they may be, can neither be the repositories nor conservers of God's revealed truth. The tree of knowledge has been the ruin of faith, ever attempting to reduce revelation to a philosophy and to measure God by people. In its pride, it puts God out and puts people into God's truth. To become babes again, on our mother's bosom, quieted, weaned, without clamor or protest, is the only position in which to know God. A calmness on the surface, and in the depths of the soul, in which God can mirror His will, His Word, and Himself, is the attitude toward Him through which He can reveal Himself, and this attitude is the right attitude of prayer.

Our Lord taught us the lesson of prayer by putting into practice in His life what He taught by His lips. Here is a simple but important statement, full of meaning: "And when he had sent the multitudes away, he went up into a mountain apart to pray: and when the evening was come, he was there alone."[7] The multitudes had been fed and were dismissed by our Lord.

The divine work of healing and teaching must be stopped awhile in order that time, place, and opportunity for prayer might be obtained. Prayer, the most divine of all labor, the most important of all ministries. Away from the eager, anxious, seeking multitudes, He has gone while the day was yet bright, to be alone with God. The multitudes tax and exhaust Him. The disciples are tossed on the sea, but calmness reigns on the mountain top where our Lord is kneeling in secret prayer—where prayer rules. "When Jesus therefore perceived that they would come and take him by force, to make him a king, he departed again into a mountain himself alone."[8]

ALONE WITH GOD

Jesus must be alone in that moment with God. Temptation was in that hour. The multitude had feasted on the five loaves and the two fishes. Filled with food and excited beyond measure, they would gladly make Him king. He flees from the temptation to secret prayer, for here is the source of His strength to resist evil. What a refuge was secret prayer even to Him! What a refuge to us from the world's dazzling and delusive crowns! What safety there is to be alone with God when the world tempts us, allures us, attracts us!

The prayers of our Lord were prophetic and illustrative of the great truth that the greatest measure of the Holy Spirit, the attesting voice, and opening heaven are only secured by prayer. This is suggested by His baptism by John the Baptist, when He prayed as He was baptized, and immediately the Holy Spirit descended upon Him like a dove.[9] More than prophetic and illustrative is this hour to Him. This critical hour is real and personal, consecrating and qualifying Him for God's highest purposes. Prayer to Him, just as it is to us, was a necessity, an absolute, invariable, condition of securing God's fullest, consecrating and qualifying power. The Holy Spirit came upon Him in fullness of measure and power in the very act of prayer.

THE HOLY SPIRIT: AN ANSWER TO PRAYER

Even so the Holy Spirit comes upon us in fullness of measure and power only in answer to ardent and intense praying. The heavens were opened to Christ, and access and communion established and enlarged by prayer. Freedom and fullness of access and closeness of communion are secured to us as the heritage of prayer. The voice attesting His Sonship came to Christ in prayer. The witness of our sonship, clear and indubitable, is secured only by praying. The constant witness of our sonship can only be retained by those who pray without ceasing. When the stream of prayer is shallow and arrested, the evidence of our sonship becomes faint and inaudible.

Endnotes

1 Luke 10:21-22
2 Hebrews 1:3
3 Probably a paraphrase of John 6:38.
4 Luke 22:42
5 James 5:16
6 2 Timothy 2:22
7 Matthew 14:23
8 John 6:15
9 Luke 3:21-22

9

Prayer Incidents in the Life of Our Lord (Continued)

SIN IS SO UNSPEAKABLY *awful in its evil that it struck down, as to death and hell, the very Son of God Himself. He had been amazed enough at sin before. He had seen sin making angels of heaven into devils of hell. Death and all its terrors did not much move or disconcert our Lord. No. It was not death: It was sin. It was hell-fire in His soul. It was the coals, and the oil, and the rosin, and the juniper, and the turpentine of the fire that is not quenched.* (Alexander Whyte, D.D.)

We note that the revelation and inspiration of a transporting prayer-hour of Christ, has as its natural sequence that gracious, encouraging, proclamation for heavy-hearted, restless, and weary souls of earth that has so impressed, captured, and drawn humanity as it fell on the ears of heavy-laden souls. Indeed, it has sweetened and relieved many people of their toils and burdens.

Come unto me, all ye that labour and are heavy laden, and I will give you rest. Take my yoke upon you, and learn of me; for I am meek and lowly in heart: and ye shall find rest unto your souls. For my yoke is easy, and my burden is light.[1]

At the grave of Lazarus, and as a condition and preparation for calling him back to life, we have our Lord calling upon His Father in heaven. "Father, I thank thee that thou hast heard me. And I know that thou hearest me always."[2] The lifting to heaven of Christ's eyes—how much was there in it! How much of confidence and plea was in that look to heaven! His very look, the lifting up of His eyes, carried His whole being heavenward, and caused a pause in that world, and drew attention and help. All Heaven was engaged, pledged, and moved when the Son of God looked up at this grave. Oh, for a people with the Christly eye, heaven lifted, and heaven arresting! As it was with Christ, so ought we to be so perfected in faith, so skilled in praying, that we could lift our eyes to heaven and say with Him, with deepest humility, and with commanding confidence, "Father, I thank thee that thou hast heard me."

YOUNG CHILDREN AND JESUS

Once more we have a very touching, beautiful, and instructive incident in Christ's praying. This time having to do with infants in their mothers' arms, parabolic as well as historical:

> And they brought young children to him, that he should touch them: and his disciples rebuked those that brought them. But when Jesus saw it, he was much displeased, and said unto them, Suffer the little children to come unto me, and forbid them not: for of such is the kingdom of God. Verily I say unto you, Whosoever shall not receive the kingdom of God as a little child, he shall not enter therein. And he took them up in his arms, put his hands upon them, and blessed them.[3]

This was one of the few times when stupid ignorance and unspiritual views aroused His indignation and displeasure. Vital principles were involved. The foundations were being destroyed, and worldly views actuated the disciples. Their temper and their words in rebuking those who brought their infants to Christ were exceedingly wrong. The very principles that He came to illustrate and propagate were being violated. Christ received the little ones. The big ones must become little ones. The old ones must become young ones before Christ will receive them. Prayer helps the little ones. The cradle must be invested with prayer. We are to pray for our little ones. The children are now to be brought to Jesus Christ by prayer, since He is in Heaven and not on earth. They are to be brought to Him early for His blessing, even when they are infants.

His blessing descends upon these little ones in answer to the prayers of those who bring them. With untiring persistence they are to be brought to Christ in earnest, persevering, prayer by their fathers and mothers. Before they know, themselves, anything about coming of their own accord, parents are to present them to God in prayer, seeking His blessing upon their offspring. At the same time, asking for wisdom, grace, and divine help to rear them that they may come to Christ of their own accord when they arrive at the years of accountability.

Holy hands and holy praying have much to do with guarding and training young lives and forming young characters for righteousness and heaven. What benevolence, simplicity, kindness, condescension, and meekness—linked with prayerfulness, are in this act of this divine teacher!

PETER'S CONFESSION OF JESUS

It was as Jesus was praying that Peter made that wonderful confession of his faith that Jesus was the Son of God.

> And it came to pass, as he was alone praying, his disciples were with him: and he asked them, saying, Whom say the people that I am? They answering said, John the Baptist; but some say, Elias; and others say, that one of the old prophets is risen again.[4]

> He saith unto them, But whom say ye that I am? And Simon Peter answered and said, Thou art the Christ, the Son of the living God. And Jesus answered and said unto him, Blessed art thou, Simon Barjona: for flesh and blood hath not revealed it unto thee, but my Father which is in heaven. And I say also unto thee, That thou art Peter, and upon this rock I will build my church; and the gates of hell shall not prevail against it. And I will give unto thee the keys of the kingdom of heaven: and whatsoever thou shalt bind on earth shall be bound in heaven: and whatsoever thou shalt loose on earth shall be loosed in heaven.[5]

It was after our Lord had made large promises to His disciples that He appointed to each of them a kingdom, and told them they would sit at His table in His kingdom and sit on thrones judging the twelve tribes of Israel. Then He gave those words of warning to Simon Peter, telling him that He had prayed for Peter. "And the Lord said, Simon, Simon, behold, Satan hath desired to have you, that he may sift you as wheat: But I have prayed for thee, that thy faith fail not: and when thou art converted, strengthen thy brethren."[6]

Happy Peter, to have such an one as the Son of God to pray for him! Unhappy Peter to be so in the toils of Satan as to demand so much of Christ's solicitude! How intense are the demands upon our prayers for some specific cases! Prayer must be personal in order to be to the fullest extent beneficial. Peter drew on Christ's praying more than any other disciple because of his exposure to greater perils, Pray for the most impulsive and imperiled ones by name. Our love and their danger give frequency, inspiration, intensity, and personality to praying.

We have seen how Christ had to flee from the multitude after the magnificent miracle of feeding the five thousand as they sought to make Him king. Then prayer was His escape and His refuge from this strong worldly temptation. He returns from that night of prayer with strength and calmness, and with a power to perform that other remarkable miracle of great wonder of walking on the sea.

EVERYTHING SANCTIFIED BY PRAYER

Even the loaves and fishes were sanctified by prayer before He served them to the multitude. "He looked up to heaven, and gave thanks."[7] Prayer should sanctify our daily bread and multiply our seed sown.

He looked up to heaven and heaved a sigh when He touched the tongue of the deaf man who had an impediment in his speech.[8] Much akin was this sigh to that groaning in spirit which He evidenced at the grave of Lazarus. "Jesus therefore again groaning in himself cometh to the grave."[9] Here was the sigh and groan of the Son of God over a human wreck, groaning that sin and hell had such a mastery over people, and troubled that such a desolation and ruin were humanity's sad inheritance. This is a lesson to be ever learned by us. Here is a fact ever to be kept in mind and heart and that must always, in some measure, weigh upon the inner spirits of God's children. We who have received the first fruit of the Spirit groan within ourselves at sin's waste, and death, and are filled with longings for the coming of a better day.

Present in all great praying, making and marking it, is the person. It is impossible to separate the praying from the person. The constituent elements of the person are the constituents of the person's praying. We flow through our praying. Only the fiery Elijah could do Elijah's fiery praying. We can get holy praying only from a holy person. Holy being can never exist without holy doing. Being is first, doing comes afterward. What we are gives being, force, and inspiration to what we do. Character, that which is graven deep, ineradicably, imperishably within us, colors all we do.

The praying of Christ, then, is not to be separated from the character of Christ. If in His praying He less weary, less selfish, more holy, more simple and direct than others, it was because these elements entered more largely into His character than into that of others.

The transfiguration marks another high point in His life, and that was preeminently a prayer time. Luke gives an account with the spirit and aim of the event:

> And it came to pass about an eight days after these sayings, he took Peter and John and James, and went up into a mountain to pray. And as he prayed, the fashion of his countenance was altered, and his raiment was white and glistering. And, behold, there talked with him two men, which were Moses and Elias: Who appeared in glory, and spake of his decease which he should accomplish at Jerusalem.[10]

The selection was made of three of His disciples for an inner circle of associates in prayer. There are few who have the spiritual tastes or aptitude for this inner circle. Even these three favored ones could scarcely stand the strain of that long night of praying. We know that He went up on that mountain to pray, not to be transfigured. But it was as He prayed, the fashion of His countenance was altered and His raiment became white and glistering. There is nothing like prayer to change character and whiten conduct. There is nothing like prayer to bring heavenly visitors and to gild with heavenly glory earth's mountain to us. Peter calls it the holy mount, made so by prayer.

THREE TIMES GOD BEARS WITNESS TO HIS SON

Three times the voice of God bore witness to the presence and person of His Son, Jesus Christ. Once at His baptism by John the Baptist. Then, again, at His transfiguration the approving, consoling, and witnessing voice of His Father was heard. He was found in prayer both of these times. The third time the attesting voice came, it was not on the heights of His transfigured glory. Neither was it as He was girding Himself to begin His conflict and to enter upon His ministry, but it was when He was hastening to the awful end. He was entering the dark mystery of His last agony, and looking forward to it. The shadows were deepening, a dire calamity was approaching, and an unknown and untried dread was before Him. Reflecting on His approaching death, prophesying about it, and forecasting the glory that would follow, in the midst of His high and mysterious discourse, the shadows came like a dread eclipse and He burst out in an agony of prayer:

Now is my soul troubled; and what shall I say? Father, save me from this hour: but for this cause came I unto this hour. Father, glorify thy name. Then came there a voice from heaven, saying, I have both glorified it, and will glorify it again. The people therefore, that stood by, and heard it, said that it thundered: others said, An angel spake to him. Jesus answered and said, This voice came not because of me, but for your sakes.[11]

But let it be noted that Christ is meeting and illuminating this fateful and distressing hour with prayer. How early the flesh reluctantly shrank from the contemplated end!

PRAYERS ON THE CROSS

How fully does His prayer on the Cross for His enemies synchronize with all He taught about love to our enemies, and with mercy and forgiveness to those who have trespassed against us! "Then said Jesus, Father, forgive them; for they know not what they do."[12] Apologizing for His murderers and praying for them, while they were jeering and mocking

Him at His death pains and their hands were reeking with His blood! What amazing generosity, pity, and love!

Again, take another one of the prayers on the Cross. How touching the prayer and how bitter the cup! How dark and desolate the hour as He exclaims, "My God, my God, why hast thou forsaken me?"[13] This is the last stroke that tears in two His heart, more exquisite in its bitterness and anguish, and more heart-piercing, than the kiss of Judas. All else was looked for, all else was put in His book of sorrows. But to have His Father's face withdrawn, God-forsaken, during the hour when these distressing words escaped the lips of the dying Son of God! Yet how truthful He is! How childlike we find Him! So when the end really comes, we hear Him again speaking to His Father: "Father, into Thy hands I commend my spirit: and having said thus, He gave up the ghost."[14]

Endnotes

1 Matthew 11:28-30
2 John 11:41-42
3 Mark 10:13-16
4 Luke 9:18-19
5 Matthew 15:16-19
6 Luke 22:31-32
7 This is a paraphrase combination from the stories of the five loaves and the seven loaves.
8 Mark 7:34
9 John 11:38
10 Luke 9:28-31
11 John 12:27-30
12 Luke 23:24
13 Mark 15:34
14 Luke 23:46

10

Our Lord's Model Prayer

W HAT SATISFACTION MUST IT *be to learn from God Himself with what words and in what manner, He would have us pray to Him so as not to pray in vain! We do not sufficiently consider the value of this prayer; the respect and attention which it requires; the preference to be given to it; its fullness and perfection; the frequent use we should make of it; and the spirit which we should bring with it. "Lord, teach us how to pray."* (Adam Clark)

Jesus gives us the pattern prayer in what is commonly known as "The Lord's Prayer." In this model of perfect prayer, He gives us a law form to be followed, and yet one to be filled in and enlarged as we may decide when we pray. The outlines and form are complete, yet it is but an outline, with many blanks, which our needs and convictions are to fill in.

Christ puts words on our lips, words that are to be uttered by holy lives. Words belong to the life of prayer. Wordless prayers are like human spirits. They may be pure and high, but too delicate and intangible for earthly conflicts and earthly needs and uses. We must have spirits clothed in flesh and blood, and our prayers must be likewise clothed in words that give them point and power, a local habitation, and a name.

This lesson of "The Lord's Prayer," drawn forth by the request of the disciples, "Lord, teach us to pray,"[1] has something in form and words like the prayer sections of the Sermon on the Mount. It is the same great lesson of praying to "Our Father which art in Heaven,"[2] and is one of insistent importunity. No prayer lesson would be complete without it. It belongs to the first and last lessons in prayer. God's fatherhood gives shape, value, and confidence to all our praying.

HALLOWING GOD'S NAME

Jesus teaches us that to hallow God's name is the first and the greatest of prayers. A desire for the glorious coming and the glorious establishment of God's glorious kingdom follows in value and in sequence the hallowing of God's name. Christians who really hallow God's name will hail the coming of the kingdom of God, and will labor and pray to bring that kingdom to pass and to establish it. Christ's pupils in the school of prayer are to be taught diligently to hallow God's name, to work for God's kingdom, and to do God's will perfectly, completely, and gladly, as it is done in heaven.

Prayer engages the highest interest and secures the highest glory of God. God's name, God's kingdom and God's will are all in it. Without prayer, His name is profaned, His kingdom fails, and His will is decried and opposed. God's will can be done on earth as it is done in Heaven. God's will done on earth makes earth like Heaven. Persistent praying is the mighty energy that establishes God's will on earth as it is established in heaven.

PRAYER SANCTIFIES OUR DAILY TOIL

Jesus is still teaching us that prayer sanctifies and makes hopeful and sweet our daily toil for daily bread. Forgiveness of sins is to be sought by prayer, and the great prayer plea we are to make for forgiveness is that we have forgiven all those who have sinned against us. It involves love for our enemies so far as to pray for them, to bless them and not curse them, and to pardon their offences against us whatever those offences may be.

We are to pray, "lead us not into temptation."[3] This is not only to be prayed, but also the tempter and the temptation are to be watched against, resisted, and prayed against.

All these things Jesus laid down in this law of prayer, but He adds to His statute law many simple lessons of comment, expansion, and expression.

"OUR FATHER" KNOWN TO MILLIONS

This prayer that He teaches His disciples became familiar to millions through the centuries since then, Many learned it at their mother's knees in childhood, others in Sunday School. The words are so childlike that children find their instruction, edification, and comfort in them as they kneel and pray. The most glowing mystic and the most careful thinker each find their own language in these simple words of prayer. Beautiful and revered as these words are, they are our words for solace, help, and learning.

Jesus led the way in prayer that we might follow His footsteps. Matchless leader in matchless praying! Lord, teach us to pray as You did yourself pray!

How marked is the contrast between the Jesus' high priestly prayer[4] and this "Lord's Prayer." He gave this copy for praying to His disciples as the first elements of prayer. How simple and childlike! No one has ever approached in composition a prayer so simple in its petitions and yet so comprehensive in all of its requests.

How these simple elements of prayer as given by our Lord commend themselves to us! This prayer is for us as well as for those to whom it was first given. It is for the child learning the ABCs of prayer, and it is for the graduate of the highest institutions of learning. It is a personal prayer, reaching to all our needs and covering all our sins. It is the highest form of prayer for others. Just as scholars can never in all their graduate studies or learning dispense with their ABCs—because the alphabet gives form, color, and expression to all graduate learning, so the learners in Christ can never dispense with the Lord's Prayer. But they may make it form the basis of their higher praying, which is the intercession for others as shown in the Lord's high priestly prayer.

The Lord's Prayer is ours and fits us in all the stages of a joyous Christian life. The high priestly prayer is ours also in the stages and office of our royal priesthood as intercessors before God. Here we have oneness with God, deep spiritual unity, and unswerving loyalty to God, living and praying to glorify God.

Endnotes

1 Luke 11:1
2 Luke 11:2
3 Luke 11:4
4 John 17

II

Our Lord's High Priestly Prayer

J<small>ESUS CLOSES</small> H<small>IS LIFE</small> *with inimitable calmness, confidence and sublimity.* *"I have glorified Thee; I have finished the work which Thou gavest me to do."* *The annals of earth have nothing comparable to it in real security and sublimity. May we come to our end thus, in supreme loyalty to Christ.* (E. M. Bounds)

We come now to consider our Lord's high priestly prayer, as found recorded in the seventeenth chapter of John's gospel.

Obedience to the Father and abiding in the Father belong to the Son, and belong to us also as partners with Christ in His divine work of intercession. How tenderly, passionate, and all-encompassing He prays for His disciples! "I pray for them I pray not for the world."[1] What a pattern of prayerfulness for God's people! For God's people are God's cause, God's Church, and God's kingdom. Pray for God's people, for their unity, sanctification, and glorification. How the subject of their unity pressed upon Jesus! Today's walls of separation, alienations, riven circles of God's family, and warring tribes of ecclesiastics—how He is torn, bleeds, and suffers anew at the sight of these divisions! Unity—that is the great burden of that remarkable high priestly prayer. "That they may be one, even as we are one."[2] The spiritual oneness of God's people—that is the heritage of God's glory to them, transmitted by Christ to His Church.

JESUS PRAYS FOR HIMSELF

First of all, in this prayer, Jesus prays for himself, not now the suppliant as in Gethsemane, not weakness, but strength now. There is not now the pressure of darkness and of hell, but passing for the time over the fearful interim, He asks that He may be glorified, and that His exalted glory may secure glory to His Father. His sublime loyalty and fidelity to God are declared, that fidelity to God that is of the very essence of interceding prayer. Our devoted lives pray. Our unswerving loyalty to God are eloquent pleas to Him and give access and confidence in our advocacy. This prayer is gemmed, but its walls are adamant. What profound and granite truths! What fathomless mysteries! What deep and rich experiences are involved in such statements as these:

> And this is life eternal, that they might know thee the only true God, and Jesus Christ, whom thou hast sent. I have glorified thee on the earth: I have finished the work which thou gavest me to do. And now, O Father, glorify thou me with thine own self with the glory which I had with thee before the world was.[3]

Let us stop and ask, have we eternal life? Do we know God experimentally, consciously, and do we know Him really and personally? Do we know Jesus Christ as a person, and as a personal Savior? Do we know Him by a heart acquaintance, and know Him well? This, this only, is eternal life. Is Jesus glorified in us? Let us continue this personal inquiry. Do our lives prove His divinity? Does Jesus shine brighter because of us? Are we opaque or transparent bodies, and do we darken or reflect His pure light? Once more let us ask: Do we seek God's glory? Do we seek glory where Christ sought it? "Glorify thou me with thy own self." Do we esteem the presence and the possession of God as our most excellent glory and our supreme good?

How closely Jesus binds Himself and His Father to His people! His heart centers upon them in this high hour of holy communion with His Father.

> I have manifested thy name unto the men which thou gavest me out of the world: thine they were, and thou gavest them me; and they have kept thy word. Now they have known that all things whatsoever thou hast given me are of thee. For I have given unto them the words which thou gavest me; and they have received them, and have known surely that I came out from thee, and they have believed that thou didst send me. I pray for them: I pray not for the world, but for them which thou hast given me; for they are thine. And all mine are thine, and thine are mine; and I am glorified in them.[4]

JESUS PRAYS FOR HIS DISCIPLES

He prays also for keeping for these disciples. Not only were they to be chosen, elected, and filled, but were to be kept by the Father's watchful eyes and by the Father's omnipotent hand. "And now I am no more in the world, but these are in the world, and I come to thee. Holy Father, keep through thine own name those whom thou hast given me, that they may be one, as we are."[5]

He prays that they might be kept by the Holy Father, in all holiness by the power of His name. He asks that His people may be kept from sin, from all sin, from sin in the concrete and sin in the abstract—from sin in all its shapes of evil, from all sin in this world. He prays that they might not only be fit and ready for heaven, but ready and fit for earth, for its sweetest privileges, sternest duties, deepest sorrows, and richest joys— ready for all of its trials, consolations, and triumphs. "I pray not that Thou shouldest take them out of the world, but that Thou shouldest keep them from the evil."[6]

Jesus prays that they may be kept from the world's greatest evil, which is sin. He desires that they may be kept from the guilt, power, pollution, and punishment of sin. The *Revised Version* makes it read, "That thou shouldst keep them from the evil one." Kept from the devil, so that he might not touch them, find them, or have a place in them—so that they might be complete owned, filled, and guarded by God. "Kept by the power of God through faith unto salvation."[7]

Jesus places us in the arms of His Father, on the care of His Father, and in the heart of His Father. He calls God into service, puts Him to the front, and places us under His Father's closer keeping—under His Father's shadow, and under the cover of His Father's wing. The Father's rod and staff are for our security, comfort, refuge, strength, and guidance.

These disciples were not to be taken out of the world, but kept from its evil, its monster evil, which is the world itself. "This present evil world."[8] How the world seduces, dazzles, and deludes people! Jesus' disciples are chosen out of the world, out of the world's bustle and earthliness, out of its all-devouring greed of gain, out of its money-desire, money-love, and money-toil. Earth draws and holds as if it were made out of gold and not out of dirt—as though it was covered with diamonds and not with graves.

DISCIPLES NOT OF THE WORLD

"They are not of the world, even as I am not of the world."[9] We are not only to be kept from sin and Satan, but also from the soil, stain, and taint of worldliness, just as Jesus was free from it Their relation to Christ was not only to free them from the world's defiling taint, its unhallowed love and criminal friendships, but the world's hatred would inevitably follow their Christlikeness. No result so necessarily and universally follows its cause as this. "The world hath hated them, because they are not of the world, even as I am not of the world."[10]

How solemn and almost awful the repetition of the declaration, "They are not of the world, even as I am not of the world." How pronounced, radical, and eternal was our Lord Christ's divorce from the world! How pronounced, radical, and eternal is that of our Lord's true followers from the world! The world hates the disciple as it hated our Lord, and will crucify the disciple just as it crucified our Lord. How pertinent the question, have we Christlike unworldliness? Does the world hate us as it hated our Lord? Are His words fulfilled in us?

If the world hate you, ye know that it hated me before it hated you. If ye were of the world, the world would love his own: but because ye are not of the world, but I have chosen you out of the world, therefore the world hateth you.[11]

Jesus puts Himself plainly before us as the full portrait of an unworldly Christian. Here is our changeless pattern. "They are not of the world, even as I am not of the world." We must be cut after this pattern.

THE UNITY OF HIS DISCIPLES

The subject of their unity pressed upon Him. Note how He called His Father's attention to it, and see how He pleaded for this unity of His followers: "And now I am no more in the world, but these are in the world, and I come to thee. Holy Father, keep through thine own name those whom thou hast given me, that they may be one, as we are."[12]

Again He returns to it as He sees the great crowds flocking to His standard as the ages pass on:

That they all may be one; as thou, Father, art in me, and I in thee, that they also may be one in us: that the world may believe that thou hast sent me. And the glory which thou gavest me I have given them; that they may be one, even as we are one: I in them, and thou in me, that they may be made perfect in one; and that the world may know that thou hast sent me, and hast loved them, as thou hast loved me.[13]

Notice how intently His heart was set on this unity. What shameful history, and what bloody annals has this lack of unity written for God's Church! These walls of separations, alienations, and riven circles of God's family warring and tearing at each other! He looks ahead and sees how Christ is torn, how He bleeds and suffers afresh in all these sad things of the future. The unity of God's people was to be the heritage of God's glory promised to them. Division and strife are the devil's bequest to the Church, a heritage of failure, weakness, shame, and woe.

The oneness of God's people was to be the one credential to the world of the divinity of Christ's mission on earth. Let us ask in all candor, are we praying for this unity as Christ prayed for it? Are we seeking the peace, welfare, glory, might, and divinity of God's cause as it is found in the unity of God's people?

THE SANCTIFICATION OF HIS DISCIPLES

Going back again, note how He puts Himself as the exponent and pattern of this unworldliness that He prays may possess His disciples. He sends them into the world just as His Father sent Him into the world. He expects them to be and do, just as He was and as He did for His Father. He sought the sanctification of His disciples that they might be wholly devoted to God and purified from all sin. He desired in them a holy life and a holy work for God. He devoted Himself to death in order that they might be devoted to God in life. He prayed for a true sanctification—a real, whole, and thorough sanctification, embracing soul, body, and mind for time and eternity. With Him the Word itself had much to do with their true sanctification. "Sanctify them through Thy truth: Thy word is truth . . . And for their sakes I sanctify myself, that they also might be sanctified through the truth."[14]

Entire devotedness was to be the type of their sanctification. His prayer for their sanctification marks the pathway to full sanctification. Prayer is that pathway. All the ascending steps to that lofty position of entire sanctification are steps of prayer—increasing prayerfulness in spirit and in fact. "Pray without ceasing"[15] is the imperative prelude to "the very God of peace sanctify you wholly."[16] Prayer is but the continued interlude and doxology of this rich grace in the heart: "I pray God your whole spirit and soul and body be preserved blameless unto the coming of our Lord Jesus Christ. Faithful is he that calleth you, who also will do it."[17]

We can only meet our full responsibilities and fulfill our high mission when we go forth sanctified as Christ our Lord was sanctified. He sends us into the world just as His Father sent Him into the world. He expects us to be as He was, to do as He did, and to glorify the Father just as He glorified the Father.

How He longed to have us with Him in heaven: "Father, I will that they also, whom Thou hast given Me, be with Me where I am; that they may behold My glory, which Thou hast given Me: for Thou lovedst me before the foundation of the world."[18] What response do our truant hearts make to this earnest, loving, Christly longing? Are we as eager for heaven as He is to have us there? How calm, majestic, and authoritative is His "I will"!

Jesus closes His life with inimitable calmness, confidence, and sublimity. "I have glorified Thee on the earth: I have finished the work which Thou gavest Me to do."

The annals of earth have nothing comparable to it in real serenity and sublimity. May we come to our end in that way—in supreme loyalty to Christ.

Endnotes

1 John 17:9
2 John 17:22
3 John 17:3-5
4 John 17:6-10
5 John 17:11
6 John 17:15
7 I Peter 1:5
8 Galatians 1:4
9 John 17:16
10 John 17:14
11 John 15:18-19
12 John 17:11
13 John 17:21-23
14 John 17:17, 19
15 I Thessalonians 5:17
16 I Thessalonians 5:23
17 I Thessalonians 5:23-24
18 John 17:24

12

The Gethsemane Prayer

THE CUP! THE CUP! THE CUP! *Our Lord did not use many words: but He used His few words again and again, till this cup! and Thy will!—Thy will be done, and this cup—was all His prayer. "The cup! The cup! The cup!" cried Christ: first on His feet: and then on His knees: and then on His face. . . . "Lord, teach us to pray!"* (Alexander Whyte, D.D.)

We come to Gethsemane. What a contrast! The high priestly prayer had been one of intense feelings of universal grasp, and unlimited worldwide sympathy and solicitude for God's Church. Perfect calmness and perfect poise reigned in Jesus. He was majestic, simple, and free from passion or disquiet. The royal intercessor and advocate for others, His petitions are like princely edicts, judicial and authoritative. How changed now! In Gethsemane, He seems to have entered another region and becomes another man. His high priestly prayer was exquisite in its tranquil flow, unruffled in its strong, deep, current. It is like the sun, moving across the sky, unsullied glory that brightens, vitalizes, ennobles, and blesses everything. The Gethsemane prayer is that same sun declining in the west, plunged into an ocean of storm and cloud. It is storm-covered, storm-eclipsed with gloom, darkness and terror on every side.

The prayer in Gethsemane is exceptional in every way. The super-incumbent load of the world's sin is upon Jesus. The lowest point of His depression has been reached. The bitterest cup of all, His bitter cup, is being pressed to His lips. The weakness of all His weaknesses, the sorrow of all His sorrows, the agony of all His agonies are now upon Him. The flesh is giving out with its fainting and trembling pulsations, like the trickling of His heart's blood. His enemies have thus far triumphed. Satan is in a jubilee and bad men are joining in the satanic carnival.

SATAN'S HOUR

Gethsemane was Satan's hour, power, and darkness. It was the hour of massing all of Satan's forces for a final last conflict. Jesus had said, "the prince of this world cometh, and hath nothing in Me."[1] The conflict for earth's mastery is before Him. The Holy Spirit led and drove Him into the stern conflict and severe temptation of the wilderness. But His Comforter, leader, and inspiration through His matchless history, seems to have left Him now. "He . . . began to be sorrowful and very heavy."[2] Under this great pressure, we hear Him exclaiming, "My soul is exceeding sorrowful, even unto death."[3] The depression, conflict, and agony had gone to the very core of His spirit, and had sunk Him to the very verge of death. He was "sore amazed."[4]

Surprise and awe depressed His soul. "Very heavy" was the hour of hell's midnight that fell upon His spirit. Very heavy was this hour when all the sins of all the world, of every person with all their stain and all their guilt, fell upon His immaculate soul.

He cannot abide the presence of His chosen friends. They cannot enter into the depths and demands of this fearful hour. His trusted and set watchers were asleep. His Father's face is hid. His Father's approving voice is silent. The Holy Spirit who had been with Him in all the trying hours of His life, seems to have withdrawn from the scene. Alone He must drink the cup, alone He must tread the winepress of God's fierce wrath, Satan's power and darkness, and human envy, cruelty, and vindictiveness. The scene is well described by Luke:

> And He came out, and went, as He was wont, to the mount of Olives; and His disciples also followed Him. And when He was at the place, He said unto them, Pray that ye enter not into temptation. And He was withdrawn from them about a stone's cast, and kneeled down, and prayed, Saying, Father, if Thou be willing, remove this cup from Me: nevertheless not My will, but Thine, be done. And there appeared an angel unto Him from heaven, strengthening Him. And being in an agony He prayed more earnestly: and His sweat was as it were great drops of blood falling down to the ground. And when He rose up from prayer, and was come to His disciples, He found them sleeping for sorrow, And said unto them, Why sleep ye? rise and pray, lest ye enter into temptation.[5]

PRAYER OF AGONY

The prayer agony of Gethsemane crowns Calvary with glory. The prayers offered by Christ on the Cross are the union of weakness and strength, deepest agony and desolation—accompanied with the sweetest calm, most divine submission, and implicit confidence.

Nowhere in prophet or priest, king or ruler, of synagogue or church, does the ministry of prayer assume such marvels of variety, power, and fragrance as in the life of Jesus Christ. It is the aroma of God's sweetest spices, aflame with God's glory, and consumed by God's will.

We find in this Gethsemane prayer what we find nowhere else in the praying of Christ. "O my Father, if it be possible, let this cup pass from Me: nevertheless, not as I will, but as Thou wilt."[6] This is different from the whole tenor and trend of His praying and doing. How different from His high priestly prayer! "Father, I will," is the law and life of that prayer. In His last directions for prayer, He makes our will the measure and condition of prayer. "If ye abide in me, and my words abide in you, ye shall ask what ye will, and it shall be done unto you,"[7] He said to the Syrophenician woman, "Great is thy faith: be it unto thee as thou wilt."[8]

PRAYER AGAINST THE WILL OF GOD

But in Gethsemane His praying was against the declared will of God. The pressure was so heavy upon Him, the cup was so bitter, the burden was so strange and intolerable, that the flesh cried out for relief. Prostrate, sinking, sorrowful into death, He sought to be relieved from that which seemed too heavy to bear. He prayed, however, not in revolt against God's will, but in submission to that will, and yet He prayed to change God's plan and to alter God's purposes. Pressed by the weakness of the flesh, and by the powers Satan hell in all their dreadful satanic malignity and might, Jesus was on this one only occasion constrained to pray against the will of God. He did it, though, with great wariness and pious caution. He did it with declared and inviolable submission to God's will. But this was exceptional.

Simple submission to God's will is not the highest attitude of the soul to God. Seeming submission may be induced by conditions, and nothing but forced surrender. It is not done cheerfully but grudgingly, and only a temporary expedient, a fitful resolve. When the occasion or calamity that called it forth is removed, the will returns to its old ways and to its old self.

CONFORMITY WITH THE WILL OF GOD

Jesus Christ prayed always with this one exception in conformity with the will of God. He was one with God's plan, and one with God's will. To pray in conformity with God's will was the life and law of Christ. The same was law of His praying. Conformity, to live one with God, is a far higher and diviner life than to live simply in submission to God. To pray in conformity—together with God—is a far higher and diviner way to pray than mere submission. At its best state, submission is non-rebellion, an acquiescence, which is good, but not the highest. The most powerful form of praying is positive, aggressive, mightily outgoing, and creative. It molds things, changes things, and brings things to pass.

Conformity means to "stand perfect and complete in all the will of God."[9] It means to delight to do God's will, to run with eagerness and ardor to carry out His plans. Conformity to God's will involves submission, patient, loving, sweet submission. But submission in itself falls short of and does not include conformity. We may be submissive but not conformed. We may accept results against which we have warred, and even be resigned to them.

Conformity means to be one with God, both in result and in processes. Submission may be one with God in the end. Conformity is one with God in the beginning and the end. Jesus had conformity, absolute and perfect, to God's will, and by that He prayed. This was the single point where there was a drawing back from God's processes, extorted by insupportable pain, fear, and weariness. His submission was abject, loyal, and confiding, as His conformity had been constant and perfect. Conformity is the only true submission, the most loyal, the sweetest and the fullest.

Gethsemane has its lessons of humble supplications as Jesus knelt alone in the garden. Lessons of burdened prostration as He fell on His face, of intense agony, of distressing dread, of hesitancy and shrinking back, of crying out for relief—yet amid it all, of cordial submission to God accompanied with a singleness of purpose for His glory.

Our hour for the bitter cup

Satan will have for each of us his hour and power of darkness and for each of us the bitter cup and the fearful spirit of gloom.

We can pray against God's will, as Moses did to enter the Promised Land, as Paul did about the thorn in the flesh, as David did for his doomed child, as Hezekiah did to live. We may pray against God's will three times when the stroke is the heaviest, sorrow is the keenest, and grief is the deepest. We may lie prostrate all night as David did through the hours of darkness. We may pray for hours as Jesus did, and in the darkness of many nights, not measuring the hours by the clock, or the nights by the calendar. It must all be, however, the prayer of submission.

When sorrow and the night and desolation of Gethsemane fall in heaviest gloom on us, we ought to submit patiently and tearfully if need be, but sweetly and resignedly, without tremor, or doubt, to the cup pressed by a Father's hand to our lips. "Not my will, but thine, be done,"[10] our broken hearts shall say. In God's own way, mysterious to us, that cup has in its bitterest dregs, as it had for the Son of God, the gem and gold of perfection. We are to be put into the crucible to be refined. Christ was made perfect in Gethsemane, not by the prayer, but by the suffering. "For it became him, ... to make the captain of their salvation perfect through suffering."[11] The cup could not pass because the suffering must go on and yield its fruit of perfection.

Through many an hour of darkness and of Satan's power, through many painful conflicts with the prince of this world, by drinking many bitter cups, we are to be made perfect. To cry out against the terrific and searching flame of the crucible of a Father's painful processes is natural and is no sin. That is, if there be perfect agreement with the answer to our prayer, perfect submission to God's will, and perfect devotion to His glory.

A PRAYER OF SUBMISSION

If our hearts are true to God, we may plead with Him about His way, and seek relief from His painful processes. But the fierce fire of the crucible and the agonizing victim with His agonizing and submissive prayer, is not the normal and highest form of majestic and all-commanding prayer. We can cry out in the crucible, and can cry out against the flame that purifies and perfects us. God allows this, hears this, and answers this, not by taking us out of the crucible, or by lessening the fierceness of the flame, but by sending more than an angel to strengthen us. Yet crying out in that manner with full submission does not answer the real high, worldwide, royal, and eternity-reaching requests of prayer.

The prayer of submission must not be so used as to reduce or substitute the higher and mightier prayer of faith. Nor must it be so stressed as to break down persistent and prevailing prayer, which would be to disarm prayer of its efficiency and uncrown its glorious results. Such a thing would encourage listless, sentimental, and feeble praying.

We are ever ready to excuse our lack of earnest and toilsome praying by a fancied and false view of submission. We often end praying just where we ought to begin. We quit praying when God waits and is waiting for us to really pray. We are deterred by obstacles from praying, or we succumb to difficulties, and call it submission to God's will. A world of beggarly faith, spiritual laziness, and half-heartedness in prayer, are covered under the high and pious name of submission. To have no plan but to seek God's plan and carry it out, is of the essence and inspiration of Christly praying. This is far more than putting in a clause of submission. Jesus did this once in seeking to change the purpose of God, but all His other praying was the output of being perfectly at one with the plans and purposes of God. It is after this order we pray when we abide in Him and when His word abides in us. Then we ask what we will and it is done. It is then our prayers fashion and create things. Our wills then become God's will and His will becomes ours. The two become one, and there is not a note of discord.

And this is the confidence that we have in him, that, if we ask any thing according to his will, he heareth us: And if we know that he hear us, whatsoever we ask, we know that we have the petitions that we desired of him.[12]

It is then that it proves true: "And whatsoever we ask, we receive of him, because we keep his commandments, and do those things that are pleasing in his sight."[13]

What restraint, forbearance, self-denial, and loyalty to duty to God, and what deference to the Old Testament Scriptures are in that statement of our Lord: "Thinkest thou that I cannot now pray to My Father, and He shall presently give Me more than twelve legions of angels? But how then shall the Scriptures be fulfilled, that thus it must be?"[14]

Endnotes

1 John 14:30
2 Matthew 26:37
3 Matthew 26:38
4 Mark 14:33
5 Luke 22:39-46
6 Matthew 26:39
7 John 15:7
8 Matthew 15:28
9 Colossians 4:12
10 Luke 22:42
11 Hebrews 2:10
12 I John 5:14-15
13 I John 3:22
14 Matthew 26:53-54

13

The Holy Spirit and Prayer

DURING THE GREAT *Welsh Revival a minister was said to be very successful in winning souls by one sermon that he preached—hundreds were converted. Far away in a valley news reached a brother minister of the marvelous success of this sermon. He desired to find out the secret of the man's great success.—He walked the long way, and came to the minister's poor cottage, and the first thing he said was: "Brother, where did you get that sermon?" He was taken into a poorly furnished room and pointed to a spot where the carpet was worn threadbare, near a window that looked out upon the everlasting hills and solemn mountains and said, "Brother, there is where I got that sermon. My heart was heavy for men. One night I knelt there—and cried for power as I never preached before. The hours passed until midnight struck, and the stars looked down on a sleeping world, but the answer came not. I prayed on until I saw a faint streak of grey shoot up, then it war silver—silver became purple and gold. Then the sermon came and the power came and men fell under the influence of the Holy Spirit."* (G. H. Morgan)

The Gospel without the Holy Spirit would be vain and trifling. The gift of the Holy Spirit was vital to the work of Jesus Christ in the atonement. As Jesus did not begin His work on earth until He was anointed by the Holy Spirit, so the same Holy Spirit is necessary to carry forward and make effective the atoning work of the Son of God. As His anointing by the Holy Ghost at His baptism was an era in His life, so also is the coming of the Holy Spirit at Pentecost a great era in the work of redemption in making effective the work of Christ's Church.

The Holy Spirit is not only the bright lamp of the Christian dispensation, its teacher and guide, He is also the divine helper.

He is the enabling agent in God's new dispensation of doing. As the ship's pilot takes a stand at the wheel to guide the vessel, so the Holy Spirit takes up His abode in the heart to guide and empower all its efforts. The Holy Spirit executes the whole gospel through the person by His presence and control of the spirit of the person.

In the execution of the atoning work of Jesus Christ, in its general and more comprehensive operation, or in its minute and personal application, the Holy Spirit is the one efficient agent—absolute and indispensable.

THE GOSPEL CANNOT BE EXECUTED EXCEPT BY THE HOLY SPIRIT

Only He has the regal authority to do this royal work. Intellect cannot execute it, neither can learning, eloquence, or truth—not even the revealed truth can execute the gospel. The marvelous facts of Christ's life told by hearts that are not anointed by the Holy Spirit will be dry and sterile, or "like a story told by an idiot, full of sound and fury, signifying nothing." Not even the precious blood can execute the gospel. Not any, or all of these, though spoken with angelic wisdom and eloquence, can execute the gospel with saving power. Only tongues set on fire by the Holy Spirit can witness the saving power of Christ with power to save others.

No one dared move from Jerusalem to proclaim or utter the message along its streets to the dying multitudes until the Holy Spirit came in baptismal power. John could not utter a word, though he had pillowed his head on Christ's bosom and caught the pulsations of Christ's heart, and though his brain was full of the wondrous facts of that life and of the wondrous words that fell from Jesus' lips. John must wait until a fuller and richer endowment than all of these came on him. Neither could Mary live the Christ-life until she was empowered by the Holy Spirit, even though she had nurtured Jesus and stored her heart and mind full of holy and motherly memories.

THE COMING OF THE HOLY SPIRIT DEPENDS UPON PRAYER

The coming of the Holy Spirit is dependent upon prayer, for prayer only can compass with its authority and demands, the realm where this person of the Godhead has His abode. Even Christ was subject to this law of prayer. With Him it is, ever has been, and ever will be, "Ask, and it shall be given you; seek, and ye shall find; knock, and it shall be opened unto you."[1] To His dejected disciples, Jesus said, "I will pray the Father, and He shall give you another Comforter."[2] This law of prayer for the Holy Spirit presses on the Master and on the disciples as well. Of so many of God's children it may truly be said, "Ye have Him not, because ye ask not."[3] Of many others it might be said, "You have Him in faint measure because you pray for Him in faint measure."

The Holy Spirit is the spirit of all grace and of each grace as well. Purity, power, holiness, faith, love, joy and all grace are brought into being and perfected by Him. Would we grow in grace in particular? Would we be perfect in all graces? We must seek the Holy Spirit by prayer.

SEEK THE HOLY SPIRIT

We urge the seeking of the Holy Spirit. We need Him, and we need to stir ourselves up to seek Him. The measure we receive of Him will be gauged by the fervor of faith and prayer with which we seek Him. Our ability to work for God, pray to God, live for God, and affect others for God, will be dependent on the measure of the Holy Spirit received by us, dwelling in us, and working through us.

Christ lays down the clear and explicit law of prayer in this regard for all of God's children. The world needs the Holy Spirit to convict it "of sin, and of righteousness, and of judgment" [4] to come, and to make it feel its guiltiness in God's sight. This spirit of conviction on sinners comes in answer to the prayers of God's people. God's children need Him more and more, need His life, His more abundant life, His super-abundant life. But that life begins and ever increases as the child of God prays for the Holy Spirit. "If ye then, being evil, know how to give good gifts unto your children: how much more shall your heavenly Father give the Holy Spirit to them that ask Him?"[5] This is the law, a condition brightened by a promise and sweetened by a relationship.

THE GIFT OF THE HOLY SPIRIT

The gift of the Holy Spirit is one of the benefits flowing to us from the glorious presence of Christ at the right hand of God, and this gift of the Holy Spirit, together with all the other gifts of the enthroned Christ, are secured to us by prayer. It is a required condition. The Bible by express statement, as well as by its general principles and clear and constant references, teaches us that the gift of the Holy Spirit is connected with and conditioned in prayer. That the Holy Spirit is in the world as God is in the world is true. That the Holy Spirit is in the world as Christ is in the world is also true. It is also true that there is nothing predicated of Him being in us and in the world that is not predicated of God and Christ being in us and in the world.

The Holy Spirit was in the world in measure before Pentecost, and in the measure of His operation then He was prayed for and sought for, and the principles are unchanged. The truth is, if we cannot pray for the Holy Spirit we cannot pray for any good thing from God, for He is the sum of all good to us. The truth is, we seek after the Holy Spirit just as we seek after God, just as we seek after Christ, "with strong crying and tears,"[6] and we are to seek always for more and more of His gifts, power, and grace. The truth is, the presence and power of the Holy Spirit at any given meeting is conditioned on praying faith.

Christ lays down the doctrine that the reception of the Holy Spirit is conditioned on prayer, and He Himself illustrated this universal law, for when the Holy Spirit came upon Him at His baptism, He was praying. The apostolic Church in action illustrates the same great truth.

DISCIPLES IN THE AGONY OF PRAYER

A few days after Pentecost, the disciples were in an agony of prayer, "and when they had prayed, the place was shaken where they were assembled together; and they were all filled with the Holy Ghost."[7] This incident destroys every theory that denies prayer as the condition of the coming and re-coming of the Holy Spirit after Pentecost. It also confirms the view that Pentecost as the result of a long struggle of prayer is illustrative and confirmatory that God's great and most precious gifts is conditioned on asking, seeking, knocking, prayer—ardent persistent prayer.

The same truth comes to the front very prominently in Philip's revival at Samaria. Though filled with joy by believing in Christ, and though received into the Church by water baptism, they did not receive the Holy Spirit until Peter and John went down there and prayed with and for them.[8]

PAUL'S PRAYING WAS PROOF

Paul's praying was God's proof to Ananias that Paul was in a state that conditioned him to receive the Holy Spirit.[9]

The Holy Spirit is not only our teacher, inspirer, and revealer in prayer. The power of our praying in measure and force is measured by the Spirit's power working in us to do the will and work of God,[10] according to God's good pleasure. After Paul's marvelous prayer for the Church at Ephesus, he seemed to be concerned that they would think he had gone beyond the ability of God in his large asking. So he closes his appeal for them with the words that God was "able to do exceeding abundantly above all that we ask or think."[11] Note, however, that the power of God to do for us was measured by the power of God in us. "According to," says the Apostle, that is, according to the measure of, "the power that worketh in us."

The projecting power of praying outwardly is the projecting power of God in us. The feeble operation of God in us brings feeble praying. The mightiest operation of God in us brings the mightiest praying. The secret of prayerlessness is the absence of the work of the Holy Spirit in us. The secret of feeble praying everywhere is the lack of God's Spirit working in us in His mighty power.

The ability of God to answer and work through our prayers is measured by the divine energy that God has been enabled to put in us by the Holy Spirit. The projecting power of praying is the measure of the

The Holy Spirit and Prayer

Holy Spirit in us. So the statement of James in the fifth chapter of his Epistle is to this effect: "The effectual fervent prayer of a righteous man availeth much."[12]

DO WE WANT TO PRAY EFFICIENTLY AND MIGHTILY?

Then the Holy Spirit must work in us efficiently and mightily. Paul makes the principle of universal application. "Whereunto I also labour, striving according to his working, which worketh in me mightily."[13] All labor for Christ that does not spring from the Holy Spirit working in us, is trifling and vain. Our prayers and activities are feeble and lacking results because He has not and cannot work His glorious work in us. Would you pray with mighty results? Seek the mighty workings of the Holy Spirit in your spirit.

Here we have the initial lesson in prayer for the Holy Spirit that was to enlarge to its full fruitage in Pentecost. In John 14:16, Jesus urges His disciples to pray for the Father to send another Comforter who would dwell with them and be in them. This is not a prayer that the Holy Spirit might do His work in making us children of God by regeneration, but it was for that fuller grace and power and person of the Holy Spirit that we can claim by virtue of our relation as children of God. His work in us to make us the children of God, and His person abiding with us and in us as children of God, are entirely different stages of the same Spirit in His relation to us. In this latter work, His gifts and works are greater, and His presence in us is greater than His works or gifts. His work in us prepares us for Himself. His gifts are the dispensations of His presence. He puts us into Christ and makes us members of His body by His work. He keeps us in that body by His presence and person. He enables us to discharge the functions as members of that body by His gifts.

ASKING FOR THE HOLY SPIRIT

The whole lesson culminates in asking for the Holy Spirit as the great objective point of all praying. In the direction in the Sermon on the Mount, we have the very plain and definite promise, "If ye then, being evil, know how to give good gifts unto your children, how much more shall your Father which is in Heaven give good things to them that ask him?"[14] In Luke we have "good things" substituted by "the Holy Spirit."[15] All good is contained in the Holy Spirit, and He is the sum and climax of all good things.

How complex, confusing, and involved is many a human direction about obtaining the gift of the Holy Spirit as the abiding Comforter—our sanctifier and the one who empowers us! How simple and direct is our Lord's direction—ASK! This is plain and direct. Ask with urgency, ask without fainting. Ask, seek, knock, until He comes. Your heavenly Father will surely send Him if you ask for Him. Wait in the Lord for the Holy Spirit. It is the child waiting, asking, urging, and praying perseveringly for the Father's greatest gift and for the child's greatest need, the Holy Spirit.

How are we to obtain the Holy Spirit so freely promised to those who seek Him believingly? Wait, press, and persevere with all the calmness and ardor of a faith that knows no fear and allows no doubt. A faith that staggers "not at the promise of God through unbelief."[16] A faith that in its darkest and most depressed hours against hope believes in hope.[17] A faith that is brightened by hope, strengthened by hope, and saved by hope.

WAIT AND PRAY

This is the key that unlocks every castle of despair, and that opens every treasure store of God. It is the simplicity of the child's asking of the Father, who gives with a largeness, liberality, and cheerfulness, infinitely above everything ever known to earthly parents. Ask for the Holy Spirit, seek for the Holy Spirit, knock for the Holy Spirit. He is the Father's greatest gift for the child's greatest need.

In these three words, "ask, seek, and knock,"[18] given to us by Jesus, we have the repetition of the advancing steps of insistency and effort. He is laying Himself out in command and promise in the strongest way, showing us that if we will lay ourselves out in prayer and will persevere, rising to higher and stronger attitudes and sinking to deeper depths of intensity and effort, that the answer must inevitably come. Truly, the stars would fail to shine before the asking, seeking, and knocking would fail to obtain what is needed and desired.

There is no elect company here, only the election of undismayed, persistent, never-fainting effort in prayer: "To him that knocketh it shall be opened."[19] Nothing can be stronger than this declaration assuring us of the answer, unless it is the promise upon which it is based, "ask, and it shall be given you."[20]

Endnotes

1 Matthew 7:7
2 John 14:16
3 James 4:2
4 John 16:8
5 Luke 11:13
6 Hebrews 5:7
7 Acts 4:31
8 Acts 8:5-17
9 Acts 9:11-17
10 Romans 8:26-27
11 Ephesians 3:20
12 James 5:16

13 Colossians 1:29
14 Matthew 7:11
15 Luke 11:3
16 Romans 4:20
17 Romans 4:18
18 Matthew 7:7
19 Matthew 7:8
20 Matthew 7:7; Luke 11:9

14

The Holy Spirit: Our Helper in Prayer

WE MUST PRAY IN *the Spirit, in the Holy Ghost, if we would pray at all. Lay this, I beseech you, to heart. Do not address yourselves to prayer as to a work to be accomplished in your own natural strength. It is a work of God, of God the Holy Ghost, a work of His in you and by you, and in which you must be fellow-workers with Him—but His work notwithstanding.* (Archbishop Trench)

One of the revelations of the New Testament concerning the Holy Spirit is that He is our helper in prayer. So we have in the following incident in our Lord's life the close connection between the Holy Spirit's work and prayer:

> In that hour Jesus rejoiced in spirit, and said, I thank thee, O Father, Lord of heaven and earth, that thou hast hid these things from the wise and prudent, and hast revealed them unto babes: even so, Father; for so it seemed good in thy sight.[1]

Here we have revelations of what God is to us. Only the child's heart can know the Father, and only the child's heart can reveal the Father. It is only by prayer that all things are delivered to us by the Father through the Son. It is only by prayer that all things are revealed to us by the Father and by the Son. It is only in prayer that the Father gives Himself to us, which is much more in every way than all other things whatsoever.

The *Revised Version* reads: "At that same hour Jesus rejoiced in the Holy Spirit." This sets forth that great truth not generally known, or if known, ignored, that Jesus Christ was generally led by the Holy Spirit, and that His joy and His praying, as well as His working, and His life, were under the inspiration, law, and guidance of the Holy Spirit.

THE HOLY SPIRIT HELPS US

> Likewise the Spirit also helpeth our infirmities: for we know not what we should pray for as we ought.[2]

This text is most significant and vital, and needs to be quoted. Patience, hope, and waiting help us in prayer. But the greatest and the most divine of all helpers is the Holy Spirit. He takes hold of things for us. We are dark and confused, ignorant and weak, in many things—in fact, in everything pertaining to the heavenly life, especially in the simple service of prayer. There is an ought on us, an obligation, a necessity to pray, a spiritual necessity upon us of the most absolute and imperative kind. But we do not feel the obligation and have no ability to meet it. The Holy Spirit helps us in our weaknesses, gives wisdom to our ignorance, turns ignorance into wisdom, and changes our weakness into strength. The Spirit himself does this. He helps and takes hold with us as we tug and toil. He adds His wisdom to our ignorance, gives His strength to our weakness. He pleads for us and in us. He quickens, illumines, and inspires our prayers. He composes and elevates the matter of our prayers, and inspires the words and feelings of our prayers. He works mightily in us so that we can pray mightily. He enables us to pray always and ever according to the will of God.

In John's first epistle we have these words:

> And this is the confidence that we have in Him, that, if we ask any thing according to His will, He heareth us: And if we know that He hear us, whatsoever we ask, we know that we have the petitions that we desired of Him.[3]

That which gives us boldness and so much freedom and fullness of approach toward God, the fact and basis of that boldness and liberty of approach, is that we are asking "according to His will." This does not mean submission, but conformity. "According to" means after the standard, conformity, agreement. We have boldness and all freedom of access to God because we are praying in conformity to His will. God records His general will in His Word, but He has this special work in praying for us to do. His things are prepared for us, as the prophet says, "that waiteth for him."[4] How can we know the will of God in our praying? What are the things that God designs specially for us to do and pray? The Holy Spirit reveals them to us perpetually.

THE HOLY SPIRIT MAKES INTERCESSION FOR US

The Spirit itself maketh intercession for us with groanings which cannot be uttered. And he that searcheth the hearts knoweth what is the mind of the Spirit, because he maketh intercession for the saints according to the will of God.[5]

Combine this text with those words of Paul in I Corinthians and what follows:

> But as it is written, Eye hath not seen, nor ear heard, neither have entered into the heart of man, the things which God hath prepared for them that love him. But God hath revealed them unto us by his Spirit: for the Spirit searcheth all things, yea, the deep things of God. For what man knoweth the things of a man, save the spirit of man which is in him? even so the things of God knoweth no man, but the Spirit of God. Now we have received, not the spirit of the world, but the spirit which is of God; that we might know the things that are freely given to us of God. Which things also we speak, not in the words which man's wisdom teacheth, but which the Holy Ghost teacheth; comparing spiritual things with spiritual. But the natural man receiveth not the things of the Spirit of God: for they are foolishness unto him: neither can he know them, because they are spiritually discerned. But he that is spiritual judgeth all things, yet he himself is judged of no man. For who hath known the mind of the Lord, that he may instruct him? But we have the mind of Christ. [6]

"Revealed unto us by His Spirit." Note those words. God searches the heart where the Spirit dwells and knows the mind of the Spirit. The Spirit who dwells in our hearts searches the deep purposes and the will of God to us, and reveals those purposes and that will of God, "that we might know the things that are freely given to us of God." Our spirits are so fully indwelt by the Spirit of God, so responsive and obedient to His illumination and to His will, that we ask with holy boldness and freedom the things that the Spirit of God has shown us as the will of God, and faith is assured. Then "we know that we have the petitions that we desired of Him."

PRAYERS OF NATURAL PEOPLE

Natural people pray, but pray according to their own will, fancy, and desire. If they have ardent desires and groanings, they are simply the fire and agony of nature, and not that of the Spirit. What a world of natural praying there is—selfish, self-contented, self-inspired! The Spirit, when He prays through us, or helps us to meet the mighty duty of right praying, trims our praying down to the will of God, and then we give heart and expression to His unutterable groanings. Then we have the mind of Christ, and pray as He would pray. His thoughts, purposes, and desires are our thoughts, purposes, and desires.

This is not a new and different Bible from that which we already have, but it is the Bible we have, applied personally by the Spirit of God. It is not new texts, but rather the Spirit's embellishing of certain texts for us at the time.

THE HOLY SPIRIT REVEALS THE WORD OF GOD TO US

It is the unfolding of the Word by the Spirit's light, guidance, and teaching that enables us to perform the great office of intercessors on earth, in harmony with the great intercessions of Jesus Christ at the Father's right hand in heaven.

We have in the Holy Spirit an illustration and an enabler of what this intercession is and ought to be. We are charged to pray in the spirit and to pray in the Holy Spirit.[7] We are reminded that the Holy Spirit "helpeth our infirmities." Intercession is an art of so divine and high a nature that though we know not what to pray for as we ought, yet the Spirit teaches us this heavenly science by making intercession in us "with groanings which cannot be uttered." How burdened these intercessions of the Holy Spirit! How profoundly He feels the world's sin, woe, and loss, and how deeply He sympathizes with the dreadful conditions, are seen in His groanings that are too deep for utterance and too sacred to be voiced by Him. He inspires us to this most divine work of intercession, and His strength enables us to sigh unto God for the oppressed, burdened, and distressed creation. The Holy Spirit helps us in many ways.

PRAYING IN THE SPIRIT

How intense will be the intercessions of the saints who supplicate in the spirit. How vain and false and how utterly fruitless and inefficient are prayers without the Spirit! Official prayers they may be, fitted for state occasions, beautiful and courtly, but worth less than nothing as God values prayer.

It is our untiring praying that will help the Holy Spirit to His mightiest work in us. At the same time, He helps us to these strenuous and exalted efforts in prayer.

We can and do pray by many inspirations and in many ways that are not of God. Many prayers are stereotyped in manner and in matter, partly if not completely. Many prayers are hearty and vehement, but it is natural heartiness and a fleshly vehemence. Much praying is done by force of habit and through form. Habit is a second nature and holds to the good when so directed, as well as to the bad. The habit of praying is a good habit, and should be early and strongly formed. But to pray by habit merely is to destroy the life of prayer and allow it to degenerate into a hollow and sham-producing form. Habit may form the bank for the river of prayer, but there must be a strong, deep, and pure current, crystal and life-giving, flowing between these two banks. Hannah multiplied her praying, "but she poured out her soul before the Lord."[8] We cannot make our prayer habits too marked and controlling if the life-waters be full and overflow the banks.

THE HOLY SPIRIT: OUR TEACHER IN PRAYER

Our divine example in praying is the Son of God. Our divine helper in praying is the Holy Spirit. He quickens us to pray and helps us in praying. Acceptable prayer must be begun and carried on by His presence and inspiration. We are enjoined in the holy Scriptures to be "praying in the Holy Ghost."[9] We are charged to be "praying always with all prayer and supplication in the Spirit."[10] We are reminded for our encouragement that:

> Likewise the Spirit also helpeth our infirmities: for we know not what we should pray for as we ought: but the Spirit itself maketh intercession for us with groanings which cannot be uttered. And he that searcheth the hearts knoweth what is the mind of the Spirit, because he maketh intercession for the saints according to the will of God.[11]

We are so ignorant in this matter of prayer, and all other teachers are so powerless to impart its lessons to our understanding and heart, that the Holy Spirit comes as the infallible and all-wise teacher to instruct us in this divine art. Someone has rightly said, "To pray with all your heart and all your strength, with the reason and the will, this is the greatest achievement of the Christian warfare on earth."

This is what we are taught to do and enabled to do by the Holy Spirit. If no person can say that Jesus is the Christ but by the Spirit's help, for the much greater reason no person can pray except by the aid of God's Spirit. For many of us, our mother's lips, now sealed by death, taught us many sweet lessons of prayer, prayers that have bound and held our hearts like golden threads. But these prayers, flowing through the natural channel of a mother's love, can not serve the purposes of our adulthood's warring, stormy life. These maternal lessons are but the ABCs of praying. For the higher and graduating lessons in prayer we must have the Holy Spirit. He only can unfold to us the mysteries of the prayer life, its duty and service.

PRAYING BY THE PRESENCE OF THE HOLY SPIRIT

To pray by the Holy Spirit we must have Him always. He does not, like earthly teachers, teach us the lesson and then withdraw. He stays to help us practice the lesson He has taught. We pray, not by the precepts and lessons He has taught, but we pray by Him. He is both teacher and lesson. We can only know the lesson because He is always with us to inspire, illumine, explain, and help us to perform it. We pray not by the truth the Holy Spirit reveals to us, but we pray by the actual presence of the Holy Spirit. He puts the desire in our hearts, and kindles that desire by His own flame. We simply give lips, voice, and heart to His unutterable groanings. Our prayers are taken up by Him and energized and sanctified by His intercession. He prays for us, through us, and in us. We pray by Him, through Him, and in Him. He puts the prayer in us, and we give it utterance and heart.

We always pray according to the will of God when the Holy Spirit helps our praying. He prays through us only according to the will of God. If our prayers are not according to the will of God, they die in the presence of the Holy Spirit. He gives such prayers no countenance or help. Discountenanced and unhelped by Him, prayers that are not according to God's will soon die out of every heart where the Holy Spirit dwells.

We must, as Jude says, "be praying in the Holy Ghost." As Paul says, "with all prayer and supplication in the Spirit." Never forgetting that "the Spirit also helpeth our infirmities: for we know not what we should pray for as we ought: but the Spirit itself maketh intercession for us with groanings which cannot be uttered." Above all, over all, and through all our praying there must be the name of Christ, which includes the power of His blood, the energy of His intercession, and the fullness of the enthroned Christ. "Whatsoever ye shall ask in my name, that will I do."[12]

Endnotes

1 Luke 10:21
2 Romans 8:26
3 1 John 5:14-15
4 Isaiah 64:4
5 Romans 8:26b-27
6 1 Corinthians 2:9-16
7 Jude 1:20
8 Paraphrase of 1 Samuel 1:15
9 Jude 1:20
10 Ephesians 6:18
11 Romans 8:26-27
12 John 14:13

15

The Two Comforters and Advocates

IF WE WERE ASKED *whose Comforter the Holy Spirit was, the answer would be—Ours. The answer is not so ready when we are asked whose Advocate He is. The Spirit is Christ's Advocate, not ours. It is Christ's place He takes, Christ's cause He pleads, Christ's name He vindicates, Christ's Kingdom He administers.* (Samuel Chadwick)

The fact that we have two divine Comforters, Advocates, Helpers, declares the richness of God's provisions in the gospel, and also declares the settled purpose of God to execute His work of salvation with effectiveness and final success. Our infirmities are many and varied in our pilgrimage and warfare for heaven. These two Comforters and Advocates attend to them all with manifold wisdom.

The richness of God's provision of two Intercessors in executing the plan of salvation finds its counterpart in the prayer promise in its unlimited nature, comprehending all things, great and small. "All things, whatsoever ye shall ask in prayer, believing, ye shall receive."[1] All things we have in Christ, all things we have in the Holy Spirit, and all things we have in prayer.

How much is ours in God's plan and purposes we have in these two Advocates, the one ascended to heaven and enthroned there to intercede for our benefit—the other, His representative and better substitute, on earth to work in us and make intercessions for us!

THE TWO ADVOCATES
The first Advocate was a person. The other Advocate also a person, but not clothed in physical form or subject to human limitations as the first

one necessarily was. Transient and local was the first Advocate. The other Advocate not limited to locality, transient, but abiding, Not dealing with the sensible, material, fleshly, but entering personally into the mysterious and imperial domain of the spirit, to emancipate and transform that waste and dark realm into more than Eden beauty. The first Advocate left His novitiates that they might enter into higher regions of spiritual knowledge. Christ withdrew that the Spirit might train and school the disciples into the deeper mysteries of God, and all the historical and physical might be transmuted into the pure gold of the spiritual. The first Advocate brought to us a picture of what we must be. The other Advocate mirrored this perfect and fadeless image on our hearts. The first Advocate, like David, gathered and furnished the material for the temple. The other Advocate forms God's glorious temple out of this material.

The possibilities of prayer, then, are the possibilities of these two divine intercessors. Where are the limitations to results when the Holy Spirit intercedes for us with groanings that cannot be uttered, when He so helps us that our prayers run parallel to the will of God, and we pray for the very things and in the very manner in which we ought to pray, schooled in and pressed to these prayers by the urgency of the Holy Spirit! How measureless are the possibilities of prayer when we are filled with all the fullness of God. When we stand "perfect and complete in all the will of God."[2] If the intercession of Moses so wondrously preserved the being and safety of Israel throughout its marvelous history and destiny, what may we not secure through our intercessor, who is so much greater than Moses? All that God has lies open to Christ through prayer. All that Christ has lies open to us through prayer.

THE TWO INTERCESSORS

If we have the two Intercessors covering the whole realm of goodness, power, purity, and glory in heaven and on earth—if we have the better Comforter with us here in this world—why is it that we sigh to know Jesus after the flesh as the disciples knew Him? Why is it that the mighty work of these two almighty Intercessors finds us so barren of heavenly fruit, so feeble in all Christly principles, so low in the Christly life, and so marred in the Christly image? Is it not because our prayers for the Holy Spirit have been so faint and few? The heavenly Christ can only come to us in full beauty and power when we have received the fullness of the present earthly Comforter, the Holy Spirit.

If we were living always the life of prayer, breathing always the spirit of prayer, being always in the fact of prayer, praying always in the Holy Spirit, the heavenly Christ would become ours by a clearer vision, a deeper love, and a more intimate fellowship than He was to His disciples in the days of His flesh.

We would not disguise or lessen the fact that there is a loss to us by our absent Christ as we will see and know Him in heaven. But in our earthly work to be done by us, and above all to be done in us, we will know Christ and the Father better, and can better utilize them by the ministry of the Holy Spirit than would have been possible under the personal, human presence of the Son. So to the loving and obedient ones who are filled with the Spirit, both the Father and the Son will come unto us and make their abode with us.[3] In the day of the fullness of the indwelling Spirit, "Ye shall know that I am in my Father, and ye in Me, and I in you."[4] Amazing oneness and harmony, wrought by the almighty power of the Holy Spirit!

There is not a note in the archangel's song to which the Holy Spirit does not attune people into sympathy, not a pulsation in the heart of God to which the Holy Spirit-filled heart does not respond with loud amens and joyful hallelujahs. Even more than this, by the other Comforter, the Holy Ghost, we "know the love of Christ, which passeth knowledge."[5] More than this, by the Holy Spirit we are "filled with all the fullness of God." More than this, God is able to do "exceeding abundantly above all that we ask or think, according to the power [of the Holy Spirit] that worketh in us."[6]

The presence and power of the other Advocate would more than compensate the disciples for the loss of Christ. His going away had filled their hearts with a strange sorrow. A loneliness and desolation like an orphan's woe had swept over their hearts and stunned and bewildered them. But He comforted them by telling them that the Holy Ghost would be like the pains of a travailing mother, all forgotten in the untold joy that a child was born into the world.

Endnotes

1 Matthew 21:22
2 Colossians 4:12
3 See Hosea 6:3
4 John 14:20
5 Ephesians 3:19
6 Ephesians 3:20

16

Prayer and the Holy Spirit Dispensation

Hᴏᴡ Gᴏᴅ ɴᴇᴇᴅs, *how the world needs, how the Church needs the flow of the mighty river more blessed than the Nile, deeper, broader and more overflowing than the Amazon's mighty current! and yet what mere rills we are! We need, the age needs, the Church needs, memorials of God's mighty power, which will silence the enemy and the avenger, dumbfound God's foes, strengthen weak saints, and fill strong ones with triumphant raptures.* (E. M. Bounds)

The dispensation of the Holy Spirit was ushered in by prayer. Read these words from the book of Acts: "And when they were come in, they went up into an upper room, where abode both Peter, and James, and John, and Andrew, Philip, and Thomas, Bartholomew, and Matthew, James the son of Alphaeus, and Simon Zelotes, and Judas the brother of James."[1]

This was the attitude that the disciples assumed after Jesus had ascended to heaven. That meeting for prayer ushered in the dispensation of the Holy Spirit to which prophets had looked forward with entranced vision. In a very marked way, this dispensation that holds in its keeping the fortune of the Gospel has been committed to prayer.

Tʜᴇ ᴀᴘᴏsᴛᴏʟɪᴄ sᴀɪɴᴛs ᴋɴᴇᴡ ᴛʜᴇ ᴡᴏʀᴛʜ ᴏғ ᴘʀᴀʏᴇʀ

Apostolic saints knew well the worth of prayer and were jealous of the most sacred offices that infringed on their time and strength and hindered them from giving themselves "continually to prayer, and to the ministry of the Word."[2] They put prayer first. The Word depends on prayer that it "may have free course, and be glorified."[3] Praying apostles make preaching apostles. Prayer gives edge, entrance, and weight to the Word. Sermons conceived by prayer and saturated with prayer are weighty sermons.

Sermons may be ponderous with thought, sparkle with the gems of genius and of taste, pleasing and popular, but without having their birth and life in prayer, for God's uses they are trifles, dull and dead.

The Lord of the harvest sends out laborers, full in number and perfect in kind, in answer to prayer. It needs no prophetic understanding to declare that if the Church had used prayer force to its utmost, the light of the gospel would have long ago circled the world.

THE GOSPEL WAITS ON MORE PRAYER

God's gospel has always waited more on prayer than on anything else for its successes. A praying Church is strong though poor in all else. A prayerless Church is weak though rich in all else. Only praying hearts will build God's kingdom. Only praying hands will put the crown on the Savior's head.

The Holy Spirit is the divinely appointed substitute for and representative of the personal and humanized Christ. How much He is to us! We are to be filled by Him, live in Him, walk in Him, and be led by Him! We are to conserve and kindle to a brighter and more consuming glow the holy flame! We must be careful to never to quench that pure flame! We must be watchful and tender, and loving so that we do not grieve His sensitive, loving, nature! We must be attentive, meek, and obedient, so we never to resist His divine impulses, always hear His voice, and always do His Divine will. This cannot be done without much and continuous prayer!

THE PERSISTENT WIDOW

The persistent widow had a great case to win against helpless, hopeless, despair, but she did it by persistent prayer. We have this great treasure to preserve and enhance, but we have a divine Person to instruct us and help. We can only be enabled to meet our duties by exceedingly much prayer.

Prayer is the only element in which the Holy Spirit can live and work. Prayer is the golden chain that happily enslaves Him to His happy work in us.

Everything depends upon our having this the Holy Spirit, and retaining Him in the fullness of His power. With the disciples, Pentecost was made by prayer. With them, Pentecost was continued by giving themselves to continued prayer. Persistent and unwearied prayer is the price we will have to pay for our Pentecost—instant and continued prayer. Abiding in the fact and in the spirit of prayer is the only surety of our abiding in Pentecostal power and purity.

Not only should the many-sided operation of the Holy Spirit in us and for us teach us the necessity of prayer for Him, but His condition with our praying assumes another attitude, the attitude of mutual dependence, that of action and reaction. The more we pray, the more He helps us to pray, and the larger the measure of Himself He gives to us. We are not only to pray and press and wait for His coming to us, but after we have received

Him in His fullness, we are to pray for a fuller and still larger bestowment of Himself to us. We are to pray for the largest and ever-increasing and constant fullness of capacity.

PAUL'S PRAYER FOR THE EPHESIAN CHURCH

"Be strengthened with might by His Spirit in the inner man,"[4] as Paul prayed for the Spirit-baptized Ephesian church. It will be remembered that He also prayed that "Christ may dwell in your hearts by faith,"[5] rooted and grounded in love, measuring up to the breadth, length, depth, and height of the most perfect sainthood, and up to the immeasurable love of Christ, being "filled with all the fullness of God."[6]

In that wonderful prayer for those Christians, Paul laid himself out to pray to God, and by prayer he sought to fathom the fathomless depths and to measure the unlimited purposes and benefits of God's plan of salvation for immortal souls by the presence and work of the Holy Spirit. Only persistent and invincible prayer can bring the Holy Spirit to us, and secure for us these indescribable gracious results. "Epaphras . . . always laboring fervently for you in prayers, that ye may stand perfect and complete in all the will of God."[7]

The Word of God provides for a mighty, consciously realized Christianity in His saints, into whose happy, shining, spirits God has been brought as a dweller, and whose heaven-toned lives have been attuned to melody by God's own hand.

THE MIGHTY FLOW OF THE HOLY SPIRIT

Then will it prove true: "He that believeth on me, . . . out of his belly shall flow rivers of living water."[8] Here is a promise concerning the indwelling and out-flowing of the Holy Spirit in us—life-giving fructifying and irresistible, a ceaseless out-flow of the river of God in us.

How God needs, how the world needs, how the Church needs, the flow of this mighty river, more blessed than the Nile, and deeper, broader, and more overflowing than the Amazon's broad and mighty current! Yet what mere rivulets we are and have been!

O that the Church, by the infilling and out-flowing of the Holy Spirit, might be able to raise up everywhere memorials of the Holy Spirit's power, which might fix the eye as well as engage the heart! We need, the age needs, the Church needs, memorials of God's mighty power, which will silence the enemy and the avenger, dumbfound God's foes, strengthen weak saints, and fill strong ones with triumphant raptures.

A glance at some more of the divine promises concerning this vital question would show us how they need to be projected into the experimental and the actual. "If any man will do his will, he shall know of the doctrine, whether it be of God, or whether I speak of myself."[9] How we need a conscious Christianity, personal and vital, unspeakable in its joy and full of glory![10] The need is for a conscious Christianity, made so by the Spirit bearing witness "that we are the children of God."[11] A Christianity of "I know," is the only powerful, vital, and aggressive Christianity. "One thing I know, that, whereas I was blind, now I see."[12] We need men and women in these loose days who can verify the above mentioned promise of Christ in their inner consciousness. Yet how many untold thousands of people are there in all of our churches who have only a dim, intangible hope so, maybe so, I trust so, kind of Christianity—all dubious, fragile, and unstable.

A GREAT NEED IN THE MODERN CHURCH

There is a great need in these days in the modern Church for Christians to see, seek, and obtain the high privilege in the Gospel of a heaven-born, clear cut, and happy Christian experience. One that is born of the presence of the Holy Spirit, and that gives an undoubted assurance of sins forgiven and adoption into the family of God.

There is also a need, subsequent to this conscious realization of divine favor in the forgiveness of sins and added to it, of the reception of the Holy Spirit in His fullness. An incoming of the Holy Spirit that purifies their hearts by faith, perfects them in love, overcomes the world, and bestows a divine, inward, power over all sin, both inward and outward. And that also gives them boldness to bear witness and qualifies them for real Christian service in the Church and in the world.

AGNOSTICISM IN THE CHURCH

There is a fearfully prevailing agnosticism along this line in the Church at this time. We greatly fear that a vast majority of our Church members are now in this school of spiritual agnosticism, and consider it to be a virtue to be there. God's Word gives no encouragement whatever to a shadowy Christianity and a vague Christian experience. It calls us definitely into the realm of knowledge. It crowns Christianity with the crown of "I know." It passes us from the darkness of sin, doubt, and inward misgiving into the marvelous light, where we see clearly and know fully our personal relations to God.

> The things unknown to feeble sense,
> Unseen by reason's glimmering ray,
> With strong, commanding confidence,
> Their heavenly origin display.

Two things may be said just here in concluding this part of our study upon this subject: First, this sort of Biblical Christianity that we have described comes directly through the action of the Holy Spirit dealing personally with each soul. Second, the Holy Spirit in all of His offices pertaining to spiritual life and Christian experience is secured by earnest, definite, prevailing prayer.

Endnotes

1 Acts 1:13
2 Acts 6:4
3 2 Thessalonians 3:1
4 Ephesians 3:16
5 Ephesians 3:17
6 Ephesians 3:19
7 Colossians 4:12
8 John 7:38
9 John 7:17
10 1 Peter 1:8
11 Romans 8:16
12 John 9:25

Book 5

The Weapon of Prayer

I

Prayer Essential to God

THEN SHALT THOU CALL, *and the LORD shall answer; thou shalt cry, and he shall say, Here I am. . . . Then shalt thou delight thyself in the LORD; and I will cause thee to ride upon the high places of the earth, and feed thee with the heritage of Jacob thy father: for the mouth of the LORD hath spoken it.* (Isaiah 58:9, 14)

It must never be forgotten that Almighty God rules this world. He is not an absentee God. His hand is ever on the throttle of human affairs. He is everywhere present in the concerns of time. "His eyes behold, his eyelids try, the children of men."[1] He rules the world just as He rules the Church—by prayer. This lesson needs to be emphasized, repeated and repeated again in the ears of men and women of modern times. It must be brought to bear with cumulative force on the consciences of this generation, whose eyes have no vision for the eternal things, whose ears are deaf toward God.

Nothing is more important to God than prayer in dealing with people. But it is likewise all-important to people to pray. Failure to pray is failure along the whole line of life. It is failure of duty, service, and spiritual progress. God must help people by prayer. Those who do not pray, therefore, rob themselves of God's help and place God where He cannot help people. Saints must pray to God if love for God is to exist. Faith, hope, and patience, and all the strong, beautiful, vital forces of piety are withered and dead in a prayerless life. The life of the individual believer, personal salvation, and personal Christian graces have their being, bloom, and fruitage in prayer.

THE NECESSITY OF PRAYER

All this and much more can be said as to the necessity of prayer to the existence and culture of piety in the individual. But prayer has a larger sphere, a more obligated duty, a loftier inspiration. Prayer concerns God, whose purposes and plans are conditioned on prayer. His will and His glory are bound up in praying. The days of God's splendor and renown have always been the great days of prayer. God's condition for great movements in this world has been prayer, and they have continued and been fashioned by prayer. God has put Himself in these great movements just as saints have prayed. Present, prevailing, conspicuous, and mastering prayer has always brought God to be present. The real and obvious test of a genuine work of God is the prevalence of the spirit of prayer. God's mightiest forces surcharge and impregnate a movement when prayer's mightiest forces are there.

God's movement to bring Israel from Egyptian bondage had its inception in prayer. Thus prayer was early established by God and praying saints as one of the granite forces upon which His world movements were to be based.

Hannah's petition for a son began a great prayer movement for God in Israel. Praying women, whose prayers like those of Hannah, can give men like Samuel to the cause of God, do more for the Church and the world than all the politicians on earth. Those born of prayer are the saviors of a country, and those saturated with prayer give life and impetus to the Church. Under God, they are saviors and helpers of both Church and country.

We must believe that the divine record of the facts about prayer and God are given in order that we might be constantly reminded of Him, and be ever refreshed by the faith that God holds His Church for the entire world, and that God's purpose will be fulfilled. His plans concerning the Church will most assuredly and inevitably be carried out. Without doubt, that record of God has been given so that we may be deeply impressed that the prayers of God's saints are a great factor, a supreme factor, in carrying forward God's work, with ease and in time. When the Church is in the condition of prayer, God's cause always flourishes and His kingdom on earth always triumphs.

WHEN THE CHURCH FAILS TO PRAY

When the Church fails to pray, God's cause decays and evil of every kind prevails. In other words, God works through the prayers of His people, and when they fail Him at this point, decline and deadness ensue. It is according to the divine plans that spiritual prosperity comes through the prayer-channel. Praying saints are God's agents for carrying on His saving and providential work on earth. If His agents fail Him, neglecting to pray, then His work fails. Praying saints of the Most High are always forerunners of spiritual prosperity.

Throughout the ages, the saints of the Church who have held the Church for God have had the ministry of prayer in affluent fullness and richness. The rulers of the Church that the Scriptures reveal have had preeminence in prayer. Eminent, they may have been, in culture, in intellect, and in all the natural or human forces. Or they may have been lowly in physical attainments and native gifts. Yet in each case prayer was the all potent force in the leadership of the Church. This was so because God was with and in what they did, for prayer always carries us back to God. It recognizes God and brings God into the world to work and save and bless. The most efficient agents in disseminating the knowledge of God, in prosecuting His work upon the earth, and in standing as breakwater against the billows of evil, have been praying Church leaders. God depends upon them, employs them, and blesses them.

PRAYER CANNOT BE SECONDARY

Prayer cannot be retired as a secondary force in this world. To do so is to retire God from the movement. It is to make God secondary. The prayer ministry is an all-engaging force. It must be so, to be a force at all. Prayer is the sense of God's need and the call for God's help to supply that need. The estimate and place of prayer is the estimate and place of God. To give prayer the secondary place is to make God secondary in life's affairs. To substitute other forces for prayer, retires God and materializes the whole movement.

Prayer is an absolute necessity to the proper carrying on of God's work. God has made it so. This must have been the principal reason why in the early Church, when the complaint that the widows of certain believers had been neglected in the daily administration of the Church's benefactions, that the twelve called the disciples together and told them to look out for seven men, "full of the Holy Ghost, and wisdom,"[2] who they would appoint over that benevolent work. They then added this important statement, "But we will give ourselves continually to prayer, and to the ministry of the Word."[3] They surely realized that the success of the Word and the progress of the Church were dependent in a preeminent sense upon their "giving themselves to prayer." God could effectively work through them in proportion as they gave themselves fully to prayer.

APOSTLES DEPENDENT UPON PRAYER

The Apostles were as dependent upon prayer as other folks. Sacred work—Church activities—may so engage and absorb us as to hinder praying, and when this is the case, evil results always follow. It is better to let the work go by default than to let the praying go by neglect. Whatever affects the intensity of our praying affects the value of our work. "Too busy to pray" is not only the keynote to backsliding, but it mars even the work done. Nothing is well done without prayer for the simple reason that it leaves God out of the account. It is so easy to be seduced by the good to the neglect of the best, until both the good and the best perish. How easily may Christians, even leaders in Zion, be led by the insidious wiles of Satan to cut short our praying in the interests of the work! How easy to neglect prayer or abbreviate our praying simply by the plea that we have Church work on our hands. Satan has effectively disarmed us when he can keep us too busy doing things to stop and pray.

"We will give ourselves continually to prayer, and the ministry of the Word." The *Revised Version* has it, "We will continue steadfastly in prayer." The implication of the word used here means to be strong and steadfast, to be devoted to and keep at it with constant care, to make a business out of it. We find the same word in Colossians 4:12, and in Romans 12:12, which is translated, "Continuing instant in prayer."

THE LAW OF PRAYER

The law of prayer recognizes God as God, and depends upon Him to do for us what He would not do without prayer. The apostles were under the necessity of prayer, just as all believers are in every age and in every place. They had to be devoted to prayer in order to make their ministry of the Word efficient. The business of preaching is worth very little without it being in direct partnership with the business of praying. Apostolic preaching cannot be carried on unless there is apostolic praying. Alas, that this plain truth has been so easily forgotten by those who minister in holy things! Without in any way passing a criticism on the ministry, we feel it is high time that somebody or other declared to its members that effective preaching is conditioned on effective praying. The preaching that is most successful comes from a ministry that has much prayer in it. Perhaps one might go so far as to say that it is the only kind that is successful. God can mightily use the preacher who prays. That person is God's chosen messenger for good, whom the Holy Spirit delights to honor. A praying preacher is God's efficient agent in saving sinners and in edifying the saints.

APOSTLES LOSING APOSTOLIC POWER

In Acts 6:1-8 we have the record of how the Apostles felt that they were losing—had lost—in apostolic power because they did not have relief from certain duties in order that they might give themselves more to prayer. So they called a halt because they discovered to their regret that they were too deficient in praying. Doubtless they kept up the form of praying, but it was seriously defective in intensity and in point of the amount of time given to it. Their minds were too much preoccupied with the finances of the Church. Just as in this day we find in many places both laypeople and ministers are so busily engaged in "serving tables" that they are glaringly deficient in praying. In fact, in present-day Church affairs Christians are looked upon as religious because they give largely of their money to the Church, and people are chosen for official positions not because they are people of prayer, but because they have the financial ability to run Church finances and to get money for the Church.

Now these Apostles, when they looked into this matter, determined to put aside these hindrances growing out of Church finances, and resolved to "give themselves to prayer." Not that these finances were to be ignored or set aside, but ordinary laypeople "full of faith and the Holy Ghost" could be found. Really religious Christians who could easily attend to this money business without in the least affecting their piety or their praying, thus giving them something to do in the Church, and at the same time taking the burden from the Apostles who would be able now to pray more. By praying more they blessed themselves in soul, and at the same time could more effectively do the work to which they had been called.

They realized too, as they had not realized before, that they were being so pressed by attention to material things, things right in themselves, that they could not give to prayer that strength, ardor, and time that its nature and importance demanded. We will discover, under close scrutiny of ourselves sometimes, that things legitimate, things right in themselves, things commendable, may so engross our attention, so preoccupy our minds, and so draw on our feelings that prayer may be omitted, or at least very little time may be given to prayer.

NEGLECT OF THE PRAYER CLOSET

How easy to slip away from the closet! Even the Apostles had to guard themselves at that point. How much we need to watch ourselves at the same place! Things legitimate and right may become wrong when they take the place of prayer. Things right in themselves may become wrong things when they are allowed to fasten themselves inordinately upon our hearts. It is not only the sinful things that hurt prayer. It is not alone questionable things that are to be guarded against. But it is things that are right in their places, but which are allowed to sidetrack prayer and shut the closet door, often with the self-comforting plea that "we are too busy to pray."

Possibly this has had as much to do with the breaking down of family prayer in this age as any other one cause. It is at this point that family Christianity has decayed, and just here is one cause of the decline of the prayer meeting. Men and women are too busy with legitimate things to "give themselves to prayer." Other things are given the right of way. Prayer is set aside or made secondary. Business comes first. This means not always that prayer is second, but that prayer is put entirely out. The Apostles drove directly at this point, and determined that even Church business should not affect their praying habits. Prayer must come first. Then would they be in deed and truth God's real agents in His world, through whom He could effectually work, because they were praying saints, and thereby put themselves directly in line with His plans and purposes, which was that He works through praying saints.

When the complaint came to their ears, the Apostles discovered that what they had been doing did not fully serve the divine ends of peace, gratitude, and unity, but discontent, complaining, and division were the result of their work, which had far too little prayer in it. So prayer was put prominently to the front.

PRAYING SAINTS ARE NECESSARY

Praying saints are a necessity in carrying out the divine plan for the salvation of sinners. God has made it so. It is He who established prayer as a divine ordinance, and this implies people are to do the praying. So that praying men and women are a necessity in the world. The fact that so often God has employed people of prayer to accomplish His ends clearly proves the proposition. It is altogether unnecessary to name all the instances where God used the prayers of righteous saints to carry out His gracious designs. Time and space are too limited for the list. Yet one or two cases might be named.

In the case of the golden calf, when God purposed to destroy the Israelites because of their great sin of idolatry, at the time when Moses was receiving the law at God's hands, the very being of Israel was imperiled, for Aaron had been swept away by the strong popular tide of unbelief and sin. All seemed lost but Moses and prayer, and prayer became more efficient and wonder-working in behalf of Israel than Aaron's magic rod. God was determined on the destruction of Israel and Aaron. His anger waxed hot. It was a fearful and a critical hour. But prayer held back heaven's desolating fury. God's hand was held fast by Moses, the mighty intercessor.

MOSES AND ISRAEL

Moses was set on delivering Israel. It was with him a long and exhaustive struggle of praying for forty days and forty nights. Not for one moment did he relax his hold on God. Not for one moment did he quit his place at the feet of God, even for food. Not for one moment did he moderate his demand or ease his cry. Israel's existence was in the balance. Almighty God's wrath must be stayed. Israel must be saved at all hazards. And Israel was saved. Moses would not let God alone. And so, today, we can look back and give the credit of the present race of the Jews to the praying of Moses centuries ago.

Persevering prayer always wins. God yields to importunity and fidelity. He has no heart to say "No" to such praying as Moses did. God's purpose to destroy Israel is actually changed by the praying of this man of God. It is but an illustration of how much just one saint praying is worth in this world, and how much depends upon that person.

DANIEL IN BABYLON

When in Babylon, Daniel refused to obey the decree of the king not to ask any petition of any god or person for thirty days, he shut his eyes to the decree that would shut him off from his praying room, and refused to be deterred from calling upon God from fear of the consequences. So he "kneeled upon his knees three times a day,"[4] and prayed as he had before done, leaving it all with God as to the consequences of thus disobeying the king.

There was nothing impersonal about Daniel's praying. It always had an objective, and was an appeal to a great God, who could do all things. There was no coddling of self, nor looking after subjective or reflex influences. In the face of the dreadful decree that is to precipitate him from place and power into the lion's den, "he kneeled upon his knees three times a day . . . and gave thanks before his God, as he did aforetime."[5] The gracious result was that prayer laid its hands upon an almighty arm, which interposed in that den of vicious, cruel, lions and closed their mouths and preserved His servant Daniel, who had been true to Him and who had called upon Him for protection. Daniel's praying was an essential factor in defeating the king's decree and in discomfiting the wicked, envious, rulers who had set the trap for Daniel in order to destroy him and remove him from place and power in the kingdom.

Endnotes

1 Psalm 11:4
2 Acts 6:3
3 Acts 6:4
4 Daniel 6:10
5 Daniel 6:10

2

Putting God to Work

F OR SINCE THE BEGINNING *of the world men have not heard, nor perceived by the ear, neither hath the eye seen, O God, beside thee, what he hath prepared for him that waiteth for him.* (Isaiah 64:4)

The assertion voiced in the title given this chapter is but another way of declaring that God has of His own motion placed Himself under the law of prayer, and has obligated Himself to answer the prayers of saints. He has ordained prayer as a means whereby He will do things through saints as they pray, which He would not otherwise do. Prayer is a specific divine appointment, an ordinance of heaven, whereby God purposes to carry out His gracious designs on earth and to execute and make efficient the plan of salvation.

When we say that prayer puts God to work, it is simply to say that saints have it in their power by prayer to move God to work in His own way among people, in which way He would not work if prayer was not made. Thus while prayer moves God to work, at the same time God puts prayer to work. As God has ordained prayer, and as prayer has no existence separate from people, but involves people, then logically prayer is the one force that puts God to work in earth's affairs through saints and their prayers.

Let these fundamental truths concerning God and prayer be kept in mind in all allusions to prayer, and in all our reading of the incidents of prayer in the Scriptures.

If prayer puts God to work on earth, then, by the same token, prayerlessness rules God out of the world's affairs, and prevents Him from working. If prayer moves God to work in this world's affairs, then prayerlessness excludes God from everything concerning people, and leaves humanity on earth the mere creature of circumstances, at the mercy of blind fate, and without help of any kind from God. It leaves people in this world with its tremendous responsibilities and its difficult problems, and with all of its sorrows, burdens and afflictions, without any God at all. In reality, the denial of prayer is a denial of God Himself, for God and prayer are so inseparable that they can never be divorced.

Prayer affects three different spheres of existence—the divine, angelic, and human. It puts God to work, it puts angels to work, and it puts people to work. It lays its hands upon God, angels, and people. What a wonderful reach there is in prayer! It brings into play the forces of heaven and earth. God, angels, and people are subjects of this wonderful law of prayer, and all these have to do with the possibilities and the results of prayer. God has so far placed Himself subject to prayer that by reason of His own appointment, He is induced to work among saints in a way in which He does not work if saints do not pray. Prayer lays hold upon God and influences Him to work. This is the meaning of prayer as it concerns God. This is the doctrine of prayer, or else there is nothing whatever in prayer.

PRAYER PUTS GOD TO WORK IN ALL THINGS PRAYED FOR

While people in their weakness and poverty wait, trust, and pray, God undertakes the work. "For since the beginning of the world men have not heard, nor perceived by the ear, neither hath the eye seen, O God, beside thee, what he hath prepared for him that waiteth for him."[1]

Jesus Christ commits Himself to the force of prayer. "Whatsoever ye shall ask in My name," He says, "that will I do, that the Father may be glorified in the Son. If ye shall ask any thing in My Name, I will do it."[2] And again, "If ye abide in Me, and My words abide in you, ye shall ask what ye will, and it shall be done unto you."[3]

To no other energy is the promise of God committed as to that of prayer. Upon no other force are the purposes of God so dependent as this one of prayer. The Word of God expounds on the results and necessity of prayer. The work of God stays or advances as prayer puts forth its strength. Prophets and apostles have urged the utility, force, and necessity of prayer. "I have set watchmen upon thy walls, O Jerusalem, which shall never hold their peace day nor night: ye that make mention of the LORD, keep not silence. And give Him no rest, till He establish, and till He make Jerusalem a praise in the earth."[4]

Prayer, with its antecedents and attendants, is the one and only condition of the final triumph of the Gospel. It is the one and only condition that honors the Father and glorifies the Son. Little and poor praying has weakened Christ's power on earth, postponed the glorious results of His reign, and retired God from His sovereignty.

PRAYER DEPENDS UPON GOD TO WORK

Prayer puts God's work in His hands and keeps it there. It looks to Him constantly and depends on Him implicitly to further His own cause. Prayer is but faith resting in, acting with, and leaning on and obeying God. This is why God loves it so well, why He puts all power into its hands, and why He so highly esteems people of prayer.

Every movement for the advancement of the Gospel must be created by and inspired by prayer. In all these movements of God, prayer precedes and attends as an invariable and necessary condition.

In this relation, God makes prayer identical in force and power with Himself and says, in essence, to those on earth who pray: "You are on the earth to carry on My cause. I am in heaven, the Lord of all, the Maker of all, the Holy One of all. Now whatever you need for My cause, ask Me and I will do it. Shape the future by your prayers, and all that you need for present supplies, command Me.[5] I made heaven and earth, and all things in them. Ask largely. 'Open thy mouth wide, and I will fill it.'[6] It is My work that you are doing. It concerns My cause. Be prompt and full in praying. Do not abate your asking, and I will not wince nor abate in My giving."

GOD CONDITIONS HIS ACTIONS ON PRAYER

Everywhere in His Word His actions and attitude are shaped by prayer. To quote all the Scriptural passages that prove the immediate, direct, and personal relation of prayer to God, would be to transfer whole pages of the Scripture to this study. Humanity has personal relations with God. Prayer is the divinely appointed means by which humanity comes into direct connection with God. By His own ordinance God holds Himself bound to hear prayer. God bestows His great good on His children when they seek it along the avenue of prayer.

When Solomon closed his great prayer that he offered at the dedication of the temple, God appeared to him, approved him, and laid down the universal principles of His action. In 2 Chronicles 7:12-15 we read as follows:

And the Lord appeared to Solomon by night, and said unto him, I have heard thy prayer, and have chosen this place to myself for an house of sacrifice. If I shut up heaven that there be no rain, or if I command the locusts to devour the land, or if I send pestilence among my people; If my people, which are called by my name, shall humble themselves, and pray, and seek my face, and turn from their wicked ways; then will I hear from heaven, and will forgive their sin, and will heal their land. Now mine eyes shall be open, and mine ears attent unto the prayer that is made in this place.[7]

In His purposes concerning the Jews in the Babylonian captivity, God asserts His unfailing principles:

> For thus saith the Lord, That after seventy years be accomplished at Babylon I will visit you, and perform my good word toward you, in causing you to return to this place. For I know the thoughts that I think toward you, saith the Lord, thoughts of peace, and not of evil, to give you an expected end. Then shall ye call upon me, and ye shall go and pray unto me, and I will hearken unto you. And ye shall seek me, and find me, when ye shall search for me with all your heart.[8]

In Bible terminology, prayer means calling upon God for things we desire—asking things of God. Thus we read: "Call onto me, and I will answer thee, and show thee great and mighty things, which thou knowest not,"[9] "Call upon me in the day of trouble: I will deliver thee."[10] "Then shalt thou call, and the LORD shall answer; thou shalt cry, and He shall say, Here I am."[11]

PRAYER IS A DIRECT APPLICATION TO GOD

Prayer is revealed as a direct application to God for some temporal or spiritual good. It is an appeal to God to intervene in life's affairs for the good of those for whom we pray. God is recognized as the source and fountain of all good, and prayer implies that all His good is held in His keeping for those who call upon Him in truth.

That prayer is an application to God, interaction with God, and communion with God, comes out strongly and simply in the praying of Old Testament saints. Abraham's intercession for Sodom is a striking illustration of the nature of prayer, interaction with God, and showing the intercessory side of prayer. The declared purpose of God to destroy Sodom confronted Abraham, and his soul within him was greatly moved because of his great interest in that fated city. His nephew and family resided there. That purpose of God must be changed. God's decree for the destruction of this evil city's inhabitants must be revoked.

ABRAHAM PRAYS FOR SODOM

It was no small undertaking that faced Abraham when he conceived the idea of beseeching God to spare Sodom. Abraham sets himself to change God's purpose and to save Sodom with the other cities of the plain. It was certainly a most difficult and delicate work for him to undertake to throw his influence with God in favor of those doomed cities so as to save them.

He bases his plea on the simple fact of the number of righteous people who could be found in Sodom, and appeals to the infinite rectitude of God not to destroy the righteous with the wicked. "That be far from thee to do after this manner, to slay the righteous with the wicked. . . . Shall not the Judge of all the earth do right?"[12] With what deep self-abasement and reverence does Abraham enter upon his high and divine work! He stood before God in solemn awe, and meditation, and then drew near to God and spoke. He advanced step by step in faith, demand, and urgency, and God granted every request that he made. It has been well said that "Abraham left off asking before God left off granting." It seems that Abraham had a kind of optimistic view of the piety of Sodom. He scarcely expected when he undertook this matter to have it end in failure. He was greatly in earnest, and had every encouragement to press his case. In his final request he surely thought that with Lot, his wife, daughters, sons, and sons-in-law, he had his ten righteous persons for whose sake God would spare the city. But alas! The count failed when the final test came. There were not ten righteous people in that large population.

But this was true. If he did not save Sodom by his persistent praying, the purposes of God were stayed for a season. It is possible that if Abraham's goodness of heart had not over-estimated the number of pious people in that devoted city, God might have saved it had he reduced his figures still further.

This is a representative case illustrative of Old Testament praying, and disclosing God's mode of working through prayer. It shows further how God is moved to work in answer to prayer in this world, even when it comes to changing His purposes concerning a sinful community. This praying of Abraham was no mere performance, no dull, lifeless ceremony, but an earnest plea, a strong advocacy, to secure a desired end—to have an influence, one person with another person.

How full of meaning is this series of remarkable intercessions made by Abraham! Here we have arguments designed to convince God, and pleas to persuade God to change His purpose. We see deep humility, but holy boldness as well. Perseverance and advances made based on victory in each petition. Here we have enlarged asking encouraged by enlarged answers. God stays and answers as long as Abraham stays and asks. To Abraham, God is existent, approachable, and all powerful, but at the same time, He defers to praying saints, acts favorably on their desires, and grants them favors asked for. Not to pray is a denial of God, a denial of His existence, a denial of His nature, and a denial of His purposes toward humanity.

God has specifically to do with prayer promises in their breadth, certainty, and limitations. Jesus Christ presses us into the presence of God with these prayer promises. He does it not only by the assurance that God will answer, but that no other being but God can answer. He presses us to God because only in this way can we move God to take a hand in earth's affairs, and induce Him to intervene in our behalf.

BELIEVING AND RECEIVING IN PRAYER

"All things, whatsoever ye ask in prayer, believing, ye shall receive,"[13] says Jesus. This all-comprehensive condition not only presses us to pray for all things, everything great and small, but it sets us on and shuts us up to God. For who but God can cover the unlimited range of universal things, and can assure us certainly of receiving the very thing for which we may ask in all the thesaurus of earthly and heavenly good?

It is Jesus Christ, the Son of God, who makes demands on us to pray, and it is He who puts Himself and all He has so fully in the answer. It is He who puts Himself at our service and answers our demands when we pray.

Just as He puts Himself and the Father at our command in prayer, to come directly into our lives and to work for our good, so also does He engage to answer the demands of two or more believers who are agreed as touching any one thing. "If two of you shall agree on earth as touching any thing that they shall ask, it shall be done for them of my Father which is in heaven."[14] None but God could put Himself in a covenant so binding as that, for only God could fulfill such a promise and could reach to its exacting and all controlling demands. Only God can answer for the promises.

GOD AND PEOPLE NEED PRAYER

God needs prayer, and people need prayer, too. It is indispensable to God's work in this world, and is essential to getting God to work in earth's affairs. So God binds people to pray by the most solemn obligations. God commands people to pray, and so not to pray is plain disobedience to an imperative command of Almighty God. Prayer is such a condition without which the graces, the salvation, and the good of God are not bestowed on people. Prayer is a high privilege, a royal prerogative—and many and eternal are the losses by failure to exercise it. Prayer is the great, universal, force to advance God's cause. It is the reverence that hallows God's name. It is the ability to do God's will, and the establishment of God's kingdom in the hearts of the children of God. These, and their coincidences and agencies, are created and affected by prayer.

One of the constitutional enforcements of the Gospel is prayer. Without prayer, the Gospel can neither be preached effectively, promulgated faithfully, experienced in the heart, or be practiced in the life. For the very simple reason that by leaving prayer out of the catalogue of Christian duties, we leave God out, and His work cannot progress without Him.

KING CYRUS

The movements that God purposed under Cyrus, king of Persia, prophesied about by Isaiah many years before Cyrus was born, are conditioned on prayer. God declares His purpose, power, independence, and defiance of obstacles that are in the way of His carrying out those purposes. His omnipotent and absolutely infinite power is set to encourage prayer. He has been ordering all events, directing all conditions, and creating all things, that He might answer prayer. Then He turns Himself over to His praying ones to be commanded. It is then that all the results and power He holds in His hands will be bestowed in lavish and unmeasured generosity to carry out prayers, and to make prayer the mightiest energy in the world.

The passage about Cyrus in Isaiah 46 is too lengthy to be quoted in its entirety, but it is well worth reading. It closes with these strong words about prayer, which are the climax of all that God has been saying concerning His purposes in connection with Cyrus:

> Thus saith the Lord, the Holy One of Israel, and his Maker, Ask me of things to come concerning my sons, and concerning the work of my hands command ye me. I have made the earth, and created man upon it: I, even my hands, have stretched out the heavens, and all their host have I commanded.[15]

In the conclusion of the history of Job, we see how God intervenes in behalf of Job and calls upon his friends to present themselves before Job that he may pray for them. "My wrath is kindled against thee, and against thy two friends," is God's statement, with the further words added, "My servant Job shall pray for you: for him will I accept."[16] This is a striking illustration of God intervening to deliver Job's friends in answer to Job's prayer.

ANGELS AND PRAYER

We have heretofore spoken of prayer affecting God, angels, and people. Christ wrote nothing while living. Memoranda, notes, sermon writing, sermon making were alien to Him. Autobiography was not to His taste. The Revelation of John was His last utterance. In that book is illustrated the great importance, priceless value, and high position that prayer obtains in the movements, history, and unfolding progress of God's Church in this world. This illustration shows the interest the angels in heaven have in the prayers of the saints and in accomplishing the answers to those prayers:

> And another angel came and stood at the altar, having a golden censer; and there was given unto him much incense, that he should offer it with the prayers of all saints upon the golden altar which was before the throne. And the smoke of the incense, which came with the prayers of the saints, ascended up before God out of the angel's hand. And the angel took the censer, and filled it with fire of the altar, and cast it into the earth: and there were voices, and thunderings, and lightnings, and an earthquake.[17]

Translated into the prose of everyday life, these words show how the capital stock by which heaven carries on the business of salvation under Christ, is made up of the prayers of God's saints on earth. It also discloses how these prayers in flaming power come back to earth and produce its mighty commotions, influences, and revolutions.

PRAYING SAINTS ARE ESSENTIAL TO GOD

Praying saints are essential to Almighty God in all His plans and purposes. God's secrets, councils, and cause have never been committed to prayerless saints. Neglect of prayer has always brought loss of faith, loss of love, and loss of prayer. Failure to pray has been the harmful and inevitable cause of backsliding and estrangement from God. Prayerless saints have stood in the way of God fulfilling His Word and doing His will on earth. They tie the divine hands and interfere with God in His gracious designs. As praying saints are a help to God, so prayerless saints are a hindrance to Him.

We press the Scriptural view of the necessity of prayer, even at the cost of repetition. The subject is too important for repetition to weaken or tire, too vital to be trite or tame. We must feel it anew. The fires of prayer have burned low. Ashes and not flames are on its altars.

No insistence in the Scriptures is more pressing than prayer. No exhortation is oftener repeated, none is more hearty, none is more solemn and stirring, than to pray. No principle is more strongly and broadly declared than that which urges us to prayer. There is no duty to which we are more strongly obliged than the obligation to pray. There is no command more imperative and insistent than that of praying. Are you praying in everything without ceasing, in the closet, hidden from the eyes of the world, and praying always and everywhere? That is the personal, pertinent, and all-important question for every soul.

GOD INTERVENES IN ANSWER TO PRAYER

Many instances occur in God's Word that show that God intervenes in this world in answer to prayer. Nothing is clearer when the Bible is consulted than that Almighty God is brought directly into the things of this world by the praying of His people. Jonah flees from duty and takes ship for a distant port. But God follows him, and by a strange providence this disobedient prophet is cast out of the vessel, and the God who sent him to Nineveh prepares a fish to swallow him. In the fish's belly he cries out to the God against whom he had sinned, and God intervenes and causes the fish to vomit Jonah out on dry land. Even the fishes of the great deep are subject to the law of prayer.

ELIJAH FED BY BIRDS

The birds of the air are also subject to this same law. Elijah had foretold to Ahab the coming of that prolonged drought, and food and water became scarce. God sent Elijah to the brook Cherith, and said to him, "It shall be, that thou shalt drink of the brook; and I have commanded the ravens to feed thee there. . . . And the ravens brought bread and flesh in the morning, and bread and flesh in the evening; and he drank of the brook."[18] Can any one doubt that this man of God, who later on shut up and opened the rain clouds by prayer, was not praying about this time, when so much was at stake? God interposed among the birds of the air this time and strangely moved them to take care of His servant so that he would not lack food and water.

DAVID'S ACTION DISPLEASED GOD

Instead of listening to the advice of his prime minister, Joab, David yielded to the suggestion of Satan, and counted the people, which displeased God. So God told him to choose one of three evils as a retribution for his folly and sin. Pestilence came among the people in violent form, and David betakes himself to prayer.

> And David said unto God, Is it not I that commanded the people to be numbered? even I it is that have sinned and done evil indeed; but as for these sheep, what have they done? let thine hand, I pray thee, O Lord my God, be on me, and on my father's house; but not on thy people, that they should be plagued.[19]

Though God had been greatly grieved at David for numbering Israel, He could not resist this appeal of a penitent and prayerful spirit. God was moved by prayer to put His hand on the springs of disease and stop the fearful plague. God was put to work by David's prayer.

Numbers of other cases could be named. These are sufficient. God seems to have taken great pains in His divine revelation to people to show how He interferes in earth's affairs in answer to the praying of His saints.

PRAYER AND THE LAWS OF NATURE

In minds of some over-critical people who are not strong believers in prayer, the question might arise just here as to the so-called "laws of nature," as if there was a conflict between what they call the "laws of nature" and the law of prayer. These people make nature a sort of imaginary god entirely separate of Almighty God. What is nature anyway? It is but the creation of God, the maker of all things. And what are the "laws of nature" but the laws of God, through which He governs the material world. As the law of prayer is also the law of God, there cannot possibly be any conflict between the two sets of laws, but all must work in perfect harmony. Prayer does not violate any natural law. God may set aside one law for the higher working of another law, and this He may do when He answers prayer. Or Almighty God may answer prayer working through the course of natural law. But whether or not we understand it, God is over and above all nature, and can and will answer prayer in a wise, intelligent, and just manner, even though we may not understand it. So in no sense is there any discord or conflict between God's several laws when God is induced to interfere with human affairs in answer to prayer.

In this connection, another word might be said. We used the form of words to which there can be no objection, that prayer does certain things. But this, of course, does not imply that prayer as a human means accomplishes anything, but that prayer only accomplishes things instrumentally. Prayer is the instrument, God is the efficient and active agent. So prayer in itself does not interfere in earth's affairs, but prayer in the hands of saints moves God to intervene and do things, which He would not otherwise do if prayer was not used as the instrument.

It is as we say, "faith has saved you," by which is simply meant that God through the faith of the sinners saves them. Faith being only the instrument used by the sinners to bring salvation to them.

Endnotes

1 Isaiah 64:4
2 John 14:13-14
3 John 15:17
4 Isaiah 62:6-7
5 Isaiah 45:11
6 Psalm 81:10
7 2 Chronicles 7:12-15
8 Jeremiah 29:10-13
9 Jeremiah 33:3
10 Psalm 50:15
11 Isaiah 58:9
12 Genesis 18:25
13 Matthew 21:22
14 Matthew 18:19
15 Isaiah 45:11-12
16 Job 42:7-8
17 Revelation 8:3-5
18 I Kings 17:4, 6
19 I Chronicles 21:17

3

The Necessity for Praying Saints

P RAYING ALWAYS WITH ALL *prayer and supplication in the Spirit, and watching thereunto with all perseverance and supplication for all saints.* (Ephesians 6:18)

Without praying also for us, that God would open unto us a door of utterance, to speak the mystery of Christ, for which I am also in bonds: that I may make it manifest, as I ought to speak. (Colossians 4:3)

One of the crying things of our day is for people whose faith, prayers, and study of the Word of God have been vitalized. Those on whose hearts is written a transcript of that Word, and who will give it forth as the incorruptible seed that lives and abides forever. Nothing more is needed to clear up the haze by which a critical unbelief has eclipsed the Word of God than the faithfulness of the pulpit in its unwavering allegiance to the Bible and the fearless proclamation of its truth. Without this, the standard-bearer fails, and wavering and confusion follow all along the ranks. The pulpit has done its mightiest work in the days of its unswerving loyalty to the Word of God.

In close connection with this, we must have people of prayer, people in high and low places who hold to and practice Scriptural praying. While the pulpit must hold to its unswerving loyalty to the Word of God, it must, at the same time, be loyal to the doctrine of prayer, which that same Word illustrates and enforces upon humanity.

Schools, colleges, and education considered simply as such, cannot be considered leaders in carrying forward the work of God's kingdom in the world. They have neither the right, the will, nor the power to do the work. This is to be accomplished by the preached Word, delivered in the power of the Holy Ghost sent down from heaven, sown with prayerful hands, and watered with the tears of praying hearts. This is the divine law. We are shut up and sealed to it—if we would follow the Lord.

Saints are demanded for the great work of soul saving, and saints must go. It is no angelic or impersonal force that is needed. Human hearts baptized with the spirit of prayer must bear the burden of this message. Human tongues on fire as the result of earnest, persistent, prayer, must declare the Word of God to dying humanity.

THE CHURCH NEEDS PRAYING SAINTS

The Church today needs praying saint to execute its solemn and pressing responsibility to meet the fearful crisis that is facing it. The crying need of the times is for saints in increased numbers—God-fearing people, praying people, Holy Ghost people. They must be people who can endure hardness, who will count not their lives dear unto themselves, but will count all things but dross for the excellence of the knowledge of Jesus Christ, the Savior. The saints who are so greatly needed in this age of the Church are those who have learned the business of praying—learned it upon their knees, learned it in the need and agony of their own hearts.

Praying saints are the one commanding need of this day, as of all other days, in which God is to have or make a showing. Saints who pray are, in reality, the only Christian saints, and it takes a full-measured person to pray. Saints of prayer are the only saints who do or can represent God in this world. No cold, irreligious, prayerless saint can claim the right. They misrepresent God in all His work, and all His plans. Praying saints are the only saints who have influence with God, the only kind of saints to whom God commits Himself and His Gospel. Praying saints are the only saints in which the Holy Spirit dwells, for the Holy Spirit and prayer go hand-in-hand. The Holy Spirit never descends upon prayerless saints. He never fills them, He never empowers them. There is nothing whatever in common between the Spirit of God and saints who do not pray. The Spirit dwells only in a prayer atmosphere.

IN DOING GOD'S WORK THERE IS NO SUBSTITUTE FOR PRAYER

The saints of prayer cannot be displaced with other kinds of saints. People of financial skill, people of education, people of worldly influence—none of these can possibly be put in substitution for the people of prayer. The life, the vigor, the motive-power of God's work is formed by praying saints. A vitally diseased heart is not a more fearful symptom of approaching death than non-praying saints are of spiritual atrophy.

The saints to whom Jesus Christ committed the fortunes and destiny of His Church were people of prayer. To no other kind of people has God ever committed Himself in this world. The Apostles were preeminently men of prayer. They gave themselves to prayer. They made praying their chief business. It was first in point of importance and first in results. God never has, and He never will, commit the weighty interests of His kingdom to prayerless saints, those who do not make prayer a conspicuous and controlling factor in their lives. Saints who do not pray never rise to any eminence of piety. People of piety are always people of prayer. Saints are never noted for the simplicity and strength of their faith who are not preeminently people of prayer. Piety flourishes nowhere so rapidly and so rankly as in the closet. The closet is the garden of faith.

INTERFERENCE AND PRAYER

The Apostles allowed no duty, however sacred, to so engage them as to infringe upon their time and prevent them from making prayer the main thing. The Word of God was ministered by apostolic faithfulness and zeal. It was spoken by saints with apostolic commissions and whose heads the fiery tongues of Pentecost had baptized. The Word was pointless and powerless if it is not freshly endued with power by continuous and mighty prayer. The seed of God's Word must be saturated in prayer to make it germinate. It grows readier and roots deeper when it is prayer-soaked.

The Apostles were praying saints, themselves. They were teachers of prayer, and trained their disciples in the school of prayer. They urged prayer upon their disciples, not only that they might attain to the loftiest eminence of faith, but that they might be the most powerful factors in advancing God's kingdom.

JESUS AND PRAYER

Jesus Christ was the divinely appointed leader of God's people, and no one thing in His life proves His eminent fitness for that office so fully as His habit of prayer. Nothing is more suggestive of thought than Christ's continual praying, and nothing is more conspicuous about Him than prayer. His campaigns were arranged, His victories gained, in the struggles and communion of His all-night praying. His praying rent the heavens. Moses and Elijah and the Transfiguration glory waited on His praying. His miracles and His teaching had their force from the same source. Gethsemane's praying crimsoned Calvary with serenity and glory. His prayer makes the history and hastens the triumphs of His Church. What an inspiration and command to prayer is Christ's life! What a comment on its worth! How He shames our lives by His praying!

Like all His followers who have drawn God nearer to the world and lifted the world nearer to God, Jesus was the man of prayer, who was made by God a leader and commander to His people. His leadership was one of prayer. A great leader He was, because He was great in prayer. All great leaders for God have fashioned their leadership in the struggles of their prayer closets. Many great people have led and molded the Church who have not been great in prayer, but they were great only in their plans, great for their opinions, great for their organization, great by natural gifts, by the force of genius or of character. They were not, however, great for God. But Jesus Christ was a great leader for God. His was the great leadership of great praying. God was in His leadership greatly because prayer was in it greatly. We might well express the wish that we be taught by Him to pray, and to pray more and more.

THE SECRET OF PRAYING SAINTS

Herein has been the secret of the saints of prayer in the past history of the Church. Their hearts were after God, their desires were on Him, their prayers were addressed to Him. They communed with Him, sought nothing of the world, sought great things of God, persisted with Him, conquered all opposing forces, and opened up the channel of faith deep and broad between them and heaven. All this was done by the use of prayer. Holy meditations, spiritual desires, heavenly drawings, swayed their intellects, enriched their emotions, and filled and enlarged their hearts. All this was so because they were first of all people of prayer.

The saints who have thus communed with God and who have sought after Him with their whole hearts, have always risen to consecrated eminence. No saints have ever risen to this eminence whose flames of holy desire have not all been dead to the world and all aglow for God and heaven. Nor have they ever risen to the heights of the higher spiritual experiences unless prayer and the spirit of prayer have been conspicuous and controlling factors in their lives.

ENTIRE CONSECRATION

The entire consecration of many of God's children stands out distinctly like towering mountain-peaks. Why is this? How did they ascend to these heights? What brought them so near to God? What made them so Christ-like? The answer is easy—prayer. They prayed much, prayed long, and drank deeper and deeper still. They asked, they sought, and they knocked, until heaven opened its richest inner treasures of grace to them. Prayer was the Jacob's Ladder by which they scaled those holy and blessed heights, and the way by which the angels of God came down to earth and ministered to them.

The saints of spiritual character and might always value prayer. They took time to be alone with God. Their praying was no hurried performance. They had many serious needs to be relieved, and many weighty pleas they had to offer. Many large supplies they must secure. They had to do much silent waiting before God, and much patient asking and asking again to speak to Him. Prayer was the only channel through which supplies came, and was the only way to utter pleas. The only acceptable waiting before God of which they knew anything was prayer. They valued praying. It was more precious to them than all jewels, more excellent than any good, more to be valued than the greatest good of earth. They esteemed it, valued it, prized it, and did it. They pressed it to its farthest limits, tested its greatest results, and secured its most glorious heritage. To them, prayer was the one great thing to be appreciated and used.

The Apostles above everything else were praying people, and left the impression of their prayer example and teaching upon the early Church. But the Apostles are dead and times and people have changed. They have no successors by official assignment or inheritance. Our times have no commission to make other apostles. Prayer is the entrance to spiritual and apostolic leadership. Unfortunately, our times are not prayerful times. God's cause just now greatly needs praying leaders. Other things may be needed, but above all else this is the crying demand of these times and the urgent first need of the Church.

PROSPERITY: A HINDRANCE TO SPIRITUAL FORCES

This is the day of great wealth in the Church and of wonderful material resources. But, unfortunately, the prosperity of material resources is a great enemy and a severe hindrance to strong spiritual forces. It is an invariable law that the presence of attractive and potent material forces creates a trust in them, and by the same inevitable law, creates distrust in the spiritual forces of the Gospel. They are two masters that cannot be served at one and the same time. For just in proportion as the mind is fixed on one, it will be drawn away from the other. The days of great financial prosperity in the Church have not been days of great spiritual prosperity. Moneyed saints and praying saints are not synonymous terms.

In I Timothy 2, Paul emphasizes the need of saints to pray. Church leaders in his estimation are to be conspicuous for their praying. Prayer should and must of necessity shape their characters, and must be one of their distinguishing characteristics. Prayer should be one of their most powerful elements in the Church, so much so that it cannot be hid. Prayer should make Church leaders notable. Character, official duty, reputation, and life should all be shaped by prayer. The mighty forces of prayer lie in its praying leaders in a marked way. The standing obligation to pray rests in a peculiar sense on Church leaders. The Church would be wise to discover this prime truth and give prominence to it.

GOD NEEDS PRAYING LEADERS

It may be laid down as an axiom, that God needs, first of all, leaders in the Church who will be first in prayer, saint with whom prayer is habitual and characteristic, saints who know the primacy of prayer. But even more than a habit of prayer, and more than prayer being characteristic of them, Church leaders are to be impregnated with prayer—Christians whose lives are made and molded by prayer, whose heart and life are made up of prayer. These are the Christians—the only Christians—God can use in the furtherance of His kingdom—and the implanting of His message in the hearts of people throughout the world.

4

God's Need of People Who Pray

W E DO WHAT HE *commands. We go where He wants us to go. We speak what He wants us to speak. His will is our law. His pleasure our joy. He is, today, seeking the lost and He would have us seek with Him. He is shepherding the lambs and He wants our cooperation. He is opening doors in heathen lands, and He wants our money and our prayers."* (Anonymous)

It demands prayer leadership to hold the Church to God's aims, and to fit it for God's uses. Prayer leadership preserves the spirituality of the Church, just as prayerless leaders make for unspiritual conditions. The Church is not spiritual simply by the mere fact of its existence, nor by its vocation. It is not held to its sacred vocation by generation, nor by succession. Like the new birth, it is "not of blood, nor of the will of the flesh, nor of the will of man, but of God."[1]

The Church is not spiritual simply because it is concerned and deals in spiritual values. It may hold its confirmations by the thousand, it may multiply its baptisms, and administer its sacraments innumerable times, and yet be as far from fulfilling its true mission as human conditions can make it.

This present world's general attitude retires prayer to insignificance and obscurity. By it, salvation and eternal life are put in the background. It cannot be too often affirmed, therefore, that the prime need of the Church is not people of money or people of brains, but people of prayer. Leaders in the realm of religious activity are to be judged by their praying habits, and not by their money or social position. Those who must be placed in

415

the forefront of the Church's business, must be, first of all, people who know how to pray.

God does not conduct His work, solely, with people of education or of wealth or of business capacity. Neither can He carry on His work through people of large intellects or of great culture, or through people of great social eminence and influence. All these can be made to count provided they are not regarded as being primary. These men and women, by the simple fact of these qualities and conditions, cannot lead in God's work or control His cause. Men and women of prayer, before anything else, are indispensable to the furtherance of the kingdom of God on earth. No other sort will fit in the scheme or do the deed. Men and women, great and influential in other things, but small in prayer, cannot do the work Almighty God has set out for His Church to do in this world.

People who represent God and who stand here in His stead, people who are to build up His kingdom in this world, must be in an eminent sense people of prayer. Whatever else they may have, whatever else they may lack, they must be men and women of prayer. Having everything else and lacking prayer, they must fall. Having prayer and lacking all else, they can succeed. Prayer must be the most conspicuous and the most potent factor in the character and conduct of men and women who undertake the divine commission. God's business requires men and women who are versed in the business of praying.

PRAYER REQUIRES COURAGEOUS MEN AND WOMEN

It must be kept in mind that the praying to which the disciples of Christ are called by Scriptural authority and enforcement, is a valiant calling for courageous men and women. Those God wants and upon whom He depends, must work at prayer just as they work at their worldly calling. They must follow this business of praying through, just as they do their secular pursuits. Diligence, perseverance, heartiness, and courage must all be in it if it is to succeed.

Everything secured by Gospel promise, defined by Gospel measure, and represented by Gospel treasure are to be found in prayer. All heights are scaled by it, all doors are opened to it, all victories are gained through it, and all grace depends on it. Heaven has all its good and all its help for those who pray.

How marked and strong is the injunction of Christ that sends men and women from the parade of public giving and praying to the privacy of their closets, where with shut doors, and in encircling silence, they are alone in prayer with God!

In all ages, those who have carried out the divine will on the earth, have been people of prayer. The days of prayer are God's prosperous days. His heart, His oath, and His glory are committed to one purpose—that every knee should bow to Christ.[2] The day of the Lord, in a preeminent sense, will be a day of universal prayer.

GOD'S WORK SUFFERS WHEN PEOPLE DO NOT PRAY

God's cause does not suffer through lack of divine ability, but by reason of the lack of prayer-ability in saints. God's action is just as much bound up in prayer at this time, as it was when He said to Abimelech, "[Abraham] shall pray for thee, and thou shalt live."[3] So it was also when God said to Job's friends, "My servant Job shall pray for you: for him will I accept."[4] God's great plan for the redemption of humanity is as much bound up to prayer for its prosperity and success as when the decree creating the movement was issued from the Father. Foremost it contained the imperative, universal, and eternal condition, "Ask of me, and I will give thee the heathen for thy inheritance, and the uttermost part of the earth for thy possession."[5]

In many places an alarming state of things has come to pass, in that the many who are enrolled in our churches are not praying men and women. Many of those occupying prominent positions in church life are not _____. It is greatly to be feared that much of the work of the _____ done by those who are perfect strangers to the prayer _____ wonder that the work does not succeed.

_____ may be true that many in the Church say prayers, it is equally _____ praying is of the stereotyped order. Their prayers may be _____ with _____timent, but they are tame, timid, and without fire or force. Even this sort of _____aying is done by a few straggling people that are found at prayer-meetings. Those whose names are to be found bulking large in our great Church assemblies are not those noted for their praying habits. Yet the entire fabric of the work in which they are engaged has, by necessity, to depend on the adequacy of prayer. This fact is similar to the crisis that would be created were a country to have to admit in the face of an invading foe that it cannot fight and knows nothing about the weapons by which war may be successfully waged.

GOD PROPOSES THAT SAINTS PRAY

In all God's plans for human redemption, He proposes that saints pray. The saints are to pray in every place—in the church, in the closet, in the home, on sacred days, and on secular days. All things and everything are dependent on the measure of the saints' praying.

Prayer is the genius and mainspring of life. We pray as we live, we live as we pray. Life will never be finer than the quality of the prayer closet. The mercury of life will rise only by the warmth of the closet. Persistent lack of prayer eventually will lower life below zero.

To measure and weigh the conditions of prayer, is readily to discover why saints do not pray in larger numbers. The conditions are so perfect, so blessed, that it is a rare character who can meet them. A heart that is all love, a heart that holds even its enemies in loving contemplation and prayerful concern, a heart from which all bitterness, revenge, and envy are purged—how rare! Yet this is the only condition of mind and heart in which a Christian can expect to command the effectiveness of prayer.

THE CONDITIONS OF AUTHENTIC PRAYING

There are certain conditions laid down for authentic praying. Saints are to pray, "lifting up holy hands"[6]—hands here being the symbol of life. Hands unsoiled by stains of evil doing are the emblem of a life unsoiled by sin. Saints are to come into the presence of God with holy lives, and thus approach the throne of the Highest where they can "obtain mercy, and find grace to help in time of need."[7] Here, then, is one reason why Christians do not pray. They are too worldly in heart and too secular in life to enter the closet. And even though they enter there, they cannot offer the "effectual fervent prayer of the righteous man [that] availeth much."[8]

Again, "hands" are the symbols of supplication. Outstretched hands stand for an appeal for help. It is the silent yet eloquent attitude of a helpless soul standing before God, appealing for mercy and grace. "Hands," too, are symbols of activity, power, and conduct. Hands outstretched to God in prayer must be "holy hands," unstained hands. The word *holy* here means undefiled, unspotted, untainted, and religiously observing every obligation. How far remote is all this from the character of the sin-loving, worldly-minded, fleshly disposed men and women, soiled by fleshly lusts, spotted by worldly indulgence, unholy in heart and conduct! "He who seeks equity must do equity," is the maxim of earthly courts. So those who seeks God's good gifts must practice God's good deeds. This is the maxim of heavenly courts.

PRAYER IS AFFECTED BY CHARACTER AND CONDUCT

Prayer is sensitive, and always affected by the character and conduct of the one who prays. Water cannot rise above its own level, and a spotless prayer cannot flow from a spotted heart. Straight praying is never born of crooked conduct. It is what Christians are behind their praying that gives character to their supplication. The cowardly heart cannot do brave praying. Soiled men and women cannot make clean, pure, supplication.

It is neither words, thoughts, ideas, or feelings that shape praying, but character and conduct. Christians must walk in upright fashion in order to be able to pray well. Bad character and unrighteous living break down praying until it becomes commonplace and without meaning. Praying takes its tone and vigor from the life of the man or woman exercising it. When character and conduct are at a low ebb, praying can barely live, much less thrive.

The man or woman of prayer, whether layperson or preacher, is God's right-hand person. In the realm of spiritual affairs, that person creates conditions, inaugurates movements, and brings things to pass.

ALL CHRISTIANS ARE OBLIGED TO PRAY

By the fact and condition of their creation and redemption, all Christians are under obligation to pray. Every Christian can pray, and every Christian should pray. But when it comes to the affairs of the Kingdom, let it be said, at once, that a prayerless saint in the Church of God is like a paralyzed organ of the physical body. That person is out of place in the communion of saints, out of harmony with God, and out of accord with His purposes for humanity. A prayerless saints handicaps the vigor and life of the whole system like a demoralized soldier is a menace to the force that he or she is a part of in the day of battle. The absence of prayer lessens all the life-forces of the soul, cripples faith, sets aside holy living, shuts out heaven. In holy Scripture, the line is sharply drawn between praying saints and non-praying saints.

FLETCHER OF MADELEY

Of Fletcher of Madeley—one of the praying saints—it is written that:

He was far more abundant in his public labours than the greater part of his companions in the holy ministry. Yet these bore but little proportion to those internal exercises of prayer and supplication to which he was wholly given up in private, which were almost uninterruptedly maintained from hour to hour. He lived in the spirit of prayer, and whatever employment in which he was engaged, this spirit of prayer was constantly manifested through them all.

Without this he neither formed any design, nor entered upon any duty. Without this he neither read nor conversed. Without this, he neither visited nor received a visitor. There have been seasons of supplications in which he appeared to be carried out far beyond the ordinary limits of devotion, when, like his Lord upon the Mount of Transfiguration, while he continued to pour out his mighty prayer, the fashion of his countenance has been changed, and his face has appeared as the face of an angel.

O God, raise up more men and women of prayer like John Fletcher! How we need in our day, praying Christians through whom God can work!

Endnotes

1 John 1:13
2 Philippians 2:10
3 Genesis 20:7
4 Job 42:8
5 Psalm 2:8
6 I Timothy 2:8
7 Hebrews 4:16
8 James 5:16

5

Prayerless Christians

*I*F THERE WAS EVER *a time when Peter, James, and John needed to remain awake it was in Gethsemane. If James had persisted in keeping awake it might have saved his decapitation a few years later. If Peter had stirred himself to really intercede for himself and others he would not have denied his Christ that night in the palace of Caiaphas.* (H. W. Hodge)

There is great need in this day for Christian business people to infuse their mundane affairs with the spirit of prayer. There is a great army of successful merchants of almost every kind who are members of Christ's Church, and it is high time they attended to this matter. This is but another version of the phrase, "putting God into business," which means the realization and restraint of His presence and of His fear in all the secular activities of life. We need the atmosphere of the prayer closet to pervade our places of business. The sanctity of prayer is needed to impregnate business. We need the spirit of Sunday carried over to Monday and continued until Saturday. But this cannot be done by prayerless Christians, but by Christians of prayer. We need business people to go about their concerns with the same reverence and responsibility with which they enter the closet. Christians are badly needed who are devoid of greed, but who, with all their hearts, carry God with them into the secular affairs of life.

Business people of the world imagine prayer to be too impotent a thing to come into rivalry with business methods and worldly practices. Against such a misleading doctrine, Paul sets the whole commands of God—loyalty to Jesus Christ, the claims of pious character, and the demands of the salvation of the world. Christians must pray, and put strength and heart into their praying. This is part of the primary business of life, and to it God has called Christians first of all.

PRAYING CHRISTIANS ARE GOD'S AGENTS

Praying Christians are God's agents on earth, the representative of government of heaven, set to a specific task on the earth. While it is true that the Holy Spirit, the angels of God, are agents of God in carrying forward the redemption of the human race, yet among them there must be praying saints. God has great use for them. He can make much of them, and in the past has done wonderful things through them. These are His instruments in carrying out God's great purposes on the earth. They are God's messengers—His watchers, shepherds, and workers who need not be ashamed. Fully equipped for the great work to which they are appointed, they honor God and bless the world.

Above all things, Christian men and women must primarily be leaders in prayer. No matter how conspicuous they may be in other activities, they fail if they are not conspicuous in prayer. They must give their brain and heart to prayer. Those who make and shape the program of Christ's Church, who map out its line of activity, should themselves be shaped and made by prayer. Those controlling the Church finances, its thought, its action—should all be people of prayer.

THE PROGRESS OF GOD'S WORK

The progress of God's work to completion in this world has two basic principles—God's ability to give and people's ability to ask. Failure in either one is fatal to the success of God's work on earth. God's inability to do or to give would put an end to redemption. People's failure to pray would, just as surely set a limit to the plan. But God's ability to do and to give has never failed and cannot fail. But people's ability to ask can fail and often does. Therefore the slow progress that is being made toward the realization of a world won for Christ lies entirely with people's limited asking. There is need for the entire Christian Church on the earth to give itself to prayer. The Church upon its knees would bring heaven upon the earth.

The wonderful ability of God to do for us is expressed by Paul in one of his most comprehensive statements, "And God is able to make all grace abound toward you; that ye, always having all sufficiency in all things, may abound to every good work."[1]

I pray you will study that remarkable statement: "God is able to make all grace abound." That is, He is able to give such sufficiency that we may abound—overflow—to every good work. Why are we not more fully overflowing? The answer is lack of prayer ability. "We have not, because [we] ask not."[2] We are feeble, weak, and impoverished because of our failure to pray. God is restrained in doing because we are restrained by reason of our non-praying. All failures in securing heaven are traceable to lack of prayer or misdirected petition.

PRAYER MUST BE BROAD IN SCOPE

Prayer must be broad in its scope—it must plead for others. Intercession for others is the hallmark of all true prayer. When prayer is confined to self and to the sphere of one's personal needs, it dies by reason of its littleness, narrowness, and selfishness. Prayer must be broad and unselfish or it will perish. Prayer is the soul of a person stirred to plead with God for people. In addition to being interested in the eternal interests of one's own soul, it must, in its very nature, be concerned for the spiritual and eternal welfare of others. Your ability to pray for yourself is only effective to the degree that you have compassion and concern for others.

In his second letter to Timothy, the apostle Paul specifically emphasizes that those who occupy positions of influence and places of authority are to give themselves to prayer. "I will therefore that the men pray every where."[3] This is the high calling of the saints of the Church, and no calling is so engaging, so engrossing, and so valuable that we can afford to relieve Christians from the all-important vocation of secret prayer. Nothing whatever can take the place of prayer. Nothing whatever can atone for the neglect of praying. This is uppermost, first in point of importance and first in point of time. No person is so high in position, or in grace, to be exempt from an obligation to pray. No person is too big to pray, no matter who he or she is, nor what office is held. The king on his throne is as much obligated to pray as the peasant in a cottage. None is so high and exalted in this world or so lowly and obscure as to be excused from praying. The help of everyone is needed in prosecuting the work of God, and the prayer of each praying Christian helps to swell the total. The leaders in place, in gifts, and in authority are to be chiefs in prayer.

CIVIL AND CHURCH LEADERS

Civil and Church rulers shape the affairs of this world. So civil and Church rulers themselves need to be shaped personally in spirit, heart, and conduct, and in truth and righteousness, by the prayers of God's people. This is in direct line with Paul's words:

> I exhort therefore, that, first of all, supplications, prayers, intercessions, and giving of thanks, be made for all men; for kings, and for all that are in authority.[4]

It is a sad day for righteousness when church politics, instead of holy praying, shapes the administration of the Kingdom and elevates Christians to place and power. Why pray for all people? Because God wills the salvation of all people. God's children on earth must link their prayers to God's will. Prayer is to carry out the will of God. God wills the salvation of all people. His heart is set on this one thing. Our prayers must be the creation and exponent of God's will. We are to grasp humanity in our praying as God grasps humanity in His love, His interest, and His plans to redeem humanity. Our sympathies, prayers, struggles, and ardent desires must run parallel with the will of God—broad, generous, world-wide, and godlike. The Christian must in all things, first of all, be conformed to the will of God, but nowhere shall this royal devotion be more evident than in the salvation of the human race. This high partnership with God, as His vicegerents on earth, is to have its fullest, richest, and most efficient exercise in prayer for all humanity.

CHRISTIANS PRAY FOR ALL PEOPLE

Christians are to pray for all people, and are to pray especially for rulers in Church and state so "that we may lead a quiet and peaceable life in all godliness and honesty."[5] Peace on the outside and peace on the inside. Praying calms disturbing forces, allays tormenting fears, brings conflict to an end. Prayer tends to do away with turmoil. But even if there be external conflicts, it is well to have deep peace within the citadel of the soul. "That we may lead a quiet and peaceable life." Prayer brings inner calm and furnishes outward tranquility. If there were praying rulers and subjects world-wide, they would allay turbulent forces, make wars to cease, and cause peace to reign.

Christians must pray for all people so that we may lead lives "in all godliness and honesty." That is, with godliness and gravity. Godliness is to be like God. It is to be godly, to have God-likeness, having the image of God stamped upon the inner nature, and showing the same likeness in conduct and in temper. Almighty God is the very highest model, and to be like Him is to possess the highest character. Prayer molds us into the image of God, and at the same time tends to mold others into the same image in proportion to our praying for them. Prayer means to be God-like, and to be God-like is to love Christ and love God, to be one with the Father and the Son in spirit, character, and conduct. Prayer means to stay with God until you are like Him. Prayer makes a godly person, and puts within that person "the mind of Christ"[6]—the mind of humility, self-surrender, service, compassion, and prayer. If we really pray, we will become more like Christ, or else we will quit praying.

PRAY EVERYWHERE

"Men [are to] pray everywhere"—in the closet, in the prayer-meeting, about the family altar—and do it "lifting up holy hands, without wrath and doubting."[7] Here is not only the obligation laid upon Christians to pray, but instructions as to how they should pray. People must pray "without wrath." That is, without bitterness against their neighbors or other Christians, without the stubbornness of a strong will, without hard feelings, without an evil desire or emotion kindled by nature's fires in the carnal nature. Praying is not to be done by these questionable things, or in company with such evil feelings, but "without" them, aloof and entirely separate from them. This is the sort of praying Christians are called upon to do—the sort of praying that God hears and the kind that prevails with God and accomplishes things. Such praying in the hands of Christians become divine agencies in God's hands for carrying on God's gracious purposes and executing His designs in redemption.

THE HIGHER ORIGIN OF PRAYER

Prayer has a higher origin than the human nature. This is true whether human nature as separate from the angelic nature, or human carnal nature unrenewed and unchanged is meant. Prayer does not originate in the realms of the carnal mind. Such a nature is entirely foreign to prayer simply because "the carnal mind is enmity against God."[8] It is by the new spirit that we pray—the new spirit sweetened by the sugar of heaven, perfumed with the fragrance of the upper world, and invigorated by a breath from the crystal sea. The new spirit is native to the skies, panting after the heavenly things, inspired by the breath of God. It is the praying temper from which all the old juices of the carnal, unregenerate, nature have been expelled, and the fire of God has created the flame that has consumed worldly lusts. The juices of the spirit have been injected into the soul, and the praying is entirely divorced from wrath.

PRAY WITHOUT DOUBTING

Christians are also to pray "without . . . doubting." The *Revised Version* puts it, "without . . . disputing." They must have faith in God and belief in God's Word "without question." No doubting or disputing must be in the mind. There must be no opinions, no hesitancy, no questioning, no reasoning, no intellectual quibbling, no rebellion, but a strict, stead-fast, loyalty of spirit to God—a life of loyalty in heart and intellect to God's Word.

God has much to do with believing people who have a living, transforming, faith in Jesus Christ. These are God's children. A father loves his children, supplies their needs, hears their cries, and answers their requests. Children believe their father, love him, trust in him, and ask him for what they need, believing without doubting that their father will hear their requests. God has everything to do with answering the prayer of His children. Their troubles concern Him, and their prayers awaken Him. Their voice is sweet to Him. He loves to hear them pray, and He is never happier than to answer their prayers.

PRAYER INTENDED FOR GOD'S EAR

It is not people but God who hears and answers prayer. Prayer covers the whole range of human needs. Hence, "in every thing by prayer and supplication with thanksgiving let your requests be made known unto God."[9] Prayer includes the entire range of God's ability. "Is any thing too hard for the LORD?"[10] Prayer does not belong to one favored part of our needs, but reaches to and embraces the entire circle of our wants, simply because God is the God of the whole person. God has pledged Himself to supply the needs of the whole person, physical, intellectual, and spiritual. "But my God shall supply all your need according to His riches in glory by Christ Jesus."[11] Prayer is the child of grace, and grace is for the whole person, and for every person in the human race.

Endnotes

1 2 Corinthians 9:8
2 James 4:2
3 I Timothy 2:8
4 I Timothy 2:1-2
5 I Timothy 2:2
6 I Corinthians 2:16
7 I Timothy 2:8
8 Romans 8:7
9 Philippians 4:6
10 Genesis 18:14
11 Philippians 4:19

6

Praying Saints at a Premium

OUR REDEEMER WAS IN *the Garden of Gethsemane. His hour was come. He felt as if He would be strengthened somewhat, if He had two or three disciples near Him. His three chosen disciples were within a stone's cast of the scene of His agony; but they were all asleep that the Scripture might be fulfilled—'I have trodden the winepress alone, and of the people there was none with Me.' The eight, in the distance, were good and true disciples; but they were only ordinary men, or men with a commonplace call.* (Alexander Whyte)

No insistence in the Bible is more pressing than the injunction it lays upon Christians to pray. No exhortation contained therein is more hearty, more solemn, and more stirring. No principle is more strongly stressed than that "men ought always to pray and not to faint."[1] In view of this command, it is pertinent to inquire as to whether the majority of Christian people are praying men and women? Is prayer a fixed course in your church? In the Sunday school, the home, the colleges, have we any graduates in the school of prayer? Is the Church producing those who have diplomas from the great university of prayer? This is what God requires, what He commands, and it is those who possess such qualifications that He must have to accomplish His purposes and carry out the work of His Kingdom on earth.

It is earnest praying that had need to be done. Lazy praying, without heart or strength, with neither fire nor tenacity, defeats its own avowed purpose. The prophet of past times laments that in a day that needed strenuous praying there was no one who "stirred up himself to take hold of [God]."[2] Christ charges us "not to faint" in our praying. Laxity and

427

indifference are great hindrances to prayer, both to the practice of praying and the process of receiving. It requires a brave, strong, fearless, and insistent spirit to engage in successful prayer. Praying for too many things also interferes with effectiveness. Too many petitions break tension and unity and breed neglect. Prayers should be specific and urgent. Too many words, like too much width, breeds shallows and sandbars. A single objective that absorbs the whole being and inflames the entire person is the properly constraining force in prayer.

It is easy to see how prayer was a decreed factor in the dispensations preceding the coming of Jesus, how that their leaders had to be people of prayer, and how that God's mightiest revelation of Himself was a revelation made through prayer. It is also easy to see how Jesus Christ, in His personal ministry, and in His relation to God, was great and constant in prayer. His labors and dispensation overflowed with fullness in proportion to His prayers. The possibilities of His praying were unlimited, and the possibilities of His ministry were in keeping with His praying. The necessity of His praying was equaled only by the consistency with which He practiced it during His early life.

DISPENSATION OF THE HOLY SPIRIT

The dispensation of the Holy Spirit is a dispensation of prayer, in a preeminent sense. Here prayer has an essential and vital relation. Without depreciating the possibilities and necessities of prayer in all the preceding dispensations of God in the world, it must be declared that it is in this latter dispensation that the engagements and demands of prayer are given their greatest authority, their possibilities rendered unlimited, and their necessity unavoidable.

These days of ours have urgent need of a generation of praying saints, a band of men and women through whom God can bring His great and greatest movements more fully into the world. The Lord our God is not restricted within Himself, but He is restricted in us, by reason of our little faith and weak praying. A breed of Christian is greatly needed who will seek tirelessly after God—who will give Him no rest day and night until He hearken to their cry. The times demand praying men and women who are thirsty for God's glory, who are broad and unselfish in their desires, quenchless for God, who seek Him late and early, and who will give themselves no rest until "the whole earth be filled with His glory."[3]

PRAYING MEN AND WOMEN NEEDED

Men and women are needed whose prayers will give to the world the utmost power of God, and who will make His promises blossom with rich and full results. God is waiting to hear us and challenges us to bring Him to do this thing by our praying. He is asking us today, as He did His ancient Israel, to "prove [Him] now herewith."[4] Behind God's Word is

428

God Himself, and we read: "Thus saith the LORD, the Holy One of Israel, and his Maker, Ask of me of things to come concerning my sons, and concerning the work of my hands command ye me."[5] It is as though God places Himself in the hands and at the disposal of His people who pray—as indeed He does.

The dominant element of all praying is faith that is conspicuous, cardinal, and emphatic. Without such faith it is impossible to please God,[6] and equally impossible to pray.

There is a current conception of spiritual duties that tends to separate the pulpit and the pew, as though the pulpit bore the entire burden of spiritual concerns, while the pew was concerned only with duties that relate to the lower sphere of the secular and worldly. Such a view needs drastic correction. God's cause, its obligations, efforts, and successes, lie with equal pressure on pulpit and pew.

But the Christians in the pews are not taxed with the burden of prayer as they ought to be, and as there must be before any new visitation of power comes to the Church. The Church never will be wholly for God until the pews are filled with praying men and women. The Church cannot be what God wants it to be until those of its members who are leaders in business, politics, law, and society are leaders in prayer.

GOD BEGAN HIS WORK WITH PEOPLE OF PRAYER

God began His early movements in the world with people of prayer. He chose Abraham to be the father of the race that became His chosen people in the world for hundreds of years. To that race He committed His oracles, and from it came the promised Messiah. Abraham, a leader of God's cause, was preeminently a praying man. When we consider his conduct and character, we readily see how prayer ruled and swayed this great leader of God's people in the wilderness. "Abraham planted a grove in Beersheba, and called there on the name of the LORD, the everlasting God."[7] It is an outstanding fact that wherever Abraham pitched his tent and camped for a season with his household, he immediately erected an altar of sacrifice and prayer. His was a personal and a family religion, in which prayer was a prominent and abiding factor.

Prayer is the medium of divine revelation. It is through prayer that God reveals Himself to the spiritual soul today—just as in the Old Testament days He made His revelations to the people who prayed. God shows Himself to the person who prays. "God is with thee in all that thou doest."[8] This was the clear conviction of those who would gladly make a covenant with Abraham. The reason for this tribute was the belief commonly held concerning the patriarch. They believed that he was not only a man of prayer, but a man whose prayers God would answer. This is the summary and secret of divine rule in the Church. In all ages God has ruled the Church by prayerful men and women. When prayer fails, the divine leadership fails.

ABRAHAM

As we have seen, Abraham, the father of the faithful, was a prince and a priest in prayer. He had remarkable influence with God. God stays His vengeance while Abraham prays. His mercy is suspended and conditioned on Abraham's praying. His visitations of wrath are removed by the praying of this ruler in Israel. The movements of God are influenced by the prayers of Abraham, the friend of God. Abraham's righteous prayerfulness permits him to share the secrets of God's counsels, while the knowledge of these secrets draws out and intensifies his praying. With Abraham, the altar of sacrifice is hard by the altar of prayer. With him the altar of prayer sanctifies the altar of sacrifice. To Abimelech God said, "[Abraham] is a prophet, and he shall pray for thee, and thou shalt live."[9]

SAMUEL

Christian people must pray for people. On one occasion, Samuel said unto the people, "Moreover as for me, God forbid that I should sin against the LORD in ceasing to pray for you."[10] It was fortunate for these sinful people who had rejected God and desired a human king that they had in Israel a man of prayer. The royal way to enlarge personal grace is to pray for others. Intercessory prayer is a means of grace to those who exercise it. We enter the richest fields of spiritual growth and gather its priceless riches in the avenues of intercessory prayer. To pray for people is of divine nomination, and represents the highest form of Christian service.

PEOPLE MUST PRAY AND BE PRAYED FOR

People must pray, and people must be prayed for. The Christian must pray for all things, of course, but prayers for people are infinitely more important, just as people are infinitely more important than things. So also prayers for people are far more important than prayers for things because people more deeply concern God's will and the work of Jesus Christ than things. People are to be cared for, sympathized with and prayed for, because sympathy, pity, compassion and care accompany and precede prayer for people, when they are not called out for things.

All this makes praying a real business, and not child's play—not a secondary affair, or a trivial matter but a serious business. The Christians who have made a success of praying have made a business of praying. It is a process demanding the time, thought, energy, and hearts of Christians. Prayer is business for time, business for eternity. It is a Christian's business to pray, transcending all other business and taking precedence over all other vocations, professions, or occupations. Our praying concerns ourselves, all people, their greatest interests, even the salvation of their immortal souls. Praying is a business that takes hold of eternity and the things beyond the grave. It is a business that involves earth and heaven. All worlds are touched and worlds are influenced by prayer. It has to do with God and people, angels and devils.

JESUS WAS A LEADER IN PRAYER

Jesus was preeminently a leader in prayer, and His praying is an incentive to prayer. How prominently prayer stands out in His life! The leading events of His earthly career are distinctly marked by prayer. The wonderful experience and glory of the Transfiguration were preceded by prayer, and were the result of the praying of our Lord. What words He used as He prayed we do not know, nor do we know what He prayed for. But doubtless it was at night and long into its hours that the Master prayed. It was while He prayed that the darkness fled, and His form was lit with unearthly splendor. Moses and Elijah came to yield to Him not only the palm of law and prophecy, but the palm of praying. None other prayed as did Jesus, had any such a glorious manifestation of the divine presence, or heard so clearly the revealing voice of the Father: "This is my beloved Son: hear him."[11] Happy disciples to be with Christ in the school of prayer![12]

How many of us have failed to come to this glorious Mount of Transfiguration because we were unacquainted with the transfiguring power of prayer! It is the going apart to pray, the long, intense seasons of prayer, in which we engage that makes the face shine, transfigures the character, and makes even dull, earthly, garments glisten with heavenly splendor. But more than this. It is real praying that makes eternal things real, close, and tangible, and that brings the glorified visitors and the heavenly visions. Transfigured lives would not be so rare if there were more of this transfigured praying. These heavenly visits would not be so few if there was more of this transfigured praying.

REDEMPTION DEPENDS UPON SAINTS WHO PRAY

How difficult it appears to be for the Church to understand that the whole scheme of redemption depends upon saints of prayer! The work of our Lord while here on the earth, as well of the apostle Paul, was by teaching and example to develop praying Christians to whom the future of the Church should be committed. How strange that instead of learning this simple and all important lesson, the modern Church has largely overlooked it! We need to turn afresh to that wondrous leader of spiritual Israel, our Lord Jesus Christ, who by example and precept enjoins us to prayer. Also to Paul, the great apostle to the Gentiles, who by virtue of his praying habits and prayer lessons is a model and an example to God's people in every age and place.

Endnotes

1 Luke 18:1
2 Isaiah 64:7
3 Psalm 72:19
4 Malachi 3:10
5 Isaiah 45:11
6 Hebrews 11:6
7 Genesis 21:33
8 Genesis 21:22
9 Genesis 20:7
10 I Samuel 12:23
11 Luke 9:35
12 For further study along this line, see *With Christ in the School of Prayer* by Andrew Murray, ©1999 by Bridge-Logos Publishers.

7

The Ministry and Prayer

O F COURSE THE PREACHER *is above all others distinguished as a man of prayer. He prays as an ordinary Christian, else he were a hypocrite. He prays more than ordinary Christians else he were disqualified for the office he has undertaken If you as ministers are not very prayerful you are to be pitied. If you become lax in sacred devotion, not only will you need to be pitied but your people also, and the day cometh in which you will be ashamed and confounded. Our seasons of fastings and prayer at the Tabernacle have been high days indeed; never has heaven's gate stood wider; never have our hearts been nearer the central glory.* (Charles Haddon Spurgeon)

Preachers are God's leaders. They are divinely called to their holy office and high purpose and primarily are responsible for the condition of the Church. Just as Moses was called of God to lead Israel out of Egypt through the wilderness into the Promised Land, so God calls His ministers to lead His spiritual Israel through this world unto the heavenly land. They are divinely commissioned to leadership, and are by precept and example to teach God's people what God would have them be. Paul's counsel to the young preacher Timothy is in point: "Let no man despise thy youth; but be thou an example of the believers, in word, in conversation, in charity, in spirit, in faith, in purity."[1]

God's ministers shape the Church's character, and give tone and direction to its life. The prefacing sentence of the letter to each of the seven churches in Asia reads, "To the angel of the Church." This seems to indicate that the angel—the minister—was in the same state of mind and condition of life as the membership, and that these "angels" or ministers were largely responsible for the spiritual condition of things existing in each Church. The "angel" in each case was the preacher, teacher, or leader. The first Christians knew full well and felt this responsibility. In their helplessness, consciously felt, they cried out, "And who is sufficient for these things?"[2] as the tremendous responsibility pressed upon their hearts and heads. The only reply to such a question was, "God only."[3] So they were necessarily compelled to look beyond themselves for help and throw themselves on prayer to secure God. More and more as they prayed they felt their responsibility, and more and more by prayer they got God's help. They realized that their sufficiency was of God.

Prayer belongs in a very high and important sense to the ministry. It takes vigor and elevation of character to administer the prayer-office. Praying prophets have frequently been at a premium in the history of God's people. In every age the demand has been for leaders in Israel who pray. God's sentinels must always and everywhere be people of prayer.

PRAYING PREACHERS

It should be no surprise for ministers to be often found on their knees seeking divine help under the responsibility of their call. These are the true prophets of the Lord, and these are they who stand as mouthpieces of God to a generation of wicked and worldly minded men and women. Praying preachers are the boldest, truest, and swiftest ministers of God. They mount up highest and are nearest to Him who has called them. They advance more rapidly and in Christian living are most like Christ.

In reading the record of the four evangelists, we cannot but be impressed by the supreme effort made by our Lord to rightly instruct the twelve Apostles in the things that would properly qualify them for the tremendous tasks that would be theirs after He had gone back to the bosom of the Father. His solicitude was for the Church that it should have believers, holy in life and in heart, who would know full well from whence came their strength and power in the work of the ministry. A large part of Christ's teaching was addressed to these chosen Apostles, and the training of the twelve occupied much of His thought and consumed much of His time. In all that training, prayer was laid down as a basic principle.

We find the same thing to be true in the life and work of the apostle Paul. While he addressed himself to the edification of the churches to whom he ministered and wrote, it was in his mind and purpose to rightly instruct and prepare ministers to whom would be committed the interests of God's people. The two epistles to Timothy were addressed to a young preacher, while that to Titus was also written to a young minister. Paul's design appears to have been to give to each of them instruction that would be needed to correctly do the work of the ministry to which they had been called by the Spirit of God. Underlying these instructions was the foundation stone of prayer, since they would not be able to "show [themselves] approved unto God, [workers] that need[ed] not to be ashamed, rightly dividing the word of truth,"[4] unless they were men of prayer.

The welfare of Church and the ministry

The highest welfare of the Church of God on earth depends largely upon the ministry, and so Almighty God has always been jealous of His sentinels—His preachers. His concern has been for the character of the men and women who minister at His altars in holy things. They must be people who lean upon Him, who look to Him, and who continually seek Him for wisdom, help, and power to effectively do the work of the ministry. So He has designed men and women of prayer for the holy office, and has relied upon them successively to perform the tasks He has assigned them.

God's great works are to be done as Christ did them. Indeed, are to be done with increased power received from the ascended and exalted Christ. These works are to be done by prayer. Believers must do God's work in God's way and to God's glory, and prayer is a necessity to its successful accomplishment.

The thing far above all other things in the equipment of the preacher is prayer. Before everything else, the preacher must be a person who makes a specialty of prayer. A prayerless preacher is a misnomer. Such preachers either missed their calling, or have grievously failed God who called them into the ministry. God wants men and women who are not ignoramuses, who "study to show [themselves] approved."[5] Preaching the Word is essential. Social qualities are not to be underestimated, and education is good. But under and above all else, prayer must be the main plank in the platform of those who go forth to preach the unsearchable riches of Christ to a lost and hungry world. The one weak spot in our Church institutions lies just here. Prayer is not regarded as being the primary factor in church life and activity, and other things, good in their places, are made primary. First things need to be put first, and the first thing in the equipment of a minister is prayer.

Jesus is the pattern for preachers

Our Lord is the pattern for all preachers, and with Him prayer was the law of life. By it He lived. It was the inspiration of His toil, the source of His strength, the spring of His joy. With our Lord, prayer was no sentimental episode, or an afterthought, or a pleasing, diverting prelude, nor an interlude, nor a parade or form. For Jesus, prayer was exacting, all-absorbing, paramount. It was the call of a sweet duty to Him, the satisfying of a restless yearning, the preparation for heavy responsibilities, and the meeting of a vigorous need. This being so, the disciples must be as their

Lord, the servants as their Master. As was the Lord Himself, so also must be those whom He has called to be His disciples. Our Lord Jesus Christ chose His twelve Apostles only after He had spent a night in praying. So we may rest assured that He sets the same high value on those He calls to His ministry, in this our own day and time.

No feeble or secondary place was given to prayer in the ministry of Jesus. It comes first—emphatic, conspicuous, controlling. Of prayerful habits, of a prayerful spirit, given to long solitary communion with God, Jesus was above all else, a man of prayer. The crux of His earthly history, in New Testament terminology is condensed to a single statement found in Hebrews 5:7:

> Who in the days of his flesh, when he had offered up prayers and
> supplications with strong crying and tears unto him that was able
> to save him from death, and was heard in that he feared.

As was their Lord and Master, whose they are and whom they serve, so let His ministers be. Let Him be their pattern, their example, their leader and teacher. Much reference is made in some quarters about "following Christ," but it is confined to the following of Him in modes and ordinances, as if salvation were wrapped up in the specific way of doing a thing. "The path of prayer thyself hath trod," is the path along which we are to follow Him, and in no other. Jesus was given as a leader to the people of God, and no leader ever exemplified more the worth and necessity of prayer. Equal in glory with the Father, anointed and sent on His special mission by the Holy Spirit, His incarnate birth, His high commission, His royal anointing—all these were His, but they did not relieve Him from the exacting claims of prayer. Rather they tended to impose these claims upon Him with greater authority. He did not ask to be excused from the burden of prayer. He gladly accepted it, acknowledged its claims, and voluntarily subjected Himself to its demands.

His leadership was preeminent, and His praying was preeminent. Had it not been, His leadership would have been neither preeminent nor divine. If, in true leadership, prayer had been dispensable, then certainly Jesus could have dispensed with it. But He did not, and none of His followers who desire effectiveness in Christian activity can do anything other than follow their Lord.

JESUS TAUGHT HIS DISCIPLES TO PRAY

While Jesus Christ practiced praying Himself, being personally under the law of prayer, and while His parables and miracles were but exponents of prayer, He labored directly to teach His disciples the specific art of praying. He said little or nothing about how to preach or what to preach. But He spent His strength and time in teaching believers how to speak to

God, how to commune with Him, and how to be with Him. He knew full well that those who have learned the craft of talking to God, will be well versed in talking to people. We may turn aside for a moment to observe that this was the secret of the wonderful success of the early Methodist preachers, who were far from being learned people. But with all their limitations, they were people of prayer, and they did great things for God.

All ability to talk to people is measured by the ability with which a preacher can talk to God for people. He "who ploughs not in his closet, will never reap in his pulpit."

The fact must ever be kept in the forefront and emphasized that Jesus Christ trained His disciples to pray. This is the real meaning of that saying, "The Training of the Twelve." It must be kept in mind that Christ taught the world's preachers more about praying than He did about preaching. Prayer was the great factor in the spreading of His Gospel. Prayer conserved and made efficient all other factors. Yet He did not discount preaching when He stressed praying, but rather taught the utter dependence of preaching on prayer.

"The Christian's trade is praying," declared Martin Luther. Every Jewish boy had to learn a trade. Jesus Christ learned two, the trade of a carpenter, and that of praying. The one trade served earthly uses, the other served His divine and higher purposes. Jewish custom committed Jesus when a boy to the trade of a carpenter. The law of God bound Him to praying from His earliest years, and remained with Him to the end.

CHRIST IS OUR EXAMPLE

Christ is the Christian's example, and every Christian must pattern after Him. Every preacher must be like our Lord and Master, and must learn the trade of praying. Those who learn well the trade of praying, master the secret of the Christian art, and become a skilled workers in God's workshop. They become those who need not to be ashamed, a worker together with their Lord and Master.

"Pray without ceasing,"[6] is the trumpet call to the preachers of our time. If the preachers will get their thoughts clothed with the atmosphere of prayer, if they will prepare their sermons on their knees, a gracious outpouring of God's Spirit will come upon the earth.

THE INDISPENSABLE QUALIFICATION FOR PREACHING

The one indispensable qualification for preaching is the gift of the Holy Spirit, and it was for the bestowal of this indispensable gift that the disciples were charged to tarry in Jerusalem. The absolute necessity there is for receiving this gift if success is to attend the efforts of the ministry, is found in the command the first disciples had to stay in Jerusalem until they received it—and also with the instant and earnest prayerfulness with which they sought it. In obedience to their Lord's command to tarry in that city until they were endued with power from on high after He left them for heaven, they immediately entered on obtaining it by continued and earnest prayer. "These all with one accord continued steadfastly in prayer, with the women, and Mary, the mother of Jesus, and with his brethren."[7] John refers to this same thing in his first epistle. "Ye have an unction from the Holy One,"[8] he says. It is this divine unction that preachers of the present day should sincerely desire, pray for, and remain unsatisfied until the blessed gift is richly bestowed.

Another allusion to this same important procedure is made by our Lord shortly after His resurrection, when He said to His disciples: "But ye shall receive power, after that the Holy Ghost is come upon you."[9] At the same time, Jesus directed the attention of His disciples to the statement of John the Baptist concerning the Spirit, the identical thing for which He had commanded them to tarry in the city of Jerusalem—"power from on high."[10] Alluding to John the Baptist's words, Jesus said, "For John truly baptized with water; but ye shall be baptized with the Holy Ghost not many days hence."[11] At a later date, Peter said of our Lord, "God anointed [Him] with the Holy Ghost and with power."[12]

These are the divine statements of the mission and ministry of the Holy Spirit to preachers of that day, and the same divine statements apply with equal force to the preachers of this day. God's ideal minister is a God-called, divinely anointed, Spirit-touched person, separated unto God's work, set apart from secularities and questionable affairs, baptized from above, marked, sealed, and owned by the Spirit, devoted to the Lord and His ministry. These are the divinely-appointed requisites for a preacher of the Word. Without them, the preacher is inadequate and inevitably unfruitful.

BRING THE CHURCH BACK TO PRAYER

Today, there is no scarcity of preachers who deliver eloquent sermons on the need and nature of revival, and advance elaborate plans for the spread of the kingdom of God, but the praying preachers are far more rare. The greatest benefactor this age can have, is a person who will bring the preachers, the Church, and the people back to the practice of real praying. The reformer needed just now is the praying reformer. The leader Israel requires is one who, with clarion voice, will call the ministry back to their knees.

There is considerable talk of the coming revival in the air, but we need to have the vision to see that the revival we need, is one that is born of the Holy Spirit. Such a revival brings deep conviction for sin, and regeneration for those who seek God's face. Such a revival comes at the end of a season of real praying, and it is utter folly to talk about or expect a revival without the Holy Spirit operating in His peculiar office, conditioned on much earnest praying. Such a revival will begin in pulpit and pew alike and will be promoted by both preacher and layperson working in harmony with God.

The heart is the vocabulary of prayer, the life the best commentary on prayer, and the outward bearing its fullest expression. The character is made by prayer, the life is perfected by prayer. The ministry needs to learn this as thoroughly as the laypeople. There is but one rule for both.

So adverse was the general body of Christ's disciples to prayer, having so little taste for it, and having so little sympathy with Him in the deep things of prayer and its mightier struggles, that the Master had to select a circle of three more apt scholars—Peter, James, and John—who had more of sympathy and relish for this divine work, and take them aside that they might learn the lesson of prayer. These men were nearer to Jesus, fuller of sympathy, and more helpful to Him because they were more prayerful.

Blessed, indeed, are those disciples whom Jesus Christ calls into a more intimate fellowship with Him in this day, and who, readily responding to the call, are found much on their knees before Him. Distressing, indeed, is the condition of those servants of Jesus who, in their hearts, are averse to the exercise of the ministry of prayer.

All the great eras of our Lord, historical and spiritual, were made or fashioned by His praying. In like manner, His plans and great achievements were born in prayer and impregnated by the spirit of it. As was the Master, so also must His servant be. As the Lord did in the great eras of His life, so should the disciple do when faced by important crises. "To your knees, O Israel!" should be the clarion-call to the ministry of this generation.

THE HIGHEST FORM OF CHRISTIAN LIFE IS ATTAINED BY PRAYER

The richest revelations of God—Father, Son, and Spirit—are made, not to the learned, the great or the "noble" of earth, but people of prayer. "For ye see your calling, brethren, that not many wise men after the flesh, not many mighty, not many noble, are called."[13] God makes known the deep things of God, and reveals the higher things of His character, to the lowly, inquiring, praying ones. It must be said again, this is as true of preachers as of laypeople. It is the spiritual person who prays, and to praying ones God makes His revelations through the Holy Spirit.

Praying preachers have always brought the greater glory to God, have moved His Gospel onward with its greatest, speediest rate and power. A non-praying preacher and a non-praying Church may flourish outwardly and advance in many aspects of their life. Both preacher and church may become synonyms for success, but unless it rests on a praying basis, all success will eventually crumble into deadened life and ultimate decay.

WHY YOU "HAVE NOT"

"Ye have not, because ye ask not,"[14] is the solution of all spiritual weakness both in the personal life and in the pulpit. Either that or it is, "Ye ask, and receive not, because ye ask amiss."[15] Real praying lies at the foundation of all real success of the ministry in the things of God. The stability, energy, and ease with which God's kingdom is established in this world are dependent upon prayer. God has made it so, and so God is anxious for Christians to pray. He is especially concerned that His chosen ministers will be people of prayer, and so gives that wonderful statement in Luke to encourage His ministers to pray:

> And I say unto you, Ask, and it shall be given you; seek, and ye shall find; knock, and it shall be opened unto you. For every one that asketh receiveth; and he that seeketh findeth; and to him that knocketh it shall be opened.[16]

Thus both command and direct promise give accent to His concern that they should pray. Pause and think on these familiar words. "Ask, and it shall be given you." That itself would seem to be enough to set us all, layperson and preachers, to praying, since it is so direct, simple, and unlimited. These words open all the treasures of heaven to us, simply by asking for them.

STUDYING THE PRAYERS OF PAUL

If we have not studied the prayers of Paul, primarily a preacher to the Gentiles, we can have but a feeble view of the great necessity for prayer, and how much it is worth in the life and the work of a minister of the Gospel. Furthermore, we shall have but a very limited view of the possibilities of the Gospel to enrich and make strong and perfect Christian character, as well as to equip preachers for their high and holy task. Oh, when will we learn the simple yet all important lesson that the one great thing needed in the life of preachers to help them in their personal life, to keep their soul alive to God, and to give effectiveness to the Word preached by them is real, constant prayer!

With prayer uppermost in his mind, Paul assures the Colossians that "Epaphras . . . [is] always labouring fervently for you in prayers, that ye may stand perfect and complete in all the will of God."[17] To this high state of grace, "complete in all the will of God," he prays they may come. So prayer was the force that was to bring them to that elevated, vigorous, and stable state of heart. This is in line with Paul's teaching to the Ephesians, "And he gave some . . . pastors and teachers; for the perfecting of the saints, for the work of the ministry, for the edifying of the body of Christ."[18] It is evident from this that the whole work of the ministry is not merely to induce sinners to repent, but it is also the "perfecting of the saints." So Epaphras labored fervently in prayers for this thing. Certainly he was himself a praying man, in praying so earnestly for these early Christians.

The Apostles put forth their efforts so that Christians would honor God by the purity and consistency of their outward lives. They were to reproduce the character of Jesus Christ. They were to perfect His image in themselves, imbibe His temper, and reflect His character in all their tempers and conduct. They were to be imitators of God as dear children, to be holy as He was holy. Thus even laypeople were to preach by their conduct and character, just as the ministry preached with their mouths.

PRAYING NIGHT AND DAY

To elevate the followers of Christ to these exalted heights of Christian experience, they were in every way true in the ministry of God's Word, in the ministry of prayer, in holy consuming zeal, in burning exhortation, in rebuke and reproof. Added to all these, sanctifying all these, invigorating all these, and making all of them salutary, they centered and exercised constantly the force of mightiest praying. "Night and day praying exceedingly"—that is, praying out of measure, with intense earnestness, superabundantly, beyond measure, exceeding abundantly.

Night and day praying exceeding that we might see your face, and might perfect that which is lacking in your faith. Now God himself and our Father, and our Lord Jesus Christ, direct our way unto you. And the Lord make you to increase and abound in love one toward another, and toward all men, even as we do toward you: to the end he may stablish your hearts unblamable in holiness before God, even our Father, at the coming of our Lord Jesus Christ with all his saints.[19]

It was after this fashion that these Apostles—the first preachers in the early Church—labored in prayer. Only those who labor after the same fashion are the true successors of these Apostles. This is the true, the Scriptural, "apostolical succession." It is the succession of simple faith, earnest desire for holiness of heart and life, and zealous praying. These are the things today the make the ministry strong, faithful, and efficient, workers "that needeth not to be ashamed, rightly dividing the word of truth."[20]

JESUS LIVED AND SUFFERED UNDER THE LAW OF PRAYER

Jesus Christ, God's leader and commander of His people, lived and suffered under this law of prayer. All His personal conquests in His life on earth were won by obedience to this law. Since He ascended to heaven, the conquests that have been won by His representatives were gained only when this condition of prayer was heartily and fully met. Christ was under this one prayer condition. His Apostles were under the same prayer condition. His saints are under it, and even His angels are under it. By every token, therefore, preachers are under the same prayer law. Not for one moment are they relieved or excused from obedience to the law of prayer. It is their very life, the source of their power, the secret of their religious experience and communion with God.

Christ could do nothing without prayer. Christ could do all things by prayer. The Apostles were helpless without prayer—and were absolutely dependent upon it for success in defeating their spiritual foes. They could do all things by prayer.

Endnotes

1 1 Timothy 4:12
2 2 Corinthians 2:16
3 Mark 2:7
4 2 Timothy 2:15
5 2 Timothy 2:15
6 1 Thessalonians 5:17
7 Acts 1:14
8 1 John 2:20
9 Acts 1:8
10 Luke 24:49
11 Acts 1:5
12 Acts 10:38
13 1 Corinthians 1:26
14 James 4:2
15 James 4:3
16 Luke 11:9-10
17 Colossians 4:12
18 Ephesians 4:11-12
19 1 Thessalonians 3:10-13
20 2 Timothy 2:15

8

Prayerlessness in the Pulpit

Henry Martyn laments that *"want of private devotional reading and shortness of prayer through incessant sermon-making had produced much strangeness between God and his soul" He judges that he had dedicated too much time to public ministrations and too little to private communion with God. He was much impressed with the need of setting apart times for fasting and to devote times to for solemn prayer. Resulting from this he records "Was assisted this morning to pray for two hours."* (E. M. Bounds)

All God's saints came to their sainthood by the way of prayer. The saints could do nothing without prayer. We can go further and say that the angels in heaven can do nothing without prayer, but can do all things by praying. These messengers of the Highest are largely dependent on the prayers of the saints for the sphere and power of their usefulness, which open avenues for angelic usefulness, and create missions for them on the earth. As it is with all the Apostles, saints, and angels in heaven, so is it with preachers. "The angels of the churches" can do nothing without prayer that opens doors of usefulness and gives power and point to their words.

How can preachers preach effectively, make impressions on hearts and minds, and have fruits to their ministries, who do not get their messages first-hand from God? How can they deliver a rightful message without having their faith quickened, their vision cleared, and their heart warmed by their communication with God?

It would be well for all of us, in this connection, to read again Isaiah's vision recorded in the seventh chapter of his prophecy when, as he waited, and confessed and prayed before the throne, the angel touched his lips with a live coal from God's altar:

> Then flew one of the seraphim unto me, having a live coal in his hand, which he had taken with the tongs from off the altar: and he laid it upon my mouth, and said, Lo, this hath touched thy lips; and thy iniquity is taken away, and thy sin is purged.[1]

Oh, the need there is for present-day preachers to have their lips touched with a live coal from the altar of God! This fire is brought to the mouths of those prophets who are of a prayerful spirit, and who wait in the secret place for the appointed angel to bring the living flame. Preachers of the same temper as Isaiah received visits from the angel who brings live coals to touch their lips. Prayer always brings the living flame to unloose tongues, to open doors of utterance, and to open great and effectual doors of doing good. This, above all else, is the great need of the prophets of God.

As far as the abiding interests of Christianity are concerned, a pulpit without a closet will always be a barren thing. Blessed is the preacher whose pulpit and closet are close by each other, and who goes from the one into the other. To consecrate no place to prayer is to make a beggarly showing, not only in praying, but in holy living, for secret prayer and holy living are so closely joined that they can never be separated. A preacher or a Christian may live a decent Christian life without secret prayer, but decency and holiness are two widely different things. And the former is attained only by secret prayer.

A preacher may preach in an official, entertaining and learned way, without prayer, but between this kind of preaching and the sowing of God's precious seed there is distance not easily covered.

PRAYER REQUIRED FOR KINGDOM SUCCESS

We cannot declare too often or too strongly that prayer, involving all of its elements, is the one prime condition of the success of Christ's kingdom, and that all else is secondary and incidental. Prayerful preachers, prayerful men and women, only can press this Gospel with aggressive power. They only can put in it conquering forces. Preachers may be sent out by the thousand, their equipments be ever so complete, but unless they are skilled in the trade of prayer, trained to its martial and exhaustive exercise, their going will be lacking in power and effectiveness. Moreover, except the men and women who are behind these preachers, who furnish their equipment, are men and women in whose characters prayer has become to be serious labor, their efforts will be vain and fruitless.

Prayer should be the inseparable accompaniment of all missionary effort, and must be the one equipment of the missionaries as they go out to their fields of labor and enter upon their delicate and responsible tasks. Prayer and missions go hand in hand. Prayerless missionaries are failure before they go out, while there are out, and when they return to their native land. A prayerless board of missions needs to learn the lesson of the necessity of prayer.

PRAYER ENTHRONES GOD AND ELEVATES CHRIST

Prayer enthrones God as sovereign and elevates Jesus Christ to sit with Him. Had Christian preachers used to its full the power of prayer, the "kingdoms of this world [would have] become the kingdoms of our Lord, and of his Christ"[2] long before this. Prayer, much prayer, must be added to all the appeals for missionaries, the money raised for missions, and to the scores being sent out to needy fields. Missions have their root in prayer, must have prayer in all of its plans, and prayer must precede, go with, and follow all of its missionaries and laborers.

In the face of all difficulties that face the Church in its great work on earth, and the almost superhuman and complex obstacles in the way of evangelizing the world, God encourages us by His strongest promises: "Call unto me, and I will answer thee, and show great and mighty things, which thou knowest not."[3] The revelations of God to those who are of a prayerful spirit go far beyond the limits of the praying. God commits Himself to answer the specific prayer, but He does not stop there. He says, "Ask of me things to come concerning my sons, and concerning the work of my hands command ye me."[4] Think over that remarkable statement of God to those who pray, "Command ye me," He actually places Himself at the command of praying preachers and a praying Church. And this is a sufficient answer to all doubts, fears, and unbelief—and a wonderful inspiration to do God's work in His own way, which means by the way of prayer.

Then, as if to still fortify the faith of His ministry and of His Church, to hedge about and fortify against any temptation to doubt or discouragement, He declares by the mouth of the great apostle to the Gentiles, "He is able to do exceeding abundantly above all that we ask or think."[5]

It is unquestionably taught that preachers in going forward with their God-appointed tasks, in their prayers, can command God, which is to command His ability, His presence, and His power. "Certainly I will be with thee"[6] is the reply to every sincere inquiring minister of God. All of God's called workers in the ministry are privileged to stretch their prayers into regions where neither words nor thought can go, and are permitted to expect from Him beyond their praying. And for their praying they can expect God Himself, and even more: "great and mighty things which thou knowest not."

GOOD PREACHING COMES FROM GOOD PRAYING

Real heart-praying, live-praying, praying by the power of the Spirit, direct, specific, ardent, simple praying—this is the kind of praying that legitimately belongs to the pulpit. This is the kind demanded just now by the ministers who stand in the pulpit. There is no school in which to learn to pray in public but in the closet. Preachers who have learned to pray in the closet, have mastered the secret of pulpit praying. It is but a short step from secret praying to effective, live pulpit-praying.

Good pulpit praying follows from good secret praying. A closed closet with the preacher makes for cold, spiritless, formal praying in the pulpit. Study how to pray, O preacher, but not by studying the forms of prayer, but by attending the school of prayer on your knees before God. Here is where we learn not only to pray before God, but learn also how to pray in the presence of people. Those who have learned the way to the closet have discovered the way to pray when they enter the pulpit.

How easily we become professional and mechanical in the most sacred undertakings! Henry Martyn learned the lesson so hard to learn, that the cultivation and perfection of personal righteousness was the great and prime factor in the preacher's true success. So likewise those that learn the lesson so hard to learn, that live, spiritual, effective pulpit praying is the outgrowth of regular secret praying, have learned their lessons well. Moreover: their work as preachers will depend upon their praying.

The great need of the hour is for good people of prayer in the pulpit as well as good preachers. Just as live, spiritual, preaching is the kind that impresses and moves people, so the same kind of pulpit praying moves and impresses God. Not only is the preacher called to preach well, but also called to pray well. Not called to pray after the fashion of the Pharisees, who love to stand in public and pray that they may be seen and heard of people. The right sort of pulpit praying is far removed from Pharisaical praying, as far distant as light is from darkness, as great as heat is from cold, as life is from death.

PREACHING IS THE LOFTIEST WORK A PERSON CAN DO

Where are we? What are we doing? Preaching is the very loftiest work possible for a person to do. And praying goes hand-in-hand with preaching. It is a mighty, a lofty work. Preaching is a life-giving work sowing the seeds of eternal life. Oh, may we do it well, do it after God's order, do it successfully! May we do it divinely well, so that when the end comes, the solemn close of earthly probation, we may hear from the Great Judge of all the earth, "Well done, good and faithful servant . . . enter thou into the joy of thy Lord."[7]

When we consider this great question of preaching, we are led to exclaim, "With what reverence, simplicity, and sincerity ought it to be done!" What truth in the inward parts is demanded in order that it be done acceptably to God and with profit to people! How real, true, and loyal those who practice it ought to be! How great the need to pray as Christ prayed, with strong cryings and tears and godly fear! Oh, may we as preachers do the real thing of preaching, with no sham, with no mere form of words, with no dull, cold, professional utterances, but give ourselves to prayerful preaching and prayerful praying! Preaching that gives life is born of praying that gives life. Preaching and praying always go together, like Siamese twins, and can never be separated without death to one or the other, or death to both.

This is not the time for kid-glove methods or sugar-coated preaching. This is no time for playing gentle as a preacher, or for putting on the garb of the scholar in the pulpit, if we propose to disciple all nations, destroy idolatry, crush the rugged and defiant forces of paganism, and overcome and destroy the tremendous forces of evil now opposing the kingdom of God in this world. Brave Christians, true Christians, praying Christians— afraid of nothing but God are the kind needed just now.

There will be no smiting the forces of evil that now hold the world in thralldom, no lifting of the degraded hordes of paganism to light and eternal life, by any but praying Christians. All others are merely playing at Christianity, make-believe soldiers with no armor and no ammunition, who are absolutely helpless in the face of a wicked and false world.

None but soldiers and bond servants of Jesus Christ can possibly do this tremendous work. "Endure hardness as a good soldier of Jesus Christ,"[8] cries the great apostle. This is no time to think of self, to consult with dignity, to confer with flesh and blood, to think of ease, or to shrink from hardship, grief, and loss. This is the time for toil, suffering, and self-denial. We must lose all for Christ in order to gain all for Christ. Saints are needed in the pulpit, and in the pew, who are "bold to take up, firm to sustain, the consecrated cross."

Here is the sort of preachers God wants. And this sort are born of much praying. For no person is sufficient for these things who is a prayerless preacher. Praying preachers alone can meet the demand and will be equal to the emergency.

PRAYERLESS LIPS AND PRAYERLESS HANDS

The Gospel of Jesus has neither relish nor life in it when spoken by prayerless lips or handled by prayerless hands. Without prayer, the doctrines of Christ degenerate into dead orthodoxy. Preaching them without the aid of the Spirit of God, who comes into the preacher's messages only by prayer, is nothing more than mere lecturing, with no life, no grip, no force in the preaching. It amounts to nothing more than live rationalism or sickly sentimentalism. "But we will give ourselves continually to prayer, and to the ministry of the Word,"[9] was the settled and declared purpose of the apostolic ministry. The kingdom of God waits on prayer, and prayer puts wings on the Gospel and power into it. By prayer it moves forward with conquering force and rapid advance.

If prayer is left out of account, the preacher rises to no higher level than the lecturer, the politician, or the secular teacher. That which distinguishes the preacher from all other public speakers is the fact of prayer. And as prayer deals with God, this means that preachers have God with them, while other speakers do not need God with them to make their public messages effective. The preachers above everything else are spiritual people, people of the Spirit, who deal with spiritual things. And this implies that preachers have to do with God in their pulpit work in a high and holy sense. This can be said of no other public speakers. And so prayer must necessarily go with the preachers and their preaching. Pure intellectuality is the only qualification for other public speakers. Spirituality that is born of prayer belongs to the preachers.

In the Sermon on the Mount, Jesus Christ often speaks of prayer. It stands out prominently in His utterances on that occasion. The lesson of prayer that He taught was one of hallowing God's name, of pushing God's kingdom. We are to long for the coming of the kingdom of God. It is to be longed for, and must be first in our interaction with God. God's will must have its royal way in the hearts and wills of those who pray. The point of urgency is made by our Lord that saints are to pray in earnest, by asking, seeking, knocking, in order to hallow God's name, bring His will to pass, and to forward His kingdom among humanity.

Let it be kept in mind that while this prayer-lesson has to do with all Christians, it has a peculiar application to the ministry, for it was the twelve would-be preachers who made the request of our Lord Jesus Christ, "Lord, teach us to pray, as John also taught his disciples."[10] So that primarily these words were spoken first to twelve saints just entering upon their work as ministers. Jesus was talking as Luke records it, to preachers. So He speaks to the preachers of this day. How He pressed these twelve men into the ministry of prayer! The present-day ministry needs the same lesson to be taught them, and needs the same urgency pressing them to prayer as their habit of life.

PREACHERS CANNOT TEACH WHAT THEY DO NOT KNOW

Notwithstanding all they may claim for themselves, nor how many good things may be put down to their credit, prayerless preachers will never learn well God's truth, which they are called upon to declare with all truthfulness and plainness of speech. Blind and blinding still will those be if they live a prayerless life. A prayerless ministry cannot know God's truth, and not knowing it, cannot teach it to ignorant people. Those who teach us the path of prayer must first of all walk in the same path. Preachers cannot teach what they do not know. Preachers who are strangers to prayer will be blind leaders of the blind. Prayer opens the preacher's eyes, and keeps them open to the evil of sin, the peril of it, and the penalty it incurs. A blind leader leading the blind will be the vocation of anyone who is prayerless in their own life.

The best and the greatest offering that the Church and the ministry can make to God is an offering of prayer. If the preachers of the this century will learn well the lesson of prayer, and use it fully in all its exhaustless efficiency, the next millennium will come to its zenith before the century closes.

BIBLE PREACHERS PRAY

They are filled with the Holy Spirit, filled with God's Word, and filled with faith. They have faith in God, faith in God's only begotten Son, their personal Savior, and they have implicit faith in God's Word. They cannot do otherwise than pray. They cannot be other than saints of prayer. The breadth of their lives and the pulsations of their hearts are prayer. Bible preachers live by prayer, love by prayer, and preach by prayer. Their bended knees in the place of secret prayer advertise what kind of preachers they are.

Preachers may lose faith in God, in Jesus Christ as their personal and present Savior, become devoid of the peace of God and let the joy of salvation go out of their hearts, and yet be unconscious of it. How needful for preachers to be continually examining themselves, and inquiring into their personal relations to God and their spiritual condition! The preachers, like the philosophers of old, may defer to a system; and earnestly contend for it after they have lost all faith in its great facts. Preachers may in the pulpit with hearts of unbelief, minister at the altars of the Church, while alien to the most sacred and vital principles of the Gospel.

It is a comparatively easy task for preachers to become so absorbed in the material and external affairs of the Church that they lose sight of their own souls, forget the necessity of prayer so needful to keep their own souls alive to God, and lose the inward sweetness of a Christian experience.

The prayer that makes much of our preaching must itself be made much of. The character of our praying will determine the character of our preaching. Serious praying will give serious weight to preaching. Prayer makes preaching strong, gives it unction and makes it stick. In every ministry, weighty for good, prayer has always been a serious business prophetic of good. It cannot be said with too much emphasis, preachers must be preeminently people of prayer.

PREACHERS MUST LEARN TO PRAY

Preachers must learn to pray, and they must have such an estimate of prayer and its great worth that they feel they cannot afford to omit it from the catalogue of their private duties. Their hearts must be attuned to prayer, while they themselves touch the highest note of prayer. Only in the school of prayer can the heart learn to preach. No gifts, no learning, no brain-force, can atone for the failure to pray. No earnestness, no diligence, no study, no amount of social service, will supply its lack. Talking to people for God may be a great thing and very commendable. But talking to God for people is far more valuable and commendable.

The power of Bible preaching lies not simply or solely in superlative devotion to God's Word, and jealous passion for God's truth. All these are essential, valuable, helpful. But above all these things, there must be the sense of the divine presence, and the consciousness of the divine power of God's Spirit on and in the preacher. Preachers must have an anointing, an empowering, a sealing of the Holy Spirit, for the great work of preaching, making them akin to God's voice, and giving them the energy of God's right hand, so that these Bible preachers can say,

> Thy words were found, and I did eat them; and thy word was unto me the joy and rejoicing of mine heart: For I am called by thy name, O LORD of hosts.[11]

Endnotes

1 Isaiah 6:6-7
2 Revelation 11:15
3 Jeremiah 33:3
4 Isaiah 45:11
5 Ephesians 3:20
6 Exodus 3:12
7 Matthew 25:23
8 2 Timothy 2:3
9 Acts 6:4
10 Luke 11:1
11 Jeremiah 15:16

9

Prayer Equipment for Preachers

GO BACK! *Back to that upper room; back to your knees; back to searching of heart and habit, thought and life; back to pleading, praying, waiting, till the Spirit of the Lord floods the soul with light, and you are endued with power from on high. Then go forth in the power of Pentecost, and the Christ-life shall be lived, and the works of Christ shall be done. You shall open blind eyes, cleanse foul hearts, break men's fetters, and save men's souls. In the power of the indwelling Spirit, miracles become the commonplace of daily living.* (Samuel Chadwick)

Almost the last words uttered by our Lord before His ascension to heaven were those addressed to the eleven disciples. They were words that really were spoken to preachers, and had to do directly with them. The words indicated very clearly the essential thing they needed to preach the Gospel, beginning at Jerusalem: "And, behold, I send the promise of My Father upon you: but tarry ye in the city of Jerusalem, until ye be endued with power from on high."[1]

Two things are very clearly set forth in these urgent directions. First, the power of the Holy Ghost for which they must tarry. This was to be received after their conversion, an indispensable requisite, equipping them for the great task set before them. Secondly, the "promise of the Father," this "power from on high," would come to them after they had waited in earnest, continuous, prayer. A reference to Acts 1:14 will reveal that these same men, with the women, "continued with one accord in prayer and supplication." They continued that way until the Day of Pentecost when the power from on high descended upon them.

This "power from on high," as important to those early preachers as it is to present-day preachers, was not the force of a mighty intellect that holds in its grasp great truths, flooding them with light, and forming them into verbal shapeliness and beauty. Nor was it the acquisition of great learning, or the result of a sermon, faultless and complete through the rules of rhetoric. It was none of these things. Nor was this spiritual power held then, nor is it held now, in the keeping of any earthly sources of power.

The effect and energy of all human forces are essentially different in source and character, and do not at all result from this "power from on high." The transmission of such power is directly from God, a bestowal in rich measure of the force and energy that pertains only to God, and which is transmitted to His messengers only in answer to a longing, struggling attitude of the soul before the Master. Only those receive it who are conscious of their own impotence and seek the omnipotence of the Lord they serve in order more fully to understand the given Word and to preach the same to dying sinners and hungry saints.

The "power from on high" may be found in combination with all sources of human power, but is not to be confounded with them, is not dependent upon them, and must never be superseded by them. Whatever human gift, talent, or force a preacher may possess it is not to be made paramount, or even conspicuous. It must be hidden, lost, overshadowed by this "power from on high." The forces of intellect and culture may all be present, but without this inward, heaven-given, power, all spiritual effort is vain and unsuccessful. Even when lacking the other equipment but having this "power from on high," a preacher cannot but succeed. It is the one essential, all-important, vital force that a messenger of God must possess to give wings to the message, put life into the preaching, and be enabled to speak the Word with acceptance and power.

Unction versus pathos

A word of explanation is necessary here. Distinctions need to be kept in mind. We must think clearly upon this question. "Power from on high" means "the unction from the Holy One"[2] resting on and abiding in the preacher. This is not so much a power that bears witness to a person being the child of God as it is a preparation for delivering the Word to others. Unction must be distinguished from pathos. Pathos may exist in a sermon while unction is entirely absent.[3] So also, unction may be present and pathos absent. Both may exist together, but they are not to be confused, or made to appear to be the same thing. Pathos promotes emotion, tender feeling, sometimes tears. Quite often it results from the relation of an affecting incident, or when the tender side is peculiarly appealed to. But pathos is neither the direct nor indirect result of the Holy Spirit resting upon the preacher while preaching, but unction is.

Unction is evidence of the workings of an indefinable agency in the preacher, which results directly from the presence of this "power from on high." It is deep, conscious, life-giving, and motivating—giving power and point to the preached Word. It is the element in a sermon that arouses, stirs, convicts, and moves the souls of sinners and saints. This is what preachers require, the great equipment for which they should wait and pray. This "unction of the Holy One" delivers from dryness, saves from superficiality, and gives authority to preaching. It is the one quality that distinguishes preachers of the Gospel from other secular public speakers. It is that which makes a sermon unique, unlike the deliverance of any other public speaker.

PRAYER IS THE LANGUAGE OF NEED

Prayer is the language of a person burdened with a sense of need. It is the voice of the beggar, conscious of personal poverty, asking of another the things that are needed. It is not only the language of lack, but of felt lack, of lack consciously realized. "Blessed are the poor in spirit,"[4] means not only that the fact of poverty of spirit brings the blessing, but also that poverty of spirit is realized, known, and acknowledged. Prayer is the language of those who need something—something which they, themselves, cannot supply but which God has promised them, and for which they ask. In the end, poor praying and prayerlessness amount to the same thing, for poor praying proceeds from a lack of the sense of need, while prayerlessness has its origin in the same soil. Not to pray is not only to declare there is nothing needed, but to admit to a non-realization of that need. This is what aggravates the sin of prayerlessness. It represents an attempt at instituting an independence of God, a self-sufficient ruling of God out of the life. It is a declaration made to God that we do not need Him, and hence do not pray to Him.

THE LAODICEAN CHURCH

This is the state in which the Holy Spirit, in His messages to the Seven Churches in Asia, found the Laodicean Church and "the Laodicean state" has come to stand for one in which God is ruled out, expelled from the life, put out of the pulpit. The entire condemnation of this church is summed up in one expression: "Because thou sayest, I . . . have need of nothing."[5] This is the most alarming state into which a person, church, or preacher can come. Trusting in its riches, in its social position, in things outward and material, the Church at Laodicea omitted God, leaving Him out of their church plans and church work, and declared, by their acts and by their omission of prayer, "I . . . have need of nothing."

No wonder the self-satisfied declaration brought forth its sentence of punishment—"Because thou art lukewarm, and neither cold nor hot, I will spue thee out of my mouth."[6] The idea conveyed is that such a backslidden state of heart is as repulsive to God as spoiled food is to the human stomach, and as the stomach expels that which is objectionable, so Almighty God threatens to "spue out of His mouth" these people who were in such a religious condition so repulsive to Him. All of it was traceable to a prayerless state of heart, for no one can read this word of the Spirit to this Laodicean Church and not see that the very core of their sin was prayerlessness. How could a Church, given to prayer, openly and arrogantly declare, "I have need of nothing," in the face of the Spirit's assertion that it needed everything, "Thou . . . knowest not that thou art wretched, and miserable, and poor, and blind, and naked"?[7] In addition to their sin of self-sufficiency and of independence of God, the Laodiceans were spiritually blind.

Oh, what dullness of sight, what blindness of soul! These people were prayerless, and did not know the consequences of such prayerlessness. They lacked everything that goes to make up spiritual life, force, and self-denying piety, and vainly supposed themselves to need nothing but material wealth, thus making temporal possessions a substitute for spiritual wealth. By this, there were leaving God entirely out of their activities, and relying upon human and material resources to do the work only possible to the divine and supernatural, and secured alone by prayer.

Do not let it be forgotten that this letter (in common with the other six letters) was primarily addressed to the preacher in charge of the church. All this strengthens the impression that the "angel of the church" was in this lukewarm state. The minister was living a prayerless life, relying upon things other than God, practically saying, "I have need of nothing." For these words are the natural expression of the spirit of a person who does not pray, who does not care for God, and who does not feel the need of Him in life, in work and in preaching. Furthermore, the words of the Spirit seem to indicate that the "angel of the church" at Laodicea was indirectly responsible for this sad condition into which the Laodicean Church had fallen.

THE MODERN CHURCH

May not this sort of a church be found in modern times? Is it not likely that we could discover some preachers of modern times who fall under a similar condemnation to that passed upon the "angel of the church" of Laodicea?

Preachers of the present age excel those of the past in many, possibly in all, human elements of success. They are well abreast of the age in learning, research, and intellectual vigor. But these things neither insure "power from on high" nor guarantee a live, thriving Christian experience or righteous life. These purely human gifts do not bring with them an insight into the deep things of God, strong faith in the Scriptures, or an intense loyalty to God's divine revelation.

The presence of these earthly talents even in the most commanding and impressive form and richest measure, do not in the least abate the necessity for the added endowment of the Holy Spirit. Herein lies the great danger menacing the pulpit of today. All around us we see a tendency to substitute human gifts and worldly attainments for that supernatural, inward power that comes from on high in answer to earnest prayer.

MODERN PREACHING

In many instances modern preaching seems to fail in the very thing that should create and distinguish true preaching, which is essential to its being and which alone can make of it a divine and powerfully aggressive agency. It lacks, in short, "the power from on high" that alone can make it a living thing. It fails to become the channel through which God's saving power can be made to appeal to people's consciences and hearts.

Quite often, modern preaching fails at this vital point, for lack of exercising a potent influence that disturbs sinners in their sleep of security, and awakens them to a sense of need and peril. There is a growing need of an appeal that will quicken and arouse the conscience from its ignoble stupor and give it a sense of wrong-doing and a corresponding sense of repentance. There is need of a message that searches into the secret places of human hearts, dividing, as it were, the joints and the marrow, and laying bare the mysterious depths before the sinner and God. Much of our present-day preaching is lacking in that quality that infuses new blood into the heart and veins of faith, that arms it with courage and skill for the battle with the powers of darkness, and secures it a victory over the forces of the world.

HOLY SPIRIT NEEDED TO ACCOMPLISH HIGH AND NOBLE ENDS

Such high and noble ends can never be accomplished by human qualifications, nor can these great results be secured by a pulpit clothed only with the human elements of power, however gracious, comfortable, and helpful they may be. The Holy Spirit is needed. He alone can equip the ministry for its difficult and responsible work in and out of the pulpit. Oh, that the present-day ministry may come to see that its one great need is to be endued with "power from on high," and that this one need can be secured only by the use of God's appointed means of grace—the ministry of prayer.

PREACHERS NEED PRAYER

Prayer is needed by preachers so that their personal relations with God may be maintained, and that because there is no difference between them and any other kind of person in so far as their personal salvation is concerned. This they must work out "with fear and trembling,"[18] just as all other people must do. Thus prayer is of vast importance to preachers so that they may possess a growing Christian experience, and be enabled to live such a life that their character and conduct will back up their preaching and give force to their message.

Preachers must have prayer in their pulpit work, for no minister can preach effectively without prayer. They also have use for prayer in praying for others. Paul was a notable example of a preacher who constantly prayed for those to whom he ministered.

But we come, now, to another sphere of prayer, that of the people praying for the preacher. "Brethren, pray for us,"[9] This is the cry that Paul set in motion, and that has been the cry of spiritually-minded preachers—those who know God and who know that value of prayer—in all succeeding ages. No condition of success or the reverse of it must abate the cry. No degree of culture, no abundance of talents, must cause that cry to cease. The learned preachers, as well as the unlearned, have equal need to call out to the people they serve, "Withal praying also for us."[10]

Such a cry voices the felt need of the hearts of preachers who feel the need for the sympathies of a people to be in harmony with their ministers. It is but the expression of the inner soul of preachers who feel their insufficiency for the tremendous responsibilities of the pulpit, who realize their weakness and their need of the divine unction, and who throw themselves upon the prayers of their congregation, and call out to them, "Praying always with all prayer and supplication in the Spirit . . . and for me, that utterance may be given unto me."[11] It is the cry of deep felt want in the hearts of preachers who feel they must have this prayer made specifically for them that they may do their work in God's own way.

When this request to a people to pray for their preacher is cold, formal, and official, it freezes instead of bearing fruit. To be ignorant of the necessity for the cry is to be ignorant of the sources of spiritual success. To fail to stress the cry and to fail to have responses to it is to sap the sources of spiritual life. Preachers must sound out the cry to God's Church. Saints everywhere of every kind and of every level of faith must speedily respond and pray for preachers. The imperative need of the work demands it. "Pray for us,"[12] is the natural cry of the hearts of God's called ministers—faithful preachers of the Word.

Saintly praying in the early Church helped apostolic preaching mightily, and rescued the apostles from many dire straits. It can do the same thing today. It can open doors for apostolic labors and apostolic lips to utter bravely and truly the Gospel message. Apostolic movements wait their ordering from prayer, and avenues long closed are opened to apostolic entrance by and through the power of prayer. The messenger receives the message and is schooled as to how to carry and deliver the message by prayer. The forerunner of the Gospel and that which prepares the way is prayer—not only by the praying of the messengers themselves, but by the praying of God's Church.

"PRAY FOR US"

Writing along this line in his second epistle to the Thessalonians, Paul is first general in his request and says, "Brethren, pray for us." Then he becomes more detailed and specific:

> Finally, brethren, pray for us, that the word of the Lord may have free course, and be glorified, even as it is with you: And that we may be delivered from unreasonable and wicked men: for all men have not faith.[13]

The *Revised Version* has for "free course" the word "run." *The Word* means doctrine, and the idea conveyed is that this doctrine of the Gospel is rapidly propagated, a metaphor taken from the running of a race, and is an exhortation to exert one's self, to strive hard, to expend strength. Thus the prayer for the spread of the Gospel gives the same energy to the Word of the Lord, as the greatest outlay of strength gives success to the racer. Prayer in the pew gives the preached Word energy, facility, and success. Preaching without the backing of mighty praying is as limp and worthless an effort as can be imagined. Prayerlessness in the pew is a serious hindrance to the running of the Word of the Lord.

The preaching of the Word of the Lord fails to run and be glorified from many causes. The difficulty may lie with preachers themselves, should their outward conduct be out of harmony with the rule of the Scriptures and their own profession. The Word lived must be in accord with the Word delivered. The life must be in harmony with the sermon. The spirit and behavior of preachers out of the pulpit must run parallel with the Word of the Lord spoken in the pulpit. Otherwise, preachers are an obstacle to the success of their own message.

Again, the Word of the Lord may fail to run, may be seriously encumbered and crippled by the inconsistent lives of those who are the hearers of it. Bad living in the pew will seriously cripple the Word of the Lord as it attempts to run on its appointed course. Unrighteous lives among the laity heavily weights down the Word of the Lord and hampers the work of the ministry. Yet prayer will remove this burden that seriously handicaps the preached Word. It will tend to do this in a direct way, or in an indirect manner. For just as you set laypeople to praying for the preacher or even for themselves, it awakens conscience, stirs the heart, and tends to correct evil ways and to promote good living. No person will pray long and continue in sin. Praying breaks up bad living, while bad living breaks down prayer. Praying goes into bankruptcy when a person goes to sinning. To obey the cry of the preacher, "Brethren, pray for us," sets people to doing that which will induce right living in them, and will tend to break them away from sin. So it comes about that it is worth considerable to get the laity to pray for the ministry. Prayer helps the preacher, is an aid to the sermon, assists the hearer, and promotes right living in the pew.

Prayer also moves those who pray for preachers and for the Word of the Lord, to use all their influence to remove any hindrance to that Word that they may see, and that lies in their power to remove.

But prayer reaches preachers directly. God hears the praying of a church for its minister. Prayer for the preached Word is a direct aid to it. Prayer for the preacher gives wings to the Gospel, as well as feet. Prayer makes the Word of the Lord go forward strongly and rapidly. It takes the shackles off the message, and gives it a chance to run straight to the hearts of sinners and saints alike. It opens the way, clears the track, furnishes a free course. The failure of many preachers may be found just here. The preacher was hampered, hindered, and crippled by a prayerless church. Non-praying officials stood in the way of the Word preached, and became veritable stumbling blocks in the way of the Word, definitely preventing its reaching the hearts of the unsaved.

UNBELIEF AND PRAYERLESSNESS

It is written of our Lord in Matthew's gospel that when He entered into His own country, "he did not many mighty works there because of their unbelief."[14] Mark puts it a little differently, but giving out the same idea:

> And he could there do no mighty work, save that he laid his hands upon a few sick folk, and healed them. And he marveled because of their unbelief.[15]

Unquestionably, the unbelief of that people hindered our Lord in His gracious work and tied His hands. If that is true, it requires no undue straining of the Scriptures when we say that the unbelief and prayerlessness of churches can tie the hands of preachers, and prevent them from doing many great works in the salvation of souls and in edifying saints.

Prayerlessness, therefore, as it concerns preachers is a very serious matter. If it exists in the preachers themselves, then they tie their own hands and make the Word as preached by them ineffective and void. If prayerless people be found in the pew, then it hurts the preachers, robs them of invaluable help, and interferes seriously with the success of their work. How great the need of a praying church to help on the preaching of the Word of the Lord! Both pew and pulpit are jointly concerned in this preaching business. It is a co-partnership. The two go hand in hand. One must help the other, one can hinder the other. Both must work in perfect accord or serious damage will result, and God's plan concerning the preacher and the preached Word will be defeated.

Endnotes

1 Luke 24:49
2 I John 2:20
3 *Pathos* brings an emotional response, *unction* (anointing) brings a spiritual reponse.
4 Matthew 5:3
5 Revelation 3:17
6 Revelation 3:16
7 Revelation 3:17
8 Philippians 2:12
9 I Thessalonians 5:25
10 Colossians 4:3
11 Ephesians 6:18-19
12 I Thessalonians 5:25
13 2 Thessalonians 3:1-2
14 Matthew 13:58
15 Mark 6:5-6

10

The Preacher's Cry: "Pray for us!"

THAT THE TRUE APOSTOLIC *preacher must have the prayers of others—good people to give to his ministry its full quota of success, Paul is a preeminent example. He asks, he covets, he pleads in an impassionate way for the help of all God's saints, He knew that in the spiritual realm as elsewhere, in union there is strength; that the consecration and aggregation of faith, desire, and prayer increased the volume of spiritual force until it became overwhelming and irresistible in its power. Units of prayer combined, like drops of water, make an ocean that defies resistance.* (E. M. Bounds)

How far does praying for preachers help preaching? It helps them personally and officially. It helps them to maintain a righteous life, it helps them in preparing their message, and it helps the Word preached by them to run to its appointed goal, unhindered and unhampered.

A praying church creates a spiritual atmosphere most favorable to preaching. What preachers knowing anything of the real work of preaching doubt the veracity of this statement? The spirit of prayer in a congregation creates an atmosphere surcharged with the Spirit of the Highest, removes obstacles, and gives the Word of the Lord right of way. The very attitude of such a congregation constitutes an environment most encouraging and favorable to preaching. It renders preaching an easy task. It enables the Word to run quickly and without friction, helped on by the warmth of souls engaged in prayer.

People in the pew praying for the preachers are like the poles that hold up the wires along which the electric current runs. They are not the power, neither are they the specific agents in making the Word of the Lord effective. But they hold up the wires along which the divine power runs to the hearts of preachers. They give liberty to the preachers, exemption from being restricted, and keep them from straying into non-scriptural areas. They make conditions favorable for the preaching of the Gospel. Preachers, not a few, who know God, have had large experience and are aware of the truth of these statements. Yet how hard they have found it to preach in some places! This was because they had no "door of utterance,"[1] were hampered in their delivery, and had no response whatever to their appeals. On the other hand, at other times thought flowed easily, words came freely, and there was no failure in utterance. The preacher "had liberty," as the old saints used to declare.

The preaching of the Word to a prayerless congregation falls at the very feet of the preacher. It has no traveling force. It stops because the atmosphere is cold, unsympathetic, unfavorable to its running to the hearts of men and women. Nothing is there to help it along. Just as some prayers never go above the head of the one who prays, so the preaching of some preachers goes no farther than the front of the pulpit from which it is delivered. It takes prayer in the pulpit and prayer in the pew to make preaching arresting, life-giving, and soul-saving.

THE WORD OF GOD LINKED TO PRAYER

The Word of God is inseparably linked with prayer. The two are solidly joined, twins from birth, and twins by life. The Apostles found themselves absorbed by the sacred and pressing duty of distributing the alms of the Church, until time was not left for them to pray. They directed that others should be appointed to discharge this task, that they might be the better able to give themselves continually to prayer and to the ministry of the Word.

So it might likewise be said that prayer for the preacher by the church is also inseparably joined to preaching. A praying church is an invaluable help to the faithful preacher. The Word of the Lord runs in such a church, and is glorified in the saving of sinners, in the reclamation of back-sliders, and in the sanctifying of believers. Paul connects the Word of God closely in prayer in writing to Timothy:

> For every creature of God is good, and nothing to be refused, if it be received with thanksgiving: For it is sanctified by the word of God and prayer.[2]

So the Word of the Lord is dependent on prayer for its rapid spread and for its full and most glorious success.

Paul indicates that prayer transforms the ills that come to the preacher: "For I know that this shall turn to my salvation through your prayer, and the supply of the Spirit of Jesus Christ."[3] It was through their prayer that these benefits would come to him. And so it is through the prayer of a church that the pastor will be the beneficiary of large spiritual things.

In the latter part of the epistle to the Hebrews, we have writer's request for prayer for himself addressed to the Hebrew Christians, basing his request on the grave and eternal responsibilities of the office of a preacher:

> Obey them that have the rule over you, and submit yourselves: for they watch for your souls, as they that must give account, that they may do it with joy, and not with grief: for that is unprofitable for you.

> Pray for us: for we trust we have a good conscience, in all things willing to live honestly.[4]

How little the Church understands the fearful responsibility attached to the office and work of the ministry! "For they watch for your souls, as they that must give account." God's appointed sentinels, to warn when danger is near. God's messengers sent to rebuke, reprove, and exhort with all long-suffering. Ordained as shepherds to protect the sheep against devouring wolves. How filled with responsibility is their position! They are to give account to God for their work, and are to face a day of reckoning. How much do such men and women need the prayers of those to whom they minister! Who should be more ready to do this praying than God's people, His own Church, those presumably who are in heart sympathy with the ministers and their all-important work, divine in its origin.

Among the last messages of Jesus to His disciples are those found in the fourteenth, fifteenth, and sixteenth chapters of John's Gospel. In the fourteenth, as well as in the others, are some very specific teachings about prayer, designed for their help and encouragement in their future work. We must never lose sight of the fact that these last discourses of Jesus Christ were given to disciples alone, away from the busy crowds, and seem primarily intended for them in their public ministry. In reality, they were words spoken to preachers, for these eleven men were to be the first preachers of the new dispensation.

With this thought in mind, we are able to see the tremendous importance given to prayer by our Lord, and the high place He gave it in the life-work of preachers, both in this day and in that day.

First our Lord proposes that He will pray for these disciples, that the Father might send them another Comforter, even the Spirit of truth, whom the world could not receive. He preceded this statement by a direct command to them to pray, to pray for anything, with the assurance that they would receive what they asked for.

If, therefore, there was value in their own praying, and it was of great worth that our Lord should intercede for them, then of course it would be worthwhile that the people to whom they would minister should also pray for them. It is no wonder then that the apostle Paul should take the key from our Lord, and several times break out with the urgent exhortation, "Pray for us."[5]

TRUE PRAYING BY LAYPEOPLE

True praying done by the laypeople helps in many ways, but in one particular way. It materially helps the preachers to be brave and true. Read Paul's request to the Ephesians:

> Praying always with all prayer and supplication in the Spirit, and watching thereunto with all perseverance and supplication for all saints; And for me, that utterance may be given unto me, that I may open my mouth boldly, to make known the mystery of the gospel, For which I am an ambassador in bonds: that therein I may speak boldly, as I ought to speak.[6]

How much of the boldness and loyalty of Paul was dependent upon the prayers of the Church, or rather how much he was helped at these two points, we may not know. But unquestionably much aid in preaching the Word must have come to him through the prayers of the Christians at Ephesus, Colossae, and Thessalonica. Aid that he would never have had if these churches had not prayed for him. In like manner, in modern times the gift of ready and effective utterance in the preachers have been bestowed upon them through the prayers of praying churches.

The apostle Paul did not desire to fall short of that most important quality in a preacher of the Gospel, namely, boldness. He was no coward, or time-server, or person-pleaser, but he needed prayer so that he might not, through any kind of timidity, fail to declare the whole truth of God, or through fear of people, declare it in an apologetic, hesitating, way. He desired to remove himself as far as possible from an attitude of this kind. His constant desire and effort was to declare the Gospel with consecrated boldness and with freedom. "That I may open my mouth boldly, to make known the mystery of the Gospel . . . that I may speak boldly, as I ought to speak," seemed to be his great desire, and it would appear that, at times, he was really afraid that he might exhibit cowardice, or be affected by the fear of the face of people.

PREACHERS LIKE PAUL NEEDED TODAY

This is a day that has urgent need of preachers after the mold of the great apostle—preachers of courage, brave, and true, who are not swayed by the fear of people, or reduced to silence or apology by the dread of consequences. And one way to secure them is for the pew to engage in earnest prayer for the preachers.

In Paul's word to the Ephesian elders, given when on his way to Jerusalem, Paul removes himself from the charge of blood-guiltiness, in that he had not failed to declare the whole counsel of God to them. To the Philippian church, also, he says that through their prayers he would prove to be neither ashamed nor afraid.

Nothing, perhaps, can be more detrimental to the advancement of the kingdom of God among sinners than a timid or doubtful statement of revealed truth. The preachers who state only the half of what they believe stand side by side with those who fully declare what they only half believe. No coward can preach the Gospel, and declare the whole counsel of God. To do that, a person must be in the battle-attitude not from passion, but by reason of deep conviction, strong conscience, and full-orbed courage. Faith is in the custody of a gallant heart, while timidity surrenders, always, to a brave spirit. Paul prayed, and prevailed on others to pray that he might be a person of resolute courage, brave enough to do everything but sin. The result of this mutual praying is that history has no finer instance of courage in a minister of Jesus Christ than that displayed in the life of the apostle Paul. He stands in the premier position as a fearless, uncompromising, God-fearing, preacher of the Gospel of his Lord.

God seems to have taken great pains with His prophets of old time to save them from fear while delivering His messages to humanity. He sought in every way to safeguard His messengers from the fear of people, and by means of command, reasoning, and encouragement sought to render them fearless and true to their high calling. One of the besetting temptations of preachers is the "fear" of the face of people. Unfortunately, not a few surrender to this fear, and either remain silent at times when they should be boldly eloquent, or temper with smooth words the stern mandate it is theirs to deliver. "The fear of man bringeth a snare."[7]

With this sore temptation, Satan often besets the preacher of the Word and few are there who have not felt the force of this temptation. It is the duty of ministers of the Gospel to face this temptation to fear the face of people with resolute courage, to steel themselves against it, and, if need be, trample it under foot. To this important end, preachers should be prayed for by their church. They need deliverance from fear, and prayer is the agency whereby it can be driven away, and freedom from the bondage of fear given to their soul.

The battle between Israel and Amalek

In Exodus 17, we have a striking picture of the need preachers have for prayer, and of what a people's prayers can do for them. Israel and Amalek were in battle, and the contest was severe and close. Moses stood on top of the hill with his rod lifted up in his hands, the symbol of power and victory. As long as Moses held up the rod, Israel prevailed, but when he let down his hand with the rod, Amalek prevailed. While the contest was in the balance, Aaron and Hur came to the rescue, and when Moses' hands were heavy, these two men "stayed up his hands . . . until the going down of the sun. And Joshua discomfited Amalek and his people."[8]

By common consent, this incident in the history of ancient Israel has been recognized as a striking illustration of how a people may sustain their preacher by prayer, and of how victory comes when the people pray for their preacher.

GOD ENCOURAGES HIS PEOPLE NOT TO BE AFRAID

Some of the Lord's very best people in Old Testament times had to be encouraged against fear by Almighty God. Moses himself was not free from the fear that harasses and compromises a leader. God told him to go to Pharaoh in these words: "Come now therefore, and I will send thee unto Pharaoh, that thou mayst bring forth my people the children of Israel out of Egypt."[9] But Moses, largely through fear, began to offer objections and excuses for not going, until God became angry with him, and said, finally, that He would send Aaron with Moses to do the talking, as long as Moses insisted that he "was slow of speech and of a slow tongue."[10] But the fact was, Moses was afraid of the face of Pharaoh, and it took God some time to circumvent his fears and nerve him to face the Egyptian monarch and deliver God's message to him.

Joshua, too, the successor of Moses, and a man seemingly courageous, had to be fortified by God against fear, lest he shrink from duty and be reduced to discouragement and timidity. God said to him: "Have not I commanded thee? Be strong and of good courage, neither be thou dismayed: for the LORD thy God is with thee whithersoever thou goest."[11] Jeremiah was a good and true man, yet he was sorely tempted to fear and had to be warned and strengthened lest he prove false to his charge. When God ordained him a prophet unto the nations, Jeremiah began to excuse himself on the ground that he could not speak, being but a child in that regard. So the Lord had to safeguard him from the temptation of fear, that he might not prove faithless: "Thou therefore gird up thy loins, and arise, and speak unto them all that I command thee: be not dismayed at their faces, lest I confound thee before them."[12]

Since these great men of old time were so beset with this temptation, and disposed to shrink from duty, we need not be surprised that preachers of our own day are to be found in similar case. The devil is the same in all ages, and human nature has not undergone any change. How needful, then, that we pray for the leaders of our Israel, especially that they may receive the gift of boldness and speak the Word of God with courage.

This was one reason why Paul insisted so vigorously that the brethren pray for him, so that a door of utterance might be given him, and that he might be delivered from the fear of people, and blessed with holy boldness in preaching the Word.

The challenge and demand of the world in our own day is that Christianity be made practical, that its precepts be expressed in practice and brought down from the realm of the ideal to the levels of everyday life. This can be done only by praying people, who being much in sympathy with their ministers will not cease to bear them up in their prayers before God.

Preachers of the Gospel cannot meet the demands made upon them alone, any more than the vine can bear grapes without branches. The Christians who sit in the pews are to be the fruit-bearing ones. They are to translate the "ideal" of the pulpit into the "real" of daily life and action. But they will not do it, they cannot do it, if are not they devoted to God and much given to prayer. Devotion to God and devotion to prayer are one and the same thing.

Endnotes

1 Colossians 4:3
2 I Timothy 4:4-5
3 Philippians 1:19
4 Hebrews 13:17-18
5 I Thessalonians 5:25; 2 Thessalonians 3:1
6 Ephesians 6:18-20
7 Proverbs 29:25
8 Exodus 17:12-13
9 Exodus 3:10
10 Exodus 4:10
11 Joshua 1:9
12 Jeremiah 1:17

II

Modern Examples of Prayer

"WHEN THE DRAGON-FLY *rends his husk and harnesses himself, in a clean plate of sapphire mail, his is a pilgrimage of one or two sunny days over the fields and pastures wet with dew, yet nothing can exceed the marvelous beauty in which he is decked. No flowers on earth have a richer blue than the pure color of his cuirass. So is it in the high spiritual sphere. The most complete spiritual loveliness may be obtained in the shortest time, and the stripling may die a hundred years old, in character and grace.*" (History of David Brainerd)

God has not confined Himself to Bible days in showing what can be done through prayer. In modern times, also, He is seen to be the same prayer-hearing God as in times past. Even in these latter days, He has not left Himself without witness. Christian biography and Church history, alike, furnish us with many noble examples and striking illustrations of prayer, its necessity, its worth, and its fruits, all tending to the encouragement of the faith of God's saints and all urging them on to more and better praying. God has not confined Himself to Old and New Testament times in employing praying saints as His agents in furthering His cause on earth, and He has placed Himself under obligation to answer their prayers just as much as He did the saints of old. A selection from these praying saints of modern times will show us how they valued prayer, what it meant to them, and what it meant to God.

SAMUEL RUTHERFORD

Take for example, the instance of Samuel Rutherford, the Scottish preacher, exiled to the north of Scotland, forbidden to preach, and banished from his home and pastoral charge. Rutherford lived between 1600 and 1661. He was a member of the Westminster Assembly, Principal of New College, and Rector of St. Andrews' University. He is said to have been one of the most moving and affectionate preachers of his time, or perhaps, in any age of the Church. People said of him, "He is always praying." Concerning his and his wife's praying, one wrote:

He who had heard either pray or speak, might have learned to bemoan his ignorance. Oh, how many times have I been convinced by observing them of the evil of insincerity before God and unsavoriness in discourse!

He so prayed for his people that he himself says, "There I wrestled with the Angel and prevailed."

Rutherford was ordered to appear before Parliament to answer the charge of high treason, although a man of scholarly attainments and rare genius. At times he was depressed and gloomy; especially was this the case when he was first banished and silenced from preaching, for there were many murmurings and charges against him. But his losses and crosses were so sanctified that Christ became more and more to him. Marvelous are the statements of his estimate of Christ. This devoted man of prayer wrote many letters during his exile to preachers, to state officers, to lords temporal and spiritual, to honorable and holy men, to honorable and holy women, all breathing an intense devotion to Christ, and all born of a life of great devotion to prayer.

Ardor and panting after God have been characteristics of great souls in all ages of the Church and Samuel Rutherford was a striking example of this fact. He was a living example of the truth that he who always prays will be enveloped in devotion and joined to Christ in bonds of holy union.

HENRY MARTYN

Then there was Henry Martyn, scholar, saint, missionary, and apostle to India. Martyn was born February 18, 1781, and sailed for India, August 31, 1805. He died at Tokal, Persia, October 16, 1812. Here is part of what he said about himself while a missionary:

What a knowledge of man and acquaintance with the Scriptures, and what communion with God and study of my own heart ought to prepare me for the awful work of a messenger from God on business of the soul.

Said one of this consecrated missionary:

Oh, to be able to emulate his excellencies, his elevation of piety, his diligence, his superiority to the world, his love for souls, his anxiety to improve all occasions to do souls good, his insight into the mystery of Christ, and his heavenly temper! These are the secrets of the wonderful impression he made in India.

It is interesting and profitable to note some of the things that Martyn records in his diary. Here is an example:

The ways of wisdom appear more sweet and reasonable than ever, and the world more insipid and vexatious. The chief thing I mourn over is my want of power, and lack of fervor in secret prayer, especially when attempting to plead for the heathen. Warmth does not increase within me in proportion to my light.

If Henry Martyn, so devoted, ardent and prayerful, lamented his lack of power and want of fervor in prayer, how ought our cold and feeble praying abase us in the very dust? Alas, how rare are such praying saints in the Church of our own day!

Again we quote a record from his diary. He had been quite ill, but had recovered and was filled with thankfulness because it had pleased God to restore him to life and health again.

Not that I have yet recovered my former strength, but I consider myself sufficiently restored to prosecute my journey. My daily prayer is that my late chastisement may have its intended effect, and make me, all the rest of my days, more humble and less self-confident.

Self-confidence has often led me down fearful lengths, and would, without God's gracious interference, prove my endless perdition. I seem to be made to feel this evil of my heart more than any other at this time. In prayer, or when I write or converse on the subject, Christ appears to me my life and my strength; but at other times I am thoughtless and bold, as if I had all life and strength in myself. Such neglects on our part are a diminution of our joys.

Among the last entries in this consecrated missionary's journal we find the following:

I sat in the orchard and thought, with sweet comfort and peace, of my God, in solitude, my Company, my Friend, my Comforter. Oh, when shall time give place to eternity!

Note the words, "in solitude,"—away from the busy haunts of people, in a lonely place, like his Lord, he went out to meditate and pray.

Brief as this summary is, it suffices to show how fully and faithfully Henry Martyn exercised his ministry of prayer. The following may well serve to end our portrayal of him:

> By daily weighing the Scriptures, with prayer, he waxed riper and riper in his ministry. Prayer and the Holy Scriptures were those wells of salvation out of which he drew daily the living water for his thirsty immortal soul. Truly may it be said of him, he prayed always with all prayer and supplication, in the Spirit, and watched thereunto with all perseverance.

DAVID BRAINERD

David Brainerd, the missionary to the North American Indians, is a remarkable example of a praying man of God. Robert Hale speaks thus of him:

> Such invincible patience and self-denial; such profound humility, exquisite prudence, indefatigable industry; such devotedness to God, or rather such absorption of the whole soul in zeal for the divine glory and the salvation of men, is scarcely to be paralleled since the age of the Apostles. Such was the intense ardor of his mind that it seems to have diffused the spirit of a martyr over the common incidents of his life.

Dr. A. J. Gordon speaks thus of Brainerd:

> In passing through Northampton, Mass., I went into the old cemetery, swept off the snow that lay on the top of the slab, and I read these simple words:

> Sacred to the memory of David Brainerd, the faithful and devoted missionary to the Susquehanna, Delaware and Stockbridge Indians of America, who died in this town, October 8th, 1717.

That was all there was on the slab. Now that great man did his greatest work by prayer. He was in the depths of those forests alone, unable to speak the language of the Indians, but he spent whole days literally in prayer. What was he praying for? He knew he could not reach these savages, for he did not understand their language. If he wanted to speak at all, he must find somebody who could vaguely interpret his thought. Therefore he knew that anything he could do must be absolutely dependent upon God. So he spent whole days in praying, simply that the power of the Holy Ghost might come upon him so unmistakably that these people would not be able to stand before him.

What was his answer? Once he preached through a drunken interpreter, a man so intoxicated that he could hardly stand up. This was the best he could do. Yet scores were converted through that sermon. We can account for it only that it was the tremendous power of God behind him.

Now this man prayed in secret in the forest. A little while afterward, William Carey read his life and by its impulse he went to India. Payson read it as a young man, over twenty years old, and he said that he had never been so impressed by anything in his life as by the story of Brainerd. Murray McCheyne read it, and he likewise was impressed by it.

But all I care is simply to enforce this thought, that the hidden life, a life whose days are spent in communion with God, in trying to reach the source of power, is the life that moves the world. Those living such lives may be soon forgotten. There may be no one to speak a eulogy over them when they are dead. The great world may take no account of them. But by and by, the great moving current of their lives will begin to tell, as in the case of this young man, who died at about thirty years of age. The missionary spirit of this nineteenth century is more due to the prayers and consecration of this one man than to any other one.

So I say. And yet that most remarkable thing is that Jonathan Edwards, who watched over him all those months while he was slowly dying of consumption, should also say: "I praise God that it was in His Providence that he should die in my house, that I might hear his prayers, and that I might witness his consecration, and that I might be inspired by his example."

When Jonathan Edwards wrote that great appeal to Christendom to unite in prayer for the conversion of the world, which has been the trumpet call of modern missions, undoubtedly it was inspired by this dying missionary.

To David Brainerd's spirit, John Wesley bore this testimony:

I preached and afterward made a collection for the Indian schools in America. A large sum of money is now collected. But will money convert heathens? Find preachers of David Brainerd's spirit, and nothing can stand before them. But without this, what will gold or silver do? No more than lead or iron.

Some selections from Brainerd's diary will be of value as showing what manner of person he was:

My soul felt a pleasing yet painful concern," he writes, "lest I should spend some moments without God. Oh, may I always live to God! In the evening I was visited by some friends, and spent the time in prayer, and such conversation as tended to edification. It was a comfortable season to my soul. I felt an ardent desire to spend every moment with God. God is unspeakably gracious to me continually. In time past, He has given me inexpressible sweetness in the performance of duty. Frequently my soul has enjoyed much of God, but has been ready to say, "Lord, it is good to be here;" and so indulge sloth while I have lived on the sweetness of my feelings. But of late God has been pleased to keep my soul hungry almost continually, so that I have been filled with a kind of pleasing pain. When I really enjoy God, I feel my desires of Him the more insatiable, and my thirstings after holiness the more unquenchable.

Oh, that I may feel this continual hunger, and not be retarded, but rather animated by every duster from Canaan, to reach forward in the narrow way, for the full enjoyment and possession of the heavenly inheritance! Oh, may I never loiter in my heavenly journey!

It seems as if such an unholy wretch as I never could arrive at that blessedness, to be holy as God is holy. At noon I longed for sanctification and conformity to God. Oh, that is the one thing, the all!

Toward night enjoyed much sweetness in secret prayer, so that my soul longed for an arrival in the heavenly country, the blessed paradise of God.

If inquiry be made as to the secret of David Brainerd's heavenly spirit, his deep consecration and exalted spiritual state, the answer will be found in the last sentence quoted above. He was given to much secret prayer, and was so close to God in his life and spirit that prayer brought forth much sweetness to his inner soul.

We have cited the foregoing cases as illustrative of the great fundamental fact that God's great servants are saints devoted to the ministry of prayer. They are God's agents on earth who serve Him in this way, and who carry on His work by this holy means.

LOUIS HARMS

Louis Harms was born in Hanover, in 1809, and then came a time when he was powerfully convicted of sin. Said he, "I have never known what fear was. But when I came to the knowledge of my sins, I quaked before the wrath of God, so that my limbs trembled." He was mightily converted to God by reading the Bible. Rationalism, a dead orthodoxy, and worldliness, held the multitudes around Hermansburgh, his native town. His father was a Lutheran minister. When his father died, he became his successor.

He began with all the energy of his soul to work for Christ, and to develop a church of a pure, strong type. The fruit was soon evident. There was a quickening on every hand, attendance at public services increased, reverence for the Bible grew, conversation on sacred things revived, and unfaithfulness, worldliness, and dead orthodoxy vanished like a passing cloud. Harms proclaimed a conscious and present Christ, the Comforter, in the full energy of His mission, the revival of apostolic piety and power. The entire neighborhood became regular attendants at church, the Sabbath was restored to its sanctity, and hallowed with strict devotion. Family altars were erected in the homes, and when the noon bell sounded every head was bowed in prayer. In a very short time, the whole aspect of the country was entirely changed. The revival in Hermansburgh was essentially a prayer revival, brought about by prayer and yielding fruits of prayer in a rich and an abundant ingathering.

WILLIAM CARVOSSO

William Carvosso, an old-time Methodist class-leader, was one of the best examples that modern times has afforded of what was probably the religious life of Christians in the apostolic age. He was a prayer-leader, a class-leader, a steward, and a trustee, but never aspired to be a preacher. Yet a preacher he was of the very first quality, and a master in the art and science of soul-saving. He was a singular instance of a person learning the simplest rudiments late in life. He had up to the age of sixty-five years never written a single sentence, yet he wrote letters that would make volumes, and a book that was regarded as a spiritual classic in the great world-wide Methodist Church.

Not a page or a letter, it is believed, was ever written by him on any other subject but Christianity. Here are some of his brief utterances that give us an insight into his religious character. "I want to be more like Jesus." "My soul thirsteth for Thee, O God." "I see nothing will do, O God, but being continually filled with Thy presence and glory."

This was the continual out-crying of his inner soul, and this was the strong inward impulse that moved the outward man. At one time we hear him exclaiming, "Glory to God! This is a morning without a cloud." Cloudless days were native to his sunny Christianity and his gladsome spirit. Continual prayer and turning all conversation toward Christ in every company and in every home, was the inexorable law he followed, until he was gathered home.

On the anniversary of his spiritual birth, he calls the time when he was born again to mind in great joyousness of spirit, and breaks forth: "Blessed be Thy name, O God! The last has been the best of the whole. I may say with Bunyan, 'I have got into that land where the sun shines night and day.' I thank Thee, O my God, for this heaven, this element of love and joy, in which my soul now lives."

Here is a sample of Carvosso's spiritual experiences, of which he had many:

I have sometimes had seasons of remarkable visitation from the presence of the Lord. I well remember one night when in bed being so filled, so over-powered with the glory of God, that had there been a thousand suns shining at noonday, the brightness of that divine glory would have eclipsed the whole. I was constrained to shout aloud for joy. It was the overwhelming power of saving grace. Now it was that I again received the impress of the seal and the earnest of the Spirit in my heart. Beholding as in a glass the glory of the Lord I was changed into the same image from glory to glory by the Spirit of the Lord. Language fails in giving but a faint description of what I there experienced. I can never forget it in time nor to all eternity.

Many years before I was sealed by the Spirit in a somewhat similar manner. While walking out one day, I was drawn to turn aside on the public road, and under the canopy of the skies, I was moved to kneel down to pray. I had not long been praying with God before I was so visited from Him that I was overpowered by the divine glory, and I shouted till I could be heard at a distance. It was a weight of glory that I seemed incapable of bearing in the body, and therefore I cried out, perhaps unwisely, Lord, stay Thy hand. In this glorious baptism these words came to my heart with indescribable power: "I have sealed thee unto the day of redemption."

Oh, I long to be filled more with God! Lord, stir me up more in earnest. I want to be more like Jesus. I see that nothing will do but being continually filled with the divine presence and glory. I know all that Thou hast is mine, but I want to feel a close union. Lord, increase my faith.

Such was William Carvosso—a man whose life was impregnated with the spirit of prayer, who lived on his knees, so to speak, and who belonged to that company of praying saints that has blessed the earth.

JONATHAN EDWARDS

Jonathan Edwards must be placed among the praying saints—one whom God mightily used through the instrumentality of prayer. As in the instance of the great New Englander, purity of heart should be ingrained in the very foundation areas of every person who is a true leader of others and a minister of the Gospel of Christ and a constant practitioner in the holy office of prayer. A sample of the utterances of this mighty man of God is here given in the shape of a resolution that he formed, and wrote down:

Resolved to exercise myself in this all my life long, viz., with the greatest openness to declare my ways to God, and to lay my soul open to God—all my sins, temptations, difficulties, sorrows, fears, hopes, desires, and everything and every circumstance.

We are not surprised, therefore, that the result of such fervid and honest praying was to lead him to record in his diary:

It was my continual strife day and night, and my constant inquiry how I should be more holy, and live more holily. The heaven I desired was a heaven of holiness. I went on with my eager pursuit after more holiness and conformity to Christ.

The character and work of Jonathan Edwards were exemplifications of the great truth that the ministry of prayer is the efficient agency in every truly God-ordered work and life. He himself gives some particulars about his life when a boy. He might well be called the "Isaiah of the Christian dispensation." There was united in him great mental powers, ardent piety, and devotion to study, unequaled save by his devotion to God. Here is what he says about himself:

When a boy I used to pray five times a day in secret, and to spend much time in religious conversation with other boys. I used to meet with them to pray together. So it is God's will through His wonderful grace, that the prayers of His saints should be one great and principal means of carrying on the designs of Christ's kingdom in the world. Pray much for the ministers and the Church of God.

The great powers of Edwards' mind and heart were exercised to procure an agreed union in extraordinary prayer of God's people everywhere. His life, efforts, and character are an exemplification of his statement.

The heaven I desire is a heaven spent with God; an eternity spent in the presence of divine love, and in holy communion with Christ.

At another time he said:

The soul of a true Christian appears like a little white flower in the spring of the year, low and humble on the ground, opening its bosom to receive the pleasant beams of the sun's glory, rejoicing as it were in a calm rapture, diffusing around a sweet fragrance, standing peacefully and lovingly in the midst of other flowers.

Again he writes:

Once as I rode out in the woods for my health, having alighted from my horse in a retired place, as my manner has been to walk for divine contemplation and prayer, I had a view, that for me was extraordinary, of the glory of the Son of God as Mediator between

God and man, and of His wonderful, great, full, pure, and sweet grace and love, and His meek and gentle condescension. This grace that seemed so calm and sweet, appeared also great above the heavens. The person of Christ appeared ineffably excellent with an excellence great enough to swallow up all thought and conception, which continued, as near as I can judge, about an hour. It kept me the greater part of the time in a flood of tears and weeping aloud. I felt an ardency of soul to be, what I know not otherwise how to express, emptied and annihilated, to lie in the dust; to be full of Christ alone, to love Him with my whole heart.

As it was with Jonathan Edwards, so it is with all great intercessors. They come into that holy and elect condition of mind and heart by a thorough self-dedication to God, by periods of God's revelation to them, making distinct marked eras in their spiritual history, eras never to be forgotten. Eras during which faith mounts up with wings as eagles, and gives a new and fuller vision of God, a stronger grasp of faith, a sweeter, clearer vision of all things heavenly and eternal, and a blessed intimacy with and access to God.

12

Modern Examples of Prayer (Continued)

EDWARD BOUNDS DID NOT *merely pray well that he might write well about prayer. He prayed for long years upon subjects to which easygoing Christians rarely give a thought. He prayed for objects which men of less faith are ready to call impossible. Yet from these continental, solitary prayer-vigils, year by year there arose a gift of prayer-teaching equaled by few men. He wrote transcendently about prayer because he was transcendent in its practice.* (C. L. Chilton Jr.)

LADY MAXWELL

Lady Maxwell was contemporary with John Wesley, and a fruit of Methodism in its earlier phases. She was a woman of refinement, culture, and deep piety. Separating herself entirely from the world, she sought and found the deepest Christian experience, and was a woman fully set apart to God. Her life was one of prayer, of complete consecration to God, living to bless others. She was noted for her systematic habits of life, which entered into and controlled her Christianity. Her time was economized and ordered for God. She arose at four o'clock in the morning, and attended preaching at five o'clock. After breakfast she held a family service. Then from eleven to twelve o'clock she observed a season of intercessory prayer. The rest of the day was given to reading, visiting, and acts of benevolence.

Her evenings were spent in reading. At night before retiring, Christian services were held for the family and sometimes in praising God for His mercies.

Rarely has God been served with more intelligence, or out of a richer experience, a nobler ardor, a richer nobility of soul. Strongly, spiritually, and ardently attached to Wesley's doctrine of entire dedication, she sought it with persistency, and a never flagging zeal. She obtained it by faith and prayer, and illustrated it in a life as holy and as perfect as is given mortals to reach. If today this great feature of Wesley's teaching had models and teachers possessed of the profound spiritual understanding and experience as had Fletcher of Madeley and Lady Maxwell of Edinburgh, it would not have been so misunderstood, but would have commended itself to the good and pure everywhere by holy lives, if not by its verbiage.

Lady Maxwell's diary yields some rich counsel for secret prayer, holy experience, and consecrated living. One of the entries runs as follows:

> Of late I feel painfully convinced that I do not pray enough. Lord, give me the spirit of prayer and of supplication. Oh, what a cause of thankfulness is it that we have a gracious God to whom to go on all occasions! Use and enjoy this privilege and you can never be miserable. Who gives thanks for this royal privilege? It puts God in everything, His wisdom, power, control, and safety. Oh, what an unspeakable privilege is prayer! Let us give thanks for it, I do not prove all the power of prayer that I wish.

Thus we see that the remedy for non-praying is praying. The cure for little praying is more praying. Praying can procure all things necessary for our good.

With this excellent woman praying embraced all things and included everything. To one of her most intimate friends she writes:

> I wish I could provide you with a proper maid, but it is a difficult matter. You have my prayers for it, and if I hear of one I will let you know.

So small a matter as the desire for a housemaid for a friend was with her an event not too small to take to God in prayer.

In the same letter, she tells her friend that if she wants "more faith. Cry mightily for it, and stir up the gift of God that is in you."

Whether the need was a small secular thing as a servant, or a great spiritual grace, prayer was the means to attain that end and supply that want. "There is nothing," she writes to a dear correspondent, "so hurtful to the nervous system as anxiety. It preys upon the vitals and weakens the whole frame, and what is more than all, it grieves the Holy Spirit." Her remedy, again, for a common evil, was prayer.

How prayer unburdens us of care by bringing God in to relieve and possess and hold?

Paul said:

Be careful for nothing; but in everything by prayer and supplication with thanksgiving let your requests he made known unto God. And the peace of God, which passeth all understanding, shall keep your hearts and minds through Christ Jesus.[1]

The figure is that of a beleaguered and distressed garrison, unable to protect the fort from the enemies that assault it, into which strong reinforcements are poured. Into the heart that is oppressed, distracted, and discouraged, true prayer brings God, who holds it in perfect peace and in perfect safety. This Lady Maxwell fully understood theoretically, but which was better, experimentally.

Christ Jesus is the only cure for undue care and anxiety of soul, and we secure God, His presence and His peace by prayer. Undue care is so natural and so strong, that none but God can eject it. It takes God, the presence and personality of God Himself, to oust the undue care and to enthrone quietness and peace. When Christ comes in with His peace, all tormenting fears are gone, trepidation and harrowing anxieties capitulate to the reign of peace, and all disturbing elements depart. Anxious thought and undue care assault the soul, and feebleness, faintness, and cowardice are within. Prayer reinforces with God's peace, and the heart is kept by Him. "Thou wilt keep him in perfect peace, whose mind is stayed on Thee."[2] All now is safety, quietness and assurance. "The work of righteousness shall be peace; and the effect of righteousness quietness and assurance forever."[3]

But to ensure this great peace, prayer must pass into strenuous, insistent, personal supplication, and thanksgiving must bloom into full flower. Our exposed condition of heart must be brought to the knowledge of God, by prayer and supplication, with thanksgiving. The peace of God will keep the heart and thoughts, fixed and fearless. Peace, deep, exhaustless, wide, flowing like a river, will come in.

Referring again to Lady Maxwell, we hear her saying:

God is daily teaching me more simplicity of spirit, and makes me willing to receive all as His unmerited gift, and to call on Him for everything I need, as I need it, and He supplies my wants according to existing needs. But I have certainly felt more of it this last eighteen months than in former periods. I wish to pray without ceasing. I see the necessity of praying always, and not fainting.

Again we hear her declaring: "I wish to be much in prayer. I greatly need it. The prayer of faith shuts or opens heaven. Come, Lord, and turn my captivity." If we felt the need of prayer as this saintly woman did, we could bear her company in her saintly ascension. Prayer truly "shuts or opens heaven." Oh, for a quality of faith that would test to the uttermost the power of prayer!

Lady Maxwell utters a great truth when she says:

When God is at work either among a people, or in the heart of an individual, the adversary of souls is peculiarly at work also. A belief of the former should prevent discouragement, and a fear of the latter should stir us up to much prayer. Oh, the power of faithful prayer! I live by prayer! May you prove its sovereign efficacy in every difficult case.

We find a record among Lady Maxwell's writings that shows us that in prayer and meditation she obtained enlarged views of the full salvation of God, and what is thus discovered, faith goes out after, and according to its strength are its returns.

I daily feel the need of the precious blood of sprinkling," she says, "and dwell continually under its influence, and most sensibly feel its sovereign efficacy. It is by momentary faith in this blood alone that I am saved from sin. Prayer is my chief employ.

If this last statement, "prayer, the chief employ" had always been true of God's people, this world would have been by this time quite another world, and God's glory, instead of being dim, and shadowy, and only in spots, would now shine with universal and unrivaled effulgence and power.

Here is another record of her ardent and faithful praying: "Lately, I have been favored with a more ardent spirit of praying than almost ever formerly."

We need to study these words—"favored with a more ardent spirit of praying"—for they are pregnant words. The spirit of prayer, the ardent spirit of prayer and its increase, and the more ardent spirit of prayer—all these are of God. They are given in answer to prayer. The spirit of prayer and the more ardent spirit are the result of ardent, persistent, secret prayer.

At another time, Lady Maxwell declared that secret prayer was the means whereby she derived the greatest spiritual benefit.

I do indeed prove it to be an especial privilege. I could not live without it, though I do not always find comfort in it. I still ardently desire an enlarged sphere of usefulness, and find it comfortable to embrace the opportunities afforded me.

An "enlarged sphere of usefulness" is certainly a proper theme of intense prayer, but that prayer must ever be accompanied with an improvement of the opportunities afforded by the present.

Many page might be filled with extracts from Lady Maxwell's diary as to the vital importance of, and the nature of the ministry of prayer, but we must forbear. For many years she was in ardent supplication for an enlargement of her sphere of usefulness, but all these years of ardent praying may be condensed into one statement:

> My whole soul has been thirsting after a larger sphere of action, agreeably to the promises of a faithful God. For these few last weeks I have been led to plead earnestly for more holiness. Lord, give me both, that I may praise Thee.

These two things, for which this godly woman prayed, must go together. They are one, and not to be separated. The desire for a larger field of work without the accompanying desire for an increase of consecration, is perilous, and may be supremely selfish, the offspring of spiritual pride.

JOHN FLETCHER

John Fletcher, also a contemporary of John Wesley, was intimately associated with the founder of Methodism. He was a scholar of courtesy and refinement, a strong, original thinker, eloquent in simplicity and truth. That which qualified him as a spiritual leader was his exceedingly great faith in God, his nearness to God, and his perfect assurance of dear unquestioned relationship to his Lord. Fletcher had profound convictions concerning the truth of God, a deep and perpetual communion with his Lord and Savior, and was profound and humble in his knowledge of God and Christian experience. He was a man of deep spiritual insight into the things of God, and his thorough earnestness, his truth, and his consecration, marked him as a man of God, well equipped by all these things for a leader in Israel.

Unceasing prayer was the sign and secret of Fletcher's sainthood, its power and influence. His whole life was one of prayer. So intently was his mind fixed on God, that he sometimes said, "I would not rise from my seat without lifting up my heart to God." A friend relates the fact that whenever they met, his first salute was, "Do I meet you praying?" If they were talking on theology, in the midst of it he would break off abruptly and say, "Where are our hearts now?" If the misconduct of any person who was absent was mentioned, he would say, "Let us pray for him."

The very walls of his room—so it was said—were stained by the breath of his prayers. Spiritually, Madeley was a dreary, desolate, desert when he went to live there, but it was so revolutionized by his prayers that it bloomed and blossomed like the garden of the Lord. A friend of his thus writes of Fletcher:

> Many of us have at times gone with him aside, and there we would continue for two or three hours, wrestling like Jacob for the blessing, praying one after another. And I have seen him on these occasions so filled with the love of God that he could contain no

more, but would cry out, "O my God, withhold Thy hand or the vessel will burst!" His whole life was a life of prayer.

JOHN FOSTER

John Foster, a man of exalted piety and deep devotion to God, while on his dying bed, thus spoke concerning prayer when he was about to depart this life:

Pray without ceasing has been the sentence repeating itself in my silent thoughts, and I am sure that it will be, it must be, my practice till the last conscious hour of my life. O why was it not my practice throughout that long, indolent, inanimate half century past! I often think mournfully of the difference it would have made in me. Now there remains so little time for a mere genuine, effective spiritual life.

MARTIN LUTHER

The Reformation of the fifteenth century owes its origin to prayer. In all his lifework, begun, continued, and ended, Martin Luther was instant in prayer. The secret of his extraordinary activity is found in this statement: "I have so much work to do that I cannot get along without giving three hours daily of my best time to prayer." Another of his sayings was, "It takes meditation and prayer to make a divine," while his every day motto was, "He that has prayed well, has studied well."

At another time he thus confessed his lack: "I was short and superficial in prayer this morning," he says. How often is this the case with us! Let it be remembered that the source of decline in religion and the proof of decline in a Christian life is found just here, in "short and superficial praying." Such praying betokens and secures strangeness with God.

WILLIAM WILBERFORCE

William Wilberforce once said of himself: "I have been keeping too late hours, and hence have had but a hurried half hour to myself. I am lean and cold and hard. I had better allow more time, say two hours, or an hour-and-a-half, daily to religious exercises."

He must be very skilled and accustomed to long praying whose short prayers are not superficial. Short prayers make shallow lives. Longer praying would work like magic in many a decayed spiritual life. A holy life would not be so difficult and rare a thing if our praying was not so brief, cold and superficial.

GEORGE MÜLLER

George Müller, that remarkable man of such simple yet strong faith in God, a man of prayer and Bible reading, founder and promoter of the noted orphanage in England, which cared for hundreds of orphan children, conducted the institution solely by faith and prayer. He never asked anyone for anything, but simply trusted in the Providence of God, and it is a notorious fact that never did the inmates of the home lack any good thing. From his paper he always excluded money matters, and financial difficulties found no place in it. Nor would he mention the sums that had been given him, or the names of those who made contributions. He never spoke of his needs to others or asked a donation. The story of his life and the history of this orphanage read like a chapter from the Scriptures.

The secret of his success was found in this simple statement made by him: "I went to my God and prayed diligently, and received what I needed." That was the simple course that he pursued. There was nothing he insisted on with greater earnestness than that, be the expenses what they might be, let them increase ever so suddenly, he must not beg for anything. There was nothing in which he took more delight and showed more earnestness in telling than that he had prayed for every want that ever came to him in his great work. His was a work of continuous and most persistent praying, and he always confidently claimed that God had guided him throughout it all. A stronger proof of a divine providence, and of the power of simple faith and of answered prayer, cannot be found in Church history or Christian biography.

JOHN WESLEY

In writing to a friend at one time. John Wesley helps, urges and prays, as we will see from the following from his own pen:

Have you received a gleam of light from above, a spark of faith? If you have, let it not go! Hold fast by His grace that earnest of your inheritance. Come just as you are, and come boldly to the throne of grace. You need not delay. Even now the bowels of Jesus yearn over you. What have you to do with tomorrow? I love you today. And how much more does He love you?

> He pities still His wandering sheep,
> And longs to bring you to His fold.

Today hear His voice, the voice of Him that speaks as never man spake.

MADAME JEANNE GUYON

The seekings of Madame Guyon[4] after God were sincere, and her yearnings were strong and earnest. She applied to a devout Franciscan friar for advice and comfort. She stated her convictions and told him of her long and fruitless seeking. After she had finished speaking to him, the friar remained silent for some time, in inward meditation and prayer. Then he said to her:

["

> Your efforts have been unsuccessful, because you have sought without what you can only find within. Accustom yourself to seek God in your heart, and you will not fail to find Him.

CHARLES G. FINNEY

Charles G. Finney said:

> When God has specially promised the thing, we are bound to believe we shall receive it when we pray for it. You have no right to put in an "if," and say, "Lord, if it be Thy will, give me Thy Holy Spirit." This is to insult God. To put an "if" in God's promise when God has put none there, is tantamount to charging God with being insincere. It is like saying, "O God, if Thou art in earnest in making these promises, grant us the blessing we pray for."

ADONIRAM JUDSON

We may fittingly conclude this chapter by quoting a word of Adoniram Judson's, the noted missionary to Burma. Speaking of the prevailing power of prayer he said:

> "Nothing is impossible," said one of the seven sages of Greece, "to industry." Let us change the word, "industry," to "persevering prayer," and the motto will be more Christian and more worthy of universal adoption. God loves importunate prayer so much that He will not give us much blessing without it. God says, "Behold I will do a new thing; now it shall spring forth; shall ye not know it? I will even make a way in the wilderness and rivers in the desert. This people have I formed for myself; they shall shew forth my praise."

Endnotes

1 Philippians 4:6-7
2 Isaiah 26:3
3 Isaiah 32:17
4 For further information about Madame Guyon and her teachings on prayer, see *Madame Jeanne Guyon*, by Jeanne Guyon, ©2001 by Bridge-Logos Publishers.

BOOK 6

THE PURPOSE OF PRAYER

I

The Power of Prayer

MY CREED LEADS ME TO *think that prayer is efficacious, and surely a day's asking God to overrule all events for good is not lost. Still there is a great feeling that when a man is praying he is doing nothing, and this feeling makes us give undue importance to work, sometimes even to the hurrying over or even to the neglect of prayer.*

Do not we rest in our day too much on the arm of flesh? Cannot the same wonders be done now as of old? Do not the eyes Of the Lord run to and fro throughout the whole earth still to show Himself strong on behalf of those who put their trust in Him? Oh that God would give me more practical faith in Him! Where is now the Lord God of Elijah? He is waiting for Elijah to call on Him. (James Gilmour of Mongolia)

The more praying there is in the world the better the world will be, the mightier the forces against evil everywhere. Prayer, in one phase of its operation, is a disinfectant and a preventive. It purifies the air, destroys the contagion of evil. Prayer is no fitful, short-lived, thing. It is no voice crying unheard and unheeded in the silence. It is a voice that goes into God's ear, and it lives as long as God's ear is open to holy pleas, and as long as His heart is alive to holy things.

God shapes the world by prayer. Prayers are deathless. The lips that uttered them may be closed in death, the heart that felt them may have ceased to beat, but the prayers live before God. God's heart is set on them, and prayers outlive the lives of those who uttered them. They outlive a generation, outlive an age, outlive a world.

That person is the most immortal who has done the most and the best praying. They are God's heroes, God's saints, God's servants, God's vicegerents. A person can pray better because of the prayers of the past. A person can live holier because of the prayers of the past. The person of many and acceptable prayers has done the truest and greatest service to the incoming generation. The prayers of God's saints strengthen the unborn generation against the desolating waves of sin and evil. Woe to the generation of sons and daughters who find their censers empty of the rich incense of prayer. Those whose fathers and mothers have been too busy or too unbelieving to pray. Because of it, their unhappy inheritance may well be perils inexpressible and consequences untold. Fortunate are those whose fathers and mothers have left them a wealthy inheritance of prayer.

The prayers of God's saints are the capital stock in heaven by which Christ carries on His great work upon earth. The great throes and mighty convulsions on earth are the results of these prayers. Earth is changed and revolutionized, angels move on more powerful and rapid wings, and God's policy is shaped as the prayers are more numerous and efficient.

It is true that the mightiest successes that come to God's cause are created and carried on by prayer. God's day of power—the angelic days of activity and power—are when God's Church comes into its mightiest inheritance of mightiest faith and mightiest prayer. God's conquering days are when the saints have given themselves to the mightiest prayer. When God's house on earth is a house of prayer, then God's house in heaven is busy and all powerful in its plans and movements. It is then that His earthly armies are clothed with the triumphs and spoils of victory and His enemies defeated on every hand.

God conditions the very life and success of His cause on prayer. The condition was put in the very existence of God's cause in this world. "Ask of Me"[1] is the one condition God puts in the advance and triumph of His cause.

THE ADVANCEMENT OF GOD'S CAUSE

Christians are to pray—to pray for the advance of God's cause. Prayer puts God in full force in the world. To a prayerful Christian, God is present in realized force. To a prayerful Church, God is present in glorious power. The second Psalm is the divine description of the establishment of God's cause through Jesus Christ. All inferior dispensations have merged in the enthronement of Jesus Christ. God declares the enthronement of His Son. The nations are incensed with bitter hatred against His cause. God is described as laughing at their enfeebled hate. "He that sitteth in the heavens shall laugh: the Lord shall have them in derision."[2] "Yet have I set my king upon my holy hill of Zion."[3] The decree has passed immutable and eternal.

I will declare the decree: the Lord hath said unto me, Thou art my Son; this day have I begotten thee. Ask of me, and I shall give thee the heathen for thine inheritance, and the uttermost parts of the earth for thy possession. Thou shalt break them with a rod of iron; thou shalt dash them in pieces like a potter's vessel.[4]

ASK OF ME

Ask of Me is the condition—a praying people willing and obedient. "Prayer . . . shall be made for Him continually; and daily shall He be praised."[5] Under this universal and simple promise men and women of old laid themselves out for God. They prayed and God answered their prayers, and the cause of God was kept alive in the world by the flame of their praying.

Prayer became a settled and only condition to move His Son's Kingdom. "Ask, and it shall be given you; seek, and ye shall find; knock, and it shall be opened unto you."[6] The strongest one in Christ's kingdom is the person who is the best knocker. The secret of success in Christ's Kingdom is the ability to pray. The one who can wield the power of prayer is the strong one, the holy one in Christ's Kingdom. The most important lesson we can learn is how to pray.

Prayer is the keynote of the most sanctified life, of the holiest ministry. They do the most for God who are the highest skilled in prayer. Jesus Christ exercised His ministry in this way.

BROTHER LAWRENCE

That we ought to give ourselves to God with regard to things both temporal and spiritual, and seek our satisfaction only in the fulfilling His will, whether He lead us by suffering, or by consolation, for all would be equal to a soul truly resigned. Prayer is nothing else but a sense of God's presence. (Brother Lawrence)[7]

PHILLIP HENRY

Be sure you look to your secret duty; keep that up whatever you do. The soul cannot prosper in the neglect of it. Apostasy generally begins at the closet door. Be much in secret fellowship with God. It is secret trading that enriches the Christian.

Pray alone. Let prayer be the key of the morning and the bolt at night. The best way to fight against sin is to fight it on our knees. (Phillip Henry)

ROBERT HALL

The prayer of faith is the only power in the universe to which the Great Jehovah yields. Prayer is the sovereign remedy. (Robert Hall)

COLERIDGE

An hour of solitude passed in sincere and earnest prayer, or the conflict with and conquest over a single passion or subtle bosom sin will teach us more of thought, will more effectually awaken the faculty and form the habit of reflection than a year's study in the schools without them. (Coleridge)

RICHARD CECIL

A man may pray night and day and deceive himself, but no man can be assured of his sincerity who does not pray. Prayer is faith passing into act. A union of the will and intellect realizing in an intellectual act. It is the whole man that prays. Less than this is wishing or lip work, a sham or a mummery.

If God should restore me again to health I have determined to study nothing but the Bible. Literature is inimical to spirituality if it be not kept under with a firm hand. (Richard Cecil)

Endnotes

1 Psalm 2:8a
2 Psalm 2:4
3 Psalm 2:6
4 Psalm 2:7-9
5 Psalm 72:15b
6 Matthew 7:7
7 For more by Brother Lawrence, see *The Practice of the Presence of God*, ©1999 published by Bridge-Logos Publishers.

2

Prayer Moves God's Hand

OUR SANCTIFICATION DOES NOT *depend upon changing our works, but in doing that for God's sake which we commonly do for our own. The time of business does not with me differ from the time of prayer. Prayer is nothing else but a sense of the presence of God.* (Brother Lawrence)[1]

Let me burn out for God. After all, whatever God may appoint prayer is the great thing. Oh that I may be a man of prayer. (Henry Martyn)

The possibilities and necessity of prayer, its power and results are manifested in stopping and changing the purposes of God, and in relieving the stroke of His power. Abimelech was smitten by God:

So Abraham prayed unto God: and God healed Abimelech, and his wife, and his maidservants; and they bare children. For the Lord had fast closed up all the wombs of the house of Abimelech, because of Sarah Abraham's wife.[2]

JOB
Job's miserable, mistaken, comforters had so deported themselves in their controversy with Job that God's wrath was kindled against them. "My servant Job shall pray for you," said God, "for him will I accept. . . . And the Lord turned the captivity of Job when he prayed for his friends."[3]

JONAH
Jonah was in dire condition when "the Lord sent out a great wind into the sea, and there was a mighty tempest."[4] When lots were cast by those

aboard ship, "the lot fell upon Jonah."[5] He was cast overboard into the Sea, but "the LORD had prepared a great fish to swallow up Jonah . . . Then Jonah prayed unto the LORD his God out of the fish's belly . . . and the Lord spake unto the fish, and it vomited out Jonah upon the dry land."[6] When the disobedient prophet lifted up his voice in prayer God heard and sent deliverance.

PHARAOH

Pharaoh was a firm believer in the possibilities of prayer, and its ability to relieve. When staggering under the woeful curses of God, he pleaded with Moses to intercede for him. "Intreat the Lord for me,"[7] was his pathetic appeal four different times when the plagues were scourging Egypt. Four times these urgent appeals were made to Moses, and four times prayer lifted the dread curse from the hard king and his doomed land.

MOSES

The blasphemy and idolatry of Israel in making the golden calf and declaring their devotions to it were a fearful crime. The anger of God waxed hot, and He declared that He would destroy the offending people. The Lord was very angry with Aaron also, and to Moses He said, "Let Me alone, that I may destroy them."[8] But Moses prayed, and kept on praying. He prayed day and night for forty days. He told the Israelites about his prayer struggle on their behalf.

And I fell down before the Lord, as at the first, forty days and forty nights: I did neither eat bread, nor drink water, because of all your sins which ye sinned, in doing wickedly in the sight of the Lord, to provoke him to anger. For I was afraid of the anger and hot displeasure, wherewith the Lord was wroth against you to destroy you. But the Lord hearkened unto me at that time also. And the Lord was very angry with Aaron to have destroyed him: and I prayed for Aaron also the same time.[9]

NINEVEH

"Yet forty days, and Nineveh shall be overthrown." It was the purpose of God to destroy that great and wicked city. But the people of Nineveh prayed, covered with sackcloth. Sitting in ashes she cried "mightily to God," and "And God saw their works, that they turned from their evil way; and God repented of the evil, that he had said that he would do unto them; and he did it not."[10]

HEZEKIAH

The message of God to Hezekiah was: "Set thine house in order: for thou shalt die, and not live."[11] Hezekiah turned his face toward the wall, and prayed to the Lord, and said:

Then Hezekiah turned his face toward the wall, and prayed unto the Lord, And said, Remember now, O Lord, I beseech thee, how I have walked before thee in truth and with a perfect heart, and have done that which is good in thy sight. And Hezekiah wept sore.

Then came the word of the Lord to Isaiah, saying, Go, and say to Hezekiah, Thus saith the Lord, the God of David thy father, I have heard thy prayer, I have seen thy tears: behold, I will add unto thy days fifteen years.[12]

These men knew how to pray and how to prevail in prayer. Their faith in prayer was no passing attitude that changed with the wind or with their own feelings and circumstances. It was a fact that God heard and answered, that His ear was ever open to the cry of His children, and that the power to do what was asked of Him was commensurate with His willingness. Thus the Old Testament men and women, strong in faith and in prayer . . .

. . . subdued kingdoms, wrought righteousness, obtained promises, stopped the mouths of lions, Quenched the violence of fire, escaped the edge of the sword, out of weakness were made strong, waxed valiant in fight, turned to flight the armies of the aliens.[13]

Everything then, as now, was possible to the men and women who knew how to pray. Prayer, indeed, opened a limitless storehouse, and God's hand withheld nothing. Prayer introduced those who practiced it into a world of privilege, and brought the strength and wealth of heaven down to the aid of finite human beings. What rich and wonderful power belonged to those who had learned the secret of victorious approach to God! With Moses it saved a nation. With Ezra it saved a church.

PRAYER SLACKENED

And yet, strange as it seems when we contemplate the wonders of which God's people had been witness, there came a slackness in prayer. The mighty hold upon God that had so often struck awe and terror into the hearts of their enemies, lost its grip. The people, backslidden and apostate, had gone off from their praying—if the bulk of them had ever truly prayed. The Pharisee's cold and lifeless praying was substituted for any genuine approach to God, and because of that formal method of praying the whole worship became a parody of its real purpose. A glorious dispensation, and gloriously executed by Moses, by Ezra, by Daniel and Elijah, by Hannah and Samuel. But the circle seems limited and short-lived. The praying ones were few and far between. They had no survivors, none to imitate their devotion to God, none to preserve the roll of the elect.

In vain had the decree established the divine order, the divine call—*Ask of Me.* From the earnest and fruitful crying to God they turned their faces to pagan gods, and cried in vain for the answers that could never come. And so they sank into that godless and pitiful state that has lost its object in life when the link with the Eternal has been broken. Their favored dispensation of prayer was forgotten—they knew not how to pray.

THE POWER OF PRAYER

What a contrast to the achievements that brighten up other pages of holy Scripture. The power working through Elijah and Elisha in answer to prayer reached down even to the very grave. In each case, a child was raised from the dead, and the powers of famine were broken. "The effectual fervent prayer of a righteous man availeth much."[14] Elijah was a man of passions like us. He prayed fervently that it might not rain, and it rained not on the earth for three years and six months. And he prayed again, and the heaven gave rain, and the earth brought forth her fruit. Jonah prayed while imprisoned in the great fish, and he came to dry land, saved from storm and sea and monsters of the deep by the mighty energy of his praying.

How wide the gracious provision of the grace of praying as administered in that marvelous dispensation They prayed wondrously. Why could not their praying save the dispensation from decay and death? Was it not because they lost the fire without which all praying degenerates into a lifeless form? It takes effort and toil and care to prepare the incense. Prayer is no laggard's work. When all the rich, spiced, graces from the body of prayer have by labor and beating been blended and refined and intermixed, the fire is needed to unloose the incense and make its fragrance rise to the throne of God. The fire that consumes creates the spirit and life of the incense. Without fire, prayer has no spirit. It is like dead spices, full of corruption and worms.

The casual, intermittent, prayer is never bathed in this divine fire. For the person who thus prays is lacking in the earnestness that lays hold of God, determined not to let Him go until the blessing comes. "Pray without ceasing,"[15] counseled the great apostle. That is the habit that drives prayer right into the mortar that holds the building stones together.

A. J. GORDON

"You can do more than pray after you have prayed," said the godly Dr. A. J. Gordon, "but you cannot do more than pray until you have prayed." The story of every great Christian achievement is the history of answered prayer.

ALEXANDER WHYTE

Alexander Whyte wrote:

The greatest and the best talent that God gives to any man or woman in this world is the talent of prayer. And the best usury that any man or woman brings back to God when He comes to reckon with them at the end of this world is a life of prayer. And those servants best put their Lord's money 'to the exchangers' who rise early and sit late, as long as they are in this world, ever finding out and ever following after better and better methods of prayer, and ever forming more secret, more steadfast, and more spiritually fruitful habits of prayer, till they literally 'pray without ceasing,' and till they continually strike out into new enterprises in prayer, and new achievements, and new enrichments.

MARTIN LUTHER

When asked what his plans for the following day were, Martin Luther answered: "Work, work, from early until late. In fact, I have so much to do that I shall spend the first three hours in prayer."

CROMWELL

Cromwell, too, believed in being much upon his knees. Looking on one occasion at the statues of famous men, he turned to a friend and said, "Make mine kneeling, for thus I came to glory."

It is only when the whole heart is gripped with the passion of prayer that the life-giving fire descends, for none but the earnest saint gets access to the ear of God.

Endnotes

1 See *The Practice of the Presence of God* by Brother Lawrence, ©1999 by Bridge-Logos Publishers.
2 Genesis 20:17-18
3 Job 42:8, 10
4 Jonah 1:4
5 Jonah 1:7
6 Jonah 1:17-2:2, 10
7 Exodus 8:8, 28; 9:28; 10:17
8 Deuteronomy 9:14
9 Deuteronomy 9:18-20
10 Jonah 3:10
11 Isaiah 38:1b
12 Isaiah 38:2-5
13 Hebrews 11:33-34
14 James 5:16
15 1 Thessalonians 5:17

3

More and Better Praying

WHEN THOU FEELEST THYSELF *most indisposed to prayer yield not to it, but strive and endeavour to pray even when thou thinkest thou canst not pray.* (Hildersam)

It was among the Parthians the custom that none was to give their children any meal in the morning before they saw the sweat on their faces, and you shall find this to be God's usual course not to give His children the taste of His delights till they begin to sweat in seeking after them. (Richard Baxter)

Of all the duties enjoined by Christianity none is more essential and yet more neglected than prayer. Most people consider the exercise a fatiguing ceremony, which they are justified in abridging as much as possible. Even those whose profession or fears lead them to pray, pray with such languor and wanderings of mind that their prayers, far from drawing down blessings, only increase their condemnation. (Fénelon)

More and better praying is the secret of the whole matter. More time for prayer, more desire and preparation to meet God, to commune with God through Christ—this has the whole of the matter in it. Our manner and matter of praying ill become us. The attitude and relationship of God and the Son are the eternal relationship of Father and Son, of asking and giving—the Son always asking, the Father always giving:

Ask of me, and I shall give thee the heathen for thine inheritance, and the uttermost parts of the earth for thy possession. Thou shalt break them with a rod of iron; thou shalt dash them in pieces like a potter's vessel.[1]

Jesus is to be always praying through His people. "For Mine house shall be called a house of prayer for all people."[2] We must prepare ourselves to pray; to be like Christ, to pray like Christ.

The access of Christians in prayer to God opens everything, and makes their impoverishment their wealth. All things are theirs through prayer. The wealth and the glory—all things are Christ's. As the light grows brighter and prophets take in the nature of the restoration, the divine record seems to be enlarged.

Thus saith the Lord, the Holy One of Israel, and his Maker, Ask me of things to come concerning my sons, and concerning the work of my hands command ye me. I have made the earth, and created man upon it: I, even my hands, have stretched out the heavens, and all their host have I commanded.[3]

CHRISTIAN AUTHORITY AND POWER IN PRAYER

To Christians it is given to pray to God with all this authority and power in the demands of God's earthly kingdom. Heaven, with all it has, is under tribute to carry out the ultimate, final, and glorious purposes of God. Why then is the time so long in carrying out these wise benedictions for humanity? Why then does sin so long reign? Why are the oath-bound covenant promises so long in coming to their gracious end? Sin reigns, Satan reigns, sighing marks the lives of many—all tears are fresh and full.

Why is all this so? Because we have not prayed to bring the evil to an end, we have not prayed as we must pray, and we have not met the conditions of prayer.

ASK OF ME

Ask of Me. Ask of God. We have not rested on prayer. We have not made prayer the sole condition. There has been violation of the primary condition of prayer. We have not prayed correctly. We have not prayed at all. God is willing to give, but we are slow to ask. The Son, through His saints, is ever praying and God the Father is ever answering.

Ask of Me. In the invitation is conveyed the assurance of answer; the shout of victory is there and may be heard by the listening ear. The Father holds the authority and power in His hands. How easy is the condition, and yet how long we are in fulfilling the conditions! Nations are in bondage, and the uttermost parts of the earth are still unpossessed. The earth groans. The world is still in bondage. Satan and evil hold sway.

The Father holds Himself in the attitude of Giver. *Ask Of Me*, and that petition to God the Father empowers all agencies, inspires all movements. The Gospel is divinely inspired. Back of all its inspirations is prayer. *Ask of Me* lies back of all movements. Standing as the endowment of the enthroned Christ is the oath-bound covenant of the Father. "Ask of me, and I shall give thee the heathen for thine inheritance, and the uttermost parts of the earth for thy possession."[4]

> And he shall live, and to him shall be given of the gold of Sheba: prayer also shall be made for him continually; and daily shall he be praised.[5]

The prayers of holy men and women are always streaming up to God as fragrant as the richest incense. And God in many ways is speaking to us, declaring His wealth and our impoverishment. "I am the Maker of all things; the wealth and glory are Mine. Command ye Me."[6]

We can do all things by God's aid, and can have the whole of His aid by asking. The Gospel, in its success and power, depends on our ability to pray. The dispensations of God depend on humanity's ability to pray. We can have all that God has. Command ye Me. This is no figment of the imagination, no idle dream, no vain fancy. The life of the Church is the highest life. Its office is to pray. Its prayer life is the highest life, the most fragrant, the most conspicuous.

The book of Revelation says nothing about prayer as a great duty, a hallowed service, but much about prayer in its aggregated force and energies. It is the prayer force ever living and ever praying. It is all saints' prayers going out as a mighty, living energy. And when the lips that uttered the words are stilled and sealed in death, the living church has an energy of faith to inherit the forces of all the past praying and make it deathless.

JOHN FOSTER

The statement by the Baptist philosopher, John Foster, contains the purest philosophy and the simple truth of God, for God has no force and demands no conditions but prayer:

> More and better praying will bring the surest and readiest triumph to God's cause. Feeble, formal, listless praying brings decay and death. The Church has its sheet-anchor in the closet; its magazine stores are there.

> I am convinced that every man who amidst his serious projects is apprized of his dependence upon God as completely as that dependence is a fact, will be impelled to pray and anxious to induce his serious friends to pray almost every hour. He will not without it promise himself any noble success any more than a mariner

would expect to reach a distant coast by having his sails spread in a stagnation of air.

I have intimated my fear that it is visionary to expect an unusual success in the human administration of religion unless there are unusual omens: now a most emphatic spirit of prayer would be such an omen; and the individual who should determine to try its last possible efficacy might probably find himself becoming a much more prevailing agent in his little sphere. And if the whole, or the greater number of the disciples of Christianity were with an earnest and unalterable resolution of each to combine that heaven should not withhold one single influence which the very utmost effort of conspiring and persevering supplication would obtain, it would be a sign that a revolution of the world was at hand.

Edward Payson

Edward Payson, one of God's own, says this of Foster's statement:

Very few missionaries since the apostles, probably have tried the experiment. He who shall make the first trial will, I believe, effect wonders. Nothing that I could write, nothing that an angel could write, would be necessary to him who should make this trial.

One of the principal results of the little experience which I have had as a Christian minister is a conviction that religion consists very much in giving God that place in our views and feelings which He actually fills in the universe. We know that in the universe He is all in all. So far as He is constantly all in all to us, so far as we comply with the Psalmist's charge to his soul, 'My soul, wait thou only upon God;' so far, I apprehend, have we advanced towards perfection. It is comparatively easy to wait upon God; but to wait upon Him only—to feel, so far as our strength, happiness, and usefulness are concerned, as if all creatures and second causes were annihilated, and we were alone in the universe with God, is, I suspect, a difficult and rare attainment.

At least, I am sure it is one which I am very far from having made. In proportion as we make this attainment we shall find everything easy; for we shall become, emphatically, men of prayer; and we may say of prayer as Solomon says of money, that it answereth all things.

JOHN FOSTER

This same John Foster said, when approaching death:

> I never prayed more earnestly nor probably with such faithful frequency. 'Pray without ceasing' has been the sentence repeating itself in the silent thought, and I am sure it must be my practice till the last conscious hour of life. Oh, why not throughout that long, indolent, inanimate, past half-century?

Yet this is the way in which we all act about prayer. Conscious as we are of its importance, of its vital importance, we yet let the hours pass away as a blank and can only lament in death the irremediable loss.

When we calmly reflect upon the fact that the progress of our Lord's Kingdom is dependent upon prayer, it is sad to think that we give so little time to the holy exercise. Everything depends upon prayer, and yet we neglect it not only to our own spiritual hurt but also to the delay and injury of our Lord's cause upon earth. The forces of good and evil are contending for the world. If we would, we could add to the conquering power of the army of righteousness, and yet our lips are sealed, our hands hang listlessly by our side, and we jeopardize the very cause in which we profess to be deeply interested by holding back from the prayer chamber.

Prayer is the one prime, eternal condition by which the Father is pledged to put the Son in possession of the world. Christ prays through His people. Had there been persistent, universal, and continuous prayer by God's people, long ago this the earth would have been possessed for Christ. The delay is not to be accounted for by the inveterate obstacles, but by the lack of the right asking. We do more of everything else than of praying. As poor as our giving is, our contributions of money exceed our offerings of prayer. Perhaps in the average congregation fifty aid in paying. But perhaps only one saintly, ardent, soul shuts itself up with God and wrestles for the deliverance of the heathen world. Official praying on set or state occasions counts for nothing in this estimate. We emphasize other things more than we do the necessity of prayer.

We are saying prayers after an orderly way, but we have not the world in the grasp of our faith. We are not praying after the order that moves God and brings all divine influences to help us. The world needs more true praying to save it from the reign and ruin of Satan.

We do not pray as Elijah prayed. John Foster puts the whole matter to a practical point. "When the Church of God," he says, "is aroused to its obligation and duties and right faith to claim what Christ has promised— 'all things whatsoever'—a revolution will take place."

But not all praying is praying. The driving power, the conquering force in God's cause is God Himself. "Call unto Me, and I will answer thee, and show thee great and mighty things, which thou knowest not,"[7] is God's challenge to prayer.

Prayer and God's work

"Ask of Me things to come, concerning My sons, and concerning the work of My hands command ye Me" is God's carte blanche to prayer. Faith is only omnipotent when on its knees, and its outstretched hands take hold of God, then it draws to the utmost of God's capacity; for only a praying faith can get God's "all things whatsoever."

Wonderful lessons are the Syrophenician woman—the persistent widow—and the friend at midnight, of what dauntless prayer can do in mastering or defying conditions, in changing defeat into victory, and triumphing in the regions of despair. Oneness with Christ, the acme of spiritual attainment, is glorious in all things. Most glorious in that we can then "ask what we will and it shall be done unto us."[8] Prayer in Jesus' name puts the crowning crown on God, because it glorifies Him through the Son and pledges the Son to give to Christians "whatsoever and anything" they shall ask.[9]

In the New Testament, the marvelous prayer of the Old Testament is put to the front that it may provoke and stimulate our praying. It is preceded with a declaration, the dynamic energy of which we can scarcely translate.

The effectual fervent prayer of a righteous man availeth much. Elias was a man subject to like passions as we are, and he prayed earnestly that it might not rain: and it rained not on the earth by the space of three years and six months. And he prayed again, and the heaven gave rain, and the earth brought forth her fruit.[10]

Our scarcity of results, the cause of all leanness, is solved by the apostle James: "ye have not, because ye ask not. Ye ask, and receive not, because ye ask amiss, that ye may consume it upon your lusts."[11]

That is the whole truth in a nutshell!

Endnotes

1 Psalm 2:8-9
2 Isaiah 56:7b
3 Isaiah 45:11-12
4 Psalm 2:8
5 Psalm 72:15
6 Paraphrase of Psalm 45:11-12
7 Jeremiah 33:3
8 Paraphrase of John 15:7
9 Paraphrase of John 14:13
10 James 5:16b-18
11 James 4:2b-3

4

Pray Always and Everywhere

THE POTENCY OF PRAYER *hath subdued the strength of fire; it had bridled the rage of lions, hushed anarchy to rest, extinguished wars, appeased the elements, expelled demons, burst the chains of death, expanded the gates of heaven, assuaged diseases, repelled frauds, rescued cities from destruction, stayed the sun in its course, and arrested the progress of the thunderbolt. Prayer is an all-efficient panoply, a treasure undiminished, a mine which is never exhausted, a sky unobscured by clouds, a heaven unruffled by the storm. It is the root, the fountain, the mother of a thousand blessings.* (Chrysostom)

The prayers of holy men appease God's wrath, drive away temptations, resist and overcome the devil, procure the ministry and service of angels, rescind the decrees of God. Prayer cures sickness and obtains pardon; it arrests the sun in its course and stays the wheels of the chariot of the moon; it rules over all gods and opens and shuts the storehouses of rain, it unlocks the cabinet of the womb and quenches the violence of fire; it stops the mouths of lions and reconciles our suffering and weak faculties with the violence of torment and violence of persecution; it pleases God and supplies all our need. (Jeremy Taylor)

Perfect prayer is only another name for love. (Fénelon)

More things are wrought by prayer
Than this world dreams of. Wherefore, let thy voice
Rise like a fountain for me night and day.
For what are men better than sheep or goats,
That nourish a blind life within the brain,
If, knowing God, they lift not hands of prayer
Both for themselves and those who call them friend?
For so the whole round earth is every way
Bound by gold chains about the feet of God.
(Tennyson)

CHARLES SPURGEON

It was said of the late C. H. Spurgeon that he glided from laughter to prayer with the naturalness of one who lived in both elements. With him the habit of prayer was free and unfettered. His life was not divided into compartments, the one shut off from the other with a rigid exclusiveness that barred all intercommunication. He lived in constant fellowship with his Father in Heaven. He was ever in touch with God, and thus it was as natural for him to pray as it was for him to breathe.

"What a fine time we have had; let us thank God for it," he said to a friend on one occasion, when, out under the blue sky and wrapped in glorious sunshine, they had enjoyed a holiday with the unfettered enthusiasm of schoolboys. Prayer sprang as spontaneously to his lips as did ordinary speech, and never was there the slightest incongruity in his approach to the divine throne straight from any scene in which he might be taking part.

THE RIGHT ATTITUDE ABOUT PRAYER

That is the attitude with regard to prayer that ought to mark every child of God. There are, and there ought to be, stated seasons of communion with God when, everything else shut out, we come into His presence to talk to Him and to let Him speak to us. Out of such seasons springs that beautiful habit of prayer that weaves a golden bond between earth and heaven. Without such stated seasons the habit of prayer can never be formed;—without them there is no nourishment for the spiritual life. By means of them the soul is lifted into a new atmosphere—the atmosphere of the heavenly city, in which it is easy to open the heart to God and to speak with Him as friend speaks with friend.

Thus, in every circumstance of life, prayer is the most natural out-pouring of the soul, the unhindered turning to God for communion and direction. Whether in sorrow or in joy, in defeat or in victory, in health or in weakness, in calamity or in success, the heart leaps to meet with God just as a child runs to its mother's arms, ever sure that with her is the sympathy that meets every need.

Dr. Adam Clarke and John Wesley

Dr. Adam Clarke, in his autobiography, records that when Mr. Wesley was returning to England by ship, considerable delay was caused by contrary winds. Wesley was reading a book when he became aware of some confusion on board, and when he asked what the matter was, he was informed that the wind was contrary. "Then" was his reply, "let us go to prayer."

After Dr. Clarke had prayed, Wesley broke out into fervent supplication that seemed to be more the offering of faith than of mere desire. "Almighty and everlasting God," he prayed, "Thou hast sway everywhere, and all things serve the purpose of Thy will, Thou holdest the winds in Thy fists and sittest upon the water floods, and reignest a King forever. Command these winds and these waves that they obey Thee, and take us speedily and safely to the haven whither we would go."

The power of this petition was felt by all. Wesley rose from his knees, made no remark, but took up his book and continued reading. Dr. Clarke went on deck, and to his surprise found the vessel under sail, standing on her right course. Nor did she change until she was safely at anchor. On the sudden and favorable change of wind, Wesley made no remark. He so fully expected to be heard that he took it for granted that he was heard.

That was prayer with a purpose—the definite and direct utterance of one who knew that he had the ear of God, and that God had the willingness as well as the power to grant the petition which he asked of Him.

Major D. W. Whittle and George Müller

Major D. W. Whittle, in an introduction to the wonders of prayer, says of George Müller, of Bristol:

I met Mr. Müller in the express, the morning of our sailing from Quebec to Liverpool. About half-an-hour before the tender was to take the passengers to the ship, he asked of the agent if a deck chair had arrived for him from New York. He was answered 'No,' and told that it could not possibly come in time for the steamer I had with me a chair I had just purchased, and told Mr. Müller of the place near by, and suggested, as but a few moments remained, that he had better buy one at once.

His reply was, 'No, my brother. Our Heavenly Father will send the chair from New York. It is one used by Mrs. Müller. I wrote ten days ago to a brother, who promised to see it forwarded here last week. He has not been prompt, as I would have desired, but I am sure our Heavenly Father will send the chair. Mrs. Müller is very sick on the sea, and has particularly desired to have this same chair, and not finding it here yesterday, we have made special prayer that our Heavenly Father would be pleased to provide it for us, and we will trust Him to do so.'

As this dear man of God went peacefully on board, running the risk of Mrs. Müller making the trip without a chair, when, for a couple of dollars, she could have been provided for, I confess I feared Mr. Müller was carrying his faith principles too far and not acting wisely. I was kept at the express office ten minutes after Mr. Müller left. Just as I started to hurry to the wharf, a team drove up the street, and on top of a load just arrived from New York was Mr. Müller's chair.

It was sent at once to the tender and placed in my hands to take to Mr. Müller, just as the boat was leaving the dock (the Lord having a lesson for me). Mr. Müller took it with the happy, pleased expression of a child who has just received a kindness deeply appreciated, and reverently removing his hat and folding his hands over it, he thanked the Heavenly Father for sending the chair.

MELANCTHON AND MARTIN LUTHER

One of Melancthon's correspondents writes of Luther's praying:

I cannot enough admire the extraordinary, cheerfulness, constancy, faith and hope of the man in these trying and vexatious times. He constantly feeds these gracious affections by a very diligent study of the Word of God. Then not a day passes in which he does not employ in prayer at least three of his very best hours.

Once I happened to hear him at prayer. Gracious God! What spirit and what faith is there in his expressions! He petitions God with as much reverence as if he was in the divine presence, and yet with as firm a hope and confidence as he would address a father or a friend. 'I know,' said he, 'Thou art our Father and our God; and therefore I am sure Thou wilt bring to naught the persecutors of Thy children. For shouldest Thou fail to do this Thine own cause, being connected with ours, would be endangered. It is entirely thine own concern. We, by Thy providence, have been compelled to take a part. Thou therefore wilt be our defence.'

Whilst I was listening to Luther praying in this manner, at a distance, my soul seemed on fire within me, to hear the man address God so like a friend, yet with so much gravity and reverence; and also to hear him, in the course of his prayer, insisting on the promises contained in the Psalms, as if he were sure his petitions would be granted.

WILLIAM BRAMWELL

Of William Bramwell, a noted Methodist preacher in England, wonderful for his zeal and prayer, the following is related by a sergeant major in the army:

> In July, 1811, our regiment was ordered for Spain, then the seat of a protracted and sanguinary war. My mind was painfully exercised with the thoughts of leaving my dear wife and four helpless children in a strange country, unprotected and unprovided for. Mr. Bramwell felt a lively interest in our situation, and his sympathising spirit seemed to drink in all the agonised feelings of my tender wife. He supplicated the throne of grace day and night in our behalf. My wife and I spent the evening previous to our march at a friend's house, in company with Mr. Bramwell, who sat in a very pensive mood, and appeared to be in a spiritual struggle all the time.
>
> After supper, he suddenly pulled his hand out of his bosom, laid it on my knee, and said: 'Brother Riley, mark what I am about to say! You are not to go to Spain. Remember I tell you, you are not; for I have been wrestling with God on your behalf, and when my Heavenly Father condescends in mercy to bless me with power to lay hold on Himself, I do not easily let Him go; no, not until I am favoured with an answer. Therefore you may depend upon it that the next time I hear from you, you will be settled in quarters.' This came to pass exactly as he said. The next day the order for going to Spain was countermanded.

PRAYING WITH A PURPOSE

These men prayed with a purpose. To them God was not far away, in some inaccessible region, but near at hand, ever ready to listen to the call of His children. There was no barrier between. They were on terms of perfect intimacy, if one may use such a phrase in relation to human beings and their Maker. No cloud obscured the face of the Father from His trusting child, who could look up into the divine countenance and pour out the longings of its heart. That is the type of prayer which God never fails to hear. He knows that it comes from a heart at one with His own; from one who is entirely yielded to the heavenly plan, and so He bends His ear and gives to the pleading child the assurance that its petition has been heard and answered.

Have we not all had some such experience when with set and undeviating purpose we have approached the face of our Father? In an agony of soul we have sought refuge from the oppression of the world in the anteroom of heaven. The waves of despair seemed to threaten destruction, and as no way of escape was visible anywhere, we fell back, like the disciples of old, upon the power of our Lord, crying to Him to save us lest we perish. Then, in the twinkling of an eye, the thing was done. The billows sank into a calm, the howling wind died down at the divine command, and the agony of the soul passed into a restful peace as over the whole being there crept the consciousness of the divine presence, bringing with it the assurance of answered prayer and sweet deliverance.

A PERSON OF GOD

"I tell the Lord my troubles and difficulties, and wait for Him to give me the answers to them," says one person of God. "And it is wonderful how a matter that looked very dark will in prayer become clear as crystal by the help of God's Spirit. I think Christians fail so often to get answers to their prayers because they do not wait long enough on God. They just drop down and say a few words, and then jump up and forget it and expect God to answer them. Such praying always reminds me of the small boy ringing his neighbor's doorbell, and then running away as fast as he can go."

When we acquire the habit of prayer we enter into a new atmosphere. "Do you expect to go to heaven?" asked some one of a devout Scotsman. "Why, man, I live there," was the quaint and unexpected reply. It was a pithy statement of a great truth, for all the way to heaven is heaven begun to the Christian who walks near enough to God to hear the secrets He has to impart.

HORACE BUSHNELL

This attitude is beautifully illustrated in a story of Horace Bushnell, told by Dr. Parkes Cadman. Bushnell was found to be suffering from an incurable disease. One evening the Rev. Joseph Twichell visited him, and, as they sat together under the starry sky, Bushnell said: "One of us ought to pray." Twichell asked Bushnell to do so, and Bushnell began his prayer; burying his face in the earth, he poured out his heart until, said Twichell, in recalling the incident, "I was afraid to stretch out my hand in the darkness lest I should touch God."

SAMUEL RUTHERFORD

To have God that near is to enter the holy of holies—to breathe the fragrance of the heavenly air, to walk in Eden's delightful gardens. Nothing but prayer can bring God and us into this happy communion. That was the experience of Samuel Rutherford, just as it is the experience of every one who passes through the same gateway. When this saint of God was confined in jail at one time for conscience sake, he enjoyed in a rare degree the divine companionship, recording in his diary that Jesus entered his cell, and that at His coming "every stone flashed like a ruby."

DAVID LIVINGSTONE

Many others have borne witness to the same sweet fellowship when prayer had become the one habit of life that meant more than anything else to them. David Livingstone lived in the realm of prayer and knew its gracious influence. It was his habit every birthday to write a prayer, and on the next to the last birthday of all, this was his prayer: "O Divine one, I have not loved Thee earnestly, deeply, sincerely enough. Grant, I pray Thee, that before this year is ended I may have finished my task." It was just on the threshold of the year that followed that his faithful men, as they looked into the hut of Ilala, while the rain dripped from the eaves, saw their master on his knees beside his bed in an attitude of prayer. He had died on his knees in prayer.

STONEWALL JACKSON

Stonewall Jackson was a man of prayer. He said, "I have so fixed the habit in my mind that I never raise a glass of water to my lips without asking God's blessing, never seal a letter without putting a word of prayer under the seal, never take a letter from the post without a brief sending of my thoughts heavenward, never change my classes in the lecture-room without a minute's petition for the cadets who go out and for those who come in."

JAMES GILMOUR

James Gilmour, the pioneer missionary to Mongolia, was a man of prayer. He had a habit in his writing of never using a blotter. He made a rule when he got to the bottom of any page to wait until the ink dried and spend the time in prayer.

In this way their whole being was saturated with the divine, and they became the reflectors of the heavenly fragrance and glory. Walking with God down the avenues of prayer we acquire something of His likeness, and unconsciously we become witnesses to others of His beauty and His grace. Professor James, in his famous work, "Varieties of Religious Experience," tells of a man of forty-nine who said:

> God is more real to me than any thought or thing or person. I feel His presence positively, and the more as I live in closer harmony with His laws as written in my body and mind. I feel Him in the sunshine or rain; and all mingled with a delicious restfulness most nearly describes my feelings. I talk to Him as to a companion in prayer and praise, and our communion is delightful. He answers me again and again, often in words so clearly spoken that it seems my outer ear must have carried the tone, but generally in strong mental impressions. Usually a text of Scripture, unfolding some new view of Him and His love for me, and care for my safety . . . That He is

mine and I am His never leaves me; it is an abiding joy. Without it life would be a blank, a desert, a shoreless, trackless waste.

SIR THOMAS BROWNE

Equally notable is the testimony of Sir Thomas Browne, the beloved physician who lived at Norwich in 1605, and was the author of a very remarkable book of wide circulation, "Religio Medici." In spite of the fact that England was passing through a period of national convulsion and political excitement, he found comfort and strength in prayer. He wrote in a journal found among his private papers after his death:

I have resolved, to pray more and pray always, to pray in all places where quietness inviteth, in the house, on the highway and on the street; and to know no street or passage in this city that may not witness that I have not forgotten God.

I purpose to take occasion of praying upon the sight of any church which I may pass, that God may be worshipped there in spirit, and that souls may be saved there; to pray daily for my sick patients and for the patients of other physicians; at my entrance into any home to say, 'May the peace of God abide here'; after hearing a sermon, to pray for a blessing on God's truth, and upon the messenger; upon the sight of a beautiful person to bless God for His creatures, to pray for the beauty of such an one's soul, that God may enrich her with inward graces, and that the outward and inward may correspond; upon the sight of a deformed person, to pray God to give them wholeness of soul, and by and by to give them the beauty of the resurrection.

What an illustration of the praying spirit! Such an attitude represents prayer without ceasing, reveals the habit of prayer in its unceasing supplication, in its uninterrupted communion, in its constant intercession. What an illustration, too, of purpose in prayer! Of how many of us can it be said that as we pass people in the street we pray for them, or that as we enter a home or a church we remember the inmates or the congregation in prayer to God?

The explanation of our thoughtlessness or forgetfulness lies in the fact that prayer with so many of us is simply a form of selfishness. It means asking for something for ourselves—that and nothing more. From such an attitude we need to pray to be delivered.

The prayer of faith is the only power in the universe to which the great Jehovah yields. "Prayer is the sovereign remedy" (Robert Hall).

5

The Greatest of All Forces

THE CHURCH, INTENT ON *the acquisition of temporal power, had well nigh abandoned its spiritual duties, and its empire, which rested on spiritual foundations, was crumbling with their decay, and threatened to pass away like an unsubstantial vision.* (Lea's Inquisition)

Are we praying as Christ did? Do we abide in Him? Are our pleas and spirit the overflow of His spirit and pleas? Does love rule the spirit—perfect love?

These questions must be considered as proper and relevant at a time like the present. We do fear that we are doing more of other things than prayer. This is not a praying age. It is an age of great activity, of great movements, but one in which the tendency is very strong to stress the seen and the material and to neglect and discount the unseen and the spiritual. Prayer is the greatest of all forces, because it honors God and brings Him into active aid.

There can be no substitute, no rival for prayer. It stands alone as the great spiritual force, and this force must be imminent and acting. It cannot be dispensed with during one generation, nor held in abeyance for the advance of any great movement—it must be continuous and particular, always, everywhere, and in everything. We cannot run our spiritual operations on the prayers of the past generation. Many people believe in the effectiveness of prayer, but not many pray. Prayer is the easiest and hardest of all things. It is the simplest and the most sublime. It is the weakest and the most powerful. Its results lie outside the range of human possibilities and are limited only by the omnipotence of God.

THE POWER OF PRAYER

Few Christians have anything but a vague idea of the power of prayer. Fewer still have any experience of that power. The Church seems almost wholly unaware of the power God puts into its hand. This spiritual carte blanche on the infinite resources of God's wisdom and power is rarely, if ever, used. It is certainly never used to the full measure of honoring God. It is astounding how poor the use, how little the benefits. Prayer is our most formidable weapon, but the one in which we are the least skilled, the most averse to its use. We do everything else for the heathen except the thing God wants us to do. In fact, the only thing that does any good, and that makes all else we do effective

To graduate in the school of prayer is to master the whole course of a Christian life. The first and last stages of holy living are crowned with praying. It is a life trade. The hindrances of prayer are the hindrances in a holy life. The conditions of praying are the conditions of righteousness, holiness, and salvation. An amateur in the trade of praying is a bungler in the trade of salvation.

Prayer is a trade to be learned. We must be apprentices and serve our time at it. Painstaking care, much thought, practice, and labor are required to be a skillful tradesman in praying.

Practice in this, as well as in all other trades, makes perfect. Only toiling hands and hearts make Christians proficient in this heavenly trade.

CHRISTIANS WHO DO NOT PRAY

In spite of the benefits and blessings that flow from communion with God, the sad confession must be made that we are not praying much. A comparatively small number lead in prayer at the meetings. Fewer still pray in their families. Fewer still are in the habit of praying regularly in their closets. Meetings specially for prayer are as rare as frost in July. In many churches there is neither the name nor the semblance of a prayer meeting. In the town and city churches the prayer meeting in name is not a prayer meeting in fact. A sermon or a lecture is the main feature. Prayer is the nominal attachment.

PRAYER AND A HOLY LIFE

Our people are not a praying people, which is evident by their lives. Prayer and a holy life mutually act and react. Neither can survive alone. The absence of the one is the absence of the other. We are in danger of substituting churchly work and a ceaseless round of showy activities for prayer and holy living. A holy life does not live in the closet, but it cannot live without the closet. If, by any chance, a prayer chamber should be established without a holy life, it would be a chamber without the presence of God in it.

Put the saints everywhere to praying is the burden of the apostolic effort and the key note of apostolic success. Jesus Christ had striven to do this in the days of His personal ministry. He was moved by infinite compassion at the ripened fields of earth perished for lack of laborers. Pausing in His own praying, He tries to awaken the sleeping sensibilities of His disciples to the duty of prayer, as He charges them: "Pray ye therefore the Lord of the harvest, that he will send forth labourers into his harvest."[1] "And he spake a parable unto them to this end, that men ought always to pray, and not to faint."[2]

Before Pentecost the apostles could only get glimpses of this great importance of prayer. But the Spirit coming and filling on Pentecost elevated prayer to its vital and all-commanding position in the Gospel of Christ. The call now of prayer to every saint is the Spirit's loudest and most demanding call. Sainthood's piety is made, refined, and perfected by prayer. The Gospel moves with slow and timid pace when the saints are not at their prayers early and late and long.

TEACHERS OF PRAYER

Where are the Christlike leaders who can teach the modern saints how to pray and put them at it? Do our leaders know we are raising up a prayerless set of saints? Where are the apostolic leaders who can put God's people to praying? Let them come to the front and do the work, and it will be the greatest work that can be done. An increase of educational facilities and a great increase of money will be the direst curse to Christianity if they are not sanctified by more and better praying than we are doing.

More praying will not come as a matter of course. The campaign for the twentieth or thirtieth century will not help our praying, but will hinder it if we are not careful. Nothing but a specific effort from a praying leadership will avail. None but praying leaders can have praying followers. Praying apostles will give birth to praying saints. A praying pulpit will give birth to praying pews. We greatly need somebody who can set the saints to this business of praying. We are a generation of non-praying saints. Non-praying saints are a beggarly gang of saints, who have neither the fire, beauty, and power of saints. Who will restore this branch? The person who can set the Church to praying will be the greatest of reformers and apostles.

In the past, holy men and women have changed the whole force of affairs, and revolutionized character and country by prayer. Such achievements are still possible to us. The power is only waiting to be used. Prayer is but the expression of faith.

MIGHTY THINGS WROUGHT BY PRAYER

Time would fail to tell of the mighty things wrought by prayer, for by it holy ones have "subdued kingdoms, wrought righteousness, obtained promises, stopped the mouths of lions, Quenched the violence of fire, escaped the edge of the sword, out of weakness were made strong, waxed valiant in fight, turned to flight the armies of the aliens."[3]

Prayer honors God, and dishonors self. It is a plea of weakness, ignorance, need. A plea that heaven cannot disregard. God delights to have us pray.

Prayer is not the enemy of work, it does not paralyze activity. It works mightily. Prayer itself is the greatest work. It springs activity, stimulates desire and effort. Prayer is not an opiate but a tonic. It does not lull to sleep but arouses anew for action. The lazy saint does not, will not, cannot pray, for prayer demands energy. Paul calls it a striving, an agony. With Jacob it was a wrestling. With the Syrophenician woman it was a struggle that called into play all the higher qualities of the soul, and which demanded great force to meet.

PRAYER AND THE LAZY CHRISTIAN

The closet is not an asylum for the lazy and worthless Christian. It is not a nursery where none but babes belong. It is the battlefield of the Church, its citadel. It's the scene of heroic and unearthly conflicts. The closet is the base of supplies for the Christian and the Church. Cut off from it there is nothing left but retreat and disaster. The energy for work, the mastery over self, the deliverance from fear, all spiritual results and graces, are much advanced by prayer. The difference between the strength, experience, and holiness of Christians is found in the contrast in their praying.

Few, short, feeble prayers, are always a sign of low spiritual condition. Christians ought to pray much and apply themselves to it with energy and perseverance. Eminent Christians have been eminent in prayer. The deep things of God are learned nowhere else. Great things for God are done by great prayers. Those who pray much, study much, love much, work much, and do much for God and humanity. The execution of the Gospel, the vigor of faith, and the maturity and excellence of spiritual graces wait on prayer.

Endnotes

1 Matthew 9:38
2 Luke 18:1
3 Hebrews 11:33-34

6

Persistence in Prayer

"NOTHING IS IMPOSSIBLE TO INDUSTRY," *said one of the seven sages of Greece. Let us change the word industry for persevering prayer, and the motto will be more Christian and more worthy of universal adoption. I am persuaded that we are all more deficient in a spirit of prayer than in any other grace. God loves importunate prayer so much that He will not give us much blessing without it. And the reason that He loves such prayer is that He loves us and knows that it is a necessary preparation for our receiving the richest blessings which He is waiting and longing to bestow.*

I never prayed sincerely and earnestly for anything but it came at some time—no matter at how distant a day, somehow, in some shape, probably the last I would have devised, it came. (Adoniram Judson)

It is good, I find, to persevere in attempts to pray. If I cannot pray with perseverance or continue long in my addresses to the Divine Being, I have found that the more I do in secret prayer the more I have delight to do, and have enjoyed more of the spirit of prayer; and frequently I have found the contrary, when by journeying or otherwise, I have been deprived of retirement. (David Brainerd)

Christ puts importunity as a distinguishing characteristic of true praying. We must not only pray, but we must pray with great urgency, intentness, and repetition. We must not only pray, but we must pray again and again. We must not get tired of praying. We must be thoroughly in earnest and deeply concerned about the things for which we ask, for Jesus

Christ made it very plain that the secret of prayer and its success lie in its urgency. We must press our prayers upon God.

In a parable of exquisite pathos and simplicity, our Lord taught not simply that people ought to pray, but that people ought to pray with full heartiness, and press the matter with vigorous energy and brave hearts.

> And he spoke a parable unto them to this end, that men ought always to pray, and not to faint; Saying, There was in a city a judge, which feared not God, neither regarded man: And there was a widow in that city; and she came unto him, saying, Avenge me of mine adversary. And he would not for a while: but afterward he said within himself, Though I fear not God, nor regard man; Yet because this widow troubleth me, I will avenge her, lest by her continual coming she weary me. And the Lord said, Hear what the unjust judge saith. And shall not God avenge his own elect, which cry day and night unto him, though he bear long with them? I tell you that he will avenge them speedily. Nevertheless when the Son of man cometh, shall he find faith on the earth?[1]

This poor woman's case was a most hopeless one, but persistence brings hope from the realms of despair and creates success where neither success nor its conditions existed. There could be no stronger case, to show how unwearied and dauntless persistence gains its ends where everything else fails. The preface to this parable says, "And he spake a parable unto them to this end, that men ought always to pray, and not to faint."[2] He knew that we would soon get faint-hearted in praying, so to hearten us He gives this picture of the marvelous power of persistence.

The widow, weak and helpless, is helplessness personified. Stripped of every hope and influence that could move an unjust judge, she yet wins her case solely by her tireless and offensive persistence. Could the necessity of persistence, its power and tremendous importance in prayer, be pictured in deeper or more impressive fashion? It surmounts or removes all obstacles, overcomes every resisting force, and gains its ends in the face of invincible hindrances. We can do nothing without prayer. All things can be done by persistent prayer.

Another parable spoken by Jesus enforces the same great truth. A man at midnight goes to his friend for a loan of bread. His pleas are strong, based on friendship and the embarrassing and exacting demands of necessity, but these all fail. He gets no bread, but he stays and presses, and waits and gains. Sheer persistence succeeds where all other pleas and influences had failed.

THE PARABLE OF THE SYROPHENICIAN WOMAN

The case of the Syrophenician woman is a parable in action. She is stopped in her approach to Christ by the information that He will not see any one. She is denied His presence, and then in His presence is treated with seeming indifference, with the chill of silence and unconcern. She presses and approaches. The pressure and approach are repulsed by the stern and crushing statement that He is not sent to her class or kind, that she is reprobated from His mission and power. She is humiliated by being called a dog. Yet she accepts all, overcomes all, and wins all by her humble, dauntless, invincible persistence.

The Son of God, pleased, surprised, and overpowered by her unconquerable persistence, says to her: "O, woman, great is thy faith: be it unto thee even as thou wilt."[3] Jesus Christ surrenders Himself to the persistence of a great faith. "And shall not God avenge His own elect, which cry day and night unto Him, though He bear long with them?"[4]

Persistence in Prayer

Jesus Christ puts ability to persist as one of the elements of prayer, one of the main conditions of prayer. The prayer of the Syrophenician woman is an exhibition of the matchless power of persistence, of a conflict more real and involving more of vital energy, endurance, and all the higher elements than was ever illustrated in the conflicts of Isthmia or Olympia.

The first lessons of persistence are taught in the Sermon on the Mount: "Ask, and it shall be given; seek, and ye shall find; knock, and it shall be opened."[5] These are steps of advance: "For every one that asketh, receiveth; and he that seeketh, findeth; and to him that knocketh it shall be opened."[6]

Without continuance, the prayer may go unanswered. Persistence is made up of the ability to hold on, to press on, to wait with unrelaxed and unrelaxable grasp—restless desire and restful patience. Persistent prayer is not an incident, but the main thing, not a performance but a passion, not a need but a necessity.

Prayer in its highest form and grandest success assumes the attitude of a wrestler with God. It is the contest, trial and victory of faith. A victory not secured from an enemy, but from Him who tries our faith that He may enlarge it—that tests our strength to make us stronger. Few things give such quickened and permanent vigor to the soul as a long exhaustive season of persistent prayer. It makes an experience, an epoch, a new calendar for the spirit, a new life to Christianity, a soldierly training.

High Spiritual Effort

The Bible never wearies in its pressure and illustration of the fact that the highest spiritual good is secured as the return of the outgoing of the highest form of spiritual effort. There is neither encouragement nor room in Bible religion for feeble desires, listless efforts, lazy attitudes. All must be strenuous, urgent, ardent. Inflamed desires, impassioned, unwearied insistence and persistence delight heaven. God would have His children incorrigibly in earnest and persistently bold in their efforts. Heaven is too busy to listen to half-hearted prayers or to respond to pop-calls.

Our whole being must be in our praying. Like John Knox, we must say and feel, "Give me Scotland, or I die." Our experience and revelations of God are born of our costly sacrifice, our costly conflicts, our costly praying. The all-nigh wrestling of Jacob made an era never to be forgotten in Jacob's life, brought God to the rescue, changed Esau's attitude and conduct, changed Jacob's character, and saved and affected his life and entered into the habits of a nation.

Our seasons of persistent prayer cut themselves, like the print of a diamond, into our hardest places, and mark with ineffaceable traces our characters. They are the salient periods of our lives! The memorial stones that endure and to which we turn.

PERSISTENCE IS A CONDITION OF PRAYER

Persistence, it may be repeated, is a condition of prayer. We are to press the matter, not with vain repetitions, but with urgent repetitions. We repeat, not to count the times, but to gain the prayer. We cannot quit praying because heart and soul are in it. We pray "with all perseverance"[7] We hang to our prayers because by them we live. We press our pleas because we must have them or die. Christ gives us two most expressive parables to emphasize the necessity of persistence in praying. Perhaps Abraham lost Sodom by failing to press to the utmost his privilege of praying. Joash, we know, lost because he stayed his smiting.

Perseverance counts much with God as well as with people. If Elijah had ceased at his first petition the heavens would have scarcely yielded their rain to his feeble praying. If Jacob had quit praying at decent bedtime he would scarcely have survived the next day's meeting with Esau. If the Syrophenician woman had allowed her faith to faint by silence, humiliation, repulse, or stop mid-way its struggles, her grief-stricken home would never have been brightened by the healing of her daughter.

Pray and never faint is the motto Christ gives us for praying. It is the test of our faith. And the severer the trial and the longer the waiting, the more glorious the results.

The benefits and necessity of persistence are taught by Old Testament saints. Praying saints must be strong in hope, faith, and prayer. They must know how to wait and to press—to wait on God and be in earnest in our approaches to Him.

Abraham has left us an example of persistent intercession in his passionate pleading with God on behalf of Sodom and Gomorrah. As already indicated, if he had not ceased in his asking, perhaps God would not have ceased in His giving. Abraham left off asking before God left off granting. Moses taught the power of persistence when he interceded for

Israel forty days and forty nights by fasting and prayer. And he succeeded in his persistence.

PLEADING AND WAITING

Jesus, in His teaching and example, illustrated and perfected this principle of Old Testament pleading and waiting. How strange that the only Son of God—who came on a mission direct from His Father, whose only heaven on earth and life and law were to do His Father's will in that mission—should be under the law of prayer. That the blessings that came to Him were impregnated and purchased by prayer. Stranger still, that persistence in prayer was the process by which His wealthiest supplies from God were gained. Had He not prayed with persistence, no transfiguration would have been in His history, no mighty works would have rendered His career divine. His all-night praying was that which filled with compassion and power His all-day work. The persistent praying of His life crowned His death with its triumph. He learned the high lesson of submission to God's will in the struggles of persistent prayer before He illustrated that submission so sublimely on the Cross.

CHARLES SPURGEON

"Whether we like it or not," said Mr. Spurgeon, "asking is the rule of the kingdom. 'Ask, and ye shall receive.'[8] It is a rule that never will be altered in anybody's case. Our Lord Jesus Christ is the elder brother of the family, but God has not relaxed the rule for Him. Remember this text: Jehovah says to His own Son, 'Ask of Me, and I shall give Thee the heathen for Thine inheritance, and the uttermost parts of the earth for Thy possession.'[9] If the Royal and Divine Son of God cannot be exempted from the rule of asking that He may have, you and I cannot expect the rule to be relaxed in our favor. Why should it be? What reason can be pleaded why we should be exempted from prayer? What argument can there be why we should be deprived of the privilege and delivered from the necessity of supplication? I can see none: can you? God will bless Elijah and send rain on Israel, but Elijah must pray for it. If the chosen nation is to prosper Samuel must plead for it. If the Jews are to be delivered, Daniel must intercede. God will bless Paul, and the nations shall be converted through him, but Paul must pray. Pray he did without ceasing; his epistles show that he expected nothing except by asking for it. If you may have everything by asking, and nothing without asking, I beg you to see how absolutely vital prayer is, and I beseech you to abound in it."

FAILURE AND LACK OF PERSISTENCE

There is not the least doubt that much of our praying fails because of a lack of persistence. It is without the fire and strength of perseverance.

Persistence is of the essence of true praying. It may not be always called into exercise, but it must be there as the reserve force. Jesus taught that perseverance is the essential element of prayer. Saints must be in earnest when they kneel at God's footstool.

Too often we get faint-hearted and quit praying at the point where we ought to begin. We let go at the very point where we should hold on strongest. Our prayers are weak because they are not impassioned by an unfailing and resistless will.

God loves persistent pleaders, and sends them answers that would never have been granted but for the persistency that refuses to let go until the petition craved for is granted.

Endnotes

1 Luke 18:1-8
2 Luke 18:1
3 Matthew 15:28
4 Luke 18:7
5 Matthew 7:7
6 Matthew 7:8
7 Ephesians 6:18
8 John 16:24
9 Psalm 2:8

7

Praying Always

I SUSPECT I HAVE BEEN *allotting habitually too little time to religious exercises as private devotion, religious mediation, Scripture reading, etc. Hence I am lean and cold and hard. God would perhaps prosper me more in spiritual things if I were to be more diligent in using the means of grace. I had better allot more time, say two hours or an hour and a half, to religious exercises daily, and try whether by so doing I cannot preserve a frame of spirit more habitually devotional, a more lively sense of unseen things, a warmer love to God, and a greater degree of hunger and thirst after righteousness, a heart less prone to be soiled with worldly cares, designs, passions, and apprehension and a real undissembled longing for heaven, its pleasures and its purity.* (William Wilberforce)

"Men ought always to pray, and not to faint."[1] The words are the words of our Lord, who not only always tried to impress upon His followers the urgency and importance of prayer, but set them an example that they have been far too slow to copy.

The always speaks for itself. Prayer is not a meaningless function or duty to be crowded into the busy or the weary ends of the day. We are not obeying our Lord's command when we content ourselves with a few minutes upon our knees in the morning rush or late at night when our faculties, tired with the tasks of the day, call out for rest. God is always within call, it is true—His ear is ever attentive to the cry of His child. But we can never get to know Him if we use the vehicle of prayer as we use the telephone—for a few words of hurried conversation. Intimacy requires development. We can never know God, to the degree it is our privilege to know Him, by brief, fragmentary, and unconsidered repetitions of intercessions that are requests for personal favors and nothing more.

That is not the way in which we can come into communication with heaven's King. Someone has well said, "The goal of prayer is the ear of God." This is a goal that can only be reached by patient, continued, and continuous waiting upon Him, and pouring out our heart to Him and permitting Him to speak to us. Only by so doing can we expect to know Him. As we come to know Him better, we shall spend more time in His presence and find that presence a constant and ever-increasing delight.

Always does not mean that we are to neglect the ordinary duties of life. What it means is that the soul that has come into intimate contact with God in the silence of the prayer-chamber is never out of conscious touch with the Father. It means that the heart is always going out to Him in loving communion, and that the moment the mind is released from the task upon which it is engaged, it returns as naturally to God as the bird does to its nest. What a beautiful conception of prayer we get if we regard it in this light, if we view it as a constant fellowship, an unbroken audience with the King. Prayer then loses every bit of dread that it may once have possessed. It is then that we no longer regard prayer as a duty that must be performed, but rather as a privilege that is to be enjoyed, a rare delight that is always revealing some new beauty.

As a result, when we open our eyes in the morning our thoughts instantly mount heavenward. To many Christians the morning hours are the most precious portion of the day, because they provide the opportunity for the hallowed fellowship that gives the keynote to the day's program. What better introduction can there be to the never-ceasing glory and wonder of a new day than to spend it alone with God? It is said that Mr. Moody, at a time when no other place was available, kept his morning watch in the coal-shed, pouring out his heart to God, and finding in his precious Bible a true "feast of fat things."[2]

GEORGE MÜLLER

George Müller also combined Bible study with prayer in the quiet morning hours. At one time his practice was to give himself to prayer in the morning after having dressed. Then his plan underwent a change. As he himself put it:

> I saw the most important thing I had to do was to give myself to the reading of the Word of God, and to meditation on it, that thus my heart might be comforted, encouraged, warned, reproved, instructed; and that thus, by means of the Word of God, whilst meditating on it, my heart might be brought into mental communion with the Lord.

I began, therefore, to meditate on the New Testament early in the morning. The first thing I did, after having asked in a few words for the Lord's blessing upon his precious Word, was to begin to meditate on the Word of God, searching, as it were, into every verse to get blessing out of it; not for the sake of the public ministry of the Word, not for the sake of preaching on what I had meditated on, but for the sake of obtaining food for my own soul.

The result I have found to be almost invariably thus, that after a very few minutes my soul has been led to confession, or to thanksgiving, or to intercession or to supplication; so that, though I did not, as it were, give myself to prayer, but to meditation, yet it turned almost immediately more or less into prayer.

The study of the Word and prayer go together, and where we find the one truly practiced, the other is sure to be seen in close alliance. But we do not pray always. That is the trouble with so many of us. We need to pray much more than we do and much longer than we do.

ROBERT MURRAY MCCHEYNE

Gifted and saintly Robert Murray McCheyne, of whom it was said, "Whether viewed as a son, a brother, a friend, or a pastor, he was the most faultless and attractive exhibition of the true Christian they had ever seen embodied in a living form," knew what it was to spend much time upon his knees, and he never wearied in urging upon others the joy and the value of holy intercession.

"God's children should pray," he said. "They should cry day and night unto Him, God hears every one of your cries in the busy hour of the daytime and in the lonely watches of the night." In every way, by preaching, by exhortation when present and by letters when absent, McCheyne emphasized the vital duty of prayer, persistent and unceasing prayer.

In his diary we find this: "In the morning was engaged in preparing the head, then the heart. This has been frequently my error, and I have always felt the evil of it, especially in prayer. Reform it then, O Lord."

While on his trip to the Holy Land he wrote, "For much of our safety I feel indebted to the prayers of my people. If the veil of the world's machinery were lifted off how much we would find done in answer to the prayers of God's children."

In an ordination sermon he said to the new ministers:

Give yourself to prayers and the ministry of the Word. If you do not pray, God will probably lay you aside from your ministry as He did me, to teach you to pray. Remember Luther's maxim, "To have prayed well is to have studied well." Get your texts from God, your thoughts, your words. Carry the names of the little flock upon your breast like the High Priest. Wrestle for the unconverted. Luther spent his last three hours in prayer.

John Welch prayed seven or eight hours a day. He used to keep a plaid on his bed that he might wrap himself in when he rose during the night. Sometimes his wife found him on the ground lying weeping. When she complained, he would say, "O, woman, I have the souls of three thousand to answer for, and I know not how it is with many of them."

McCheyne exhorted and charged the future congregations of these new ministers:

> Pray for your pastor. Pray for his body, that he may be kept strong and spared many years. Pray for his soul, that he may be kept humble and holy, a burning and shining light. Pray for his ministry, that it may be abundantly blessed, that he may be anointed to preach good tidings, Let there be no secret prayer without naming him before your God, no family prayer without carrying your pastor in your hearts to God.

McCheyne's biographer says, "Two things he seems never to have ceased from—the cultivation of personal holiness and the most anxious efforts to win souls."

Those two things are the inseparable attendants on the ministry of prayer. Prayer fails when the desire and effort for personal holiness fail. No person is a soul-winner who is not an adept in the ministry of prayer.

"It is the duty of ministers," said holy Robert Murray McCheyne, "to begin the reformation of religion and manner with themselves, families, etc., with confession of past sin, earnest prayer for direction, grace and full purpose of heart." He begins with himself under the head of "Reformation in Secret Prayer," and he resolves:

> I ought not to omit any of the parts of prayer—confession, adoration, thanksgiving, petition, and intercession. There is a fearful tendency to omit confession proceeding from low views of God and His law, slight views of my heart, and the sin of my past life. This must be resisted. There is a constant tendency to omit adoration when I forget to Whom I am speaking, when I rush heedlessly into the presence of Jehovah without thought of His awful name and character. When I have little eyesight for his glory, and little admiration of His wonders, I have the native tendency of the heart to omit giving thanks, and yet it is specially commanded.

> Often when the heart is dead to the salvation of others I omit intercession, and yet it especially is the spirit of the great Advocate

Who has the name of Israel on His heart. I ought to pray before seeing anyone. Often when I sleep long, or meet with others early, and then have family prayer and breakfast and forenoon callers, it is eleven or twelve o'clock before I begin secret prayer. This is a wretched system; it is unscriptural. Christ rose before day and went into a solitary place.

David says, "Early will I seek Thee[3] . . . Thou shalt early hear my voice."[4] Mary Magdalene came to the sepulcher while it was yet dark. Family prayer loses much of its power and sweetness; and I can do no good to those who come to seek from me. The conscience feels guilty, the soul unfed, the lamp not trimmed. I feel it is far better to begin with God, to see His face first, to get my soul near Him before it is near another. "When I awake, I am still with Thee."[5] If I have slept too long, or I am going on an early journey, or my time is in any way shortened, it is best to dress hurriedly and have a few minutes alone with God than to give up all for lost. But in general it is best to have at least one hour alone with God before engaging in anything else. I ought to spend the best hours of the day in communion with God. When I awake in the night, I ought to rise and pray as David and John Welch did.

McCheyne believed in being always in prayer, and his fruitful life, short though that life was, affords an illustration of the power that comes from long and frequent visits to the secret place where we meet with our Lord.

People of McCheyne's caliber are needed today—praying saints, who know how to give themselves to the greatest task demanding their time and their attention. Saints who can give their whole heart to the holy task of intercession—saints who can pray through. God's cause is committed to His people. God commits Himself to people. Praying Christians are the vicegerents of God. They do His work and carry out His plans.

We are obliged to pray if we are citizens of God's Kingdom. Prayerlessness is expatriation, or worse, from God's Kingdom. It is outlawry, a high crime, a constitutional breach. Christians who relegate prayer to a subordinate place in their life soon lose whatever spiritual zeal they may have once possessed. The Church that makes little of prayer cannot maintain vital piety, and is powerless to advance the Gospel. The Gospel cannot live, fight, and conquer without prayer—prayer unceasing, instant, and ardent.

Little prayer is the characteristic of a backslidden age and of a backslidden Church. Whenever there is little praying in the pulpit or in the pew, spiritual bankruptcy is imminent and inevitable.

The cause of God has no commercial age, no cultured age, no age of education, no age of money. But it has one golden age, and that is the age of prayer. When its leaders are people of prayer, when prayer is the prevailing element of worship, like the incense giving continual fragrance to its service, then the cause of God will be triumphant.

A CALL TO MORE AND BETTER PRAYING

Better praying and more of it, that is what we need. We need holier men, and more of them, holier women, and more of them to pray— women like Hannah, who, out of their greatest griefs and temptations brewed their greatest prayers. Through prayer Hannah found her relief. Everywhere the Church was backslidden and apostate, its foes were victorious. Hannah gave herself to prayer, and in sorrow she multiplied her praying. She saw a great revival born of her praying. When the whole nation was oppressed, prophet and priest, Samuel was born to establish a new line of priesthood, and her praying warmed into life a new life for God. Everywhere religion revived. and flourished. God, true to His promise, "Ask of Me," though the praying came from a woman's broken heart, heard and answered, sending a new day of holy gladness to revive His people.

So once more, let us apply the emphasis and repeat that the great need of the Church in this and all ages is saints of such commanding faith, of such unsullied holiness, of such marked spiritual vigor and consuming zeal, that they will work spiritual revolutions through their mighty praying. Someone has said truly:

> Natural ability and educational advantages do not figure as factors in this matter; but a capacity for faith, the ability to pray, the power of a thorough consecration, the ability of self-littleness, an absolute losing of one's self in God's glory and an ever present and insatiable yearning and seeking after all the fullness of God. Men who can set the Church ablaze for God, not in a noisy, showy way, but with an intense and quiet heat that melts and moves every thing for God.

SECRET PRAYER

To return to the vital point, secret praying is the test, the gauge, the conserver of a Christian's relation to God. The prayer-chamber, while it is the test of the sincerity of our devotion to God, becomes also the measure of the devotion. The self-denial, the sacrifices that we make for our prayer-chambers, the frequency of our visits to that hallowed place of meeting with the Lord, the lingering to stay, the reluctance to leave, are values that we put on time alone with God. It is the price we pay for the Spirit's visiting hours of heavenly love.

The prayer-chamber conserves our relation to God. It hems every raw edge, tucks up every flowing and entangling garment, and girds up every fainting loin. The sheet-anchor does not hold the ship more surely and safely than the prayer-chamber holds to God. Before Satan can break our hold on God or close up our way to heaven, he has to close up the way to our prayer-chamber and break our hold on it.

Be not afraid to pray; to pray is right;
Pray if thou canst with hope, but ever pray,
Though hope be weak or sick with long delay;
Pray in the darkness if there be no light;
And if for any wish thou dare not pray
Then pray to God to cut that wish away.

Endnotes

1 Luke 18:1
2 Isaiah 25:6
3 Psalm 63:1
4 See Psalm 5:3
5 Psalm 139:18

8

Praying Saints

IN GOD'S NAME I BESEECH *you let prayer nourish your soul as your meals nourish your body. Let your fixed seasons of prayer keep you in God's presence through the day, and His presence frequently remembered through it be an ever-fresh spring of prayer. Such a brief, loving recollection of God renews a man's whole being, quiets his passions, supplies light and counsel in difficulty, gradually subdues the temper, and causes him to possess his soul in patience, or rather gives it up to the possession of God.* (Fénelon)

Devoted too much time and attention to outward and public duties of the ministry. But this is a mistaken conduct, for I have learned that neglect of much and fervent communion with God in meditation and prayer is not the way to redeem the time nor to fit me for public ministrations.

I rightly attribute my present deadness to want of sufficient time and tranquillity for private devotion. Want of more reading, retirement and private devotion, I have little mastery over my own tempers. An unhappy day to me for want of more solitude and prayer. If there be anything I do, if there be anything I leave undone, let me be perfect in prayer.

After all, whatever God may appoint, prayer is the great thing. Oh that I may be a man of prayer! (Henry Martyn)

That the Christians had quit praying in Paul's time we cannot say for certain. They have, in the main, quit praying now. They are too busy to pray. Time and strength and every faculty are laid under tribute to money, to business, to the affairs of the world. Few Christians lay themselves out in great praying. The great business of praying is a hurried, petty, starved, beggarly business with most Christians.

St. Paul calls a halt, and lays a levy on the saints for prayer. Put the saints to praying is Paul's unfailing remedy for great evils in Church, government, politics, business, and home. Put the saints to praying and politics will be cleansed, business will be godlier, the Church will be holier, and the home will be sweeter.

> I exhort therefore, that, first of all, supplications, prayers, intercessions, and giving of thanks, be made for all men; For kings, and for all that are in authority; that we may lead a quiet and peaceable life in all godliness and honesty. For this is good and acceptable in the sight of God our Saviour; . . . I will therefore that men pray every where, lifting up holy hands, without wrath and doubting.[1]

Praying women and children are invaluable to God, but if their praying is not supplemented by praying men, there will be a great loss in the power of prayer—a great breach and depreciation in the value of prayer, great paralysis in the energy of the Gospel. Jesus Christ spoke a parable unto the people, telling them that men ought always to pray and not faint. Men who are strong in everything else ought to be strong in prayer, and never yield to discouragement, weakness, or depression. Men who are brave, persistent, redoubtable in other pursuits ought to be full of courage, unfailing, and strong-hearted in prayer.

Men are to pray; all are to pray. Men, as distinguished from women, men in their strength in their wisdom. There is an absolute, specific, command that the men pray. There is an absolute imperative necessity that men pray. The first of human beings was a man, so they should also be first in prayer.

The men are to pray for men. The direction is specific and classified. Just underneath we have a specific direction with regard to women. About prayer, its importance, wideness, and practice the Bible here deals with the men in contrast to, and distinct from, the women. The men are definitely commanded, seriously charged, and warmly exhorted to pray. Perhaps in Paul's day it was that men were averse to prayer, or indifferent to it. It may be that they deemed it a small thing, and gave to it neither time, value, or significance. But God would have all men pray, and so the great Apostle lifts the subject into prominence and emphasizes its importance.

PRAYER IS OF TRANSCENDENT IMPORTANCE

Prayer is the mightiest agent to advance God's work. Only praying hearts and hands can do God's work. Prayer succeeds when all else fails.

Prayer has won great victories, and rescued, with notable triumph, God's saints when every other hope was gone. Christians who know how to pray are the greatest boon God can give to earth—they are the richest gift earth can offer heaven. Christians who know how to use this weapon of prayer are God's best soldiers, His mightiest leaders.

Praying Christians are God's chosen leaders. The distinction between the leaders that God brings to the front to lead and bless His people, and those leaders who owe their position of leadership to a worldly, selfish, unsanctified selection, is this, God's leaders are preeminently people of prayer. This distinguishes them as the simple, divine, evidence of their call, the seal of their separation by God. Whatever of other graces or gifts they may have, the gift and grace of prayer towers above them all. In whatever else they may share or differ, in the gift of prayer they are one.

What would God's leaders be without prayer? Strip Moses of his power in prayer, a gift that made him eminent in pagan estimate, and the crown is taken from his head, the food and fire of his faith are gone. Elijah without his praying would have neither record nor place in the divine legation. His character would have been insipid, cowardly, its energy, defiance, and fire gone. Without Elijah's praying the Jordan would never have yielded to the stroke of his mantle, nor would the stern angel of death have honored him with the chariot and horses of fire. The argument that God used to quiet the fears and convince Ananias of Paul's condition and sincerity is the epitome of his history, the solution of his life and work—"Behold he prayeth."[2]

WITHOUT PRAYER THERE WOULD BE NO GREAT SAINTS OF GOD

Paul, Luther, Wesley—what would these chosen ones of God be without the distinguishing and controlling element of prayer? They were leaders for God because mighty in prayer. They were not leaders because of brilliancy in thought, because exhaustless in resources, because of their magnificent culture or native endowment, but leaders because by the power of prayer they could command the power of God. Praying saints mean much more than saints who say prayers, much more than saints who pray by habit. It means saints with whom prayer is a mighty force, an energy that moves heaven and pours untold treasures of good on earth.

Praying saints are the safety of the Church from the materialism that is affecting all its plans and polity, and which is hardening its life-blood. The insinuation circulates as a secret, deadly, poison that the Church is not so dependent on purely spiritual forces as it used to be—that changed times and changed conditions have brought it out of its spiritual straits and dependencies and put it where other forces can bear it to its climax. A fatal snare of this kind has allured the Church into worldly embraces, dazzled her leaders, weakened its foundations, and shorn it of much of its beauty and strength. Praying saints are the saviors of the Church from this material tendency. They pour into it the original spiritual forces, lift it off the sand-bars of materialism, and press it out into the ocean depths of spiritual power. Praying saints keep God in the Church in full force, keep His hand on the helm, and train the Church in its lessons of strength and trust.

The number and efficiency of the laborers in God's vineyard in all lands is dependent on the people of prayer. The mightiness of these people of prayer increases, by the divinely arranged process, the number and success of the consecrated labors. Prayer opens wide their doors of access, gives holy aptness to enter, and holy boldness, firmness, and fruitage. Praying people are needed in all fields of spiritual labor. There is no position in God's Church, high or low, that can be well filled without instant prayer. No position where Christians are found that does not demand the full play of a faith that always prays and never faints. Praying Christians are needed in the house of business, as well as in the house of God, so that they may order and direct the business, not according to the principles of this world, but according to Bible precepts and the principles of the heavenly life.

The need of the Chruch

People of prayer are needed especially in the positions of Church influence, honor, and power. These leaders of Church thought, of Church work, and of Church life should be people of signal power in prayer. It is the praying heart that sanctifies the toil and skill of the hands, and the toil and wisdom of the head. Prayer keeps work in the line of God's will, and keeps thought in the line of God's Word. The solemn responsibilities of leadership, in a large or limited sphere, in God's Church should be so hedged about with prayer that between it and the world there should be an impassable gulf. The leadership should be so elevated and purified by prayer that neither cloud nor night should stain the radiance nor dim the sight of a constant meridian view of God. Many Church leaders seem to think if they can be prominent as people of business, money, influence, intelligence, plans, scholarly attainments, eloquent gifts, and conspicuous activities, that these are enough, and will win atone for the absence of the higher spiritual power that only much praying can give. But how vain and paltry are these in the serious work of bringing glory to God, controlling the Church for Him, and bringing it into full accord with its divine mission.

Praying saints do the most for God

Praying saints are the saints that have done so much for God in the past. They are the ones who have won the victories for God, and spoiled

His foes. They are the ones who have set up His Kingdom in the very camps of His enemies. There are no other conditions of success in this day. This century has no relief statute to suspend the necessity or force of prayer—no substitute by which its gracious ends can be secured. We are shut up to this—only praying hands can build for God. They are God's mighty ones on earth, His master-builders. They may be destitute of all else, but with the wrestlings and prevailings of a simple-hearted faith they are mighty, the mightiest for God. Church leaders may be gifted in all else, but without this greatest of gifts they are as Samson shorn of his locks, or as the Solomon's temple without the divine presence or the divine glory—on whose altars the heavenly flame has died.

The only protection and rescue from worldliness lie in our intense and radical spirituality. Our only hope for the existence and maintenance of this high, saving, spirituality, under God, is in the purest and most aggressive leadership—a leadership that knows the secret power of prayer. Prayer alone is the sign by which the Church has conquered and given it conscience, conviction, and courage to hold true to its symbols, true to its traditions, and true to the hidings of its power. We need this prayerful leadership. We must have it—so that by the perfection and beauty of its holiness, by the strength and elevation of its faith, by the potency and pressure of its prayers, by the authority and spotlessness of its example, by the fire and contagion of its zeal, by the singular sublimity, and unworldliness of its piety, it may influence God and hold and mold the Church to its heavenly pattern.

Praying leaders, how mightily they are felt. How their flame arouses the Church! How they stir it by the force of their Pentecostal presence! How they embattle and give victory by the conflicts and triumphs of their own faith! How they fashion it by the pressure and persistence of their prayers! How they inoculate it by the contagion and fire of their holiness! How they lead the march in great spiritual revolutions! How the Church is raised from the dead by the resurrection call of their sermons! Holiness springs up in their wake as flowers at the voice of spring, and where they tread the desert blooms as the garden of the Lord. God's cause demands such leaders along the whole line of official position from deacon to superior. How feeble, aimless, or worldly are our efforts, how demoralized and vain for God's work without them!

The gift of these leaders is not in the range of ecclesiastical power. They are God's gifts. Their being, presence, number, and ability are the tokens of His favor. Their lack of these are the sure sign of His disfavor, the witness of His withdrawal. Let God's Church be on its knees before the Lord of hosts, that He may more mightily endow the leaders we already have, and put others in rank, and lead all along the line of our embattled front.

The world is coming into the Church at many points and in many ways. It oozes in, pours in, comes in with brazen front or soft, insinuating, disguise. It comes in at the top and comes in at the bottom, and percolates through many a hidden way.

THE HEART OF THE MATTER

We are looking for praying saints—saints whose presence in the Church will make it like a censer of holiest incense flaming up to God. With God the person counts for everything. Rites, forms, organizations are of small consequences. Unless they are backed by the holiness of the person they are offensive in His sight. "Bring no more vain oblations; incense is an abomination unto me; the new moons and sabbaths, the calling of assemblies, I cannot away with; it is iniquity, even the solemn meeting."[3]

Why does God speak so strongly against His own ordinances? Personal purity had failed. The impure person tainted all the sacred institutions of God and defiled them. God regards the person in so important a way as to put a kind of discount on all else. People have built Him glorious temples and have striven and exhausted themselves to please God by all manner of gifts. But in lofty strains He has rebuked these proud worshippers and rejected their princely gifts.

Thus saith the Lord, The heaven is my throne, and the earth is my footstool: where is the house that ye build unto me? and where is the place of my rest? For all those things hath mine hand made, and all those things have been, saith the Lord: but to this man will I look, even to him that is poor and of a contrite spirit, and trembleth at my word. He that killeth an ox is as if he slew a man; he that sacrificeth a lamb, as if he cut off a dog's neck; he that offereth an oblation, as if he offered swine's blood; he that burneth incense, as if he blessed an idol. Yea, they have chosen their own ways, and their soul delighteth in their abominations.[4]

Turning away in disgust from these costly and profane offerings, He declares: "But to this man will I look, even to him that is poor and of a contrite spirit, and trembleth at My word."

PERSONAL PURITY

This truth that God regards the personal purity of the person is fundamental. This truth suffers when ordinances are made much of and forms of worship multiply. Christians and their spiritual character decline as Church ceremonials increase. The simplicity of worship is lost in religious aesthetics, or in the gaudiness of religious forms.

This truth that the personal purity of the individual is the only thing God cares for is lost sight of when the Church begins to estimate people for what they have. When the Church eyes a person's money, social standing, and belongings in any way, then spiritual values are at a fearful discount, and the tear of penitence and heaviness of guilt are never seen at its portals. Worldly bribes have opened and stained its pearly gates by the entrance of the impure.

This truth that God is looking after personal purity is swallowed up when the Church has a greed for numbers. "Not numbers, but personal purity is our aim," said the fathers of Methodism. The parading of Church statistics is mightily against the grain of spiritual religion. Eyeing numbers greatly hinders the looking after personal purity. The increase of quantity is generally at a loss of quality. Bulk abates preciousness.

A LACK OF PERSONAL PIETY

The age of Church organization and Church machinery is not an age noted for elevated and strong personal piety. Machinery looks for engineers and organizations for generals, and not for saints, to run them. The simplest organization may aid parity as well as strength but beyond that narrow limit organization swallows up the individual, and is careless of personal purity. A push for activity, enthusiasm, and zeal for an organization come in as the vicious substitutes for spiritual character. Holiness and all the spiritual graces of hardy culture and slow growth are discarded as too slow and too costly for the progress and rush of the age. By dint of machinery, new organizations, and spiritual weakness, results are vainly expected to be secured that can only be secured by faith, prayer, and waiting on God.

Christians and their spiritual character is what God is looking after. If saints, holy saints, can be turned out by the easy processes of Church machinery readier and better than by the old-time processes, we would gladly invest in every new and improved patent. But we do not believe it. We adhere to the old way—the way the holy prophets went, the king's highway of holiness.

WILLIAM WILBERFORCE

An example of this is afforded by the case of William Wilberforce. High in social position, a member of Parliament, the friend of Pitt the famous statesman, he was not called of God to forsake his high social position nor to quit Parliament, but he was called to order his life according to the pattern set by Jesus Christ and to give himself to prayer. To read the story of his life is to be impressed with its holiness and its devotion to the dams of the quiet hours alone with God. His conversion was announced to his friend—to Pitt and others—by letter.

In the beginning of his religious career he records:

My chief reasons for a day of secret prayer are, (I) That the state of public affairs is very critical and calls for earnest deprecation of the Divine displeasure. (2) My station in life is a very difficult one, wherein I am at a loss to know how to act. Direction, therefore, should be specially sought from time to time. (3) I have been graciously supported in difficult situations of a public nature.

I have gone out and returned home in safety, and found a kind reception has attended me. I would humbly hope, too, that what I am now doing is a proof that God has not withdrawn His Holy Spirit from me. I am covered with mercies.

The recurrence of his birthday led him again to review his situation and employment.

I find that books alienate my heart from God as much as anything. I have been framing a plan of study for myself, but let me remember but one thing is needful, that if my heart cannot be kept in a spiritual state without so much prayer, meditation, Scripture reading, etc., as are incompatible with study, I must seek first the righteousness of God.

Everything was to be surrendered for his spiritual advance.

I fear that I have not studied the Scriptures enough. Surely in the summer recess I ought to read the Scriptures an hour or two every day, besides prayer, devotional reading and meditation. God will prosper me better if I wait on Him. The experience of all good Christians shows that without constant prayer and watchfulness the life of God in the soul stagnates. Doddridge's morning and evening devotions were serious matters. Colonel Gardiner always spent hours in prayer in the morning before he went forth. Bonnell practiced private devotions largely morning and evening, and repeated Psalms dressing and undressing to raise his mind to heavenly things.

I would look up to God to make the means effectual. I fear that my devotions are too much hurried, that I do not read Scripture enough. I must grow in grace; I must love God more; I must feel the power of Divine things more. Whether I am more or less learned signifies not. Whether even I execute the work which I deem useful is comparatively unimportant. But beware my soul of lukewarmness.

The New Year began with the Holy Communion and new vows.

I will press forward and labor to know God better and love Him more. Assuredly I may, because God will give His Holy Spirit to them that ask Him, and the Holy Spirit will shed abroad the love of God in the heart. O, then, pray, pray; be earnest, press forward and follow on to know the Lord. Without watchfulness, humiliation and prayer, the sense of Divine things must languish.

To prepare for the future he said he found nothing more effectual than private prayer and the serious perusal of the New Testament.

I must put down that I have lately too little time for private devotions. I can sadly confirm Doddridge's remark that when we go on ill in the closet we commonly do so everywhere else. I must mend here. I am afraid of getting into what Owen calls the trade of sinning and repenting . . . Lord help me, the shortening of private devotions starves the soul; it grows lean and faint. This must not be. I must redeem more time. I see how lean in spirit I become without full allowance of time for private devotions; I must be careful to be watching unto prayer.

At another time Wilberforce wrote this:

I must try what I long ago heard was the rule of E—the great upholsterer, who, when he came from Bond Street to his little villa, always first retired to his closet. I have been keeping too late hours, and hence have had but a hurried half hour to myself. Surely the experience of all good men confirms the proposition, that without due measure of private devotions, the soul will grow lean.

To his son he wrote:

Let me conjure you not to be seduced into neglecting, curtailing or hurrying over your morning prayers. Of all things, guard against neglecting God in the closet. There is nothing more fatal to the life and power of Christianity. More solitude and earlier hours—prayer three times a day at least. How much better might I serve if I cultivated a closer communion with God.

Wilberforce knew the secret of a holy life. Is that not where most of us fall? We are so busy with other things, so immersed even in doing good and in carrying on the Lord's work, that we neglect the quiet seasons of prayer with God, and before we are aware of it our soul is lean and impoverished.

CHARLES SPURGEON

Spurgeon said:

One night alone in prayer might make us new Christians, changed from poverty of soul to spiritual wealth, from trembling to triumphing. We have an example of it in the life of Jacob. Aforetime the crafty shuffler, always bargaining and calculating, unlovely in almost every respect, yet one night in prayer turned the supplanter into a prevailing prince, and robed him with celestial grandeur. From that night he lives on the sacred page as one of the nobility of heaven.

Could not we, at least now and then, in these weary earthbound years, hedge about a single night for such enriching traffic with the skies? What, have we no sacred ambition? Are we deaf to the yearnings of Divine love? Yet, my brethren, for wealth and for science men will cheerfully quit their warm couches, and cannot we do it now and again for the love of God and the good of souls? Where is our zeal, our gratitude, our sincerity? I am ashamed while I thus upbraid both myself and you. May we often tarry at Jabbok, and cry with Jacob, as he grasped the angel—

> With thee all night I mean to stay,
> And wrestle till the break of day.

Surely, brethren, if we have given whole days to folly, we can afford a space for heavenly wisdom. Time was when we gave whole nights to chambering and wantonness, to dancing and the world's revelry; we did not tire then; we were chiding the sun that he rose so soon, and wishing the hours would lag awhile that we might delight in wilder merriment and perhaps deeper sin. Oh, wherefore, should we weary in heavenly employments? Why grow we weary when asked to watch with our Lord? Up, sluggish heart, Jesus calls thee! Rise and go forth to meet the heavenly friend in the place where He manifests Himself.

We can never expect to grow in the likeness of our Lord unless we follow His example and give more time to communion with the Father. A revival of real praying would produce a spiritual revolution.

Endnotes

1 I Timothy 2:1-3, 8
2 Acts 9:11
3 Isaiah 1:13
4 Isaiah 66:1-3

9

The Possibilities of Prayer

B EAR UP THE HANDS *that hang down, by faith and prayer; support the tottering knees. Have you any days of fasting and prayer? Storm the throne of grace and persevere therein, and mercy will come down.* (John Wesley)

We must remember that the goal of prayer is the ear of God. Unless that is gained the prayer has utterly failed. The uttering of it may have kindled devotional feeling in our minds, the hearing of it may have comforted and strengthened the hearts of those with whom we have prayed, but if the prayer has not gained the heart of God, it has failed in its essential purpose

A mere formalist can always pray so as to please himself. What has he to do but to open his book and read the prescribed words, or bow his knee and repeat such phrases as suggest themselves to his memory or his fancy? Like the Tartarian Praying Machine, give but the wind and the wheel, and the business is fully arranged. So much knee-bending and talking, and the prayer is done. The formalist's prayers are always good, or, rather, always bad, alike. But the living child of God never offers a prayer which pleases himself; his standard is above his attainments; he wonders that God listens to him, and though he knows he will be heard for Christ's sake, yet he accounts it a wonderful instance of condescending mercy that such poor prayers as his should ever reach the ears of the Lord God of Sabaoth. (C. H. Spurgeon)

It may be said with emphasis that no lazy saint prays. Can there be a lazy saint? Can there be a prayerless saint? Does not slack praying cut short sainthood's crown and kingdom? Can there be a cowardly soldier? Can there be a saintly hypocrite? Can there be virtuous vice? It is only when these impossibilities are brought into being that we then can find a prayerless saint.

To go through the motion of praying is a dull business, though not a hard one. To say prayers in a decent, delicate, way is not heavy work. But to pray really, to pray until Satan feels the ponderous stroke, to pray until the iron gates of difficulty are opened, until the mountains of obstacles are removed, until the mists are exhaled and the clouds are lifted, and the sunshine of a cloudless day brightens—this is hard work. But it is God's work and a Christian's best labor. Never was the toil of hand, head, and heart less spent in vain than when praying. It is hard to wait and press and pray, and hear no voice, yet stay until God answers. The joy of answered prayer is the joy of a travailing mother when a child is born into the world, the joy of a slave whose chains have been burst asunder and to whom new life and liberty have just come.

A bird's eye view of what has been accomplished by prayer shows what we lost when the dispensation of real prayer was substituted by Pharisaical pretence and sham. It shows, too, how imperative is the need for holy men and women who will give themselves to earnest, Christlike praying.

IT IS NOT AN EASY THING TO PRAY

Back of the praying there must lie all the conditions of prayer. These conditions are possible, but they are not to be seized in a moment by the prayerless. They may always be present to the faithful and holy, but cannot exist in or be met by a frivolous, negligent, lazy spirit. Prayer does not stand alone. It is not an isolated performance. Prayer stands in closest connection with all the duties of an ardent piety. It is the issuance of a character that is made up of the elements of a vigorous and commanding faith. Prayer honors God, acknowledges His being, exalts His power, adores His providence, secures His aid. A sneering half-rationalism cries out against devotion, that it does nothing but pray. But to pray well is to do all things well. If it be true that devotion does nothing but pray, then it does nothing at all. To do nothing but pray fails to do the praying, for the antecedent, coincident, and subsequent conditions of prayer are but the sum of all the energized forces of a practical, working piety.

The possibilities of prayer run parallel with the promises of God. Prayer opens an outlet for the promises, removes the hindrances in the way of their execution, puts them into working order, and secures their gracious ends. More than this, prayer, like faith, obtains promises, enlarges their operation, and adds to the measure of their results. God's promises were to

Abraham and to his seed, but many a barren womb, and many a minor obstacle, stood in the way of the fulfillment of these promises. Prayer, however, removed them all, made a highway for the promises, added to the facility and speediness of their realization, and by prayer the promise shone bright and perfect in its execution.

The possibilities of prayer are found in its allying itself with the purposes of God, for God's purposes and the Church's praying are the combination of all potent and omnipotent forces. More than this, the possibilities of prayer are seen in the fact that it changes the purposes of God. It is in the very nature of prayer to plead and give directions. Prayer is not a negation. It is a positive force. It never rebels against the will of God, never comes into conflict with that will, but that it does seek to change God's purpose is evident. Christ said, "The cup which My Father hath given Me, shall I not drink it?"[1] and yet He had prayed that very night, "If it be possible, let this cup pass from Me."[2] Paul sought to change the purposes of God about the thorn in his flesh. God's purposes were fixed to destroy Israel, and the prayer of Moses changed the purposes of God and saved Israel. In the time of the Judges, the people of Israel were apostate and greatly oppressed. They repented and cried to God and He said: "Ye have forsaken Me, and served other gods: wherefore I will deliver you no more:"[3] But they humbled themselves, put away their strange gods, and God's "soul was grieved for the misery of Israel,"[4] and he sent them deliverance by Jephthah.

HEZEKIAH

God sent Isaiah to say to Hezekiah, "Set thine house in order; for thou shalt die, and not live;"[5] and Hezekiah prayed, and God sent Isaiah back to say, "I have heard thy prayer, I have seen thy tears: behold . . . I will add unto thy days fifteen years."[6]

"Yet forty days and Nineveh shall be overthrown,"[7] was God's message by Jonah. But Nineveh cried mightily to God, and "God repented of the evil, that He had said that He would do unto them; and He did it not."[8] The possibilities of prayer are seen from the various conditions it reaches and the different ends it secures. Elijah prayed over a dead child, and it came to life. Elisha did the same thing. Christ prayed at Lazarus's grave, and Lazarus came forth. Peter knelt down and prayed beside dead Dorcas, and she opened her eyes and sat up, and Peter presented her alive to the distressed company. Paul prayed for Publius, and healed him. Jacob's praying changed Esau's murderous hate into the kisses of the tenderest brotherly embrace. God gave Jacob and Esau to Rebecca because Isaac prayed for her. Joseph was the child of Rachel's prayers. Hannah's praying gave Samuel to Israel. John the Baptist was given to Elizabeth, barren and past age as she was, in answer to the prayer of Zacharias. Elisha's praying brought famine or harvest to Israel—as he prayed so it was. Ezra's praying carried the Spirit of God in heart-breaking conviction to the entire city of Jerusalem, and brought them in tears of repentance back to God. Isaiah's praying carried the shadow of the sun back ten degrees on the dial of Ahaz.

In answer to Hezekiah's praying, an angel slew one hundred and eighty-five thousand of Sennacherib's army in one night. Daniel's praying opened to him the vision of prophecy, helped him to administer the affairs of a mighty kingdom, and sent an angel to shut the lions' mouths. The angel was sent to Cornelius, and the Gospel opened through him to the Gentile world, for the angel said to him "Thine prayers and alms are come up for a memorial before God."

"And what shall I more say? for the time would fail me to tell of Gedeon, and of Barak, and of Samson, and of Jephthae; of David also, and Samuel, and of the prophets."[9] Also of Paul and Peter, and John and the Apostles, and the holy company of saints, reformers, and martyrs, who, through praying "subdued kingdoms, wrought righteousness, obtained promises, stopped the mouths of lions, Quenched the violence of fire, escaped the edge of the sword, out of weakness were made strong, waxed valiant in fight, turned to flight the armies of the aliens."[10]

PRAYER PUTS GOD INTO THE PROBLEM

Prayer puts God in the matter with commanding force: "Ask of Me things to come concerning My sons," says God, "and concerning the work of My hands command ye Me."[11] We are charged in God's Word "always to pray,"[12] "in every thing by prayer,"[13] "continuing instant in prayer,"[14] to "pray every where,"[15] "praying always."[16]

The promise is as illimitable as the command is comprehensive. "All things, whatsoever ye shall ask in prayer, believing, ye shall receive,"[17] "whatever ye shall ask,"[18] "if ye shall ask any thing."[19] "Ye shall ask what ye will, and it shall be done unto you."[20] "Whatsoever ye ask the Father . . . He will give it to you."[21]

If there is anything not involved in all things whatsoever, or not found in the phrase ask anything, then these things may be left out of prayer. Language could not cover a wider range, nor involve more fully all of the smallest details. These statements are but samples of the all-comprehending possibilities of prayer under the promises of God to those who meet the conditions of right praying.

These passages, though, give but a general outline of the immense regions over which prayer extends its sway. Beyond these, the effects of prayer reaches and secures good from regions that cannot be traversed by language or thought. Paul exhausted language and thought in praying, but conscious of necessities not covered and realms of good not reached he covers these impenetrable and undiscovered regions by this general statement, "unto Him that is able to do exceeding abundantly above all that we ask or think, according to the power that worketh in us."[22] The promise is, "Call upon Me, and I will answer thee, and show thee great and mighty things, which thou knowest not."[23]

ELIJAH'S PRAYERS

James declared that "the effectual fervent prayer of a righteous man availeth much."[24] How much he could not tell, but illustrates it by the power of Old Testament praying to stir up New Testament saints to imitate, by the fervor and influence of their praying, the holy prophets of old, and duplicate and surpass the power of their praying. Elijah, he says, "was a man subject to like passions as we are, and he prayed earnestly that it might not rain: and it rained not on the earth by the space of three years and six months. And he prayed again, and the heaven gave rain, and the earth brought forth her fruit."[25]

ALL OF HEAVEN WAITS ON THE PRAYERS OF THE SAINTS

In the Revelation of John, the whole lower order of God's creation and His providential government, the Church and the angelic world, are in the attitude of waiting on the efficiency of the prayers of the saintly ones on earth to carry on the various interests of earth and heaven. The angel takes the fire kindled by prayer and casts it earthward, "and there were voices, and thunderings, and lightnings, and an earthquake."[26] Prayer is the force that creates all these alarms, disturbances, and struggles. "Ask of Me," says God to His Son, and to the Church of His Son, "and I shall give thee the heathen for Thine inheritance, and the uttermost parts of the earth for Thy possessions."[27]

The saints who have done mighty things for God have always been mighty in prayer, have well understood the possibilities of prayer, and made most of these possibilities. The Son of God, the first of all the mightiest of all, has shown us the all-powerful and far-reaching possibilities of prayer. Paul was mighty for God because he knew how to use, and how to get others to use, the mighty spiritual forces of prayer.

The seraphim, burning, sleepless, adoring, is the figure of prayer. It is resistless in its ardor—devoted and tireless. There are hindrances to prayer that nothing but pure, intense, flame can surmount. There are toils and outlays and endurance that nothing but the strongest, most ardent flame can abide. Prayer may be low-tongued, but it cannot be cold-tongued. Its words may be few, but they must be on fire. Its feelings may not be impetuous, but they must be white with heat. It is the "effectual fervent prayer" that influences God.

THE HOUSE OF PRAYER

God's work is the work of prayer. It is the zeal for God's house and the zeal for God's work that makes God's house glorious and His work abide.

When the prayer-chambers of saints are closed or are entered casually or coldly, then Church rulers are secular, fleshly, and materialized. It is then that spiritual character sinks to a low level, and the ministry becomes restrained and weakened.

When prayer fails, the world prevails. When prayer fails, the Church loses its divine characteristics, its divine power. The Church is swallowed up by a proud ecclesiasticism, and the world scoffs at its obvious impotence.

Endnotes

1 John 18:11
2 Matthew 26:39
3 Judges 10:13
4 Judges 10:16
5 2 Kings 20:1
6 2 Kings 20:5-6
7 Jonah 3:4
8 Jonah 3:10
9 Hebrews 11:32
10 Hebrews 11:33-34
11 Isaiah 45:11
12 Luke 18:1
13 Philippians 4:6
14 Romans 12:12
15 1 Timothy 2:8
16 Ephesians 6:18
17 Matthew 21:22
18 John 14:13
19 John 14:14
20 John 15:7
21 John 16:23
22 Ephesians 3:20
23 Jeremiah 33:3
24 James 5:16
25 James 5:17-18
26 Revelation 8:5
27 Psalm 2:8

10

Prayerless Praying

I TOOK UPON ALL THE *four Gospels as thoroughly genuine, for there is in them the reflection of a greatness which emanated from the person of Jesus and which was of as Divine a kind as ever was seen on earth.* (Goethe)

There are no possibilities, no necessity for prayerless praying, a heartless performance, a senseless routine, a dead habit, a hasty, careless performance—it justifies nothing. Prayerless praying has no life, gives no life, is dead, breathes one death. Not a battle-axe but a child's toy, for play not for service. Prayerless praying does not come up to the importance and aims of a recreation. Prayerless praying is only a weight, an impediment in the hour of struggle, of intense conflict a call to retreat in the moment of battle and victory. (E. M. Bounds)

Why do we not pray? What are the hindrances to prayer? This is not a curious nor trivial question. It goes not only to the whole matter of our praying, but to the whole matter of our Christianity. Christianity is bound to decline when praying is hindered. That which hinders praying, hinders Christianity. Saints who are too busy to pray will be too busy to live a holy life.

Other duties become pressing and absorbing and crowd out prayer. If an inquest could be secured on this dire, spiritual, calamity, the coroner's verdict in many cases of dead praying would be "starved to death." This way of hindering prayer becomes so natural, so easy, so innocent that it comes on us all unawares. If we will allow our praying to be crowded out, it will always be done. Satan had rather we let the grass grow on the path to our prayer-chamber than anything else. A closed chamber of prayer means gone out of Christian business. Or what is worse, made an assignment and carrying on our Christianity in some other name than God's and to somebody else's glory. God's glory is only secured in the business of Christianity by carrying that Christianity on with a large capital of prayer. The apostles understood this when they declared that their time must not be employed in even the sacred duties of alms-giving. They must give themselves, they said, "continually to prayer and to the ministry of the Word."[1] Prayer was put first with them and the ministry of the Word gained its efficiency and life from prayer.

The process of hindering prayer by crowding out is simple and goes by advancing stages. First, prayer is hurried through. Unrest and agitation, fatal to all devout exercises, come in. Then the time is shortened, desire for the exercise weakens. Then it is crowded into a corner and depends on the fragments of time for its exercise. Its value depreciates. The duty has lost its importance. It no longer commands respect or brings benefit. It has fallen out of estimate, out of the heart, out of the habits, and out of the life. We cease to pray and cease to live spiritually.

There is nothing that stops the desolating floods of worldliness and business and cares but prayer. Christ meant this when He charged us to "watch and pray."[2] There is no pioneering corps for the Gospel but prayer. Paul knew that when he declared that "night and day [we pray] exceedingly that we might see your face, and might perfect that which is lacking in your faith."[3] There is no arriving at a high state of grace without much praying, and no staying in those high states without great praying. Epaphras knew this when he labored "fervently . . . in prayers" for the Colossian Church, "that [they might] stand perfect and complete in all the will of God."[4]

PRESERVING OUR PRAYING

The only way to preserve our praying from being hindered is to estimate prayer at its true and great value. Estimate it as Daniel did, who, when he "knew that the writing was signed he went into his house; and his windows being opened to Jerusalem, he kneeled upon his knees three times a day and prayed and gave thanks before his God, as he did aforetime."[5] Put praying into the high values as Daniel did, above place, honor, ease, wealth, and life. Put praying into the habits as Daniel did. "As he did aforetime" has much in it to give firmness and faithfulness in the hour of trial—much in it to remove hindrances and master opposing circumstances.

One of Satan's wiliest tricks is to destroy the best by the good. Business and other duties are good, but we are so filled with these that they crowd out and destroy the best. Prayer holds the citadel for God, and if Satan can by any means weaken prayer he is a gainer so far. And when prayer is dead, the citadel is taken. We must keep prayer as the faithful sentinel keeps

guard, with sleepless vigilance. We must not keep it half-starved and feeble as a baby, but we must keep it in giant strength. Our prayer-chamber should have our freshest strength, our calmest time, its hours unhindered, without intrusion, and without haste. Private place and plenty of time are the life of prayer. To kneel upon our knees three times a day and pray and give thanks before God as we did aforetime, is the very heart and soul of Christianity, and makes saints, like Daniel of "an excellent spirit,"[6] and "greatly beloved"[7] in heaven.

The greatness of prayer, involving as it does the whole person, in the intense form, is not realized without spiritual discipline. This makes it hard work, and before this exacting and consuming effort our spiritual sloth or feebleness stands abashed.

THE SIMPLICITY OF PRAYER

The simplicity of prayer, its child-like elements, form a great obstacle to true praying. Intellect gets in the way of the heart. Only the child-spirit is the spirit of prayer. It is no holiday occupation to make the person a child again. In song, in poetry, in memory a saints may wish to be a child again, but in prayer the saint must be a child again in reality. It must be as though we are at our mother's knee, artless, sweet, intense, direct, and trustful. With no shade of doubt, no temper to be denied. A desire that burns and consumes that can only be voiced by a cry. It is no easy work to have this child-like spirit of prayer.

If praying were but an hour in the closet, difficulties would face and hinder even that hour. But praying is the whole life preparing for the closet. How difficult it is to cover home and business, all the sweets and all the bitters of life, with the holy atmosphere of the closet! A holy life is the only preparation for prayer. It is just as difficult to pray as it is to live a holy life. In this we find a wall of exclusion built around our closets. Christians do not love holy praying, because they do not love and will not do holy living. Montgomery sets forth the difficulties of true praying when he declares the sublimity and simplicity of prayer.

> Prayer is the simplest form of speech
> That infant lips can try.
> Prayer is the sublimest strains that reach
> The Majesty on high.

This is not only good poetry, but a profound truth as to the loftiness and simplicity of prayer. There are great difficulties in reaching the exalted, angelic, strains of prayer. The difficulty of coming down to the simplicity of infant lips is not much less.

Prayer in the Old Testament is called wrestling. Conflict and skill, strenuous, exhaustive, effort are involved. In the New Testament we have the terms striving, laboring fervently, fervent, effectual, agony, all indicating putting forth intense effort, and overcoming difficulties. We sing in our praises.

> What various hindrances we meet
> In coming to a mercy seat.

We also have learned that the gracious results secured by prayer are generally proportioned to the outlay in removing the hindrances that obstruct our soul's high communion with God.

SATAN TREMBLES WHEN CHRISTIANS PRAY

Christ spoke a parable to this end, that "men ought always to pray, and not to faint."[8] The parable of the persistent widow teaches the difficulties in praying, how they are to be surmounted, and the happy results that follow from noble praying. Difficulties will always obstruct the way to the closet as long as it remains true . . .

> That Satan trembles when he sees
> me weakest saint upon his knees.

Courageous faith is made stronger and purer by mastering difficulties. These difficulties but focus the eye of faith on the glorious prize that is to be won by the successful wrestler in prayer. Saints must not faint in the contest of prayer. They must give themselves to this high and holy work, defying the difficulties in the way, and experience more than an angel's happiness in the results. Luther said, "To have prayed well is to have studied well." More than that, to have prayed well is to have fought well. To have prayed well is to have lived well. To pray well is to die well.

PRAYER IS A GIFT

Prayer is a rare gift, not a popular, ready, gift. Prayer is not the fruit of natural talents. It is the product of faith, holiness, and a deeply spiritual character. Christians learn to pray as they learn to love. Perfection in simplicity, in humility in faith—these form its chief ingredients. Novices in these graces are not adept in prayer. It cannot be seized upon by untrained hands. Graduates in heaven's highest school of art can alone touch its finest keys, raise its sweetest, highest notes. Fine material, fine finish are required. Master workers are required, for mere beginners cannot execute the work of prayer.

The spirit of prayer should rule our spirits and our conduct. The spirit of the prayer-chamber must control our lives or the closest hour will be dull and sapless. Always praying in spirit; always acting in the spirit of praying—these make our praying strong. The spirit of every moment is that which imparts strength to the closet communion. It is what we are out of the closet that gives victory or brings defeat to the closet. If the spirit of the world prevails in our non-closet hours, the spirit of the world will prevail in our closet hours, and that will make it a vain and idle farce.

We must live for God out of the closet if we would meet God in the closet. We must bless God by praying lives if we would have God's blessing in the closet. We must do God's will in our lives if we would have Gods ear in the closet. We must listen to God's voice in public if we would have God listen to our voice in private. God must have our hearts out of the closet, if we would have God's presence in the closet. If we would have God in the closet, God must have us out of the closet. There is no way of praying to God, but by living to God. The closet is not simply a confessional, but a place of holy communion and high, of sweet communion, and of intense intercession.

PRAYER AND HOLY LIVING

They would get more from God if they lived more obedient and well pleasing to God. We would have more strength and time for the divine work of intercession if we did not have to expend so much strength and time setting up old scores and paying our delinquent taxes. Our spiritual liabilities are so greatly in excess of our spiritual assets that our closet time is spent in taking out a decree of bankruptcy instead of being the time of great spiritual wealth for us and for others. Our closets are too much like the sign, "Closed for Repairs."

John said of primitive Christian praying, "Whatsoever we ask, we receive of Him, because we keep His commandments, and do those things that are pleasing in His sight."[9] We should note what unlimited grounds were covered, what unlimited gifts were received by their strong praying: "Whatsoever"—how comprehensive the range and reception of mighty praying; how suggestive the reasons for the ability to pray and to have prayers answered. Obedience, but more than mere obedience, doing the things that please God well. They went to their closets made strong by their strict obedience and loving faithfulness to God in their conduct. Their lives were not only true and obedient, but they were thinking about things above obedience, searching for and doing things to make God glad. These can come with eager step and radiant countenance to meet their Father in the closet, not simply to be forgiven, but to be approved and to receive.

It makes much difference whether we come to God as a criminal or a child, to be pardoned or to be approved, to settle scores or to be embraced, for punishment or for favor. Our praying to be strong must be buttressed by holy living. The name of Christ must be honored by our lives before it will honor our intercessions. The life of faith perfects the prayer of faith.

OUR LIVES GIVE COLOR AND BODY TO OUR PRAYING

Our lives not only give color to our praying, but they give body to it as well. Bad living makes bad praying. We pray feebly because we live feebly. The stream of praying cannot rise higher than the fountain of living. The closet force is made up of the energy that flows from the converging streams of living. The feebleness of living throws its weakness into closet homes. We cannot talk to God strongly when we have not lived for God strongly. The closet cannot be holy to God when the life has not been holy to God. The Word of God emphasizes our conduct as giving value to our praying. "Then shalt thou call, and the LORD shalt answer; Thou shalt cry, and He shall say, Here I am. If thou take away from the midst of thee the yoke, the putting forth of the finger, and speaking vanity."[10]

Saints are to pray "lifting up holy hands, without wrath and doubting."[11] We are to pass the time of our time here in fear if we would call on the Father. We cannot divorce praying from conduct. "Whatsoever we ask, we receive of Him, because we keep His commandments, and do those things that are pleasing in His sight."[12] "Ye ask, and receive not, because ye ask amiss, that ye may consume it upon your lusts."[13] The injunction of Christ, "Watch and pray,"[14] is to cover and guard conduct that we may come to our closets with all the force secured by a vigilant guard over our lives.

CHRISTIANITY AND BAD LIVING

Our Christianity breaks down most often and most sadly in our conduct. Beautiful theories are marred by ugly lives. The most difficult as well as the most impressive point in piety is to live it. Our praying suffers as much as our Christianity from bad living. Preachers were charged in primitive times to preach by their lives or preach not at all. So Christians everywhere ought to be charged to pray by their lives or pray not at all. Of course the prayer of repentance is acceptable. But repentance means to quit doing wrong and learn to do well. A repentance that does not produce a change in conduct is a sham. Praying that does not result in pure conduct is a delusion. We have missed the whole office and virtue of praying if it does not rectify conduct. It is in the very nature of things that we must quit praying or quit bad conduct. Cold, dead praying may exist with bad conduct, but cold, dead praying is no praying in God's estimate. Our praying advances in power as it rectifies the life. A life growing in its purity and devotion will be a more prayerful life.

The pity is that so much of our praying is without object or aim. It is without purpose. How much praying there is by men and women who never abide in Christ—hasty praying, sweet praying full of sentiment, pleasing praying, but not backed by a life wedded to Christ. Popular praying! How much of this praying is from unsanctified hearts and unhallowed lips! Prayers spring into life under the influence of some great excitement, by some pressing emergency, through some popular clamor, some great peril. But the conditions of prayer are not there. We rush into God's presence and try to link Him to our cause, inflame Him with our passions, move Him by our peril. All things are to be prayed for—but with clean hands, with absolute deference to God's will, and abiding in Christ. Prayerless praying by lips and hearts untrained to prayer, by lives out of harmony with Jesus Christ—prayerless praying, which has the form and motion of prayer but is without the true heart of prayer—never moves God to an answer. It is of such praying that James says: "Ye ask, and receive not, because ye ask not. Ye ask, and receive not, because ye ask amiss."[15]

The two great evils—not asking, and asking in a wrong way. Perhaps the greater evil is wrong asking, for it has in it the show of duty done, of praying when there has been no praying—a deceit, a fraud, a sham. The times of the most praying are not really the times of the best praying. The Pharisees prayed much, but they were actuated by vanity. Their praying was the symbol of their hypocrisy by which they made God's house of prayer a den of robbers. Theirs was praying on state occasions—mechanical, perfunctory, professional, beautiful in words, fragrant in sentiment, well ordered, well received by the ears that heard, but utterly devoid of every element of real prayer.

THE CONDITIONS OF PRAYER

The conditions of prayer are well ordered and clear—abiding in Christ and in His name. One of the first necessities, if we are to grasp the infinite possibilities of prayer, is to get rid of prayerless praying. It is often beautiful in words and in execution. It has the drapery of prayer in rich and costly form, but it lacks the soul of praying. We fall so easily into the habit of prayerless service, of merely filling a program.

If Christians only prayed on all occasions and in every place where they go through the motion! If there were only holy inflamed hearts back of all these beautiful words and gracious forms! If there were always uplifted hearts in these erect Christians who are uttering flawless but vain words before God! If there were always reverent bended hearts when bended knees are uttering words before God to please people's ears!

There is nothing that will preserve the life of prayer; its vigor, sweetness, obligations, seriousness and value, so much as a deep conviction that prayer is an approach to God, a pleading with God, an asking of God. Reality will then be in it, reverence will then be in the attitude, in the place, and in the air. Faith will draw, kindle, and open. Formality and deadness cannot live in this high and all-serious home of the soul.

PRAYERLESS PRAYING

Prayerless praying lacks the essential element of true praying—it is not based on desire, and is devoid of earnestness and faith. Desire burdens the chariot of prayer, and faith drives its wheels. Prayerless praying has no burden, because it has no sense of need. There is no fire because there is none of the vision, strength, or glow of faith. No mighty pressure to prayer, no holding on to God with the deathless, despairing, grasp, "I will not let Thee go, except thou bless me."[16] No utter self-abandon, lost in the throes of a desperate, pertinacious, and consuming plea: "Yet now, if Thou wilt forgive their sin—; if not, blot me, I pray thee, out of Thy book;"[17] or, "Give me Scotland, or I die."

Prayerless praying stakes nothing on the issue, for it has nothing to stake. It comes with empty hands, indeed, and they are listless hands as well as empty. They have never learned the lesson of empty hands clinging to the Cross. This lesson to them has no form nor comeliness.

Prayerless praying has no heart in its praying. The lack of heart deprives praying of its reality, and makes it an empty and unfit vessel. Heart, soul, life must be in our praying. The heavens must feel the force of our crying, and must be brought into oppressed sympathy for our bitter and needy state. A need that oppresses us, and has no relief but in our crying to God, must voice our praying.

Prayerless praying is insincere. It has no honesty at heart. We name in words what we do not want in heart. Our prayers give formal utterance to the things for which our hearts are not only not hungry, but for which they really have no taste. We once heard an eminent and saintly preacher, now in heaven, come abruptly and sharply on a congregation that had just risen from prayer, with the question and statement, "What did you pray for? If God should take hold of you and shake you, and demand what you prayed for, you could not tell Him to save your life what the prayer was that has just died from your lips."

So it always is, prayerless praying has neither memory nor heart. A mere form, a heterogeneous mass, an insipid compound, a mixture thrown together for sound and to fill up, but with neither heart nor aim, is prayerless praying. A dry routine, a dreary drudge, a dull and heavy task is this prayerless praying.

But prayerless praying is much worse than either task or drudge, it divorces praying from living. It utters its words against the world, but with heart and life runs into the world. It prays for humility, but nurtures pride. Prays for self-denial, while indulging the flesh. Nothing exceeds in gracious results true praying, but better not to pray at all than to pray prayerless prayers, for they are but sinning, and the worst of sinning is to sin on our knees.

PRAYING BY HABIT

The prayer habit is a good habit, but praying by dint of habit only is a very bad habit. This kind of praying is not conditioned after God's order, nor generated by God's power. It is not only a waste, a perversion, and a delusion, but it is a prolific source of unbelief. Prayerless praying gets no results. God is not reached, self is not helped. It is better not to pray at all than to secure no results from praying. Better for the one who prays, better for others. People hear of the grand results that are to be secured by prayer—the matchless good promised in God's Word to prayer. These keen-eyed worldlings or timid little faith ones mark the great discrepancy between the results promised and results realized, and are led necessarily to doubt the truth and worth of that which is so big in promise and so beggarly in results. Christianity and God are dishonored, and doubt and unbelief are strengthened by much asking and no getting.

In contrast with this, what a mighty force prayerful praying is. Real prayer helps God and humanity. God's Kingdom is advanced by it. The greatest good comes to humanity by it. Prayer can do anything that God can do. The pity is that we do not believe this as we ought, and we do not put it to the test.

DR. A. J. GORDON

The deepest need of the Church today is not for any material or external thing, but the deepest need is spiritual. Prayerless work will never bring in the kingdom. We neglect to pray in the prescribed way. We seldom enter the closet and shut the door for a season of prayer. Kingdom interests are pressing on us thick and fast and we must pray. Prayerless giving will never evangelize the world. (Dr. A. J. Gordon)

Endnotes

1 Acts 6:4
2 Matthew 26:41
3 1 Thessalonians 3:10
4 Colossians 4:12
5 Daniel 6:10
6 Daniel 5:12, 6:3
7 Daniel 10:11
8 Luke 18:1
9 1 John 3:22
10 Isaiah 58:9
11 1 Timothy 2:8
12 1 John 3:22
13 James 4:3
14 Matthew 26:41
15 James 4:2-3
16 Genesis 32:26
17 Exodus 32:32

II

Prayer Can Do Anything

THE GREAT SUBJECT OF *prayer, that comprehensive need of the Christian's life, is intimately bound up in the personal fullness of the Holy Spirit. It is "by the One Spirit we have access unto the Father"* (Ephesians. 2:18), *and by the same Spirit, having entered the audience chamber through the "new and living way" we are enabled to pray in the will of God* (Romans 8:15, 26-27; Galatians 4:6; Ephesians. 6:18; Jude 20-21).

Here is the secret of prevailing prayer, to pray under a direct inspiration of the Holy Spirit, whose petitions for us and through us are always according to the Divine purpose, and hence certain of answer. "Praying in the Holy Ghost" is but cooperating with the will of God, and such prayer is always victorious. How many Christians there are who cannot pray, and who seek by effort, resolve, joining prayer circles, etc., to cultivate in themselves the "holy art of intercession," and all to no purpose. Here for them and for all is the only secret of a real prayer life—"Be filled with the Spirit," who is "the Spirit of grace and supplication." (Rev. J. Stuart Holden, M.A.)

The preceding chapter closed with the statement that prayer can do anything that God can do. It is a tremendous statement to make, but it is a statement borne out by history and experience. If we are abiding in Christ—and if we abide in Him we are living in obedience to His holy will—and approach God in His name, then there lies open before us the infinite resources of the divine treasure-house.

557

The saint who truly prays gets from God many things denied to the prayerless person. The aim of all real praying is to get the thing prayed for, as the child's cry for bread has for its end the getting of bread. This view removes prayer clean out of the sphere of religious performances. Prayer is not acting a part or going through religious motions. Prayer is neither official nor formal nor ceremonial, but direct, hearty, intense. Prayer is not religious work that must be gone through, and succeeds because it is well done. Prayer is the helpless and needy child crying to the compassion of the Father's heart and the bounty and power of a Father's hand. The answer is as sure to come as the Father's heart can be touched and the Father's hand moved.

ASK, SEEK, KNOCK

The object of asking is to receive. The aim of seeking is to find. The purpose of knocking is to arouse attention and get in, and this is Christ's repeated assurance that the prayer without doubt will be answered, its end without doubt secured. Not by some round-about way, but by getting the very thing asked for.

The value of prayer does not lie in the number of prayers, or the length of prayers, but its value is found in the great truth that we are privileged by our relations to God to unburden our desires and make our requests known to God, and He will relieve by granting our petitions. The child asks because the parent is in the habit of granting the child's requests. As the children of God we need something and we need it badly, and we go to God for it. Neither the Bible nor the child of God knows anything of that half-infidel declaration, that we are to answer our own prayers. God answers prayer. True Christians do not pray to stir themselves up, but their prayers are the stirring up of themselves to take hold of God. The heart of faith knows nothing of that specious skepticism that stays the steps of prayer and chills its ardor by whispering that prayer does not affect God.

D. L. MOODY

D. L. Moody used to tell a story of a little child whose father and mother had died, and who was taken into another family. The first night she asked whether she could pray as she used to do. They said: "Oh, yes!" So she knelt down and prayed as her mother had taught her; and when that was ended, she added a little prayer of her own: "O God, make these people as kind to me as father and mother were." Then she paused and looked up, as if expecting the answer, and then added: "Of course you will." How sweetly simple was that little one's faith! She expected God to answer and "do," and "of course" she got her request, and that is the spirit in which God invites us to approach Him.

Daniel Quorm

In contrast to that incident is the story told of the quaint Yorkshire class leader, Daniel Quorm, who was visiting a friend. One morning he came to the friend and said, "I am sorry you have met with such a great disappointment."

"Why, no," said the man, "I have not met with any disappointment."

"Yes," said Daniel, "you were expecting something remarkable today."

"What do you mean?" said the friend.

"Why you prayed that you might be kept sweet and gentle all day long. And, by the way things have been going, I see you have been greatly disappointed."

"Oh," said the man, "I thought you meant something particular."

Prayer is mighty in its operations, and God never disappoints those who put their trust and confidence in Him. They may have to wait long for the answer, and they may not live to see it, but the prayer of faith never misses its object.

Dr. J. Wilbur Chapman

"A friend of mine in Cincinnati had preached his sermon and sank back in his chair, when he felt impelled to make another appeal to sinners," says Dr. J. Wilbur Chapman. "A boy at the back of the church lifted his hand.

"My friend left the pulpit and went down to him, and said, 'Tell me about yourself.'

"The boy said, 'I live in New York. I am a prodigal. I have disgraced my father's name and broken my mother's heart. I ran away and told them I would never come back until I became a Christian or they brought me home dead.' That night there went from Cincinnati a letter telling his father and mother that their boy had turned to God.

"Seven days later, in a black-bordered envelope, a reply came which read: 'My dear boy, when I got the news that you had received Jesus Christ the sky was overcast; your father was dead.' Then the letter went on to tell how the father had prayed for his prodigal boy with his last breath, and concluded, 'You are a Christian tonight because your old father would not let you go.'"

A steadfast father

A fourteen-year-old boy was given a task by his father. It so happened that a group of boys came along just then and wiled the boy away with them, and so the work went undone. But the father came home that evening and said, "Frank, did you do the work that I gave you?"

"Yes, sir," said Frank. He told an untruth, and his father knew it, but said nothing. It troubled the boy, but he went to bed as usual.

Next morning his mother said to him, "Your father did not sleep all last night."

"Why didn't he sleep?" asked Frank.

His mother said, "He spent the whole night praying for you."

This sent the arrow into his heart. He was deeply convicted of his sin, and knew no rest until he had got right with God. Long afterward, when the boy became Bishop Warne, he said that his decision for Christ came from his father's prayer that night. He saw his father keeping his lonely and sorrowful vigil praying for his boy, and it broke his heart. Said he, "I can never be sufficiently grateful to him for that prayer."

AN EVANGELIST

An evangelist, much used of God, has put on record that he commenced a series of meetings in a little church of about twenty members who were very cold and dead, and much divided. A little prayer meeting was kept up by two or three women. "I preached, and closed at eight o'clock," he says. "There was no one to speak or pray. The next evening one man spoke.

"The next morning I rode six miles to a minister's study, and kneeled in prayer. I went back, and said to the little church: 'If you can make out enough to board me, I will stay until God opens the windows of heaven. God has promised to bless these means, and I believe He will.'

"Within ten days there were so many anxious souls that I met one hundred and fifty of them at a time in an inquiry meeting, while Christians were praying in another house of worship. Several hundred, I think, were converted. It is safe to believe God."

JOHN B. GOUGH

A mother asked the late John B. Gough to visit her son to win him to Christ. Gough found the young man's mind full of skeptical notions, and impervious to argument. Finally, the young man was asked to pray, just once, for light. He replied: "I do not know anything perfect to whom or to which I could pray."

"How about your mother's love?" said the orator. "Isn't that perfect? Hasn't she always stood by you, and been ready to take you in, and care for you, when even your father had really kicked you out?"

The young man chocked with emotion, and said, "Y-e-s, sir; that is so."

"Then pray to Love—it will help you. Will you promise?" He promised.

That night the young man prayed in the privacy of his room. He kneeled down, closed his eyes, and struggling a moment uttered the words: "O Love." Instantly as by a flash of lightning, the old Bible text came to him: "God is love," and he said, brokenly, "O God!"

Then another flash of divine truth, and a voice said, "God so loved the world, that He gave His only begotten Son,"—and there, instantly, he exclaimed, "O Christ, Thou incarnation of divinest love, show me light and truth." It was all over. He was in the light of the most perfect peace. He ran downstairs, adds the narrator of this incident, and told his mother that he was saved. That young man is today an eloquent minister of Jesus Christ.

Miss Dickerson

A water famine was threatened in Hakodate, Japan. Miss Dickerson, of the Methodist Episcopal Girls' School, saw the water supply growing less daily, and in one of the fall months appealed to the Board in New York for help. There was no money on hand, and nothing was done. Miss Dickerson inquired the cost of putting down an artesian well, but found the expense too great to be undertaken.

On the evening of December 31st, when the water was almost exhausted, the teachers and the older pupils met to pray for water, though they had no idea how their prayer was to be answered. A couple of days later a letter was received in the New York office that ran something like this: "Philadelphia, January 1st. It is six o'clock in the morning of New Year's Day. All the other members of the family are asleep, but I was awakened with a strange impression that someone, somewhere is in need of money that the Lord wants me to supply." Enclosed was a cashier's check for an amount that just covered the cost of the artesian well and the piping of the water into the school buildings.

Ramabai

"I have seen God's hand stretched out to heal among the heathen in as mighty wonder-working power as in apostolic times," once said a well known minister to the writer. "I was preaching to two thousand famine orphan girls, at Kedgaum, India, at Ramabai's Mukti (salvation) Mission. A swarm of serpents as venomous and deadly as the reptile that smote Paul, suddenly raided the walled grounds, 'sent of Satan,' Ramabai said, and several of her most beautiful and faithful Christian girls were smitten by them, two of them bitten twice. I saw four of the very flower of her flock in convulsions at once, unconscious and apparently in the agonies of death.

"Ramabai believes the Bible with an implicit and obedient faith. There were three of us missionaries there. She said: 'We will do just what the Bible says, I want you to minister for their healing according to James 5:14-18.' She led the way into the dormitory where her girls were lying in spasms, and we laid our hands upon their heads and prayed, and anointed them with oil in the name of the Lord. Each of them was healed as soon as anointed and sat up and sang with faces shining. That miracle and marvel among the heathen mightily confirmed the word of the Lord, and was a profound and overpowering proclamation of God."

HUDSON TAYLOR

Some years ago, the record of a wonderful work of grace in connection with one of the stations of the China Inland Mission attracted a good deal of attention. Both the number and spiritual character of the converts had been far greater than at other stations where the consecration of the missionaries had been just as great as at the more fruitful place.

This rich harvest of souls remained a mystery until Hudson Taylor on a visit to England discovered the secret. At the close of one of his addresses a gentleman came forward to make his acquaintance. In the conversation that followed, Mr. Taylor was surprised at the accurate knowledge the man possessed concerning this inland China station. "But how is it," Mr. Taylor asked, "that you are so conversant with the conditions of that work?"

"Oh!" he replied, "the missionary there and I are old college-mates. For years we have regularly corresponded. He sends me names of enquirers and converts, and these I daily take to God in prayer."

At last the secret was found! A praying saint at home, praying definitely, praying daily, for specific cases among the heathen. That is the real intercessory missionary.

Hudson Taylor himself, as all the world knows, was a man who knew how to pray and whose praying was blessed with fruitful answers. In the story of his life, told by Dr. and Mrs. Howard Taylor, we find page after page aglow with answered prayer.

On his way out to China for the first time, in 1853, when he was only 21 years of age, he had a definite answer to prayer that was a great encouragement to his faith. "They had just come through the Dampier Strait, but were not yet out of sight of the islands. Usually a breeze would spring up after sunset and last until about dawn. The utmost use was made of it, but during the day they lay still with flapping sails, often drifting back and losing a good deal of the advantage gained at night." The story continues in Hudson Taylor's own words:

"This happened notably on one occasion when we were in dangerous proximity to the north of New Guinea. Saturday night had brought us to a point some thirty miles off the land, and during the Sunday morning service, which was held on deck, I could not fail to see that the Captain looked troubled and frequently went over to the side of the ship. When the service was ended I learned from him the cause. A four-knot current was carrying us toward some sunken reefs, and we were already so near that it seemed improbable that we should get through the afternoon in safety. After dinner, the long boat was put out and all hands endeavored, without success, to turn the ship's head from the shore.

"After standing together on the deck for some time in silence, the Captain said to me:

"'Well, we have done everything that can be done. We can only await the result.'

"A thought occurred to me, and I replied: 'No, there is one thing we have not done yet.'

"'What is that?' he queried.

"'Four of us on board are Christians. Let us each retire to his own cabin, and in agreed prayer ask the Lord to give us immediately a breeze. He can as easily send it now as at sunset.'

"The Captain complied with this proposal. I went and spoke to the other two men, and after prayer with the ship's carpenter, we all four retired to wait upon God. I had a good but very brief season in prayer, and then felt so satisfied that our request was granted that I could not continue asking, and very soon went up again on deck. The first officer, a godless man, was in charge. I went over and asked him to let down the clews or corners of the mainsail, which had been drawn up in order to lessen the useless flapping of the sail against the rigging.

"'What would be the good of that?' he answered roughly.

"I told him we had been asking a wind from God, that it was coming immediately, and we were so near the reef by this time that there was not a minute to lose.

"With an oath and a look of contempt, he said he would rather see a wind than hear of it.

"But while he was speaking I watched his eye, following it up to the royal, and there, sure enough, the corner of the top most sail was beginning to tremble in the breeze.

"'Don't you see the wind is coming? Look at the royal!' I exclaimed.

"'No, it is only a cat's paw,' he rejoined (a mere puff of wind).

"'Cat's paw or not,' I cried, 'pray let down the mainsail and give us the benefit.'

"This he was not slow to do. In another minute the heavy tread of the men on deck brought up the Captain from his cabin to see what was the matter. The breeze had indeed come! in a few minutes we were plowing our way at six or seven knots an hour through the water . . . and though the wind was sometimes unsteady, we did not altogether lose it until after passing the Pelew Islands.

"Thus God encouraged me," adds this praying saint, "before landing on China's shores to bring every variety of need to Him in prayer, and to expect that He would honor the name of the Lord Jesus and give the help each emergency required."

S. D. GORDON

In an address at Cambridge some time ago (reported in "The Life of Faith," April 3rd, 1912) Mr. S. D. Gordon told in his own inimitable way the story of a man in his own country, to illustrate from real life the fact of the reality of prayer, and that it is not mere talking.

"This man," said Mr. Gordon, "came of an old New England family, a bit farther back an English family. He was a giant in size, and a keen man mentally, and a university-trained man. He had gone out West to live, and represented a prominent district in our House of Congress, answering to your House of Commons. He was a prominent leader there. He was reared in a Christian family but he was a skeptic, and used to lecture against Christianity. He told me he was fond, in his lectures, of proving, as he thought, conclusively, that there was no God. That was the type of his infidelity.

"One day he told me he was sitting in the Lower House of Congress. It was at the time of a Presidential Election, and when party feeling ran high. One would have thought that was the last place where a man would be likely to think about spiritual things. He said: 'I was sitting in my seat in that crowded House and that heated atmosphere, when a feeling came to me that the God, whose existence I thought I could successfully disprove, was just there above me, looking down on me, and that He was displeased with me, and with the way I was doing.

I said to myself, 'This is ridiculous, I guess I've been working too hard. I'll go and get a good meal and take a long walk and shake myself, and see if that will take this away.'

He got his extra meal, took a walk, and came back to his seat, but the impression would not be shaken off that God was there and was displeased with him. He went for a walk, day after day, but could never shake the feeling off.

Then he went back to his constituency in his State, he said, to arrange matters there. He had the ambition to be the Governor of his State, and his party was the dominant party in the State, and, as far as such things could be judged, he was in the line to become Governor there, in one of the most dominant States of our Central West.

He said: 'I went home to fix that thing up as far as I could, and to get ready for it. But I had hardly reached home and exchanged greetings, when my wife, who was an earnest Christian woman, said to me that a few of them had made a little covenant of prayer that I might become a Christian.'

He did not want her to know the experience that he had just been going through, and so he said as carelessly as he could, 'When did this thing begin, this praying of yours?' She named the date. Then he did some very quick thinking, and he knew, as he thought back, that it was the day on the calendar when that strange impression came to him for the first time.

He said to me: 'I was tremendously shaken. I wanted to be honest. I was perfectly honest in not believing in God, and I thought I was right. But if what she said was true, then merely as a lawyer sifting his evidence in a case, it would be good evidence that there was really something in their prayer.

I was terrifically shaken, and wanted to be honest, and did not know what to do. That same night I went to a little Methodist chapel, and if somebody had known how to talk with me, I think I should have accepted Christ that night.'

Then he said that the next night he went back again to that chapel, where meetings were being held each night, and there he kneeled at the altar, and yielded his great strong will to the will of God.

Then he said, 'I knew I was to preach,' and he is preaching still in a Western State.

That is half of the story. I also talked with his wife—I wanted to put the two halves together, so as to get the bit of teaching in it all—and she told me this. She had been a Christian—what you call a nominal Christian—a strange confusion of terms. Then there came a time when she was led into a full surrender of her life to the Lord Jesus Christ.

Then she said, 'At once there came a great intensifying of desire that my husband might be a Christian, and we made that little compact to pray for him each day until he became a Christian. That night I was kneeling at my bedside before going to rest, praying for my husband, praying very earnestly and then a voice said to me, 'Are you willing for the results that will come if your husband is converted?'

The little message was so very distinct that she said she was frightened; she had never had such an experience. But she went on praying still more earnestly, and again there came the quiet voice, 'Are you willing for the consequences?' And again there was a sense of being startled, frightened. But she still went on praying, and wondering what this meant, and a third time the quiet voice came more quietly than ever as she described it, 'Are you willing for the consequences?'

"Then she told me she said with great earnestness, 'O God, I am willing for anything Thou dost think good, if only my husband may know Thee, and become a true Christian man.' She said that instantly, when that prayer came from her lips, there came into her heart a wonderful sense of peace, a great peace that she could not explain, a 'peace that passeth understanding,' and from that moment—it was the very night of the covenant, the night when her husband had that first strange experience—the assurance never left her that he would accept Christ. And all those weeks she prayed with the firm assurance that the result was coming.

What were the consequences? They were of a kind that I think no one would think small. She was the wife of a man in a very prominent political position. She was the wife of a man who was in the line of becoming the first official of his State, and she officially the first lady socially of that State, with all the honor that that social standing would imply.

Now she is the wife of a Methodist preacher, with her home changed every two or three years, she going from this place to that, a very different social position, and having a very different income than she would otherwise have had. Yet I never met a woman who had more of the wonderful peace of God in her heart, and of the light of God in her face, than that woman."

Mr. Gordon's comment on that incident is this: "Now you can see at once that there was no change in the purpose of God through that prayer. The prayer worked out His purpose; it did not change it. But the woman's surrender gave the opportunity of working out the will that God wanted to work out. If we might give ourselves to Him and learn His will, and use all our strength in learning His will and bending to His will, then we would begin to pray, and there is simply nothing that could resist the tremendous power of the prayer. Oh for more saints who will be simple enough to get in touch with God, and give Him the mastery of the whole life, and learn His will, and then give themselves, as Jesus gave Himself, to the sacred service of intercession!"

To the man or woman who is acquainted with God and who knows how to pray, there is nothing remarkable in the answers that come. They are sure of being heard, since they ask in accordance with what they know to be the mind and the will of God.

DR. WILLIAM BURT

Dr. William Burt, Bishop of Europe in the Methodist Episcopal Church, tells that a few years ago, when he visited their Boys' School in Vienna, he found that although the year was not up, all available funds had been spent. He hesitated to make a special appeal to his friends in America. He counseled with the teachers. They took the matter to God in earnest and continued prayer, believing that He would grant their request.

Ten days later Bishop Burt was in Rome, and there came to him a letter from a friend in New York, which read substantially thus: "As I went to my office on Broadway one morning (and the date was the very one on which the teachers were praying), a voice seemed to tell me that you were in need of funds for the Boys' School in Vienna. I very gladly enclose a check for the work." The check was for the amount needed. There had been no human communication between Vienna and New York. But while they were yet speaking God answered them.

Some time ago there appeared in an English religious weekly the report of an incident narrated by a well-known preacher in the course of an address to children. For the truth of the story he was able to vouch.

A child lay sick in a country cottage, and her younger sister heard the doctor say, as he left the house, "Nothing but a miracle can save her." The little girl went to her money-box, took out the few coins it contained, and in perfect simplicity of heart went to shop after shop in the village street, asking, "Please, I want to buy a miracle." From each she came away disappointed. Even the local chemist had to say, "My dear, we don't sell miracles here."

But outside his door two men were talking, and had overheard the child's request. One was a great doctor from a London hospital, and he asked her to explain what she wanted. When he understood the need, he hurried with her to the cottage, examined the sick girl, and said to the mother: "It is true—only a miracle can save her, and it must be performed at once." He got his instruments, performed the operation, and the patient's life was saved.

D. L. MOODY

D. L. Moody gives this illustration of the power of prayer: "While in Edinburgh, a man was pointed out to me by a friend, who said: 'That man is chairman of the Edinburgh Infidel Club' I went and sat beside him and said, 'My friend, I am glad to see you in our meeting. Are you concerned about your welfare?'

"'I do not believe in any hereafter.'

"'Well, just get down on your knees and let me pray for you.'

"'No, I do not believe in prayer.'

"I knelt beside him as he sat, and prayed. He made a great deal of sport of it. A year after I met him again I took him by the hand and said: 'Hasn't God answered my prayer yet?'

"'There is no God. If you believe in one who answers prayer, try your hand on me.'

"'Well, a great many are now praying for you, and God's time will come, and I believe you will be saved yet.'

"Some time afterwards I got a letter from a leading barrister in Edinburgh telling me that my infidel friend had come to Christ, and that seventeen of his club men had followed his example.

"I did not know how God would answer prayer, but I knew He would answer. Let us come boldly to God."

ROBERT LOUIS STEVENSON

Robert Louis Stevenson tells a vivid story of a storm at sea. The passengers below were greatly alarmed, as the waves dashed over the vessel. At last one of them, against orders, crept to the deck, and came to the pilot, who was lashed to the wheel that he was turning without flinching. The pilot caught sight of the terror-stricken man, and gave him a reassuring smile. Below went the passenger, and comforted the others by saying, "I have seen the face of the pilot, and he smiled. All is well."

That is how we feel when through the gateway of prayer we find our way into the Father's presence. We see His face, and we know that all is well, since His hand is on the helm of events, and "even the winds and the waves obey Him." When we live in fellowship with Him, we come with confidence into His presence, asking in the full confidence of receiving and meeting with the justification of our faith.

Let your hearts be much set on revivals of religion. Never forget that the churches have hitherto existed and prospered by revivals; and that if they are to exist and prosper in time to come, it must be by the same cause which has from the first been their glory and defense. (John Hawes)

If any minister can be satisfied without conversions, he shall have no conversions. (C. H. Spurgeon)

12

Prayer and Revival

I DO NOT BELIEVE THAT *my desires for a revival were ever half so strong as they ought to be; nor do I see how a minister can help being in a "constant fever" when his Master is dishonored and souls are destroyed in so many ways.* (Edward Payson)

An aged saint once came to the pastor at night and said: "We are about to have a revival." He was asked why he knew so. His answer was, "I went into the stable to take care of my cattle two hours ago, and there the Lord has kept me in prayer until just now. And I feel that we are going to be revived." It was the commencement of a revival. (H. C. Fish)

It has been said that the history of revivals is the history of Christianity, and no one can study their history without being impressed with their mighty influence upon the destiny of the race. To look back over the progress of the divine kingdom upon earth is to review revival periods that have come like refreshing showers upon dry and thirsty ground, making the desert to blossom as the rose, and bringing new eras of spiritual life and activity just when the Church had fallen under the influence of the apathy of the times, and needed to be aroused to a new sense of her duty and responsibility.

"From one point of view, and that not the least important," writes Principal Lindsay, in The Church and the Ministry in the Early Centuries, "the history of the Church flows on from one time of revival to another, and whether we take the awakenings in the old Catholic, the medieval, or the modern Church, these have always been the work of Christians specially gifted with the power of seeing and declaring the secrets of the deepest Christian life, and the effect of their work has always been proportionate to the spiritual receptivity of the generation they have spoken to."

As God, from the beginning, has worked prominently through revivals, there can be no denial of the fact that revivals are a part of the divine plan. The Kingdom of our Lord has been advanced in large measure by special seasons of gracious and rapid accomplishment of the work of conversion, and it may be inferred, therefore, that the means through which God has worked in other times will be employed in our time to produce similar results.

Wrote one writer on the subject:

> The quiet conversion of one sinner after another, under the ordinary ministry of the Gospel, must always be regarded with feelings of satisfaction and gratitude by the ministers and disciples of Christ. But a periodical manifestation of the simultaneous conversion of thousands is also to be desired, because of its adaptation to afford a visible and impressive demonstration that God has made that same Jesus, Who was rejected and crucified, both Lord and Christ;[1] and that, in virtue of His divine mediatorship, He has assumed the royal scepter of universal supremacy, and "must reign, till all enemies are under His feet."[2]

It is, therefore, reasonable to expect that, from time to time, He will repeat that which on the day of Pentecost formed the conclusive and crowning evidence of His Messiahship and Sovereignty; and, by so doing, startle the slumbering souls of careless worldlings, gain the attentive ear of the unconverted, and in a remarkable way, break in upon those brilliant dreams of earthly glory, grandeur, wealth, power, and happiness, which the rebellious and God-forgetting multitude so fondly cherish. Such an outpouring of the Holy Spirit forms at once a demonstrative proof of the completeness and acceptance of His once offering of Himself as a sacrifice for sin, and a prophetic "earnest" of the certainty that He "shall . . . appear the second time without sin unto salvation," to "judge the world with righteousness."[3]

CHARLES G. FINNEY

That revivals are to be expected, proceeding, as they do from the right use of the appropriate means, is a fact that needs not a little emphasis in these days, when the material is exalted at the expense of the spiritual, and when ethical standards are supposed to be supreme. That a revival is not a miracle was powerfully taught by Charles G. Finney. There might, he said, be a miracle among its antecedent causes, or there might not. The Apostles employed miracles simply as a means by which they arrested attention to their message, and established its divine authority.

But the miracle was not the revival. The miracle was one thing; the revival that followed it was quite another thing. The revivals in the Apostles' days were connected with miracles, but they were not miracles.

All revivals are dependent upon God, but in revivals, as in other things, He invites and requires the assistance of people, and the full result is obtained when there is cooperation between the divine and the human. In other words, to employ a familiar phrase, God alone can save the world, but God cannot save the world alone. God and saints unite for the task, the response of the divine being invariably in proportion to the desire and the effort of the human.

This cooperation then, being necessary, what is the duty which we, as co-workers with God, require to undertake? First of all, and most important of all—the point that we desire particularly to emphasize—we must give ourselves to prayer.

Dr. J. Wilbur Chapman

"Revivals," as Dr. J. Wilbur Chapman reminds us, "are born in prayer. When Wesley prayed England was revived. When Knox prayed, Scotland was refreshed. When the Sunday School teachers of Tannybrook prayed, 11,000 young people were added to the Church in a year. Whole nights of prayer have always been succeeded by whole days of soul-winning."

D. L. Moody

When D. L. Moody's Church in Chicago lay in ashes, he went over to England in 1872, not to preach, but to listen to others preach while his new church was being built. One Sunday morning he was prevailed upon to preach in a London pulpit. But somehow the spiritual atmosphere was lacking. He confessed afterwards that he never had such a hard time preaching in his life. Everything was perfectly dead, and, as he vainly tried to preach, he said to himself, "What a fool I was to consent to preach! I came here to listen, and here I am preaching." Then the awful thought came to him that he had to preach again at night, and only the fact that he had given the promise to do so kept him faithful to the engagement.

But when Mr. Moody entered the pulpit at night, and faced the crowded congregation, he was conscious of a new atmosphere. "The powers of an unseen world seemed to have fallen upon the audience."

As he drew towards the close of his sermon he became emboldened to give out an invitation, and as he concluded he said, "If there is a man or woman here who will tonight accept Jesus Christ, please stand up." At once about 500 people rose to their feet. Thinking that there must be some mistake, he asked the people to be seated, and then, in order that there might be no possible misunderstanding, he repeated the invitation, couching it in even more definite and difficult terms. Again the same number rose.

Still thinking that something must be wrong, Mr. Moody, for the second time, asked the standing men and women to be seated, and then he invited all who really meant to accept Christ to pass into the vestry. Fully 500 people did as requested, and that was the beginning of a revival in that church and neighborhood, which brought Mr. Moody back from Dublin, a few days later, that he might assist the wonderful work of God.

The sequel, however, must be given, or our purpose in relating the incident will be defeated. When Mr. Moody preached at the morning service there was a woman in the congregation who had an invalid sister. On her return home she told the invalid that the preacher had been a Mr. Moody from Chicago, and on hearing this she turned pale.

"What," she said, "Mr. Moody from Chicago! I read about him some time ago in an American paper, and I have been praying God to send him to London, and to our church. If I had known he was going to preach this morning I would have eaten no breakfast. I would have spent the whole time in prayer. Now, sister, go out of the room, lock the door, send me no dinner; no matter who comes, don't let them see me. I am going to spend the whole afternoon and evening in prayer."

And so while Mr. Moody stood in the pulpit that had been like an ice-chamber in the morning, the bed-ridden saint was holding him up before God, and God, who ever delights to answer prayer, poured out His Spirit in mighty power.

Professor Thomas Nicholson

The God of revivals who answered the prayer of His child for Mr. Moody, is willing to hear and to answer the faithful, believing, prayers of His people today. Wherever God's conditions are met there the revival is sure to fall. Professor Thomas Nicholson, of Cornell College in America, relates an experience on his first circuit that impresses anew the old lesson of the place of prayer in the work of God.

There had not been a revival on that circuit in years, and things were not spiritually hopeful. During more than four weeks the pastor had preached faithfully, visited from house to house, in stores, shops, and out-of-the-way places, and had done everything he could. The fifth Monday night saw many of the official members at lodges, but only a corporal's guard at the church.

From that meeting the pastor went home, cast down, but not in despair. He resolved to spend that night in prayer. Locking the door, he took Bible and hymn book and began to inquire more diligently of the Lord, though the meetings had been the subject of hours of earnest prayer. Only God knows the anxiety and the faithful, prayerful study of that night.

Near dawn, a great peace and a full assurance came that God would surely bless the plan which had been decided upon, and a text was chosen which he felt sure was of the Lord. Dropping upon the bed, the pastor slept about two hours, then rose, hastily had breakfast, and went nine miles to the far side of the circuit to visit some sick people. All day the assurance increased.

"Toward night," the pastor reported, "a pouring rain set in, the roads were heavy and we reached home, wet, without supper, and a little late, only to find no fire in the church, the lights unlit, and no signs of service. The janitor had concluded that the rain would prevent the service. We changed the order, rang the bell, and prepared for war."

Three young men formed the congregation, but in that "full assurance" the pastor delivered the message that had been prayed out on the preceding night, as earnestly and as fully as if the house had been crowded, then made a personal appeal to each young man in turn. Two yielded, and testified before the meeting closed.

The tired pastor went to a sweet rest, and next morning, rising a little later than usual, learned that one of the young men was going from store to store throughout the town telling of his wonderful deliverance, and exhorting the people to salvation. Night after night conversions occurred, until in two weeks we heard 44 people testify in 45 minutes. All three points of that circuit saw a blaze of revival that winter, and family after family came into the church, until the membership was more than trebled.

Out of that meeting, one convert is a successful pastor in the Michigan Conference, another is the wife of one of the choicest of our pastors, and a third was in the ministry for a number of years, and then went to another denomination, where he is faithful to this day. Probably none of the members ever knew of the pastor's night of prayer, but he truly believes that God somehow does for the saint who thus prays, what He does not do for the saint who does not pray, and he is certain that "more things are wrought by prayer than this world dreams of."

All the true revivals have been born in prayer. When God's people become so concerned about the state of Christianity that they lie on their faces day and night in earnest supplication, the blessing will be sure to fall.

Revival in Shotts, Scotland

It is the same all down the ages. Every revival of which we have any record has been bathed in prayer. Take, for example, the wonderful revival in Shotts (Scotland) in 1630. The fact that several of the then persecuted ministers would take a part in solemn convocation having become generally known, a vast concourse of godly persons assembled on this occasion from all quarters of the country, and several days were spent in social prayer, preparatory to the service.

In the evening, instead of retiring to rest, the multitude divided themselves into little bands, and spent the whole night in supplication and praise. The Monday was consecrated to thanksgiving, a practice not then common, and proved the great days of the feast. After much entreaty, John Livingston, chaplain to the Countess of Wigtown, a young man and not ordained, agreed to preach. He had spent the night in prayer and conference—but as the hour of assembling approached his heart quailed at the thought of addressing so many aged and experienced saints, and he actually fled from the duty he had undertaken.

But just as the church of Shotts was vanishing from his view, those words, "Was I ever a barren wilderness or a land of darkness?"[4] were borne in upon his mind with such force that it compelled him to return to the work. He took for his text Ezekiel 36:25-26, and discoursed with great power for about two hours. Five hundred conversions were believed to have occurred under that one sermon, which had been prefaced by prayer.

"It was the sowing of a seed through Clydesdale, so that many of the most eminent Christians of that country could date their conversion, or some remarkable confirmation of their case, from that day."

RICHARD BAXTER

Of Richard Baxter it has been said that "he stained his study walls with praying breath; and after becoming thus anointed with the unction of the Holy Ghost, he sent a river of living water over Kidderminster."

GEORGE WHITFIELD

George Whitfield once prayed, "O Lord, give me souls or take my soul." After much closet pleading, "he once went to the devil's fair and took more than a thousand souls out of the paw of the lion in a single day."

CHARLES G. FINNEY

Mr. Finney says: "I once knew a minister who had a revival fourteen winters in succession. I did not know how to account for it till I saw one of his members get up in a prayer meeting and make a confession. 'Brethren,' he said, 'I have been long in the habit of praying every Saturday night till after midnight for the descent of the Holy Ghost among us. And now, brethren (and he began to weep), I confess that I have neglected it for two or three weeks.' The secret was out. That minister had a praying church."

And so we might go on multiplying illustration upon illustration to show the place of prayer in revival and to demonstrate that every mighty movement of the Spirit of God has had its source in the prayer-chamber. The lesson of it all is this, that as workers together with God we must regard ourselves as in not a little measure responsible for the conditions that prevail around us today. Are we concerned about the coldness of the

Church? Do we grieve over the lack of conversions? Does our soul go out to God in midnight cries for the outpouring of His Spirit?

If not, part of the blame lies at our door. If we do our part, God will do His. Around us is a world lost in sin, above us is a God willing and able to save. It is our responsibility to build the bridge that links heaven and earth, and prayer is the mighty instrument that does the work.

And so the old cry comes to us with insistent voice, "Pray, brethren, pray."

Endnotes

1 Acts 2:36
2 I Corinthians 15:25
3 Psalm 96:13
4 Jeremiah 2:31

13

The Purpose of All Real Prayer

*L*ORD JESUS, CAUSE ME *to know in my daily experience the glory and sweetness of Thy name, and then teach me how to use it in my prayer, so that I may be even like Israel, a prince prevailing with God. Thy name is my passport, and secures me access; Thy name is my plea, and secures me answer; Thy name is my honor and secures me glory. Blessed Name, Thou art honey in my mouth, music in my ear, heaven in my heart, and all in all to all my being!* (C.H. Spurgeon)

I do not mean that every prayer we offer is answered exactly as we desire it to be. Were this the case, it would mean that we would be dictating to God, and prayer would degenerate into a mere system of begging. Just as an earthly father knows what is best for his children's welfare, so does God take into consideration the particular needs of His human family, and meets them out of His wonderful storehouse. If our petitions are in accordance with His will, and if we seek His glory in the asking, the answers will come in ways that will astonish us and fill our hearts with songs of thanksgiving. God is a rich and bountiful Father, and He does not forget His children, nor withhold from them anything which it would be to their advantage to receive. (J. Kennedy MacLean)

The example of our Lord in the matter of prayer is one that His followers might well copy. Christ prayed much and He taught much about prayer. His life and His works, as well as His teaching, are illustrations of the nature and necessity of prayer. He lived and labored to answer prayer. But the necessity of persistence in prayer was the emphasized point in His teaching about prayer. He taught not only that we must pray, but that we must persevere in prayer.

He taught in command and precept the idea of energy and earnestness in praying. He gives to our efforts gradation and climax. We are to ask, but to the asking we must add seeking, and seeking must pass into the full force of effort in knocking. The pleading soul must be aroused to effort by God's silence. Denial, instead of abating or abashing, must arouse its latent energies and kindle anew its highest ardor.

The sermon on the Mount

In the Sermon on the Mount, in which He lays down the cardinal duties of His Christianity, He not only gives prominence to prayer in general and secret prayer in particular, but He sets apart a distinct and different section to give weight to persistent prayer. To prevent any discouragement in praying He lays as a basic principle the fact of God's great fatherly willingness—that God's willingness to answer our prayers exceeds our willingness to give good and necessary things to our children— the same way that God's ability, goodness, and perfection exceed our infirmities and evil. As a further assurance and stimulant to prayer Christ gives the most positive and repeated assurance of answer to prayers. He declares: "Ask, and it shall be given you; seek, and ye shall find; knock and it shall be opened unto you." And to make assurance doubly sure, He adds: "For every one that asketh, receiveth; and he that seeketh, findeth; and to him that knocketh it shall be opened"(Matthew 7:7-8).

Why does He unfold to us the Father's loving readiness to answer the prayer of His children? Why does He affirm so strongly that prayer will be answered? Why does He repeat that positive affirmation six times? Why does Christ on two distinct occasions go over the same strong promises, repeat, and repeat again in regard to the certainty of prayer being answered? Because He knew that there would be delay in many answers that would call for persistent pressing, and that if our faith did not have the strongest assurance of God's willingness to answer, delay would break it down. Also, that our spiritual laziness would come in under the guise of submission and say it is not God's will to give what we ask, and so cease praying and lose our case.

God's willingness to answer prayer

After Christ had put God's willingness to answer prayer in a very clear and strong light, He then urges to persistence, and that every unanswered prayer, instead of abating our pressure, should only increase intensity and energy. If asking does not get, let asking pass into the settled attitude and spirit of seeking. If seeking does not secure the answer, let seeking pass on to the more energetic and clamorous plea of knocking. We must persevere till we get it. No failure here if our faith does not break down.

As our great example in prayer, our Lord puts love as a primary condition—a love that has purified the heart from all the elements of hate, revenge, and ill will. Love is the supreme condition of prayer, a life inspired by love. The 13th chapter of First Corinthians is the law of prayer as well as the law of love. The law of love is the law of prayer, and to master this chapter from the epistle of St. Paul is to learn the first and fullest condition of prayer.

Praying in Jesus' name

Christ taught us also to approach the Father in His name. That is our passport. It is in His name that we are to make our petitions known.

Verily, verily, I say unto you, He that believeth on me, the works that I do shall he do also; and greater works than these shall he do; because I go unto my Father. And whatsoever ye shall ask in my name, that will I do, that the Father may be glorified in the Son. If ye shall ask any thing in my name, I will do it (John 14:12-14).

How wide and comprehensive is that "whatsoever." There is no limit to the power of that name. "Whatsoever ye shall ask." That is the divine declaration, and it opens up to every praying child a vista of infinite resource and possibility.

That is our heritage. All that Christ has, may become ours if we obey the conditions. The one secret is prayer. The place of revealing and of equipment, of grace and of power, is the prayer-chamber. As we meet there with God we shall not only win our triumphs, but we shall also grow in the likeness of our Lord and become His living witnesses to lost humanity.

Without prayer, the Christian life is robbed of its sweetness and its beauty, and becomes cold and formal and dead. Rooted, however, in the secret place where God meets and walks and talks with His own, it grows into such a testimony of Divine power that all humanity will feel its influence and be touched by the warmth of its love. Thus, resembling our Lord and Master, we shall be used for the glory of God and the salvation of our many. And that, surely, is the purpose of all real prayer and the end of all true service.

BOOK 7

THE POWER OF PRAYER

I

Praying People Needed

STUDY UNIVERSAL HOLINESS OF *life. Your whole usefulness depends on this, for your sermons last but an hour or two; your life preaches all the week. If Satan can only make a covetous minister a lover of praise, of pleasure, of good eating, he has ruined your ministry. Give yourself to prayer, and get your texts, your thoughts, your words from God. Luther spent his best three hours in prayer.* (Robert Murray McCheyne)

We are constantly striving and straining to devise new methods, plans, and organizations to advance the Church and become more active and efficient in spreading the gospel. This trend of the day has a tendency to lose sight of the person or sink the person in the plan or organization. God's plan is to make much of people, far more of them than of anything else. People are God's method. The Church is looking for better methods. God is looking for better people. "There was a man sent from God, whose name was John."[1] The period that heralded and prepared the way for Christ was bound up in that man John. "Unto us a child is born, unto us a son is given."[2] The world's salvation comes out of that cradled Son.

When Paul appeals to the personal character of the Christians who rooted the gospel in the world, he solves the mystery of their success. The glory and efficiency of the gospel is staked on the people who proclaim it. When God declares that "the eyes of the Lord run to and fro throughout the whole earth, to show himself strong in the behalf of them whose heart is perfect toward Him,"[3] he declares the necessity of people and His dependence on them as a channel through which to exert His power upon the world. This vital, urgent truth is one that this age of technology is apt

583

to forget. The forgetting of it is as harmful to the work of God as the removal of the sun from its place would be. Darkness, confusion, and death would result.

THE CHURCH'S NEEDS

What the Church needs today is not more machinery or better, not new organizations or more and novel methods, but men and women whom the Holy Ghost can use—people of prayer, people mighty in prayer. The Holy Ghost does not flow through methods, but through people. He does not come on machinery, but on people. He does not anoint plans, but people—people of prayer.

An eminent historian has said that the accidents of personal character have more to do with the revolutions of nations than either philosophic historians or democratic politicians will allow. This truth has its full application to the gospel of Christ and the character and conduct of the followers of Christ. Christianize the world, and you transfigure nations and individuals. This is eminently true of the preachers of the gospel.

The character as well as the fortunes of the gospel is committed to the preacher, who makes or mars the message from God to humanity. The preacher is the golden pipe through which the divine oil flows. The pipe must not only be golden, but open and flawless so that the oil may have a full, unhindered, and unwasted flow.

The person makes the preacher. God must make the person. The messenger is, if possible, more than the message. The preacher is more than the sermon. The preacher is the life of the sermon. Even as the life-giving milk from the mother's bosom is basically the mother's life, so all the preacher says is infused and impregnated by what the preacher is. The treasure is in earthen vessels, and the taste of the vessel impregnates and may discolor the treasure. The person, the whole person, lies behind the sermon. Preaching is not the performance of an hour. It is the outflow of a life. It takes twenty years to make a sermon because it takes twenty years to make the person. The true sermon is a thing of life. The sermon grows because the person grows. The sermon is forceful because the person is forceful. The sermon is holy because the person is holy. The sermon is full of divine unction because the person is full of divine unction.

PAUL'S GOSPEL

Paul called it "my gospel."[4] It wasn't that he had slanted it to agree with his personal eccentricities or changed it by selfish promotion. It was that the gospel was put into the heart and lifeblood of Paul as a personal trust to be executed by his Pauline traits, and set aflame and empowered by the fiery energy of his fiery soul. What were Paul's sermons? Where are they? Skeletons, scattered fragments, afloat on the sea of inspiration! But the man Paul, greater than his sermons, lives forever, in full form, feature and stature, with his molding hand on the Church. The preaching is but a voice. The voice in silence dies, the text is forgotten, the sermon fades from memory; the preacher lives.

The sermon cannot rise in its life-giving forces above the person. Dead people give out dead sermons, and dead sermons kill. Everything depends on the spiritual character of the preacher. Under the Jewish dispensation the high priest had inscribed in jeweled letters on a golden frontlet: "Holiness to the Lord." So every preacher in Christ's ministry must be molded into and mastered by this same holy motto. It is a crying shame for the Christian ministry to fall lower in holiness of character and holiness of aim than the Jewish priesthood. Jonathan Edwards said, "I went on with my eager pursuit after more holiness and conformity to Christ. The heaven I desired was a heaven of holiness."

WHEN THE GOSPEL MOVES

The gospel of Christ does not move by popular waves. It has no self-propagating power. It moves as the people who have charge of it move. The preacher must impersonate the gospel. Its divine, most distinctive, features must be embodied in the person who proclaims it. The constraining power of love must be in the preacher as a projecting, eccentric, all-commanding, self-oblivious force. The energy of self-denial must be the preacher's being, heart, blood, and bones. The preacher who goes forth among people must be clothed with humility, filled with meekness, wise as a serpent, and harmless as a dove. The preacher must wear the bonds of a servant with the spirit of a king—a high, royal, king with an independent bearing, yet with the simplicity and sweetness of a child. Preachers must throw themselves with all the abandon of perfect, self-emptying, faith and self-consuming zeal into their work for the salvation of humanity. Those who would take hold of a generation and shape it for God must be hearty, heroic, compassionate, and fearless martyrs. They cannot take hold of the Church or the world for God If they are timid time servers, place seekers, or if they be people pleasers or afraid of people. It is the same if their faith has a weak hold on God or His Word, or if their denial of the things of the world can be broken by any change of self or the world.

PREACHERS SHOULD PREACH TO THEMSELVES

Preachers should preach sharpest and strongest to themselves. Their most difficult, delicate, laborious, and thorough work must be with themselves. The training of the twelve was the great, difficult, and enduring work of Christ. Preachers are not sermon makers, but people shapers and saint makers. The only ones well-trained for this business are those who have made themselves a courageous person and a saint. It is not great talents, great learning, or great preachers that God needs, but men and women who are great in holiness, faith, love, and faithfulness—in other words, great for God. They should always be preaching by holy sermons in the pulpit, and by holy lives out of it. These can mold a generation for God.

The early Christians were formed after this manner. They were people of solid mold, preachers after the heavenly type—heroic, stalwart, soldierly, saintly. Preaching with them meant self-denying, self-crucifying, serious, toilsome, martyr business. They applied themselves to it in a way that told on their generation, and formed in its womb a generation yet unborn for God. The preaching person is to be the praying person. Prayer is the preacher's mightiest weapon. An almighty force in itself, it gives life and force to all.

The real sermon is made in the closet. The person—God's person—is made in the closet. A Christian's life and profoundest convictions are born in secret communion with God. The burdened and tearful agony of the preacher's spirit, and the most powerful and sweetest messages were gotten when alone with God. Prayer makes the Christian. Prayer makes the preacher. Prayer makes the pastor.

THE PRIDE OF LEARNING

The pride of learning is against the dependent humility of prayer. Prayer is with the pulpit too often only official—a performance for the routine of service. Prayer is not to the modern pulpit the mighty force it was in Paul's life or Paul's ministry. Preachers who do not make prayer a mighty factor in their own life and ministry are weak as a factor in God's work and are powerless to project God's cause in this world.

Endnotes

1 John 1:6
2 Isaiah 9:6
3 2 Chronicles 16:9
4 Romans 2:16, 16:25; 2 Timothy 2:8

2

Our Sufficiency is of God

B UT ABOVE ALL HE *excelled in prayer. The inwardness and weight of his spirit, the reverence and solemnity of his address and behavior, and the fewness and fullness of his words have often struck even strangers with admiration as they used to reach others with consolation. The most awful, living, reverent frame I ever felt or beheld, I must say, was his prayer. And truly it was a testimony. He knew and lived nearer to the Lord than other men, for they that know him most will see most reason to approach him with reverence and fear.* (William Penn of George Fox)[1]

By a slight perversion the sweetest graces may bear the bitterest fruit. The sun gives life, but sunstrokes are death. Preaching is to give life, but it may kill. Preachers hold the keys—they may lock as well as unlock.[2] Preaching is God's great institution for the planting and maturing of spiritual life. When properly executed, its benefits are untold. When wrongly executed, no evil can exceed its damaging results. It is an easy matter to destroy the flock if the shepherd is unwary or the pasture is destroyed. It is easy to capture the fortress if the watchmen is asleep or the food and water is poisoned. Invested with such gracious prerogatives, exposed to so great evils, involving so many grave responsibilities, it would be a parody on the shrewdness of the devil and a libel on his character and reputation if he did not use his wily influences to weaken the preacher and the preaching. In face of all this, Paul's exclamatory question, "who is sufficient for these things?"[3] is always appropriate.

Paul says, "our sufficiency is of God; Who also hath made us able ministers of the new testament; not of the letter, but of the spirit: for the letter killeth, but the spirit giveth life."[4]

TRUE MINISTRY IS OF GOD

The true ministry is God-touched, God-enabled, and God-made. The Spirit of God is on the preacher in anointing power. The fruit of the Spirit is in the preacher's heart. The Spirit of God has vitalized the preacher and the Word. Anointed preaching gives life—gives life as the spring gives life, gives life as the resurrection gives life, gives ardent life as the summer gives ardent life, gives fruitful life as the autumn gives fruitful life. The life-giving preacher is a person of God whose heart is ever thirsty for God, whose soul is always following hard after God, whose eye is single to God, and in whom by the power of God's Spirit the flesh and the world have been crucified. The anointed preacher's ministry is like the generous flood of a life-giving river.

The preaching that kills is non-spiritual preaching. The ability of the preaching is not from God. Lower sources than God have given it energy and stimulant. The Spirit is not evident in the preacher or the preaching. Many kinds of forces may be projected and stimulated by preaching that kills, but they are not spiritual forces. They may resemble spiritual forces, but are only the shadow, the counterfeit. They may seem to have life, but the life is bewitched. The preaching that kills is the letter. It may be shapely and orderly, but it is the letter still—the dry, husky, letter; the empty, bald, shell. The letter may have the germ of life in it, but it has no breath of spring to energize it. The words are winter seeds, as hard as the winter's soil, as icy as the winter's air. There is no power in them to thaw or germinate the seed.

LETTER-PREACHING

This letter-preaching has the truth. But even divine truth has no life-giving energy alone. It must be energized by the Spirit, with all God's forces at its back. Truth that is not quickened by God's Spirit deadens as much as or more than error. It may be the truth, but without the Spirit its shade and caress are deadly. Without the Spirit its truth is error and its light is darkness. The letter-preaching is without unction, and is neither mellowed nor oiled by the Spirit. There may be tears, but tears cannot run God's machinery. Tears may be nothing but summer's breath on a snow-covered iceberg, nothing but surface slush. There may be emotion and earnestness, but it is the emotion of the actor and the earnestness of the attorney.

Preachers may feel warm from the kindling of their own sparks, be eloquent over their own exegesis, earnest in delivering the product of their own brain. The professor may usurp the place and imitate the fire of the apostle, and brains and nerves may serve the place and fake the work of

God's Spirit. By these forces the letter may glow and sparkle like an illumined text, but the glow and sparkle will be as barren of life as the field sown with pearls. The death-dealing element lies back of the words, back of the sermon, back of the occasion, back of the manner, back of the action. The great hindrance is in the preacher. There is not in the preacher the mighty life-creating forces of the Spirit. There may be no discount on the preacher's orthodoxy, honesty, cleanness, or earnestness. But somehow the person, the inner person, in its secret places has never broken down and surrendered to God. The inner life is not a great highway for the transmission of God's message and power.

Somehow self and not God rules in the holy of holies. Somewhere, all unconscious to the preacher, some spiritual nonconductor has touched the inner person and the divine current has been arrested. The inner person has never felt its thorough spiritual bankruptcy and utter powerlessness. The preacher has never learned to cry out with an unutterable cry of self-despair and self-helplessness until God's power and God's fire comes in and fills, purifies, and empowers. Self-esteem, self-ability in some deadly shape has defamed and violated the temple that should be held sacred for God.

LIFE-GIVING PREACHING

Life-giving preaching costs the preacher much—death to self, crucifixion to the world, travail of the soul. Crucified preaching only can give life. Crucified preaching can come only from a crucified preacher.

Endnotes

1 English religious leader who founded the Society of Friends, or Quakers. Born 1624, died 1691.
2 Matthew 16:19
3 2 Corinthians 2:16
4 2 Corinthians 3:5b-6

3

The Letter Kills

DURING THIS AFFLICTION *I was brought to examine my life in relation to eternity closer than I had done when in the enjoyment of health. In this examination relative to the discharge of my duties toward my fellow creatures as a man, a Christian minister, and an officer of the Church, I stood approved by my own conscience; but in relation to my Redeemer and Saviour the result was different. My returns of gratitude and loving obedience bear no proportion to my obligations for redeeming, preserving, and supporting me through the vicissitudes of life from infancy to old age. The coldness of my love to Him who first loved me and has done so much for me overwhelmed and confused me; and to complete my unworthy character, I had not only neglected to improve the grace given to the extent of my duty and privilege, but for want of improvement had, while abounding in perplexing care and labor, declined from first zeal and love. I was confounded, humbled myself, implored mercy, and renewed my covenant to strive and devote myself unreservedly to the Lord.* (Bishop McKendree)

The preaching that kills may be, and often is, orthodox[1]— dogmatically,[2] inviolably orthodox. We love orthodoxy. It is good. It is the best. It is the clean, clear-cut teaching of God's Word. It is the trophies won by truth in its conflict with error, the levees that faith has raised against the desolating floods of honest or reckless misbelief or unbelief. But orthodoxy, clear and hard as crystal, suspicious and militant, may be nothing but the well-shaped, well-named, and well-learned letter that kills.

Nothing is so dead as a dead orthodoxy—too dead to speculate, think, study, or pray.

The preaching that kills may have insight and grasp of principles. It may be scholarly and critical in taste. It may have every small detail of the derivation and grammar of the letter. It may be able to trim the letter into its perfect pattern, and illuminate it as the teachings of Plato and Cicero may be illuminated. It may study it as a lawyer studies his text-books to form his brief or to defend his case. Yet it may be like a frost, a deadly, killing frost.

Letter-preaching may be eloquent, adorned with poetry, sprinkled with prayer, spiced with sensation, and illumined by genius. Yet these may but the massive and costly casket and rare and beautiful flowers that encase the corpse. The preaching that kills may be without scholarship. It may be unmarked by any freshness of thought or feeling. It may be clothed in tasteless generalities or dull specialties. It may be sloppy and without style. It may have no flavor of the prayer closet or of study—graced neither by thought, expression, or prayer. Under such preaching how wide and utter the desolation, and how profound the spiritual death!

LETTER-PREACHING DEALS WITH THE SURFACE

This letter-preaching deals with the surface and shadow of things, and not the things themselves. It does not penetrate the inner part. It has no deep insight into, no strong grasp of, the hidden life of God's Word. It is true to the outside, but the outside is the hull that must be broken and penetrated for the kernel. The letter may be dressed so as to attract and be fashionable, but the attraction is not toward God and the fashion is not for heaven.

The failure is in the preachers. God has not made them. They have never been in the hands of God like clay in the hands of the potter. They have been busy about their sermon, its thought and finish, its drawing and impressive forces. But the deep things of God have never been sought, studied, fathomed, and experienced. They have never stood before "the throne high and lifted up,"[3] never heard the seraphim song. They have never seen the vision nor felt the rush of that awful holiness, and cried out in utter abandon and despair under the sense of weakness and guilt. They have never had their life renewed, their heart touched, purged, inflamed by the live coal from God's altar. Their ministry may draw people to them, to the Church, to the form, and the ceremony. But there are no true drawings to God—no sweet, holy, divine communion is brought about.

The Church has been painted but not edified, pleased but not sanctified. Life is suppressed, a chill is on the summer air, and the soil is baked. The city of our God becomes the city of the dead, and the Church a graveyard and not an embattled army. Praise and prayer are stifled and worship is dead. The preachers and the preaching have helped sin, not holiness. They have peopled hell, not heaven.

PREACHING THAT KILLS

Preaching that kills is prayerless preaching. Without prayer preachers create death, and not life. Preachers who are feeble in prayer are feeble in life-giving forces. Preachers who have put aside prayer as a conspicuous and largely prevailing element in their own character have stripped their preaching of its distinctive life-giving power. Professional praying there is and will be, but professional praying helps the preaching do its deadly work. Professional praying chills and kills both preaching and praying.

Much of the lax devotion and lazy, irreverent, attitudes in congregational praying are attributable to professional praying in the pulpit. In many pulpits, prayers are long, rambling, dry, and empty. Without unction or heart, they fall like a killing frost on all the graces of worship. They are death-dealing prayers. Every trace of devotion has perished under their breath. The deader they are the longer they grow. A plea for short praying, live praying, real heart praying, praying by the Holy Spirit—direct, specific, ardent, simple, unctuous in the pulpit—is in order. A school to teach preachers how to pray, as God counts praying, would be more beneficial to true piety, true worship, and true preaching than all theological schools.

WHAT ARE WE DOING?

Stop! Pause! Consider! Where are we? What are we doing? Preaching to kill? Praying to kill? Praying to God—the great God, the maker of all worlds, the judge of all humanity! What reverence! What simplicity! What sincerity! What truth in the inward parts is demanded![4] How real we must be! How hearty! Prayer to God is the noblest exercise, the loftiest effort of people, the most real thing! Shall we not forever discard accursed preaching that kills and prayer that kills, and do the real thing, the mightiest thing— prayerful praying, life-creating preaching? By this we will bring the mightiest force to bear on heaven and earth and draw on God's exhaustless and open treasure for the need and spiritual poverty of humanity!

Endnotes

1 *Orthodoxy*: Adhering to the accepted or traditional and established faith, especially in religion.
2 *Dogma*: Theology. A doctrine or a corpus of doctrines relating to matters such as morality and faith, set forth in an authoritative manner by a church.
3 Isaiah 6:1
4 Psalm 51:6

4

Tendencies to Be Avoided

*L*ET US OFTEN LOOK *at Brainerd in the woods of America pouring out his very soul before God for the perishing heathen without whose salvation nothing could make him happy. Prayer—secret fervent believing prayer—lies at the root of all personal godliness. A competent knowledge of the language where a missionary lives, a mild and winning temper, a heart given up to God in closet religion—these, these are the attainments which, more than all knowledge, or all other gifts, will fit us to become the instruments of God in the great work of human redemption.* (Carrey's Brotherhood, Serampore)

There are two extreme tendencies in the ministry. The one is to shut itself out from intercourse with the people. The monk and the hermit were illustrations of this—they shut themselves out from people to be more with God. They failed, and do fail, of course. Our being with God is of use only as we expend its priceless benefits on humanity. This age, neither with preacher nor with people, is much intent on God. Our desire is not that way. Church leaders shut themselves in their study, become students, bookworms, Bible worms, sermon makers, noted for literature, thought, and sermon. But where are the people and God? Out of heart, out of mind. Preachers who are great thinkers and students must be the greatest people of prayer. If they are not, they will be the greatest of backsliders—heartless professionals, rationalistic, less than the least of preachers in God's estimate.

The other tendency is to thoroughly popularize the ministry. The preacher is no longer God's person, but a person of affairs, of the people.

Such preachers do not pray, because their mission is to the people, not to God. If they can move the people, create an interest, a sensation in favor of religion, and an interest in church work—they are satisfied. Their personal relation to God is no factor in their work. Prayer has little or no place in their plans. The disaster and ruin of such ministries cannot be computed by earthly arithmetic. What the preachers are in prayer to God, for themselves and for their people, determines the degree of their power for real good to humanity. It also determines their true fruitfulness and faithfulness to God and people—for time and eternity.

It is impossible for preachers to keep their spirit in harmony with the divine nature of their high calling without much prayer. It is a serious mistake for preachers to think that they can keep themselves spiritually trim and fit by laboring faithfully in the word and routine of the ministry. Even sermon-making—unceasing and difficult as an art, duty, work, or even pleasure—will occupy, harden, and alienate the heart from God by neglect of prayer. The scientist loses God in nature. Preachers may lose God in their sermon.

PRAYER FRESHENS THE HEART

Prayer freshens the heart of a preacher, keeps it in tune with God and in sympathy with the people, lifts the ministry out of the chilly air of a profession. It makes routine fruitful and moves every wheel with the ease and power of a divine unction.

Charles Spurgeon says: "Of course preachers are above all others distinguished as people of prayer. They pray as ordinary Christians, else they were hypocrites. They pray more than ordinary Christians, else they were disqualified for the office they have undertaken. If you as ministers are not very prayerful, you are to be pitied. If you become lax in sacred devotion, not only will you need to be pitied but your people also, and the day cometh in which you shall be ashamed and confounded. All our libraries and studies are mere emptiness compared with our closets. Our seasons of fasting and prayer at the Tabernacle have been high days indeed; never has heaven's gate stood wider; never have our hearts been nearer the central Glory."

The praying that makes a prayerful ministry is not a little praying put in as we put flavor to give it a pleasant smack. The praying must be in the body and form its very blood and bones. Prayer is no petty duty to be put into a corner. It is no piecemeal performance made out of the fragments of time that have been snatched from business and other engagements of life. Prayer means that the best of our time, and the heart of our time and strength, must be given. It does not mean the closet being absorbed in Bible studies or swallowed up in the activities of ministerial duties. It means the closet first and studies and activities second. Both studies and activities are freshened and made efficient by the closet.

PRAYER AFFECTS MINISTRY AND LIFE

Prayer that affects one's ministry must give tone to one's life. The praying that gives color and bent to character is no pleasant, hurried, pastime. It must enter as strongly into the heart and life as Christ's "strong crying and tears" did (Hebrews 5:7). It must draw out the soul into an agony of desire as Paul's did. It must be an internal fire and force like the "effectual fervent prayer" of James (James 5:16). It must be of the quality that when put into the golden censer and incensed before God works mighty spiritual struggles and revolutions.

Prayer is not a little habit pinned on to us while we were tied to our mother's apron strings. Neither is it a little decent quarter of a minute's grace said over an hour's dinner. It is a most serious work of our most serious years. It engages more of time and appetite than our longest dining or richest feast. The prayer that makes much of our preaching must itself be made much of. The character of our praying will determine the character of our preaching. Light praying will make light preaching. Prayer makes preaching strong, gives it unction, and makes it stick. In every ministry that has accomplished good, prayer has always been a serious business.

PREACHERS MUST BE PEOPLE OF PRAYER

Preachers must be preeminently people of prayer. Their heart must graduate in the school of prayer. Only in the school of prayer can the heart learn to preach. No learning can make up for the failure to pray. No earnestness, no diligence, no study, no gifts will supply its lack.

Talking to people for God is a great thing, but talking to God for people is greater still. Those who have not learned well how to talk to God for people will never talk well and with real success to people for God. More than this, prayerless words in and out of the pulpit are deadening words.

5

Prayer Is the Great Essential

Y OU KNOW THE VALUE *of prayer: it is precious beyond all price. Never, never neglect it.* (Sir Thomas Buxton)

Prayer is the first thing, the second thing, the third thing necessary to a minister. Pray, then, my dear brother: pray, pray, pray. (Edward Payson)

In the preacher's life, study, and pulpit, prayer must be a conspicuous and an all-impregnating force and an all-coloring ingredient. It must play no secondary part, be no mere coating. To preachers it is given to be with their Lord "all night in prayer."[1] To train themselves in self-denying prayer, preachers are charged to look to their Master, who, "rising up a great while before day, he went out, and departed into a solitary place, and there prayed."[2]

A preacher's study should be a closet, a Bethel, an altar, a vision, and a ladder. Every thought must ascend to heaven before it goes to humanity. Every part of the sermon must be scented by the air of heaven and made serious, because God was in the study.

As a steam engine never moves until the fire is kindled, so preaching—with all its machinery, perfection, and polish—is at a dead standstill on the track of spiritual results until prayer has kindled and created the steam. The texture, fineness, and strength of the sermon is just so much rubbish unless the mighty force of prayer is in it, through it, and behind it. Preachers must put God in the sermon by prayer. They must by prayer move God toward the people before they can move people to God by their words. Preachers must have had audience and ready access to God before they can have access to the people. An open way to God for a preacher is the surest pledge of an open way to the people.

It is necessary to say and say again that prayer as a mere habit, as a performance gone through by routine or in a professional way, is a dead and rotten thing. Such praying has no connection with the praying for which we plead. We are stressing true praying that engages and sets on fire every high element of the preacher's being. Prayer that is born of vital oneness with Christ and the fullness of the Holy Ghost. Prayer that springs from the deep, overflowing, fountains of tender compassion and never-ending concern for humanity's eternal good. Prayer must come from a consuming zeal for the glory of God;, and a thorough conviction of a preacher's difficult and delicate work and the imperative need of God's mightiest help. Praying grounded on these solemn and profound convictions is the only true praying. Preaching backed by such praying is the only preaching that sows the seeds of eternal life in human hearts and builds people up for heaven.

POPULAR PREACHING WITH NO PRAYING

It is true that with little or no praying there may be popular preaching, pleasant preaching, taking preaching, preaching of much intellectual, literary, and brainy force that does a bit of good. But the preaching that secures God's end in preaching must be born of prayer from text to pulpit. It must be delivered with the energy and spirit of prayer. Then it must be followed, made to germinate, and kept in vital force in the hearts of the hearers by the preacher's prayers, long after the occasion has past.

We may excuse the spiritual poverty of our preaching in many ways, but the true secret will be found in the lack of urgent prayer for God's presence in the power of the Holy Spirit. There are preachers innumerable who can deliver masterful sermons, but the effects are short-lived. They do not enter as a factor at all into the regions of the spirit where the fearful war between the Church and Satan, heaven and hell, is being waged. They do not do so because they are not made powerfully militant and spiritually victorious by prayer.

The preachers who gain mighty results for God are those who have prevailed in their pleadings with God before venturing to plead with people. The preachers who are the mightiest in their closets with God are the mightiest in their pulpits with people.

Preachers are human folks, and are exposed to and often caught by the strong changes of human currents. Praying is spiritual work, and human nature does not like tiring spiritual work. Human nature wants to sail to heaven under a favoring breeze and a full, smooth sea. Prayer is humbling work. It abases intellect and pride, crucifies self-glory, and signs our spiritual bankruptcy. All these are hard for flesh and blood to bear. It is easier not to pray than to bear them. So we come to one of the crying evils of these times, maybe of all times—little or no praying. Of these two evils, perhaps little praying is worse than no praying. Little praying is a kind of make-believe, a salve for the conscience, a farce and a delusion.

LITTLE VALUED PRAYER

The little value we put on prayer is evident from the little time we give to it. The time given to prayer by the average preacher scarcely counts in the sum of the daily total. Not infrequently the only time preachers pray is by their bedside in their nightclothes, ready for bed and soon in it. Perhaps they also say a few hasty snatches of prayer before their dressed in the morning, and over their breakfast. How feeble, vain, and little is such praying compared with the time and energy devoted to praying by holy men and women in and out of the Bible! How poor and mean our petty, childish praying is beside the habits of the true saints of God in all ages! God only commit the keys of His kingdom to those who think praying is their main business and devote time to it according to this high estimate of its importance. By them He works His spiritual wonders in this world. Great praying is the sign and seal of God's great leaders, and the forerunner of the conquering forces with which God will crown their labors.

Preachers are commissioned to pray as well as to preach. Their mission is incomplete if they do not do both well. Preacher may speak with all the eloquence of human beings and of angels. But unless they can pray with a faith that draws all heaven to their aid, their preaching will be "as sounding brass or a tinkling cymbal"[3] for permanent God-honoring, soul-saving, uses.

Endnotes

1 Luke 6:12
2 Mark 1:35
3 I Corinthians 13:1

6

Prayer Makes A Ministry Spiritually Successful

T HE PRINCIPAL CAUSE OF *my leanness and unfruitfulness is owing
to an unaccountable backwardness to pray. I can write or read or
converse or hear with a ready heart; but prayer is more spiritual and inward
than any of these, and the more spiritual any duty is the more my carnal heart
is apt to start from it. Prayer and patience and faith are never disappointed.
I have long since learned that if ever I was to be a minister faith and prayer
must make me one. When I can find my heart in frame and liberty for prayer,
everything else is comparatively easy.*(Richard Newton)

It may be put down as a spiritual axiom that in every ministry that is
spiritually successful, prayer is an evident and controlling force—evident
and controlling in the life of the preacher, evident and controlling in the
deep spirituality of the work. A ministry may be a very thoughtful ministry
without prayer. The preacher may secure fame and popularity without
prayer. The whole machinery of the preacher's life and work may be run
without the oil of prayer or with scarcely enough to grease one cog. But no
ministry can be a spiritual one, securing holiness in the preacher and in the
congregation, without prayer being made an evident and controlling force.

The preacher that prays truly puts God into the work. God does not
come into the preacher's work as a matter of course or on general
principles. He comes by prayer and special urgency. That God will be
found by us in the day that we seek Him with our whole heart is as true
of the preacher as of the penitent. A prayerful ministry is the only ministry
that brings the preacher into sympathy with the people. Prayer unites the

603

preacher with the congregation as essentially as it does with God. A prayerful ministry is the only ministry qualified for the high offices and responsibilities of the preacher. Colleges, learning, books, theology, preaching cannot make a preacher, but praying does.

Apostles' commission to preach

The apostles' commission to preach was empty until filled up by the Pentecost that praying brought. Praying ministers have passed beyond the regions of the popular, beyond being persons of mere affairs, of secularities, of pulpit attractiveness. They have passed beyond the ecclesiastical organizers or leaders into a more sublime and mightier region—the region of the truly spiritual. Holiness results from their work. Transfigured hearts and lives demonstrate the reality, trueness, and substantial nature of their work. God is with them. Their ministry is not projected on worldly or surface principles. They are schooled in the things of God and deeply filled with them. The agony of their prayers and their long, deep ,communing with God about His people have crowned them as princes in the things of God. The iciness of the mere professional has long since melted under the intensity of their praying.

The reason for the superficial results of many ministries and the deadness of others are to be found in the lack of praying. No ministry can succeed without much praying, and this praying must be fundamental, ever-abiding, ever-increasing. The text, the sermon, should be the result of prayer. The study should be bathed in prayer. All the duties of the ministry should so saturated with prayer that its whole spirit is the spirit of prayer.

"I am sorry that I have prayed so little," was the deathbed regret of one of God's chosen ones. That is a sad and remorseful regret for a preacher. "I want a life of greater, deeper, truer prayer," said the late Archbishop Tait. This we should all say, preacher and layperson, and we should all determine to secure it.

God's true preachers

God's true preachers have been distinguished by one great feature: they were people of prayer. Though they have differed often in many things, they have always had a common center. They may have started from different points, and traveled by different roads, but they converged to one point—they were men and women of prayer. God to them was the center of attraction, and prayer was the path that led to God. They did not pray occasionally, or a little at regular or odd times. They prayed in a way that their prayers entered into and shaped their character, vastly changed their own lives, and changed the lives of others. Their prayers made the history of the Church and influenced the events of their times. They spent much time in prayer, not because they marked the shadow on the dial or the hands on the clock, but because it was to them so momentous and engaging a business that they could hardly stop.

Prayer was to them what it was to Paul, a striving with earnest effort of soul. What it was to Jacob, a wrestling and prevailing. What it was to Christ, "strong crying and tears."[1] They "prayed always with all prayer and supplication in the Spirit, and watching thereunto with all perseverance."[2] "The effectual fervent prayer"[3] has been the mightiest weapon of God's mightiest soldiers. The statement in regard to Elijah, that he "was a man subject to like passions as we are, and he prayed earnestly that it might not rain: and it rained not on the earth by the space of three years and six months. And he prayed again, and the heaven gave rain, and the earth brought forth her fruit,"[4] encompasses all prophets and preachers who have moved their generation for God, and shows the instrument by which they worked their wonders.

Endnotes

1 Hebrews 5:7
2 Ephesians 6:18
3 James 5:16b
4 James 5:17-18

7

Examples of Praying Saints

THE GREAT MASTERS AND *teachers in Christian doctrine have always found in prayer their highest source of illumination. Not to go beyond the limits of the English Church, it is recorded of Bishop Andrews that he spent five hours daily on his knees. The greatest practical resolves that have enriched and beautified human life in Christian times have been arrived at in prayer.* (Canon Liddon)

The act of praying is the very highest energy of which the human mind is capable; praying, that is, with the total concentration of the faculties. The great mass of worldly men and of learned men are absolutely incapable of prayer. (Samuel Taylor Coleridge)

Many private prayers must of necessity be short, public prayers should normally be short and condensed, and there is often need for spontaneous prayer. But in our private communion with God, time is essential to the value of our prayer. Much time spent with God is the secret of all successful praying. Prayer that is a mighty force is the product of much time spent with God. Our short prayers owe their point and efficiency to the long ones that have preceded them. The short prevailing prayer cannot be prayed by a person who has not prevailed with God in a mightier struggle of long continuance. Jacob's victory of faith could not have been gained without that all-night wrestling. God's acquaintance is not made by pop in and pop out calls. God does not bestow his gifts on the casual or hasty. Much time with God alone is the secret of knowing Him and having influence with Him. He yields to the persistency of a faith that knows Him. He bestows His richest gifts upon those who declare their desire for and appreciation of those gifts by the constancy as well as earnestness of their importunity.

Christ is our example in this and many other things. He spent many whole nights in prayer. His custom was to pray much. He had His habitual place to pray. Many long seasons of praying make up His history and character. Paul prayed day and night. It took time from very important interests for Daniel to pray three times a day. David's morning, noon, and night praying were doubtless on many occasions very drawn out. While we have no specific account of the time these Bible saints spent in prayer, the indications are that they spent much time in prayer, and on some occasions long seasons of praying was their custom.

We would want anyone to think that the value of their prayers is to be measured by the clock. Our purpose is to impress on our minds the necessity of being much alone with God. If this feature has not been produced by our faith, then our faith is feeble and shallow.

PRAYING SAINTS

The saints who have most fully illustrated Christ in their character, and have most powerfully affected the world for Him, have been men and women who spent so much time with God as to make it a notable feature of their lives.

Charles Simeon devoted the hours from four till eight in the morning to God.

John Wesley spent two hours daily in prayer. He began at four in the morning. A person who knew him well said about him, "He thought prayer to be more his business than anything else, and I have seen him come out of his closet with a serenity of face next to shining."

John Fletcher stained the walls of his room by the breath of his prayers. Frequently he would pray with great earnestness all night. His whole life was a life of prayer. "I would not rise from my seat," he said, "without lifting my heart to God." His greeting to a friend was always, "Do I meet you praying?"

Martin Luther said: "If I fail to spend two hours in prayer each morning, the devil gets the victory through the day. I have so much business I cannot get on without spending three hours daily in prayer." He had a motto: "He that has prayed well has studied well."

Archbishop Leighton was so much alone with God that he seemed to be in a perpetual meditation. "Prayer and praise were his business and his pleasure," says his biographer.

Bishop Ken was so much with God that his soul was said to be captivated and inspired by God. He was with God before the clock struck three every morning.

Bishop Asbury said: "I propose to rise at four o'clock as often as I can and spend two hours in prayer and meditation."

Samuel Rutherford, the fragrance of whose piety is still rich, rose at three in the morning to meet God in prayer.

Joseph Alleine arose at four o'clock for his business of praying till eight. If he heard other tradesmen plying their business before he was up, he would exclaim: "O how this shames me! Doth not my Master deserve more than theirs?" He who has learned this trade well draws at will, on sight, and with acceptance of heaven's unfailing bank.

Robert Murray McCheyne, one of the holiest and among the most gifted of Scotch preachers, says: "I ought to spend the best hours in communion with God. It is my noblest and most fruitful employment, and is not to be thrust into a corner. The morning hours, from six to eight, are the most uninterrupted and should be thus employed. After tea is my best hour, and that should be solemnly dedicated to God. I ought not to give up the good old habit of prayer before going to bed; but guard must be kept against sleep. When I awake in the night, I ought to rise and pray. A little time after breakfast might be given to intercession." This was his praying plan.

John Wesley's memorable Methodist band shame us in their praying. "From four to five in the morning, private prayer. From five to six in the evening, private prayer."

John Welch, the holy and wonderful Scotch preacher, thought the day ill-spent if he did not spend eight or ten hours in prayer. He kept a plaid[1] close by so that he might wrap himself when he arose to pray at night. His wife would complain when she found him lying on the ground weeping. He would reply: "O woman, I have the souls of three thousand to answer for, and I know not how it is with many of them!"

Bishop Wilson says, "In Henry Martyn's journal the spirit of prayer, the time he devoted to the duty, and his fervor in it are the first things that strike me."

Payson wore the hard-wood boards into grooves where his knees pressed so often and so long. His biographer says: "His continuing instant in prayer, be his circumstances what they might, is the most noticeable fact in his history, and points out the duty of all who would rival his eminency. To his ardent and persevering prayers must no doubt be ascribed in a great measure his distinguished and almost uninterrupted success."

The Marquis DeRenty, to whom Christ was most precious, ordered his servant to call him from his devotions at the end of half an hour. The servant at the time saw his face through an opening in the door. It was marked with such holiness that he hated to arouse him. His lips were moving, but he was perfectly silent. The servant waited until three half hours had passed, then he called to him. He arose from his knees saying that the half hour was so short when he was communing with Christ.

David Brainerd said: "I love to be alone in my cottage, where I can spend much time in prayer."

William Bramwell is famous in Methodist annals for personal holiness, for his wonderful success in preaching, and for the marvelous answers to his prayers. For hours at a time he would pray. He almost lived on his knees. He went over his circuits like a flame of fire. The fire was kindled by the time he spent in prayer. He often spent as much as four hours in a single season of prayer in retirement.

Bishop Andrewes spent the greatest part of five hours every day in prayer and devotion.

Sir Henry Havelock always spent the first two hours of each day alone with God. If the encampment was struck at 6 A.M., he would rise at four.

Earl Cairns rose daily at six o'clock to have an hour and a half to study the Bible and pray before conducting family worship at a quarter to eight.

Dr. Judson's success in India and in prayer is attributable to the fact that he gave much time to prayer. He says on this point: "Arrange thy affairs, if possible, so that thou canst leisurely devote two or three hours every day not merely to devotional exercises but to the very act of secret prayer and communion with God. Endeavor seven times a day to withdraw from business and company and lift up thy soul to God in private retirement. Begin the day by rising after midnight and devoting some time amid the silence and darkness of the night to this sacred work. Let the hour of opening dawn find thee at the same work. Let the hours of nine, twelve, three, six, and nine at night witness the same. Be resolute in his cause. Make all practicable sacrifices to maintain it. Consider that thy time is short, and that business and company must not be allowed to rob thee of thy God."

Impossible, we say, fanatical directions! Dr. Judson impressed an empire for Christ and laid the foundations of God's kingdom with imperishable granite in the heart of Burma. He was successful, one of the few saints who mightily impressed the world for Christ. Many people of greater gifts and genius and learning than he have made no such impression. Their religious work is like footsteps in the sands, but he has engraved his work on the adamant.[2] The secret of its great depth and endurance is found in the fact that he gave time to prayer. He kept the iron red-hot with prayer, and God's skill fashioned it with enduring power. No one can do a great and enduring work for God who is not a person of prayer, and no one can be a person of prayer who does not give much time to praying.

Is it true that prayer is simply the compliance with habit, dull and mechanical? A petty performance into which we are trained until tameness, shortness, superficiality are its chief elements?

CANON LIDDON

"Is it true," asks Canon Liddon, "that prayer is, as is assumed, little else than the half-passive play of sentiment that flows languidly on through the minutes or hours of easy reverie? Let those who have really prayed give the answer."

Sometimes they describe prayer with the patriarch Jacob as a wrestling together with an unseen power that may often last for those praying earnestly late into the night hours, or even to the break of day. Sometimes they refer to common intercession with St. Paul as a concerted struggle. When praying, they have their eyes fixed on the Great Intercessor in Gethsemane, upon the drops of blood that fall to the ground in that agony of resignation and sacrifice. Importunity is of the essence of successful prayer. Importunity means not dreaminess but sustained work. It is through prayer especially that "the kingdom of heaven suffereth, violence and the violent take it by force."[3]

BISHOP HAMILTON

It was a saying of the late Bishop Hamilton that, "No one is likely to do much good in prayer who does not begin by looking upon it in the light of a work to be prepared for and persevered in with all the earnestness that we bring to bear upon subjects that are in our opinion at once most interesting and most necessary."

Endnotes

1 A rectangular woolen scarf of a tartan pattern worn over the left shoulder by Scottish Highlanders.
2 A stone once believed to be impenetrable in its hardness.
3 Matthew 11:12

8

Begin the Day with Prayer

I OUGHT TO PRAY BEFORE *seeing any one. Often when I sleep long, or meet with others early, it is eleven or twelve o'clock before I begin secret prayer. This is a wretched system. It is unscriptural. Christ arose before day and went into a solitary place. David says: "Early will I seek thee"; "Thou shalt early hear my voice." Family prayer loses much of its power and sweetness, and I can do no good to those who come to seek from me. The conscience feels guilty, the soul unfed, the lamp not trimmed. Then when in secret prayer the soul is often out of tune, I feel it is far better to begin with God—to see his face first, to get my soul near him before it is near another.* (Robert Murray McCheyne)

The saints who have done the most for God in this world have been early on their knees. Those who squander the early morning opportunity and freshness in other pursuits than seeking God will make poor headway seeking Him the rest of the day. If God is not first in our thoughts and efforts in the morning, He will be in the last place the remainder of the day.

Behind this early rising and early praying is the ardent desire that presses us into this pursuit after God. Morning listlessness is a sign of a listless heart. The heart that is slow in seeking God in the morning has lost its relish for God. David's heart was ardent after God. He hungered and thirsted after God, and so he sought God early before daylight. Bed and sleep could not chain his soul in its eagerness after God.

Jesus longed for communion with God. So, "rising up a great while before day," (Mark 1:35) he would go out into the mountain to pray. When the disciples were fully awake and ashamed of their indulgence they would know where to find him. If we went through the list of men and women who have mightily impressed the world for God, we would find them early after God.

A desire for God that cannot break the chains of sleep is a weak thing and will do but little good for God after it has indulged itself fully. The desire for God that stays far behind the devil and the world at the beginning of the day will never catch up.

It is not simply getting up that puts Christians to the front and makes them captains and generals in God's army. It is the ardent desire that stirs and breaks all self-indulgent chains. But getting up gives release, increase, and strength to the desire. If they had lain in bed and indulged themselves, the desire would have been quenched. The desire aroused them and put them on the stretch for God, and this heeding and acting on the call gave their faith its grasp on God and gave to their hearts the sweetest and fullest revelation of God. The resulting strength of faith and fullness of revelation made them saints by eminence. The halo of their sainthood has come down to us, and we have entered on the enjoyment of their conquests. We take our fill in enjoyment, however, and not in productions. We build their tombs (Luke 11:48) and write their epitaphs, but are careful not to follow their examples.

We need a generation of preachers who seek God and seek Him early. We need men and women who give the freshness and dew of effort to God, and in return obtain the freshness and fullness of His power so that he may be as the dew to them, full of gladness and strength through all the heat and labor of the day. Our laziness after God is our crying sin. The children of this world are far wiser than we. They are at it early and late. We do not seek God with ardor and diligence. No one gets God who does not follow hard after Him, and no soul follows hard after God who is not after Him in the early morning.

9

Prayer and Devotion United

THERE IS A MANIFEST *lack of spiritual influence on the ministry of the present day. I feel it in my own case and I see it in that of others. I am afraid there is too much of a low, managing, contriving, maneuvering temper of mind among us. We are laying ourselves out more than is expedient to meet one person's taste and another person's prejudices. The ministry is a grand and holy affair, and it should find in us a simple habit of spirit and a holy but humble indifference to all consequences. The leading defect in Christian ministers is lack of a devotional habit.* (Richard Cecil)

There was never greater need for saintly men and women. But even more imperative is the call for saintly, God-devoted preachers. The world moves with gigantic and rapid strides. Satan has his hold and rule on the world, and labors to make all its movements serve and promote his purposes. Christianity must do its best work and present its most attractive and perfect models. Modern sainthood must be inspired by the loftiest ideals and largest possibilities through the Holy Spirit. Paul lived on his knees so that the Ephesian Church might measure the heights, breadths, and depths of an immeasurable saintliness, and "be filled with all the fullness of God."[1] Epaphras laid himself out with the exhaustive toil and strenuous conflict of fervent prayer so that the Colossian Church might "stand perfect and complete in all the will of God."[2]

Everything everywhere in apostolic times was pressing forward so that the people of God might each and "all come in the unity of the faith, and of the knowledge of the Son of God, unto a perfect man, unto the measure of the stature of the fullness of Christ."[3] No premium was given to those who came short of God's calling. No encouragement was given to an old babyhood. The babies were to grow to adulthood, and the old were to bear fruit in old age and be fat and flourishing, instead of feeble and infirmed. The godliest thing in Christianity is holy men and women.

HOLINESS ENERGIZES THE SOUL

No amount of money, genius, or culture can move things for God. Holiness energizes the soul. It sets the whole person aflame with love and with desire for more faith, prayer, zeal, and consecration. This is the secret of power. These we need and must have, and Christians must be the incarnation of this God-inflamed devotedness. God's advance has been stopped, his cause crippled, and His name dishonored because of their lack. Genius—though the loftiest and most gifted education—though the most learned and refined position, dignity, place, honored names, and high ecclesiastics cannot move this chariot of our God. It is a fiery one, and fiery forces only can move it. The genius of a Milton fails. The imperial strength of a Leo fails. Brainerd's spirit can move it. Brainerd's spirit was on fire for God, on fire for souls. There was nothing earthly, worldly, or selfish about him that could lessen in the least the intensity of his all-impelling and all-consuming force and flame.

Prayer is the creator as well as the channel of devotion. The spirit of devotion is the spirit of prayer. Prayer and devotion are united as soul and body are united, as life and the heart are united. There is no real prayer without devotion, no devotion without prayer. Preachers must be surrendered to God in the holiest devotion. They are not professional people, their ministry is not a profession. It is a divine institution, a divine devotion. They are devoted to God. Their aim, aspirations, ambitions are for God and to God. To them, prayer is as essential as food is to life.

DEVOTION TO GOD

Preachers must be devoted to God above everything else. Their relations to God are the insignia and credentials of their ministry. These must be clear, conclusive, unmistakable. No common, surface type of piety must be theirs. If they do not excel in grace, they do not excel at all. If they do not preach by life, character, conduct, they do not preach at all. If their piety is light, their preaching may be as soft and sweet as music, but its weight will be a feather's weight—visionary and fleeting as the morning cloud or the early dew. There is no substitute for devotion to God in the preacher's character and conduct. Devotion to a church, opinions, organizations, orthodoxy are paltry, misleading, and vain when they become the source of inspiration.

God must be the mainspring of the preacher's effort, the fountain and crown of all the work. The name and honor of Jesus Christ, the advance of His cause, must be all in all. The preacher must have no inspiration but the name of Jesus Christ, no ambition but to have him glorified, no toil but for him. Then prayer will be a source of illuminations, the means of perpetual advance, and the gauge of success. The perpetual aim, the only ambition, preachers can cherish is to have God with them.

A POOR MODEL OF DIVINE POWER

Never did the cause of God need perfect illustrations of the possibilities of prayer more than in this age. No age, no person, will be examples of the gospel power except the ages or persons of deep and earnest prayer. A prayerless age will have but scant models of divine power. Prayerless hearts will never rise to Alpine heights. The age may be a better age than the past. But there is an infinite distance between the betterment of an age by the force of an advancing civilization, and its betterment by the increase of holiness and Christlikeness by the energy of prayer. The Jews were much better when Christ came than in the ages before. It was the golden age of their Pharisaic religion. Their golden religious age crucified Christ. Never more praying, never less praying. Never more sacrifices, never less sacrifice. Never less idolatry, never more idolatry. Never more temple worship, never less God worship. Never more lip service, never less heart service—imagine, God worshiped by those whose hearts and hands crucified His Son. Never more churchgoers, never fewer saints.

It is prayer-power that makes saints. Holy characters are formed by the power of real praying. The more of true saints, the more of praying—the more of praying, the more of true saints.

Endnotes

1 Ephesians 3:19
2 Colossians 4:12
3 Ephesians 4:13

10

Examples of Devotion

I URGE UPON YOU COMMUNION *with Christ, a growing communion. There are curtains to be drawn aside in Christ that we never saw, and new foldings of love in Him. I despair that I shall ever win to the far end of that love, there are so many plies in it. Therefore dig deep, and sweat and labor and take pains for him, and set by as much time in the day for Him as you can. We will be won in the labor.* (Samuel Rutherford)

God has now, and has always had, many of these devoted, prayerful, preachers—men and women in whose lives prayer has been a mighty, controlling, conspicuous force. The world has felt their power, God has felt and honored their power. God's cause has moved mightily and swiftly by their prayers. Holiness has shone out in their characters with a divine radiances.

God found one of the men He was looking for in David Brainerd, whose work and name have gone into history. He was no ordinary man, but was capable of shining in any company. He was the peer of the wise and gifted ones, eminently suited to fill the most attractive pulpits and to labor among the most refined and cultured—most of whom were highly anxious to secure him for their pastor. President Edwards said that he was, "a young man of distinguished talents, had extraordinary knowledge of men and things, had rare conversational powers, excelled in his knowledge of theology, and was truly, for one so young, an extraordinary divine, and especially in all matters relating to experimental religion. I never knew his equal of his age and standing for clear and accurate notions of the nature and essence of true religion. His manner in prayer was almost inimitable, such as I have very rarely known equaled. His learning was very considerable, and he had extraordinary gifts for the pulpit."

DAVID BRAINERD

No nobler story has been recorded in earthly annals than that of David Brainerd. No miracle attests with diviner force the truth of Christianity than the life and work of this man. Alone in the savage wilds of America, struggling day and night with a mortal disease, unschooled in the care of souls, having access to the Indians for a large portion of time only through the bungling medium of a pagan interpreter, with nothing but the Word of God in his heart and in his hand, his soul fired with the divine flame, and a place and time to pour out his soul to God in prayer, he fully established the worship of God and secured all its gracious results. The Indians were changed with a great change. Many were converted from immoral pagan ways and became pure, devout, intelligent Christians. All vice as reformed, and the external duties of Christianity were at once embraced and acted on. Family prayer was set up. Church meetings were instituted and religiously observed. The internal graces of Christianity were exhibited with growing sweetness and strength.

The source of these results is found in David Brainerd himself, not in the conditions or events but in the man Brainerd. He was God's man, for God first and last and all the time. God could flow unhindered through him. The omnipotence of grace was neither arrested nor stopped by the conditions of his heart. The whole channel was broadened and cleaned out for God's fullest and most powerful passage, so that God with all his mighty forces could come down on the hopeless, savage, wilderness, and transform it into His blooming and fruitful garden. For nothing is too hard for God to do if He can get the right kind of person to do it with.

Brainerd lived a life of holiness and prayer. His diary is full and monotonous with the record of his seasons of fasting, meditation, and retirement. The time he spent in private prayer amounted to many hours daily. "When I return home," he said, "and give myself to meditation, prayer, and fasting, my soul longs for mortification, self-denial, humility, and divorcement from all things of the world."

"I have nothing to do," he said, "with earth but only to labor in it honestly for God. I do not desire to live one minute for anything which earth can afford." After this high order he prayed:

Feeling somewhat of the sweetness of communion with God and the constraining force of His love, and how admirably it captivates the soul and makes all the desires and affections to center in God, I set apart this day for secret fasting and prayer, to entreat God to direct and bless me with regard to the great work which I have in view of preaching the gospel, and that the Lord would return to me and show me the light of His countenance.

I had little life and power in the forenoon. Near the middle of the afternoon God enabled me to wrestle ardently in intercession for my absent friends, but just at night the Lord visited me marvelously in prayer. I think my soul was never in such agony before. I felt no restraint, for the treasures of divine grace were opened to me. I wrestled for absent friends, for the ingathering of souls, for multitudes of poor souls, and for many that I thought were the children of God, personally, in many distant places. I was in such agony from sun half an hour high till near dark that I was all over wet with sweat, but yet it seemed to me I had done nothing. O, my dear Savior did sweat blood for poor souls! I longed for more compassion toward them. I felt still in a sweet frame, under a sense of divine love and grace, and went to bed in such a frame, with my heart set on God.

It was prayer that gave to his life and ministry their marvelous power. People of mighty prayer are people of spiritual might. Prayers never die. Brainerd's whole life was a life of prayer. By day and by night he prayed. Before preaching and after preaching he prayed. Riding through the endless solitudes of the forests he prayed. On his bed of straw he prayed. Retiring to the dense and lonely forests, he prayed. Hour by hour, day after day, early morning and late at night, he was praying and fasting, pouring out his soul, interceding, communing with God. He was with God mightily in prayer, and God was with him mightily. By it he being dead yet speaks and works (Hebrews 11:4b). And he will speak and work until the end comes. When it does, he will be one of the first among the glorious ones of that glorious day.

JONATHAN EDWARDS

Jonathan Edwards said of Brainerd: "His life shows the right way to success in the works of the ministry. He sought it as the soldier seeks victory in a siege or battle; or as a man that runs a race for a great prize. Animated with love to Christ and souls, how did he labor? Always fervently. Not only in word and doctrine, in public and in private, but in prayers by day and night, wrestling with God in secret and travailing in birth with unutterable groans and agonies, until Christ was formed in the hearts of the people to whom he was sent. Like a true son of Jacob, he persevered in wrestling through all the darkness of the night, until the breaking of the day!"

II

Heart Preparation Necessary

FOR NOTHING REACHES THE *heart but what is from the heart or pierces the conscience but what comes from a living conscience.* (William Penn)

In the morning I was more engaged in preparing the head than the heart. This has been frequently my error, and I have always felt the evil of it especially in prayer. Reform it then, O Lord! Enlarge my heart and I shall preach. (Robert Murray McCheyne)

A sermon that has more head infused into it than heart will not borne home with efficacy to the hearers. (Richard Cecil)

With its manifold and many-sided forces, prayer helps the mouth to utter the truth in its fullness and freedom. The preacher is to be prayed for, the preacher is made by prayer. The preacher's mouth is to be prayed for— made open and filled by prayer. A holy mouth is made by praying, by much praying. A brave mouth is made by praying, by much praying. The Church and the world, God and heaven, owe much to Paul's mouth. Paul's mouth owed its power to prayer.

How manifold, unlimited, valuable, and helpful prayer is to preachers in so many ways, at so many points—in every way! One great value is that it helps the heart.

Praying makes the preacher a heart preacher. Prayer puts the preacher's heart into the preacher's sermon. Prayer puts the preacher's sermon into the preacher's heart.

The heart makes the preacher. Men and women of great hearts are great preachers. Those of bad hearts may do a measure of good, but this is rare. The hireling and the stranger may help the sheep at some points, but it is the good shepherd with the good shepherd's heart who will bless the sheep and fill the full measure of the shepherd's place.

We have emphasized sermon preparation until we have lost sight of the important thing to be prepared—the heart. A prepared heart is much better than a prepared sermon. A prepared heart will make a prepared sermon.

Volumes have been written laying down the mechanics and form of sermon-making, until we have become possessed with the idea that this scaffolding is the building. Young preachers have been taught to lay out all their strength on the form, taste, and beauty of their sermon as a mechanical and intellectual product. We have thereby cultivated a vicious taste among the people and raised the clamor for talent instead of grace, eloquence instead of piety, rhetoric instead of revelation, reputation and brilliancy instead of holiness. By it, we have lost the true idea of preaching, lost preaching power, and lost strong conviction of sin that it develops. We have also lost the rich experience and elevated Christian character, and the authority over consciences and lives that always results from genuine preaching.

It would not do to say that preachers study too much. Some of them do not study at all, and others do not study enough. Numbers do not study the right way to show themselves workmen approved of God (2 Timothy 2:15). But our great problem is not lack of head culture, but of heart culture. Not lack of knowledge, but lack of holiness. That is our sad and telling defect. It is not that we know too much, but that we do not meditate on God and His word and watch and fast and pray enough. The heart is the great hindrance to our preaching. Words pregnant with divine truth find no open pathway in our hearts. Stumbling, they fall stripped and powerless.

WORLDLY AMBITION

Can ambition that lusts after praise and position preach the gospel of the one who made Himself of no reputation and took on Himself the form of a servant (Philippians 2:7)? Can the proud, vain, and egotistical preach the gospel of He who was meek and lowly? Can the bad-tempered, passionate, selfish, hard, worldly person preach a Christianity that teems with long-suffering, self-denial, and tenderness—a Christianity that authoritatively demands separation from hatred and crucifixion to the world? Can the hireling official, heartless and disinterested, preach the gospel that demands shepherds give their life for the sheep? Can the covetous who count salary and money preach the gospel until their have purged their heart and can say in the spirit of Christ and Paul the words of John Wesley: "I count it dung and dross; I trample it under my feet; I (yet not I, but the grace of God in me) esteem it just as the mire of the streets, I desire it not, I seek it not?"

God's revelation does not need the light of human genius, the polish and strength of human culture, the brilliancy of human thought, the force of human brains to adorn or enforce it. But it does demand the simplicity, docility, humility, and faith of a child's heart.

It was this surrender and subordination of intellect and genius to the divine and spiritual forces that made Paul peerless among the apostles. It was this that gave Wesley his power and engraved his labors in the history of humanity. Our great need is heart-preparation. Luther held it as an axiom: "He who has prayed well has studied well."

We are not saying that preachers are not to think and use their intellects. But those will use their intellect best who cultivate their heart most. We do not say that preachers should not be students. But we do say that their great study should be the Bible, and those study the Bible best who have kept their heart with diligence. We do not say that preachers should not know people, but they who have fathomed the depths and intricacies of their own heart will be the most skilled in human nature.

A FOUNTAIN OF PREACHING

We are saying that while the channel of preaching is the mind, its fountain is the heart. You may broaden and deepen the channel, but if you do not look well to the purity and depth of the fountain, you will have a dry or polluted channel. We do say that almost any person of common intelligence has sense enough to preach the gospel, but very few have grace enough to do so. We do say that those who have struggled with their own heart and conquered it, who have taught it humility, faith, love, truth, mercy, sympathy, and courage, and who can pour through a strong intellect the rich treasures of a heart thus trained and filled with the power of the gospel on the consciences of their hearers—such preachers will be the truest and most successful preachers in the esteem of their Lord.

12

Grace from the Heart Rather than the Head

STUDY NOT TO BE A *fine preacher. Jerichos are blown down with rams' horns. Look simply unto Jesus for preaching food; and what is wanted will be given, and what is given will be blessed, whether it be a barley grain or a wheaten loaf, a crust or a crumb. Your mouth will be a flowing stream or a fountain sealed, according as your heart is. Avoid all controversy in preaching, talking, or writing; preach nothing down but the devil, and nothing up but Jesus Christ.* (Berridge)

The heart is the savior of the world. Heads do not save. Genius, brains, brilliancy, strength, and natural gifts do not save. The gospel flows through hearts. All the mightiest forces are heart forces. All the sweetest and loveliest graces are heart graces. Great hearts make great characters—great hearts make divine characters. God is love. There is nothing greater than love, nothing greater than God. Hearts make heaven, heaven is love. There is nothing higher and sweeter than heaven. It is the heart and not the head that makes God's great preachers. The heart counts much every way in Christianity. The heart must speak from the pulpit. The heart must hear in the pew. In fact, we serve God with our hearts. Head homage does not pass current in heaven.

We believe that one of the serious and most popular errors of the modern pulpit is more thought than prayer, more head than heart, in its sermons. Big hearts make big preachers, and good hearts make good preachers. A theological school to enlarge and cultivate the heart is the golden and highest desire of the gospel. It is the heart that binds a congregation to a pastor and enables the pastor to govern them.

Congregations may admire a pastor's gifts, may be proud of a pastor's ability, may be affected for a time by a pastor's sermons, but the stronghold of a pastor's power is the heart. The pastor's scepter is love, and the throne of power is the pastor's heart.

GOOD SHEPHERDS GIVE THEIR LIFE FOR THE SHEEP

Heads never make martyrs. It is the heart that surrenders the life to love and faithfulness. It takes great courage to be a faithful pastor, and the heart alone can supply this courage. Gifts and genius may be brave, but it is the gifts and genius of the heart and not of the head.

It is easier to fill the head than it is to prepare the heart. It is easier to make a brain sermon than a heart sermon. It was heart that drew the Son of God from heaven. It is heart that will draw people to heaven. Men and women of heart is what the world needs to sympathize with its woe, to kiss away its sorrows, to empathize with its misery, and to alleviate its pain. Christ was eminently a man of sorrows, because he was preeminently a man of heart.

"GIVE ME YOUR HEART"

"Give Me your heart," is God's demand of people. "Give me your heart!" is humanity's demand of humanity.

A professional ministry is a heartless ministry. When salary plays a great part in the ministry, the heart plays little part. We may make preaching our business, and not put our hearts into the business. Those who put self to the front in their preaching put heart to the rear. Those who do not sow with their heart in their study will never reap a harvest for God. The closet is the heart's study. We will learn more about how to preach and what to preach there than we can learn in our libraries. "Jesus wept" (John 11:35) is the shortest and biggest verse in the Bible. It is those who go forth weeping (not preaching great sermons), bearing precious seed, who will come again rejoicing, bringing their sheaves with them (Psalm 126:6).

Praying gives sense, brings wisdom, broadens and strengthens the mind. The closet is a perfect schoolteacher and schoolhouse for the preacher. Thought is not only brightened and clarified in prayer, but thought is born in prayer. We can learn more in an hour praying, when praying indeed, than from many hours in the study. Books are in the closet that can be found and read nowhere else. Revelations are made in the closet that are made nowhere else.

13

Unction a Necessity

ONE BRIGHT BLESSING THAT *private prayer brings down upon the ministry is an indescribable and inimitable something—an unction from the Holy One. . . . If the anointing that we bear come not from the Lord of hosts, we are deceivers, since only in prayer can we obtain it. Let us continue instant constant fervent in supplication. Let your fleece lie on the thrashing floor of supplication until it is wet with the dew of heaven.* (Charles Haddon Spurgeon)

ALEXANDER KNOX

Alexander Knox was a Christian philosopher in the days of John Wesley. He was not an supporter of Wesley's beliefs, but a strong personal friend, and had a great deal of spiritual sympathy with the Wesleyan movement. He wrote: "It is strange and lamentable, but I verily believe the fact to be that except among Methodists and Methodistic clergyman, there is not much interesting preaching in England. The clergy, too generally have absolutely lost the art. There is, I conceive, in the great laws of the moral world a kind of secret understanding like the affinities in chemistry, between rightly promulgated religious truth and the deepest feelings of the human mind. Where the one is duly exhibited, the other will respond. Did not our hearts burn within us?—but to this devout feeling is indispensable in the speaker.

Now, I am obliged to state from my own observation that this unction, as the French not unfitly term it, is beyond all comparison more likely to be found in England in a Methodist conventicle (i.e. religious meeting) than in a parish church. This, and this alone, seems really to be that which fills the Methodist houses and thins the churches. I am, I verily think, no enthusiast; I am a most sincere and cordial churchman, a humble disciple of the school of Hale and

Boyle, of Burnet and Leighton. Now I must aver that when I was in this country, two years ago, I did not hear a single preacher who taught me like my own great masters but such as are deemed Methodists. And I now despair of getting an atom of heart instruction from any other quarter.

The Methodist preachers (however I may not always approve of all their expressions) do most assuredly diffuse this true religion and undefiled. I felt real pleasure last Sunday. I can bear witness that the preacher did at once speak the words of truth and soberness. There was no eloquence—the honest man never dreamed of such a thing—but there was far better: a cordial communication of vitalized truth. I say vitalized because what he declared to others it was impossible not to feel he lived on himself.

This unction is the art of preaching. Preachers who never had this unction never had the art of preaching. Preachers who have lost this unction have lost the art of preaching. Whatever other arts preachers may have and retain—the art of sermon-making, the art of eloquence, the art of great, clear thinking, the art of pleasing an audience—they have lost the divine art of preaching. This unction makes God's truth powerful and interesting, draws and attracts, edifies, convicts, saves.

This unction vitalizes God's revealed truth, makes it living and life-giving. Even God's truth spoken without this unction is light, dead, and deadening. Though abounding in truth, though weighty with thought, though sparkling with rhetoric, though pointed by logic, though powerful by earnestness, without this divine unction it issues in death and not in life.

CHARLES SPURGEON

Mr. Spurgeon says:

I wonder how long we might beat our brains before we could plainly put into word what is meant by preaching with unction. Yet he who preaches knows its presence, and he who hears soon detects its absence. Samaria in famine typifies a discourse without it. Jerusalem with her feast of fat things, full of marrow, may represent a sermon enriched with it. Every one knows what the freshness of the morning is when orient pearls abound on every blade of grass, but who can describe it, much less produce it of itself? Such is the mystery of spiritual anointing. We know, but we cannot tell to others what it is. It is as easy as it is foolish to counterfeit it. Unction is a thing that you cannot manufacture, and its counterfeits are worse than worthless. Yet it is in itself priceless, and beyond measure needful if you would edify believers and bring sinners to Christ.

14

The Mark of True Gospel Preaching

SPEAK FOR ETERNITY. *Above all things, cultivate your own spirit. A word spoken by you when your conscience is clear and your heart full of God's Spirit is worth ten thousand words spoken in unbelief and sin. Remember that God, and not man, must have the glory. If the veil of the world's machinery were lifted off, how much we would find is done in answer to the prayers of God's children.* (Robert Murray McCheyne)

Unction is that indefinable, indescribable, something that an old, renowned, Scotch preacher describes this way: "There is sometimes somewhat in preaching that cannot be ascribed either to matter or expression, and cannot be described what it is, or from whence it cometh, but with a sweet violence it pierceth into the heart and affections and comes immediately from the Word; but if there be any way to obtain such a thing, it is by the heavenly disposition of the speaker."

We call it unction. It is this unction that makes the word of God "quick, and powerful, and sharper than any two-edged sword, piercing even to the dividing asunder of soul and spirit, and of the joints and marrow . . . a discerner of the thoughts and intents of the heart" (Hebrews 4:12). It is this unction that gives the words of the preacher such point, sharpness, and power, and that creates such friction and stir in many dead congregations. The same truths have been told in the strictness of the letter, smooth as human oil could make them. But they resulted in no signs of life, not even a pulse throb. All remains as peaceful as the grave and as dead. But when the same preacher receives a baptism of this unction, there is now divine inspiration in the preaching. The letter of the Word has been enhanced and fired by this mysterious power. The actions of life now begin, actions that either receive or resist. The unction pervades and convicts the conscience and breaks the heart.

This divine unction is the feature that separates and distinguishes true gospel preaching from all other methods of presenting the truth. It creates a wide spiritual chasm between the preacher who has it and the one who does not. It supports and impregnates revealed truth with all the energy of God. Unction is simply putting God in His own Word and on His own preachers. The potential and personal nature of the unction to the preacher come from mighty and great prayerfulness and by continual prayerfulness. Unction inspires and clarifies the intellect, and gives insight, understanding, and projecting power. It gives to the preacher heart power, which is greater than head power. Tenderness, purity, and force flow from the heart by it. Enlargement, freedom, fullness of thought, directness, and simplicity of utterance are the fruits of this unction.

EARNESTNESS IS NOT UNCTION

Often earnestness is mistaken for this unction. Those who have the divine unction will be earnest in the very spiritual nature of things, but there may be a vast deal of earnestness without the least mixture of unction.

Earnestness and unction look alike from some points of view. Earnestness may be readily and without detection substituted or mistaken for unction. It requires a spiritual eye and a spiritual taste to discriminate.

Earnestness may be sincere, serious, ardent, and persevering. It goes at a thing with good will, pursues it with perseverance, and urges it with ardor—that is, puts force into it. But all these forces do not rise higher than the mere human. The person is in it—the whole person, with all that the person has of will and heart, of brain and genius, of planning and working and talking. Such people set themselves to some purpose that has mastered them, and then pursue to master it. There may be none of God in it. There may be little of God in it, because there is so much of the person in it.

The person may present pleas in advocacy of the earnest purpose that please or touch and move or overwhelm with conviction of their importance. In all this, earnestness may move along earthly ways, being propelled by human forces only, its altar made by earthly hands and its fire kindled by earthly flames. It is said of a rather famous preacher of gifts, whose construction of Scripture was to his fancy or purpose, that he "grew very eloquent over his own exegesis." So people grow exceedingly earnest over their own plans or movements. Earnestness may be selfishness simulated.

WHAT IS UNCTION?

It is the indefinable in preaching that makes it preaching. It is that which distinguishes and separates preaching from all mere human addresses. It is the divine in preaching. It makes the preaching sharp to those who need sharpness. It distills as the dew to those who need to he refreshed. It is well described in the following stanzas.

It was a two-edged sword
Of heavenly temper keen,
And double were the wounds it made
Wherever it glanced between.

'Twas death to sin; 'twas life
To all who mourned for sin.
It kindled and it silenced strife,
Made war and peace within.

This unction comes to the preacher not in the study but in the closet. It is heaven's distillation in answer to prayer. It is the sweetest exhalation of the Holy Spirit. It impregnates, floods, softens, saturates, cuts, and soothes. It carries the Word like dynamite, like salt, like sugar. It makes the Word a soother, an arranger, a revealer, a searcher. It makes the hearers culprits or saints, makes them weep like children and live like giants. It opens the heart and the wallet as gently and strongly as the spring opens the leaves. This unction is not the gift of genius. It is not found in the halls of learning. No eloquence can woo it. No industry can win it. No prelate's hands can confer it. It is the gift of God—the signet set to His own messengers. It is heaven's knighthood given to the chosen true and brave ones who have sought this anointed honor through many hours of tearful, agonizing prayer.

Earnestness is good and impressive. Genius is gifted and great. Thought kindles and inspires. But it takes a diviner endowment, a more powerful energy than earnestness, genius, or thought to break the chains of sin, to win estranged and depraved hearts to God, to repair the breaches and restore the Church to its old ways of purity and power. Nothing but holy unction can do this.

15

The Price of Unction

A LL THE MINISTER'S EFFORTS *will be vanity or worse than vanity if he does not have unction. Unction must come down from heaven and spread a savor and feeling and relish over his ministry; and among the other means of qualifying himself for his office, the Bible must hold the first place, and the last also must be given to the Word of God and prayer.* (Richard Cecil)

In the Christian system, unction is the anointing of the Holy Ghost, separating men and women unto God's work and qualifying them for it. This unction is the one divine enablement by which the preacher accomplishes the peculiar and saving ends of preaching. Without this unction there are no true spiritual results accomplished. The results and forces in preaching do not rise above the results of unsanctified speech. Without unction there is no more power in the preaching than there is in the wood of the pulpit.

This divine unction on the preacher generates through the Word of God the spiritual results that flow from the gospel. Without this unction, these results are not secured. Many pleasant impressions may be made, but these all fall far below the goals of gospel preaching. This unction may be simulated. There are many things that look like it, there are many results that resemble its effects. But all of them are foreign to its intended results and to its nature. The fervor or softness excited by a pathetic or emotional sermon may look like the movements of the divine unction, but they have no strong, perpetrating, heart-breaking force. There is no heart-healing balm in these surface, sympathetic, emotional movements. They are not radical, sin-searching, or sin-curing.

This divine unction is the one distinguishing feature that separates true gospel preaching from all other methods of presenting truth. It backs and interpenetrates the revealed truth with all the force of God. It illumines the Word and broadens and enriches the intellect and enables it to grasp and apprehend the Word. It qualifies the preacher's heart, and brings it to that condition of tenderness, purity, force, and light that are necessary to secure the highest results. This unction gives to the preacher liberty and enlargement of thought and soul. This is a freedom, fullness, and directness of utterance that can be secured by no other process.

NO POWER WITHOUT UNCTION

Without this unction on the preacher the gospel has no more power to propagate itself than any other system of truth. This is the seal of its divinity. Unction in the preacher puts God in the gospel. Without the unction, God is absent, and the gospel is left to the low and unsatisfactory forces that the ingenuity, interest, or talents of people can devise to enforce and project their doctrines.

It is in this element that the pulpit fails in more often than in any other element. It is at this all-important point that it lapses. It may have learning, brilliancy, and eloquence, and may delight and charm. Sensation or less offensive methods may bring in crowds. Mental power may impress and enforce truth with all its resources. But without this unction, each and all these will be but as the restless assault of the waters on a Gibraltar. Spray and foam may cover and spangle, but the rocks are still there, unimpressed and immoveable. The human heart can no more be swept of its hardness and sin by these human forces than these rocks can be swept away by the ocean's ceaseless flow.

This unction is the consecration force, and its presence the continuous test of that consecration. It is this divine anointing on the preacher that secures consecration to God and His work. Other forces and motives may call the preacher to the work, but this only is consecration. A separation to God's work by the power of the Holy Spirit is the only consecration recognized by God as legitimate.

THE PULPIT NEEDS UNCTION

The unction, the divine unction, this heavenly anointing, is what the pulpit needs and must have. This divine and heavenly oil put on it by the imposition of God's hand must soften and lubricate the whole person—heart, head, spirit—until it separates the preacher with a mighty separation from all earthly, secular, worldly, selfish motives and aims—separating to everything that is pure and godlike.

It is the presence of this unction on the preacher that creates the stir and friction in many congregations. The same truths have been told in the strictness of the letter, but no ruffle has been seen, no pain or pulsation felt. All is quiet as a graveyard. Another preacher comes, and is filled with this mysterious influence. The letter of the Word is fired by the Spirit, and the throes of a mighty movement are felt. It is the unction that pervades and stirs the conscience and breaks the heart. Unctionless preaching makes everything hard, dry, acrid, dead.

This unction is not a memory or an era of the past only. It is a present, realized, conscious fact. It belongs to the experience of the preachers as well as to their preaching. It is that which transforms them into the image of their divine Master, as well as that by which they declare the truths of Christ with power. It is so much the power in the ministry as to make all else seem feeble and vain without it. Its presence atones for the absence of all other and feebler forces.

This unction is not an inalienable gift. It is a conditional gift, and its presence is perpetuated and increased by the same process by which it was at first secured—by unceasing prayer to God, by impassioned desires after God, by esteeming it, by seeking it with tireless ardor, by deeming all else loss and failure without it.

WHERE UNCTION COMES FROM

Where does this unction come from and how? Direct from God in answer to prayer. Only praying hearts are filled with this holy oil, and only praying lips are anointed with this divine unction.

Prayer, much prayer, is the price of preaching unction. Prayer, much prayer, is the sole condition of keeping this unction. Without unceasing prayer the unction never comes to the preacher. Without perseverance in prayer, the unction, like the over-kept manna, breeds worms.

16

Prayer Marks Spiritual Leadership

GIVE ME ONE HUNDRED *preachers who fear nothing but sin and desire nothing but God, and I care not a straw whether they be clergymen or laymen; such alone will shake the gates of hell and set up the kingdom of heaven on earth. God does nothing but in answer to prayer.* (John Wesley)

The apostles knew the necessity and worth of prayer to their ministry. They knew that their high commission as apostles, instead of relieving them from the necessity of prayer, committed them to it by a more urgent need. Consequently, they were exceedingly careful that some other important work should not exhaust their time and prevent their praying as they should. So they appointed laymen to look after the delicate and engrossing duties of ministering to the poor, that they (the apostles) might, unhindered, "give themselves continually to prayer, and to the ministry of the word."[1] Prayer is put first, and their relation to prayer is put most strongly—"give themselves to it." They made a business of it, surrendering themselves to praying, putting fervor, urgency, perseverance, and time in it.

How holy, apostolic men devoted themselves to this divine work of prayer! "Night and day praying exceedingly," says Paul.[2]

"We will give ourselves continually to prayer" is the consensus of apostolic devotion. How these New Testament preachers laid themselves out in prayer for God's people! How they put God in full force into their churches by their praying! These holy apostles did not vainly fancy that they had met their high and solemn duties by delivering God's word faithfully, but their preaching was made to stick and tell by the heat and insistence of their praying. Apostolic praying was as taxing, toilsome, and imperative as apostolic preaching. They prayed mightily night and day to bring their people to the highest regions of faith and holiness. They prayed mightier still to hold them to this high spiritual altitude. Preachers who have never learned in the school of Christ the high and divine art of intercession for God's people will never learn the art of preaching. Not even if homiletics be poured into them by the ton, and though they be the most gifted geniuses in sermon-making and sermon-delivery.

The prayers of apostolic, saintly leaders do much in making saints of those who are not apostles. If the Church[3] leaders had remained as particular and fervent in praying for their people as the apostles were, the sad, dark times of worldliness and apostasy would not have marred the history and eclipsed the glory and slowed the advance of the Church. Apostolic praying makes apostolic saints, and keeps apostolic times of purity and power in the Church.

What loftiness of soul, what purity and elevation of motive, what unselfishness, what self-sacrifice, what exhaustive toil, what ardor of spirit, what divine tact are necessary to be an intercessor for humanity!

Preachers are to lay themselves out in prayer for their people. Not that they might be simply saved, but that they be mightily saved. The apostles laid themselves out in prayer that their saints might be perfect. Not that they should have a little relish for the things of God, but that they "might be filled with all the fullness of God."[4] Paul did not rely on his apostolic preaching to secure this end, but for this cause he bowed his knees "unto the Father of our Lord Jesus Christ."[5] Paul's praying carried Paul's converts further along the highway of sainthood than Paul's preaching did. Epaphras did as much or more by prayer for the Colossian saints than by his preaching. He labored fervently always in prayer for them that they might "stand perfect and complete in all the will of God."[6]

Preachers are preeminently God's leaders. They are primarily responsible for the condition of the Church. They shape its character, and give tone and direction to its life.

SPIRITUAL SUCCESS AND THE CHURCH

Everything in the Church depends upon these leaders. They shape the times and the institutions. The Church is divine, the treasure it incases is heavenly, but it bears the imprint of the human. The treasure is in earthen vessels, and it smacks of the vessel. The Church of God makes, or is made by, its leaders. Whether it makes them or is made by them, it will be what its leaders are—spiritual if they are so, secular if they are, conglomerate if its leaders are. Israel's kings gave character to Israel's piety. A church rarely revolts against or rises above the religion of its leaders. Strongly spiritual leaders, men and women of holy might, at the lead are tokens of God's favor. Disaster and weakness follow the wake of feeble or worldly leaders. Israel had fallen low when God gave children to be their princes and babes to rule over them. No happy state is predicted by the prophets when children oppress God's Israel and weak leaders rule over them. Times of strong spiritual leadership are times of great spiritual prosperity to the Church.

Prayer is one of the eminent characteristics of strong spiritual leadership. Leaders of mighty prayer are leaders of might and mold things. Their power with God has the conquering tread.

How can those preach who do not get their message fresh from God in the closet? How can they preach without having their faith quickened, their vision cleared, and their heart warmed by their closeting with God? Alas, for the pulpit lips that are untouched by this closet flame. They will always be dry and unctionless, and truths divine will never come with power from them. As far as the real interests of Christianity are concerned, a pulpit without a closet will always be a barren thing.

A preacher may preach in an official, entertaining, or learned way without prayer, but between this kind of preaching and sowing God's precious seed with holy hands and prayerful, weeping hearts there is an immeasurable distance.

PRAYERLESS MINISTRY

A prayerless ministry is the undertaker for all God's truth and for God's Church. It may have the most costly casket and the most beautiful flowers, but it is a funeral, regardless of the charming decorations. A prayerless Christian will never learn God's truth. A prayerless ministry will never be able to teach God's truth. Ages of millennial glory have been lost by a prayerless Church. The coming of our Lord has been postponed indefinitely by a prayerless Church. Hell has enlarged itself and filled its dire caves in the presence of the dead service of a prayerless Church.

The best and greatest offering is an offering of prayer. If the preachers of this century will learn well the lesson of prayer, and use fully the power of prayer, the next millennium will come to its highest point before the century closes. "Pray without ceasing"[7] is the trumpet call to the preachers of this century. If the preachers will get their texts, thoughts, words, and sermons in their closets, the next century will find a new heaven and a new earth. The old sin-stained and sin-eclipsed heaven and earth will pass away under the power of a praying Church.

Endnotes

1 Acts 6:4
2 I Thessalonians 3:10
3 Whenever reference is made to the universal Church, we have capitalized the word. When the reference is to a local church, we have lowercased the word.

4 Ephesians 3:19
5 Ephesians 3:14
6 Colossians 4:12
7 I Thessalonians 5:17

17

Preachers Need the Prayers of the People

IF SOME CHRISTIANS THAT *have been complaining of their ministers had said and acted less before people and had applied themselves with all their might to cry to God for their ministers—had, as it were, risen and stormed heaven with their humble, fervent, and incessant prayers for them— they would have been much more in the way of success.* (Jonathan Edwards)

Somehow the practice of praying especially for the preacher has fallen into disuse or become discounted. We have occasionally heard the practice spoken of as being a discredit to the ministry. Some say that to pray for the preacher is to publicly declare the inefficiency of the ministry. Perhaps, it offends the pride of learning and self-sufficiency of some preachers. But these should be offended and rebuked if a ministry is so neglectful as to allow them to exist.

Prayer is not simply the duty or privilege of the preacher's profession, it is a necessity. Air is not more necessary to the lungs than prayer is to the preacher. It is absolutely necessary for the preacher to pray. It is an absolute necessity that the preacher be prayed for. These two propositions are wedded into a union that should never be divorced: the preacher must pray, the preacher must be prayed for. It will take all the praying preachers can do, and all the praying they can get done for them, to meet the fearful responsibilities and gain the largest, truest success in God's great work. Next to the cultivation of the spirit and fact of intense prayer in themselves, true preachers covet with a great covetousness the prayers of God's people.

HOLY PREACHERS ESTEEM PRAYER

The holier the preachers are and the more they esteem prayer, the clearer they see that God gives himself to the praying ones, and that the measure of God's revelation to the soul is the measure of the soul's longing, persistent prayer for God. Salvation never finds its way to a prayerless heart. The Holy Spirit never abides in a prayerless spirit. Preaching never edifies a prayerless soul. Christ knows nothing of prayerless Christians. The gospel cannot be projected by prayerless preachers. Gifts, talents, education, eloquence, God's call, cannot lessen the demand of prayer. It can only intensify the necessity for preachers to pray and to be prayed for. The more the preachers' eyes are opened to the nature, responsibility, and difficulties in their work, the more they will see. If they are true preachers, the more they will feel the necessity of prayer—not only the increasing demand to pray themselves, but to call on others to help them by their prayers.

Paul is an illustration of this. If any person could project the gospel by reason of personal force, by brain power, by culture, by personal grace, by God's apostolic commission, God's extraordinary call, that man was Paul. Paul is an eminent example that the preacher must be a person given to prayer. Further, that true apostolic preachers must have the prayers of other good people to give to their ministry its full quota of success, Paul is a preeminent example. He asks, he covets, he pleads in an impassioned way for the help of all God's saints. He knew that in the spiritual realm, as elsewhere, in union there is strength. And that the concentration and aggregation of faith, desire, and prayer increased the volume of spiritual force until it became overwhelming and irresistible in its power. Units of prayer combining like drops of water make an ocean that defies resistance. So Paul, with his clear and full apprehension of spiritual dynamics, determined to make his ministry as impressive, eternal, and irresistible as the ocean, by gathering all the scattered units of prayer and precipitating them on his ministry.

PAUL'S LABORS AND RESULTS

The reason for Paul's preeminence in labors and results, and his impression on the Church and the world, can be found in the fact that he was able to center on himself and his ministry more of prayer than others. To his brethren at Rome he wrote, "Now I beseech you, brethren, for the Lord Jesus Christ's sake, and for the love of the Spirit, that ye strive together with me in prayers to God for me."[1]

To the Ephesians he says, "Praying always with all prayer and supplication in the Spirit, and watching thereunto with all perseverance and supplication for all saints; and for me, that utterance may be given unto me, that I may open my mouth boldly, to make known the mystery of the gospel."[2]

To the Colossians he says, "Withal praying also for us, that God would open unto us a door of utterance, to speak the mystery of Christ, for which I am also in bonds: that I may make it manifest, as I ought to speak."[3]

To the Thessalonians he says sharply and strongly: "Brethren, pray for us."[4]

Paul calls also on the Corinthian church to help him: "Ye also helping together by prayer for us."[5] This was to be part of their work. They were to lay to the helping hand of prayer. In an additional and closing charge to the Thessalonian church about the importance and necessity of their prayers, he says, "Finally, brethren, pray for us, that the word of the Lord may have free course, and be glorified, even as it is with you: and that we may be delivered from unreasonable and wicked men."[6]

He impresses the Philippians that all his trials and opposition can be made subservient to the spread of the gospel by the efficiency of their prayers for him.

Philemon was to prepare a lodging for him, for through Philemon's prayer Paul was to be his guest.

Paul's attitude on this question illustrates his humility and deep insight into the spiritual forces that project the gospel. More than this, it teaches a lesson for all times. If Paul was so dependent on the prayers of God's saints to give his ministry success, how much greater the necessity that the prayers of God's saints be centered on the ministry of today!

Paul did not feel that this urgent plea for prayer was to lower his dignity, lessen his influence, or depreciate his piety. What if it did? Let dignity go, let influence be destroyed, let his reputation be marred—he must have their prayers. Called, commissioned, chief of the Apostles as he was, all his equipment was imperfect without the prayers of God's people. He wrote letters everywhere, urging them to pray for him. Do you pray for your pastor? Do you pray for your pastor in secret? Public prayers are of little worth unless they are founded on or followed up by private praying. The praying ones are preachers as Aaron and Hur were to Moses. They hold their hands and decide the issue that is so fiercely raging around them.

APOSTLES URGED THE CHURCH TO PRAY

The plea and purpose of the apostles were to motivate the Church to praying. They did not ignore the grace of cheerful giving. They were not ignorant of the place that religious activity and work occupied in the spiritual life. But not one or all of these in apostolic estimate or urgency could at all compare in necessity and importance with prayer. The apostles used the most sacred and urgent pleas, the most fervid exhortations, the most comprehensive and arousing words to enforce the all-important obligation and necessity of prayer.

"Put the saints everywhere to praying" is the burden of the apostolic effort and the keynote of apostolic success. Jesus Christ had striven to do this in the days of His personal ministry. As He was moved by infinite compassion at the ripened fields of earth perishing for lack of laborers, He paused in his own praying and tried to awaken the dull sensibilities of His disciples to the duty of prayer. He commanded them: "Pray ye therefore the Lord of the harvest, that He will send forth labourers into His harvest."[7] "And He spake a parable unto them to this end, that men ought always to pray, and not to faint."[8]

Endnotes

1 Romans 15:30
2 Ephesians 6:18-19
3 Colossians 4:3-4
4 1 Thessalonians 5:25
5 2 Corinthians 1:11
6 2 Thessalonians 3:1-2
7 Matthew 9:38
8 Luke 18:1

18

Time in Prayer

THIS PERPETUAL HURRY OF *business and company ruins me in soul if not in body. More solitude and earlier hours! I suspect I have been allotting habitually too little time to religious exercises, as private devotion and religious meditation, Scripture-reading, etc. Hence I am lean and cold and hard. I had better allot two hours or an hour and a half daily. I have been keeping too late hours, and hence have had but a hurried half hour in a morning to myself. Surely the experience of all good men confirms the proposition that without a due measure of private devotions the soul will grow lean. But all may be done through prayer—almighty prayer, I am ready to say—and why not? For that it is almighty is only through the gracious ordination of the God of love and truth. O then, pray, pray, pray!* (William Wilberforce)

Our devotions are not measured by the clock, but time is essential to them. The ability to wait and stay and press belongs essentially to our communion with God. Undue haste is always inappropriate and damaging, and is so to an alarming extent in the great business of communion with God. Short devotions are the ruin of deep piety. Calmness, understanding, and strength are never the companions of haste. Short devotions deplete spiritual vigor, slow down spiritual progress, sap spiritual foundations, and poison the root and bloom of spiritual life. They are the prolific source of backsliding, the sure indication of a superficial piety. They deceive, poison, rot the seed, and impoverish the soil.

It is true that Bible prayers in word and print are short, but the praying saints of the Bible were with God through many a sweet and holy hour. They won by few words but long waiting. The prayers Moses records may be short, but Moses prayed to God with fasting and mighty crying forty days and nights.

The statement of Elijah's praying may be condensed to a few brief paragraphs, but doubtless Elijah, who when praying he prayed, spent many hours of fiery struggle and lofty communion with God before he could say to Ahab with assured boldness, "There shall not be dew nor rain these years, but according to my word."[1]

The Scripture record of Paul's prayers is short, but Paul prayed exceedingly night and day.[2]

THE LORD'S PRAYER

The prayer called The Lord's Prayer is a divine example for infant lips, but many times the man Jesus prayed all night before His work was done. His all night and long-sustained devotions gave His work its finish and perfection, and gave to His character the fullness and glory of its divinity.

Spiritual work is taxing work, and people are loath to do it. Praying, true praying, costs an outlay of serious attention and time, which flesh and blood do not relish. Few people are made of such strong fiber that they will make a costly outlay when surface work will pass as well in the market. We can habituate ourselves to our poor praying until it looks well to us— at least it keeps up a decent form and quiets conscience—the deadliest of opiates! We can slight our praying and not realize the peril until the foundations are gone. Hurried devotions make weak faith, feeble convictions, and questionable piety. To be little with God is to be little for God. To cut short our praying makes our whole Christian character short, small, improvised, and careless.

It takes good time for the full flow of God into the spirit. Short devotions cut the pipe of God's full flow. It takes time in the secret places to get the full revelation of God. Little time and hurry mar the picture.

HENRY MARTYN

Henry Martyn laments that "want of private devotional reading and shortness of prayer through incessant sermon-making had produced much strangeness between God" and his soul. He judged that he had dedicated too much time to public ministering and too little in private communion with God. He was much impressed to set apart times for fasting and to devote times for solemn prayer. Because of this he says he "was assisted this morning to pray for two hours."

WILLIAM WILBERFORCE

Said William Wilberforce, the peer of kings, "I must secure more time for private devotions. I have been living far too public for me. The shortening of private devotions starves the soul; it grows lean and faint. I have been keeping too late hours." Of a failure of his in Parliament he says: "Let me record my grief and shame, and all, probably, from private devotions having been contracted, and so God let me stumble." More solitude and earlier hours was his remedy.

More time and early hours for prayer would act like magic to revive and invigorate many a decayed spiritual life. More time and early hours for prayer would result in holy living. A holy life would not be so rare or so difficult a thing if our devotions were not so short and hurried. A Christly temper in its sweet and passionless fragrance would not be so alien and hopeless a heritage if our closet times were lengthened and intensified. We live shabbily because we pray meagerly. Plenty of time to feast in our closets will bring marrow and fatness to our lives.

IN AND OUT OF THE CLOSET

Our ability to stay with God in our closet measures our ability to stay with God out of the closet. Hasty closet visits are deceptive, defaulting. We are not only deluded by them, but we are losers by them in many ways and in many rich legacies. Tarrying in the closet instructs and wins. We are taught by it, and the greatest victories are often the results of great waiting—waiting until words and plans are exhausted, and silent and patient waiting gains the crown. Jesus Christ asks with an affronted emphasis, "Shall not God avenge His own elect, which cry day and night unto Him?"[3]

To pray is the greatest thing we can do. To do it well there must be calmness, time, and deliberation. Otherwise, it is degraded into the smallest and poorest of things. True praying has the largest results for good, and poor praying, the least. We cannot do too much of real praying, and we cannot do too little of false praying. We must learn anew the worth of prayer, and enter anew the school of prayer. There is nothing that takes more time to learn. If we would learn the wondrous art, we must not give a fragment here and there—"A little talk with Jesus," as the tiny saintlets sing. Instead, we must demand and hold with iron grasp the best hours of the day for God and prayer, or there will be no praying worth the name.

TODAY IS NOT A DAY OF PRAYER

This, however, is not a day of prayer. There are saints who pray. Prayer is defamed by preacher and priest. In these days of hurry and bustle, of electricity and steam, people will not take time to pray. There are preachers who "say prayers" as part of their program on regular or state occasions. But who "stirreth himself up to take hold of" God?[4]

Who prays as Jacob prayed—until he is crowned as a prevailing, princely, intercessor? Who prays as Elijah prayed—until all the locked-up forces of nature were unsealed and a famine-stricken land bloomed as the garden of God? Who prayed as Jesus Christ prayed—as out upon the mountain he "continued all night in prayer to God?"[5] The apostles gave themselves "continually to prayer."[6]

But the most difficult thing today is to get men and women, or even the preachers, to pray in the same way. There are laypeople who will give their money—some of them in rich abundance—but they will not give themselves to prayer, without which their money is just a curse. There are plenty of preachers who will preach and deliver great and eloquent addresses on the need of revival and the spread of the kingdom of God. But there are not many who will pray, and without it all preaching and organizing are worse than vain. Prayer is out of date, almost a lost art, and the greatest benefactor this age could have is the person who will bring the preachers and the Church back to prayer.

Endnotes

1 1 Kings 17:1
2 1 Thessalonians 30
3 Luke 18:7
4 Isaiah 64:7
5 Luke 6:12
6 Acts 6:4

19

Prayer in the Pulpit and Prayer in the Pew

I JUDGE THAT MY PRAYER *is more than the devil himself; if it were otherwise, Luther would have fared differently long before this. Yet men will not see and acknowledge the great wonders or miracles God works in my behalf. If I should neglect prayer but a single day, I should lose a great deal of the fire of faith.* (Martin Luther)

Before Pentecost the apostles could only get a glimpse of the great importance of prayer. But the Spirit coming and filling on Pentecost elevated prayer to its vital and all-commanding position in the gospel of Christ. Since then the call of prayer to every saint is the Spirit's loudest and most demanding call. Sainthood's piety is made, refined, and perfected by prayer. The gospel moves with slow and timid pace when the saints are not at their prayers early and late and long.

Where are the Christly leaders who can teach the modern saints how to pray and put them at it? Do we know we are raising up a prayerless set of saints? Where are the apostolic leaders who can put God's people to praying? Let them come to the front and do the work and it will be the greatest work that can be done. An increase of educational facilities and a great increase of money power will be the darkest curse to Christianity if they are not sanctified by more and better praying than we are doing.

Campaigns to raise money or build churches will not help our praying, but will hinder it if we are not careful. Nothing but a specific effort from a praying leadership will avail. The chief ones must lead in the apostolic effort to engrave the vital importance and fact of prayer in the heart and life of the Church. None but praying leaders can have praying followers. Praying apostles will result in praying saints. A praying pulpit will result in praying pews. We greatly need somebody who can set the saints to this business of praying. We are not a generation of praying saints. Non-praying saints are a paltry gang of saints who have neither the zeal, beauty, or power of saints. Who will restore this breach? The greatest will of reformers and apostles will be those who can set the Church to praying.

We put it as our most sober judgment that the great need of the Church in this and all ages is men and women of commanding faith, unsullied holiness, and marked spiritual vigor and consuming zeal. The prayers, faith, lives, and ministry of such men and women will be of so radical and aggressive a form as to work spiritual revolutions in individual lives and in the Church.

We do not mean those who create a sensation by novel devices. Or those who attract by pleasing entertainment. But men and women who can stir things and work revolutions by the preaching of God's Word and by the power of the Holy Ghost—revolutions that change the whole current of things.

Natural ability and educational advantages do not figure as factors in this matter. Only the capacity for faith, the ability to pray, the power of thorough consecration, the ability of self-littleness, and an absolute losing of one's self in God's glory. These things, coupled with an ever-present and insatiable yearning and seeking after all the fullness of God, will develop saints who can set the Church ablaze for God. Not in a noisy, showy way, but with an intense and quiet heat that melts and moves everything for God.

GOD CAN WORK WONDERS

God can work wonders if He can get a suitable man or woman. Men and women can work wonders if they can get God to lead them. The full endowment of the spirit that turned the world upside down would be eminently useful in these latter days. Christians who can stir things mightily for God, whose spiritual revolutions change the whole aspect of things, are the universal need of the Church.

The Church has never been without these saints. They adorn its history. They are the standing miracles of the divinity of the Church. Their example and history are an unfailing inspiration and blessing. An increase in their number and power should be our prayer.

WHAT HAS BEEN DONE CAN BE DONE AGAIN

That which has been done in spiritual matters can be done again, and be better done. This was Christ's view. He said, "Verily, verily, I say unto you, He that believeth on me, the works that I do shall he do also; and greater works than these shall he do; because I go unto my Father" (John 14:12).

The past has not exhausted the possibilities or demands for doing great things for God. The Church that is dependent on its past history for its miracles of power and grace is a fallen Church.

God wants elect saints—saints out of whom self and the world have gone by a severe crucifixion—gone by a bankruptcy that has so totally ruined self and the world that there is neither hope nor desire of recovery. Saints who by this insolvency and crucifixion have turned toward God perfect hearts.

Let us pray ardently that God's promise of prayer may be more than realized.

BOOK 8

PRAYER AND PRAYING SAINTS

I

Praying Saints of the Old Testament

THE HOLY SPIRIT WILL *give to the praying saint the brightness of an immortal hope, the music of a deathless song, in His baptism and communion with the heart, He will give sweeter and more enlarged visions of heaven until the taste for other things will pall, and other visions will grow dim and distant. He will put notes of other worlds in human hearts until all earth's music is discord and songless.* (Rev. E. M. Bounds)

Old Testament history is filled with accounts of praying saints. The leaders of Israel in those early days were noted for their praying habits. Prayer is the one thing which stands out prominently in their lives.

JOSHUA

To begin with, note the incident in the tenth chapter of Joshua where the very heavenly bodies were made subject to prayer. A prolonged battle was on between the Israelites and their enemies. Just before dark it was discovered that a few more hours of daylight were needful to ensure victory for the Lord's hosts. Joshua, that sturdy man of God, stepped into the breach with prayer. The sun was too rapidly declining in the west for God's people to reap the full fruits of a noted victory Seeing how much depended upon the occasion, Joshua cried out in the sight and hearing of Israel, "Sun, stand thou still upon Gibeon, and thou, Moon, in the Valley of Ajalon."[1] And the sun stood still and the moon stopped on her course at the command of this praying man of God, until the Lord's people had avenged themselves upon the Lord's enemies.

JACOB

Jacob was not a strict pattern of righteousness prior to his all-night praying. Yet he was a man of prayer and believed in the God of prayer. So we find him swift to call upon God in prayer when he was in trouble. Afraid of Esau, he left home and headed for the home of Laban, a kinsman. As night came on, he stopped at a certain place to refresh himself with sleep. As he slept, he had a wonderful dream in which he saw the angels of God ascending and descending on a ladder that stretched from earth to heaven. It was no wonder when he awoke he was compelled to exclaim, "Surely the LORD is in this place; and I knew it not."[2]

It was then that he entered into a specific and definite covenant with Almighty God. In prayer, "Jacob vowed a vow, saying, If God will be with me, and will keep me in this way that I go, and will give me bread to eat, and raiment to put on, So that I come again to my father's house in peace; then shall the Lord be my God: And this stone, which I have set for a pillar, shall be God's house: and of all that thou shalt give me I will surely give the tenth unto thee."[3]

With a deep sense of his utter dependence upon God, and desiring above everything the help of God, Jacob conditioned his prayer for protection, blessing, and guidance by a solemn vow. Thus Jacob supported his prayer to God by a vow.

Twenty years passed while Jacob tarried at the house of Laban. During that time, he married two of Laban's daughters and God gave him children. He also increased largely in wealth, and so he resolved to leave that place and return home to where he had been reared.

Nearing home, it occurred to him that he must meet his brother Esau, whose anger had not lessened regardless of the passage of many years. God, however, had said to Jacob, "Return unto the land of thy fathers; and to thy kindred, and I will be with thee."[4] In this dreadful emergency, no doubt God's promise and his vow made long ago came to his mind, and he gave himself to an all-night season of prayer. Now comes that strange, inexplicable, incident of the man wrestling with Jacob all night long, until Jacob at last obtained the victory. "I will not let thee go, except thou bless me."[5] And then and there, in answer to his earnest, pressing, importunate praying, he was richly blessed personally and his name was changed. But even more than that, God went ahead of Jacob's desire, and strangely moved upon the angry nature of Esau, and lo and behold, when Jacob met him next day, Esau's anger had entirely abated, and he vied with Jacob in showing kindness to his brother who had wronged him. No explanation of this remarkable change in the heart of Esau is satisfactory which leaves out prayer.

HANNAH

Samuel, the mighty man of God and intercessor in Israel, was the product of his mother's prayer. Hannah is a memorable example of the nature and benefits of persistent praying. No son had been born to her and she yearned for a man child. Her whole soul was in her desire. So she went to the house of worship where Eli the priest of God was. Staggering under the weight that bore down on her heart she was beside herself and seemed to be intoxicated. Her desires were too intense for praying out loud. She poured out her soul in prayer before the Lord. Insuperable natural difficulties were in the way, but she multiplied her praying until her God-lightened heart and her bright face recorded the answer to her prayers, and Samuel was hers by a conscious faith and a nation was restored by faith.[6]

Samuel was born in answer to the vow and prayers of Hannah, for the solemn covenant that she made with God if He would grant her request must not be left out of the account in investigating this incident of a praying woman and the answer she received. Prayer in its highest form of faith is the prayer that carries the whole person as a sacrificial offering. Thus devoting the whole person and all they have to God in a definite, intelligent vow. A vow that is never to be broken, that goes on with never-ending thirst and impassioned desire for heaven. Such an attitude of self-devotion to God mightily helps praying.

SAMSON

Samson is somewhat of a paradox when we examine his religious character. But amid all his faults, which were extremely grave, he knew the God who hears prayer and he knew how to talk to God.

It matters not how far Israel had gone from God or to what depth it had fallen, there were no chains with which Israel was bound but that their cry to God easily spanned the distance, fathomed the depths, and broke the chains. It was the lesson they were always learning and always forgetting—prayer always brought God to their deliverance, and that there was nothing too hard for God to do for His people. We find all of God's saints in difficulties at different times in some way or another. Their difficulties are, however, often the heralds of their great triumphs. But for whatever cause their troubles come, or of what kind they were, there is no trouble of any degree of difficulty, or from any source or nature that prayer could not deliver them. It was not the great strength of Samson that delivered him out of his troubles. Read what the Scriptures say.

> And when he came unto Lehi, the Philistines shouted against him: and the Spirit of the Lord came mightily upon him, and the cords that were upon his arms became as flax that was burnt with fire, and his bands loosed from off his hands. And he found a new jawbone of an ass, and put forth his hand, and took it, and slew a thousand

men therewith. And Samson said, With the jawbone of an ass, heaps upon heaps, with the jaw of an ass have I slain a thousand men. And it came to pass, when he had made an end of speaking, that he cast away the jawbone out of his hand, and called that place Ramath-lehi.

And he was sore athirst, and called on the Lord, and said, Thou hast given this great deliverance into the hand of thy servant: and now shall I die for thirst, and fall into the hand of the uncircumcised? But God clave an hollow place that was in the jaw, and there came water thereout; and when he had drunk, his spirit came again, and he revived.[7]

We have another incident in the case of this strange Old Testament character, showing that when they were in great difficulties their minds involuntarily turned to God in prayer. However irregular in life they were, however far from God they departed, however sinful they might be when trouble came upon these people, they invariably called upon God for deliverance. As a rule, when they repented God heard their cries and granted their requests. This incident in Samson's life shows us how his life ended.

Read the record as found in Judges 16. Samson had formed an alliance with Delilah, a heathen woman, and in conspiracy with the Philistines she sought to discover the source of his immense strength. Three successive times she failed, and at last by her persistence and womanly arts persuaded Samson to divulge to her the wonderful secret. So in an unsuspecting hour he disclosed to her the fact that the source of his strength was in his hair, which had never been cut. While he slept, she deprived him of his great physical power by cutting off his hair. Then she called for the Philistines, and they came and bound him and put out his eyes and otherwise mistreated him.

On an occasion when the Philistines were gathered together to offer a great sacrifice to their idol god Dagon, they called for Samson to make sport for them. The following is the account as he stood there presumably the laughing-stock of these enemies of his and of God.

And Samson said unto the lad that held him by the hand, Suffer me that I may feel the pillars whereupon the house standeth, that I may lean upon them. Now the house was full of men and women; and all the lords of the Philistines were there; and there were upon the roof about three thousand men and women, that beheld while Samson made sport. And Samson called unto the Lord, and said, O Lord God, remember me, I pray thee, and strengthen me, I pray thee, only this once, O God, that I may be at once avenged of the

Philistines for my two eyes. And Samson took hold of the two middle pillars upon which the house stood, and on which it was borne up, of the one with his right hand, and of the other with his left. And Samson said, Let me die with the Philistines. And he bowed himself with all his might; and the house fell upon the lords, and upon all the people that were therein. So the dead which he slew at his death were more than they which he slew in his life.[8]

Endnotes

1 Joshua 10:12
2 Genesis 28:16
3 Genesis 28:20-22
4 Genesis 31:3
5 Genesis 32:26
6 1 Samuel 1:1-20
7 Judges 15:14-19a
8 Judges 16:26-30

2

Praying Saints of the Old Testament
(Continued)

Bishop Lambeth and Wainwright *had a great M. E. Mission in Osaka, Japan. One day the order came from high up that no more meetings would be allowed in the city by Protestants. Lambeth and Wainwright did all they could but the high officials were obstinate and unrelenting. They then retired to the room of prayer. Supper time came and the Japanese girl came to summon them to their meal, but she fell under the power of prayer. Mrs. Lambeth came to find what the matter was and fell under the same power. They then rose and went to the mission hall and opened it: and at once commenced meeting. God fell upon the assembly and two of the sons of the city officials came to the altar and were saved. Next morning one of the officials in authority came to the mission and said, "Go on with your meetings, you will not be interrupted." The Osaka daily paper came out with box car letters saying, "*THE CHRISTIAN'S GOD CAME TO TOWN LAST NIGHT.*"*(Rev. H. C. Morrison)

JONAH

Jonah, the man who prayed in the great fish's belly, brings to view another remarkable instance of these Old Testament worthies who were given to prayer. This man Jonah was a prophet of the Lord and a fugitive from God and from the place of duty. He had been sent on a mission of warning to wicked Nineveh, and had been commanded to cry out against them, "for their wickedness is come up before me," [1]said God. But because of fear or something else, Jonah declined to obey God, and took passage on a ship for Tarshish—fleeing from God. He seems to have overlooked the plain fact that the same God who had sent him on that alarming mission had His eye upon him as he hid himself on board that vessel. A storm arose as the vessel was on its way to Tarshish, and it was decided to throw Jonah overboard in order to appease God and to prevent the destruction of the boat and of all on board. But God was there as He had been with Jonah from the beginning. He had prepared a great fish to swallow Jonah in order to stop him, defeat him in his flight from the post of duty, and to save him so he might help to carry out the purposes of God.

It was Jonah who was in the fish's belly in that great difficult, passing through a strange experience, who called upon God. And God heard him and caused the fish to vomit him out on dry land. What possible force could rescue him from this fearful place? He seemed hopelessly lost, in "the belly of hell," as good as dead and damned. But he prays—what else can he do? And this is just what he had been accustomed to do when in trouble before.

> I cried by reason of mine affliction unto the Lord, and he heard me; out of the belly of hell cried I, and thou heardest my voice.[2]

> And the Lord spake unto the fish, and it vomited out Jonah upon the dry land.[3]

Like others, he joined prayer to a vow he had made, for he says in his prayer, "But I will sacrifice unto thee with the voice of thanksgiving; I will pay that that I have vowed. Salvation is of the Lord."[4]

Prayer was the mighty force that brought Jonah from "the belly of hell." Prayer, mighty prayer, has secured the end. Prayer brought God to the rescue of unfaithful Jonah, despite his sin of fleeing from duty, and God could not deny his prayer. Nothing is too hard for prayer because nothing is too hard for God.

That answered prayer of Jonah in the fish's belly in its mighty results became an Old Testament type of the miraculous power displayed in the resurrection of Jesus Christ from the dead. Our Lord puts His seal of truth upon the fact of Jonah's prayer and resurrection.

Nothing can be simpler than these cases of God's mighty deliverance. Nothing is plainer than that prayer has to do with God directly and simply. Nothing is clearer than that prayer has its only worth and significance in the great fact that God hears and answers prayer. This the Old Testament saints strongly believed. It is the one fact that stands out continuously and prominently in their lives. They were essentially men and women of prayer.

How greatly we need a school to teach the art of praying! This simplest of all arts and mightiest of all forces is always in danger of being forgotten or perverted. The further we get away from our mother's knees, the further we get away from the true art of praying. All our after-schooling and our after-teachers unteach us the lessons of prayer. People prayed well in Old Testament times because they were simple people and lived in simple times. They were childlike, lived in childlike times, and had childlike faith.

DAVID

In citing the Old Testament saints noted for their praying habits, David must by no means be overlooked. He was preeminently a man of prayer. With him prayer was a habit, for we hear him say, "Evening, and morning, and at noon, will I pray, and cry aloud: and He shall hear my voice."[5]

Prayer with the sweet psalmist of Israel was no strange occupation. He knew the way to God and was often found in that way. It is no wonder we hear his call so dear and impressive, "O come, let us worship and bow down: let us kneel before the Lord our maker."[6]

He knew God as the one being who could answer prayer: "O Thou that hearest prayer, unto Thee shall all flesh come."[7]

When God smote the child born of Bathsheba, because David had by his grievous sins given occasion of the enemies of God to blaspheme, it is no surprise that we find him engaged in a week's prayer, asking God for the life of the child. The habit of his life asserted itself in this great emergency in his home, and we find him fasting and praying for the child to recover. The fact that God denied his request does not at all affect the question of David's habit of praying. Even though he did not receive what he asked for, his faith in God was not in the least affected. The fact is that while God did not give him the life of that baby boy, He afterward gave him another son—Solomon. So that possibly the latter son was a far great blessing to him than would have been the child for whom he prayed.

In close connection with this season of prayer we must not overlook David's penitential praying when Nathan, by command of God, uncovered David's two great sins of adultery and murder. At once David acknowledged his wickedness, saying unto Nathan, "I have sinned."[8] To see his deep grief over his sin, his heart-broken spirit and genuine repentance, it is only necessary to read Psalm 51 where confession of sin, deep humiliation, and prayer are the chief ingredients of the psalm.

David knew where to find a sin-pardoning God, and was received back again and had the joys of salvation restored to him by earnest, sincere, penitential praying. In the same way are all sinners brought into the divine favor, find pardon, and find a new heart.

The entire book of Psalms brings prayer to the front, and prayer fairly bristles before our eyes as we read this devotional book of the Scriptures.

SOLOMON

Neither must Solomon be overlooked in the famous catalogue of saints who prayed in Old Testament times. Whatever their faults, they did not forget the God who hears prayer, or stop seeking the God of prayer. While this wise man in his later life departed from God, and his sun set under a cloud, we find him praying at the beginning of his reign.

Solomon went to Gibeon to offer sacrifice, and prayer always went in close companionship with it. While Solomon was there, the Lord appeared to him in a dream by night, and said to him, "Ask what I shall give thee."[9] The sequel shows the material out of which Solomon's character was formed. What was his request?

> And now, O Lord my God, thou hast made thy servant king instead of David my father: and I am but a little child: I know not how to go out or come in. And thy servant is in the midst of thy people which thou hast chosen, a great people, that cannot be numbered nor counted for multitude. Give therefore thy servant an understanding heart to judge thy people, that I may discern between good and bad: for who is able to judge this thy so great a people?[10]

Reading that prayer carefully with an open heart, we do not wonder at its results.

> And the speech pleased the Lord, that Solomon had asked this thing. And God said unto him, Because thou hast asked this thing, and hast not asked for thyself long life; neither hast asked riches for thyself, nor hast asked the life of thine enemies; but hast asked for thyself understanding to discern judgment; Behold, I have done according to thy words: lo, I have given thee a wise and an understanding heart; so that there was none like thee before thee, neither after thee shall any arise like unto thee. And I have also given thee that which thou hast not asked, both riches, and honour: so that there shall not be any among the kings like unto thee all thy days.[11]

What praying this was! What self-deprecation and simplicity! "I am but a little child." How he specified the one thing needed! And see how much more he received than that for which he asked!

Take the remarkable prayer at the dedication of the temple. Possibly this is the longest recorded prayer in God's Word. How comprehensive, pointed, intensive, it is! Solomon could not afford to lay the foundations of God's house in anything else but in prayer. And God heard this prayer as he heard him before, "Now when Solomon had made an end of praying, the fire came down from heaven, and consumed the burnt offering and the sacrifices; and the glory of the Lord filled the house."[12] Thus God attested to the acceptance of this house of worship and of Solomon, the praying king.

The list of these Old Testament saints given to prayer grows as we proceed, and is too long to notice at length all of them. But the name of Isaiah, the great evangelical prophet, and that of Jeremiah, the weeping prophet, must not be left out of the account. Still others might be mentioned. These are sufficient, and with their names we may close the list. Let careful readers of the Old Scriptures keep the prayer question in mind, and they will see how great a place prayer occupied in the minds and lives of the men and women of those early days.

Endnotes

1 Jonah 1:2
2 Jonah 2:2
3 Jonah 2:10
4 Jonah 2:9
5 Psalm 55:17
6 Psalm 95:6
7 Psalm 65:2
8 2 Samuel 12:13
9 1 Kings 3:5
10 1 Kings 3:7-9
11 1 Kings 3:10-13
12 2 Chronicles 7:1

3

Abraham, the Man of Prayer

OH FOR DETERMINED MEN *and women, who will rise early and really burn out for God. Oh for a faith that will sweep into heaven with the early dawning of the morning and have ships from a shoreless sea loaded in the soul's harbor ere the ordinary laborer has knocked the dew from his scythe or the huckster has turned from his pallet of straw to spread nature's treasures of fruit before the early buyers.* (Rev. Homer W. Hodge)

Abraham, the friend of God, was a striking illustration of one of the Old Testament saints who believed strongly in prayer. Abraham was not a shadowy figure by any means. In the simplicity and dimness of the patriarchal dispensation, as illustrated by him, we learn the worth of prayer as well as discover its antiquity. Prayer reaches back to the first ages of humanity on earth. We see how the energy of prayer is absolutely required in the simplest as well as in the most complex dispensations of God's grace.

When we study Abraham's character, we find him responding to God's command to go out into an unknown country. He took his family and household servants with him—and his nephew, Lot. Wherever he stopped on his journey for a night or longer, he always erected an altar and "called on the name of the Lord."[1] This man of faith and prayer was one of the first to erect a family altar around which to gather his household and offer the sacrifices of praise, worship, and prayer. These altars were essentially altars about which he gathered his household, as distinguished from secret prayer.

As God's revelations became fuller and more perfect, Abraham's praying increased, and it was at one of these spiritual eras that "Abraham fell on his face: and God talked with him."[2] On still another occasion we find this father of the faithful[3] on his face before God, astonished almost to disbelief at the purposes and revelations of Almighty God to him in promising him a son in his old age,[4] and the wonderful promises that God made concerning that son.

Even Ishmael's destiny is shaped by Abraham's prayer when he prayed, "O that Ishmael might live before thee!"[5]

INTERCEDING FOR SODOM

What a remarkable story is that of Abraham's standing before God repeating his intercessions for the wicked city of Sodom, the home of his nephew Lot, which was doomed by God's decision to destroy it! Sodom's fate was for a while held back by Abraham's praying. In fact, it was almost entirely relieved by the humility and insistence of the praying of this man who believed strongly in prayer and who knew how to pray. No other recourse was opened to Abraham to save Sodom but prayer. Perhaps the failure to ultimately rescue Sodom from her doom of destruction was due to Abraham's optimistic view of the spiritual condition of things in that city. It might have been possible—who knows?—that if Abraham had entreated God once more, and asked Him to spare the city if even one righteous man was found there, for Lot's sake, He might have heeded Abraham's request.

INTERCEDING FOR ABIMELECH

Note another instance in the life of Abraham that showed how he was a man of prayer and had power with God. Abraham had journeyed to Gerar and was staying there for a while. Fearing that Abimelech might kill him and take Sarah his wife for his own lustful uses, he deceived Abimelech by claiming that Sarah was his sister. God appeared to Abimelech in a dream and warned him not to touch Sarah, telling him that she was the wife of Abraham, and not his sister. Then he said unto Abimelech, "Now restore therefore the man his wife; for he is a prophet, and he shall pray for thee, and thou shalt live."[6]

The conclusion of the incident is recorded in this way: "So Abraham prayed unto God: and God healed Abimelech, and his wife, and his maidservants; and they bare children. For the Lord had fast closed up all the wombs of the house of Abimelech, because of Sarah Abraham's wife."[7]

This was a case somewhat on the line of that of Job at the close of his fearful experience and his terrible trials. Not understanding Job or God's dealings with this servant of His, his friends falsely charged Job with being in sin as the cause of all his troubles. God said to these friends of Job, "My servant Job shall pray for you: for him will I accept. . . And the Lord turned the captivity of Job, when he had prayed for his friends."[8]

Almighty God knew His servant Job as a man of prayer, and He could afford to send these friends of Job to him to pray in order to carry out and fulfill His plans and purposes.

It was Abraham's rule to stand before the Lord in prayer. His life was surcharged with prayer and Abraham's days were sanctified by prayer. For wherever he halted in his pilgrimage, prayer was his inseparable companion. Side by side with the altar of sacrifice was the altar of prayer. He got up early in the morning and went to the place where he stood before the Lord in prayer.

Endnotes

1 Genesis 13:4
2 Genesis 17:3
3 Romans 4:11; Galatians 3:9
4 Genesis 17:1-19
5 Genesis 17:18
6 Genesis 20:7
7 Genesis 20:17-18
8 Job 42:8, 10

4

Moses, the Mighty Intercessor

INTERCESSORY PRAYER IS A *powerful means of grace to the praying person. Martyn observes that at times of inward dryness and depression, he had often found a delightful revival in the act of praying for others for their conversion, or sanctification, or prosperity in the work of the Lord. His dealings with God for them about these gifts and blessings were for himself the divinely natural channel of a renewed insight into his own part and lot in Christ, into Christ as his own rest and power, into the "perfect freedom" of an entire yielding of himself to his Master for His work.* (Bishop Handley C. G. Moule)

Prayer unites with the purposes of God and lays itself out to secure those purposes. How often would the wise and benign will of God fail in its rich and beneficial ends by the sins of the people if prayer had not come in to stop His wrath and make the promise sure! Israel as a nation would have met their just destruction and their just fate after their apostasy with the golden calf had it not been for the intervention and unceasing praying of Moses' for forty days and forty nights.

Moses' character was marvelously affected by his marvelous praying. His near and sublime communion with God in the giving of the law did not transfigure his character as much as those tireless forty days in prayer with God. It was when he came down from that long struggle of prayer that his face shone with such dazzling brightness. Our mounts of transfiguration and the heavenly shining in character and conduct are born of seasons of wrestling prayer. All-night praying has changed many a supplanting Jacob into a princely Israel who has power with God and with people.

No mission was more majestic in purpose and results than that of Moses, and none was more responsible, diligent, and difficult. In it we are taught the sublime ministry and rule of prayer. Not only is it the medium of supply and support, but it is a compassionate agency through which the pitying long-suffering of God has an outflow. Prayer is a medium to restrain God's wrath, that mercy might rejoice against judgment.

MOSES AND HIS MISSION

It is recorded: "When Jacob was come into Egypt, and your fathers cried unto the Lord, then the LORD sent Moses and Aaron, which brought your fathers out of Egypt, and made them dwell in this place."[1] This is the beginning of the great movement for the deliverance of the Hebrews from Egyptian bondage.

The great movements of God have had their origin and energy in and were shaped by prayers of people. Prayer deals directly with God. Many needful things are obtained by prayer but mainly and almost solely prayer is concerned with God's dealings with His people. He is pleased to direct His methods and base His actions on the prayers of His saints. Prayer influences God greatly. Even though God commissioned, Moses cannot do God's great work without much praying. Moses cannot govern God's people and carry out the divine plans without having his censer filled full of the incense of prayer. The work of God cannot be done without the fire and fragrance always burning, ascending, and perfuming.

MOSES AND PHARAOH

Moses' prayers are often found removing or holding back the terrible stroke of God's wrath. Four times Moses' prayers were solicited by Pharaoh to relieve him of the fearful stroke of God's wrath. "Intreat the LORD."[2] Pharaoh most earnestly begged Moses while the loathsome frogs were upon him. "Moses cried unto the Lord because of the frogs which he had brought against Pharaoh. And the Lord did according to the word of Moses."[3]

When the grievous plague of flies had corrupted the whole land, Pharaoh again piteously cried out to Moses, "intreat for me."[4] Moses went out from Pharaoh and entreated the Lord, and the Lord again did according to the word of Moses.

The mighty thunderings and hail in their alarming and destructive fury extorted from this wicked king the very same earnest appeal to Moses, "Intreat the LORD."[5] Moses went out from the city into privacy, and alone with Almighty God he "spread abroad his hands unto the LORD: and the thunders and hail ceased, and the rain was not poured upon the earth."[6]

Though Moses was the man of law, yet with him prayer asserted its mighty force. as in the more spiritual times of the New Testament, Moses could have said, "My house is the house of prayer."[7]

Moses accepts at its full face value the foundation principle of praying that prayer has to do with God. With Abraham we saw this dearly and strongly pronounced. With Moses it is dearer and stronger still if possible. The events in his life declared that prayer affected God, that God was influenced in His conduct by prayer, and that God hears and answer prayer even when the hearing and answering might change His conduct and reverse His action. Stronger than all other laws, and more inflexible than any other decree, is the decree, "Call unto Me and I will answer thee."[8]

Moses lived close to God

Moses lived near God, and had the freest and most unhindered and boldest access to God. Instead of lessening the necessity of prayer, this fact made it more necessary, obvious, and powerful. Familiarity and closeness to God gives relish, frequency, point, and potency to prayer. Those who know God the best are the richest and most powerful in prayer. Little acquaintance with God, and strangeness and coldness to Him, make prayer a rare and feeble thing.

There were conditions of extremity to which Moses was reduced that prayer did not relieve, but there is no position of extremity that baffles God when prayer puts God into the matter.

Moses' Divine mission

It was planned, ordered, and directed, by God. The more there is of God in a movement, the more there is of prayer—conspicuous and controlling prayer. Moses' prayer rule of the church illustrates the necessity of courage and persistence in prayer. For forty days and forty nights Moses was pressing his prayer for the salvation of the Lord's people. In his long season of praying he was so concerned for God's people that bodily infirmities and appetites did not bother him. How strangely the prayers of a righteous man affect God is evident from the exclamation of God to Moses, "Now therefore let me alone, that my wrath may wax hot against them, and that I may consume them: and I will make of thee a great nation."[9] The presence of such an influence over God fills us with astonishment, awe, and fear. How lofty, bold and devoted must be such a pleader!

> And Moses returned unto the Lord, and said, Oh, this people have sinned a great sin, and have made them gods of gold. Yet now, if thou wilt forgive their sin—; and if not, blot me, I pray thee, out of thy book which thou hast written. And the Lord said unto Moses, Whosoever hath sinned against me, him will I blot out of my book. Therefore now go, lead the people unto the place of which I have spoken unto thee: behold, mine Angel shall go before thee: nevertheless in the day when I visit I will visit their sin upon them.[10]

THE REBELLION OF KORAH

The rebellion of Korah was the occasion of God's anger flaming out against all those of the congregation of Israel who sympathized with these rebels. Again Moses appears on the stage of action, this time with Aaron joining him in intercession for these sinners against God. But it only shows that in a serious time like this Moses knew to whom to go for relief, and was encouraged to pray that God would hold His wrath and spare Israel. Here is what is said about the matter:

> And the Lord spake unto Moses and unto Aaron, saying, Separate yourselves from among this congregation, that I may consume them in a moment. And they fell upon their faces, and said, O God, the God of the spirits of all flesh, shall one man sin, and wilt thou be wroth with all the congregation?[11]

MIRIAM'S PUNISHMENT

The assumption, pride, and rebellion of Miriam, Moses' sister, in which she had the presence and sympathy of Aaron, put the praying and the spirit of Moses in the noblest and most amiable light. Because of her sin God smote her with leprosy. But Moses made tender and earnest intercession for his sister who had so grievously offended God, and his prayer saved her from the fearful and incurable disease.

The record is intensely interesting, listen:

> And the anger of the Lord was kindled against them; and he departed. And the cloud departed from off the tabernacle; and, behold, Miriam became leprous, white as snow: and Aaron looked upon Miriam, and, behold, she was leprous. And Aaron said unto Moses, Alas, my lord, I beseech thee, lay not the sin upon us, wherein we have done foolishly, and wherein we have sinned. Let her not be as one dead, of whom the flesh is half consumed when he cometh out of his mother's womb. And Moses cried unto the Lord, saying, Heal her now, O God, I beseech thee.

> And the Lord said unto Moses, If her father had but spit in her face, should she not be ashamed seven days? let her be shut out from the camp seven days, and after that let her be received in again.[12]

THE WATERS OF MARAH

The murmurings of the children of Israel furnished conditions that called into play the full forces of prayer. They impressively bring out the intercessory feature of prayer and disclose Moses in his great office as an intercessor before God in behalf of others. It was at Marah that the waters were bitter and the people grievously murmured against Moses and God.

And when they came to Marah, they could not drink of the waters of Marah, for they were bitter: therefore the name of it was called Marah. And the people murmured against Moses, saying, What shall we drink? And he cried unto the Lord; and the Lord shewed him a tree, which when he had cast into the waters, the waters were made sweet: there he made for them a statute and an ordinance, and there he proved them.[13]

The records of eternity alone will disclose how many of the bitter places of the earth have been sweetened by prayer.

The people complained again at Taberah, and God became angry with them. Moses came again to the front and stepped into the breach and prayed for them. Here is the brief account:

And when the people complained, it displeased the Lord: and the Lord heard it; and his anger was kindled; and the fire of the Lord burnt among them, and consumed them that were in the uttermost parts of the camp. And the people cried unto Moses; and when Moses prayed unto the Lord, the fire was quenched.[14]

Moses got what he asked for. His praying was specific and God's answer was likewise specific. He was always heard by Almighty God when he prayed, and he was always answered by God. Once the answer was not specific. He had prayed to go into Canaan. The answer came but not what he asked for. He was given a vision of the Promised Land, but he was not allowed to go across the Jordan River into that land of promise. It was a prayer like Paul's when he prayed three times for the removal of the thorn in his flesh. But the thorn was not removed. Grace, however, was granted, which made the thorn a blessing.

It must not be thought that because Psalm 90 is incorporated with what is known as the "Psalms of David," that David was the author of it. By general consent it is attributed to Moses, and it gives us a sample of the praying of this giver of the law of God to the people. It is a prayer worth studying. It is sacred to us because it has been the requiem uttered over our dead for years that are past and gone. It has blessed the grave of many sleeping saints. But its very familiarity may cause us to lose its full meaning. We will be wise if we digest it, not for the dead, but for the living, that it may teach us how to live, how to pray while living, and how to die. "So teach us to number our days, that we may apply our hearts to wisdom. . . Establish thou the work of our hands, yea, the work of our hands establish thou it."[15]

Endnotes

1 I Samuel 12:8
2 Exodus 8:8
3 Exodus 8:12-13a
4 Exodus 8:28b
5 Exodus 9:28
6 Exodus 9:33
7 Luke 19:46
8 Jeremiah 33:3
9 Exodus 32:10
10 Exodus 32:31-34
11 Numbers 16:20-22
12 Numbers 12:9-14
13 Exodus 15:23-25
14 Numbers 11:1-2
15 Psalm 90:12, 17b

5

Elijah, the Praying Prophet

"**I** HAVE KNOWN MEN," *says Goodwin—it must have been himself—"who came to God for nothing else but just to come to Him, they so loved Him. They scorned to soil Him and themselves with any other errand than just purely to be alone with Him in His presence. Friendship is best kept up, even among people, by frequent visits; and the more free and defecate those frequent visits are, and the less occasioned by business, or necessity, or custom they are, the more friendly and welcome they are."* (Rev. Alexander Whyte)

Elijah is preeminently the elder of the prophets. The crown, the throne, and the scepter are his. His garments are white with flame. He seems exalted in his fiery and prayerful nature, as a being seemingly superhuman. The New Testament, however, places him alongside of us as a person with the same nature as we have. Instead of placing himself outside the sphere of humanity, in the marvelous results of his praying, it points to him as an example to be imitated and as inspiration to stimulate us. To pray like Elijah, and to have results like Elijah, is the crying need of the times.

Elijah had learned the lesson of prayer, and had graduated in that divine school, before Scripture mentions him. Somewhere in the secret places, on mountain or in plain, he had been alone with God, an intercessor against the debasing idolatry of Ahab. His prayers had mightily prevailed with God. He was confident and well assured that he would receive the answers to his prayers.

He had been talking with God about vengeance. He was the embodiment of his times. Those times were times of vengeance. The intercessor was not to be clothed with an olive branch with its strip of wood, the symbol of a suppliant for mercy, but with fire, the symbol of justice and the messenger of wrath. Elijah comes abruptly before us in the presence of Ahab! Well assured and with holy boldness does he declare before the astonished, cowering, king his message of fearful import. It was a message gained by his earnest praying. Someone has said about him, "in praying he prayed that it might not rain." God did not deny his prayer. "As the LORD God of Israel liveth, before whom I stand, there shall not be dew nor rain these years, but according to my word."[1]

ELIJAH'S SECRET OF PRAYER

The secret of his praying and the character of the man are found in the words, "Before whom I stand." We are here reminded of Gabriel's words to Zacharias in informing this priest of the coming of a son to him and his wife in their old age: "I am Gabriel that standeth in the presence of God."[2] The archangel Gabriel had scarcely more unflinching devotion, more courage, and more readiness of obedience, and more jealously of God's honor, than Elijah. What projecting power we see in his prayer! "And it rained not on the earth by the space of three years and six months."[3]

What omnipotent forces that can command the powers of nature! "Not dew nor rain." What man is this who dares utter such a claim or assert such a power? If his claim is false, he is a fanatic or a madman. If his claim is true, he has stayed the benevolent arm of Omnipotence, and put himself, by God's grace, in God's place. The accursed and burnt-up land and the fiery, rainless, and dewless days and nights, attest the truth of his saying. They also prove the sternness, strength, firmness, and passion of the man who holds back the clouds and stays the blessed visitation of the rain. Elijah is his name, and this attests the truth of that name, "My God is Jehovah."

His prayers have the power to stay the beneficial course of nature. He stands in God's stead in this matter. The sober, passionless, unimaginative James, the brother of our Lord, says to us in his Epistle: "See what prayer can do, prayer by an Elijah! Pray as Elijah prayed. Let the righteous person put forth the energy of prayer to its fullest extent. Let saints and sinners, angels and devils, see and feel the mighty power of prayer. See how the prayer of a good person has power and influence and avails with God!"

NO PRETENSE IN ELIJAH'S PRAYING

No sham praying was that of Elijah. It was no mere performance, no spiritless, soulless, official praying. Elijah was in Elijah's praying. The whole man, with all his fiery forces, was in it. Almighty God to him was real. Prayer to him was the means of projecting God in full force on the world in order to vindicate His name, establish His own being, avenge His blasphemed name and violated law, and vindicate His servants.

Instead of "prayed earnestly" in James 5:17, the *Revised Version* has it, "In his prayer he prayed," or "with prayer he prayed." That is, with all the combined energies of prayer he prayed.

Elijah's praying was strong, insistent, and resistless in its elements of power. Feeble praying secures no results and brings neither glory to God nor good to humanity.

Elijah learned new and higher lessons of prayer while hidden away by God and with God when he was by the brook Cherith. He was doubtless communing with God while Ahab was searching everywhere for him. After a while he was ordered to Sarepta, where God had commanded a widow to sustain him. He went there for the widow's good as well as for his own. A benefit to Elijah and a special good to the widow were the results of Elijah's going. While this woman provided for him, he provided for the woman. Elijah's prayers did more for the woman than the woman's hospitality did for Elijah. Great trials awaited the widow and great sorrows, too. Her widowhood and her poverty tell of her struggles and her sorrows. Elijah was there to relieve her poverty and to lessen her griefs.

ELIJAH AND THE WIDOW'S SON

Here is the interesting account:

> And it came to pass after these things, that the son of the woman, the mistress of the house, fell sick; and his sickness was so sore, that there was no breath left in him. And she said unto Elijah, What have I to do with thee, O thou man of God? art thou come unto me to call my sin to remembrance, and to slay my son? And he said unto her, Give me thy son. And he took him out of her bosom, and carried him up into a loft, where he abode, and laid him upon his own bed. And he cried unto the Lord, and said, O Lord my God, hast thou also brought evil upon the widow with whom I sojourn, by slaying her son? And he stretched himself upon the child three times, and cried unto the Lord, and said, O Lord my God, I pray thee, let this child's soul come into him again. And the Lord heard the voice of Elijah; and the soul of the child came into him again, and he revived. And Elijah took the child, and brought him down out of the chamber into the house, and delivered him unto his mother: and Elijah said, See, thy son liveth.

> And the woman said to Elijah, Now by this I know that thou art a man of God, and that the word of the Lord in thy mouth is truth.[4]

Elijah's prayer enters regions where prayer had never gone before. The awful, mysterious, and powerful regions of the dead are now invaded by the presence and demands of prayer. Jesus Christ refers to Elijah's going to this widow as mainly, if not solely, for her good. Elijah's presence and praying keep the woman from starving and brings her son back from death. Surely no sorrow is like the bitterness of the loss of an only son. With what assured confidence Elijah faces the conditions! There is no hesitancy in his actions, and there is no pause in his faith. He takes the dead son to his own room, and alone with God he makes the issue. In that room God meets him and the struggle is with God alone. The struggle is too intense and too sacred for companionship or for spectator. The prayer is made to God and the issue is with God. The child has been taken by God, and God rules in the realms of death. In His hands are the issues of life and death. Elijah believed that God had taken the child's spirit, and that God could as well restore that spirit. God answered Elijah's prayer. The answer was the proof of Elijah's mission from God, and of the truth of God's Word. The dead child brought to life was a sure conviction of this truth: "Now by this I know that thou art a man of God, and that the word of the Lord in thy mouth is truth."[5] Answers to prayer are the evidences of the being of God and of the truth of His Word.

ELIJAH AND THE ALTAR

The immortal test of Elijah made in the presence of an apostate king, and in the face of a backslidden nation and an idolatrous priesthood on Mount Carmel, is a sublime exhibition of faith and prayer. In the contest, the prophets of Baal had failed. No fire from heaven falls from heaven in answer to their frantic cries. Elijah, in great quietness of spirit and with confident assurance, calls Israel to him. He repairs the wasted altar of God, the altar of sacrifice and of prayer, and puts the pieces of the bullock in order on the altar. He then uses every means possible to prevent any charge of deception. Every thing is flooded with water. Then Elijah prays a model prayer, remarkable for its clearness, simplicity, and sincerity. It is noted for its brevity and its faith.

Read the account given in the Scriptures:

> And it came to pass at the time of the offering of the evening sacrifice, that Elijah the prophet came near, and said, Lord God of Abraham, Isaac, and of Israel, let it be known this day that thou art God in Israel, and that I am thy servant, and that I have done all these things at thy word. Hear me, O Lord, hear me, that this people may know that thou art the Lord God, and that thou hast turned their heart back again. Then the fire of the Lord fell, and consumed the burnt sacrifice, and the wood, and the stones, and the dust, and licked up the water that was in the trench. And when all the people saw it, they fell on their faces: and they said, The Lord, he is the God; the Lord, he is the God. [6]

Elijah had been dealing directly with God as before. True prayer always deals with God. This prayer of Elijah was to determine the existence of the true God, and the answer direct from God settles the question. The answer is also the credentials of Elijah's divine mission and the evidence that God deals with people. If we had more of Elijah's praying, marvels would not be the marvels that they are now to us. God would not be so strange, so far away in being, and so feeble in action. Everything is tame and feeble because our praying is so tame and feeble.

God said to Elijah, "Go show thyself to Ahab; and I will send rain on the earth."[7] Elijah acted promptly on the divine order, and showed himself to Ahab. He had made his issue with Ahab, Israel, and Baal. The whole current of national feeling had turned back to God. The day was fading into the evening shades. No rain had come. But Elijah did not fold his arms and say the promise had failed. Instead, he gave purpose and fulfillment to the promise.

ELIJAH BRINGS RAIN

Here is the Scripture record with the result given:

And Elijah said unto Ahab, Get thee up, eat and drink; for there is a sound of abundance of rain. So Ahab went up to eat and to drink. And Elijah went up to the top of Carmel; and he cast himself down upon the earth, and put his face between his knees, And said to his servant, Go up now, look toward the sea. And he went up, and looked, and said, There is nothing. And he said, Go again seven times. And it came to pass at the seventh time, that he said, Behold, there ariseth a little cloud out of the sea, like a man's hand. And he said, Go up, say unto Ahab, Prepare thy chariot, and get thee down, that the rain stop thee not. And it came to pass in the mean while, that the heaven was black with clouds and wind, and there was a great rain. And Ahab rode, and went to Jezreel. And the hand of the Lord was on Elijah; and he girded up his loins, and ran before Ahab to the entrance of Jezreel.[8]

Then it was, as James records, "And he prayed again, and the heaven gave rain, and the earth brought forth her fruit."[9]

Elijah's persistent, fiery, praying and God's promise brought the rain. Prayer carries the promise to its gracious fulfillment. It takes persistent and persevering prayer to give to the promise its largest and most gracious results. In this instance it was expectant prayer, watchful of results, looking for the answer. Elijah had the answer in the small cloud like a person's hand. He had the inward assurance of the answer even before he had the rain. How Elijah's praying shames our feeble praying! His praying brought things to pass. It vindicated the existence and being of God, brought conviction to dull and sluggish consciences, and proved that God was still God in the nation. Elijah's praying turned a whole nation back to God, ordered the moving of the clouds, and directed the falling of the rain. It called down fire from heaven to prove the existence of God or to destroy God's enemies.

The praying of the Elder Prophet of Israel was clothed in his robes of fire. The golden crown was on his head, and his censer was full and fragrant with the flame, melody, and perfume of prayer. What wonderful power clothed him on this occasion! It was no wonder that Elisha cried out as he saw this fiery prophet of the Lord enter the chariot for his heavenly ride, "My father, my father, the chariot of Israel, and the horsemen thereof."[10] But chariots and armies could not begin to do as much for Israel as did this praying Elijah. Prayers are omnipotent forces, worldwide and heaven-reaching.

Where are the praying saints of fiery faith today who can ignite Elijah's prayers? We need at this time rulers in the Church who can add to the force, flame, and fragrance of Elijah's praying by their own prayers.

Elijah could touch nothing but by prayer. God was with him mightily because he was mighty in prayer.

In the contest with the prophets of Baal, he makes the issue clearly and positively that the way to determine the true God is by prayer. Does God live? Is the Bible a revelation from Him? How often in these days are those questions asked? How often do they need to be settled? An appeal by prayer is the only settlement to them. Where is the trouble? Not in God, but in our praying.

ANSWERS AND THE REALITY OF GOD

The proof of God and of His being is that He answers prayer. It takes the faith and prayer of Elijah to settle the question. Where are the Elijahs in the Church today? Where are the saints of like passions as Elijah—those who can pray as he prayed? We have thousands of saints of like passions, but where are the saints of like praying as he was? Notice with what calm, assured, confidence he stakes the issue and builds the altar. How calm and pointed is his prayer on that occasion!

Instead of such praying being out of the range of New Testament principles and moderation, Elijah's praying is given as an example to be imitated, and as an illustration of what prayer can do when performed by the right people in the right way. Elijah's results could be secured if we had more Elijah saints to do the praying.

Elijah prayed really, truly, and earnestly. There is much praying today that is not real praying, only a mere shell and mere words! Much of it might well be termed non-praying. The world is full of such praying. It goes nowhere, avails nothing, and brings no returns. In fact, no returns or results are expected.

The requirements of true prayer are the requirements of scriptural, vital, personal Christianity. They are the requirements of real Christian service in this life. Primary among these requirements is that in serving we serve. And in praying we must pray. Truth and heart reality, these are the core, substance, sum, and heart of prayer. There are no possibilities in prayer unless we really pray in all simplicity, reality, and trueness. Prayerless praying—how common, how popular, how delusive and vain!

Endnotes

1 I Kings 17:1
2 Luke 1:19
3 James 5:17
4 I Kings 17:17-24
5 I Kings 17:24
6 I Kings 18:36-39
7 I Kings 18:1
8 I Kings 18:41-46
9 James 5:18
10 2 Kings 2:12

6

Hezekiah, the Praying King

ONE CAN FORM A *habit of study until the will seems to be at rest and only the intellect is engaged, the will having retired altogether from exercise. This is not true of real praying. If the affections are laggard, cold, indifferent, if the intellect is furnishing no material to clothe the petition with imagery and fervor, the prayer is a mere vaporing of intellectual exercise, nothing being accomplished worth while.* (Rev. Homer W. Hodge)

The great religious reformation under King Hezekiah and the prophet Isaiah was thoroughly impregnated with prayer in its various stages. King Hezekiah of Judah will serve as an illustration of a praying elder of God's Church, white-robed and gold-crowned. He had genius and strength, wisdom and piety. He was a statesman, general, poet, and religious reformer. He is a distinct surprise to us, not so much because of his strength and genius—they were to be expected—but in his piety under all the circumstances connected with him. The rare statement, "He did that which was right in the sight of the LORD,"[1] is a glad and thrilling surprise when we consider all his those before him and his environments. Where did he come from? Under what circumstances was his childhood life spent? Who were his parents and what were their religious character?

Worldliness, half-heartedness, and utter apostasy marked the reign of his father, grandfather, and his great-grandfather. His home surroundings as he grew up were far from being favorable to godliness and faith in God. One thing, however, favored him. He was fortunate in having Isaiah for his friend and counselor when he assumed the crown of Judah. How much there is in a ruler's having a God-fearing person for a counselor and an associate!

The familiar and successful praying he did to intercede with God is seen in the Passover feast in which a number of the people were unfit to participate. They had not prepared themselves by the required ceremonial cleansing, and it was important that they be allowed to eat the Passover feast with all the others.

Here is the brief account with special reference to the praying of Hezekiah and the result:

> For there were many in the congregation that were not sanctified: therefore the Levites had the charge of the killing of the passovers for every one that was not clean, to sanctify them unto the Lord. For a multitude of the people, even many of Ephraim, and Manasseh, Issachar, and Zebulun, had not cleansed themselves, yet did they eat the passover otherwise than it was written. But Hezekiah prayed for them, saying, The good Lord pardon every one that prepareth his heart to seek God, the Lord God of his fathers, though he be not cleansed according to the purification of the sanctuary. And the Lord hearkened to Hezekiah, and healed the people.[2]

So the Lord heard him as he prayed, and even the violation of the most sacred law of the Passover was forgiven in answer to the prayer of this praying, God-fearing, king. Law must yield its scepter to prayer.

The strength, directness, and foundation of his faith and prayer are found in his words to his army. The are memorable words, stronger and mightier than all the hosts of Sennacherib:

> Be strong and courageous, be not afraid nor dismayed for the king of Assyria, nor for all the multitude that is with him: for there be more with us than with him: With him is an arm of flesh; but with us is the Lord our God to help us, and to fight our battles. And the people rested themselves upon the words of Hezekiah king of Judah.[3]

His defense against the mighty enemies of God was prayer. His enemies quailed and were destroyed by his prayers when his own armies were powerless. God's people were always safe when their princes were princes in prayer.

An occasion of serious import came to the people of God during his reign that was to test his faith in God and furnish opportunity to try prayers to obtain deliverance. Judah was sorely pressed by the Assyrians, and humanly speaking defeat and captivity seemed imminent. The King of

Assyria sent a commission to defy and blaspheme the name of God and to insult King Hezekiah. They spoke their insults and blasphemy publicly. Note what Hezekiah immediately did without hesitation:

> And it came to pass, when king Hezekiah heard it, that he rent his clothes, and covered himself with sackcloth, and went into the house of the Lord.[4]

His very first impression was to turn to God by going to the "the house of the Lord," the house of prayer. God was in his thoughts, and prayer was the first thing to be done. So he sent messengers to Isaiah to join him in prayer. In such an emergency God must not be left out of the account. God must be appealed to for deliverance from these blasphemous enemies of God and His people.

Just at this particular point in time, the forces of the King of Assyria, which were besieging Hezekiah, were diverted from an immediate attack on Jerusalem. The King of Assyria, however, sent to Hezekiah a defaming and blasphemous letter.

For the second time, as he is insulted and beset by the forces of this heathen king, he enters the house of the Lord, the house of prayer. Where else should he go? To whom else should he appeal but to the God of Israel?

And Hezekiah received the letter from the hand of the messengers, and read it: and Hezekiah went up unto the house of the Lord, and spread it before the Lord.

> And Hezekiah prayed unto the Lord, saying, O Lord of hosts, God of Israel, that dwellest between the cherubims, thou art the God, even thou alone, of all the kingdoms of the earth: thou hast made heaven and earth.[5]

> Now therefore, O Lord our God, save us from his hand, that all the kingdoms of the earth may know that thou art the Lord, even thou only.[6]

Note the speedy answer and the marvelous results of such praying by this God-fearing king. First, Isaiah gave the King full assurance that he need fear nothing. God had heard the prayer, and would give a great deliverance.

Second, the angel of the Lord came with swift wings and smote 185,000 Assyrians. The king was vindicated, God was honored, and the people of God were saved.

The united prayer of the praying king and the praying prophet were almighty forces in bringing deliverance and destroying God's enemies. Armies lay at their mercy, defenseless. And angels, swift-winged and armed with almighty power and vengeance, were their allies.

Hezekiah had ministered in prayer in destroying idolatry and in reforming his kingdom. In meeting his enemies, prayer had been his chief weapon. He now comes to try its efficiency against the set and declared purposes of Almighty God. Will it avail in this new field of action? Let us see.

Hezekiah's sickness

Hezekiah was very sick, and God sends his own familiar friend and wise counselor and prophet, Isaiah, to warn him of his approaching end, and to tell him to arrange all his affairs for his final departure. This is the scriptural statement:

> In those days was Hezekiah sick unto death. And the prophet Isaiah the son of Amoz came to him, and said unto him, Thus saith the Lord, Set thine house in order; for thou shalt die, and not live.[7]

The decree came direct from God that he should die. What can set aside or reverse that divine decree of heaven? Hezekiah had never been in a condition so insurmountable, with a decree so direct and definite from God. Can prayer change the purposes of God? Can prayer snatch from the jaws of death one who has been decreed to die? Can prayer save a man from an incurable sickness? These were the questions that his faith now had to deal with. But his faith does not pause one moment. His faith is not staggered one minute at the sudden and definite news conveyed to him by the Lord's prophet. No such questions that modern unbelief or disbelief would raise are started in his mind. At once he gives himself to prayer. Immediately, without delay, he applies to God who issued the edict. To whom else could he go? Cannot God change His own purposes if He chooses?

Note what Hezekiah did in this emergency, sorely pressed, and see the gracious result:

> Then he turned his face to the wall, and prayed unto the Lord, saying, I beseech thee, O Lord, remember now how I have walked before thee in truth and with a perfect heart, and have done that which is good in thy sight. And Hezekiah wept sore.[8]

He did not offer a self-righteous plea to God for recovery. He was only pleading his faithfulness, just as Christ did hundreds of years later: "Father I have glorified thee on earth."[9] Jesus is reminding God, and is putting Him in mind as to His sincerity, faithfulness, and service, which was in every way legitimate. His prayer was directly in line with that of David in Psalm 26:1, "Judge me, O Lord; for I have walked in my integrity." Elijah's prayer is not a prayer test, or a faith cure, but it is a testing of God. It must be God's cure if a cure comes at all.

GOD HEALS HEZEKIAH

Hezekiah had hardly finished his prayer, and Isaiah was just about to go home when God gave him another message for Hezekiah, this time one more pleasant and encouraging. The mighty force of prayer had affected God, and had changed His edict and reversed Him in His purpose concerning Hezekiah. What is there that prayer cannot do? What is there that a praying person cannot accomplish through prayer?

> And it came to pass, afore Isaiah was gone out into the middle court, that the word of the Lord came to him, saying, Turn again, and tell Hezekiah the captain of my people, Thus saith the Lord, the God of David thy father, I have heard thy prayer, I have seen thy tears: behold, I will heal thee: on the third day thou shalt go up unto the house of the Lord. And I will add unto thy days fifteen years; and I will deliver thee and this city out of the hand of the king of Assyria; and I will defend this city for mine own sake, and for my servant David's sake.[10]

The prayer was to God. It was that God should reconsider and change His mind. Doubtless Isaiah returned to his house with a lighter heart than he did when he delivered his original message. God had been prayed to by this sick king, and had been asked to revoke His decree, and God had condescended to grant the request. God sometimes changes His mind. He has a right to do so. The reasons for Him to change His mind are strong reasons. His servant Hezekiah wants it done. Hezekiah had been a dutiful servant and had done much for God. Truth, perfection, and goodness have been the elements of Hezekiah's service and the rule of his life. Hezekiah's tears and prayer are in the way of God's executing His decree to take away the life of His servant. Prayer and tears are mighty things with God. They are to Him much more than consistency and much more to Him than decrees. "I have heard thy prayer, I have seen thy tears: behold, I will heal thee."

SICKNESS AND HEALTH

Sickness dies before prayer. Health comes in answer to prayer. God answered more than Hezekiah asked for. Hezekiah prayed only for his life, and God gave him life and promised him protection and security from his enemies.

But Isaiah had something to do with the recovery of this praying king. There was something more than prayer in it. Isaiah's praying was changed into the skill of the physician. "And Isaiah said, Take a lump of figs. And they took and laid it on the boil, and he recovered."[11]

It frequently takes a stronger faith to rise above means and not to trust in them, than it does to wholly reject all means. Here was a simple remedy that all might know that it did not cure the deadly disease, and yet was a means to aid or to test faith. But still more praying was to be done. Isaiah and Hezekiah could not do things without much praying:

> And Hezekiah said unto Isaiah, What shall be the sign that the Lord will heal me, and that I shall go up into the house of the Lord the third day? And Isaiah said, This sign shalt thou have of the Lord, that the Lord will do the thing that he hath spoken: shall the shadow go forward ten degrees, or go back ten degrees? And Hezekiah answered, It is a light thing for the shadow to go down ten degrees: nay, but let the shadow return backward ten degrees. And Isaiah the prophet cried unto the Lord: and he brought the shadow ten degrees backward, by which it had gone down in the dial of Ahaz.[12]

Hezekiah meets the occasion and covers the answer to his prayer with thanksgiving. The fragrance of the sweet spices are there, and the melody of the harp also.

Let us ever keep four things in mind: God hears prayer, God heeds prayer, God answers prayer, and God delivers by prayer. These things cannot be too often repeated. Prayer breaks all bars, dissolves all chains, opens all prisons, and widens all channels by which God's saints have been restricted.

Life was sweet to Hezekiah and he desired to live, but what can change God's decree? Nothing but the energy of faith. Hezekiah's heart was broken under the strain, and its waters flowed and added force and volume to his praying. He pleaded with great strivings and with strong arguments. And God heard Hezekiah praying, saw his tears, and changed his mind. Hezekiah lived to praise God and to be an example of the power of mighty praying.

PAUL'S WAY OF PRAYING

Like Hezekiah, the decent, soulless, way of praying did not suit Paul. He puts himself in the attitude of a wrestler, and charges his brethren to join him in the agony of a great conflict. He writes, "Now I beseech you, brethren, for the Lord Jesus Christ's sake, and for the love of the Spirit, that ye strive together with me in your prayers to God for me."[13] Paul was too much in earnest to touch the praying business gently or with gloved hands. He was in it as an agony, and he desired Christians to be his partners in this conflict and wrestling of his soul.

EPAPHRAS PRAYS

Epaphras was doing this same kind of praying for the Colossians: "always laboring fervently for you in prayers, that ye may stand perfect and complete in all the will of God."[14] This was an end worth agonizing for always. This kind of praying by these early pastors of the Apostolic Church was one secret of the purity and power of the Church. This was the kind of praying that was done by Hezekiah.

Hezekiah's prayer was born in the fire of a great desire, and pursued through the deepest agony of conflict and opposition to success. Our spiritual cravings are not strong enough to give life to the mighty conflicts of prayer. They are not absorbing enough to stop business, put off worldly pursuits, awaken us before day, and send us to the closet, to solitude, and to God. That there in our closets we might conquer every opposing force and win our victories from the very jaws of hell. We want preachers and men and women who can illustrate the uses, forces, blessings, and utmost limits of prayer.

TAKING HOLD OF GOD

Isaiah laments that there was no one who stirred himself up to take hold of God. Much praying was done, but it was too easy, indifferent, complacent. There were no mighty movements of the soul toward God, no array of all the sanctified energies to reach out and take hold of God and draw out His treasures for spiritual uses. Forceless prayers have no power to overcome difficulties, no power to win marked results, or gain a complete and wonderful victory.

Endnotes

1 2 Chronicles 29:2
2 2 Chronicles 30:17-20
3 2 Chronicles 32:7-8
4 Isaiah 37:1
5 Isaiah 37:14-16
6 Isaiah 37:20
7 2 Kings 20:1
8 2 Kings 20:2-3
9 John 17:4
10 2 Kings 20:4-6
11 2 Kings 20:7
12 2 Kings 20:8-11
13 Romans 15:20
14 Colossians 4:12

7

Ezra, the Praying Reformer

Befoore the Civil War *there were many signs of a new interest in prayer and new hope from its exercise. How these signs have multiplied is known to every one. This one thing at least that is good the war has done for us already. Let us not miss our opportunity. Prayer is not an easy exercise. It requires encouragement, exposition, and training. There never was a time when men and women were more sincerely anxious to be told how to pray. Prayer is the mightiest instrument in our armory, and if we are to use it as God has given the encouragement, we must do everything in our power to bring it into exercise.* (Rev. James Hastings)

Ezra the priest, and one of God's great reformers, comes before us in the Old Testament as a praying person who uses prayer to overcome difficulties and bring good things to pass. He had returned from Babylon under the patronage of the King of Babylon, who had been strangely moved toward Ezra and who favored him in many ways. Ezra had been in Jerusalem but a few days when the princes came to him with the distressing information that the people had not separated themselves from the people of that country. In fact, they were engaged in all the abominations of the heathen nations about them. Even worse, was that the princes and rulers in Israel were foremost in the trespass.

It was a sad state of affairs facing Ezra as he found the Church almost hopelessly involved with the world. God demands of His Church in all ages that it should be separated from the world, a separation so sharp that it amounts to an antagonism. To effect this very end, He put Israel in the

Promised Land, and cuts them off from other nations by mountains, deserts, and seas. Then He immediately charged them that they should not form any relation with alien nations, neither marital, social, or business.

THE CHURCH AT JERUSALEM

But when Ezra returns from Babylon, he finds the Church at Jerusalem paralyzed and hopelessly and thoroughly prostrated by the violation of this principle. They had intermarried, and had formed the closest and most sacred ties in family, social, and business life with the Gentile nations. All were involved in it—priests, Levites, princes, and people. The family, the business, and the religious life of the people were filled with this violation of God's law. What was to be done? What could be done? Here were the important questions that faced this leader in Israel, this man of God.

Everything appeared to be against the recovery of the Church. Ezra could not preach to them, because the whole city would be inflamed, and would hound him out of the place. What force was there that could recover them to God so that they would dissolve business partnerships, divorce wives and husbands, cut acquaintances, and dissolve friendships?

The first noteworthy thing about Ezra was that he saw the situation and realized how serious it was. He was not a blind-eyed optimist who never sees anything wrong in the Church. By the mouth of Isaiah, God had expressed the very pertinent question, "Who is blind but my servant?"[1]

But it could not possibly be made to apply to Ezra. Nor did he minimize the condition of things or seek to excuse the sins of the people or to minimize the enormity of their crimes. Their offense appeared in his eyes to be serious in the extreme. It is worth not a little to have leaders in Zion who have eyes to see the sins of the Church as well as the evils of the times. One great need of the modern Church is for leaders after the style of Ezra, who are not blind in their seeing department, who are willing to see the state of things in the Church, and who are not reluctant to open their eyes to the real situation.

Very naturally, seeing these dreadful evils in the Church and in the society of Jerusalem, Ezra was distressed. The sad condition of things grieved him, so much so that he rent his garments, plucked his hair, and sat down astonished. All these things are evidences of his great distress of soul at the terrible state of affairs. Then it was in that frame of mind—concerned, solicitous and troubled in soul—that he gave himself to prayer, to confession of the sins of the people, and to pleading for pardoning mercy at the hands of God. To whom should he go in a time like this but to the God who hears prayer, who is ready to pardon, and who can bring the unexpected thing to pass?

Ezra was amazed beyond expression at the wicked conduct of the people, was deeply moved, and began to fast and pray. Prayer and fasting always accomplish something. He prays with a broken heart, for there is nothing else that he can do. He prays to God, deeply burdened, prostrate on the ground, and weeping while the whole city unites with him in prayer.

EZRA'S ACCESS TO GOD Prayer was the only way to appease God, and Ezra became a great mover in a great work for God, with marvelous results. The whole work, its principles, and its results are summarized by just one verse:

> Now when Ezra had prayed, and had confessed, weeping and casting himself down before the house of God, there assembled unto him out of Israel a very great congregation of men and women and children: for the people wept sore.[2]

There had been mighty, simple, and persevering prayer. Intense and prevailing prayer had accomplished its end. Ezra's praying had brought into being and brought forth results in a great work for God. It was mighty praying because it brought Almighty God to do His own work, which was absolutely hopeless from any other source except by prayer and by God. But nothing is hopeless to prayer because nothing is hopeless to God.

Again we must say that prayer has only to do with God, and is only brings results as it has to do with God. Whatever influence the praying of Ezra had upon himself, its chief, if not its only, results followed because it affected God and moved Him to do the work.

A great and general repentance followed this praying of Ezra, and there occurred a wonderful reformation in Israel. Ezra's mourning and his praying were the great factors that had to do with bringing these great things to pass.

So thorough was the revival, that as evidences of its genuineness it is noted that the leaders in Israel came to Ezra with these words:

> We have trespassed against our God, and have taken strange wives of the people of the land: yet now there is hope in Israel concerning this thing. Now therefore let us make a covenant with our God to put away all the wives, and such as are born of them, according to the counsel of my lord, and of those that tremble at the commandment of our God; and let it be done according to the law. Arise; for this matter belongeth unto thee: we also will be with thee: be of good courage, and do it.[3]

Endnotes

1 Isaiah 42:19
2 Ezra 10:1
3 Ezra 10:2-4

8

Nehemiah, the Praying Builder

WE CARE NOT FOR *your splendid abilities as a minister, or your natural endowment as an orator before men. We are sure that the truth of the matter is this: No one will or can command success and become a real praying soul unless intense application is the price. I am even now convinced that the difference between the saints like Wesley, Fletcher, Edwards, Brainerd, Bramwell, Bounds, and ourselves is energy, perseverance, invincible determination to succeed or die in the attempt. God help us.* (Rev. Homer W. Hodge)

In listing the praying saints of the Old Testament, we must not leave out Nehemiah, the builder. He stands out on an equal footing with the others who have been considered. In the story of the reconstruction of Jerusalem after the Babylonian captivity, he plays a prominent part, and prayer is prominent in his life during those years. He was a captive in Babylon, and had an important position in the palace of the king—he was the king's cup bearer. There must have been considerable merit in him to cause the king to take a Hebrew captive and place him in such an office, where he really had the life of the king in his charge. It was his responsibility to make certain that the wine the king drank wasn't poisoned.

It was while Nehemiah was in Babylon in the king's palace, that one day some Israelites arrived from Jerusalem. Naturally, Nehemiah desired news from the people there and information concerning the city itself. The distressing information was given him that the walls were broken down, the gates were burned with fire, and the remnant who were left there at the beginning of the captivity were in great affliction and reproach.

Just one verse gives the effect of this sad news upon this man of God: "And it came to pass when I heard these words, that I sat down and wept, and mourned certain days, and fasted, and prayed before the God of heaven."[1]

Here was a man whose heart was in his own native land far away from where he now lived. He loved Israel, was concerned for the welfare of Zion, and was true to God. Deeply distressed by the information concerning the conditions at Jerusalem, he mourned and wept.

FEW TODAY WEEP AT EVIL

How few in these days who weep at the evils and abominations of the times! How rare are there those who see the desolations of Zion and are sufficiently interested and concerned for the welfare of the Church to mourn! Mourning and weeping over the decay of Christianity, the decline of revival power, and the fearful inroads of worldliness in the Church are almost an unknown quantity. There is so much of so-called optimism that leaders have no eyes to see the breaking down of the walls of Zion and the low spiritual state of the Christians of the present day—and have less heart to mourn and cry about it.

Nehemiah was a mourner in Zion. Possessing this state of heart, distressed beyond measure, he does that that other praying saints had done—he goes to God and makes it a subject of prayer. The prayer is recorded in Nehemiah I, and is a model after which to pattern our prayers.

He begins with adoration, makes confession of the sins of his nation, pleads the promises of God, mentions former mercies, and begs for pardoning mercy. Then with an eye to the future—for unquestionably he had planned that the next time he was summoned into the King's presence he would ask permission to visit Jerusalem and to do there what was possible to remedy the distressing state of affairs. We hear him pray for something very special: "And prosper, I pray Thee, thy servant this day, and grant him mercy in the sight of this man. Then he adds by way of explanation, "For I was the king's cup bearer."[2]

It seemed all right to pray for his people, but how was a heathen king to be so favorably affected that he would consent to give up his faithful cup bearer and allow him to be gone for months? No doubt the king of Babylon had little sympathy for the sad condition of Jerusalem and its people, and had no real interest in the matter, But Nehemiah believed in a God who could touch even the mind of a heathen ruler and move him favorably toward the request of his praying servant.

NEHEMIAH SUMMONED BEFORE THE KING

Nehemiah was summoned into the king's presence, and God used even the appearance of Nehemiah's countenance as an entering wedge to gain the consent of Artaxerxes. This started the inquiry of the king as to its cause, and the final result was that the king not only permitted Nehemiah to go back to Jerusalem, but furnished him with everything he needed for the journey and for the success of the enterprise.

Nehemiah rested his case when he first prayed about this matter, but he stated this significant fact as he was talking to the king: "So I prayed unto the God of heaven."[3] This gives the impression that while the king was inquiring about his request and the length of time he would be gone, Nehemiah was then and there talking silently to God about the matter.

The intense, persistent praying of Nehemiah prevailed. God can even affect the mind of a heathen ruler, and this He can do in answer to prayer without in the least overturning or forcing the person's free will.

It was a parallel case with that of Esther when she called upon her people to fast and pray for her as she went uninvited into the king's presence. As a result, the king's mind was touched by the Spirit of God at a very critical moment, and he was favorably moved toward Esther and held out the golden scepter to her.

Nehemiah's praying did not stop when he had succeeded this far. In building the wall of Jerusalem, he met with great opposition from Sanballat and Tobiah, who ridiculed the efforts of the people to rebuild the city's walls. Unmoved by their ridicule and the intense opposition of these wicked opponents of what was for God's cause, he pursued the task that he had undertaken. But he mixes prayer with all he does: "Hear, O our God, for we are despised: and turn their reproach upon their own head, and give them for a prey in the land of our captivity."[4] In continuing the account he says, "Nevertheless we made our prayer unto our God."[5]

All along in the accounts of the high and noble work he was doing, we find prayer comes out prominently to the front. Even after the walls were completed, these same enemies of his and of the people of God again opposed him in his task. But he renews his praying, and he himself records this significant prayer: "Now therefore, O God, strengthen my hands."[6]

OPPONENTS TRY TO FRIGHTEN NEHEMIAH

Still further on, when Sanballat and Tobiah hired an emissary to frighten and hinder Nehemiah, we find him setting himself directly against this new attack, and again turning to God in prayer: "My God, think Thou upon Tobiah and Sanballat according to these their works, and on the prophetess Noadiah, and the rest of the prophets, that would have put me in fear."[7] God answered His faithful laborer, and defeated the counsels and the plans of these wicked opponents of Israel.

Nehemiah discovered to his dismay that the Levites had not been given their portions, and as a result the house of God was forsaken. He took steps to see that the lawful tithes were forthcoming so that God's house would be opened to all religious services, and appointed treasurers to give attention to this business. But prayer must not be overlooked, so we find his prayer recorded at this time: "Remember me, O my God, concerning this, and wipe not out my good deeds that I have done for the house of my God, and for the offices thereof."[8]

Do not think that this was the plea of self-righteousness as was that of the Pharisee in our Lord's time who went up to the temple to pray and paraded his self-righteous claims in God's sight. It was a prayer like that of Hezekiah, who reminded God of his faithfulness to Him and of his heart's being right in His sight.

Once more Nehemiah finds evil among the people of God. Just as he corrected the evil that caused the closing of the house of God, he discovers practices of Sabbath breaking. In this, he not only counsels the people and seeks to correct them by mild means, but he proposes to exercise his authority if they do not cease their buying and selling on the Sabbath Day. He closes this part of his work also with prayer, and so he records his prayer on that occasion: "Remember me, O my God, concerning this also, and spare me according to the greatness of Thy mercy."[9]

Lastly, as a reformer, he discovers another great evil among the people. They had intermarried with the men and women of Ashdod, Ammon, and Moab. Contending with them, he caused them to reform in this matter, and the close of his record has a prayer in it: "Remember them, O my God, because they have defiled the priesthood, and the covenant of the priesthood, and of the Levites."[10]

Cleansing them from all strangers, he appointed the wards of the priests and the Levites. His recorded career closes with this brief prayer: "Remember me, O my God, for good."[11]

LEADERS WHO PRAY

Fortunate is that church whose leaders are people of prayer. Happy is that congregation who are contemplating the erection of a church and have leaders who will lay its foundations in prayer, and whose walls go up side by side with prayer. Prayer helps to build churches and to erect the walls of houses of worship. Prayer defeats the opponents of those who are prosecuting God's enterprises. Prayer touches favorably the minds even of those not connected with the Church, and moves them toward Church matters. Prayer helps mightily in all matters concerning God's cause and wonderfully aids and encourages the hearts of those who have His work in hand in this world.

Endnotes

1 Jeremiah 1:4
2 Jeremiah 1:11
3 Nehemiah 2:4

4 Nehemiah 4:4
5 Nehemiah 4:9
6 Nehemiah 6:9
7 Nehemiah 6:14
8 Nehemiah 13:14
9 Nehemiah 13:22
10 Nehemiah 13:29
11 Nehemiah 13:31

9

Samuel, the Child of Prayer

THAT WAS A GRAND *action by Jerome, one of the Roman fathers. He laid aside all pressing engagements and went to fulfill the call God gave him, viz., to translate the Holy Scriptures. His congregations were larger than many preachers of today but he said to his people, "Now it is necessary that the Scriptures be translated; you must find you another minister: I am bound for the wilderness and shall not return until my task is finished." Away he went and labored and prayed until he produced the Latin Vulgate which will last as long as the world stands. So we must say to our friends, "I must away and have time for prayer and solitude." And though we did not write Latin Vulgates yet our work will be immortal: Glory to God.* (C. H. Spurgeon)

Samuel came into this world and was given life in direct answer to prayer. He was born of a praying mother whose heart was full of earnest desire for a son. He came into life under prayer surroundings, and his first months in this world were spent in direct contact with a woman who knew how to pray. It was a prayer accompanied by a solemn vow that if he would be given he would be "lent unto the Lord."[1]

True to that vow, this praying mother put him directly in touch with the minister of the sanctuary and under the influence of the house of prayer. It was no wonder he developed into a man of prayer. We could not have expected otherwise with such a beginning in life and with such early environments. Such surroundings always make impressions upon children and tend to make character and determine destiny.

He was in a favorable place to hear God when He spoke to him, and was in an atmosphere conducive to his heeding the divine call that came to him. It was the most natural thing in the world when at the third call from heaven, when he recognized God's voice, that his childish heart responded so promptly, "Speak; thy servant heareth."[2] There was a quick response of submission, willingness, and prayer from his boyish spirit.

Had he been born of a different sort of mother, had he been placed under different surroundings, had he spent his early days in contact with different influences, there is no doubt that he would not have easily heard the voice of God calling him to His service and so readily yielded his young life to God. No child separated from the Church of God by a worldly home, worldly surroundings, and a worldly-minded mother would develop a godly character like Samuel's. It takes such influences and agencies in early life to produce praying men and women like Samuel.

PRAY FOR YOUR CHILDREN

Would you have one or more of your children called early into divine service and separated from the world unto God? Would you have them so situated that they will be called in childhood by the Spirit of God? Put them under prayer influences. Place them near to and directly under the influence of the person of God and in close touch with that house that is called the house of prayer.

Samuel knew God in boyhood. As a consequence he knew God in adulthood. He recognized God in childhood, and obeyed Him and prayed to Him. The result was that he recognized God in adulthood, obeyed Him, and prayed to Him. If more children were born of praying mothers, brought up in direct contact with the house of prayer, and reared under prayer environments, more children would hear the voice of God's spirit speaking to them, and would more quickly respond to those divine calls to a Christian life. Do we want praying young people in our churches? We must have praying mothers to give them birth, praying homes to flavor their lives, and praying surroundings to impress their minds and to lay the foundations for praying lives. Praying Samuels come from praying Hannahs. Praying priests come from "the house of prayer." Praying leaders come from praying homes.

For years Israel had been under bondage to the Philistines, and the ark was housed in the home of Abinadab, whose son Eleazer was appointed to keep this sacred testimony of God. The people had gone into idolatry and Samuel was disturbed about the religious condition of the nation. The ark of God was absent, the people were given to the worship of idols, and there had been a grievous departure from God. Calling upon them to put away their strange gods, he urged them to prepare their hearts unto the Lord and to begin again to serve Him—promising them that the Lord would deliver them out of the hands of the Philistines. His plain preaching made a deep impression on the people and bore rich fruits, as such preaching always does. "Then the children of Israel did put away Baalim and Ashtoreth, and served the Lord only."[3]

PRAYER AND REFORMATION

But this was not enough. Prayer must be accompanied by their reformation. So true to his convictions about prayer, Samuel says to the people, "Gather all Israel to Mizpeh, and I will pray for you unto the Lord."[4] While Samuel was offering up prayer for these wicked Israelites, the Philistines prepared to war against the nation. The Lord intervened at the critical moment, however, and thundered with a great thunder, and discomfited these enemies of Israel, "and they were smitten before Israel."[5]

Fortunately, the nation had a leader who could pray, who knew the place and the worth of prayer, and who had the ear of God and could influence Him.

But Samuel's praying did not stop there. He judged Israel all the days of his life. Every year he traveled to Bethel, Gilgal, and Mizpeh. Then he returned home to Ramah where he resided. "And there he built an altar unto the Lord."[6] It was an altar of sacrifice and an altar of prayer.

While the altar may have been for the benefit of the community where he lived, somewhat like a local church, it must have also been a family altar. As such, it was a place where sacrifice for sin was offered and where his household gathered for worship, praise, and prayer. Here Almighty God was acknowledged in the home, here was the advertisement of a religious home, and here father and mother called upon the name of the Lord, differentiating this home from all the worldly and idolatrous homes about them.

A RELIGIOUS HOME

Here is an example of a religious home, the kind so greatly needed in this irreligious, godless age. Blessed is that home that has in it an altar of sacrifice and prayer where daily thanksgivings ascend to heaven and where morning and night praying is done.

Samuel was not only a praying priest, a praying leader, and a praying teacher and leader, he was also a praying father. Anyone who knows what family Christianity is like today, knows full well that the great demand of these modern times is Christian homes and praying fathers and mothers. Here is where the breakdown in Christianity occurs, where the Christian life of a community first begins to decay, and where we must go first to create praying men and women in God's Church. It is in the home that the revival must commence.

A crisis came in the history of Samuel's nation. The people were infatuated by the glory of a kingdom with a human king, and were prepared to reject God as their king, which He had always been. So they came to Samuel with the bold request, "Make us a king to judge us like all the nations."[7] The request displeased Samuel, who was jealous for the name, honor, and pleasure of the Lord God. How could it be otherwise? Who would not have been likewise displeased if they had the godly character of Samuel? It grieved him in his soul.

It was then that Samuel followed the bent of his mind, "and Samuel prayed unto the Lord."[8] It seemed that in every matter concerning this people with which Samuel was connected, he must pray over it. How much more now when there was to be an entire revolution in the form of government, and God was to be displaced as the ruler of the people, and a human king was to be set up? National affairs need to be prayed over. Praying people are demanded to carry to God in prayer the affairs of government. Government leaders and lawmakers need to be prayed for. There would be fewer mistakes in government if there was more praying done in civil matters?

The Lord answered Samuel's prayer with a somewhat comforting personal assurance: "Hearken unto the voice of the people, in all that they say unto thee: for they have not rejected thee, but they have rejected Me, that I should not reign over them."[9]

But this was not the end of this matter. God must show so definitely and plainly His displeasure at the request for a human king, that the people would know what a wicked thing they had done, even though God consented to their request. They must know God still existed and was active in their lives, with their king, and in the affairs of the government. So the prayers of Samuel must again be brought into play to carry out the divine purposes.

GOD SENDS A STORM AND RAIN

Samuel calls upon the people to stand still, and he will show them what the Lord will do before their eyes. So he calls upon God, and in answer God sends a tremendous storm of thunder and rain that exceedingly terrified the people, and caused them to acknowledge their great sin in asking for a king. They were so afraid that they hastily called upon Samuel to pray for them and to spare them from what seemed to be destruction. Samuel again prayed, and God heard and answered, and the thunder and rain ceased.

One more incident in the prayer life of Samuel is worth noticing. King Saul had been ordered to destroy all the Amalekites, young and old, and all their goods. But contrary to divine instructions, Saul had spared King Agag and the best of the sheep and the cattle. He justified it by claiming that the people wanted it done.

So God brought spoke this to Samuel: "It repenteth me that I have set up Saul to be king: for he is turned back from following me, and hath not performed my commandments. And it grieved Samuel; and he cried unto the LORD all night."[10]

Such a sudden declaration was enough to produce grief of soul in a man like Samuel, who loved his nation, who was true to God, and who above everything else desired the prosperity of Zion. Such grief of soul over the evils of the Church and the sight of the abominations of the times always drive true saints to their knees in prayer. Of course Samuel carried the case to God. It was a time for prayer. The case was too serious for him not to be deeply moved to pray. Samuel's soul was so greatly disturbed that he prayed all night about it. Too much was at stake for him to shut his eyes to the affair, to treat it indifferently, and to let it pass without taking God into the matter. The future welfare of Israel was in the balance.

Endnotes

1 I Samuel 1:28
2 I Samuel 3:10
3 I Samuel 7:4
4 I Samuel 7:5
5 I Samuel 7:10
6 I Samuel 7:17
7 I Samuel 8:5
8 I Samuel 8:6
9 I Samuel 8:7
10 I Samuel 15:11

10

Daniel, the Praying Captive

IT IS A WONDERFUL *historical fact that the men of prayer have always been the men of power in the world. I want to convince you about this. Some of you men—and I am glad to see such a large number of men here tonight—if you are arguing with some friend in the workshop, be sure and ask him why it is that the men of power in the world have been the men of prayer. Take only one instance: Where did they go always to find men for the forlorn hope in Havelock's days? They went to Havelock's prayer meeting; that is where they found men who had courage to come out for the forlorn hope.* (Bishop Winnington Ingram)

It was a notable experience in the life of Daniel when he was ordered by the king in Babylon not to ask any petition of any God or king for thirty days, or he would be cast into the lions' den. He paid no attention to the edict, for it is recorded, "Now when Daniel knew that the writing was signed, he went into his house; and his windows being open in his chamber toward Jerusalem, he kneeled upon his knees three times a day, and prayed, and gave thanks before his God, as he did aforetime."[1]

This was the regular habit of this man of God. "He kneeled upon his knees . . . and prayed . . . as he did aforetime." What was the result? Just as expected. He was thrown into the lion's den. But God sent an angel into the lion's den with Daniel and shut the lion's mouths so that not a hair on his head was touched, and he was wonderfully delivered. Even so today, deliverance always come to God's saints who tread the path of prayer as did the saints of old.

Daniel did not forget his God while he was in a foreign land away from the house of God and its religious services, and deprived as he was of many religious privileges. He was a striking illustration of a young man who was decidedly religious under the most unfavorable surroundings. He proved conclusively that true servants of God can remain consistent in their relations with God even though their environments are anything else than religious. He was among heathens so far as a God-fearing nation was concerned. There was no temple worship, Sabbath day, or Word of God to be read. But he had one help there that remained with him, and of which he could not be deprived—his secret prayers.

Determining in his heart that he would not eat of the king's meat or drink the king's wine, he did not debate the matter or comprise on any one point. By so doing, he stood out in that ungodly country as a striking illustration of a young man who feared God and resolved to remain faithful to Him regardless of the cost. But he was not to have a flowery bed on which to rest or a smooth road on which to travel. The whimsical, tyrannical, and unreasonable king, Nebuchadnezzar, put him to the test and proved the strength of his faith in God. This king had a strange dream. He could not remember the details of the dream, but the fact of the dream remained. He was so troubled about the dream that he called for all his soothsayers, astrologers, and sorcerers to determine what his dream was about, which was an impossible task for any human, and then to interpret it. He put Daniel and his three companions, Shadrach, Meshach and Abednego, into the same class with these men, though they really had nothing in common with them. When none of his soothsayers, astrologers, and sorcerers could tell him what his dream was, and told him that it was impossible for anyone to uncover a dream like that. They then told the king that if he would tell the dream to them, they would interpret it. At that, the king became very angry and ordered them to be put to death. This sentence of death included Daniel and his three companions, though they had not been present with the others who could not discover and interpret the king's dream.

DANIEL TAKES ACTION

But Daniel took action. At his suggestion the execution of the rash edict was held up, and he immediately called his three companions into counsel. He urged them to unite with him in prayer that God would reveal to Daniel the dream and its interpretation. In answer to this united praying, it is recorded: "Then was the secret revealed unto Daniel in a night vision. Then Daniel blessed the God of heaven."[2]

As a sequel to this incident of the praying by the four men, Daniel revealed to the king his dream and its interpretation. As a result, the king acknowledged the God of Daniel and elevated Daniel and his three associates to high positions. It all came about because there was a praying person there just at a critical time. Blessed is the nation that has praying men and women who can come to the help of civil rulers who are greatly perplexed and in great difficulties, and who can be depended upon to pray for rulers of state and Church.

THE ANGEL GABRIEL

Years afterward, while still in a foreign land, Daniel still had not forgotten the God of his fathers, and he was given the noted vision of the "Ram and the He Goat."[3] But Daniel did not understand this strange vision, and yet he knew it was from God and had a deep and future meaning for nations and people. So, of course, he followed the bent of his religious mind and prayed about it.

> And it came to pass, when I, even I Daniel, had seen the vision, and sought for the meaning, then, behold, there stood before me as the appearance of a man. And I heard a man's voice between the banks of Ulai, which called, and said, Gabriel, make this man to understand the vision.[4]

So Gabriel made him understand the full meaning of this remarkable vision. But it came in answer to Daniel's praying. So puzzling questions may often find an answer in the closet. And as elsewhere, God employs angelic intelligences to convey information in response to prayers. Angels have much to do with prayer. Praying saints and the angels of heaven are in close touch with each other.

Some years after, Daniel was studying the records of the nation, and he discovered that it was about time for the seventy years of captivity of his people to end. So he gave himself to prayer: "And I set my face unto the Lord God, to seek by prayer and supplications, with fasting, and sackcloth, and ashes: And I prayed unto the Lord my God, and made my confession."[5]

Then follows the record in those Old Testament Scriptures of Daniel's prayer, so full of meaning, so simple in its utterances, so earnest in its spirit, so direct in its confession and requests, worthy of being used as a pattern.

It was while Daniel was speaking in prayer that the same archangel Gabriel, who seemed to have a direct interest in the praying of this man of God, "being caused to fly swiftly, touched me about the time of the evening oblation. And he informed me, and talked with me."[6] Gabriel then gave Daniel highly valuable information.

ANGELS NEAR TO US

The angels of God are much nearer to us in our seasons of prayer than we imagine. God employs these glorious heavenly intelligences in the blessed work of hearing and answering prayer. Especially when the prayer, as in the case of Daniel on this occasion, has to do with the present and future welfare of His people.

One other incident in the prayer life of this captive man in Babylon. Another revelation was made to Daniel, but the time of its fulfillment appeared to be far in the future. "In those days I, Daniel was mourning three full weeks. I ate no pleasant bread, neither came flesh nor wine in my mouth, neither did I anoint myself at all, till three whole weeks were fulfilled."[7]

THE KING OF PERSIA

It was then that he had a very strange experience and a still stranger revelation was made to him by some angelic being. It is worth reading the Scripture account:

> And, behold, an hand touched me, which set me upon my knees and upon the palms of my hands. And he said unto me, O Daniel, a man greatly beloved, understand the words that I speak unto thee, and stand upright: for unto thee am I now sent. And when he had spoken this word unto me, I stood trembling. Then said he unto me, Fear not, Daniel: for from the first day that thou didst set thine heart to understand, and to chasten thyself before thy God, thy words were heard, and I am come for thy words. But the prince of the kingdom of Persia withstood me one and twenty days: but, lo, Michael, one of the chief princes, came to help me; and I remained there with the kings of Persia.[8]

What all this means is difficult to comprehend, but enough appears on its face to lead us to believe that the angels in heaven are deeply interested in our praying, and are sent to tell us the answers to our prayers. Further, it is very clear that some unseen forces or invisible spirits are operating to hinder the answers to our prayers. Who the Prince of Persia was who withstood this great angelic being is not revealed, but enough is revealed to know that there must be a contest in the unseen world about us between those spirits sent to minister to us in answer to our prayers and the devil and his evil spirits who seek to defeat these good spirits.

The passage also gives us some indication as to the cause of delayed answers to prayer. For "three full weeks" Daniel mourned and prayed, and for "one and twenty days" the divinely appointed angel was opposed by the "Prince of the Kingdom of Persia."

It was well for Daniel that he had the courage, fortitude, and determination to persist in his praying for three weeks while the fearful conflict between good and evil spirits was going on about him unseen by mortal eyes. It will be for us if we do not give up in our praying when God seems not to hear and the answer is not immediate. It takes time to pray, and it takes time to get the answer to prayer.

Delays in answering prayer are not denials. Failure to receive an immediate answer is no evidence that God does not hear prayer. It takes not only courage and persistence to pray successfully, it also requires much patience. "Wait on the Lord: be of good courage, and he shall strengthen thine heart: wait, I say, on the Lord."9

Endnotes

1 Daniel 6:10
2 Daniel 2:19
3 Daniel 8:5-8
4 Daniel 8:15-16
5 Daniel 9:3-4a
6 Daniel 21b-22a
7 Daniel 10:2-3
8 Daniel 10:10-13
9 Psalm 27:14

II

Faith of Sinners in Prayer

A CERTAIN PREACHER WHOSE SERMONS *converted many souls received a revelation from God that it was not his sermons or works by all means but the prayers of an illiterate lay brother who sat on the pulpit steps pleading for the success of the sermon. It may be in the all-revealing day so with us. We may believe after laboring long and wearily that all honor belongs to another builder whose prayers were gold, silver, and precious stones, while our sermonizings being apart from prayer are but hay and stubble.* (C. H. Spurgeon)

One of the peculiar features of prayer as we study the Old Testament on this subject is the faith of unrighteous and backslidden people in prayer, and the great confidence they had in the prayers of praying saints of that day. They knew certain people as people of prayer who believed in God, who were favored of God, and who prayed unto God. They recognized these people as having influence with God in averting wrath and in delivering from evil.

Frequently when in trouble, when God's wrath was threatened, and even when there were visitations of evil upon them for their iniquities, they showed their faith in prayer by appealing to the ones who prayed to beg God to avert His displeasure and turn aside His wrath against them. Recognizing the value of prayer as a divine agency to save people, they asked the ones who prayed to intercede with God for them.

It is one of the strange paradoxes of those early days that while people departed from God, and went into grievous sin, they did not become either atheists nor unbelievers when it came to the question of the existence of a prayer-answering God. Wicked people held fast to a belief in God's existence, and to faith in the power of prayer to secure pardon for sin and to deliver them from God's wrath. It is worth something in showing the influence of the Church on sinners, when the latter believe in prayer and beg Christian people to pray for them. It is an item of interest and an event of importance when a sinner on a dying bed calls for a praying saint to come and pray. It means something when penitent sinners, under a sense of their guilt, feeling the displeasure of God, approach a church altar and say, "Pray for me, you praying men and women."

THE CHURCH'S LACK OF UNDERSTANDING

The Church little understands its full import, and still less appreciates and takes in the full import of praying, especially for the unsaved men and women who ask them to pray for their immortal souls. If the Church was fully alive to God and awake to the real peril of the unconverted all about it, and was in a thriving state, more sinners would be found seeking the altars of the Church and crying out to praying people, "Pray for my soul."

There may be much so-called praying for sinners, but it is cold, formal, official praying that goes nowhere, never reaches God, and accomplishes nothing. Revivals begin when sinners seek the prayers of praying people.

Several things stand out in bold relief as we look at those Old Testament days:

First, the disposition of sinners against God to almost involuntarily turn to praying people for help and refuge when trouble draws near, and to invoke their prayers for relief and deliverance. "Pray for us" was their cry.

Second, the readiness with which those praying people responded to these appeals and prayed to God for those who desired this thing. Moreover, we are impressed with the fact that these praying saints were always in the spirit of prayer and ready at any time to inquire of God. They were always keyed up on prayer.

Third, we note the wonderful influence these men and women of prayer had with God whenever they made their appeal to Him. God nearly always quickly responded and heard their praying for others. So intercessory prayer predominated in those early days of the Church.

It is a question worthy of earnest consideration—how much is the Church responsible for the unbelief of sinners today in the value of prayer as an agency in averting God's wrath, in sparing barren lives, and in giving deliverance? How much is the Church responsible for the precious few mourners in Zion in these times—those who ignore your altar calls and treat with indifference your appeals to come and be prayed for?

SINNERS ASKING FOR PRAYER

One of the first illustrations we see that shows the faith of wicked men and women in prayer and their appeal for a person of God to intercede for them is the case of the fiery serpents sent upon the Israelites. They were journeying from Mount Hor by way of the Red Sea, seeking to circle the land of Edom, when they spoke against God and Moses: "Wherefore have ye brought us up out of Egypt to die in the wilderness? for there is no bread, neither is there any water; and our soul loatheth this light bread."[1]

The thing so sorely displeased God that He sent fiery serpents among the people, and many of the people of Israel died.

> Therefore the people came to Moses, and said, We have sinned, for we have spoken against the Lord, and against thee; pray unto the Lord, that he take away the serpents from us. And Moses prayed for the people.[2]

As far as these people had departed from God, and as great as their sin was in complaining against God's dealings with them, they had not lost faith in prayer. They also did not forget that there was a leader in Israel who had influence with God in prayer, and who could by that means avert disaster and bring deliverance to them.

JEROBOAM

Jeroboam, first King of the ten tribes when the kingdom was divided, is another case in point. This was a most noted case because of the notoriety of his departure from God, which was often referred to in the history of Israel as "the sin of Jeroboam the son of Nebat,"[3] It shows that despite his great wickedness in the sight of God, he did not lose his faith in the effectiveness of prayer. This king on one occasion presumed to take the place of the high priest, and stood by the altar to burn incense. A man of God came out of Judah and cried against the altar and proclaimed, "Behold, the altar shall be rent, and the ashes that are upon it shall be poured out."[4] This angered Jeroboam, who saw that it was intended as a public rebuke for him because he had done contrary to the Levitical law in assuming the office of God's priest. So he put forth his hand with the apparent purpose of arresting or doing violence to the man of God who spoke against him, and said at the same time to those about him, "Lay hold on him."[5]

God immediately smote the king with leprosy, so that he could not pull his hand back again, and at the same time the altar was rent. Astonished beyond measure at this sudden retribution for his sin, coming like lightning from heaven, and very much afraid, Jeroboam cried out to the man of God, "Intreat now the face of the Lord thy God for me, that my hand may be restored me again." And it is recorded that "the man of God besought the

Lord, and the king's hand was restored him again, and became as it was before."[6]

Let us keep in mind that we are not now considering the praying habits of the man of God nor the possibilities of prayer, though both face us here. But rather we are finding just here that when God's wrath falls upon a ruler in Israel, who has departed from God and is guilty of a grievous sin, he immediately calls upon a praying man to intercede with God in his behalf. It is but another case where a sinner against God showed his faith in the virtue of the prayers of a saint of God.

WHEN PRAYER DECAYS

Sad is the day in a Christian land, not only where there is the decay of prayer in the Church, but where sinners are so unaffected by the religion of the Church that they have no faith in prayer and care little about the prayers of praying saints.

Another illustration follows this case very quickly. The son of King Jeroboam fell sick and was about to die. So this wicked, indifferent, king, sent his wife to Ahijah, the prophet of God, to ask him to say what would be the result of the illness of the child. She attempted to practice a deception upon the old prophet who was nearly blind, intending not to make herself known to him. But he had the vision of a prophet even though dim in sight, and immediately revealed to her that she was known to him. After telling her many things of vast importance concerning the kingdom and charging her husband that he had not kept God's commandments, but had gone into idolatry, he said to her: "Arise thou therefore, get thee to thine own house: and when thy feet enter into the city, the child shall die."[7]

How natural for a father in trouble to appeal to a praying prophet for relief? As in the first mentioned case, his sin did not blind his eyes to the value of having a person of God intercede for him. It availed nothing as was proved, but it did prove our contention that in Old Testament times sinners, while they were not themselves praying people, believed strongly in the prayers of praying saints.

JOHANAN

Take the instance of Johanan, when the children of Israel began their life of captivity in Babylon. Johanan and Jeremiah, with a small company, were left in their native land. Ishmael had conspired against Gedaliah, the appointed governor of the country, and had slain him. Johanan came to the rescue and delivered the people from Ishmael who was taking them away from their land. But Johanan wanted to flee down into Egypt, which was contrary to the God's plan. At this particular juncture of affairs, he assembled all the people, and they went to Jeremiah with the earnest appeal:

We beseech thee, our supplication be accepted before thee, and pray for us unto the Lord thy God, even for all this remnant; (for we are left but a few of many, as thine eyes do behold us:) That the Lord thy God may shew us the way wherein we may walk, and the thing that we may do.[8]

Like all other appeals to good people for prayer, Jeremiah interceded for these inquirers after the right way, and after ten days the answer came. They were told by Jeremiah what God would have them do. They should not go down to Egypt, but remain in and about Jerusalem. But the people and Johanan played Jeremiah false, and refused to do as God had told them in answer to prayer. Nevertheless, it did not disprove the fact that they had faith in prayer and in praying saints.

MANY SINNERS HAVE FAITH IN PRAYER

Another case may be noted that shows the truth of our proposition that sinners had faith in prayer in Old Testament times, thus indirectly proving the preeminence of prayer in those days. Prayer certainly must have had a prominent place and its necessity must have received general recognition when even sinners by their actions endorsed its virtue and necessity. Surely if sinners bore testimony to its worth, and at that time displayed their need of prayer, even by someone else, church people of this day should have a deep sense of its need, and should have strong faith in prayer and its virtue. If the men and women of Old Testament times were such people of prayer, and had such a reputation as praying people, then in this favored day, Christian men and women should be so given to prayer that they also would have a wide reputation as praying people.

ZEDEKIAH

Zedekiah was king of Judah just as the captivity of God's people began. He was in charge of the kingdom when Jerusalem was besieged by the King of Babylon. It was just about this time that Zedekiah sent two chosen men to Jeremiah saying: "Enquire, I pray thee, of the Lord for us; for Nebuchadrezzar king of Babylon maketh war against us; if so be that the Lord will deal with us according to all his wondrous works, that he may go up from us."[9]

God told Jeremiah in answer to this inquiry what to do and what would occur. But as in the case of Johanan, Zedekiah proved false and would not do as God instructed Jeremiah to tell him. At the same time, however, it proved conclusively that Zedekiah had not lost his faith in prayer as a means of finding out the mind of God, and it did not affect him in his belief in the virtue of the prayers of a praying person.

Truly, prayer must have had a preeminent place in all Old Testament history when not only the men and women of God were noted for their praying habits, but even those who departed from God and proved false bore testimony to its virtue by appealing to the people of prayer to make intercessions for them. This is so obvious in Old Testament history that no careful reader of these old Scriptures can fail to see and understand it.

Endnotes

1 Numbers 21:5
2 Numbers 21:7
3 2 Kings 10:29
4 I Kings 13:3
5 I Kings 13:4
6 I Kings 13:6
7 I Kings 14:12
8 Jeremiah 42:2-3
9 Jeremiah 21:2

12

Paul, the Teacher of Prayer

FLETCHER OF MADELEY, *a great teacher of a century and a half ago, used to lecture to the young theological students. He was one of the fellow-workers with Wesley and a man of most saintly character. When he had lectured on one of the great topics of the Word of God, such as the Fullness of God's Holy Spirit or on the power and blessing that He meant His people to have, he would close the lecture and say, "That is the theory; now will those who want the practice come along up to my room!" And again and again they closed their books and went away to his room, where the hour's theory would be followed by one or two hours of prayer.* (Rev. Hubert Brooke)

How instant, strenuous, persistent, and pathetic was Paul's urgency of prayer upon those to whom he wrote and spoke! "I exhort, therefore," he says, writing to Timothy, "that, first of all, supplications, prayers, intercessions, and giving of thanks be made for all men."[1] This he meant was to be the primary action and truth for the Church. First of all, before all things, to the front of all things, the Church of our Lord was to be a praying Church. It was to pray for people—all people.

To the Philippians he wrote, "Be careful for nothing; but in every thing by prayer and supplication with thanksgiving let your requests be made known unto God."[2]

The Church must be anxious about nothing. In everything prayer must be made. Nothing was too small about which to pray. Nothing was too great for God to overcome.

Paul lays it down as a vital, all-essential, injunction in writing to the Church at Thessalonica, "Rejoice evermore. Pray without ceasing. In every thing give thanks: for this is the will of God in Christ Jesus concerning you."[3]

The Church must give itself to unceasing prayer. Never was prayer to stop in the Church. This was the will of God concerning His Church on earth.

Paul was not only given to prayer himself, but he continually and earnestly urged it in a way that showed its vital importance. He was not only insistent in urging prayer upon the Church in his day, but he urged persistent praying. "Continue in prayer, and watch in the same with thanksgiving,"[4] was the keynote of all his exhortations on prayer. "Praying always with all prayer and supplication,"[5] was the way he pressed this important matter upon the people. He exhorted, "I will therefore that men pray every where, lifting up holy hands, without wrath and doubting."[6] Because he prayed after this fashion himself, he could afford to press it upon those to whom he ministered.

Paul was a leader by appointment and by universal recognition and acceptance. He had many mighty forces in this ministry. His conversion, so conspicuous and radical, was a great force, a perfect manual of aggressive and defensive warfare. His call to the apostleship was clear, bright, and convincing. But these forces were not the most divine energies that brought the largest results to his ministry. Paul's course was more distinctly shaped and his career rendered more powerfully successful by prayer than by any other force.

It is no surprise then that he should give such prominence to prayer in his preaching and writing. We could not expect it to be otherwise. As prayer was the highest exercise in his personal life, so also prayer assumed the same high place in his teaching. His example of prayer added force to his teaching on prayer. His practice and his teaching ran in parallel lines. There was no inconsistency in the two things.

Paul was the chiefest of the apostles as he was chief in prayer. If he was the first of the apostles, prayer conspired to that end. He was, therefore, all the better qualified to be a teacher on prayer. His praying fitted him to teach others what prayer was and what prayer could do. For this reason, he was competent to urge upon the people that they must not neglect prayer. Too much depended upon it.

PAUL: FIRST IN PRAYER

He was first in prayer for this cause. On him centered more saintly praying than on any one else, and so he became the first in apostleship. The crown of martyrdom was the highest crown in the royalty of heaven, but prayer put this crown of martyrdom on his head.

Those who would teach the people to pray must first themselves be given to prayer. Those who urge prayer on others must first tread the path of prayer themselves. To the same proportion that they pray, preachers will be disposed to urge prayer upon those to whom they preach. Moreover, just in proportion as preachers pray, will they be fitted to preach on prayer. If that course of reasoning be true, would it be legitimate to draw the conclusion that the reason why there is so little preaching on prayer in these modern times is because preachers are not praying people?

We might stake the whole question of the absolute necessity and the possibilities of prayer in this dispensation on Paul's attitude toward prayer. If personal force, if the energy of a strong will, if profound convictions, if personal culture and talents, and if the divine call and the divine empowerment,—if any one of these, or all of them united, could direct the God's Church without prayer, then logically prayer would be unnecessary. If profound piety and unswerving consecration to a high purpose, if impassioned loyalty to Jesus Christ, if any or all of these could exist without devoted prayer, or lift a Church leader above the necessity of prayer, then Paul was above its use. But if the great and gifted, favored and devoted, Paul felt the necessity of unceasing prayer, and realized that it was urgent and pressing in regard to its claims and necessity, and if he felt that it was clamorous and insistent that the Church should pray without ceasing, then he and his brethren in the apostolate should be aided by universal and mighty praying.

Paul's praying and his commands and the urgency with which he pressed upon the Church to pray, is the most convincing proof of the absolute necessity of prayer as a great moral force in the world. It is an indispensable and inalienable factor in the progress and spread of the Gospel, and in the development of personal piety. In Paul's view, there was no Church success without prayer, and no piety without prayer—in fact, without much prayer. A Church out of whose life streams prayer as the incense flames went out of the censer, and a leadership out of whose character, life, and habits flames prayer as imposing, conspicuous, and spontaneous as the fragrant incense flamed, this was the leadership for God.

PRAY EVERYWHERE IN EVERYTHING

To pray everywhere, to pray in everything, to continue instant in prayer, and to pray without ceasing were Paul's words as a commentator on the divine uses and the nature of prayer.

Timothy was very dear to Paul, and the attachment was mutual and intensified by all their affinities. Paul found in Timothy those elements that fitted him to be his spiritual successor, at least the depository and the leader of the great spiritual principles and forces that were essential to the establishment and prosperity of the Church. These primary and vital truths he would enforce and establish in Timothy. Paul regarded Timothy as one to whom fundamental and vital truths might be committed, who would preserve them truly, and who would commit them inviolate to the future. So he gives to Timothy this deposit of prayer for all ages as found in I Timothy 2:1.

Let it be noted before we go any further that Paul wrote directly under the supervision of the Holy Spirit, who guarded Paul against error, and who inspired the truths that Paul taught. We hold definitely without compromise in the least to the plenary inspiration of the Scriptures, and as Paul's writings are part and parcel of those sacred writings, then Paul's Epistles are portions of the Scriptures or the Word of God. This being true, the doctrine of prayer that Paul affirmed is the doctrine of the Holy Spirit. His epistles are the Word of God—inspired, authentic, and of divine authority. So prayer as taught by Paul is the doctrine that Almighty God would have His Church accept, believe, and practice.

These words to Timothy, therefore, were divinely inspired words. This section of Holy Writ is much more than merely suggestive, and is far more than a broad, bare outline on prayer. It is so instructive about prayer, about how people ought to pray, how business people should pray, and so forceful about the reasons why people should pray, that it needs to be strongly and insistently pressed.

PAUL'S WORDS TO TIMOTHY ABOUT PRAYER
Here are Paul's words to Timothy on prayer:

> I exhort therefore, that, first of all, supplications, prayers, intercessions, and giving of thanks, be made for all men; For kings, and for all that are in authority; that we may lead a quiet and peaceable life in all godliness and honesty. For this is good and acceptable in the sight of God our Saviour; Who will have all men to be saved, and to come unto the knowledge of the truth. For there is one God, and one mediator between God and men, the man Christ Jesus; Who gave himself a ransom for all, to be testified in due time. . . . I will therefore that men pray every where, lifting up holy hands, without wrath and doubting.[7]

In this prayer passage we have set forth by Paul the inheritance and practice of every Christian in all ages. In the great business of praying, it gives us a view of the energy and many-sidedness of prayer. First in point of time in all excellence of all duties is prayer. It must be first in all occupations. So exacting and imperative in its import and power is prayer that it stands first among spiritual values. Those who pray not, are not at all. They are nothing, less than nothing. They are below zero so far as Christ and God and heaven are concerned. Not simply among the first things does prayer stand on a level with other things, but first of the first, to the very forefront, does Paul put prayer with all his heart. "I exhort that first of all."

Praying is the most important thing on earth

His teaching is that praying is the most important of all things on earth. All else must be restrained, retired, to give it primacy. Put it first, and keep its primacy. The conflict is about the primacy of prayer. Defeat and victory lie in this one thing. To make prayer secondary is to uncrown it. It is to bind and destroy prayer. If prayer is put first, then God is put first, and victory is assured. Prayer must either reign in the life or must abdicate. Which shall it be?

According to Paul, "supplications, prayers, intercessions, and giving of thanks" all these elements of prayer and forms of prayer are to be offered for people. Prayer is offered for things, for all things, for all temporal good, and for all spiritual good and grace. But in these directions Paul rises to the highest results and purposes of prayer. People are to be affected by prayer. Their good, their character, conduct, and destiny are all involved in prayer. In this regard, prayer moves along the highest way, and pursues its loftiest end. We are cognizant and consonant with things, with blessings, and bestowments, with matters and things that touch people—but people themselves are here set forth as the objects of prayer. This broadens and ennobles prayer. People, through the whole sweep and range of their conditions, are to be held in the mighty grasp of prayer.

Paul's teaching is to the effect that prayer is essentially a thing of the inner nature. The spirit within us prays. So note Paul's directions: "I will therefore that men pray everywhere . . . without wrath."[8] *Wrath* is a term that denotes the natural, internal, motion of plants and fruits, swelling with juice. The natural juices are warmed into life, and rise by the warmth of Spring. People have in them natural juices that rise as does the sap. Warmth, heat, all stages of passions and desires, every degree of feeling, these spontaneously rise under provocation. Guard against and suppress them. Saints cannot pray with these natural feelings rising in them and cultivated, cherished, and continued there. Prayer is to be without these. "Without wrath." Higher, better, nobler inspiration are to lift prayer upward. "Wrath" depresses prayer, hinders it, suppresses it.

The word "without" means making no use of, having no association with, apart from, aloof from. The natural, unrenewed, heart has no part in praying. Its heat and all its natural juices poison and destroy praying. The nature of prayer is deeper than nature. We cannot pray by nature, even by the kindliest and the best nature.

Prayer is the true test of character

Faithfulness to our conditions and trueness to our relations are often evidenced by our prayerfulness. Some conditions give birth to prayer. They are the soil that germinates and perfects prayer. To pray under some circumstances seems very fitting. Not to pray in some conditions seems heartless and discordant. The great storms of life, when we are helpless and without relief, or are devoid of comfort, are the natural and providential conditions of prayer.

Widowhood is a great sorrow. It comes to saintly women as well as to others. True widows there are who are saintly. They are to be honored and their sorrow is divine. Their piety is aromatic and lightened by their bruised hearts. Here is Paul's description of such widows:

> Now she that is a widow indeed, and desolate, trusteth in God, and continueth in supplications and prayers night and day. But she that liveth in pleasure is dead while she liveth.[9]

Here is the striking contrast between two classes of women. One gives herself to supplications night and day. The other lives in pleasure and is spiritually dead. So Paul describes a true widow as being great in prayer. Her prayers, born of her faith and desolation, are a mighty force. Day and night her prayers go up to God unceasingly. The widowhood heart is a mighty appeal to God when that heart is found in the way of prayer, intense, unwearied prayer.

One of Paul's striking injunctions worthy of study is this one, "continuing instant in prayer,"[10] or as the *Revised Version* reads, "Continuing steadfast in prayer," which is his description of prayer. The term means to tarry, to remain, to be steadfast and faithful in prayer, to stick strongly to it, to stay at it with strength to the end, to give attention to it with vigor, devotion, and constancy, to give unremitting care to it.

THE BUSINESS OF PRAYER

Praying is a business, a life-long business, one to be followed with diligence, fervor, and toil. The Christian's business by way of preeminence is prayer. It is the saint's most engaging, most heavenly, most lucrative business. Prayer is a business of such high and deserved dignity and import that it is to be followed "without ceasing." That is, with no let up or break down, followed diligently and without intermission. To prayer we are to give all strength. It must cover all things, be in every place, find itself in all seasons, and embrace everything, always, and everywhere.

In Paul's remarkable prayer in Ephesians 3, he is praying for wide reaches of religious experience. He is there bowing his knees to God, in the name of Jesus Christ, and asking that God would grant that these Ephesian believers would in their experiences go far beyond the utmost stretches of past sainthood. "Filled with all the fullness of God"[11] is an experience so great and so glorious that it makes the head of modern saints so dizzy that they are afraid to look up to those supernal heights or peer down into the fathomless depths. Paul just passes us on to "Him that is able to do exceeding abundantly above all that we ask or think."[12] This is a specimen of his teaching on prayer.

In writing to the Philippian church, Paul recounts the situation and shows the transmuting power of prayer as follows:

> Some indeed preach Christ even of envy and strife; and some also of good will: The one preach Christ of contention, not sincerely, supposing to add affliction to my bonds: But the other of love, knowing that I am set for the defence of the gospel. What then? notwithstanding, every way, whether in pretence, or in truth, Christ is preached; and I therein do rejoice, yea, and will rejoice. For I know that this shall turn to my salvation through your prayer, and the supply of the Spirit of Jesus Christ, According to my earnest expectation and my hope, that in nothing I shall be ashamed, but that with all boldness, as always, so now also Christ shall be magnified in my body, whether it be by life, or by death.[13]

Boldness was to be secured by him and defeat and shame prevented by their prayers. Christ was to be gloriously magnified by and through Paul, whether he lived or died.

Note that in all these quotations in Corinthians, Ephesians, and Philippians, the *Revised Version* of the Bible gives us the most intense form of prayer, "supplications." It is the intense, personal, strenuous, persistent praying of the saints that Paul requests, and they must give special strength, interest, time, and heart to their praying to make it bear its largest and most golden fruit.

The general direction about prayer to the Colossian Christians is made specific and sharpened to the point of a personal appeal: "Continue in prayer, and watch in the same with thanksgiving; Withal praying also for us, that God would open unto us a door of utterance, to speak the mystery of Christ, for which I am also in bonds: That I may make it manifest, as I ought to speak."[14]

Paul is accredited with the authorship of the Epistle to the Hebrews. We have it in a reference to the character of Christ's praying that illustrates the elements and ways of true praying. How rich are His words! How heart-affecting and how sublime was His praying—this One who prayed as never a person prayed before, and yet prayed in order to teach people how to pray. It is written about Him, "Who in the days of his flesh, when he had offered up prayers and supplications with strong crying and tears unto him that was able to save him from death, and was heard in that he feared."[15]

The praying of Jesus Christ drew on the mightiest forces of His being. His prayers were His sacrifices, which He offered before He offered Himself on the Cross for the sins of humanity. Prayer-sacrifice is the forerunner and pledge of self-sacrifice. We must die in our closets before we can die on the cross.

Endnotes

1 I Timothy 2:1
2 Philippians 4:6
3 I Thessalonians 5:16-18
4 Colossians 4:2
5 Ephesians 6:18a
6 I Timothy 2:8
7 I Timothy 2:1-6, 8
8 I Timothy 2:8
9 I Timothy 5:5-6
10 Romans 12:12b
11 Ephesians 3:19
12 Ephesians 3:20
13 Philippians 1:15-20
14 Colossians 4:2-4
15 Hebrews 5:7

13

Paul and His Praying

IN THE LIFE OF *Frank Crossley it is told how one day in 1888 he had said good-bye at the station to his friends, General and Mrs. Booth; but before they steamed out he handed a letter to them giving details of a sacrifice he had resolved to make for the Army. He came home and was praying alone. "As I was praying," he said, "there came over me the most extraordinary sense of joy. It was not exactly in my head, nor in my heart, it was almost a grasping of my chest by some strange hand that filled me with an ecstasy I never had before. It was borne in on me that this was the joy of the Lord." So this servant of God made in his pilgrimage to God an advance from which he never fell back. He thought it likely at the time that the Booths had read this letter in the train and this was an answer to prayer of theirs; afterwards he heard they had prayed for him in the train just after getting well out of Manchester. (Rev. Edward Shillito)*

Those who study Paul's praying, both his prayers and his commands about prayer, will find what a wide, general, minute, and diversified area it covers. It will appear that men like Wesley, Brainerd, Luther, and all their holy successors in the spiritual realms, were not guilty of fanaticism or superstition when they ordered all things by prayer great and small, and committed all thing, secular and religious, natural and spiritual, to God in prayer. In this they were but following the great example and authority of the apostle Paul.

To seek God as Paul did by prayer, to commune with God as Paul did, to supplicate Jesus Christ as Paul did, to seek the Holy Spirit by prayer as

Paul did, to do this without ceasing, to be always a racer, and to win Christ as Paul did by prayer—all this makes a saint, an apostle, and a leader for God. This kind of a life engages, absorbs, enriches, and empowers with God and for God. Prayer, if successful, must always engage and absorb us. This kind of praying brings Pauline days and secures Pauline gifts. Pauline days are good, Pauline gifts are better. But Pauline praying is best of all, for it brings Pauline days, and secures Pauline gifts. Pauline praying costs much. It is death to self, the flesh, and the world. Pauline praying is worth all it costs. Prayer that costs nothing gets nothing. It is beggarly business at best.

Paul's estimate of prayer is seen and enforced by the fact that Paul was a person of prayer. His high position in the Church was not one of dignity and position to enjoy and luxuriate in. It was not one of officialism, nor was it one of arduous and exhaustless toil, for Paul was preeminently a praying man.

He began his great career for Christ in the great struggle and school of prayer. Christ's convincing and wonderful argument to calm Ananias was, "Behold, he prayeth."[1] He was three days without sight, neither eating nor drinking, but the lesson was learned well.

Paul went out on his first great missionary trip under the power of fasting and prayer. Paul and Barnabas together established every Church by the very same means, by fasting and prayer. Paul began his work in Philippi "where prayer was wont to be made."[2] As "they went to prayer,"[3] a spirit of divination was cast out of the young woman. And when Paul and Silas were put in prison, they prayed and sang praises to God at midnight.

PAUL'S PRAYING HABIT

Paul made praying a habit, a business, and a life. He literally gave himself to prayer. So with him praying was not an outer coating, a mere coloring, a paint, a polish. Praying made up the substance, bone, marrow, and very being of his religious life. His conversion was a marvel of grace and power. His apostolic commission was full and royal. But he did not vainly expect to make full proof of his ministry by the marvels of conditions and by wonderful results in the conversion. Nor did he attempt to do it by the apostolic commission signed and sealed by divine authority, and carrying with it all highest gifts and apostolic enrichments. He did it by prayer—by ceaseless, wrestling, agonizing, and Holy Spirit praying. Thus did Paul work his work, and crown his work, life, and death with martyr principles and with martyr glory.

Paul had a spiritual trait that was very marked and especially promised, and it was that of prayer. He had a profound conviction that prayer was a great as well as a solemn duty. That prayer was a royal privilege. That prayer was a mighty force. That prayer gauges piety and makes faith mighty and mightier. That much prayer was necessary to Christian success. That prayer was a great factor in the ongoing of God's kingdom on earth. And that God and heaven expected followers of Christ to pray.

WE ARE DEPENDENT ON PRAYER

Somehow we are dependent on prayer for great triumphs of holiness over sin, of heaven over hell, and of Christ over Satan. Paul took it for granted that saints who knew God would pray, saints who lived for God would pray much, and saints could not live for God who did not pray. So Paul prayed much. He was in the habit of praying. He was used to praying, and that formed the habit of prayer. He estimated prayer so greatly that he fully knew its value, and that fastened the habit on him. Paul was in the habit of praying because he loved God, and such love in the heart always finds its expression in regular habits of prayer. He felt the need of much grace, and of more and more grace, and grace only comes through the channels of prayer. And grace only abounds more and more as prayer abounds more and more.

Paul was in the habit of praying, but he prayed not by mere force of habit. Human beings are such creatures of habit that they are always in danger of doing things simply by heart in a routine, indifferent manner. Paul's habit was regular and hearty. To the Romans he wrote, "For God is my witness . . . that without ceasing I make mention of you always in my prayers."[4] Prison doors are opened and earthquakes take place by the kind of praying Paul did. All things are opened to the kind of praying that was done by Paul and Silas. All things are opened by prayer. They could shut up Paul from preaching, but this could not shut him up from praying. And the Gospel could win its way by Paul's praying as well as by Paul's preaching. The apostle might be in prison, but the Word of God was free, and went like the mountain air, while the apostle is bound in prison and abounds in prayer.

Their joy in Jesus was so profound that it expressed itself happily and sweetly in praise and prayer under extremely painful and depressing conditions. Prayer brought them into full communion with God, which made all things radiant with the Divine presence, and which enabled them to be "rejoicing that they were counted worthy to suffer shame for His name,"[5] and to "count it all joy when they fell into divers temptations."[6] Prayer sweetens all things and sanctifies all things. Prayerful saints will be suffering saints. Suffering prayerfully they will be sweet saints. Praying saints will be praising saints. Praise is but prayer set to music and song.

PAUL'S CHARGE TO EPHESUS

After Paul's notable charge to the elders at Ephesus, as he tarried there while on his way to Jerusalem, this characteristic record is made: "And when he had thus spoken, he kneeled down, and prayed with them all. And they all wept sore, and fell on Paul's neck, and kissed him."[7]

"He kneeled down, and prayed." Note those words. Kneeling in prayer was Paul's favorite attitude, the fitting posture of an earnest, humble, suppliant. Humility and intensity are in such a position in prayer before Almighty God. It is the proper attitude of people before God, of a sinner before a Savior, and of a beggar before a benefactor. To seal his sacred and living charge to those Ephesian elders by prayer was that which made the charge efficient, beneficial, and abiding.

Paul's religion was born in the throes of that three days' struggle of prayer, while he was in the house of Ananias. There he received a divine impetus that never slackened until it brought him to the gates of the eternal city. That spiritual history and religious experience, projected along the line of unceasing prayer, brought him to the highest spiritual altitudes and yielded the largest spiritual results. Paul lived in the very atmosphere of prayer. His first missionary trip was projected by prayer. It was by prayer and fasting that he was called into the foreign missionary field, and by the same means the Church at Antioch was moved to send forth Paul and Barnabas on their first missionary journey. Here is the Scripture record of it:

> Now there were in the church that was at Antioch certain prophets and teachers; as Barnabas, and Simeon that was called Niger, and Lucius of Cyrene, and Manaen, which had been brought up with Herod the tetrarch, and Saul. As they ministered to the Lord, and fasted, the Holy Ghost said, Separate me Barnabas and Saul for the work whereunto I have called them. And when they had fasted and prayed, and laid their hands on them, they sent them away.[8]

A MODEL FOR MISSIONS

Here is a model for all missionary outgoings, a presage of success. Here was the Holy Spirit directing a prayerful Church obedient to the divine leadership. This condition of things brought forth the very largest possible results in the mission of these two men of God. We may confidently assert that no Church in which Paul was prominent was a prayerless Church. Paul lived, toiled, and suffered in an atmosphere of prayer. To him, prayer was the very heart and life of religion, its bone and marrow, the motor of the Gospel, and the sign by which it conquered. We are not left in ignorance, for that spirit of prayer established churches and put in them the everlasting requisite of self-denial in the shape of fasting and the practice of prayer. Here is the divine record of Paul's work on this line:

> Confirming the souls of the disciples, and exhorting them to continue in the faith, and that we must through much tribulation enter into the kingdom of God. And when they had ordained them

elders in every church, and had prayed with fasting, they commended them to the Lord, on whom they believed.[9]

In obedience to a heavenly vision, Paul lands in Europe, and finds himself at Philippi. There is no synagogue, and few if any Jews are there. A few pious women, however, have a meeting place for prayer, and Paul is drawn by spiritual attraction and spiritual affinities to the place "where prayer is wont to be made."[10] Paul's first planting of the Gospel in Europe is at that little prayer meeting. He is there the chief prayer and man of prayer and speaker. Lydia was the first convert at that prayer meeting. They protracted the meeting. They called it a meeting for prayer.

DEMON OF DIVINATION

It was while they were going to that protracted prayer meeting that Paul performed the miracle of casting the demon of divination out of a poor demon-possessed girl, who had been made a source of gain by some covetous men. Because of it, the magistrate ordered Paul to be scourged and imprisoned. The result by God's orders was the conversion of the jailer and his whole household. To the praying apostle no discouragements are allowed. A few praying saints are enough for an apostolic field of labor.

PAUL AND SILAS IN PRISON

In this last incident, we have a picture of Paul at midnight. He is in the inner prison, dark and deadly. He has been severely and painfully scourged, his clothing is covered with blood, and there are blood clots on his gnashed and torn body. His feet are in the stocks, every nerve is feverish and swollen, sensitive, and painful. But we find him under these very unfavorable and suffering conditions at his favorite pursuit. Paul is praying with Silas, his companion, in a joyous, triumphant strain.

> And at midnight Paul and Silas prayed, and sang praises unto God: and the prisoners heard them. And suddenly there was a great earthquake, so that the foundations of the prison were shaken: and immediately all the doors were opened, and every one's bands were loosed. And the keeper of the prison awaking out of his sleep, and seeing the prison doors open, he drew out his sword, and would have killed himself, supposing that the prisoners had been fled. But Paul cried with a loud voice, saying, Do thyself no harm: for we are all here.[11]

Never was prayer so beautiful, never more productive. Paul was an expert at prayer, a lover of prayer, a wondrous devotee of prayer. He could pursue it with joyous strains even under depressing and difficult conditions. What a mighty weapon of defense prayer was to Paul. How songful! The angels doubtless stilled their highest and sweetest notes to listen to the music that bore those prayers to heaven. The earthquake trod along the path made by the mighty forces of Paul's praying. He did not go out when his chains were loosed and the stocks fell off. His praying taught him that God had nobler purposes that night than his own individual freedom. His praying and the earthquake alarm were to bring salvation to that prison, freedom from the prison house of sin that was foreshadowed by his physical emancipation. God's mighty providence had opened his prison door and broken his prison bonds. But it was not to give freedom to Paul and Silas, but to give freedom to the jailer. God's providential openings are often to test our ability to stay rather than to go. It tested Paul's ability to stay.

Endnotes

1 Acts 9:11
2 Acts 16:13
3 Acts 16:16
4 Romans 1:9
5 Acts 5:41
6 James 1:2
7 Acts 20:36-37
8 Acts 13:1-3
9 Acts 14:22-23
10 Acts 16:13
11 Acts 16:25-28

14

Paul and His Praying (Continued)

WILLIAM LAW HAS THIS *very pertinent word in his "Devout Life":*
"When you begin your petitions use such various expressions of the
attributes of God as may make you most sensible of the greatness and power
of the Divine nature?" And then William Law gives various examples, which
I am bound to say would not be helpful to me, as they would imprison my
spirit in a coat of mail. But I want to emphasize and commend the principle
of it, which is, that our fellowship should begin with the primary elements of
adoration and praise. (Rev. J. H. Jowett)

There are two occasions with wonderful results where Scripture does
not state specifically that Paul was in prayer. But the circumstances and the
results, and Paul's universal and intense praying habit, make it most evident
that the key to the results of both occasions is prayer. The first occasion is
when Paul sailed away from Philippi and came to Troas, where he abode
seven days. On the first day of the week, when the disciples came together
to break bread, Paul preached to them, expecting to depart on the morrow,
and continued his preaching until late in the night.

There was a young man named Eutychus sitting in the window. Paul
talked long into the night, and the young man fell asleep and tumbled out
the high window, and was taken up for dead. Paul went down to the place
where the young man had fallen, and embracing him told the people that
they need not be troubled for life was still in the body. Paul returned to the
upper room where he had been preaching and talked with the disciples
until the break of day. The young man was brought back in alive, and as a
result all were greatly comforted.

The very natural conclusion without the fact being specially stated is that Paul must have prayed for the young man when he embraced him, and his prayer was answered in the quick recovery of the young man.

The second occasion was in the perilous and protracted storm that overtook the vessel in which Paul was being carried as a prisoner to Rome. They were being exceedingly tossed about with the great storm, and neither sun nor stars appeared as they struggled against the wind and stormy sea. All hope that they would be saved seemed gone.

> But after long abstinence Paul stood forth in the midst of them, and said, Sirs, ye should have hearkened unto me, and not have loosed from Crete, and to have gained this harm and loss. And now I exhort you to be of good cheer: for there shall be no loss of any man's life among you, but of the ship. For there stood by me this night the angel of God, whose I am, and whom I serve, Saying, Fear not, Paul; thou must be brought before Caesar: and, lo, God hath given thee all them that sail with thee. Wherefore, sirs, be of good cheer: for I believe God, that it shall be even as it was told me.[1]

It requires no strained interpretation to read into this simple record the fact that Paul must have been praying when the angel appeared to him with that message of encouragement and assurance of safety. Paul's habit of prayer and his strong belief in prayer must have driven him to his knees. Such an emergency with him would necessarily move him to pray under such crucial circumstances.

THE ISLAND OF MELITA

While Paul and his companions are on the island of Melita after the shipwreck, there is recorded another representation of Paul at prayer. He is at his work of praying for a very ill man. While a fire was being made, a deadly poisonous viper fastened itself on his hand, and the barbarians immediately concluded it was a case of retribution for some crime Paul had committed. But they soon discovered that Paul did not die, and changed their minds and concluded that he was a sort of god.

In the same quarter at the time was the father of Publius, who was very ill of a fever and bloody flux, approaching seemingly his end. Paul went to him, laid his hands upon him, and with simple confidence in God prayed. Immediately the disease was rebuked and the man was healed. When the natives of the island saw this remarkable incident, they brought others to Paul, and they were healed in the same way, by Paul's praying.

PAUL AT EPHESUS

Turning back in Paul's life to the time he was at Ephesus on his way to Jerusalem, we find him stopping at Tyre after he departed from Ephesus. Before leaving Ephesus he had prayed with them all. But he did not trust in his words however strong, fitting, and solemn they might have been. God must be recognized, invoked, and sought. Paul did not take it for granted after he had done his best that God as a matter of course would bless his efforts to do good, but he sought God. God does not do things in a matter-of-course sort of way. God must be invoked, sought upon, and put into things by prayer.

Paul at Tyre

Following his visit to Ephesus, Paul arrived at Tyre where he stopped a few days. Here he found some disciples, who begged him not to go to Jerusalem, saying through the Spirit that he should not go up to that city. But Paul adhered to his original purpose to go to Jerusalem. The account says:

> And when we had accomplished those days, we departed and went our way; and they all brought us on our way, with wives and children, till we were out of the city: and we kneeled down on the shore, and prayed.[2]

What a sight to behold on that seashore! Here is a family picture of love and devotion, where husbands, wives, and even children are present, and prayer is made out in the open air. What an impression it must have made upon those children! The vessel was ready to depart, but prayer must cement their affections and sanctify wives and children, and bless their parting—a parting that was to be final so far as this world was concerned. The scene is beautiful and does honor to the head and heart of Paul, to his person and his piety, and shows the tender affection in which he was held. His devoted habit of sanctifying all things by prayer comes directly to the light. "We kneeled down on the shore, and prayed." Never did sea waves see a grander picture or witness a lovelier sight—Paul on his knees on the sands of that shore, invoking God's blessing upon these men, women, and children.

When Paul was arraigned at Jerusalem and made his public defense, he referred to two instances of his praying. One was when he was in the house of Judas in Damascus, after he had been stricken to the earth and brought under conviction. He was there three days, and Ananias was sent to him to lay his hand upon Paul at the time of his blindness and darkness. It was during those three days of prayer that Ananias was sent to Paul. This is the scriptural record, and the words are those of Ananias speaking to him: "And now why tarriest thou? arise, and be baptized, and wash away thy sins, calling on the name of the Lord."[3]

Prayer precedes pardon

The Lord had emboldened the timid Ananias to go and minister to Paul by telling him, "Behold, he prayeth." So we have in this reference Paul's prayerfulness intensified by the exhortation of Ananias. Prayer precedes pardon of sins. Prayer becomes those who seek God. Prayer belongs to the earnest, sincere inquirer after God. Pardon of sin and acceptance with God always come at the end of earnest praying. The evidence of sincerity in true seekers of Christ is that it can be said of them, "Behold, [they] prayeth."

The other reference in his defense lets us into the prayerful intenseness into which his whole religious life had been fashioned. It also shows us how in the absorbing ecstasy of prayer, the vision came and directions were received by which Paul's toilsome life was to be guided. Also, we see the familiar terms on which he stood and talked with his Lord:

And it came to pass, that, when I was come again to Jerusalem, even while I prayed in the temple, I was in a trance; And saw him saying unto me, Make haste, and get thee quickly out of Jerusalem: for they will not receive thy testimony concerning me. And I said, Lord, they know that I imprisoned and beat in every synagogue them that believed on thee: And when the blood of thy martyr Stephen was shed, I also was standing by, and consenting unto his death, and kept the raiment of them that slew him. And he said unto me, Depart: for I will send thee far hence unto the Gentiles.[4]

PRAYER BRINGS DIRECTION FROM HEAVEN

Prayer always brings directions from heaven as to what God would have us do. If we prayed more and more directly, we would make fewer mistakes in life as to duty. God's will concerning us is revealed in answer to prayer. If we prayed more and prayed better and sweeter, then clearer and more entrancing visions would be given us, and our communion with God would be the most intimate, free, and bold.

It is difficult to itemize or classify Paul's praying. It is so comprehensive, divergent, and detailed that it is no easy task to do so. Paul teaches much about prayer in his instructions. He specifically enforces the duty and necessity of prayer upon the Church. But what was better for Paul and better for us is that he himself prayed much and illustrated his own teaching. He practiced what he preached. He put to the test the exercise of prayer that he urged upon the people of his day.

THE CHURCH AT ROME

To the Church at Rome, Paul plainly and specifically declared solemnly his habit of praying. This is what he wrote to those Roman believers: "For God is my witness, whom I serve with my spirit in the gospel of his Son, that without ceasing I make mention of you always in my prayers."[5]

Paul not only prayed for himself. He made a practice of praying for others. He was preeminently an intercessor. As he urged intercessory prayer on others, so he interceded himself for others beside himself.

He begins that remarkable Epistle to the Romans in the spirit of prayer: He closes it with this solemn charge: "Now I beseech you, brethren, for the Lord Jesus Christ's sake, and for the love of the Spirit, that ye strive together with me in your prayers to God for me."[6]

But this is not all. In the very heart of that epistle he commands them to be "continuing instant in prayer."[7] That is, give constant attention to prayer. Make it the business of life. Be devoted to it. Just what he did himself, for Paul was a standing example of the doctrine of prayer that he advocated and pressed upon the people.

THESSALONIANS

In his epistles to the Thessalonians, how all-inclusive and wonderful the praying! He says in writing his first epistle to this Church: "We give thanks to God always for you all, making mention of you in our prayers; Remembering without ceasing your work of faith, and labour of love, and patience of hope in our Lord Jesus Christ, in the sight of God and our Father."[8]

Not to quote all he says, but it is worthwhile to read his words to this same Church of true believers further on:

Night and day praying exceedingly that we might see your face, and might perfect that which is lacking in your faith? Now God himself and our Father, and our Lord Jesus Christ, direct our way unto you. And the Lord make you to increase and abound in love one toward another, and toward all men, even as we do toward you: To the end he may stablish your hearts unblameable in holiness before God, even our Father, at the coming of our Lord Jesus Christ with all his saints.[9]

This sort of praying for these Thessalonian Christians is in direct line with that closing prayer for these same believers in this Epistle, where he records that striking prayer for their entire sanctification: "And the very God of peace sanctify you wholly; and I pray God your whole spirit and soul and body be preserved blameless unto the coming of our Lord Jesus Christ."[10]

PRAYING MEN AND WOMEN NEEDED

How Paul prayed for those early Christians! They were in his mind and on his heart and he was continually at it, "night and day praying exceedingly."[11] Oh, if we had a legion of preachers in these days of superficial piety and these times of prayerlessness, who were given to praying for their churches as Paul did for those to whom he ministered in his day! Praying men and women are needed. Likewise praying preachers are demanded in this age.

At the conclusion of that remarkable prayer in the third chapter of Ephesians, Paul declared that "God is able to do exceeding abundantly above all that we ask or think."[12] Now he declares he is praying exceeding abundantly, striving after the most earnest order, to have his prayers run parallel with God's power. He prays also that they may not limit that power nor exhaust that power, but get all there is in it to bless and greatly enrich God's Church.

Paul and his disciples prayed for the saints everywhere. It may be referred to again. With what solemnity Paul calls the attention of the Roman Christians to the important fact of praying for them, believers whom he had never seen! "God is my witness, . . . that without ceasing I make mention of you always in my prayers."[13]

To the Colossians he says, "Praying always for you."[14]

Again on the same line, we hear him say clearly, "Always in every prayer of mine for you all making request with joy."[15]

Again he writes: "I do not cease to pray for you."[16]

Once more we read, "Wherefore also we pray always for you."[17]

And again it is written, "Cease not to give thanks for you, making mention of you in my prayers."[18]

And yet again he says, "Remembrance of thee in my prayers night and day."[19]

Paul's declaration, "night and day praying exceedingly," is a condensed record of the engrossing nature of the praying done by this praying apostle. It shows conclusively how important prayer was in his estimate and in his ministry. It further shows how prayer was to him an agony of earnest striving in seeking from God blessings that could be secured in no other way.

The unselfishness of his praying is seen in his writing to the Romans where he tells them, "Making request, if by any means now at length I might have a prosperous journey by the will of God to come unto you. For I long to see you, that I may impart unto you some spiritual gift, to the end ye may be established."[20]

The object of his desire to visit Rome was not for selfish gratification, the pleasure of a trip, or for other reasons, but that he might be the means under God of imparting to them "some spiritual gift." This he desired so that they "may be established." It was that his visit might give to them some spiritual gift that they had not received, and that they might be established at those points where they needed to be rooted and grounded in faith, in love, and in all that made up Christian life and character.

Endnotes

1 Acts 27:21-25
2 Acts 21:5
3 Acts 22:16
4 Acts 22:17-21

5 Romans 1:9
6 Romans 15:30
7 Romans 12:12
8 I Thessalonians 1:2-3
9 I Thessalonians 3:10-13
10 I Thessalonians 5:23
11 I Thessalonians 3:10
12 Ephesians 3:12
13 Romans 1:9
14 Colossians 1:3
15 Philippians 1:4
16 Colossians 1:9
17 2 Thessalonians 1:11
18 Ephesians 1:16
19 2 Timothy 1:3
20 Romans 1:10-11

15

Paul and His Requests for Prayer

I DESIRE ABOVE ALL THINGS *to learn to pray. We want to sound the reveille for the Christian warriors. We desire to find truth of the lack of real praying. What is it? Why is it? Why so little time spent in prayer when Christ, who had command of His time, chose to spend great part of it in* INTERCESSION? *"He ever liveth to make intercession for us." We believe the answer to be the desire is in the heart, but the will is undisciplined, the motive is present, but the affections have not melted under hours of heavenly meditation; the intellect is keen, yet not for hours of tireless research. The intellect and the affections have never been linked together by the sealing of the blessed Holy Ghost to do or die for God's glory in the secret places, with doors shut, lusts crucified.* (Rev. Homer W. Hodge)

The many requests of Paul for prayer for himself, made to those to whom he ministered, put prayer to the front in Paul's estimate of its possibilities. Paul prayed much himself, and tried hard to arouse Christians to the imperative importance of the work of prayer. He so deeply felt the need of prayer that he was given to the habit of personal praying. Realizing this for himself, he pressed this invaluable duty upon others. Intercessory prayer, or prayer for others, occupied a high place in his estimate of prayer. It is no surprise, therefore, when we find him throwing himself upon the prayers of the churches to whom he wrote.

By all their devotion to Jesus Christ, by all their interest in the advance of God's kingdom on earth, by all the ardor of their personal attachment to Jesus, he charges them to pray much, to pray unceasingly, to pray at all times, to pray in all things, and to make praying a business of praying. Then realizing his own dependence upon prayer for his difficult duties, his sore trials, and his heavy responsibilities, he urges those to whom he wrote to pray especially for him.

THE CHIEF OF THE APOSTLES NEEDED PRAYER

Paul needed the prayers of others, for this he practically admitted in asking for their prayers. His call to the apostleship did not lift him above this need. He realized and acknowledged his dependence on prayer. He craved and prized the prayers of all good people. He was not ashamed to solicit prayers for himself and to urge Christians everywhere to pray   for him.

In writing to the Hebrews, Paul bases his request for prayer on two reasons—his honesty and his anxiety to visit them. If he were insincere, he could lay no claim to their prayers. Praying for him, it would be a powerful agent in facilitating his visit to them. They would touch the secret place of the wind and the waves, and arrange all secondary agencies and make them minister to this end. Praying puts God in haste to do for us the things that we wish at His hands.

Paul's frequent request of Christians was that they would "pray for him." We are to judge of the value of a thing by the frequency of asking for it, and by the special and urgent plea made for it. If that is true, then with Paul the prayers of the saints were among his greatest assets. By the urgent and constant request, "Pray for me," Paul showed conclusively the great value he put upon prayer as a means of grace. Paul had no need so pressing as the need of prayer. There were no values so appreciated and appreciable as the prayers of the faithful.

Paul put the great factor of prayer as the great factor in his work. The most powerful and far-reaching energy in Paul's estimate is prayer. He covets it and hoards it as he seeks the prayers of God's people. The earnestness of his soul goes out in these requests. Hear him in this entreaty for prayer he writes to the Romans: "Now I beg you, brethren, through the Lord Jesus Christ, and through the love of the Spirit, that you strive together with me in prayers to God for me."[1]

STRENGTH THROUGH OTHER'S PRAYERS

Prayers by others for Paul were valuable because they helped him. Prayers are great helpers. Nothing gives so much aid to us in our needs as real prayers. They supply needs and deliver from difficulties. Paul's writes to the Corinthians that his faith had been much tried, and he had been much helped and much strengthened by God's deliverance. "Ye also helping by prayer."[2] What marvelous things has God done for His favored saints through the prayers of others! The saints can help the saints more by fervent praying than in any other way.

In the midst of envy and detraction, and in perils by false brethren, Paul writes to the Philippians:

> For I know that this shall turn to my salvation through your prayer, and the supply of the Spirit of Jesus Christ, According to my earnest expectation and my hope, that in nothing I shall be ashamed, but that with all boldness, as always, so now also Christ shall be magnified in my body, whether it be by life, or by death.[3]

Shame was taken away, holy boldness secured, and life and death made glorious by the prayers of the saints at Philippi for Paul.

Paul had many mighty forces in his ministry. His remarkable conversion was a great force, a point of mighty projecting and propelling power, and yet he did not in his ministry secure its results by the force of his amazing conversion. His call to the apostleship was clear, luminous, and all-convincing, but he did not depend on that for the largest results in his ministry.

Paul's course was more clearly marked out and his career rendered more powerfully successful by prayer than by any other force.

ROMAN CHRISTIANS

Paul urges the Roman Christians to pray for him that he may be delivered from unbelieving people. Prayer is a defense and protection against the malignity and machinations of evil people. It can affect people because God can affect them. Paul had not only unbelieving enemies with whom to contend, but many Christians were prejudiced against him to an extent that rendered it questionable whether they would accept any Christian service at his hands. Especially was this the case at Jerusalem, and so prayer, powerful prayer, must be used to remove the mighty and deadly force of inflamed and deep-seated prejudice.

Prayer on their part for him must be used for his safety, and also that a prosperous journey and God's will might bring him speedily and surely to them, in order to bless and refresh mutually the Roman Christians.

PAUL'S PRAYER REQUESTS

These prayer requests of Paul are many-sided and all-comprehensive. His request to the Roman Church includes many things. The request for their prayers, like the Church to whom it is directed, is cosmopolitan. He beseeches them, entreats them—a term indicating intensity and earnestness, that for the sake of Jesus Christ they strive with him in their prayers for him. This he desires that he may be delivered from evil and designing people, who might hinder and embarrass him in his mission. Also, that his service for the poor saints might be accepted by the saints, and that he might ultimately come to them with joy so that they may be refreshed.

How full of heart earnestness is his request! How tender and loving is his appeal! How touching and high is the motive to the highest and truest form of prayer, "for the Lord Jesus Christ's sake!" Also for the love we bear for the Spirit, or for the love that the Spirit bears to us, and by the ties of holy Christianity. By these lofty and constraining motives he urges them to pray for him and to "strive with him" in their mutual praying. Paul is in the great prayer struggle, a struggle in which the mightiest issues are involved and imperiled—and he is in the midst of this struggle. He is committed to it because Christ is in it. He needs help, help that comes through prayer alone. So he pleads with the Christians to pray for him and with him.

PRAYER SWEEPS ENEMIES OUT OF THE WAY

By prayer, enemies are to be swept out of the way. By prayer, prejudices are driven out of the hearts of good people. Paul's way to Jerusalem would be cleared of difficulties, the success of his mission would be secured, and the will of God and the good of the saints would be accomplished. All these marvelous ends would be secured by marvelous praying.

Wonderful and world-wide are the results to be gained by mighty praying. If all apostolic successors had prayed as Paul did, if all Christians in all these ages had been one with apostolic times in the mighty work of prayer, how marvelous and divine would have been the history of God's Church! How unparalleled would have been its success! The glory of its millennium would have brightened and blessed the world ages ago.

We see in Paul's requests his estimate of the far-reaching power of prayer. Not that prayer has in it any magical force, but that it moves God to do things that it expresses. Prayer has no magic, powerful, charm in itself, but is only all power because it gets the omnipotent God to grant its request. A basic principle in all prayer as expressed or understood by Paul is that "Ye strive together with me in your prayers to God for me."[4] It is of the nature of a severe conflict in which Paul's soul is engaged. The strain is severe and exhaustive to all the energies of the soul, and the issue is tossed in uncertainty. Paul in this prayer struggle needs reinforcements and divine help in his striving. He is in the midst of the struggle, and will bear the brunt, but he solicits and pleads for the help of others. Their prayers are urgently needed. He needs help to offer intense prayers.

WRESTLING IN PRAYER

Prayer is not wrongly called "wrestling," because it is a most intense struggle. There are great hindrances to prayer and the most persistent foes. Mighty evil forces surge around the closets of prayer. Enemies strong and strongly entrenched are about the closets where praying is done. No feeble, listless act is this praying done by Paul. In this thing he has "put away childish things."[5]

The commonplace and the tame have been retired. Paul must do this praying mightily or not do it at all. The enemy must feel and stagger under the mightiness of his prayer stroke, or he strikes not at all. The strongest graces and the most courageous efforts are required here. Strength is demanded in the praying done by Paul. Courage is at a premium in it. Timid touches and faint-hearted desires avail nothing in the mind of Paul. Enemies are to be faced and routed and fields are to be won. The most untiring and invincible bravery and the highest qualities of Christian warriors are demanded for prayer. It is a trumpet call to prayer, a chieftain's clarion note, sounded out for earnest, persistent prayer as the great spiritual conflict rages.

Endnotes

1 Romans 15:30
2 2 Corinthians 1:11
3 Philippians 1:19-20
4 Romans 15:30
5 1 Corinthians 13:11

16

Paul and His Requests for Prayer (Continued)

W E ANNOUNCE THE LAW OF *prayer as follows: A Christian's prayer is a joint agreement of the will and his cabinet, the emotions, the conscience, the intellect, working in harmony at white heat, while the body co-operates under certain hygienic conditions to make the prayer long enough sustained at high voltage to insure tremendous results, supernatural and unearthly.* (Rev. Homer W. Hodge)

We come to the request of Paul made to the church at Ephesus:

Praying always with all prayer and supplication in the Spirit, and watching thereunto with all perseverance and supplication for all saints; And for me, that utterance may be given unto me, that I may open my mouth boldly, to make known the mystery of the gospel, For which I am an ambassador in bonds: that therein I may speak boldly, as I ought to speak.[1]

Paul had labored for this church and prayed night and day, with many concerns, tears, and much humility. As he drew a vivid picture of the Christian soldier, with his foes besetting him, he gave them this charge of praying specially for him.

To these Ephesian Christians he gave a comprehensive statement of the necessity, nature, and special benefits of prayer. It was to be urgent, covering all times and embracing all manner of places. Supplication must be intense, the Holy Spirit must be invoked, vigilance and perseverance must be added, and the whole family of saints must be involved.

The force of his request for prayer centered on him, that he might be able to talk with force, fluency, directness, and courage. Paul did not depend upon his natural gifts, but on those which came to him in answer to prayer. He was afraid he would be a coward, a dull, dry speaker, or a hesitating stammerer. So he urged these believers to pray that he might have courage, not only to speak clearly, but freely and fully.

Prayer for boldness

He desired them to pray that he might have boldness. No quality seems more important to the preacher than that of boldness. It is a positive quality that does not reckon consequences, but with freedom and fullness meets the crisis, faces a present danger, and performs a required duty without concern. It was one of the marked characteristics of apostolic preachers and apostolic preaching. They were bold men, they were bold preachers. The reference to the manifestation of the principle by them is almost the record of their trials. It is the applause of their faith.

Their very tenderness makes them weak. Their attachments to the people tend to bring them into bondage. Their personal fellowship, obligations to his people, and love for them, all tend to hamper their freedom and restrain their pulpit deliverances. What great need to be continually praying for boldness to speak boldly as they should speak!

The prophets of old were charged not to be afraid of the faces of people. Undaunted by the frowns of people, they were to declare the truth of God without apology, timidity, hesitancy, or compromise. The warmth and freedom of conviction and of sincerity, the fearlessness of a vigorous faith, and above all the power of the Holy Ghost, are all wonderful helpers and elements of boldness. How all this should be coveted and sought with all earnestness by ministers of the Gospel in this day!

Meekness and humility

Meekness and humility are high virtues of the first importance in the preacher, but these qualities do not at all militate against boldness. This boldness is not the freedom of passionate utterances. It is not scolding nor rashness. It speaks the truth in love. Boldness is not rudeness. Roughness dishonors boldness. It is as gentle as a mother with a babe, but as fearless as a lion standing before a foe. Fear, in the mild and innocent form of timidity, or in the criminal form of cowardice, has no place in the true ministry. Humble but holy boldness is of the very first importance.

What hidden, mysterious, mighty force can add courage to apostolic preaching, and give bolder utterances to apostolic lips? There is one answer, and it is that prayer can do the deed.

What force can so affect and dominate evil that the very results of evil will be changed into good? We have the answer in Paul's words again, in connection with prayers made for him:

Who delivered us from so great a death, and doth deliver: in whom we trust that he will yet deliver us; Ye also helping together by prayer for us.[2]

What then? notwithstanding, every way, whether in pretence, or in truth, Christ is preached; and I therein do rejoice, yea, and will rejoice.[3]

We can see how the promises of God are made real and personal by prayer. "All things work together for good to them that love God."[4] Here is a jeweled promise. Paul loved God, but he did not leave the promise alone, as a matter of course, to work out its blessed results. So he wrote to the Corinthians as we have seen before—in effect: "I am in trouble. I trust in God to deliver. Ye also helping together by prayer." Helping me by prayer, you help God to make the promise strong and rich in realization.

SUPPLICATION FOR ALL SAINTS

Paul's prayer requests embraced "supplication for all saints,"[5] but especially for apostolic courage for himself. How much he needed this courage, just as all true preachers, called of God, need it! Prayer was to open doors for apostolic labors, but at the same time it was to open apostolic lips to utter bravely and truly the apostolic message.

Hear him as he speaks to the Church at Colosses:

Withal praying also for us, that God would open unto us a door of utterance, to speak the mystery of Christ, for which I am also in bonds: That I may make it manifest, as I ought to speak.[6]

How appropriate such a request would be for present-day preachers to make to their congregation! How great the need of those things by present-day preachers that Paul desired for himself!

As in the request to the Ephesians, Paul wants a "door of utterance" given him so that he may preach with the liberty of the Spirit, be delivered from being restricted in thought or hampered in delivery. Furthermore, he desires the ability to make manifest in the clearest terms, without confusion of thought, and with force of utterance, the Gospel "as he ought to speak"—just as every preacher should speak. Happy the preachers who minister to people who pray that way for them!

Happier still if they realize how much they need these things to preach clearly, forcibly, and effectively, and urge their people to pray for them!

Prayer changes crosses, trials, and oppositions into blessings and causes them to work together for good. "This shall turn to my salvation through your prayer,"[7] says Paul. The same things today in the life of preachers are changed into gracious blessings in the end by, "ye also helping together by prayer."[8] Saintly praying mightily helped Apostolic preaching and rescued apostolic saints from many difficult situations. In the same way, such praying in these days will cause similar results in faithful preaching done by brave, fearless ministers.

PRAYERS FOR AND BY PREACHERS

Prayers for preachers avail just as prayers by preachers avail. Two things are always factors in the life and work of true preachers. First, when they pray constantly, fervently, and persistently for those to whom they preach. Second, when those to whom they minister pray for their preacher. Happy and blessed are the congregation and preacher who pray for each other.

To the Church at Thessalonica, Paul sent this urgent request—pointed, clear, and forceful:

> Finally, brethren, pray for us, that the word of the Lord may have free course, and be glorified, even as it is with you: And that we may be delivered from unreasonable and wicked men.[9]

Paul has in mind a race-course, on which the runners are exerting themselves to reach the goal. Hindrances are in the way of their success and must be removed, so that the best racer may finally succeed and obtain the reward. The "Word of the Lord" is this racer, as preached by Paul. This Word is personified and there are serious impediments that embarrass the running of the Word. It must have "free course." Everything in the way and opposing its running must be taken out of its roadway.

These impediments in the way of the Word of the Lord "running and being glorified" are found in the preachers themselves, in the church to whom they minister, and in the sinners around them. The Word runs and is glorified when it has unobstructed access to the minds and hearts of those to whom it is preached, when sinners are convicted for sin, when they seriously consider the claims of God's Word on them, and when they are induced to pray for themselves, asking for pardoning mercy. It is glorified when saints are instructed in Christian experience, corrected of errors of doctrine and mistakes in practice, and when they are led to seek for higher things and to pray for deeper experiences in the divine life.

Mark you. It is not when the preachers are glorified because of the wonderful success wrought by the Word. It is not when people praise them unduly, and make much of them because of their wonderful sermons, their great eloquence, and their remarkable gifts. The preachers are kept in the background in all this work of glorification, even though they are foremost as the object of all this praying.

PRAY FOR US

Prayer is to do all these things. So Paul urges, entreats, insists, "Pray for us." It is not so much prayer for Paul personally in his Christian life and experience. All this needed much prayer. It was really for him officially, prayer for him in the office and work of a Gospel minister. His tongue must be unloosed in preaching, his mouth unstopped, and his mind set free.

Prayer must help in his Christian life not so much because it would help to "work out his own salvation," but rather because right living would give strength to the Word of the Lord, and would save him from being a hindrance to the Word that he preached. In the same way that he desires that no hindrance be in himself that would defeat his own preaching, so he wants all hindrances taken away from the churches to whom he ministers.

This is so that Church people would not stand in the way or weigh down the Word as it runs on the race-course attempting to reach the goal, which is the minds and hearts of the people. Furthermore, he wishes hindrances in the unsaved to be set aside so that God's Word as preached by him may reach their hearts and be glorified in their salvation.

With all this before him, Paul sends this urgent request to these believers at Thessalonica, "Pray for us," because praying by true Christians would greatly help in the running of the Word of the Lord.

PRAYERS FOR PREACHERS

It is wise preachers who have the eyes to see these things, and who realize that their success largely depends upon praying of this kind for them on the part of their people. How much do we need churches now who, having the preachers in mind and the preached Word on their hearts, pray for them so that "the Word of the Lord may have free course, and be glorified."[10]

One other item in this request is worth noting: "That we may be delivered from wicked and unreasonable men."[11] Such people are hindrances in the way of the Word of the Lord. There are few preachers who are not harassed by them and need to be delivered from them. Prayer helps to bring such a deliverance to preachers from "unreasonable and wicked men." Paul was annoyed by such characters, and for this very reason he urged prayer for him that he might find deliverance from them.

Summing it all up, we find that Paul feels that the success of the Word, its liberty and largeness, are bound up in their prayers, and that their failure to pray would restrict its influence and its glory. He assets that his deliverance from unreasonable and wicked men and his safety, are in some way dependent upon their prayers. These prayers, while they greatly helped him to preach, would at the same time protect him from the cruel purposes of wicked and unreasonable men.

Endnotes

1 Ephesians 6:18-20
2 2 Corinthians 1:10-11a
3 Philippians 1:18
4 Romans 8:28
5 Ephesians 6:18
6 Colossians 4:3-4
7 Philippians 1:9
8 2 Corinthians 1:11
9 2 Thessalonians 3:1-2
10 2 Thessalonians 3:1
11 2 Thessalonians 3:2

Topical Index